CONSTITUTIONAL SECULARISM IN AN AGE OF RELIGIOUS REVIVAL

Constitutional Secularism in an Age of Religious Revival

Edited by

SUSANNA MANCINI

and

MICHEL ROSENFELD

OXFORD

UNIVERSITY PRESS

OXFORD
UNIVERSITY PRESS

Great Clarendon Street, Oxford, OX2 6DP,
United Kingdom

Oxford University Press is a department of the University of Oxford.
It furthers the University's objective of excellence in research, scholarship,
and education by publishing worldwide. Oxford is a registered trade mark of
Oxford University Press in the UK and in certain other countries

First Edition published in 2014

Impression: 2

Published in the United States of America by Oxford University Press
198 Madison Avenue, New York, NY 10016, United States of America

British Library Cataloguing in Publication Data
Data available

Library of Congress Control Number: 2013946679

ISBN 978–0–19–966038–4

Printed and bound in Great Britain by
CPI Group (UK) Ltd, Croydon, CR0 4YY

To our children,
Lucrezia and Federico (SM),
Maia and Alexis (MR)

Acknowledgments

This book is the culmination of a project that benefitted from great interaction and productive cooperation among numerous individuals and institutions. The project was initiated as part of the research agenda associated with the Blaise Pascal Research Chair administered by the Ecole Normale Superieure in Paris that Michel Rosenfeld held in 2007–2008. An interdisciplinary group of scholars from a number of countries and religious traditions was formed and met several times under the auspices of the academic host of the Pascal Chair, Professor (and subsequently Dean) Helene Ruiz-Fabri of the University of Paris I (Pantheon-Sorbonne) who acted as the co-covenor of the group and hosted and co-iorganized many meetings, conferences and symposia on the subject-matter of the present work. Special thanks are due to professor Ruiz-Fabri for her leadership, vision and generosity in connection with this project. Among the various conferences that resulted from this project, we wish to single out the out the symposium held in 2008 at the Cardozo School of Law under the auspices of Cardozo's Floersheimer Center for Constitutional Democracy. The *Cardozo Law Review* published the proceeds of the symposium in its Volume 30, n.6 (June 2009) which included the works of John Borneman, Karlheinz Ladeur and Andrew March which are included respectively as Chapters-12, 3, and 16 of the present volume. We thank the *Cardozo Law Review* for granting us the permission to reprint these three chapters. Thanks are also due to *Constellations* and to the *International Journal of Constitutional Law (I.CON)* for granting us permissions relating to earlier versions of chapters 2 and 18 and 4 respectively.

Many of the authors in this volume presented early versions of their chapters at a Colloquium on "Religion, The Constitution, and the State: Contemporary Controversies" that the two of us co-convened at the Cardozo School of Law in the Spring 2012 semester. We wish to thank Cardozo's Dean Matthew Diller and Vice-Dean Edward Stein for making the Colloquium possible and for their generous support and encouragement.

Finally, we also wish to give very special thanks to Elena L. Cohen, Cardozo School of Law JD, 2010 and Doctoral candidate at CUNY Graduate Center for her invaluable and superb editorial and general organizational work on this volume as well as for her excellent translation from Italian to English of Chapter 14 by Gustavo Zagrebelsky.

Contents

III. RELIGION, SECULARISM, AND WOMEN'S EQUALITY

IV. RELIGIOUS PERSPECTIVES AND THE LIBERAL STATE

V. THE CONFRONTATION BETWEEN SECULARISM AND RELIGION IN SPECIFIC CONTEXTS: EDUCATION AND FREE SPEECH

List of Contributors

Lama Abu-Odeh is a Professor of Law, Georgetown Law Center, and writes on Law and Economic Development, Law and Gender, and Constitutional Law. Her scholarship includes the following articles: "Of Law and the Revolution," "Of Law and the Transition to the Market: the Case of Egypt," and "Of Law and the Domestic Servant".

Daphne Barak-Erez is a Justice of the Supreme Court of Israel. Formerly she was the Stewart and Judy Colton Professor of Law at Tel Aviv University, where she also served as the Dean of the Faculty of Law.

Pierre Birnbaum is a retired professor at the University of Paris, and has taught for many years in New York universities. He has published several books on the State, including *Sociology of the State* with B. Badie (Chicago University Press, 1992) and on the historical sociology of Jews, including *The Jews of the Republic* (Stanford University Press, 1995). He recently published *Les Deux maisons. Essai sur la citoyenneté des Juifs* (Gallimard 2012), a comparison of the relations between the state and the Jews in France and in the United States.

John Borneman is a Professor of Anthropology at Princeton University. He has conducted fieldwork in Germany, Lebanon, and Syria, and focused primarily on the relation of kinship to identification with political authority. His publications include *Belonging in the Two Berlins: Kin, State, Nation* (1992); *Death of the Father: Toward an Anthropology of the End in Political Authority* (2003); *Syrian Episodes: Sons, Fathers, and an Anthropologist in Aleppo* (2008); *Political Crime and the Memory of Loss* (2011); and (as co-editor with Abdellah Hammoudi) *Being There: The Fieldwork Encounter and the Making of Truth* (2009). His forthcoming book is *Cruel Attachments: The Ritual Rehab of Child Molesters.*

Dieter Grimm teaches Constitutional Law at Humboldt University Berlin and at the Yale Law School. He is a Permanent Fellow of the Wissenschaftskolleg zu Berlin (Institute for Advanced Study) whose Rector he was from 2001 to 2007. From 1987 to 1999 he served as Justice of the Federal Constitutional Court of Germany. He is a member of the Berlin-Brandenburgische Akademie der Wissenschaften, the Academia Europaea and the American Academy of Arts and Sciences.

Ran Hirschl is a Professor of Political Science and Law, and holds a Canada Research Chair in Constitutionalism, Democracy and Development at the University of Toronto. He is the author of three books: *Towards Juristocracy: The Origins and Consequences of the New Constitutionalism* (Harvard University Press, 2004 and 2007), *Constitutional Theocracy* (Harvard University Press, 2010)—winner of the 2011 Mahoney Prize in Legal Theory, and *Comparative Matters* (Harvard University Press, forthcoming in 2014), as well as over 70 articles and book chapters on comparative constitutional law, constitutional law and religion, and the intellectual history of comparative constitutional studies. He is an Editorial Board Member of the Journal of Law & Courts, and the International Journal of Constitutional Law (I-CON), and a founding co-editor of a book series on comparative constitutional law and policy published by Cambridge University Press.

Karl-Heinz Ladeur studied law at the universities of Cologne and Bonn, and worked as a professor at the University of Bremen from 1982 to 1994. He is a professor emeritus at the University of Hamburg, and has also taught at the European Graduate School of Florenz.

Susanna Mancini is a Professor of Law at the University of Bologna School of Law. She has written extensively in the field of comparative constitutionalism and particularly on law and religion, gender and the law, reproductive rights, language rights, federalism and secession.

Andrew F. March (DPhil, Oxford) is an Associate Professor of Political Science at Yale University, where he teaches classes on Islamic law, Islamic political thought and political theory. He is the author of *Islam and Liberal Citizenship* (Oxford University Press, 2009) and numerous articles on Islamic law and political thought. He is presently working on a book on Islamic conceptions of political sovereignty, which focuses on the dual commitment in much Islamic thought to divine as well as popular sovereignty.

Robert Post is the Dean and Sol. & Lillian Goldman Professor of Law at Yale Law School. Before coming to Yale, he taught at the University of California, Berkeley, School of Law (Boalt Hall). Dean Post's subject areas are constitutional law, First Amendment, legal history, and equal protection.

Michel Rosenfeld is the Justice Sydney L. Robins Professor of Human Rights and director of the Program on Global and Comparative Constitutional Theory at the Benjamin N. Cardozo School of Law. He is the co-editor-in-chief of the International Journal of Constitutional Law (I-CON), and was president of the International Association of Constitutional Law (1999–2004). He is the author of *The Identity of the Constitutional Subject* (Routledge, 2010), *Law, Justice, Democracy and the Clash of Cultures* (Cambridge Uuniversity Press, 2011), and co-editor of *the Oxford Handbook of Comparative Constitutional Law* (Oxford Uuniversity Press, 2012).

András Sajó is a judge at the European Court of Human Rights, Strasbourg. He is a University Professor and the founding dean of Legal Studies at Central European University, and a Global Visiting Professor of Law at New York University Law School. He has been extensively involved in legal drafting throughout Eastern Europe and he participated and/or advised in drafting the Ukrainian, Georgian, and South African constitutions.

Gideon Sapir is a Professor of Law at Bar-Ilan University, Israel. He received his law degree from Bar-Ilan University, an LL.M. and S.J.D. from Northwestern University, and Rabbinical Ordination from the Israeli Chief Rabbinate. His teaching and research areas of interest are constitutional law (with an emphasis on religion and state) and constitutional theory.

Ayelet Shachar is a Professor of Law, Political Science, and Global Affairs at the University of Toronto, and holder of the Canada Research Chair in Citizenship and Multiculturalism. She has published and lectured widely on citizenship theory, immigration law, multiculturalism and women's rights. Shachar is the author of *Multicultural Jurisdictions: Cultural Differences and Women's Rights* (Cambridge University Press, 2001), for which she won the Best First Book Award from the American Political Science Association Foundations of Political Theory Section; and *The Birthright Lottery: Citizenship and Global Inequality* (Harvard University Press, 2009).

Daniel Statman is a professor of philosophy at the University of Haifa and research fellow at the Shalom Hartman Institute, Jerusalem. His areas of specialization are ethics, moral psychology, philosophy of law, and Jewish philosophy. He is author and editor of many books and articles, including *Moral Dilemmas, Moral Luck, Virtue Ethics* and (as co-author) *Religion and Morality* and *State and Religion in Israel.*

Gila Stopler is a senior lecturer at the Academic Center of Law and Business, and was a 2011–12 Tikvah Fellow at the Tikvah Center for Law and Jewish Civilization at the NYU School of Law. She obtained an LL.B from the Tel Aviv University School of Law (1995), and LL.M (2001) and J.S.D (2004) degrees from the NYU School of Law. At NYU she was awarded the David H. Moses Memorial Prize as the member of the LL.M class with the highest cumulative average, and served as a Public Service Scholar and a Hauser Research Scholar. Her areas of expertise are constitutional and comparative constitutional law, religion—state relations, multiculturalism and women's rights. She has published articles in leading transnational law and feminist journals of top universities such as Columbia, Duke, and Texas, as well as in philosophical journals, and serves as editor-in-chief of the international law journal "Law & Ethics of Human Rights."

Michel Troper taught Constitutional Law and Legal Theory at the University of Rouen until 1978, when he transferred to the University of Paris X at Nanterre. In 1993 he received an appointment to a chair at the Institut Universitaire de France and has been emeritus professor since 2006. He has been a visiting professor or scholar and gave lectures in a number of universities across the world. He held the "chaire Chaim Perelman" at the Université Libre de Bruxelles in 2008–09 and was a fellow at the Straus Institute for Law and Justice (NYU) in 2011–12).

Nadia Urbinati is a professor of political theory in the Department of Political Science, Columbia University. Her new forthcoming books are *Free and Equals* (Yale University Press) and *Democracy Disfigured: Truth, Opinion, and the People* (Harvard University Press).

Patrick Weil is a senior research fellow at the French National Research Center in the University of Paris1, Pantheon-Sorbonne. Professor Weil's work focuses on comparative immigration, citizenship, and Church states law and policy. His most recent book is *The Sovereign Citizen: Denaturalization and the Origins of the American Republic* (Penn Press, 2013). In France, Professor Weil has participated in a 2003 Presidential Commission on secularism, established by Jacques Chirac. In 1997, he completed a mission and a report on immigration and nationality policy reform for Prime Minister Lionel Jospin which led to the implementation of new immigration and citizenship laws adopted the following year.

Gustavo Zagrebelsky is a professor of Constitutional Law and Legal Theory at the University of Turin. He has served as the Chief Justice of the Constitutional Court of Italy. He regularly writes editorials for La Repubblica and other Italian newspapers.

Introduction

Susanna Mancini and Michel Rosenfeld

Constitutional secularism, as framed within the abstract confines of the realm of ideas, emerges as a necessary concomitant to the ideal of the Enlightenment—the latter being, in turn, encapsulated in two imperatives: separation of Faith from Reason and equal liberty for all. Indeed, to the extent that the prescriptions emanating from religious faith remain impervious to the strictures of public reason,[1] they stand in the way of the full deployment of reason be it in politics, scientific research, or education. Moreover, so long as all do not share the same faith, official embrace or endorsement of one faith to the exclusion or detriment of others would inevitably undermine adherence to the principle of equal liberty for all. Accordingly, by setting aside religion from the public sphere, where members of different faith-based communities must interact, constitutional secularism is meant to institutionally guarantee the dual aims of the Enlightenment. Separation of Faith from Reason is fostered by entrusting the public sphere to the latter and by allowing full expression of the former within the private sphere. Equal liberty is sustained, on the other hand, by official neutrality as between religions in the public sphere and by securing the same freedom for all religions within the private sphere. Furthermore, constitutional secularism may be construed variously as requiring outright expulsion of religion from the public sphere, as customarily understood in the context of French *laïcité*, or as merely called upon to insure that the state remains equidistant as between all religions within the polity. In either case, what remains imperative for constitutional secularism is that religion be depoliticized.

I. The Repoliticization of Religion and the Challenge to Secularism

In more recent times, however, constitutional secularism has had to confront a series of daunting challenges stemming from the repoliticization of religion. Some link this phenomenon to the migration of large numbers of adherents to Islam to Western European countries.[2] Others paint a broader picture encompassing a larger number of religions, spanning across several continents.[3] Thus, Jose Casanova has provided a comprehensive account of what he terms the "deprivatization" of religion[4] which combines the "repoliticization of the private religious and moral sphere" and the "renormativization of the

[1] See John Rawls, *Political Liberalism: Expanded Edition* (New York: Columbia University Press, 2005), 212ff. At its core, the concept of public reason elaborated by Rawls requires that propositions relating to constitutional ordering or ordinary law and politics be in principle accessible for purposes of critical evaluation to all concerned. Propositions exclusively grounded on a faith not shared by all seem bound to remain inaccessible to some of those concerned.

[2] See e.g. the Grimm and Ladeur chapters below.

[3] See Jose Casanova, *Public Religions in the Modern World* (Chicago: University of Chicago Press, 1994).

[4] Casanova, *Public Religions in the Modern World* 3.

public economic and political spheres."[5] The deprivitization in question encompasses such diverse historical events as the 1979 Islamic revolution in Iran, the political rise of fundamentalist Protestantism during the 1980's in the United States, and the prominent role of Catholicism in social and political movements spanning from Poland's Solidarity Movement, which played a key role in that country's transition from communism to constitutional democracy in the late 1980's, to liberation theology which originated and spread in Latin America going as far back as the 1960's. To this list, one should also add the prominent political role played by Judaism in Israel's attempts to forge a constitutional path consistent with its identity as a Jewish and democratic state proclaimed in its 1948 Declaration of Independence.[6] Finally, reference must be made to the most recent instances in this sequence, the Arab Spring revolutionary movements in countries such as Egypt and Tunisia where Islam has been in the forefront of transitions aimed at replacing authoritarian regimes with constitutionally grounded democracies.[7]

The repoliticization of religion has triggered a political and institutional struggle against secular constitutionalism,[8] but even more importantly in the context of ideas, it has lead to a two-pronged assault on the very legitimacy and viability of the concept at stake. On the one hand, constitutional secularism has been attacked as inherently hostile rather than neutral toward religion; and, on the other hand, constitutional secularism has been criticized as inevitably favoring one religion (or set of religions) over others. Moreover, although these two charges are seemingly inconsistent with one another, they ultimately emerge as two sides of the same coin. This is perhaps best exemplified in the case of French *laïcité,* which has been widely chastised as downright hostile to religion as evinced by its ban on students wearing the Islamic veil in public schools,[9] while at the same time perceived as remaining particularly well suited to accommodate Catholicism (though not necessarily on the latter's own terms), thus making for a mutually convenient joint project neatly encapsulated in the coined term "*catho-laique.*"[10] Consistent with this, it is precisely by projecting an aura of hostility to religion in general under a veil of neutrality that secularism can better align itself with one religion—almost always the country's majority religion—to carry out a more effective largely camouflaged war against a disfavored religion that in most cases happens to be a minority one. Furthermore, in one variant of this kind of analysis, secularism itself is cast as a religion, that of "secular humanism," which is then perceived as institutionally buttressed so as to achieve dominance over all others. A telling example of this latter variant is provided by the case brought in the United States by Protestant fundamentalist parents against a state school for teaching their children in English class a literary text that characterized a tsunami as a dramatic

[5] Casanova, *Public Religions in the Modern World* 5–6.

[6] On the contested area of state/religion relations in Israel, see various contributions in Gideon Sapir, Daphne Barak-Erez, and Aharon Barak (eds), *Israeli Constitutional Law in the Making* (Oxford: Hart Publishing, 2013).

[7] See Abu Odeh chapter below focusing on the case of Egypt.

[8] To cite but one example, some Orthodox Jews in Israel have asserted that Israel does not need a constitution because it can rely on the *Torah*. See Ervin Birnbaum, *The Politics of Compromise: State and Religion in Israel* (Rutherford: Fairleigh Dickinson University Press, 1970), 75.

[9] Susanna Mancini and Michel Rosenfeld, "Unveiling the Limits of Tolerance: Comparing the Treatment of Majority and Minority Religious Symbols in the Public Sphere," in Lorenzo Zucca and Camil Ungureanu (eds), *Law, State and Religion in the New Europe: Debates and Dilemmas* (Cambridge: Cambridge University Press, 2012), 160–91.

[10] See Jean Baubérot, *Laïcité 1905–2005: Entre passion et raison* (Paris: SEUIL, 2004), 185. For a critique of "*catho-laïcité*" as a means to favor Catholicism to better fight against Islam, see Guy Haarscher, "La laïcité falsifiée," *Observatoire des religions et de la laïcité* (17 July 2012), <http://www.o-re-la.org/index.php?option=com_k2&view=item&id=315:jean-baub%C3%A9rot-la-la%C3%AFcit%C3%A9-falsifi%C3%A9e&Itemid=85&lang=fr>.

example of the mysterious forces of nature. According to the parents who brought suit, the teaching of the text in question was in violation of the US Constitution's prohibition against the establishment of a religion as it inculcated the religion of "secular humanism" to the exclusion of the plaintiffs' religion which holds that all natural phenomena are the products of the will of God.[11]

II. Placing the Secular and Secularism in Historical Context

When placed in its proper historical context, the concept of "secularism" [12] or "the secular" evokes a very different set of connotations. This concept derives from the Christian tradition and its origin traces back to the reference made in the New Testament to Jesus' dictum to render unto Caesar what is Caesar's and to God what is God's.[13] Augustine further elaborated this distinction through the contrast he drew between the "City of God" and the "City of Man."[14] Later in the medieval era the term "*secularis*" was used to designate those members of the clergy who worked with people within society in contrast to their brethren who were exclusively devoted to spiritual pursuits within the confines of monastic life.[15] What is most striking about all three of these historical references is that the secular is wholly encompassed within a single religion[16] and that from its very beginnings Christianity sets a divide between the spiritual realm and the arena of politics.

A different conception of secularism became prevalent after the sixteenth century Protestant Reformation split Western Christianity into two. At first, the newly religiously divided Europe embraced the slogan *cuius regio, eius religio* also referred to as "one king, one faith, one law,"[17] which required weaving together religion, the state and politics to secure the hegemony of the dominant religion throughout the realm. After a series of fierce and bloody wars of religion pitting Catholics against Protestants in several European realms throughout the sixteenth and seventeenth centuries, however, secularism reentered the scene in a new guise as a buffer *among* religions. Indeed, it became apparent that war would not eradicate the split within Western Christianity and that reaching a *modus vivendi* among Catholics and Protestants was preferable to ongoing violence. Accordingly, support grew for the idea that there ought to be room for tolerance of the religion that happened to be in the minority within a particular polity by the latter's majority religion. Moreover, for there to be the requisite locus for

[11] See *Smith v. Bd of Sch. Comm'rs* 827 F.2d 684 (U.S. Fed. Ct. of App. for the 11th Cir. 1987) (the Court rejected the parents' claim and held that the state had not engaged in any propagation of religion).

[12] The term "secularism" was first used in the mid-nineteenth-century (see George Jacob Holyoake, *The Origin and Nature of Secularism Showing that Where Freethought Commonly Ends Secularism Begins* (London: Watts, 1896), 51), but the concept associated with this term traces back to antiquity.

[13] Matthew 22:21; see March chapter in this book at 293.

[14] Augustine, *De Civitate Dei Contra Paganos*, translated into English as *The City of God Against the Pagans* (5th century CE).

[15] See A. Boudinhon, "Secular Clergy," *The Original Catholic Encyclopedia*, available at <http://oce.catholic.com/index.php?title=Secular_Clergy>.

[16] Giving to Cesar what is Cesar's does not necessarily derive from any religion, but doing so to conform to the Word of Jesus does fully incorporate obedience to a worldly non-Christian ruler within the edicts of Christianity. For an incisive theoretical discussion of the concept of secularism and its relation to culture and ideology, see Etienne Balibar, *Saeculum: Culture, religion, idéologie* (2012). For the view that not only secularism but also the term "religion" itself derived from the latin "*religio*" is of "romano-christian" origin and is as such "untranslatable" into any other culture, see id. at 52 (discussing the analysis of Derrida).

[17] See Urbinati chapter.

tolerance without compromising on the subject of theological truth, it was necessary to effectuate some disentanglement of the realm of politics from that of religion. In this setting, secularism could keep the antagonistic religions at arm's length so long as neither of them could muster a decisive victory over the other. The secularism involved had to remain within Christianity, but had to avoid favoring Catholicism or Protestantism so it could serve as a buffer between them. Furthermore, the instantiation of secularism under consideration was amenable to being located *within* Christianity in two mutually reinforcing ways. First, the kind of disentangled politics necessary for coexistence could certainly promote Christianity (and that would be fully consistent with the standpoint of the antagonistic Christian religions) so long as it left sufficient room for tolerance of all Christian religions within the realm.[18] And second, this newly minted brand of secularism could build upon the distinction between the sacred and the secular found in the formerly united Christian religion. In other words, even in united Christianity the spiritual is separated from the political, and therefore this already entrenched separation can readily be adapted in order to accommodate a plurality of Christian spiritual perspectives coupled with a separate political sphere shared in common by all Christians regardless of their religious differences.[19]

The next important turn in the historical journey of secularism coincided with the deployment of the philosophy of the Enlightenment and was molded by the two late eighteenth-century revolutions, the American and the French, which set the stage for the advent of modern constitutional democracy. Although these two revolutions were certainly imbued by general Enlightenment ideas regarding secularism, they each left a distinct historical imprint on the evolving connotations of the concept. The French Revolution was strongly anti-clerical rather than anti-religious[20] and its anti-clericalism combined with its antagonism against the aristocracy are to be placed in the context of its struggle to topple feudal privilege to establish rule by the Third Estate.[21] Moreover, the French Revolution brought forth a republican ideal inspired by Rousseau's political philosophy, which promoted democratic self-government for a polity of equal citizens bound together by a social contract. Drawing on Rousseau's distinction between the citizen and the *bourgeois*,[22] the French Revolution's constitutional vision left no room for group-based allegiances or interests in the public sphere. This was dramatically illustrated by the famous dictum of Clermont-Tonnerre in connection with the

[18] The actual history of relationships between Catholics and Protestants in the various European realms in which they were in conflict during the sixteenth and seventeenth centuries veered at times far afield from the above mentioned theoretical conception of mutual tolerance as a means of peaceful coexistence. For example, in France the Edict of Nantes proclaimed in 1598 by King Henry IV accorded substantial rights to French Protestants in order to promote mutual tolerance at the end of a century that saw bloody wars of religion. This Edict was revoked, however, by King Louis XIV in 1685 prompting France's Protestants to flee in massive numbers. See Michel Grandjean and Bernard Roussel (eds), *Coexister dans l'intolérance* (Genève: Labor et Fides, 1998).

[19] It may well be that the Christian divide between the sacred and the secular may be better suited to Protestantism than to Catholicism given the unique institutional and political role played by the Catholic Church since the consolidation of Christianity in medieval Europe. On this last point, see Zagrebelsky's chapter below, and especially his discussion of secularism and the contrast he draws between the more accomodationist Catholic Church in the period following Vatican II and the more interventionist turn the latter has taken more recently consistent with the views of Pope Benedict XVI. Be that as it may, the concept of the divide in question, however interpreted or implemented, is a truly Christian one that has no equivalent in the other Abrahamic religions. See below.

[20] See Michael Collins and Matthew A. Price, *The Story of Christianity: A Celebration of 2,000 Years of Faith* (Wheaton, IL: Tyndale House Publishers, 2003), 176ff.

[21] See Emmanuel Joseph Sieyès, *What is the Third Estate?* (orig., 1789, New York: Praeger, 1964).

[22] See Jean-Jacques Rousseau, *The Social Contract* II (orig., 1762, New York: Hafner Publishing Co., 1947), 16–18.

emancipation of the Jews during the French Revolution: "Everything must be refused to the Jews as a nation and everything must be accorded to the Jews as individuals... they must be individual citizens... It would be repugnant to have groupings of non-citizens within the state, a nation within the nation."[23] In short, the two salient features of secularism in the context of the French Revolution were an attack against the political power and privileges of the dominant institutionalized organized majority religion combined with a call to every citizen to suppress the calls of his or her religious allegiance when called upon to fulfill the republican duty of self-government within the political sphere. Although the secularism in question differs from *laïcité* which originated in the nineteenth century,[24] it certainly prefigures the latter.

The American Revolution—which was above all a war of independence—also rejected the aristocratic ways and the dominant religion, which in this case was (and continues to be) the official state religion, of its English colonizer. Beyond that, however, the US Constitution set out a late eighteenth-century secularism that differs markedly from its contemporaneous French counterpart. American constitutional secularism is encapsulated in the First Amendment's "Religion" clauses, namely the "Establishment Clause" and the "Free Exercise Clause."[25] On the surface these two religion clauses may seem to call for a public sphere purged of religion combined with a private sphere constitutionally protected to allow for optimal religious flourishing. But when placed in their historical context and in light of the conflicting interpretations they have fostered throughout American constitutional history, the clauses in question project a rather different image of secularism. It has often been observed that the two clauses are in tension with one another, with the Establishment Clause calling for state disengagement from religion while at the same time the Free Exercise Clause requiring state involvement to provide meaningful sustenance to religious practice and expression.[26]

These tensions reflect an ambivalence concerning the optimal relationship between the state and religion which is traceable to America's colonial period when it became an immigration haven for minority, persecuted and dissident religions and religious movements. For example, in the seventeenth century the 13 American colonies saw significant immigration of Huguenots who fled from persecution in France[27] and of Puritans who as dissenters within the Church of England felt increasingly socially ostracized at home and therefore opted to resettle across the Ocean.[28] This pattern of immigration by religious minorities persecuted within their country of origin has continued throughout the history of the United States and has led to the following still ongoing conundrum: how to find an optimal balance between inclusion and exclusion of religion in the public sphere without fostering subjugation or subordination of some religions to others. At a minimum, exclusion should prevent the functional equivalent of a state religion which would recreate conditions similar to those that prompted large waves of immigrants to leave their country of origin. Conversely, given American society's steadfast commitment to

[23] Cited in Pierre Birnbaum, *Un Mythe Politique: "La République Juive"* (Paris: Fayard, 1988), 44–5 (our translation).

[24] See Birnbaum chapter below.

[25] The relevant language is: "Congress shall make no law respecting an establishment of religion, or prohibiting the free exercise thereof." US Const., Amend. I (1791).

[26] See e.g. Norman Redlich, John Attanasio, and Joel K. Goldstein, *Understanding Constitutional Law* (Newark, N.J.: LexisNexis, 2005), 510–29.

[27] See John Butler, *The Huguenots in America: A Refugee People in New World Society* (Cambridge, Mass.: Harvard University Press, 1983).

[28] See Sydney E. Ahlstrom, *A Religious History of the American People* (New Haven: Yale University Press, 1972), 121ff.

religion[29] —at least in theory in all its manifold manifestations, but largely in sustained opposition to the antireligious and the irreligious[30] —at a maximum, the public sphere should be inclusive of all that the various religions within the country share together. Ideally, therefore, consistent with this vision, American secularism should at once favor religion over irreligion and prohibit discrimination among religions.

As a matter of history and of constitutional jurisprudence, however, the American concept of secularism has been much more contested than its French counterpart. Although the ideal of non-discrimination among religions has remained a constant, its meaning and scope has fluctuated due to the changing and contested dynamic between inclusion and exclusion framed by the two religion clauses of the US Constitution. Thus, Jefferson's famous proclamation of the need for "a wall of separation" between Church and state has been variously interpreted as requiring a complete separation between state and religion[31] and as merely banning official state preference of one religion over others.[32] Underlying this divergence, were several factors that led to fluctuation of the scope of non-discrimination and to shifting attitudes concerning the ratio of benefits to detriments linked to greater or lesser state involvement or promotion of religion. In the earlier days of the American republic, the country regarded itself by and large as a Protestant one, and constitutional non-discrimination was understood by many as applicable to the various Protestant denominations within the polity, but not necessarily to other (minority) religions.[33] Although since then Catholicism and Judaism have been included within the effective non-discrimination purview, there still is a current debate among US Supreme Court Justices concerning including religions that do not revere a transcendent Supreme Being, thus potentially leaving out such religions as Buddhism and Hinduism.[34] Consistent with this, moreover, those who have advocated strict separation between the state and religion fall generally into three categories: agnostics or atheists whose freedom *from* religion may be trampled by a state endorsed religion;[35] minority religions which feel *de facto* discriminated against by falling outside the scope of non-discrimination or excluded from state endorsement or promotion of what the latter presents as a common denominator among all religions, but is in fact contrary to the precepts of the minority religions involved;[36] and, religions, whether belonging to the majority cluster that fully benefits from constitutional non-discrimination or within the minority, which are convinced that any state involvement, no matter how benign, is bound to result in state meddling which would inevitably lead to unacceptable compromising of sacred religious principles or practices.[37]

In sum, American secularism is by no means anti-religious or even irreligious as it boils down to state acceptance or even endorsement of what is perceived as shared in

[29] See Birnbaum chapter in this book. [30] See Birnbaum chapter in this book.

[31] See Leonard W. Levy, *The Establishment Clause: Religion and the First Amendment* (New York: Macmillan, 1986), 188.

[32] See Robert L. Cord, *Separation of Church and State: Historical Fact and Current Fiction* (New York: Lambeth Press, 1982), 213–15.

[33] See Ahlstrom, *A Religious History of the American People* 330ff.

[34] See *McCreary County v. ACLU of Kentucky* 545 U.S. 844 (2005) (Justice Scalia, dissenting).

[35] See e.g. the opinion of the court and Justice O'Connor's concurring opinion in *McCreary County* 545 U.S. 844.

[36] See e.g. *Lynch v. Donnelly* 465 U.S. 668 (1984), (Court majority depicts state display of the *crèche* as non-exclusionary notwithstanding that it symbolizes Jesus' divine nature which is rejected by Judaism and Islam).

[37] See e.g. *Testimony of J. Brent Walker, General Counsel and Assoc. Dir., Baptist Joint Committee on Public Affairs Before the Senate Committee on the Judiciary*, Federal Document Clearing House (25 Oct. 1995).

common by all protected religions combined with an ongoing contestation of the proper bounds of the dynamic between inclusion and exclusion. Thus, the inscription "In God We Trust" on official US currency,[38] or the recitation of the pledge of allegiance to "one nation under God" by public school children,[39] or official prayers characterized as generic at the opening of parliamentary sessions[40] are all arguably justifiable as falling within the common religious denominator shared by a vast majority of Americans.[41] At the same time, however, such state endorsements of religion remain contested as objectors charge that what purports to be inclusionary, such as what a majority regards as a generic prayer is in fact a Christian or a Judeo-Christian prayer, is in fact exclusionary as it effectively casts non-believers and members of other religions as outsiders.[42] Furthermore, a similar dynamic has predominated with respect to American secularism's constitutional mission to equally protect everyone's religious freedom. Here again, there has been an ongoing debate about the proper bounds of inclusion and exclusion. Most notoriously, the US Supreme Court has set a sharp divide between religious faith and acts or practices commanded by religion, in apparent accord with what could be understood as a Christian if not a downright Protestant concept. This is reflected in decisions rejecting claims to constitutional protection of acts commanded by religion[43] and has led to the assertion that the Religion Clauses jurisprudence has been modeled on a Protestant conception of religion.[44]

The preceding brief historical review of the broad outlines of the evolution of the concept of secularism from the Middle Ages until the Enlightenment highlights the latter as being distinctly Christian in nature. Moreover, this remains the case whether the secular is viewed as operating within a unified Christian religion; or to allow for peace and tolerance among Christian religions previously at war against one another; or else to preserve a Christian divide between the realm of the spirit and that of politics while purging the latter from perceived excessive intrusion by the Catholic Church as occurred during the French Revolution; or even to preserve the peace and promote coexistence among Christians and non-Christian religions pursuant to a juridical model built upon a Protestant postulation of a sharp divide between religious beliefs and religious practices or deeds. Secularism, however, does not seem equally suited to the needs of the other two major Western religions, Islam and Judaism. Indeed, these latter religions do not adhere to an internal division akin to the Christian distinction between the sacred and the secular, but instead embrace all encompassing approaches requiring

[38] See *Lynch v. Donnelly* 465 U.S. 668.

[39] *See Newtow v. The Congress, et al,* 292 F.3d. 597,609 (2009) ("[T]he words 'under God' [added to the Pledge of Allegiance in 1954] were intended to recognize a 'Supreme Being,' at a time when the Government was inveighing against atheistic Communism").

[40] See *Marsh v. Chambers* 463 U.S. 783 (1983) (Nebraska legislature prayer by state paid chaplain held constitutional).

[41] As the US Supreme Court jurisprudence on the Religion Clauses has been evolving and as Justices on the Court have generally been divided on many relevant issues, the actual justifications offered for constitutional acceptance of these state endorsements of religion have varied from religious common denominators ones to others based on the argument that these propositions or practices are so widely accepted within the country as to become part of its culture beyond any religious connotation. See the various opinions in the cases cited in the preceding three footnotes.

[42] See n. 34 above.

[43] See *Reynolds v. United States* 98 U.S. 145 (1878) (Mormons' religious duty to practice polygamy does not require a Free Exercise based exemption from state law making it a crime to be married to more than one woman) .

[44] See Marci Hamilton, "Religious Institutions, the No-Harm Doctrine, and the Public Good" (2004) *Brigham Young University Law Review* 1099.

that religious rule extend over (what in Western constitutional democracies is apportioned among) the private, the public, and the political spheres.[45]

To the extent that secularism may be inherently biased against non-Christian religions, constitutional secularism would seem vulnerable and at odds with the Enlightenment ideal of equal liberty prior to, and independently from, deprivatization or repoliticization of religion. As a matter of fact, once secularism extends beyond the bounds of a single unified religion—as occurred after the onset of the sixteenth-century European wars of religion—three major problems arise and each of them poses a serious threat to the legitimacy of constitutional secularism. The first of these is the already mentioned one regarding bias against non-Christian religions. Thus, for example, if Christian religions predominantly valorize faith and worship whereas for Islam and Judaism deeds such as male circumcision rank among the most sacred of religious obligations, then a secularism that accords priority to beliefs over deeds would inherently disadvantage the non-Christian religions involved—a situation bound to be aggravated if the latter religions happen to be minority ones within the relevant polity.[46] The second problem, in turn, is the one posed by secularism to Christianity itself as it evolves from a purely internal concept within a unified Western Christian religion all the way to present day French *laïcité* which has been characterized by many as being downright hostile to all religions, including the Christian ones.[47] More generally, secularism not only evolves away from Christianity but it also, in the course of its historical journey, carves out an ideology of its own that may turn irreligious or anti-religious and that may bestow an aura of legitimacy on agnosticism and atheism. Therefore, if one adds up the two problems thus far discussed, namely that of a Christian bias combined with legitimation of anti-religious and hence anti-Christian perspectives, then everyone who lives in a religiously or ideologically pluralistic polity where constitutional secularism is at work would seem justified in being frustrated by the institutional setting in which she must operate. Finally, the third major problem is that concerning the viability of constitutionalism in countries that are non-Christian and that may hence not be suited for any secularism deriving from Christianity. This last problem arises in Israel where Judaism is the majority religion and in Muslim countries where Islam is inscribed in the constitution, such as in the case of the constitution of Egypt adopted in 2012 after the electoral victory of the Muslim Brotherhood Party in the aftermath of the country's Arab Spring experience.[48] This last problem, raises, moreover, two key questions: Can there be a secularism fit for Judaism or Islam that is sufficiently purged of its Christian features? Or, if the answer to this last question is in the negative, can a polity comply with the basic precepts of modern constitutionalism while doing away with secularism? The first of these questions is equally pertinent in the context of Islam or Judaism as minority religions as in that of either

[45] See E. Gregory Wallace, "Justifying Religious Freedom: the Western Tradition" (2009) 114 *Penn State Law Review* 485; Benjamin Blech, *Understanding Judaism: The Basics of Deed and Creed* (Northvale, N.J.: J. Aronson, 1992).

[46] Minority religions are doubly vulnerable to the extent that they deviate from mainstream culture and that they are permanently subject to being disadvantaged (unless specifically constitutionally protected) through the democratic lawmaking process. That said, a minority religion may nevertheless be integrated within the mainstream over time by becoming more open to the polity's culture and by in turn making inroads into that culture in the course of a two-way dynamic. Thus, Jews who figured as the "other" in nineteenth-century Europe have now joined mainstream religions and been replaced as the "other" by Muslims. See Maleiha Malik, Comment, "Muslims Are Now Getting the Same Treatment Jews Had a Century Ago," *The Guardian* (2 Feb. 2007), 35.

[47] See Michel Rosenfeld, *Law, Justice, Democracy and the Clash of Cultures* (Cambridge: Cambridge University Press, 2011), 156–7.

[48] See Abu Odeh chapter below.

of these religions figuring as the majority or the state religion. On the other hand, the second question at stake seems most pressing in cases where religions such as Islam and Judaism figure as the majority or state religion.

In order to be in a better position to assess these problems both generally and in connection with the repoliticization of religion, it is useful to briefly canvass the principal existing models of constitutional regulation of the relationship between religion and the state and to compare some of the key features that they have respectively generated.

III. The Constitutional Models for Regulation of the Relationship Between the State and Religion

Under current constitutional practice, there are essentially five different models for managing the relationship between the state and religion. These are (1) the militant secularist model bent on keeping religion completely out of the public sphere (e.g. French and Turkish *laïcité*); (2) the agnostic secularist model, which seeks to maintain a neutral stance among religions but does not shy away from favoring religion over atheism and other non-religious perspectives (e.g. this is close to current American constitutional jurisprudence briefly mentioned above); (3) the confessional secular model, which incorporates elements of the polity's mainstream majority religion, primarily for identitarian purposes, and projects them as part of the polity's constitutional secularism rather than as inextricably linked to the country's main religion (e.g. Italy's or Bavaria's adoption of the crucifix as a secular symbol of national identity); (4) the official religion with institutionalized tolerance for minority religions model (e.g. the United Kingdom, Scandinavian countries, Greece); and (5) the *millet*-based model in which high priority is given to collective self-government by each religious community within the polity (e.g. Israel).

There are significant variants in relation to each of these models. For example, although both fall within model 1, French *laïcité* differs from its Turkish counterpart in that the former was adopted in a social and political setting that was already significantly secularized,[49] whereas the latter was imposed to trigger a shift toward modernism and secularism in a polity where religion was overwhelmingly predominant.[50] As a consequence, as evinced by two countries' bans on the Islamic headscarves, French *laïcité* is mainly directed against minority religions whereas Turkish *laïcité* is squarely turned against the country's dominant majority religion.[51] Moreover, as already pointed out, there is disagreement within the United States where model 2 is in operation whether secularism requires a full "wall of separation" between state and religion, or whether the state can prefer religion over non-religion so long as it does not single out any religion for preferential treatment. There can also be significant variants within model 3, the confessional secular model, depending, among other things, on whether the polity at stake has one dominant religion, as is the case in Italy, or whether it has more than one traditionally implanted religion, as is the case in Germany where Catholicism is predominant in some regions and Protestantism in others. In the context of a single dominant religion, model 3 seems in substance quite close to model 4, which is itself open to a wide range of variants. Indeed, some established religions, such as the Church of England, seem to

[49] See chapter by Michel Troper in this book.

[50] See Murat Borovali, "Islamic Headscarves and Slippery Slopes" (2009) 30 *Cardozo Law Review* 2593.

[51] See Susanna Mancini, "The Power of Symbols and Symbols as Power: Secularism and Religion as Guarantors of Cultural Convergence" (2009) 30 *Cardozo Law Review* 2629.

have little more than a ceremonial presence in the public sphere and may impinge on secularism less than some versions of the separatist approach under model 2.[52] In other cases, such as that of Greece, in contrast, the established religion can have a much more dominant role, tending to relegate minority religions close to the status of being merely tolerated. Finally, there are also many conceivable variants in connection with model 5. For instance, currently in Israel, recognized religious communities have a monopoly over marriage and divorce with respect to those whom they deem to be members of their community.[53] One could conceive, and there is much discussion about this in Israel,[54] of a *millet* system in which a secular civil libertarian alternative is available for those who wish to opt out from the religious community to which they belong.

Even from this cursory account, it becomes quite obvious that all five models discussed are beset by serious shortcomings. Not only do all these models completely fail to equally accommodate all ideologies within the relevant polity, but they also variously frustrate the aims of the religious or of the non-religious or of minority religions or, in some cases, the aims of all three. Model 1 purports to be neutral toward religion, but militant brands of *laïcité* often seem downright hostile to religion. Model 2 may well put the non-religious at a disadvantage, and may also, in spite of its professed neutrality *among* religions, privilege mainstream religion against its minority counterparts. Model 3 seems particularly problematic as confessional secularism is likely to be found wanting by most, if not all, religions within the polity and by all those who are genuinely committed toward secularism. Indeed, "confessionalized" secularism is likely to offend both the very religious who would consider their deeply held religious convictions trivialized, and the committed secularists who would feel their position being undermined through saturation of the public space with religious symbols and practices relabeled as secular.[55] In addition, Model 3 and Model 4 are bound to disfavor minority religions, thus altogether foreclosing the equal treatment all religions within the polity. Finally, Model 5, based on the *millet* system, not only is prone to disadvantaging secularism as already mentioned, but also to unduly privileging the group over the individual as well as recognized religions and certain denominations within the latter (e.g. in Israel, Orthodox Judaism to the exclusion of Conservative or Reform Judaism).

IV. Organization of the Book: Diagnoses, Critiques, and Prescriptions

The authors whose contributions are included in this volume represent a number of different disciplines including law, anthropology, history, philosophy, and political theory. These authors variously tackle a number of issues deriving from the most salient contemporary controversies regarding the relationship between the state and religion within the bounds of constitutional democracy. Taken together the contributions below provide accounts of, and explanations for, present predicaments; critiques of contemporary institutional, political and cultural arrangements, justifications and practices; and suggestions with a view to overcoming or circumventing several of the seemingly intractable or insurmountable current controversies and deadlocks. Moreover, the several contributions that follow tackle the subjects that they examine respectively from a number of

[52] See Kent Greenawalt, "Secularism, Religion, and Liberal Democracy in the United States" (2009) 30 *Cardozo Law Review* 2383, 2386–7.

[53] See Statman and Sapir chapter in this book.

[54] See Statman and Sapir chapter in this book.

[55] See Mancini, *The Power of Symbols* 2634–5.

different perspectives, some secular, others from within religion, including, in particular, from within Christianity, Islam, and Judaism.

The book is divided into five parts. Part I provides theoretical perspectives on the present day conflicts between secularism and religion. Part II focuses on the relationship between religion, secularism, and the public sphere. Part III examines the nexus between religion, secularism, and women's equality. Part IV concentrates on religious perspectives on constraints on, and accommodations of, religion within the precincts of the liberal state. Finally, Part V zeroes in on conflicts between religion and secularism in specific contexts, namely education and freedom of speech.

A. Theoretical perspectives on the conflicts between secularism and religion

The challenges posed to the Enlightenment approach to the relationship between secularism, religion, and the state are manifold and in several key respects elusive. These challenges are triggered by the repoliticization of religion noted above and by a number of other factors. The latter range widely, from mass migration of adherents of religions that seemingly differ markedly from those traditionally accommodated within the relevant secular polity to an ever greater push for society wide gender based and sexual orientation based equality. In addition, postmodern ways of thinking based on what Max Weber coined the "disenchantment of reason"[56] have undermined trust in the epistemic soundness of the divide between Faith and Reason crucial to the Enlightenment and to the modern conceptual and institutional apparatus to which it has given rise. Do these developments require recasting the relationship between constitutional secularism and religion? Updating it? Abandoning it? And if the latter question is answered in the affirmative, replacing the relationship in question or superseding it?

The five contributions comprised in this part of the book address a number of the most salient theoretical issues relating to the questions referred to above. These are dealt with respectively from the standpoint of a legal scholar who has been a constitutional judge in Germany, Dieter Grimm; from that of a political theorist, Nadia Urbinati, who places the positions of the two most prominent political philosophers of the second half of the twentieth century on the relation between religion and the secular liberal state, namely John Rawls and Jürgen Habermas, in the context of a particular twenty-first century constitutional democracy; from that of a legal scholar, Karlheinz Ladeur, who tackles simultaneously the theoretical challenges posed by postmodernism and by incorporation of a large number of immigrants who are adherents to a religion that is seemingly at serious odds with the already integrated religions and culture of the country of immigration; from that of a sitting transnational human rights judge and comparative constitutionalism scholar, Andras Sajo, who confronts the theoretical challenges posed by a search for the discovery or preservation of common judicial standards suited to harmonization of several dozens of national jurisprudences operating under different versions of the five constitutional models for dealing with the relation between the state and religion discussed above; and from that of a comparative constitutionalism scholar, Michel Rosenfeld, who explores the theoretical challenges and implications of depriving secularism of all the institutional advantages it can garner in the liberal state and

[56] See George E. McCarthy, *Dreams in Exile: Rediscovering Science and Ethics in Nineteenth-Century Social Theory* (Albany: SUNY Press, 2009), ch. 4; H.H. Gerth and C.W. Mills (eds), *From Max Weber: Essays in Sociology* (New York: Oxford University Press, 1946), 129–56, 267–301.

reintroducing it within a post-secular constitutional order as one conception of the good that competes against others, including those carved out by various religions.

B. Religion, secularism, and the public square

As both the conceptual and spatial boundaries between secularism and religion erected by liberal theory have been subjected to persistent and relentless attack, several key questions arise concerning what would be acceptable or not, desirable or not, uses of the public square in light of the current controversies and divisions among secularism and religion as well as among proponents of different religions. Susanna Mancini examines legal and political responses to the growing presence of Islam in Europe through the lens of Carl Schmitt's thought. She points out how such responses draw on an essentialist and idealized notion of the people, and aim at artificially reinforcing the cultural and religious homogeneous character of the European public sphere, thus pursuing an "identitarian" model of democracy. Pierre Birenbaum offers a historical and sociological perspective on the role of Jews in building a secular public sphere in France and in the United States. He focuses on the different strategies used by French and American Jews to dismantle the trappings of Christian dominance and concludes that, in spite of the different models for managing Church/State relations in these two countries, both American and French Jews were able to promote a secular conception of the public realm, without thereby abandoning their cultural and religious specificities. Michel Troper argues that from the standpoint of constitutional logic that the fact that Egypt is ruled by the *Sharia*, and France is governed by the principles of freedom of religion and religious neutrality of the state, does not affect in either case the power of state over religion. Whether a state imposes a religious rule or a secular one, it does so through its own constitution and laws which means that state authorities always have the last word. Lama Abu Odeh focuses on the conflict among various political actors concerning the proper constitutional role of religion in Egypt after the 2011 revolution. On the one hand, the non-Islamist camp has promoted an interpretation of "*Sharia*" aimed at removing it from the interpretive strictures of religious authorities in order to place it in official hands with a more secular and universalist bent. On the other hand, the post-revolutionary project of the Islamists has been premised on reversing the prior displacement of Islamic law in order to return it to its "proper" place as the official law of the land. Ran Hirschl and Ayelet Shachar analyze the responses to two set of claims for religious accommodation in Canada and South Africa: those claims of religion or culture that can reasonably be construed as accepting the ultimate authority and supremacy of the constitutional order and the altogether different claims to insulation from the purview of the state's constitutional ordering in order to allow for full adherence to alternative, sacred sources of authority and identity. Hirschl and Shachar conclude that notwithstanding their constitutional commitment to multiculturalism, neither Canada nor South Africa are ready to accept claims perceived as challenge to the superiority of the constitutional order.

C. Religion, secularism and women's equality

One of the most important and most troubling areas of confrontation between secularism and religion concerns the widely perceived role and impact of religion in opposing, slowing down, reversing, or circumventing the achievement of full equality for women. The liberal feminist discourse reasons in terms of equality, individual freedom, and oppression. It views traditional religious cultures as suffused with practices and ideologies concerning gender that endorse and facilitate the control of men over women.[57] The disparities of power between the sexes within traditional religions determine that male members are those who are in a position to determine and articulate the group's beliefs, practices, and interests. This limits the possibility of women belonging to such cultures to live with human dignity equal to that of men, and to live as freely chosen lives as they can. Thus, for example, certain types of traditional Muslim clothing represent unjust in-group power dynamics.[58]

In the past two decades, liberal feminism arguments have been the target of much postmodern, postcolonial and, broadly speaking, "multicultural" criticism. Roughly, liberal feminism has been accused of being culturally imperialistic,[59] of viewing women's equality as a singularly Western value,[60] of reenacting the errors of orientalist thoughts,[61] of obscuring the forces that actually shape culture, and denying that women have agency within patriarchy;[62] of not taking into account that all cultures are differently patriarchal, as well as characterized by resistance to patriarchy.[63] Thus, liberal feminism does not do justice to the heterogeneity of minority women, ignoring, for example, the rich theological work being done by female scholars. It should also be pointed out that, politically, liberal feminism is hardly a successful strategy in addressing "women's issues" in Islam, due to the taint, imparted to it by colonizers, of having served as an instrument of domination, which rendered it "suspect in Arab eyes,"[64] and produces the automatic placement of feminists on the uncomfortable side of the "West."

To be sure, there are barriers to women's equality erected by religion, or, more precisely, by traditional interpretation of religious law, such as the exclusion of women from the clergy. Other apparent religion-based impediments to women's equality, in contrast, are much more difficult to link directly or exclusively to religion. Moreover, this may be due either because what may appear as a religiously induced inequality between the sexes to a proponent of liberal secularism need not be understood as such by women within the relevant religious tradition. Or the difficulty in question may be traceable to a cause or set of circumstances broadly shared between religions and secular liberalism. Imagine, for example, that in spite of the patriarchic grounding of a religious tradition, such as Orthodox Judaism, a woman within that tradition—who happens to be familiar with the role of women in a secular liberal society as she works side by side with many such women—proclaims that her way of life promotes greater mutual respect and equality between the sexes than does secular liberalism. Should such claim be rejected out of hand

[57] Susan Moller Okin, "Is Muliculturalism Bad for Women?," *Boston Review* (October–November 1997).

[58] See e.g. the letter in the *Elle* magazine in December 2003, signed by 60 prominent French women (intellectuals, actresses, academics, and politicians), including the former Minister for Women's Rights Yvette Roudy, in support of a ban on the veil. The letter stated that "[t]o accept the Islamic veil at school and in the public administration is to legitimize a visible symbol of the submission of women in the places where the state must be the guarantor of strict equality between the sexes." "Le magazine Elle lance un appel contre le voile," *Elle* (5 Dec. 2003).

[59] Iris Marion Young, *Justice and the Politics of Difference* (Princeton, N.J.: Princeton University Press, 1990).

[60] Azizah Y. Al-Hibri, "Is Western Patriarchal Feminism Good for Third World/Minority Women? (A response to Susan Okin's 'Is Multiculturalism Bad for Women?')," *Boston Review* (October–November 1997).

[61] Mayda Yegenoglou, *Colonial Fantasies: Towards a Feminist Reading of Orientalism* (Cambridge: Cambridge University Press, 1998).

[62] Leti Volpp, "Feminism versus Multiculturalism" (2001) 101 *Columbia Law Review* 1181.

[63] Volpp, "Feminism versus Multiculturalism."

[64] Leyla Ahmed, *Women and Gender in Islam: Historical Roots of a Modern Debate* (New Haven: Yale University Press, 1992), 153, 155; Al-Hibri, "Is Western Patriarchal Feminism Good for Third World/ Minority Women?"

because there appears to be greater differentiation of gender specific roles within the religious way of life at stake than within its liberal counterpart? Or, should an informed and heartfelt claim of spiritual equality between the sexes from within a religious tradition be taken seriously and be accorded *prima facie* plausibility? On the other hand, what is often portrayed as emblematic of the subordination of women within religion, such as traditional Muslim clothing, may end up being the semantic equivalent of secular insistence in "unveiled" attire for women: in both cases, women's bodies are constructed as a "natural limitation of a woman's life."[65]

The three chapters that make up Part III of the book account for the difficulty, complexity, diversity, and controversy that characterize the interplay between religion and women's equality in the context of constitutional secularism. The first two chapters deal with the controversies surrounding the Islamic veil from very different perspectives. Patrick Weil is a legal scholar who was a member of the Stasi Commission that recommended what would become France's 2004's law banning the wearing of the Islamic veil in French public schools. Weil offers a subtle and spirited defense of this law which is firmly steeped in French republicanism, but he also accounts for his opposition to France's 2010 law forbidding wearing the full-face veil in public places. The second chapter on "the veil" is by John Borneman, an anthropologist who has lectured extensively in Europe and the Middle East. Borneman stresses that the veil is worn not only by Muslims, but also by Christian nuns and certain Orthodox Jewish women, and that its meaning differs from one religious tradition to another and from one culture to the next. Borneman underscores that the veil is imposed in some settings, permitted in others, and banned in yet others, and that what it expresses about women and what women express by choosing to wear it differ greatly throughout the various regions where its presence or absence are noteworthy. The third chapter, on the other hand, by Daphne Barak-Erez, an Israeli Supreme Court Justice and legal scholar, focuses on women's reproductive rights—abortion and assisted procreation—in Israel, a state that is meant at once to be Jewish and democratic. As Barak-Erez amply illustrates the aim to satisfy at once women's equality concerns and Jewish precepts derived from religion leads to a wealth of tensions and complexities. At times, the patriarchal nature of Judaism leads to prescriptions and constraints that seem clearly contrary to the values and aims of feminism, but at other times, religion and feminism appear as more aligned. Moreover, religion in the setting canvassed by the chapter relates in complex ways to politics: on certain occasions, religion drives politics, but on others, politics invokes religion for its own purposes. In short, attempts to reconcile religion and constitutional secularism in Israel lead to a complex and dynamic dialectic that oscillates between mutual accommodation and seemingly irresoluble confrontation.

4. Religious perspectives and the liberal state

On the surface, religion looms primarily as an obstacle to those committed to the pursuit of secularism just as, conversely, state constitutional embrace of secularism often frustrates the aims and goals of those who wish to fulfill the prescriptions of their chosen religion. Thus, secular Jews in Israel may well be frustrated by the shutdown of public

[65] Marnia Lazreg, *Questioning the Veil: Open Letters to Muslim Women* (Princeton: Princeton University Press, 2009), 122. Also see Susanna Mancini, "Patriarchy as the Exclusive Domain of the Other: The Veil Controversy, False Projection and Cultural Racism" (2012) 10(2) *International Journal of Constitutional Law* 411–28, analyzing the misuse of feminist rhetoric in anti-veil measures.

transportation on the Sabbath consistent with the dictates of Orthodox Judaism[66] whereas practicing Jews and Muslims may feel threatened by secular initiatives to ban ritual male circumcision to the extent that they do not involve the informed consent of the infant or boy concerned.[67] Upon closer examination, however, the interrelationship between secularism and religion seems bound to emerge as much more complex and nuanced than familiar instances of confrontation would suggest. There are many cases in which secular and religious aims converge such as, for example, when the Catholic Bishops and secular political progressives in the United States criticized the harshness of the unrestrained capitalist policies promoted by the Reagan Administration in the 1980's.[68] There are also circumstances in which freedom *of* religion may depend on the deployment of constitutional secularism as where a religion fears being co-opted by the state that purports to officially endorse or promote it or as a minority religion feels threatened by pervasive spread of the polity's majority religion.[69]

Secular values may also be promoted, at least in part, from within religion, that is, from the internal perspective institutionalized by a particular religion. Judaism, for instance, provides for a comprehensive legal code, the *Halakha*, for regulation of the life of its adherents, but it nonetheless commands obedience by Jews in the Diaspora to the laws of the land in which they reside provided the latter adhere to the Noahide law—i.e. the biblical commandments addressed to Jews and non-Jews alike.[70] Furthermore, whereas tolerance is primarily a secular concept or one designed to mediate among religions, it also happens in some cases to arise from within religion.[71] More generally, secularism and religions can overlap to significant extents, they can coincide on some points and they can foster parallel paths that can promote various degrees of harmony or coexistence. When all points of convergence and divergence between secularism and religion and among the various religions present within a polity are added up, both the possible scope of peaceful coexistence and the vulnerabilities to which it is exposed are likely to become more apparent.

The three chapters included in Part IV of this book all address the complex interrelationship between secularism and religion and they do so respectively from the standpoint of Christianity, Judaism, and Islam. The three chapters complement one another, moreover, in as much as the one on Christianity concentrates on the latter's current strategy to have an "external" impact on the world beyond Christianity; the one on Judaism is focused on "internal" concerns relating to the imposition of Judaism on secular Jews in Israel; and the one on Islam provides a perspective of an "outsider" religion in polities where other religions or secularism predominate. Gustavo Zagrebelsky provides an account of Catholicism's current effort, based on the views of Pope Benedict XVI and moving

[66] See e.g. Gavriel Brown, "Shabbat: A Time of Rest or Unrest?," *Kol Hamevaser* (23 Nov. 2011), available at <http://www.kolhamevaser.com/2011/11/shabbat-a-time-of-rest-or-unrest/>.

[67] Blake Sobczak, "Germany Circumcision Ban: Israeli Parliament Slams Decision by Cologne Court," *The Huffington Post* (9 July 2012), available at <http://www.huffingtonpost.com/2012/07/09/germany-circumcision-ban-_n_1659423.html>.

[68] See Casanova, *Public Religions in the Modern World* 202–203.

[69] For example, while the Egyptian government during the Muslim Brotherhood presidency of Mohamed Morsi increased the protections accorded to Islam, it did little to stem religious violence against the country's Christians. See Steven Lee Myers, "State Dept. Report Says Countries Have Repressed Religious Freedom with Laws," *The New York Times* (21 May 2013), A9.

[70] See Suzanne L. Stone, "Sinaitic and Noahide Law: Legal Pluralism in Jewish Law" (1991) 12 *Cardozo Law Review* 1157.

[71] See Suzanne L. Stone, "Tolerance and Pluralism in the Jewish Tradition," in Rusmir Mahmutćehajić (ed.), *Religious Perspectives on Tolerance* (Forum Bosnia, 2001) (discussing the concept of tolerance as molded from within the Jewish religious tradition).

away from the views that emerged from the 1965 Vatican II Council, to blur the divide between Faith and Reason and to recast the universal applicability of Catholicism and its grounding in reason to all societies secular and not, on all moral, communal, and political issues. Gideon Sapir and Daniel Statman explore the impact of Israel's religious marriage law on secular Jews within the country. Many of the latter may find it objectionable that only religious marriage is available for any Jew wishing to marry in Israel. But beyond the very *thought* of a religious marriage being offensive, what, if anything, about Jewish religious marriage could as a matter of substance be contrary to what secular marriage imposes or offensive to one who readily accepts the institution of secular marriage? Finally, Andrew March provides an account of the various views held by Islamic clerics in the Diaspora concerning the permissibility under Islam for Muslims who are members of a minority religion to collaborate with the non-Muslim state authorities or the largely non-Muslim civil society. Is it better to withhold cooperation as much as possible? Or is it preferable to restrict contact, on the one hand, to adherents to other Abrahamic religions or, on the other hand, to those who are secular on the grounds that the latter are not worshippers of false religion?

E. The confrontation between secularism and religion in specific contexts: education and free speech

A large portion of the constitutional disputes pitting the secular state against proponents of particular religions arise in the context of education. Whether the subject is the wearing of the Islamic veil by teachers or pupils in public schools, or the teaching of evolution theory or of creationism in science classes offered in state schools, or else the state mandated display of the crucifix in state school classrooms, education is a particularly vivid recurring locus of contention. Education is especially important to the contemporary secular state, the nation and civil society, on the one hand, and to religion, on the other. What ought to be included or excluded from the curriculum of secular state schools? Should there be any limitations or constraints on private religious education at the primary or secondary level? Does the answer to these questions depend on which or how many religions are involved in a particular setting?

Also thorny and exceptionally contentious are the conflicts that pit freedom of religion rights against other fundamental constitutional rights, such as free speech or equality rights. Some of the principal tensions and conflicts that emerge in the context of the relation between freedom of religion and equality rights are broached in the chapters in Part III that focus on religion and its impact on women's equality. Free speech rights are similarly frequently at odds with the kinds of rights or protections sought under the rubric of freedom of religion. This conflict arises most obviously in the context of blasphemy laws which after a period of decline are currently proliferating.[72] Increasingly, moreover, religions have embraced the language of dignity, "hate speech" and discrimination against minorities in a seemingly mounting struggle to silence their critics and detractors. Is it possible to draw lines between a minority religion and the ethnic, national, or linguistic group formed by the majority of its adherents in a country of immigration? Does a muscled attack on the truth of a given religion necessarily compromise the dignity or integrity of those who are deeply committed to it and to its precepts?

The two chapters included in this last part of the book are by constitutional scholars. Gila Stopler tackles Israel's handling of education in schools run by the Ultra-Orthodox

[72] See Myers, "State Dept. Report Says Countries have Repressed Religious Freedom with Laws" A9.

Jewish (*"Haredi"*) community. She provides a critical comparison between the Israeli approach to religious education and the regulation of such education in liberal democracies as well as in democracies with a "thickly" established religion, such as Malaysia which is an Islamic federation. Robert Post, on the other hand, addresses the seeming conflict between freedom of speech rights and freedom of religion rights or rights closely associated with the latter in the context of the controversy that surrounded the "Danish Cartoons" which caused uproar throughout the Muslim world as a consequence of their irreverent and demeaning portrayal of the Prophet Muhammad.

PART I

THEORETICAL PERSPECTIVES ON THE CONFLICTS BETWEEN SECULARISM AND RELIGION

1

Conflicts Between General Laws and Religious Norms

*Dieter Grimm**

I. Freedom of Religion in the Secular Constitutional State

A. The return of religion

For quite some time, freedom of religion was not among the most controversial fundamental rights, at least not in Germany or other European countries. The controversies between the Christian denominations faded away, partly because an increasingly secular society cared less and less about them, and partly because the growing secularization of society prompted the Christian churches to move closer to each other and to emphasize their commonalities instead of insisting on the differences. In addition, the state, which is the addressee of fundamental rights, rarely gave religious communities cause to worry about their freedom. The churches, in turn, had made their peace with the secular state and were even prepared to accept it as part of God's world plan.

This state of affairs was reflected in constitutional law and jurisprudence. With very few exceptions, the great social and political controversies that reached the German Constitutional Court did not emerge from the field of religion. There were some cases concerning education that drew a lot of interest: school prayer is an example, and there was the famous case about the crucifixes in classrooms of Bavarian elementary schools.[1] But it seems significant that the largest number of cases concerning freedom of religion dealt with the monetary aspect of this right, the church tax, which members of the Christian churches have to pay in Germany and which the state collects together with the income tax.

However, this situation has changed since the late 1980's. With the disappearance of the East–West divide, which had pushed all other conflicts into the background, religion and religious communities reappeared on the public scene and began to insist more vigorously on respect for their beliefs and on living according to the commandments of their creed. As has often been observed, a process of re-politicization of religion is taking place that goes along with a corresponding process of de-secularization of society. Religious issues play an increasing role in the public debate.[2]

* Professor of Law, Humboldt University Berlin; former Justice, Federal Constitutional Court of Germany.

[1] See BVerfGE 52, 223 (1979)—School Prayer; BVerfGE 93, 1 (1995)—(Crucifix). Excerpts of the cases in English in Donald P. Kommers and Russell A. Miller (eds), *The Constitutional Jurisprudence of the Federal Republic of Germany* (Durham, N.C.: Duke University Press, 3d edn, 2012), 567 and 577. For a general overview over the jurisprudence in matters of religious freedom and church and state relations see 538 *et seq.*

[2] See Pippa Norris and Ronald Inglehart, *Sacred and Secular: Religion and Politics Worldwide* (Cambridge: Cambridge University Press, 2nd edn, 2011); Peter Berger, Grace Davie, and Effie Fokas, *Religious America, Secular Europe?: A Theme and Variations* (Aldershot, England; Burlington, VT: Ashgate, 2008).

This development does not leave the law unaffected. European societies face a growing number of conflicts with a religious background. The courts, including the German Constitutional Court, are increasingly concerned with claims based on freedom of religion. Yet this is not a revival of the old inner-Christian controversies, nor is the reason a new hostility of the state *vis-à-vis* religion or a new identification with a single denomination as was the tradition in many European countries. Rather, the conflicts have their source in the growing multiculturalism of European societies, caused by the immigration of members of non-Christian beliefs.

Quite often, these are beliefs that, like the Christian denominations, claim possession of a divine and therefore absolute truth, but, unlike the Christian denominations, have not undergone the process of historicization and contextualization of God's revelation that permits the Christian churches to adopt a more distant attitude *vis-à-vis* sacred texts and the commandments following from them. Moreover, some religious communities do not distinguish between the error and the erring person, such that it is difficult for them to bridge the incompatibility of religious dogmas by a spirit of tolerance *vis-à-vis* believers of a different faith. Finally, the immigrants often are not accustomed to the secular state, a pluralistic society, and a law independent from religion.[3]

All this is particularly true for the Islamic religion, albeit not for Islam altogether and certainly not only for Islam. But for a number of reasons the Islamic religion is at the center of the controversies in Europe. The most obvious reason is, of course, that here the vast majority of immigrants are Muslims. For many of them, the confrontation with Western norms and life styles and the ensuing experience of the contingency of one's own beliefs and ways of life is deeply disturbing. In addition, many Islamic societies not only remain unaffected by Western modernization, but rather reject it explicitly, and draw the justification for this attitude from their religious beliefs. They are accustomed to a state that proclaims itself as an Islamic state, meaning that no clear distinction is made between religion, politics, and law.

As a consequence, new lines of conflicts appear. General laws that do not have religious implications in Western countries or reflect the Christian tradition of the Western world enter into conflict with the religious norms of the immigrants. The German society, like some other societies in Europe, has not yet found a consensus as to how to respond to this challenge. It is torn between the postulate of assimilation on the one hand and an unconditioned acceptance of otherness on the other hand, whereas the immigrants often react by insolating themselves within their host societies. There are also some who prefer to fight the Western way of life and do not always rule out the use of force.

One should not forget, however, that for Western countries, formed by Christianity, this is an encounter with their own history. For many centuries, Christian denominations confronted heretics and pagans with a similar attitude. The history of these countries is full of crusades, inquisitions, ordeals, censorship, etc. It took a long time until a peaceful coexistence of the Christian denominations became a normality, before Christians and non-Christians enjoyed equal rights, and before a pluralism of ideas, religious as well as political, was regarded as legitimate. However, in order to understand the present situation, one has to realize that this historical development, which is interpreted as progress in the West, often appears as relativism or decadence to the immigrants. It is this difference that gives the current conflict its particular severity.

[3] See e.g. Rainer Grote and Tilmann J. Röder (eds), *Constitutionalism in Islamic Countries: Between Upheaval and Continuity* (Oxford: Oxford University Press, 2012); Abdullahi Ahmed An-Naim, *Islam and the Secular State: Negotiating the Future of Shari'a* (Cambridge, MA: Cambridge University Press, 2008).

B. The secular constitutional state

This leads to the question of how the West succeeded in overcoming the inter-Christian conflicts. The answer is, in short, by establishing the secular constitutional state.[4] Its emergence is part of a long process whose beginnings date back to the Middle Ages. The decisive turn occurred, however, in the wake of the Reformation of the sixteenth century. Far from being a spiritual event only, it destroyed the religious foundation of the existing social and political order—not because the relevance of God's revelation for the worldly order and for individual behavior was now questioned, but because the content of the revelation and of God's will was no longer uncontested. The immediate consequences of the dispute about the truth were the devastating religious wars of the sixteenth and seventeenth centuries.

In this situation, the restoration of internal peace became the most important political task of the time. The solution was the secular constitutional state. This is not to say that the three elements of the notion of a "secular constitutional state" came about simultaneously. Neither were they necessarily linked to each other. But only together did they form the achievement that enabled the peaceful coexistence of persons of different beliefs in one polity and the recognition of the diversity as legitimate. All in all, it was a protracted process, full of deviations and setbacks, producing different solutions from country to country. All this cannot be described here. Suffice it to describe the product on a rather high level of abstraction, leaving aside the many regional and national differences.

(1) The *state*—By "state" we understand a political entity in which the various prerogatives that had been dispersed in medieval times among many independent bearers and that did not refer to a territory, but to persons, were united in one hand (historically in that of the prince) and condensed into the public power in the singular to which all inhabitants of a territory were subjected. In order to fulfill his pacifying function, the bearer of this unprecedented public power claimed the right to make law regardless of divine revelation and to enforce it against everybody, a right that presupposed the monopoly of legitimate force, the consequence of which was the privatization of civil society. In short, an autonomous political system emerged.

(2) The *secular* state—The secular state is the state that dissolves its bonds with religion and claims independence from religious truths. This state no longer derives its legitimacy from God, but instead bases its power on worldly grounds. It does not serve a divine destination and does not feel responsible for the eternal salvation of its subjects. Rather, it pursues a common good of a worldly nature whose core consists in the security and welfare of its inhabitants. This does not mean that religious truths lose their right to exist, but they are privatized. They become a matter for the individual and the associations that the individual chooses to join. They are regarded as compatible with the secular state as long as they do not claim absolute validity for society as a whole and stay within the framework of the public order.

(3) The secular *constitutional* state—The secular constitutional state, finally, is the state that derives its legitimacy from a consent of the governed. In short, it is the democratic state, in which a paramount law regulates the establishment and exercise of political power. Political power is regarded as a mandate, limited in time and scope, the bearers

[4] Cf. e.g. Charles Taylor, *A Secular Age* (Cambridge, MA: Belknap Press, 2007); José Casanova, *Public Religions in the Modern World* (Chicago: University of Chicago Press, 1994); Ernst-Wolfgang Böckenförde, "Die Entstehung des Staates als Vorgang der Säkularisation," in *Recht, Staat, Freiheit: Studien zur Rechtsphilosophie, Staatstheorie und Verfassungsgeschichte* (Frankfurt: Suhrkamp, 1991), 92.

of which are accountable to the people for the way they use their power. Moreover, it is the state in which the legal order is determined in a discursive public process, subject to change, and in which participation of the citizens in the formation of the collective will is guaranteed, as well as is their individual liberty and equality *vis-à-vis* government.

One of these liberties is freedom of religion, yet, not understood as freedom of one single religion with the exclusion of others. For in this case, it would be a privilege instead of equal freedom for all religious beliefs. Freedom of religion is an essential part of the constitutional state. The secular constitutional state should therefore not be confused with a secular society. Both are not in contradiction. The more multi-religious a society, the more important it is that the state remain neutral in religious matters. A state that would take sides in religious matters would lose its capability to guarantee liberty for all religious faiths.

However, different secular constitutional states may have quite different attitudes toward religion.[5] There is a militant secularism that denies religious beliefs any public role and insists on their belonging strictly to the private sphere. There is also a secularism that separates church and state: the state accepts the role religion plays in society, but is prohibited from promoting religious activities or giving material or immaterial subsidies to religious communities. There is finally a type of secularism that recognizes religion as an elementary human urge that seeks public expression, an urge that the state not only has to respect, but also must protect and maybe even promote—altogether the opposite of a secular fundamentalism.

C. Scope and limits of religious freedom

The scope of religious freedom can vary with the type of secularism that prevails in a country. However, the core of this freedom is fundamentally the same in each secular constitutional state. In most constitutions, freedom of religion is framed as an individual right. But the object of the protection, religion, refers to a supra-individual phenomenon: a set of beliefs and practices that are shared by a plurality of individuals. Religion presupposes a community that is united in its belief in some truths of a transcendental nature and that develops common forms of worship and interaction. One would call neither a worldview without a transcendental reference nor the transcendental assumptions of a single person a religion. This is why freedom of religion has not only an individual but also a collective side.

In individual terms, freedom of religion guarantees everybody the right to decide about his religious faith, to join a community of like-minded people, to confess and propagate his belief, and to lead his life according to his belief's commandments. But the freedom also includes the opposite: the right to not adhere to a religion or to leave a religious community, to hide one's religious beliefs and to not follow religious commandments. In collective terms, freedom of religion is the freedom of religious communities to determine autonomously the content of their creed, to lay down what they consider as sacred, to define the requirements that follow from the creed, and to practice their religion in common.

[5] See Rainer Grote and Thilo Marauhn, *Religionsfreiheit zwischen individueller Selbstbestimmung, Minderheitenschutz und Staatskirchenrecht: Völker- und verfassungsrechtliche Perspektiven* (Berlin: Springer, 2001); Peter Cane, Carolyn Evans, and Zoe Robinson (eds), *Law and Religion in Theoretical and Historical Context* (Cambridge: Cambridge University Press, 2011).

This has a number of consequences for the state as the addressee of freedom of religion. Since religious freedom means equal freedom, the state may neither privilege nor discriminate against certain religious groups. This is also true with regard to those religious communities that are traditionally supported by the native society—the state is not entitled to treat them preferentially. Yet, preferential treatment of a religion as such must be distinguished from protection of the values, traditions, and customs that, although originally rooted in a country's predominant religion, have lost their religious connotations and are no longer viewed as specific expressions of a religion but rather have become a part of the country's general culture that includes believers and non-believers.

Moreover, the state may not presume to declare what the content of a religious creed is or requires. Whatever a religious group understands as the meaning or the commandment of its religion, the state must take it as such. The state is not entitled to instruct a religious group as to what its religion truly means or does not mean, or what it requires or forbids. Likewise, the state may not reproach a religious group for diverging from the official teachings of its belief. Religious freedom must not be turned into a protection of orthodoxy. Yet the state has the right to determine whether a certain belief is religious in nature in the first place, and whether a group is truly a religious community—as opposed to a group seeking to hide other purposes behind a religious façade.

However, self-determination of religious communities as to the content and requirements of their religion does not mean that the state has to tolerate every behavior that is religiously motivated. Freedom of religion is not an absolute right, and religious communities are not extraterritorial. Like all fundamental rights, religious freedom may be limited by the state. The need for limitations follows, firstly, from the fact that freedom of religion is equal freedom for all individuals and all religious groups. Since the transcendent truths or divine revelations that religious groups claim to practice mutually exclude each other, the state must respect a group's creed, but prevent the group from making it binding for society as a whole.

This requires a distinction between the internal and the external sphere. Claims based on an allegedly absolute truth may be raised within the religious group only. They may not be imposed on the external world. The freedom of religious groups to follow their religious commandments can be recognized only when the state rejects any claim to make these commandments universally binding. This does not exclude missionary activities of religious groups, but they must rely on means of convincing others of the preferability of a creed; all sorts of force, be they direct or subtle, are unacceptable.

The need for limitations follows, secondly, from the fact that religious freedom is neither the only constitutionally guaranteed liberty nor the highest one. Neither are the various liberties necessarily in harmony with each other. They often collide. If no hierarchy among them is established, it must be decided which one prevails and which one has to give way in case of conflict. Hence, next to the limits ensuing from the equal allocation of one and the same liberty to many bearers are limits ensuing from the existence of other equally important liberties.

Because of the imperative character of religious beliefs, limitations of religious freedom for the sake of the same freedom of others or for the sake of other liberties are a serious matter for believers. It is the very nature of religion that its commandments are not negotiable as mere interests would be. If this is so, the state's power to restrain religiously determined or motivated behavior cannot be unlimited in itself. Not only must every limitation have a basis in general laws, but these laws must also strike a proper balance between religious freedom on the one hand and the good in whose interest freedom of religion is restricted on the other. This requirement of proportionality is valid for the formulation as well as for the application of the law.

However, the immense variety of conflicts does not allow a valid single solution for all of them. On the other hand, the specific contribution of the law to solving problems of this kind is that it offers rules that apply to more than one case and are based on broader principles. This presupposes an overview of the sorts of conflicts that used to appear in a secular constitutional state. The attempt of this chapter is, therefore, to facilitate the solution of individual cases by developing a typology of conflicts between religious norms and general laws. This typology is based on a number of cases that courts in various countries have had to decide.[6] The purpose is not, however, to discuss the judgments on their merits, but rather to use them as examples that illustrate the abstract categories.

II. Religiously Motivated Conflicts of Norms

A. Typology of conflicts

It is impossible to give a substantive definition of religious norms or general laws. Anything can be the object of a religious commandment as well as of a secular law. A religious commandment is whatever a religious community regards as ordered by some supernatural, transcendental authority. This indeterminacy is what increases the conflicts between religious norms and general laws in multicultural societies. General laws, in turn, are understood here as laws that are not directed against religion as such or against specific religious faiths, but which pursue a legitimate public interest. In doing so, however, they may collide with the religious requirements of certain groups—often those of immigrants, but also the norms of indigenous religious groups.

Basically, a believer or a religious group may claim a *liberty* that is not granted by the general laws, or they may claim *equality* rights that are not designated by the general laws. Freedom claims and equality claims do not mutually exclude each other. Questions of liberty can be reformulated in terms of equality and vice versa. The classification depends on whether this or that principle is emphasized. Each of these two basic categories, freedom-centered and equality-centered claims, has two sub-categories, and in each subcategory two modalities appear. This means that altogether eight types of conflicts can be distinguished which cover the field of conflicts between general laws and religious norms.

Within the group of *freedom claims*, the demand is either to extend or to restrict the generally guaranteed freedom in the interest of freedom of religion.

An *extension* of freedom can be requested in order to allow members of a religious community to do something in pursuance of their religion that is generally prohibited (*type 1*). Examples are the ritual killing of animals, polygamy, consumption of drugs in a ritual context, and interruption of work for purposes of prayer. An enlargement may also be requested to allow believers not to do something that is generally required (*type 2*). Examples are the legal obligation of motorcyclists to wear a helmet, which is incompatible with the religious commandment to wear a turban, the duty to send children to school, and military service.

A *restriction* of the generally guaranteed freedom for members of a certain religious community is at stake if a religion forbids believers a certain behavior that is generally

[6] For a collection of cases concerning these conflicts, see W. Cole Durham and Brett G. Scharffs (eds), *Law and Religion* (New York, NY: Aspen Publishers, 2010); Walter Kälin, *Grundrechte im Kulturkonflikt: Freiheit und Gleichheit in der Einwanderungsgesellschaft* (Zürich: NZZ-Verl., 2000). For the jurisprudence of the U.S. Supreme Court in particular, see Kent Greenawalt, *Religion and the Constitution* (Princeton, NJ: Princeton University Press, 2 vols, 2006 and 2008).

allowed, be it a total prohibition or a prohibition under certain circumstances (*type 3*). Examples are the right to obtain a divorce, the choice of one's spouse, blood transfusions, and swimming in public places. A restriction of the generally existing liberty is also at stake when a religious community requires something from its members that is optional for everybody else (*type 4*). Examples are dress and food codes, the duty to marry a person not chosen by the believer himself or herself, and forced divorce against the will of both spouses.

In the group of *equality* claims the issue is either equal treatment of various religious groups or the application of the equality principle within a religious group. In this context it is important to realize that the principle of equality not only applies when the law treats different groups of persons differently, but also when it treats different groups equally although the differences between them are such that a differentiation would be necessary.

Equal protection of religious groups usually raises the question whether all religious communities enjoy the same rights or whether indigenous religious beliefs may be privileged (*type 5*). Examples are the construction of mosques in non-Islamic countries, the call of the Muezzin (just as the Christian churches ring their bells), public display of religious symbols of all faiths, state subsidies for religious activities, the recognition of the holidays of immigrants, and the equal treatment of various religious heritages in education.

The demand for *unequal treatment* is raised if equal treatment would prevent believers from fulfilling their religious duties or would amount to a de facto discrimination against the members of a certain religious community (*type 6*). Examples are kosher food for Jewish inmates of prisons, closing a major road for traffic on the Sabbath in an area mainly populated by orthodox Jews, permission for Jewish merchants to open their shops on Sundays as a compensation for the religious obligation to close on Saturdays, depicting or ridiculing the prophet Mohammed, and handling family law issues not in the general civil courts, but in Sharia courts.

The application of the principle of *equality within* religious groups is at stake if a religion requires unequal treatment whereas the general laws prescribe equal treatment (*type 7*). In almost all cases these are questions of gender equality. Examples are the reservation of certain professions (eg priests) for men, granting the right to claim a divorce to the husband only, and the exclusion of daughters from higher education. But it is also possible that a religion requires equal treatment where the general laws differentiate (*type 8*). This type comes as a consequence of the scheme, but it is not easy to find examples. A religiously motivated permission to have sex with children, as is sometimes reported in the media, may serve as an example.

For a better survey, here again is the scheme:

- I. Freedom claims
    - 1. More freedom in favor of religion
        - (a) Permission to do what is generally prohibited
        - (b) Permission not to do what is generally required
    - 2. Less freedom in favor of religion
        - (a) Permission to prohibit what is generally allowed
        - (b) Permission to require what is generally optional
- II. Equality claims
    - 1. Equal treatment of religious groups
        - (a) Equal treatment of all religions
        - (b) Privileges for some religious groups
    - 2. Equality within religious groups
        - (a) Permission to differentiate where equal treatment is generally required
        - (b) Permission to treat equally where differentiation is generally required

B. Accomodation of freedom claims

There are no uniform answers to these problems. On the one hand, the fact that freedom of religion is a constitutionally guaranteed fundamental right excludes an unconditional application of the general laws. On the other hand, the fact that freedom of religion is not a preferred freedom that always trumps other freedoms excludes the unconditional recognition of religious claims. Hence, the solution of each conflict depends on a balancing of the competing legally protected values.[7] Sometimes freedom of religion will prevail; other times the good protected by the general law will prevail. The typology can be helpful in getting the balance correct, but it does not determine the outcome.

The extension of the generally existing freedom in order to make fulfillment of a religious duty possible (to do what is generally forbidden; not to do what is generally prescribed—types 1 and 2) is the typical case for balancing. Two preparatory steps are necessary. On the one hand, the importance of the religious commandment for the believers and the loss of religious freedom if they have to obey the general law are to be ascertained. On the other hand, the importance of the good that is protected by the general law and the danger it would face if freedom of religion prevailed are to be determined. In a third and final step, the question as to what weighs heavier must be answered.

In many cases belonging to these two types, a dispensation from obeying the general laws will be possible. The legal order is full of exemptions for various reasons and such exemptions do not lead to a legal chaos or an undermining of the trust in the law. An exemption will usually be possible if the general law does not protect third persons or society as a whole or important communal interests, but instead the individual against himself. Here the religious duty will usually be given higher weight. The same is true if the general laws protect certain habits or customs of the host society by prohibiting alternative ways of life. A protection of the host society against mere irritation would not be a sufficiently strong ground to suppress religious freedom.

If the general law serves an interest of third persons or society as a whole, the importance of the good protected, the potential danger if an exemption is granted, and the likelihood and degree of the danger will play a role. If the law regulates the relationship between private persons (as in the case of praying during work), the question will usually be whether one can reasonably expect the other side to tolerate the fulfillment of a religious duty. If the general law wants to maintain communal values, it will be necessary to ascertain their importance for the community and its identity. One may be inclined to grant an exception from the prohibition on ritually killing animals, but less so from the duty to send children to school or from monogamous marriage.

The more difficult case is, however, the restriction of a generally existing freedom for believers in a certain religion (prohibiting what is generally allowed; requiring what is generally optional—types 3 and 4). Here, differently from the two previous types of conflicts, it is not the relationship between members of a religious community and third persons or society at large that is at stake, but the relationship between a religious community and its members. The problem is not whether a religious community may determine duties that curtail the believers' freedom—it is not the business of the state to decide which duties follow from a religious creed. Nor can a religious community be prevented from sanctioning the violation of religious duties, provided the sanctions are of a religious nature only (such as excommunication).

[7] Cf. Aharon Barak, *Proportionality: Constitutional Rights and their Limitations* (Cambridge, UK: Cambridge University Press, 2012).

This is different, however, when the sanctions affect not only the religious, but also the civil status of a person (e.g. his or her right to marry), and when the sanctions cannot be implemented without the state's assistance. The secular constitutional state is under no obligation to implement religious norms or commandments. The state may not lend its enforcement power to religious norms without a sufficient secular ground. Purely religious norms have to be distinguished, however, from norms that have a religious origin but have been adopted into the secular legal order, or norms that are simultaneously valid within the state and a group of believers (e.g. many prohibitions of the Decalog, blasphemy laws, where they still exist, for the sake of the public peace).

In this context it is important that, within the secular constitutional state, religious freedom cannot be recognized unconditionally, even within a religious community. There are two main reasons for this. First, unlike the general laws, which are binding independently of the addressee's consent, religious norms depend on voluntary compliance. The state's monopoly of legitimate force does not allow compulsory means in the hands of religious communities. Consequently, the state must prevent attempts by a religious community to enforce religious norms against an unwilling believer. Since freedom of religion includes the right not to join a religious community, the state must also guarantee the right to exit.

Secondly, fundamental rights, at least in the German understanding, are considered not only as negative rights, but have a positive aspect as well.[8] They do not only obligate the state to refrain from certain actions, but also require the state to actively protect constitutionally guaranteed liberties against intrusions by private actors. This duty to protect may be a duty in favor of religious freedom (if, for example, an employer unduly limits an employee in complying with his religious duties). But it can as well be a duty to protect a believer from a religious community (e.g. the dismissal of an employee in a church-owned institution for violating a religious norm).

Moreover, the secular constitutional state cannot tolerate a religiously required behavior even if the believer complies voluntarily with the commandments of his creed, if the behavior contradicts the very essentials of the constitutional order. There is no obligation to sacrifice the identity of civil society to religious demands. The question of what belongs to these essentials will be answered by every society for itself. In Germany, human dignity and the dignity core of most fundamental rights, as well as the principle of equality, would count among the essentials; so would the physical and psychic integrity, and the right to participate in public discourse and in the formation of the public will.

C. Accommodation of equality claims

As far as *equality* claims are concerned, the easiest case is the one in which immigrant religious groups request rights that the indigenous religious groups or churches already enjoy (type 5). But this must be distinguished from state activities favoring traditions that may have Christian roots, but which developed a formative effect for society without retaining a specific religious connotation. In cases like these, freedom of religion would not serve as a basis for equal treatment of the cultural heritage of immigrants. Holidays are an example. Although most holidays that are observed in Germany and other European countries have Christian roots and are still meaningful for believers, this does not support a claim of other religious groups for a similar amount of their holidays.

[8] Cf. Dieter Grimm, "The Protective Function of the State," in Georg Nolte (ed.), *European and US Constitutionalism* (Cambridge, UK: Cambridge University Press, 2005), 137.

The same applies to the treatment of religious matters in education. The state is entitled to promote those traditions that have developed in its history and had a formative effect on its own identity. One of the tasks of education is enculturalization, and this refers to the domestic culture as it emerged over time, including, of course, all the foreign influences to which cultural development is exposed. The state may not deny immigrant religious groups the right to promote their own cultural and religious traditions—this is part of their religious freedom—but it is under no duty to make this its own concern.

Claims of religious communities or individual believers for privileges in order to be able to live according to the commandments of their religions (type 6) can normally be solved with proportionality or balancing means. The problem typically arises when persons are under the special tutelage of the state (e.g. as inmates in a state institution), and therefore unable to take care of themselves. The question in these instances will be one of the importance of the religious commandments for the believer on the one hand and the burden for the state to provide the demanded facilities on the other. If it is not an undue burden to provide a believer with the means to comply with his religious obligations in a foreign environment, the state will be obligated to assist the person.

This may be different, however, when the fulfillment of such claims causes a disadvantage for other groups. Thus, the permission for Jewish merchants to open their shops on Sundays did not lead to equal treatment with the non-Jewish competitors, but to preferential treatment. The state has no obligation to compensate for every disadvantage that may flow from compliance with religious duties. This is all the more true if the religiously motivated claim can only be fulfilled by limiting the fundamental rights of others. This would be the case, for instance, if criticism of certain religious beliefs, persons, or symbols prohibited by a certain religion were also denied to non-believers.

The same is true regarding claims to withdraw certain areas of the law from application of the general laws and from the jurisdiction of state courts. This would mean at the same time that they are exempted from the control of the constitution and the protection it renders to individual freedom, regardless of the religious affiliation of a person. The most important realm in this regard is, of course, family law, which some Muslim groups would like to take away from the ordinary courts and hand over to the Sharia courts. This can certainly not be done if the decisions of such courts are not subject to review by state courts whose duty it is to enforce the basic guarantees of the constitution.

As far as exemptions from the general requirement of equal treatment are requested on the ground of religious freedom (type 7), the question is which constitutionally protected interest deserves higher weight. The question cannot be answered in a uniform way. Freedom of religion is affected in its very core if religious services, cults, and worship are concerned. In this field, the intervention of the state is therefore limited. If, for instance, cultic activities of a religious community may be performed by men only, it would be a violation of religious freedom if the state obligated a religious community to also accept women as priests, rabbis, mullahs, etc.

There is a difference, however, if the enforcement of religious norms has consequences for the civil status of believers. If, for example, ritual services may be performed by unmarried persons only, a religious group cannot prevent such persons from engaging in marriage. But the person may, as a consequence, lose the capacity to perform religious rituals. If a religious norm regulates the relationship between members of their group, such as marital relations, in a manner contradicting constitutional principles, this norm cannot be enforced in a state court, with the consequence that the decision of the religious community cannot take civil effect.

Finally, the answer to the question whether religiously motivated or required equal treatment where the general laws differentiate (type 8) can be tolerated on grounds of freedom of religion depends on the reasons that support the differentiation. If the differentiation is the consequence of a protective duty of the state, an exemption seems impossible. In this way, the hypothetical case of sex with minors would be solved. In cases where the differentiation does not follow from a duty of the legislature to protect fundamental rights, the religious claim would be submitted to a proportionality test.

Balancing is a non-hierarchical way to solve conflicts between constitutionally protected rights or interests. It requires the legislator and the judge to take the colliding rights and interests seriously, weigh them against each other and try to preserve as much as possible of both. Thereby it can mitigate religious conflicts and create an atmosphere of mutual consideration. But balancing does not save the legislator or the judge from deciding which right or interest shall ultimately prevail in which situation. This means that religious freedom may be on the losing side regardless of the importance of a religious requirement for the believer. There are situations in which the only alternative is adaptation to the secular norm or emigration.

2

The Context of Secularism: A Critical Appraisal of the Post-Secular Argument

Nadia Urbinati[1]

Laïcité, which the English language renders as "secularism," is an attitude of the civil authority toward religious practices. It is not in itself an indication of the form of government or the liberal nature of a regime. It is recalcitrant to abstract theorizing, because context is a crucial factor for evaluating it. These three characteristics are essential in the understanding of *laïcité*. While the first two pertain to the identity and function of secularism, the latter brings us directly to the assessment of the role of religion in the public sphere. As an attitude of civil authority toward religious practices, secularism is a way of simplifying a complex social reality and a practical guide for making political decisions. It is not identifiable with the liberal nature of politics or a form of government but pertains to the affirmation of the authority of the state over all social practices prior to, and autonomous from, any form of government (for example, the ideals that motivated the political regime that Atatürk imposed on Turkey defined an authoritarian regime, although secularist in character[2]). It is crucial we keep sovereignty separate from the form of government if we want to appreciate the differences among secular projects, even *within* democratic societies.

Secularism can, of course, open the state to a liberal transformation of its political regime. But in order for this transformation to occur, other vindications are needed that endow individuals with prerogatives that limit the power of the state. Beginning in the eighteenth century, this function was filled by the bills of rights and the constitutional organization of state powers. In relation to this political and juridical frame, we should evaluate the role of religion in the public sphere of today's democratic societies. The issue can be phrased in the following question: "What does a secular state need in order to be respectful of its citizens' equal rights, or for its politics to make decisions that honor individual freedom against political and religious authority if needed?" This question serves to introduce the topic of this chapter. The argument I propose makes two claims: first, the fact of *religious pluralism* is an unavoidable condition for giving secularism a liberal nature; and second, a bill of rights and a constitution may not be sufficient conditions, although they are essential. The ethical or cultural identity of a given society is the unavoidable context that circumscribes the evaluation of the role of religion in the public sphere. Does this mean that the historical context determines the political identity of a country? Perhaps, but this is not the problem that interests me, which can hardly have a falsifiable answer anyway. What I intend to do instead is to stress the link between

[1] Columbia University.

[2] Akeel Bilgrami, "Secularism: Its Content and Context," *The Immanent Frame* (2011), available at <http://blogs.ssrc.org/tif/2011/10/20/secularism-its-content-and-context/>.

secularism or *laïcité* and religious pluralism. I will do it by using the Italian case, the case of a constitutional democracy whose society does not have a capacious religious pluralism, but one dominant religion. Through the Italian case, I would like to argue that a mono-religious society has the chance (or perhaps the need) to produce a secularist project but less or weaker chances to produce a full liberal society, even when the state embraces a democratic form of government with constitutionalized rights.

This suggests the following generalization: in mono-religious societies, secularism may be destined to be or become more radical than in religious-pluralist societies because the theocratic risk is higher. In mono-religious democratic societies, liberalism has more chances to be or remain permanently of a *modus vivendi* kind because the state needs to be more energetic in asserting the prerogative of the civil law. In this kind of society, the presence of religion in the public sphere can be problematic and actually a hindrance. To use John Rawls' terminology, in mono-religious democratic states, political liberalism has fewer chances to reach the hegemonic status of an overlapping consensus that shapes the public opinion of the society. Thus secularism per se is not an issue that we have to pay attention to when we want to discuss how intense the presence of religion in the public sphere can be, but *the fact* of religious-pluralism. The issue of pluralism is sensitive above all in a constitutional democracy, because in this form of government, although the public sphere and civil society are naturally open to host ideas and opinions of any kind (including religious), the majority has a heavier role, not only in the decision-making process, but also in the culture of the general public which shapes political opinions.

I will structure my argument as follows: first, I will critically discuss the main political conceptions that deal with the place of religion in the public sphere and show why they are unsatisfactory; and second, I will argue the need of a stronger secularism in proportion to how monadic the religious composition of a society is. The discussion of a specific judicial case—that of the exposition of the crucifix in an Italian public school—will conclude.[3]

I. A Distinction within Liberal Democratic Societies

A few years ago, the Speaker of the Italian Low Chamber, Gianfranco Fini, felt in need of specifying something that might seem redundant in a constitutional democracy. Mr. Fini declared that "the Parliament should not pass laws that are inspired by religious precepts." Monsignor Elio Sgreccia, a prominent Catholic theologian very active in the public debate, replied immediately: "The issues on which Catholics intend to be active in politics are not definable as "religious precepts" because they pertain to fundamental rights that are written in human nature, demonstrable by reason, and endorsed by the Italian constitution... Catholics are in the right position for actively participating in the public and parliamentary debate against abortion and euthanasia and to protect family."[4] In his answer to Mr. Fini, Monsignor Sgreccia adopted a style of reasoning that Rawls' revisited public reason would consider legitimate. Indeed, while publicly proclaiming principles that he derived from his comprehensive doctrine, Monsignor Sgreccia made an effort to reach out to non-religious citizens by arguing that those

[3] The main argument discussed in this chapter is derived from the article "Laïcité in reverse: Mono-religious Democracies and the Issue of Religion in the Public Sphere," (2010) 17(1) *Constellations* 4–21.

[4] See the Italian newspaper *La Repubblica*, 18 May 2009.

principles can also be accepted by them because they are in agreement with the principles of public reason contained in the Italian constitution, although expressed not in the form of public reason (or constitutional rights) but in the philosophical language of natural rights according to the Thomistic tradition. Endorsing this discursive style would seem to be a secure passport for citizens with comprehensive doctrines to actively participate in the public sphere of deliberation. Hence, Jürgen Habermas has concluded that, in post-secular democracy, religious citizens have the right to participate in public discourse with their own principles and convictions. In fact, Habermas is even more generous than Rawls and thinks that the limits on individual liberty contemplated by Rawls in his rejection of the translation of "private" reasons into "public" ones is still too demanding and, moreover, unequally demanding since it demands more on religious citizens than non-religious ones. In Habermas' view, thus, Monsignor Sgreccia should be allowed to claim publicly that the law of the Italian state should be consistent with his "religious precepts" without bothering to engage in any sort of stylistic translation, a work that only the representatives seating in the parliament should do. Indeed, as an ordinary citizen who participates in public opinion formation but not lawmaking, Monsignor Sgreccia should not be asked, not even in the name of what Rawls would call an informal or moral "duty of civility," to rephrase his religious arguments so as to make them in agreement with the language of civil rights.[5]

I would like to criticize this view. In particular, I intend to criticize Habermas' position and, to a lesser degree, Rawls' revised public reason. Both positions are tailored to a philosophical reflection of liberalism that pertains to liberal societies that are the home of factual religious pluralism, although in different ways. They are however—Habermas' more than Rawls'—hardly suitable and safe if extended or applied to constitutional democracies in which one religion enjoys a strong majority and pluralism is only predicated in the constitution and the bill of rights but is not a lived experience in society. In relation to the place of religion in the public sphere, it would be important that along with Rawls' distinction between liberal societies and despotic societies (whether decent or not) we make also *a distinction within liberal societies*, among those in which religious pluralism is both a juridical and a social reality, and those in which religious pluralism is proclaimed and protected by the law but is not a social reality or an ethical culture that shapes the public reasoning of ordinary citizens. This distinction between the juridical and the contextual level is meant to suggest that we must always regard the norm of constitutional democracy in its porous relationship to the actual cultural life of a society, and democracy always as both a set of principles and procedures and an actualization that is contextually specific and reflects itself in the general opinion of the public (ordinary citizens as well as public officers).

My conclusion can be rendered as follows: In matters that have a direct impact on the individual freedom of religion and social peace such as the presence of religion in the public sphere, political theorists should pay close attention to the ethical and historical context of a given society instead of applying to it practical conclusions that have been derived from an ideal conception of democratic societies as religious-pluralist *de facto* and *de iure*. This pragmatic suggestion of going back and forth from the ideal

[5] John Rawls, "The Idea of Public Reason Revisited," in Samuel Freeman (ed), *Collected Papers* (1999) and Jürgen Habermas, "Religion in the Public Sphere" (2006) 14(1) *European Journal of Philosophy* 1; Habermas' article has been recently republished with minor changes under the title "Cognitive Presuppositions for the 'Public Use of Reason' by Religious and Secular Citizens" in *Between Naturalism and Religion* (Cambridge, UK: Polity Press, 2008), 114 (in this chapter I shall refer primarily to the 2006 article).

norm to the context is an admission of the fact that a political practice that is liberal in a religious-pluralistic environment may be anti-liberal in a mono-religious society. Religious-pluralism is the essential condition within which we should situate any discourse on the role of religions in the public sphere. Without pluralism (as a social fact or as an actual plurality of religions, not only as a formal declaration of rights), a constitutional democracy may generate decisions that are not more liberal or inclusive and tolerant than those made in a non-constitutional democracy (or in a decent illiberal society, to paraphrase Rawls).

The advice to pay critical attention to the historical and social context is particularly urgent in the case of Habermas' position, which is rationalistic and optimistic to the point of underestimating the actual fact (or *a contrario* the lack) of pluralism in the making of a safe and open public sphere. The Italian case is exemplary of the weakness (indeed, the danger) of post-secularism as a recipe that is deduced from an ideal deliberative conception of democracy (which is, in fact, ethnocentric itself).

II. Deliberation and the Place of Political Decision

The first step of my argument focuses on the interpretation of *the issue at stake* when we deal with religion in the public sphere. I propose the following maxim: "Any reflection on the place of religions in the public sphere should be situated within the context of an authoritative political decision or the domain of civil lawmaking because, contrary to a dialogue among friends or private discussion, public debates are always performed, directly or indirectly, in the view of making new laws or changing existing laws." What makes deliberation public is not only the style and principles that define it but also the goal, which consists in *making decisions* that affect all citizens. The place of decision in democratic politics is the crucial issue at stake in the dialogue between Mr. Fini and Monsignor Sgreccia. The issue is the relationship between *civil* or *secular law* (I am going to use these two adjectives as synonyms) and *religious* or *canonic law* (but the same can also be said of the Islamic and the Judaic law). The making of decisions is a crucial domain because it goes straight to the foundation of the legitimacy of the law (and thus of authoritative decisions) in a constitutional democracy. Unfortunately, the deliberative theory of democracy seems to underrate the place of decision.

The theory of deliberative democracy lessens the role of decision in order to exalt the informal process of reasoned discourse and justification. Its goal is to prove that since any democratic decision is open to revision, the process of critical understanding and informal deliberation reflects the character of democratic politics much more genuinely than the act of decision or voting per se. The claim that democracy has a moral legitimacy along with an institutional one is of course well-established and important. Deliberation is an extended process of public justification, an exercise in intellectual honesty, reciprocal recognition of one another's dignity and equality, and a sign of true autonomy.[6] These three moral characteristics make democracy more than simply institutionally legitimate because any decision that fulfills them may be universalizable and thus contains a validity claim addressed to humanity as a whole, not merely the will of

[6] "A communicatively achieved agreement has a rational basis; it cannot be imposed by either party, whether instrumentally through intervention in the situation directly [force], or strategically through exerting influence on the decisions of one party on the basis of a calculation of success [rhetoric]." Jürgen Habermas, "Social Action, Purposive Activity, and Communication" (1981), in Maeve Cooke (ed.), *On the Pragmatics of Communication* (Cambridge, MA: MIT Press, 1998), 120.

the specific community that made it. Post Kant, the moderns are capable of achieving what the Athenians could not: a truly universalistic and egalitarian perspective and the emendation of arbitrariness from politics in a way that democracy as decision-making procedure (majority rule) cannot do. It is not hard to predict that this achievement is primed to have enormous consequences. Certainly, it may encourage an expansion of the meaning of democracy from politics to morality, from an organized and regulated public behavior whose goal is to make laws to an ethical way of collective participation. Per effect of deliberative theory, democracy is not simply the name of a form of government; its meaning is unavoidably *prescriptive*, enriched by a moral content that ascribes to participation and people's self-determination an ethical, educational, and cognitive efficacy. In the end, democracy is the name of a holistic project, not simply a matter of popular consent and majority rule. In fact, it exceeds voting and decision and makes proceduralism a lower rendering when compared to deliberation.

However, lowering the domain of decision to stress the informal and moral aspect of deliberation may encourage misleading conclusions, particularly in the case of religion. What I propose is that we think and locate all political deliberation in relation to lawmaking. This means highlighting the *political* character of *all* public deliberation, including that involving citizens with religious creed. Only if we presume a law-oriented perspective we can understand and fully evaluate the role and place of religion in the public sphere. Religious citizens (as ordinary believers, intellectuals, and members of the clergy) question and criticize existing laws or propose new laws when they enter the public sphere. This bare fact should invite theorists of democracy to keep in mind the central role of decision and identify democracy with a free process of opinion formation *whose end* is voting (by citizens and their representatives as well). The final station and natural goal of the public sphere of deliberation is decision; and civil law is the form decision takes in modern constitutional states. Within the context of lawmaking, the issue of the place of religion in the public sphere of a democratic society acquires a feature that is directly tied to the distinction between civil authority and religious authority.

The distinction between secular law and any religious law played a crucially important role in the political history of modern Europe. Its ethnocentric origin does not make it less valuable because democracy's public life is hardly possible outside or against this distinction. History and daily news prove abundantly that religions can be an intractable source of war, illiberty, and incivility whenever they claim an authority over civil law or try to blur the distinction between secular jurisprudence and sacred jurisprudence.

In *Federalist 10*, James Madison explained the nefarious (as illiberal and bellicose) potential of religions by resorting directly to the nature of religious passion, which he thought capable of predisposing human beings toward intolerance because its main goal is that of making the social order in agreement with its own principles. Because of their insatiable nature, passions (first of all those associated with God and property) are "the latent causes" of factions, which in turn are the direct causes of intolerance because of their monopolistic tendency. As we know, the solution Madison advanced was pluralism (*divide et impera*) rather than the repression of factions or their expulsion from the social domain in the attempt of depressing passions, because his goal was to achieve and preserve *civil peace and liberty together*, not civil peace alone. The state, he argued, must not embrace or bend toward any faction but guard instead over a society that should be the home of many factions that act freely and limit one another while co-existing under the same civil law. *Social and religious pluralism* on the one hand and *a monistic civil power* on the other (the source of legitimate law must be only one, the government) are the twin strategies that secure individual liberty and social peace in a constitutional democracy.

III. The Immanent Character of Democratic Authority

In modern Europe, the process of secularization (by which we should first of all mean the process of emancipation of civil authority from religious authority) has coincided with the full affirmation of religious liberty, that is to say the end of continental Christian uniformity (*Concordia Christiana*) and the overcoming of any civil restriction on minority religions (religious pluralism). The sixteenth-century formula *cuius regio, eius religio* (often translated as "one king, one faith, one law"[7]) was overcome only after the civil order succeeded in emancipating itself from the task of fulfilling goals that were external to it, such as deciding which faith was the right one or using the coercive power of the state to prepare its subjects for the eternal life or the salvation of the soul. The politics of rights put an end to toleration as state politics (or the political decision of which faith is the right one). In a constitutional state, citizens are not tolerated by the civil authority, they are—all of them without distinction—the recipients of rights and thus treated by civil authority with equality and impartiality.[8]

In a 1966 seminal article on the history of the idea of "freedom of conscience," Joseph Lecler showed that freedom of conscience, as freedom of a person and not simply of a Christian, advanced along with the recognition of religious pluralism.[9] It is in this sense entirely correct to link the history of religious freedom and political secularization to the history of the democratic and constitutional transformation of European modern states.[10] As for the secular character of modern states, what Max Weber called the "privatization of religions" did not simplistically entail that religions were confined within the believers' inner life with no social visibility, or that freedom of religion and conscience meant invisibility of one's creed from outside. It is doubtful that this could even be possible since any religion is composed of rituals and social practices along with individual faith.[11] It did not even mean that civil codes and religious codes stopped interacting the moment that the former became autonomous and hierarchically superior (according to Harold Berman they were actually in a relationship of "separation" and "competition" and in this sense "interaction").[12] Secularization meant, on the contrary, that religious contents and principles were expelled from states' apparatuses, and in particular from civil and criminal legal codes.

The state extricating itself and disassociating its legitimacy from religion resulted in two ideal projects: (a) that the state renounced expressing its preference for one religion

[7] Joseph Lecler, "Les origins et le sens de la formule: *Cujus Regio, Ejus Religio*" (1951) 38 *Recherches de Science Religieuse* 119. For an excellent historical analysis of the formation of the politics of toleration in a Catholic country (i.e. France) see R.M. Golden (ed.), *Church, State and Society under the Bourbon Kings of France* (Lawrence, Kan.: Coronado Press, 1982).

[8] "With the establishment of modern liberal states,... equality before the law and respect for the rights of individuals and minority groups tend to make toleration politically redundant." David Heyd, "Is Toleration a Political Virtue?," in Melissa S. Williams and Jeremy Waldron (eds), *Nomos XLVIII: Toleration and Its Limits* (New York and London: New York University Press, 2008), 175.

[9] Joseph Lecler, "Liberté de Conscience. Origines et sens divers de l'expression" (1966) 54 *Recherches de Science Religieuse* 370. But see also Rainer Forst, "Pierre Bayle's Reflexive Theory of Toleration," in Williams and Waldron, *Toleration and Its Limits* 78.

[10] Joseph Lecler, *Histoire de la tolérance au siècle de la Réforme*, 2 vols (Paris: Aubier, 1955), vol. 2, chs 2 and 3. See also Mario Turchetti, "Religious Concord and Political Tolerance in Sixteenth- and Seventeenth-Century France" (1991) 22(1) *The Sixteenth Century Journal* 15.

[11] On the thesis of privatization of religion as one of the salient characters of modernity see José Casanova, "Rethinking Secularization: A Global Comparative Perspective," *The Hedgehog Review* special issue on "After Secularization" (Spring/Summer 2006).

[12] Harold J. Berman, *Law and Revolution: The Formation of the Western Legal Tradition* (Cambridge, MA: Harvard University Press, 1999).

instead of (or against) another; and (b) that religions (or more precisely, churches) renounced their prerogatives on civil law (concerning Italy, the first ideal was formally actualized with the 1984 revision of the Concordat between the state and the Catholic Church, while the second ideal is still far from being actualized as the law limiting artificial procreation shows). The separation of civil law and religious law (in Europe it was essentially a separation of civil law from canonic law) was a tormented process perhaps never fully achieved (until recently on some European states' passports religious denomination appeared as an identification of the citizen along with the color of her eyes or her sex). However, this separation becomes a destination of all countries in the moment their constitutions make the foundation of civil law immanent (people's will), and not transcendent (God's will). Eighteenth-century American and French constitutionalism epitomized the apex of a process of liberalization from religious sovereignty that had started in the sixteenth century with the end of *Europae Concordia Christiana*.

The meaning and implication of the separation of civil law and religious law was effectively captured in 1938 by R.G. Renard, a Dominican and Law Professor in the University of Nancy:

> French, Italian, Spanish and even Japanese legal codes, different as they are, walk in the same direction, which is very different from the direction taken by canonic law. Indeed, while civil law disciplines society according to a perspective and within a horizon that is temporally limited, canonic [religious] law treats mundane society as the home of spiritual society, which has eternity as its destiny. The comparison [between civil law and religious law] is possible on the condition that we understand this great divide.[13]

Renard was right to think that the divide goes straight to the foundation of legitimacy: in the one case, the foundation is *within* humanity itself and its finite temporal dimension; in the other, the foundation is God, who is *outside* human temporality and history. This divide acquired its most eloquent and effective expression with the gradual democratization of the political order, which eroded the last remnants of transcendence from the polis (like nobility and honor or any other principle that claimed to be above or outside the will of the subjects).[14] Democracy's procedures of decision-making presume a permanent legal changeability because they assume that citizens' opinions are the core of political legitimacy. Democracy's political order cannot tolerate any ultimate foundation that is outside of itself—i.e. outside the principles of consent and majority rule—although this does not mean that democratic citizens (also public officers) do not experience the tension between their public identity and their private or religious one. This casts light on the meaning of the immanent character permanently *in fieri* of democratic politics.

The process that brought about the separation of secular authority and religious authority has not resulted in a society in which religion is confined within the inner life of the individual, as sociologists have simplistically suggested (thus helping create the blatant confusion between the secular character of civil law and the ideology of secularism).[15] Rather, it is a society in which a judge like the Catholic R.G. Renard is required to silence his religious faith when making an authoritative judgment (the unavoidable tension between the judge's *foro interno* and *foro externo* must never be allowed to resolve in the victory of the former over the latter). In addition, however, democratic society is also a society in which the tension between these two domains is neither repressed nor,

[13] R.G. Renard, "La contribution du droit canonique à la science du droit comparé," in *Introduction à l'étude du droit comparé: Recueil d'études en l'honneur d'Edouard Lambert* (Paris: Sirey, 1938), 109.

[14] Silvio Ferrari, *Lo spirito dei diritti religiosi: ebraismo, cristianesimo e islam a confronto* (Bologna: Il mulino, 2002), 46–7.

[15] For a critical reinterpretation of secularism see Jose Casanova, *Public Religions in the Modern World* (Chicago: University of Chicago Press, 1994).

above all, solved once and for all. The dialectic and tension between the civil and the religious is permanent and never resolved. This *permanence*—not the repression or the privatization of one's religious belief—is what makes for the character of a society that is democratic and secular at once.

In sum, the fact that religion does not have a directly political role does not mean that it does not have any role in the process of public judgment formation, a process that takes place outside state institutions as an expression of freedom of speech and of religion. The liberation of the political from the religious had the unintended consequence of making reason and autonomy (the most distinctive products of the secular age) also instruments in the service of faith. As a result, religious faith is glorified as the fruit of individual free choice instead of as the result of imposition by state authority or an un-reflected tradition. The creation of this favorable condition went hand in hand with the construction of a "public space" as a domain that is autonomous from both the sphere of the coercive norms of the State and the discretionary will of the individual's belief and interest.[16]

Two conclusions can be drawn from this: historically, the formation of a civil public sphere took place along with the distinction/hierarchy between legal-civil codes and religious codes; and in addition, in a democratic society, lawmaking is not a work that is made in isolation by elected representatives but is the result of a complex political process of communication within the public sphere between institutional domains and extra-institutional ones. Civil society movements, pressure groups, media, and parties are all active voices in the democratic decision-making process although only indirectly involved in lawmaking. Hence, in a democratic society, the secularization of the public (the law) does not entail necessarily the privatization of religion and the secularization of the public sphere of opinion formation, which is inhabited also by discourses that have religious character.

IV. Habermas' Critique of Rawls and the Issue of the Burden on Religious Citizens

In his "Religion in the Public Sphere," Habermas advanced several critical reflections on the nature of secularism in modern democracy and on Rawls' revised public reason. He asked whether the republican constitution (i.e. Rawls' political liberalism) does not in fact impose itself at the expense of other loyalties, as for instance religious loyalty, and does not become itself a new kind of religion. Habermas' revision of political liberalism evolves from a critique of the classical liberal dualism between public and private as it appears in Rawls' famous distinction between comprehensive doctrines (among them religions) and political reasoning (the state and its institutions) and reflects the continental model of co-participation, which, contrary to liberal (Rawls') dualism, rests on three legs rather than two: not only the individuals and the state but also the communities of faith (as established churches). Applied to religion, Habermas' model of co-participation entails that the juridical conflicts between individual freedom and church prerogatives are not unfailingly solved by giving priority to individual freedom. The goal that Habermas ascribes to his revision of the dualistic liberal model of separation between religion and politics is that of expanding the role of religion by fully incorporating it in the public sphere of opinion formation or deliberation. This solution, one might surmise, is actually more secularistic than Rawls' because it presumes that an open discussion would have

[16] Charles Taylor, *A Secular Age* (Cambridge, MA: Belknap Press, 2007), 1–21.

the power of transforming doctrinal or dogmatic distinctions into differences of interpretation to be evaluated and judged by reason.[17] The actors of the public sphere in a democratic society are individuals that associate in order to pursue their mundane interests or ideals but also their religious aspirations and world views. The outcome of Habermas' revision of liberal dualism is meant to offer a view of democratic society that is more inclusive than Rawls' political liberalism.[18] The issue is that Habermas' proposal may at the same time be less friendly to individual freedom.

This problem becomes more clearly visible in the case of constitutional democracies in mono-religious, rather than pluralistic, societies. Societies like the Italian one are an important test to probe the weakness of Habermas' theoretical view of post-secular public sphere. The paradox is that, on the one hand, Habermas' theory gains its normative or *a priori* status at the cost of becoming blind to empirical specificity (for instance to non-religious pluralist democracies), and, on the other, it elevates to theory what is a factual reality, which is that religions *do* play a role in democratic public sphere.

Habermas revisits the critical arguments of political liberalism in the name of what he calls a "post-secular conception" of the public sphere. In a democratic public sphere, he argues, religions are no longer compelled to exist only as private creeds but are recognized as full participants in political opinion and will formation. As we have explained above, in a democratic society, the public sphere, although formally distinct and separated from the authoritative power of lawmaking, is deeply intertwined with it.

Habermas' unacknowledged yet important assumption—with no factual demonstration—is that in Western societies, religions have now come to accept the liberal constitutional state (they are beyond liberalism as *modus vivendi*), and for this reason the public can allow itself to be less restrictive with the presence of religions in the public spheres; it can allow itself not to endorse French *laïcité*. It seems that as far as religion is concerned, advanced and mature democratic societies can be less traditionally liberal and more trustworthy in the educating effects of democratic participation.[19] But Habermas' post-secular conception rests on an unexamined assumption that is highly contextual and not generalizable. His theory is an idealization or theoretical reflection of the most secular among Western societies. In other words, Habermas' post-secularism presupposes societies within which religious pluralism *is* an existing and an accepted fact (reasonable pluralism). But pluralism (even reasonable pluralism) entails more than two religions and moreover it entails religions that are equipollent or similar in size and strength, so that one major religion does not cover the entire geo-political space of a country.[20] Habermas' idealization would be hardly applicable to democratic mono-religious societies.

[17] In a Hegelian perspective, Habermas sees religions as not-yet manifested philosophies, the expressions in a not fully rational form of principles and values that rational deliberation among open minded citizens will gradually enlighten: "I defend Hegel's thesis that the major world religions belong to the history of reason itself" (Habermas, Introduction to *Between Naturalism and Religion*, 6). On Habermas' secularist philosophy see Simone Chambers, "How Religion Speaks to the Agnostic: Habermas on the Persistent Value of Religion" (2007) 14(2) *Constellations* 220.

[18] On the contradiction between Rawls' idea of "translation" and Habermas' deliberative theory see Maeve Cooke, "A Secular State for a Postsecular Society? Postmetaphysical Political Theory and the Place of Religion" (2007) 14(2) *Constellations* 224.

[19] "[S]ecular citizens or those of other religious persuasions can under certain circumstances learn something from religious contributions; this is, for example, the case if they recognize in the normative truth content of a religious utterance hidden intuitions of their own." Habermas, "Religion in the Public Sphere" 10.

[20] This argument (which Madison made paradigmatic) was already developed by Jean Bodin, who, as I shall mention below, claimed that the peaceful coexistence of more than two religions is easier because of the self-limitation that only two religions make hard to obtain.

Let us briefly revisit the main argument of Rawls' political liberalism before discussing Habermas' criticism. In his "The Idea of Public Reason Revisited," Rawls argues that a religious doctrine can be interpreted in such a manner that it may be correlative with a constitutional conception of rights and according to styles of reasoning that, although not in the ordinary form of public reason, may legitimately participate in the formation of public judgment. These forms of reasoning are: from declaration, from conjecture, and from testimony or as "witnessing." Rawls insists that none of these three styles of judgment prefigures a pure translation from private reasons into public ones.[21] In the first case, religious citizens declare (without assuming that their fellow citizens will do the same) the principles of their faith while showing that these principles contain a constellation of moral conceptions that citizens holding different religious beliefs or no religious belief at all could accept. In the second case, non-religious citizens conjecture what religious citizens could infer from within their own faith (thus reasoning according to an *as if* model of judgment), with the goal of showing to religious citizens that they too could accept the reasonability of public reason. The clause of this *as if* reasoning is that it is sincerely performed, not made with manipulating intention or in order to obtain religious citizens' consent on a given policy. In the third case, finally, religious citizens, whose creed brings them to disagree with the opinion of the majority and thus also with the law, express publicly their disagreement in the name of their faith, although they are not allowed to transform their critical testimony into a practice of civil disobedience.[22]

These three forms of reasoning presume that citizens can resort to their specific *cultural background* in their public discourse and are compelled neither to divorce their private reason from their public reason ("the man" from "the citizen") nor to translate one into the other. According to Rawls, reasonable pluralism of this kind can contribute to strengthening toleration and public reasoning itself because it is primed to involve all citizens regardless of their faith in an exercise that is sincerely oriented toward finding good reasons to make decisions that are in the general interest.

A critical analysis of these non-public reasoning styles of public discourse exceeds the goal of this chapter. As a quick example, Italy is a good illustration of Rawls' argument of declaration because, as I have explained, Monsignor Sgreccia used an argument from St. Thomas' *jus naturalis* in order to make his case for a revision of the Italian law regulating procreation. From Rawls' perspective (and even more so Habermas') this would be a legitimate articulation of public reason and the sign of a culture of toleration that is deeper than a merely legalistic one.[23] This would be so even if the voice of the Catholic Church is in Italy the only one, and no religious pluralism exists that limits naturally the power of the Catholic voice in influencing political power.

In a mono-religious scenario, the fact that Catholic citizens make their anti-abortion claims in the name of the Thomistic conception of *ius naturalis* does not give any certainty that Catholic citizens will not form a voting bloc and employ their arguments in order to influence representatives in Parliament. In a country in which there is one major religion

[21] Rawls, "The Idea of Public Reason Revisited" s. 4.3.

[22] Rawls contemplates the solution of civil disobedience only if the latter appeals to constitutional foundations and not "external" reasons such as religious principles; disobeying civil laws in order to be faithful to one's creed—religious or ideological—does not denote civil disobedience but unlawful behavior or subversion of the law. John Rawls, "The Justification of Civil Disobedience," in Hugo Adam Bedau (ed.), *Civil Disobedience: Theory and Practice* (New York: Pegasus, 1969), 240–55.

[23] Even more optimistic are Rawlsian interpreters, e.g. Daniel A. Dombrowski, who thinks that while "[u]ntil the development of liberalism, the fair terms of cooperation among Catholics and Protestants were extremely narrow," today however "pluralism" is seen as "quite normal" to both and this is so because toleration and liberalism "grew hand in hand" and won the challenge. *Rawls and Religion: The Case for Political Liberalism* (Albany: State University of New York Press, 2001), 6.

(baptized Catholics comprise approximately 90 percent of the Italian population), this possibility cannot be ignored. Using arguments of natural rights instead of "religious precepts" directly is no guarantee that the outcome will not be a confessional law, or the violation of the separation between civil law and religious law. This is especially true if we take into account the character of democratic society as one in which—as I shall explain below—it is not only unlikely but moreover *undesirable* that the informal sphere of opinion formation and the formal sphere of lawmaking are kept separate and not in communication. The democratic character of representation rests on the fact that the elected are not an elite that is self-referential and sheltered from society.

Foreseeing this, Rawls added two important conditions, one empirical and one prescriptive, to his revisited public reason: first of all, that civil society enjoys an effective plurality of religions and second, that religious citizens—like any other citizen—should feel the moral "duty of civility" to look in their own religious culture for those ideas that are more in agreement with basic civil rights, among them those rights that guarantee freedom of conscience and full toleration. Without these two conditions, the above-mentioned revision of public reason can be a threat to constitutional democracy.[24] Yet Habermas criticizes precisely the prescription of the moral "duty of civility," while he undervalues pluralism as a fundamental condition for a safe presence of religions in the public sphere.[25]

I shall illustrate how crucial Rawls' conditions are by returning to the Italian case. In commenting on Mr. Fini's argument in favor of the autonomy of civil law from "religious precepts," a Catholic member of the Italian Parliament, Roberto Buttiglione, made a sibylline declaration. Mr. Buttiglione asserted that Catholics do not deem something as true because the Pope said so; to the contrary, they think that if the Pope deems something as true it is because it really is true. Since Catholic citizens commit themselves only to the authority of Truth, their critique of civil laws cannot be accused of violating the principle of toleration and the separation of state and the church. Catholic citizens should thus be engaged in articulating the Truth with "reasonable arguments" in order to convince their fellow citizens that they should shape their civil law accordingly. In this way, Mr. Buttiglione invited his fellow Catholic citizens to use "reasonable arguments" in a strategic and non-deliberative manner, or in order to smuggle a dogmatic and *a priori* Truth by means of a deliberative process.

To be clear, the strategic use of reason is not a characteristic that belongs only to religious or Catholic citizens. To paraphrase Madison, this is the way in which individuals holding a faith or a particular interest behave when they are active in the public sphere. Yet the strategic use of reason is particularly in tune with the character of religion, which does not approach Truth as something to be reached by human reason through a trial and error method, but as something that is given to us by God and revealed through faith. Reason is ancillary to Religion since is employed to deduce from the Truth those good precepts that ought to guide human conduct in general, not only that of the Catholics.

[24] Following the principle of reciprocity, and hence the duty of civility, would allow people to make claims from reasonable comprehensive doctrines as long as they observe *the proviso* that they then justify these claims with reasoning that other participants could in principle (although not actually) accept. Rawls, "The Idea of Public Reason Revisited" 576.

[25] Even more radical are the critiques by Nicholas Wolterstorff, "The Role of Religion in Decision and Discussion of Political Issues," in Robert Audi and Nicholas Wolterstorff (eds), *Religion in the Public Square: The Place of Religious Convictions in Political Debate* (Lanham, Md.: Rowman & Littlefield Publishers, 1997) and Paul J. Weithman, *Religion and the Obligations of Citizenship* (Cambridge, UK: Cambridge University Press, 2002), 155–60. Both of them have accused Rawls of pursuing a true secularist project.

Here, civil law is conceived as a means to achieve an end that is beyond it or, as we have said above, beyond human temporality and in view of the salvation of the soul. The city of man is in the service of the city of God; it is neither autonomous nor, therefore, properly democratic.[26]

Habermas' idea of the public role of religion and Rawls' revision of public reason to make room for styles of reasoning that are not directly political or civil presume some conditions without which those revisions may be detrimental to individual freedom of religion and primed to jeopardize the liberal character of society: pluralism of faiths, or a society in which no religion enjoys a de facto position of monopoly or primacy. Thus pluralism is essential, not optional, because it is the natural check on the instrumental use of deliberative reasoning and the monopolistic tendency that religious beliefs possess no less than economic interests. The essential correlation between security of social peace and individual freedom of conscience was captured long ago by Jean Bodin in his *Colloquium of the Seven about Secrets of the Sublime* (1588), a fundamental work concerning religious concord-discord that has unfortunately been neglected in this literature. Without religious pluralism or, Bodin made Curtius to say, with either one or only two dominant and rival religions, political society lacks a constraint that is effective enough to curb the instrumentalist use of the public sphere by religious citizens and churches without resorting to state repression.[27] "Otherwise, if one opposite were joined to another opposite with no middle ground between, there would necessarily be continual battle."[28]

I can now return to Habermas' critical remarks on Rawls' political liberalism. In order to justify the public presence of churches or religious communities (and not merely individuals with religious beliefs, as I anticipated above), Habermas advances three critiques of political liberalism: (a) it violates the principle of equality because it imposes disproportionate requirements on particular (religious) citizens; (b) it jeopardizes pluralism because it makes one identity (the political one) superior in value; and as a consequence (c) it impoverishes the moral culture of democratic society.[29]

I shall focus on Habermas' first critique. This critique materializes in the objection of pretentiousness and an unequal distribution among religious and non-religious citizens of the moral "duty of civility" to follow the norms of public reason: this is, according to Habermas, an *asymmetrical burden*. Rawls, in other words, was too demanding of all citizens in general (his view of citizenship was quasi-republican and echoed a kind of secular religion) and of some citizens (i.e. religious ones) more than others. Indeed, the idea of citizenship as public reason asks all citizens to sacrifice their personal culture (interests and values) and endlessly engages them in a work of translation from their

[26] "Canonic fairness is the opposite of fairness in civil law: the latter is all internal to the legal order and its deep and positive exigencies to be actualized; the former is capable instead of setting aside the positive legal order and make room for norms that come from elsewhere." Pio Fedele, "Equitá canonica," in *Enciclopedia del diritto* XV (Milano: Giuffrè, 1966), 159 (my translation); see on this issue Helmuth Pree, "The Divine and the Human of the Ius Divinum," in *In diversitate unitas* (Leuven: Peeters, 1997). Thus, regardless of the different interpretations of God's word in the Abrahamic religions, all of them presume that God is the source of the law; see Ferrari, *Lo spirito dei diritti religiosi* 133–4.

[27] "CURTIUS: Nothing is more destructive in a state than for citizens to be split into two factions, whether the conflict is about laws, honors, or religion. If, however, there are many factions, there is no danger of civil war, since the groups, each acting as a check on the other, protect the stability and harmony of the state." Jean Bodin, *Colloquium of the Seven about Secrets of the Sublime* (1588) translated with an Introduction, Annotations, and Crtical Readings by Marion Leather Kuntz (Princeton, NJ: Princeton University Press, 1975), 151 (IV, 117).

[28] Bodin, *Colloquium of the Seven about Secrets of the Sublime* 148 (IV, 116).

[29] For an interpretation of Habermas' thought see Alessandro Ferrara, "The Separation of Religion and Polis in a Post-secular Society" (2009) 35(1)–(2) *Philosophy and Social Criticism* 77.

private languages to a public political language. This, according to Habermas, is asking too much of liberal citizens. In addition, and in violation of the democratic principle of equality, it asks too much to those who want to live consistently with the precepts of their religious creed. "In a constitutional State [or political liberalism] religious communities are expected not only to adapt to the unstable modus vivendi of the secular contest, but moreover to accept the secular principles of legitimacy."[30] As I mentioned above, unlike Rawls, Habermas does not speak of individual citizens solely, but also of religious communities. This terminological shift is clearly unbalanced on the side of an ethical model of democracy structured not according to individual citizens but individual citizens *and* groups. Along with individuals, it includes groups such as religious communities and churches that are more organic than mere civil associations.

Habermas acknowledges Rawls' commitment to go beyond a "*de facto* pluralism," as well as his awareness that this may entail asking the conscience of a religious person to make a remarkable sacrifice. He appreciates Rawls' awareness of the burden that political liberalism implies.[31] Habermas' criticism of Rawls' revisited public reason as imposing an *asymmetrical burden* intersects with his critique that it sponsors an abstract dualism between the private and public sphere. In a word, Rawls would ask citizens (religious and non-religious) to split into two identities (private and public reason), although it is not clear how this split would not engender epistemic and moral contradictions. Habermas' critique of Rawls' dualism recalls Karl Marx's critique of republican citizenship splitting the "social man" and the "public man" in order to create an abstract general interest. But as Anna Elisabetta Galeotti has observed, Habermas' critique of liberal dualism neglects the fact that according to Rawls the two spheres overlap precisely because they operate within a space that is dense with moral and political culture, not empty of any culture.[32]

The separation of, and tension between, spheres of life is ingrained in constitutional democracy as both a condition for impartiality of judgment by public officers, and for citizens' ability to reason in general terms, rising above their own private interests or passions. In effect, the request of separation pertains to all the spheres of life, not only the spiritual one. As a matter of fact, all modern constitutions contain articles declaring that all citizens are *de iure* equal regardless of their empirical specificity. Clearly the injunction of separation involves the economic sphere (interests) and the sphere of family (values). In these cases, moreover, the violation of the principle of separation is signified with negative adjectives like "patrimonialism" and "familism." Now, if we follow the logic of Habermas' critique of an "asymmetrical burden," we should conclude that in all these cases, too, political liberalism asks too much of its citizens, and moreover that it asks more of some than of others. For instance, it asks more to those who have more substantive economic interests to defend or to those with children and a family. But clearly, this is not a conclusion that Habermas would endorse. Why, then, should the request that political liberalism makes of religious beliefs be treated differently than the request it makes of economic interests or family values? Why should a religious perspective receive a different treatment, and why should its request to participate in the public debate enjoy less constraint? Why is our effort to transcend economic interest or family values and translate them into the political language of rights to be seen as a good or desirable thing but the same effort is judged too onerous when applied to religious beliefs?

[30] Jürgen Habermas, "La voce pubblica della ragione" (2007) 104 *Reset* 6.

[31] "How is it possible for those of faith, as well as the nonreligious, to endorse a secular regime even when their comprehensive doctrines may not proposer under it, and indeed may decline?" Rawls, "The Idea of Public Reason Revisited" s. 3.1.

[32] Anna Elisabetta Galeotti, "Ma c'è laicità e laicità" (2007) 104 *Reset* 22.

These questions are not rhetorical, particularly if we pay attention to the nature of representative democracy as I have anticipated above. Representative democracy is a political system in which the power of judgment plays a crucial and weighty role in the making of political decisions, although does not command obedience since it belongs in the realm of opinion not the law. Moreover, such questions are especially relevant in light of the fact that the separation of spheres is difficult to achieve and, as we shall see below, somehow undesirable. Starting from these very considerations, however, Habermas concludes that *because* of modern democracy's complex system of indirectness, citizens should not be required (not even with a solely moral request such as Rawls' "duty of civility") to make the sacrifice of translation. It would seem as if Rawls' request would make sense only in a direct democracy, because only there do citizens act directly as lawmakers and thus can never be exonerated from thinking politically. But representative democracy circumvents this problem, and allows the large majority to retain their private beliefs at all times since politics is organized so as to create a distance between state power and the mind of the citizens, or the will and opinion.

But Habermas seems to suggest that elections and representation have inaugurated a welcome division of labor thanks to which citizens with religious beliefs can avoid "translating" their faiths into public reason while perceiving themselves "part of the *civitas terrene*" no less than citizens without religious beliefs. Representative democracy engenders a new kind of civic cooperation that makes it possible for religious citizens to choose not to renounce making arguments from within their religious principles, because they know that someone else (the representatives) will do the job of translation (that they participate in the *civitas terrena* indirectly). As a matter of fact, Habermas argues, participating in the political game even indirectly and through our personal beliefs is in itself a tacit recognition of the rules of the political game; and this is enough for the preservation of the liberal society.[33]

In substance, representative democracy has contributed to the birth of a post-secular society by offering the best solution to the problem of the relationship between politics and religion. Indeed, modern democracy has opened public space to religions by allowing religious citizens to participate in political life without putting the liberal state in jeopardy.

V. Influence, Distance, and Translation

Habermas' proposal to emend liberalism of an abstract dualism is interesting; however it opens a discussion that introduces a set of new problems. Certainly, his optimistic depiction of public space in post-secular democracy does not help us to face hard cases like the Italian one or any mono-religious society. Yet, it is precisely in relation to intractable cases that we are most in need of normative guidance. The issue is that while Habermas' position is a reflective idealization of the way the public sphere operates in democratic pluralistic societies, it is heavily problematic when we apply it to democratic societies that have no religious pluralism. In these societies, Habermas' revision of liberalism may create new risks to representative democracy precisely because this system of government—as Habermas himself has acknowledged—is one in which formal sovereignty (the act of voting) is only a minimal component of politics, while the role of the soft

[33] Habermas, "Cognitive Presuppositions for the 'Public Use of Reason' by Religious and Secular Citizens" 129.

power of judgment and public influence is of fundamental importance. At the same time, the latter are hardly controllable without putting civil liberty at risk.

As I illustrated through the Italian case, the fact that religious citizens use deliberative strategies does not make their influence less pervasive or less problematic from the point of view of minorities' protection. It may actually make it more problematic. It is the density and pervasiveness of public discourse in a representative democracy that makes important and timely Rawls' injunction that all citizens should feel the *moral duty* not to use the public sphere as a means to fulfill or sponsor their own private visions or beliefs. Contra Habermas, this is anything but an excessively burdensome request. In most societies—except for the exceptional and few societies in which religious pluralism is effective—it is the necessary condition for preserving constitutional democracy.

It is actually the nature of the representative system that amplifies the problem of the relationship between religion and politics. As Monsignor Sgreccia's clever use of *jus naturalis* argument demonstrates, the pervasive soft power of public judgment is a crucial component of religion's continued potential to present fundamental challenges to civil constitutionalism. The source of the problem lies in the relationship between electors and elected. The problem is not translation per se, because thanks to the device of elections and representation all private languages pass through a sort of translation or filtering process before and in order to enter the institutional sphere. The problem is that in the case of religion the discrepancy of viewpoints between ordinary citizens (who are not required to translate) and representatives (who are required to translate) may create a sense of duplicity, insincerity, or a distance between electors and elected that is itself corrosive to representative democracy.

Let us try to explain this crucial point. Habermas writes: "This strict demand [to justify political statements] can only be laid at the door of politicians, who within state institutions are subject to the obligation to remain neutral in the face of competing world views; in other words it [a Rawlsian proviso] can only be made of anyone who holds a public office or is a candidate for such."[34] But if it is sufficient that *only* the representatives embark in translation, we are in the paradoxical situation that those citizens who can make the translation (and thus enter politics) have presumably less strong religious beliefs than those who prefer not to make the translation and thus not to run for election. Following Habermas' logic, it would seem that representatives have religious beliefs that are neither strong nor perhaps truly sincere or, and this is even worse, that they are Machiavellian enough to be willing to practice the art of translation in view of achieving consent on proposals that are inspired by their religious precepts.

The problems and moral ambiguities implied in Habermas' formula (only public officials should be required to translate, not ordinary citizens) bring to light the nature of representative democracy and its difficult relation with rational deliberation. Indeed, democratic representation is not a form of delegation because representatives do not simplistically sit in the Parliament in the place of citizens but act along with them and by their authorization in order to make laws that all must obey. The distinction between elected and electors designates a form of *inter-dependence* rather than a separation or

[34] Habermas, "Religion in the Public Sphere" 9, referencing Rawls: "It is imperative to realize that the idea of public reason does not apply to all political discussions of fundamental questions, but only to discussions of those questions in what I refer to as the public political forum. This forum may be divided into three parts: the discourses of the judges in their decisions, and especially of the judges of a supreme court; the discourse of government officials, especially chief executives and legislators; and finally, the discourse of candidates for public office and their campaign managers, especially in their public oratory, party platforms, and political statements." "The Idea of Public Reason Revisited" 575.

dualism because those who make the translation from within the institutions are or should be *in a permanent relationship* with those who are, in Habermas' words, not required to translate because they operate outside of the institutions. Thus, even in the case that decision-making procedures are honoured and the Parliament is not like a Babel tower made of representatives of corporate groups, the influence of public judgment (and religious opinions) on lawmaking is hardly containable and controllable. As I said, it is representative democracy itself that presumes that the extra-institutional domain exercises a permanent influence on representative institutions. Yet, as Habermas himself implicitly suggests, particularly in the case of religion, it would be desirable that representatives do not listen too much or too closely to their electors because if they did, religion would directly enter the lawmaking process and jeopardize civil law (in parliament, he writes, "the standing rules of procedure of the house must empower the house leader to have religious statements expunged from the minutes."[35]) The issue is that, unless state institutions are sealed from or impermeable to civil society (something not only impossible but also *undesirable* in a representative democracy that aspires to be more than a form of elite authorization by the people), the presence of religious ideas will never be only among those who can avoid translation (ordinary citizens). It will unavoidably also be among those who sit in state institutions and pass laws.[36]

It is not hard to foresee the truly concrete risk (and the Italian case is exemplary) that religious groups construct factions and lobbies and use their representatives in order to translate "religious precepts" into arguments of public reason so as to attain the goals of reshaping civil law and making it more in agreement with their religious codes, and thus less civil. This confirms that *ordinary citizens*, and not only public officials, ought to be inspired by the *civil duty* of translation, and not the astute will to transfer their belief in their political discourses even if, one must stress, that duty is and must be only moral, not legal. Particularly in societies in which there is no religious pluralism, citizenship should be felt by the large majority of citizens as a civil identity that requires a sacrifice of personal views from all members. All in all, precisely because religious pluralism within society cannot play a deterrent role against the monopolistic temptation of religious faiths, the presence of religions in the public sphere would require more, not less constitutional ethos.

To summarize my main argument, I would say that the issue of translation from religious arguments into public deliberation arguments is not an abstract activity without any practical dimension. Rather, it brings to the fore the relationship between the sociological position of religious institutions on the one hand, and the discourse its intellectuals and spokespeople use in public on the other. The problem is not just that we should pay attention to both of these levels as Habermas suggests, but also that, precisely *because* of the nature of political representation, the former plays an important role in determining the character of the latter. In other words, in genuine religious pluralism, the "translation" attempts of religious public speech may be initially strategic, but they have to aim at *political* persuasion as a matter of fact since they are not already a majority. However, in a mono-religious society, translation can be skin-deep and superficial or even absent because there is no real need to persuade anyone who doesn't already share the same comprehensive doctrine. Therefore, the rationality of the political translation is not so much a question of "strategic" versus "communicative" orientation. It is a

[35] Habermas, "La voce pubblica della ragione" 6.

[36] Thus Ferrara argues that there is no justification in censuring representatives' speech: "Should minutes of parliamentary debates be subject to censorship and reflect less than faithfully what has been said on the floor?" "The Separation of Religion" 87.

function of social conditions, of whether or not religion is in the position of having to actually persuade those who do not share its comprehensive doctrine, i.e. make a political translation.[37]

VI. A Case of Post-Secular Democracy

I would like to corroborate the argument I have been making by proposing a concrete example of what a post-secular democracy might look like in a mono-religious constitutional democracy. In 2000, the Italian Court of Cassation stated the principle that the public space should be neutral in order to be friendly to all religions (in fact to non-Catholic religions). But in Italy, the discussion about the meaning of *laïcité* has never been easily resolved. In 2005, the Administrative Tribunal of the Veneto Region (TAR) rejected a request by some parents to remove the crucifix from a classroom of a public elementary school. On that occasion, the Constitutional Court, asked to intervene, declared that the issue belonged to the domain of administration since the issue of the crucifix in public spaces depends not on a law but on old statutes (older than Italian Constitution of 1948) and can thus be resolved by the local administration in question, in that case, by the elementary public school of Abano (in the Province of Padua). Clearly, the Constitutional Court endorsed a position that was friendly to the notoriously strong federalist sentiments and Catholic public sensitivity of the Veneto Region (in which the Northern League is a majority in local government). But it is not the issue that I would like to discuss. I would like instead to focus on the argument that the TAR of Veneto Region devised in order to justify the legitimacy of the crucifix in a public school. Before proceeding I need to offer some background information.

We need to know that the Italian Constitution guarantees equality, freedom of individual conscience and pluralism of religion (Articles 3, 8, 19, 20) and moreover that, with the 1984 Revision of the Concordat between the State and the Vatican (originally sealed in 1929 under the Fascist regime), Italy no longer recognizes Catholicism as the official religion of the state. In 1984, Italy ceased to have an official religion. Since then, many important efforts have been made to make civil and criminal codes consistent with the new Concordat between the state and the Church, although with a mix of success and timidity. The recent conservative turn in national politics has increased this ambiguity. The decline of ideological political parties and the growth of the Church's direct influence in politics are the essential components of the ambiguity. However, my aim here is not to offer a political analysis of the transformations of the Italian society; it is to contextualize a case study so as to prove how cautious we should be in welcoming the presence of religion in the public sphere.[38]

Let us turn to the argument in defense of the crucifix in the classroom. The TAR argued that the display of the crucifix does not violate the principle of *laïcité* sanctioned by the Constitution and is not in disagreement with the norms of the 1984 revision of the Concordat because the crucifix "expresses, in a symbolic yet adequate way the religious origins of toleration, of reciprocal respect, of the valorization of persons, their rights, respect of freedom, and the autonomy of individual conscience in relation to the

[37] I thank Ian Zuckerman for helping me clarify this crucial point.

[38] I owe most of the observations on the Italian laïcité to Tania Groppi, "Le principe de laïcité comme création jurisprudentielle en Italie," rapport présenté dans le colloque sur "Constitution et laïcité" Le 80éme anniversaire de la laïcité constitutionelle en Turquie, Université de Marmara (10 April 2008) (unpublished paper).

secular authority, and the rejection of any form of discrimination."[39] A civil tribunal interpreted the crucifix as an argument or a symbol of toleration and freedom of conscience because it would show that Christ was crucified as a consequence of the violation of toleration and freedom of religious conscience. Religious citizens—actually public magistrates who reflect (unavoidably as we saw) the background culture of their fellow citizens—have here translated their private precepts of faith into public reasons. They have declared that while it "connotes Italian civilization," the crucifix is also in perfect agreement with the civil values and the norms expressed by and contained in the democratic constitution.[40]

The argument by the TAR of Veneto Region was consciously framed in an attempt to prove that civil language and religious language may cooperate and on some occasions overlap; that the language of religion coincides, in the case of the crucifix, with both universal rights (individual or human rights) and the cultural, juridical, and ethical tradition of the Italian democratic society. Legal scholars have pointed out instead that this revisionist argument signifies a confessionalization of the principle of *laïcité*. The method of the judges was opposite to the method that Rawls thought political officials should adopt in a liberal state: trying to translate non-political languages, and in particular language belonging to comprehensive conceptions, into a language in which all citizens can recognize themselves, regardless of their personal belief. But the Italian judges situated themselves fully within the religious ethical culture of the majority in order to prove that *this* language can be used along with and instead of the civil or political language that the Italian constitution contains. In this way, they transformed the crucifix into a secular symbol, making it trespass its naturally religious meaning in order to become a national-cultural symbol incorporated within the civil law. The public role of religion turned out to be an explicit threat to the secular interpretation of the constitution as a civil law document.

In fact, a Christian believer should feel irritated with the transfiguration of a religious value produced by a secular authority in order to achieve a political goal, namely, making a decision in tune with the majority culture. *Laïcité* Italian style is a kind of *laïcité* that refuses to proclaim indifference to religious phenomena; it wants to be *not equidistant* from all existing religions but *equiclose* to them (but in fact to the majority religion). Rather than a-confessional pluralism, Italian democracy claims to endorse a kind of pluralism that is confessional-friendly. This *laïcité in reverse*, which expresses a favorable attitude toward religion in the public sphere, would encounter no opposition from Habermas' proposal (although Habermas would not approve of a state institution that does not make the translation). If we apply Habermas' conception of post-secular public sphere to a mono-religious democracy such as Italy, post-secularism becomes a pretext to bypass the liberal dualism between private reason and public reason and to directly recognize the cultural patrimony of the large majority of the population; in fact, to translate into institutional language the influence that religion exercises in the public sphere free from religious pluralism's constraint. Italian democracy is a post-secular democracy

[39] Consiglio di Stato in sede giurisdizionale, Sezione sesta, sentenza n 556/2006.

[40] Voting 15 to 2, the Grand Chamber of the European Court of Human Rights ruled on 18 March 2011 confirming the TAR decision with the similar argument: while the crucifix is a religious symbol, the presence of the crucifix did not breach the rights of non-Catholics or atheists: "There is no evidence before the Court that the display of a religious symbol on classroom walls may have an influence on pupils," the ruling stated. In similar vein, a defense of the TAR judgment was made by Alessandro Ferrara, *The Force of the Example: Explorations in the Paradigm of Judgment* (New York: Columbia University Press, 2008), 198–203.

that employs constitutional rights to pursue an agenda that, if fully implemented, would challenge the constitutional democratic state in its foundations. It proves that post-secularism obscures the political threat to constitutional democracy itself in the very moment it does not make the context paradigmatic, i.e. does not make religious pluralism a necessary precondition for the admission of religion in the public sphere.

3

The Myth of the Neutral State and the Individualization of Religion: The Relationship Between State and Religion in the Face of Fundamentalism

Karl-Heinz Ladeur

I. Introduction

A. What is the "neutrality principle"?

Around the world, we are witnessing a revitalization of religious issues, which includes, in particular with respect to contemporary Islam, a re-politicization of religion. Religion has become, once again, a political *topos*.[1] The secularized western world is thus facing a new challenge for which it appears to be inadequately prepared. The idea of freedom of faith, guaranteed as a fundamental right, obliges the western democratic states to respect the religious activities of their citizens and to secure their free development. Therefore, the state is principally neither allowed to favor nor discriminate against certain denominations. This concept of equidistance is known as the principle of state neutrality. It commits the state to generally withdrawing from religious issues and, particularly, to not defining what can legitimately be classified as religion and religiously connoted behavior.[2]

The leeway given to the self-conception of religious groups by the German Federal Constitutional Court and its wide understanding of what kind of behavior has a direct relationship with faith, and therefore deserves protection as freedom of religion, is to be understood against this background. However, with regard to the new challenges mentioned above, the neutrality principle increasingly serves yet another purpose. The courts use it as an escape-option in order to avoid dealing directly with problems which appear to be too complex under the law, but rather seem to be issues for the sociology of religion. In this context, neutrality merely functions as a *chiffre* for indifference. But this strategy of avoidance, though understandable in the face of the public sensitivity, undermines the

[1] See Karl-Heinz Ladeur and Ino Augsberg, *Tolerenze-Religione-Recht. Die Herausforderung des "neutralen" Staates durch neue Formen der Religiosität in der postmodernen Gesellschaft* (Tübingen, Germany: Mohr Siebeck, 2007), 1. On the (misleading) concept of a "revival of the religious," see Gianni Vattimo, "Die Spur der Spur," Gianni Vattimo and Jacques Derrida (eds), *Die Religion* (Frankfurt am Main: Suhrkamp, 2007), 107; Gianni Vattimo, *Jenseits des Christentums. Gibt es eine welt ohne gott?* (München: Hanser, cop., 2004), 29; Jürgen Habermas, *Zwischen Naturalismus und Religion. Philosophische Aufsätze* (Frankfurt am Main: Suhrkamp, 2004), 7.

[2] For a case discussing kosher butchering, see Bundesverfassungsgerichts [BVerfGE] [Federal Constitutional Court] 15 January 2002, 104 Entscheidungen des Bundesverfassungsgerichts [BVerfGE] 337 (353) (F.R.G.).

law's function of conflict resolution. Furthermore, it corresponds to neither the historical development nor to the functional aspects of the idea of religious freedom.

B. A historical and a sociological approach to the idea of freedom of faith

Historically, the state's withdrawal from religion corresponds to the withdrawal of religion from politics.[3] This evolution modifies the idea of religion—that is here to say: Christianity. Religion now demands an internalization by one's own conscience, the *forum internum*, which is primarily constituted by an observation not of others, but of the Other, i.e. God. The liberalization of conscience correlates with the internalization of faith, the public ceremonial exercise of which is limited to non-political aspects. From this individualist perspective, religious tolerance is a rather pragmatic concept: since the individual conscience cannot be forced to the right decision, any act of violence becomes futile. This justifies abstention from using state power in order to enforce religious commands. So, according to John Locke, the state, while still receiving its tasks directly from God, is limited to those tasks that have a non-spiritual character.[4] The state, so conceived, has the secular purpose to guarantee the life of its citizens, but—for theological reasons—it cannot enforce their inner belief in certain confessions.[5] A deviance from specific religious commands, which a majority of the population might still regard as an absolute truth, then no longer calls for persecution, but can be tolerated instead. This explains the continuing reservations to Catholicism: its capacity as an institutionalized decoupling of individual faith and politics has been called into question.[6] Accordingly, there are voices today claiming that, within the Islamic world, this step from a "collective" to an "individual" subject, making tolerance in the modern sense possible, has not yet been taken.[7] Hence the de-politicization of the Islamic world—if possible at all—is still to come.

What can be interpreted as a historical confinement of freedom of faith in this sense has its theoretical counterpart in a functionalistic theory of fundamental rights. According to Niklas Luhmann's sociological analysis, fundamental rights are not only

[3] See Jacob Taubes, "Statt einer Einleitung. Leviathan als sterblicher Gott. Zur Aktualität von Thomas Hobbes," in Jacob Taubes (ed), *Der Fürst dieser Welt. Carl Schmitt und die Folgen: Herausgegeben Von Jacob Taubes* (1985), 9, 14.

[4] Ian Harris, "Eglise et etat chez Locke," in Yves Charles Zarka et al (eds), *Les fondements philosophiques de la tolérance en France et en Angleterre au XVIIe siècle: Tome I, Études* (Paris: Presses universitaires de France, 2002), 175, 202.

[5] Therefore Habermas's concept of tolerance as a "Gunsterweis," i.e. performance of a favor, deduced from the historical example of French absolutism and serving as a mere prologue of "true" tolerance merging in the rules of public discourse, is one-sided. See Jürgen Habermas and Jacques Derrida, *Philosophie in Zeiten des Terrors. Zwei Gespräche* (Berlin: Philo, 2004), 66–8. The same critique applies to the "Erlaubniskonzeption," i.e. the concept of concession, developed in Rainer Forst, *Toleranz im Konflikt. Geschichte, Gehalt und Gegenwart eines umstrittenen Begriffs* (Frankfurt am Main: Suhrkamp, 2003).

[6] For a discussion of Catholicism in the United States see Philip Hamburger, *Separation of Church and State* (Cambridge, MA: Harvard University Press, 2002), 481. For the development of the Catholic idea of the state, see Rudolf Uertz, *Vom Gottesrecht zum Menschenrecht. Das katholische Staatsdenken in Deutschland von der Französischen Revolution bis zum II. Vatikanischen Konzil (1789–1965)* (Paderborn: Schöningh, 2005). Hegel still considered Catholicism to be incompatible with the idea of the modern state. See Georg Wilhelm Friedrich Hegel, *Vorlesungen über die Philosophie der Geschichte*, vol. XI (Stuttgart: Bad Cannstatt, 5th edn, 1971), 530.

[7] See Yves Charles Zarka and Cynthia Fleury, *Difficile tolérance* (Paris: Presses universitaires de France, 2004), 179, 213. For a psychoanalysis of Islam referring to this idea, see Josef H. Ludin, "Zwischen Allmacht und Hilflosigkeit. Über okzidentales und orientalisches Denken" (1994) 542 *Merkur* 404–12.

personal freedoms. Rather, within a poly-contextual world without a central point of observance, but only intelligible by multiple second-order perspectives,[8] fundamental rights guarantee the differentiation of society in several relatively autonomous social spheres.[9] Thus they serve as barriers against totalitarian tendencies of certain societal subsystems. This theory applies almost perfectly to the new phenomena of religiously motivated and politically ambitious movements. Their tendency to a total molding of an entire society creates the general conflict concerning the relationship between state and religion. In this respect, Islam demonstrates with particular distinctiveness a structural problem concerning all types of religion. But it can be observed that Christian confessions increasingly tend to exert influence on the political process, too. By contrast, one goal of fundamental rights is to secure an independent sphere of action for each societal subsystem. Therefore, the guarantee of freedom of faith can reach no farther than ensuring that the exertion of faith does not encroach upon the activities of the other social spheres. Hence, advocating rules of the Islamic *sharia* or the Jewish *halaka* as religiously determined legal orders or a religiously motivated refusal of certain scientific theories reaching beyond the private realm, e.g. at school, is not backed by basic German law. Neutrality of the state, in this perspective, does not mean exempting religion from the challenges of the modern world. On the contrary, it expects religious communities to come to terms with them. Neutrality, then, is but a symbol of the instability of the differentiation of societal subsystems, which has to be continually reproduced as a *process* of neutralization. It therefore calls upon the state as a political system to set up variable demarcations *vis-à-vis* other social systems, including religion.

II. Fundamentalism And The Fragmentation of the Subject In Postmodern Society

A. The "return of religion" as a postmodern phenomenon

The worldwide phenomena of a "return of religion," in western countries in particular, demonstrate the fact that both religion and the public realm into which it returns have undergone considerable change. The postmodern state, which might be described as a state which has lost the capacity to promote stable "ideal-egos" and to function as a public institutionalization of a "super-ego,"[10] tends to boil down its basic structure to a reduced version of the protection of individual "rights." A process of multiplication of "ego-ideals," which are offered for "autonomous" internalization, has been brought about; it finds its repercussions in the transformation of civil rights. Civil rights are

[8] See Niklas Luhmann, *Beobachtungen Der Moderne* (Opladen: Westdeutscher Verlag, 1990), 100.

[9] See Karl-Heinz Ladeur, *Der Staat gegen die Gesellschaft. Zur Verteidigung der Rationalität der "Privatrechtsgesellschaft"* (2006), 194–6, 348; Niklas Luhmann, *Grundrechte als Institution. Ein Beitrag zur politischen Soziologie* (Berlin: Duncker & Humblot, 2nd edn, 1975); Helmut Willke, *Stand und Kritik der neueren Grundrechtstheorie. Schritte zu einer normativen Systemtheorie* (Berlin: Duncker und Humblot, 1975), 21–3, 157–71; Gunther Teubner, "Globale Zivilverfassungen. Alternativen zur staatszentrierten Verfassungstheorie" (2003) 63 Zeitschrift für Ausländisches Öffentliches Recht und Völkerrecht 1–28. For a particular focus on religion, see Niklas Luhmann, *Die Religion der Gesellschaft* (Frankfurt am Main: Suhrkamp, 2000), 315; Friedrich Wilhelm Graf, *Die Wiederkehr der Götter: Religion in der modernen Kultur* (München: Beck, 2004), 239–41.

[10] Eugène Enriquez and Claudine Haroche, *La face obscure des démocraties modernes* (Ramonville Saint-Agne: Erès, 2002), 22.

no longer related to and embedded in stable legal or social institutions that structure a trans-subjective process of self-organization of freedom and create networks of inter-relationships in society (markets, mass communication, religion, art, etc.),[11] but they are regarded as protecting individual "identities," which can be readily generated in a multiplicity of versions and which can be freely chosen by persons following their preferences.[12] These seemingly autonomous choices are manipulated by special bureaucracies[13] and are, at the same time, failures of autonomous choice procedures, which are cured by the therapeutic state.

Meaning is no longer derived from religion or identification with a traditional nation-state.[14] As a consequence, religious freedom as a public, mainly collective, institution has been transformed into a fragment of a diffuse "right to identity" that blurs the line between the public and private domains. The public dimension of "civil rights" shrinks and re-emerges as a diffuse "right to recognition" of the freely chosen identity by public authorities and, finally, by every individual. "Recognition" is an extremely open formula whose volatility can be demonstrated by the fact that the classical liberal "harm principle," which was referred to when it came to the determination of the limits of the exercise of freedom, has lost its relevance in decision-making processes, both in public procedures and in private firms. This principle has an element of "social epistemology" to it, which was used as a frame of reference for the definition of social and normative rules. "Harm" refers to a social knowledge basis, which is implicit in a multiplicity of fields of practice, from which "experience," as a product of a distributed "culture of improvement," emerges—as opposed to a state-centered "polizeywissenschaft" (in Germany), which pre-supposes the centrality of the state and its privileged position as an observer of society.

This general cognitive framework is also based upon a kind of meta-decision on what one can expect from others, in general, and the more personal feelings which belong to the private sphere.

As Marcel Gauchet has convincingly argued, religious fundamentalism is a new phenomenon that challenges postmodern societies, particularly those which have done everything to demonstrate that religion is not necessary for them.[15] Religious fundamentalism is closely linked to its antidote, a weak, narcissistic personality, in a paradoxically symmetric way. Fundamentalism asserts an understanding of religion as a personal preference of the individual. The heteronomy of religion has been transformed into the autonomy of individual identity. The postmodern version of religious fundamentalism is focused on a personal expressive interiority of *feelings*, not of religious behavior, attitudes, or an attachment to a collective religious order.[16] This evolution has brought state schools, in particular, into troubled waters: one need only refer to the Crucifix-case in Bavaria (and in Italy), the "headscarf" affairs,

[11] Dany-Robert Dufour, *L'Art de réduire les têtes: Sur la nouvelle servitude de l'homme libéré à l'ère du capitalisme total* (Paris: Denoël, 2003), 127; Michel Schneider, *La confusion des sexes* (Paris: Flammarion, 2007), 77.

[12] Kenneth J. Gergen, *The Saturated Self: Dilemmas of Identity in Contemporary Life* (New York: Basic Books, 1991), 146.

[13] Jeffery Stout, *Ethics after Babel: The Languages of Morals and their Discontents* (1988), 207.

[14] Samuel Weber, *Benjamin's -abilities* (Cambridge, MA: Harvard University Press, 2008), 254.

[15] Marcel Gauchet, *Un monde désenchanté?* (Paris: Éditions de l'Atelier, 2004), 147.

[16] Gauchet, *Un monde désenchanté?* 169,183.

sexual instruction, school prayers, home education, etc. It is much more difficult to strike a balance between conflicting *collective* understandings of religion and public "therapeutic" engagements with a view to the harmonization of conflicting "personal identities."

Against this background, it should be very important for postmodern secularized societies to reflect more on the fate of their *institutions* and try to find a way to re-establish a stable "binding" core element of the law,[17] not in the sense of a limit imposed on the imaginary autonomy of an individual that tries to assert its "identity," but of the law's constitutive character as a symbolic order of the "Other."[18] The recognition of this perplexing alien "Other" allows for the understanding of rules as a "grid for action"[19] and prepares the ground for the basic structure of a "communal setting among and between *selves*, rather than what is experienced within the *self*." Institutions are sets of anonymous rules, which blur the boundaries between normative and cognitive rationalities. Accepting the limits of autonomy and transparency, on the one hand, and the illusionary sovereignty of the nation-state and its claim to guarantee identity, on the other, opens up a trans-subjective structure generated and retained from the intergenerational process of observation of the patterns of coordination that limit the narcissism and the destructive fantasies of man, on the one hand, and make possible the emergence of trust in society (beyond inter-subjective relationships), on the other.

This consideration brings us back to religion. For a secularized society, it may be valuable to make more room for religion in public education in particular. Religion may remind even non-religious persons of the inescapability of a heterogeneous order that does not dissolve into a collection of identity choices that demand mutual recognition. Religion, in the sense referred to here, preserves the feeling of "perplexity" that emerges from the challenge of transcendence that has left its traces in the cultural infrastructure of (post)modern societies.[20] It may, then, be easier to look for some meta-rules of the "collision" of divergent religions in public institutions. Also, this approach may allow for a more differentiated observation of colliding religious orders. A distinction can be made, for example, between practical moral rules (sexuality) or cultural preferences in subjects of literature to be treated in courses and doctrinal "propositions" in theology, etc. Fundamentalism is itself based upon expressive cults of illusionary communities of *selves*, which try to escape from the inevitable involvement in the social realm of rules and practices that traditional religions have always accepted. The new versions of "me-religions" are no different from other understandings of "individual rights" regarded as asserting personal feelings against alienating heterogeneous social constraints.

[17] Myriam Revault d'Allonnes, *Le pouvoir des commencements: Essai sur l'autorité* (Paris: Éd. du Seuil, 2006), 250.

[18] Weber, *Benjamin's -abilities* 54.

[19] Adam B. Seligman, *Modernity's Wager: Authority, the Self and Transcendence* (Princeton: Princeton University Press, 2000), 93.

[20] Richard Velkley, "On the Roots of Rationalism: Strauss's Natural Right and History as Response to Heidegger" (2008) 70 *Review of Politics* 245, 250.

III. Individualization And Privatization of The Legal Status of Religion In Germany

A. The recent evolution of constitutional doctrine and court practice

In Germany, there is an increasing tendency to regard the privatization of religion[21] and the principle of the "neutrality" of the state in religious matters[22] as the central elements of the constitutional status of religion. At the same time, it is undeniable that constitutional norms that integrate religion into the public realm are reduced to mere exceptions to the rule.[23] The right of religious communities to provide for religious instruction in public schools as an equal part of the teaching program (including in examinations), which is guaranteed by Article 7 paragraph 4 of the Federal Constitution (Grundgesetz), is one of the elements that grants religious communities a special "public status." The right itself has the character of a constitutional freedom to act, and, at the same time, remains a social right in as much as it includes the right to financial subventions for teachers and the equality of religious instruction in the school curriculum.

The recent tendency to downplay the public role of religion within the state seems to be not without consequence if one considers the norms of the federal constitution alone. But, in a systematic and historical interpretation, one has to pay tribute to the fact that the major norms on the constitutional basis of public instruction according to the division of competencies in the federal order are to be found in the constitutions of the *Länder*. In the earlier constitutions (not in the constitutions of the eastern *Länder*), one finds general norms about the Christian character of public instruction in general (beyond religious instruction in the stricter sense). These norms can be explained as part of a compromise between the state and the Christian churches, which demanded influence over public schooling in exchange for self-restraint in the field of private schools.[24] The Federal Constitutional Court has regarded these constitutional norms, for example, of the *Land-Baden*-Württemberg, on the Christian character of public schools as being in conformity with the federal constitutional requirements—this decision[25] was published

[21] See Ansgar Hense, "Zwischen Kollektivität und Individualität. Einige geschichtliche Aspekte der Religionsfreiheit," in Hans Michael Heinig and Christian Walter (eds), *Staatskirchenrecht oder Religions-verfassungsrecht?, Ein begriffspolitischer Grundsatzstreit* (Tübingen: Mohr Siebeck, 2007), 7, 26; Marcel Gauchet, *La religion dans la démocratie: Parcours de la laïcité* (Paris: Gallimard, 2001), 105–10; Gauchet, *Un monde désenchanté?* 182–4 (taking the view that religion in postmodern times has necessarily become individualistic); Oliver Lepsius, "Die Religionsfreiheit als Minderheitenrecht in Deutschland, Frankreich und den USA" (2006) 34 *Leviathan* 321 (describing the transformation in a historical and comparative perspective).

[22] For a discussion of the concept of "neutrality," see Stefan Huster, *Die ethische Neutralität des States. Eine liberale Interpretation der Verfassung* (Tübingen: Mohr Siebeck, 2002), 112–15; Stefan Huster, "Die Bedeutung des Neutralitätsgebotes für die verfassungstheoretische und verfassungsrechtliche Einordnung des Religionsrechts," in Walter and Heinig, *Religionsverfassungsrecht* 107, 109, 121.

[23] Huster, "Die Bedeutung" 120.

[24] This sector of schooling is to this day underdeveloped, though the reticence of the churches to establish private religious schools is declining.

[25] For the constitutional status of religion in the "Christian community schools" in Baden-Württemberg, see Bundesverfassungsgerichts [BVerfGE] [Federal Constitutional Court] 17 Dec. 1975, 41 Entscheidungen des Bundesverfassungsgerichts [BVerfGE] 29 (F.R.G.); and in Nordrhein-Westfalen, see Bundesverfassungsgerichts [BVerfGE] [Federal Constitutional Court] 17 Dec. 1975, 41 Entscheidungen des Bundesverfassungsgerichts [BVerfGE] 88 (F.R.G.).

in 1975, before the rise of the more recent above-mentioned tendency toward privatization of religion.[26]

In its 1995 decision about the restriction of the exhibition of the Christian crucifix in public classrooms,[27] the court paid little attention to an earlier judgment on the separation of powers in a federal system and discussed the importance of the negative right to religious freedom, i.e. the right not to be confronted with religious symbols or rituals (school prayers) in the public realm.[28]

This constitutional freedom, whose status is not beyond doubt, has become increasingly the "Grundnorm" (the centerpiece) of the "constitution of religion" (*Religions verfassungsrecht*),[29] which is regarded as one of the pillars of the principle of neutrality of the state (federal and *Länder*). This new concept tends to replace the older version of the law on the relationship between the state and the churches (*Staatskirchenrecht*). This evolution is one of the symptoms of an increasing individualization of religious freedom,[30] which increasingly undermines the former public status of the churches, and, as a consequence, the collective and organizational dimension of religion as opposed to the individual rights of man. This collective dimension had the repercussion of allowing churches to make binding contracts with the state in religious matters, including the recognition that the Holy See could use international law for its contracts (*Konkordat*).

B. Which role for "constitutional preconditions" in doctrine?

This new development towards a "constitution of religion" as an individualistic paradigm has recently been given a representative form by Christoph Möllers[31] —a rising star of constitutional law—at the annual conference of the association of German professors of "state law."[32] As a first step, Möllers denies the constitutional status of the "principle of neutrality" of the modern state[33] as the antidote of a more traditional principle of

[26] Bundesverfassungsgerichts [BVerfGE] [Federal Constitutional Court] 17 Dec. 1975, 41 Entscheidungen des Bundesverfassungsgerichts [BVerfGE] 29 (F.R.G.). The Federal Constitutional Court refers to the Christian "values of education and culture" as a legitimate framing of public education by the legislator and the constitutions of the Länder. See Bundesverfassungsgerichts [BVerfGE] [Federal Constitutional Court] 16 May 1995, 93 Entscheidungen des Bundesverfassungsgerichts [BVerfGE] 1 (F.R.G.); see also Winfried Brugger and Stefan Huster (eds), *Der Streit um das Kreuz in der Schule. Zur* religiös-weltanschaulichen Neutralität des Staates (Baden-Baden: Nomos Verlagsgesellschaft, 1998) (providing documentation of the controversy that was raised by this decision). For a discussion of this matter under Italian law, see Corte Cost., 13 Dec. 2004, n 389. See also Claus Dieter Classen, *Religionsrecht* (Tübingen: Mohr Siebeck, 2006), paras 185–7; Hans Michael Heinig, "The Headscarf of a Muslim Teacher in German Public Schools," in Winfried Brugger and Michael Karayanni (eds), *Religion in the Public Sphere: A Comparative Analysis of German, Israeli, American and International Law* (Berlin, New York: Springer, 2007), 181.

[27] See 93 BVerfGE 1; see also Brugger and Stefan Huster, *Der Streit* (providing documentation of the controversy that was raised by this decision).

[28] See Classen, *Religionsrecht* paras 161–3, 291.

[29] For the evolution of the recent change towards "Religionsverfassungsrecht" instead of "Staatskirchenrecht," see the contributions in Walter and Heinig, *Religionsverfassungsrecht*, in particular the overview by Hans Michael Heinig, "Kritik und Selbstkritik," at 357.

[30] See Stefan Korioth, "Die Entwicklung des Staatskirchenrechts in Deutschland seit der Reformation," in Walter and Heinig, *Religionsverfassungsrecht* 53, 59–60 (discussing the individualization of religious freedom); Gauchet, *La religion dans la démocratie*.

[31] Christoph Möllers, "Religiöse Freiheit als Gefahr?," 2 Oct. 2008 (Report at the annual conference of the Association of German Professors of Public Law at Erlangen).

[32] This self-description had in itself a symbolic value in the past, because it distances itself from the more open concept of "constitutional law" with its comprehensive perspective on society.

[33] Möllers, "Religiöse Freiheit als Gefahr?," thesis no 4.

"coordination" of state and churches in the public realm because it cannot claim to add legal value to the protection of the individual guaranteed by constitutional liberties. As a second step, he denies the legal value of the western Christian culture as "constitutional presupposition" (*Verfassungsvoraussetzung*)[34] as a supposedly historical resource that might give orientation to the understanding of constitutional norms. According to Möllers, such an assumption would neglect the "plurality and the contradictions inherent in existing traditions and their darker side."[35] Religious traditions can be part of a liberal constitutional order—and have, in fact, been integrated in the German constitution—but this is only due to the positive constitutional *decisions* to make them the objects of positive law. This construction follows in a problematic way the tradition of the subject philosophy and its "foundational function" in claiming to frame our experience of reality. By its supposedly self-reflexive transparency, it claims to be able to lay a foundation for knowledge, and, by its sovereignty, it posits itself as the founder of normativity.[36] One could read Jacques Derrida's reference to the "Christian scansion" of the history of fraternity as the precondition of democracy in "Politics of Friendship"[37] in the perspective taken here. Democracy seems to be "called forth by a tradition that precedes, overshadows, and sustains it."[38] The ongoing process of rewriting and rereading culture is a consequence of the inescapable experience of a recognition of the *Other*, a heritage we cannot reject—a recognition that is reflected in dialogue with the others as "neighbors." This, in turn, requires first an understanding of the *Other's* tradition, community, and conception of individuality.[39] In other words, identity needs a "social footing" as a precondition for communicability and as a basis for personality to which rights and obligations can be attributed.[40]

[34] German constitutional doctrine traditionally refers to "constitutional preconditions" in order to legitimize the assumption that an institution (like the state or, according to some, a church) has to be attributed a constitutional status beyond the wording of constitutional norms. This assumption is rejected in recent literature (with good reasons). See Möllers, "Religiöse Freiheit als Gefahr?," thesis no 4; Christian Walter, *Religionsverfassungsrecht. In vergleichender und internationaler Perspektive* (Tubingen: Mohr Siebeck, 2006), 551, 553; Huster, "Die Bedeutung" 124. The position that is taken in this article does in fact invoke a "prepolitical conception" of culture (critique in Huster, *Die Bedeutung* 128) that does not reduce the collective dimension of the constitution to democratic decision-making, but regards culture as a frame of reference for public schools in particular. As such, it is characterized by "structural variety," Dirk Baecker, *Wozu Kultur?* (Berlin: Kulturverlag Kadmos, 2000), 157, and "indefinitely extended, historical revisions," Joseph Margolis, *The Arts and the Definition of the Human: Towards a Philosophical Anthropology* (Stanford, Calif.: Stanford University Press, 2009), 94. This is what one may call, with Margolis, "objectivity... in play." The "cultural world... is subject to indefinitely extended, historicized revisions but it cannot be treated as an obsolete remainder of the past." Margolis, *The Arts and the Definition of the Human* 94. This process is structured by deference to trans-subjective historical constraints that have to be interpreted in public schooling in a paradoxical manner: scholars have to be taught their cultural heritage (including its varieties) and at the same time be prepared to continue the play.

[35] Möllers, "Religiöse Freiheit als Gefahr?," thesis no 5.

[36] Vincent Descombes and Charles Larmore, *Derniéres nouvelles du moi* (Paris: Presses universitaires de France, 2008), 180, 182.

[37] Jacques Derrida, *Politics of Friendship* (George Collins trans.; London, New York: Verso, 1997), 156.

[38] Hent de Vries, *Religion and Violence: Philosophical Perspectives from Kant to Derrida* (Baltimore: Johns Hopkins University Press, 2001), 364 (attenuating this assumption with a question mark).

[39] Leora Batnitzky, *Idolatry and Representation: The Philosophy of Franz Rosenzweig Reconsidered* (Priceton, N.J.: Princeton University Press, 2000), 193; Eric L. Santner, *On the Psychotheology of Everyday Life: Reflections on Freud and Rosenzweig* (Chicago; University of Chicago Press, 2001), 5, 24.

[40] Harrison C. White, *Identity and Control: How Social Formations Emerge* (Princeton: Princeton University Press, 2005), 1.

This version would follow the line drawn by Ernst-Wolfgang Böckenförde in his oft-quoted hypothesis that the modern secularized state lives on preconditions that it cannot create itself.[41] However, the argument that is given here would focus on the inescapability of the theologico-political founding of culture that is transformed and punctuated by a discontinuity of historical processes, but cannot be left behind. This would not end up in a religious mythology but in the Derridean "grammatological" displacement of the "voice" that pretends to (re)present reality to "scripture" and its semiological networks of relationships as its substitute.[42]

C. The withering of the "public sphere"

The concept of the "public sphere" as a paradigm had attained a certain prominence in the 1960's, when the liberal constitutional model of the "society of individuals" was greatly remodeled by the creation of a new layer within a multi-level order of constitutional paradigms that impose a certain structure to constitutional norms and their understanding. This evolution was part of the transformation of the liberal society to the "society of organizations" that attributed not only empirical relevance but also normative value to groups, associations, organizations, media, etc., not only to the individual.[43] The contribution of certain groups to the interpretation of the public sphere as a domain of discussion and filtering or bundling of political alternatives (political parties)—between the individual, on the one hand, and the state as the public decision-maker, on the other—was regarded as essential for the reproduction of culture and political orientation. Among the central actors in this public realm, the churches played a privileged role.[44]

Christoph Möllers's paper tries to formulate a new line of compromise that no longer puts the emphasis on the public status of religion as a collective phenomenon according to its own rationality and following the "positive" freedom of religion. On the contrary, the specifically public constitutional momentum of religion[45] and its collective dimension is, albeit not shifted in a one-sided approach towards the "negative" freedom of religion of the individual, primarily attributed to the state as the organized public actor. This gives the state broad discretionary leeway, for example in deciding the problem of the legitimacy of presenting religious symbols in public schools (the Muslim headscarf, the exhibition of the crucifix in classrooms) as part of a self-interpretation of the "democratic state." This is regarded as part of the "democratic *raison d'état*"—a symptomatic formulation—that can be referred to whenever the state wants to reject the widespread

[41] Ernst-Wolfgang Böckenförde, *Staat, Gesellschaft, Freiheit. Studien zur Staatstheorie und zum Verfassungsrecht* (Frankfurt am Main: Suhrkamp, 1976), 60.

[42] This goes back to Sigmund Freud's devaluation of the voice and the "presence" of words. See Jacques le Rider, *Freud, de l'acropole au sinaï: le retour a l'antique des modernes viennois* (Paris: PUF, 2002), 258.

[43] See Ulrich K. Preuß, *Zum staatsrechtlichen Begriff des Öffentlichen. Untersucht am Beispiel des verfassungsrechtlichen Status kultureller Organisationen* (Stuttgart, E. Klett 1969); Helmut K.J. Ridder, *Die öffentliche Aufgabe der Presse im System des modernen Verfassungsrechtes* (Wien: Verband Österr. Zeitungsherausgeber, 1962); Alfred Rinken, *Das Öffentliche als verfassungstheoretisches Problem. Dargestellt am Rechtsstatus der Wohlfahrtsverbände* (Berlin: Duncker & Humblot, 1971).

[44] See Rudolf Smend, *Verfassung undVverfassungsrecht* (München: Leipzig, Duncker & Humblot, 1928), 80 (providing a historical perspective); Korioth, "Die Entwicklung des Staatskirchenrechts in Deutschland seit der Reformation" 39, 59 (discussing the evolution of the public dimension of churches in Germany).

[45] For a discussion of the *individual* self-interpretation in the process of doctrinal structuring of the limits of constitutional liberties, see Martin Morlok, *Selbstverständnis als Rechtskriterium* (Tübingen: J.C.B. Mohr, 1993).

invocation of negative religious freedom against any unwelcome confrontation with religious symbols in the public sphere.

The problem of the argumentative weight of "constitutional preconditions" beyond the text of constitutional norms[46] as such is solved in a reductionist way: it is reformulated as the necessity to consider the self-interpretation of individuals, as in the domain of the arts, science, etc., on the one hand, while the collective dimension of this problem is boiled down by the recognition of the state itself as "the constitutional precondition *par excellence*."

According to a recent decision of the Federal Constitutional Court, in the event of a collision between the general obligation to attend schools and the religious freedom of parents who intend to teach their children at home[47] the former prevails because the state has a legitimate concern for the general capability to enter into dialogue with others that is taken to be a "basic precondition" (*Grundvoraussetzung*) of democratic decision-making and involvement in a public sphere.[48] Thus, religious freedom cannot be invoked to call the general obligation to attend schools into question. The knowledge-generating function of schools and their contribution to the formation of personal identities as a precondition of the exercise of constitutional liberties is reduced in quite a symptomatic way to the reproduction of the democratic *state*. One might ask whether the basic conditions of instruction cannot be guaranteed by parents themselves if certain requirements are fulfilled—as is the case in the United States—and attenuate the general obligation to attend public or private schools. This argumentation also includes a characteristic tendency to evade the collective dimension of religious freedom, which refers to different modes of coupling religion and western society.[49] This paradox seems to disappear when it is turned into the object of a democratic majority decision. At this point, it is no longer the entanglement of a historical form of life and constitutional law that is at stake, but merely a public decision that is, as such, beyond the constraint of justification. The productive societal tension between law, society, and religion is being cooled off. The cultural-linguistic symbolic dimension of a form of life that has dominated, and still dominates, the lives of individuals and societies[50] becomes a "competency" within the domain of state actions that seems to be able to absorb the collective character of what was formerly part of a separate societal public sphere. What is left to society is the individual option (a decision in itself) for religious freedom.

However, the collective dimension of the constitutive character of religion, which shapes the identity of individuals by paradoxical societal means—there is no self-construction of identity—is brought to bear when George Lindbeck assumes that "open societies" need religious communities in the process of inculcating "moral abstraction" in individuals, which is paradoxically necessary for the preservation of the openness and plurality of society.[51] In the same vein, Eric P. Santner takes the view that the biblical (in particular, the Jewish) tradition is the beginning of a form of life, and

[46] See Walter, *Religiongsverfassungsrecht* 76–8 (discussing the historical evolution).

[47] Because of ethical concerns for sexual instruction and lax moral standards of behavior.

[48] Bundesverfassungsgerichts [BVerfGE] [Federal Constitutional Court] 6 Jun. 2006, 2 Entscheidungen des Bundesverfassungsgerichts [BVerfGE] 1693 (F.R.G.).

[49] See Classen, *Religionsrecht* paras 76–9 (providing a discussion of the collective dimension of religious freedom (which is increasingly being played down)); Hense, "Zwischen Kollektivität und Individualität" 14; see also Louis Dumont, "Religion, Politics and Society in the Individualistic Universe" (1971) 7 (N.S.) *Proceedings of the Royal Anthropological Institute* 31, 32 (providing a comparative perspective).

[50] George A. Lindbeck, *The Nature of Doctrine: Religion and Theology in a Postliberal Age* (Philadelphia: Westminster Press, 1984), 22.

[51] Lindbeck, *The Nature of Doctrine* 66.

not only of reflection, which is the foundation of an opening towards the *Other*, the strangeness, as the reference to a "universality-in-becoming."[52] "Universality" is, in this perspective, regarded as a "possibility of a shared opening to the . . . turbulence *immanent* to the very construction of identity."[53] The "human being becomes a 'subject' by acts of foundation, preservation, and augmentation"[54] —with this conception, Santner builds a bridge between the psychoanalytic notion of the unconscious and the (not only Jewish) view of God and religion. From a similar perspective, Hans Joas regards religion as being founded in the "experience of transcendence."[55] This "experience of transcendence" is an experience in which the person also transcends himself or herself, not in the sense of a moral overcoming of the individual moral judgment, but in the sense of being thrown outside the limits of the self, of a being captured by something which lies beyond one's individual self, a movement that liberates from the fixation on one's self. The believers offer the non-believers the possibility of making this discovery of the *Other* for themselves—an offer that can, of course, miss the addressees.[56]

IV. Religion without Culture—Culture Without Religion?

A. The conflict between trans-subjective and subjective components of religious freedom

Under this construction, religion is attributed a basic function that, in Möllers' view, is encapsulated in a circular self-referential reflection of the state by a public decision. His argument that the plurality and ambivalence of religious forms (their potential destructive side) tended to be ignored in a reference to religion as a "constitutional precondition," as a societal non-state based "foundation," is itself erroneous; the openness and plurality of the Judeo-Christian tradition[57] is not an impediment to the construction of identity-building as a kind of appropriation of one's part in a collective culture.[58] On the contrary, it is the form that gives historical viability to the paradox of the collective venture of founding individual freedom. It goes without saying that this is not a plea for a "state religion." The state is not allowed to identify with religious ideas or discriminate against minority beliefs or non-believers—this is the true kernel of the "neutrality principle."[59]

This is different for those elements of religion that extend beyond "belief" in the stricter sense, and that have found their expression or repercussions in literature, morality, or Christian symbols—including the crucifix.[60] At this point, a clarification is necessary: these remarks should not be misunderstood as a conception that denigrates the religious content

[52] Santner, *On the Psychotheology of Everyday Life* 5.

[53] Santner, *On the Psychotheology of Everyday Life*.

[54] Santner, *On the Psychotheology of Everyday Life* 26.

[55] Hans Joas, *Braucht der Mensch Religion? Über Erfahrungen der Selbsttranszendenz* (Freiburg im Breisgau: Herder, 2004), 17.

[56] Joas, *Braucht der Mensch Religion?* 17, 31, 35.

[57] Stéphane Mosès, *Eros und Gesetz. Zehn Lektüren der Bibel* (Paderborn: Wilhelm Fink Verlag, 2004), 91.

[58] Dror Wahrman, *The Making of the Modern Self: Identity and Culture in Eighteenth Century England* (New Haven: Yale University Press, 2004), 168.

[59] See Karl-Heinz Ladeur and Ino Augsberg, "The Myth of the Neutral State: The Relationship Between State and Religion in the Face of New Challenges" (2007) 8 *German Law Journal* 2, available at <http://www.germanlawjournal.com/article.php?id=795> (providing an English summary of Ladeur and Augsberg, *Tolerenze-Religione-Recht*).

[60] For the communicative message of the crucifix, see Huster, *Die Ethische* 152, and the dissenting opinion of three judges in Bundesverfassungsgerichts [BVerfGE] [Federal Constitutional Court] 16 May 1995, 93 Entscheidungen des Bundesverfassungsgerichts [BVerfGE] 1 (F.R.G.).

of this symbol in favor of its cultural meaning,[61] as has been argued in the conflict over the constitutional acceptability of a crucifix in Bavarian or Italian state schools with the intention of reducing the emotional tensions that came to the fore in the public debate by formulating a compromise. However, the crucifix is a symbol that allows for different readings; it is a Christian religious symbol for some, and it can be a cultural symbol for others, which may be interpreted in a positive or a negative way. The state may well allow this conflict of interpretation to be deployed in the public domain. The principle of "neutrality of the state" implies that the state is not allowed to define "the religious"[62] but can only establish meta-rules for the management of a regime conflict that may open the regime of public education for a "reentry" of "the religious" as it is defined by religious institutions into the realm of public education as far as it is compatible with culture as the "collective memory."

Here, a parallel may be drawn with the decision of the Federal Constitutional Court on the legality of school prayers in state schools.[63] According to the view taken by the Court, an identification of the state, on the one hand, and a constraint imposed on the pupils, on the other, would be incompatible with the freedom of religion, even if "exceptions" for both teachers and pupils were accepted. However, giving the opportunity to both groups to say a prayer *before* the beginning of school instruction (early in the morning) is a constitutional option which follows the model of religious instruction according to the German understanding of "neutrality," which is not equivalent to the French "laïcité." The role of the so-called negative freedom of religion, which may appear to be infringed by the public exhibition of religious symbols that can be attributed to "state acts," should not be overstated. It should not be invoked with the intention of imposing restrictions on that positive religious freedom of pupils and teachers which is the core of this civil right. In this respect, the German distinction between the positive and the negative version of this freedom may be misleading.

B. Reenter the cultural dimension of religion

The coupling of religion and the evolution of collective cultural traditions that play a role in the formation of individual identities is also the means for legitimacy of the privileged position of the established Christian denominations. The dominant, more individualized interpretation of religion reinforces in a normative perspective a tendency to separate not only the state and religion but *culture* and religion.[64] This distinction opens the legitimate space for tolerance as the meta-norm for the management of conflicts with other minority religions or non-believers.[65] Their position *vis-à-vis* the objective collective and cultural weight of religious traditions in the public sphere has to be guaranteed

[61] The crucifix is a religious symbol, but this does not exclude the possibility of a public authority as such—in a polycontextual setting of different systems—to observe the symbol as a cultural one.

[62] In fact, this obviously happens more often than not in state practice. See Olivier Rey, *La sainte ignorance: le temps de la religion sans culture* (Paris: Editions du Seuil, 2008), 252.

[63] Bundesverfassungsgerichts [BVerfGE] [Federal Constitutional Court] 16 Oct. 1973, 52 Entscheidungen des Bundesverfassungsgerichts [BVerfGE] 223 (F.R.G.); Classen, *Religionsrecht* paras 161–3.

[64] Rey, *La sainte ignorance: le temps de la religion sans culture* passim.

[65] Bundesverfassungsgerichts [BVerfGE] [Federal Constitutional Court] 16 Oct. 1979, 93 Entscheidungen des Bundesverfassungsgerichts [BVerfGE] 1 (8) (F.R.G.); Bundesverfassungsgerichts [BVerfGE] [Federal Constitutional Court] 16 Oct. 1979, 52 Entscheidungen des Bundesver fassungsgerichts [BVerfGE] 223 (241) (F.R.G); Volker Wick, *Die trennung von staat und kirche* (München: Beck, 2006), 82.

by the individual components of religious freedom, which have to be recognized in state schools in particular. This element is primarily embodied in the negative religious freedom, but is also present in the principle of respect for cultural diversity in public instruction in general. This is the counterpart of the collective momentum of religion and religious values in the process of forming identities in state schools.

The impact of religious traditions on the common culture and the reproduction of a shared knowledge basis in state schools is a consequence of the inscription of the trans-subjective element of the symbolic-linguistic forms of life, which must be inculcated in the process of the cultural reproduction of a society. The tendency toward a decoupling of religion and society is equivalent to an "exculturation" of religion, or alternatively a reduction in the meaning of culture.[66] In this respect, there cannot be an unlimited range of options offered to individuals; there is always a "heritage" that, in itself, includes a reference to the future openness and plurality of culture for the adolescent or adult individual. A formal equality of religions cannot be expected or established at this stage of identity construction in the domain of public schools. However, a specific "structural tolerance" ("structure *tolérance*")[67] in the public sphere has to be determined by the fact that, at a first stage of public education (of younger pupils), the "heritage" character of culture, the reproduction of a "collective memory,"[68] can take a privileged position to the detriment of cultural and religious divergence and plurality. As mentioned above, at this stage, the following stage of cultural reproduction already has to be anticipated and prepared for,[69] i.e. the transition from a presupposed, un-chosen model of identity to a culture of choice, of diversity and plurality that opens the path toward a self-reflexive position *vis-à-vis* the multiplicity of options inherent in the "pool of variety" of a liberal culture.[70] This hypothesis does not imply the assumption that it is only through religion that access to the "common pool of ideas" of shared knowledge, which should open a space of individual choice and self-construction, is imaginable. But it can be assumed that an alternative is not easy to formulate, which is demonstrated by the irritating and uncertain role of state schooling in postmodern fragmented societies. The position taken in this chapter only favors the hypothesis that it is difficult to renounce the contribution of religion to the formation of identities by schools in liberal societies.[71] This is why one can, in fact, speak of the role of established religious denominations in

66 Rey, *La sainte ignorance: le temps de la religion sans culture* 153, 156.

67 Zarka and Fleury, *Difficile tolérance.*

68 Cf Baecker, *Wozu Kultur?* 158; Margolis, *The Arts and the Definition of the Human* 24, 94. See generally Jan Assmann, *Das kulturelle Gedächtnis: Schrift, Erinnerung und Identität in frühen Hochkulturen* (München: C.H. Beck, 1997), 29, 34; Maurice Halbwachs, *Das Gedächtnis und seine sozialen Bedingungen* (Frankfurt am Main: Suhrkamp, 1985).

69 Zarka and Fleury, *Difficile tolerance* 148–9; cf Jean-Claude Kaufmann, *Quand je est un autre: pourquoi et comment ça change en nous* (Paris: Armand Colin, 2008), 89–90.

70 Zarka and Fleury, *Difficile tolerance* 148–9; see also Kaufmann, *Quand je est un autre* 89–90.

71 For the "blind spot" of the *becoming* of a person in theories of the public rationality of communication, see Jill Gentile, "Between Private and Public: Towards a Conception of the Transitional Subject" (2008) 89 *International Journal of Psychoanalysis* 959, 960, 970. "Through the creation of symbols... we actually create ourselves as symbols, becoming part of material and cultural life." The individual "truly belong[s] *between* private and public," which creates a paradoxical challenge for public schooling, which, in a sense, has to *generate* individuals and refer to liberty in the future. Gentile, "Between Private and Public: Towards a Conception of the Transitional Subject" 959, 960, 970. The concept of the "transitional *subject*," which elaborates upon Winnicott's seminal idea of the "transitional object," might indicate the "not yet" of the adolescent's being a person. See d'Allonnes, *Le pouvoir des commencements* 251 (providing a view to the trans-subjective "symbolic system," which structures a series of events and establishes a "longue durée" of meaning).

a collective culture as being a "precondition of the constitution" that, unlike an explicit decision, allows for a broad interpretation of the constitutional norms concerning the status of religion in state schools. This role cannot be attributed to religion solely by positive law in the stricter sense, as Möllers assumes, because of its inscription in a distributed knowledge base that finds its repercussions in literature, in practices of teaching, moral standards, and conventions of respect and politeness, etc., all of which are mainly implicit to a culture and can be reflected upon only in a limited and case-by-case way. This can be demonstrated by the case of the crucifix. What is the normative value of a norm that allows for the exhibition of the crucifix in state schools? There is no clear rule that might be imposed by positive law, but only the reference to a precondition of schooling, which loses its sense once it no longer resonates with the practice of learning. "Constitutional preconditions" have mainly an unconscious character; they are the "traces" of the past, which have to be interpreted and adapted again and again to the changing conditions of cultural reproduction, but they are not norms in the stricter sense that always presuppose the adult individual as the subject of choice and the addressee of obligations.

V. "Collision Rules" Instead of the "Neutrality Principle"

A. The paradox of a public obligation to form free individuals

One should not be misled by the fact that, naturally, a (school) administration is the addressee of an obligation to exhibit the crucifix in classrooms (if such a norm exists). However, the explicit binding element *vis-à-vis* teachers and pupils is something different; it is, in fact, very limited. In this respect, it should be repeated that the role of civil liberties is not exhausted by its functions as a guarantee of individual choices in different social systems (arts, economics, science, etc.)[72] and a limit imposed on state acts that intend to reduce this liberty (*Abwehrrecht*), and a supplementary component of civil rights exists in the guarantee of the societal self-organization of norms, conventions, patterns of action, values, and practices. This relational rationality of civil rights, which is concerned with the networks of relationships among individuals (and organizations), also finds its expression in institutions, such as state schools, which are meant to reproduce the possibilities of access to, and participation in, these networks. This is the background condition of the state school as the trans-subjective institution that has a constitutional status in Germany. This paradoxical trans-subjective component of public education cannot be reduced in a one-sided way to an individual right to public assistance because of its enabling role in the process of becoming a subject of choices. Neither can it be dissolved in the positive competency of the state to make decisions on the organization of public instruction (this would be Möllers' position).

A restriction of this collective element of schooling in the process of reproducing the "individual of society"[73] in a merely self-referential perspective on the reproduction of democracy as a form of the state and its entrenchment in a public realm of debate would not be viable either. The preliminary question of the paradoxical generation of the subject of liberties would be evaded. It should be stressed again that the reference

[72] See Luhmann, *Die Religion der Gesellschaft*; Willke, *Stand und Kritik der nereren Grundrechtstheorie*; Karl-Heinz Ladeur, *Postmoderne Rechtstheorie. Selbstreferenz—Selbstorganisation—Prozeduralisierung* (Berlin: Duncker & Humblot, 2nd edn 1995), 176–90.

[73] See Markus Schroer, *Das Individuum der Gesellschaft. Synchrone und diachrone Theorieperspektiven* (Frankfurt am Main: Suhrkamp, 2001).

to a concept of "identity" does not imply the assumption that a homogeneous unity of the individual could, or should, be the "goal" of public schooling. On the contrary! It is, instead, the *problématique* of the collective conditions of the constitution of the subject both *of* and *in* a liberal constitutional order that is at stake, and that is missed by the reference to the reproduction of a democratic citizen as the goal of public education.[74] The question of a societal identity of the "individual of society" has to be raised first. "Identity" in this sense refers to the paradoxical question of the beginning of individuality, which cannot, by itself, be the object of "choice"[75] but does remain a precondition for making choices. The far-spread tendency to ignore this paradoxical unconscious or trans-subjective *Other* of the individual, its permanent "shadow," which haunts the individual even after having attained the reflexive capacity to make choices by its continuous processing of cultural revisions and reinterpretations,[76] misses the division in the subject. The individual is merely the self-determination that is emancipated even from the *Other* of the law or the judgment of others (the famous "man within" of Adam Smith) only when it dissolves in the purely ephemeral volatility of a continuously changing combinatory of expressive clichés that are "sampled" in the immediate self-experience offered by the postmodern consumer society.[77] In a less emotional way, individuality becomes the malleable object of permanent "bargaining" with both *Others* and *the state* about the construction of a self.[78]

The consequences of this evolution can be observed in the transformation of the legal system, whose objective abstract and universal structures are increasingly replaced or supplemented by situational "balancing" on a case-by-case basis, in which individual and general elements are entangled in a horizontal network of new "rights" to self-fulfillment and satisfaction of needs, instead of constitutional rights to participate in the trans-subjective networks of the differentiated social systems. The foundational character of the law is replaced by more complex procedural elements of ad hoc coordination of private and public interests that do not allow for the formation of social expectations, norms, conventions, and patterns of action by self-organized institutions that generate a shared "common knowledge," and, on this basis, trust in the stability of society, on the one hand, and a movement of self-observation and self-control, on the other. Religion stands for the inevitable retention of the "split" in the subject,[79] which is the basis of the self-transformation of society and the opening for its diversity and the universality of the *Other* and of the *Others* (the "neighbors"). This is why religion and churches have, with good reason, been the cornerstones of the "public sphere" situated between the state as the organized public actor and the private individuals in civil society. The *problématique*

[74] It is also a widespread illusion to assume that public education can be steered "democratically"—in European countries this illusion takes on the form of the never ending cycle of "reforms" and "reforms of reform." The well-known book by Amy Gutmann, *Democratic Education* (Princeton, N.J.: Princeton University Press, 1987), 54–6, follows the concept of "value clarification," which ends up paying deference to a kind of self-discovery of the individual. See Sidney B. Simon, Leland W. Howe, and Howard Kirschenbaum, *Values Clarification: The Classic Guide to Discovering Your Truest Feelings, Beliefs and Goals* (New York: Warner Books, 1995); see also Marie-Claude Blais, Marcel Gauchet, and Dominique Ottavi, *Conditions de l'education* (Paris: Stock, 2008) (providing a pertinent critique of postmodern public education).

[75] Wahrman, *The Making of the Modern Self* 168.

[76] Margolis, *The Arts and the Definition of the Human* 94–6.

[77] See Olivier Rey, *Une folle solitude: le fantasme de l'homme auto-construit* (Paris: Éditions du Seuil, 2006), 233; Dany-Robert Dufour, *L'art de reduire les têtes: sur la nouvelle servitude de l'homme libéré à l'ère du capitalisme total* (Paris: Denoël, 2003), 127.

[78] Lucien Jaume, *La liberté et la loi: les origins philosophiques du libéralisme* (Paris: Fayard, 2000); Charles Melman, *L'homme sans gravite: jouir à tout prix* (Paris: Denoël, 2005), 129–31 (providing a psychoanalyst's perspective).

[79] Slavoj Žižek, *Das Unbehagen im Subjekt* (Wien: Passagen-Verl., 1998), 124–6.

of post-modernity is mirrored by the rise of the negative freedom of religion—beyond the limits of the obvious legitimacy of protection from constraint in a stricter sense—that has increasingly been transformed into a right not to be confronted with the *Other* of transcendency transfigured by religious symbols in the public sphere.[80] This is one of the phenomena of the transformation of religion in post-modernity, a replacement of transcendence with a need for an immediate expressive feeling of the *Other*, who is the object of a projection of a wish for recognition.[81] The other side of this immediacy of emotional self-affirmation is to be seen in the transformation of the trans-subjective character of religion into a "personal conviction"[82] that rejects any abstract and objective bindingness, including any meta-norms for the coordination of the rules of religion and public norms. This also has consequences for the legal and constitutional determination of what "religion" means: it has been pointed out above that the role of constitutional rights also consists of the self-organization of trans-subjective functional systems in society, including religion.[83] This idea has had repercussions in the earlier judgment of the Federal Constitutional Court, which tried to restrict the protection of the civil right to religious freedom to traditional religions (not just Christianity).[84]

This approach of giving religion more contours went, perhaps, too far, but at least it paid tribute to the trans-subjective component of religion, while the more recent jurisprudence has abandoned all attempts to determine a concept of religion that would reach beyond the subjective feeling of individuals who invoke the right to religious freedom. Civil rights in general, and religious freedom in particular, are reduced to different versions of the same right to personal self-expression and self-affirmation, whereas the unavoidable limits that the use of these rights has to accept is abstracted from the *eigen-rationality* of social systems, and take on the character of a generalized reservation for the requirements of "community" (*Gemeinschaftsbindung*) that is, more or less, defined by the state authorities, and balanced with the self-interpretation of individuals.[85] This evolution cannot be avoided once the *eigen-rationality* of the trans-subjective social systems and their potential self-organization and production of self-imposed constraints is played down. In the end, a definition of what a religion and its specific rationality are, according to a collective practice and its dogmatization, is no longer possible. At the same time, the criteria for the formulation of limits to religious freedom cannot be formulated in a specific manner that could be adapted to the collective understanding of its organizations and traditions. Rather, we are left with personal feelings, which cannot be evaluated in a rational way from the "outside."

B. The legal management of a "regime collision"

The development of Christianity, Judaism, Islam, and other traditional religions has been accompanied by reflections on the "conflict of norms" of religious rules and state

[80] Slavoj Žižek, "Neighbors and Other Monsters: A Plea for Ethical Violence," in Slavoj Žižek, Eric L. Santner, and Kenneth Reinhard, *The Neighbor: Three Inquiries in Political Theology* (Chicago: University of Chicago Press, 2005), 134, 184.

[81] Lindbeck, *The Nature of Doctrine* 22.

[82] Gauchet, *Un monde désenchanté?* 169, 175; Leora Batnitzky, *From Politics to Law: Modern Jewish Thought and the Invention of Jewish Law* (unpublished manuscript) (on file with author), 19.

[83] Luhmann, *Die Religion der Gesellschaft*.

[84] Bundesverfassungsgerichts [BVerfGE] [Federal Constitutional Court] 8 Nov. 1960, 12 Entscheidungen des Bundesverfassungsgerichts [BVerfGE] 1 (4) (F.R.G.); Classen, *Religionsrecht* para 79.

[85] Bundesverfassungsgerichts [BVerfGE] [Federal Constitutional Court] 8 Nov. 1960, 12 Entscheidungen des Bundesverfassungsgerichts [BVerfGE] 1 (F.R.G.); Classen, *Religionsrecht* para 79.

law. This "collision of regimes,"[86] the clash of religion and politics in particular, has led to a number of ways of internalizing the rules generated in other social systems within the *eigen-rationality* of religion. All traditional religions have also been shaped in the past by meta-norms, which allowed for a "structural coupling" of politics and religion. This cooperative approach, and as a consequence the search for "rules of collision," changes fundamentally when religions are increasingly personalized, or, as in the case of Islam, the individualization is used to escape from the legal requirements formulated by a non-traditional western state, while the coordination of religion and politics in Islamic countries poses no serious problems. This is another phenomenon that mirrors the deep transformation that religion has undergone in post-modernity.

The evolution of a personalized understanding of religion corresponds to the above-mentioned tendency to expand the role of negative religious freedom because it may protect the "inner forum" of the believer, who does not refer to symbols in public in the same vein as non-believers. The invocation of the positive version of religious freedom still contains the remnants of a trans-subjective and collective role of religion in the public sphere. The individualization of the principle of tolerance and its coupling with a strong conception of "negative" religious freedom results in the recognition of the right of each individual to live according to his or her own values and preferences, and consequently, the protagonists of a relativistic morality have to refrain from communicating their hypotheses in a multi-cultural society because this would hurt the identity of the adherents of religions.[87]

The complex differentiated status of religion *vis-à-vis* the postmodern western state can be demonstrated with reference to religious instruction in state schools:[88] the right is granted to all religious communities in the same way but the specific relationships between Christian churches and the state have left their traces in the formulation of the conditions that have to be fulfilled by claimants. The right can only be invoked by "religious communities" that have organized themselves in a "church-like" manner, i.e. they have to be autonomous and separate from secular organizations. This condition cannot easily be met by Islamic associations, which do not, in general, acknowledge this principle of clear separation. In addition to this requirement, the constitution presupposes a religious doctrinal self-reflection of spiritual communities that guarantee a certain unity and consistency of the "denomination." This requirement is, again, not easily fulfilled by many of the "new" religious "sects" or by Islam. Notwithstanding the constitutional guarantee of religious instruction, this interpretation of the right of religious communities appears to be adequate because a regime of cooperation between the state and the religious community is at stake, not the self-affirmation of a religion. This is not just freedom of religion but its role in public instruction, which was to adopt certain standards of systematicity, doctrinal reflection for religious instruction, and, as a consequence, an academic education of the teachers. These requirements need not, of course, be met in the autonomous reproduction of faith in churches or equivalent organizations.

This link between a religious constitutional right and state authority is an example of the complexity of the relationship between religion and politics, which cannot be managed by "balancing" alone. It shows that, even in other fields of conflicts, the *problématique*

[86] See Andreas Fischer-Lescano, "Kritik der praktischen Konkordanz" (2008) 41 *Kritische Justiz* 166. See generally Andreas Fischer-Lescano and Gunther Teubner, *Regime-Kollisionen. Zur Fragmentierung des globalen Rechts* (Frankfurt am Main: Suhrkamp, 2006), 57–65, 170–1.

[87] Vincent Descombes, *Le raisonnement de l'ours: Et autres essais de philosophie pratique* (Paris: Éditions du Seuil, 2007), 202.

[88] See Werner Heun, "Integration des Islam," in Walter and Heinig, *Religionsverfassungsrecht* 339.

of the "principle of neutrality" in the public sphere in particular, the question has to be raised of which "collision rules"[89] have to be formulated for the coordination of the trans-subjective collective role of religion and its contributions to the reproduction of culture, on the one hand, and the requirements of respect and tolerance for individual "dissenters," on the other.[90]

A similar "rule of collision" that differentiates between religions and allows for a multilevel order following the conflict line that is at stake might be formulated for the regime of private schools, and religious private schools in particular. According to Article 7 paragraph 4 of the German Constitution, private schools have to be controlled and evaluated by the state. For primary schools, there is still a further requirement that there be a specific pedagogical interest in the establishment of a new type of private school (including a religious one), while, for secondary schools, it is the other way around: pedagogical or other public interest must not conflict with the task of the school. With respect to religious schools, a differentiation is possible, which would favor a cognitive or proof rule that privileges religions which have a long tradition of theological thinking and pedagogical practice. In contrast, new, "fundamentalist" religions should not be able to profit from these procedural rules and the underlying strict administrative scrutiny, which would not, in principle, exclude such religions from organizing private schools. It does not go without saying that fundamentalist religions that favor the emotional-expressive side of religion as opposed to the transcendental *Other* can refer to a rule of presumption that has been tested for traditional religions over the course of centuries.[91] It should not be neglected that this "multilevel" order of "collision rules" does not at all exclude the individual freedom to follow such a religion. At this point, the fundamental traditional "limit of damage,"[92] which can be regarded as a liberal test-standard for public restrictions imposed on individual liberties, can be brought into play. This limit has a protective effect in as much as the presence of the "danger" for a private or public good—not just any interest—is to be valued upon the basis of societal distributed "common knowledge," and not upon a privileged "state (or police) science" on which the state authorities my be tempted to base their decisions, as was the case during the absolutist reign in Europe. As mentioned above, the Federal Constitutional Court in an earlier decision[93] had, in principle, drawn a legal distinction between traditional ("familiar") religions and "alien," or new, religions. In this general form, the distinction is not compatible with religious freedom, although this distinction can be useful within a system of "rules of collision" when it comes to the point where trans-subjective networks of cultural relations have to be referred to, for example, in the conception of state education, or when the protection of children and younger persons from detrimental influences and the presumptive effect of a procedural "rule of freedom" does not count. Against

[89] Fischer-Lescano, "Kritik der praktischen Konkordanz" 166.

[90] If one bears in mind that rules of collision for the conflict of opinions or religions should not primarily harmonize conflicts, but structure a controversy or a clash of values, the exclusion of religious symbols from public schools should only be the last measure taken; to avoid the conflict with the otherness of others should not be a primary goal of public education. See Žižek, "Neighbors and Other Monsters" 178.

[91] Karl-Heinz Ladeur, "Genehmigung privater Konfessionsschulen" (1993) 41 *Recht der Jugend und des Bildungswesens* 282.

[92] See Nadia Urbinati, *Mill on Democracy: From the Athenian Polis to Representative Government* (Chicago: University of Chicago Press, 2002), 134, 162–4.

[93] Bundesverfassungsgerichts [BVerfGE] [Federal Constitutional Court] 8 Nov. 1960, 12 Entscheidungen des Bundesverfassungsgerichts [BVerfGE] 1 (4) (F.R.G.); Classen, *Religionsrecht* para 79.

the background of this distinction between individual freedom and the reproduction of "identity" in the above-mentioned way, the reproduction of a distributed "collective memory" and the link to the movement of the "self- transcendence" of the individual in educational processes does have an institutional standing in the multi-level management of the "collision of rules" (here, politics and religion).

C. For a differentiated typology of conflicts

1. The Islamic "headscarf" in particular

This consideration leads to the question—which has already been raised with reference to school prayers[94] —of whether the role of the state in the process of enabling individuals (pupils, parents, teachers) and organizations to introduce certain subjects of instruction, symbolic forms, or rituals as part of the collective cultural dimension into state schools should not be kept separate from the "official" identification of the state with religious doctrines that might threaten the individual component of religious freedom. These ideas are not equivalent. There seems to be a whole range of relationships between religion and the state in public education. While the state merely offers a framework for personal encounters between teachers and pupils or for pupils among themselves by allowing time to be spent on prayer before the beginning of the official teaching, the state does not identify with religion, which would establish something like a state religion. The possibility of a spillover in the form of discrimination against non-believers cannot be completely discarded, but this is more a pedagogical than legal question.

The necessity of drawing a distinction between different modes of public involvement in religious questions can also be demonstrated for the question of whether a Muslim female teacher is allowed to wear the "Islamic headscarf"[95] or, more generally, whether clearly visible religious symbols may be worn by teachers in public schools. It is clearly not the neutrality of the state, as such, that is at stake—nobody in a Christian or Jewish country would assume that the state identifies with Islam.[96] Instead, it can legitimately be asked whether the teacher as an individual identifies with a version of Islam that does not accept the implicit "collision norms" that are applied in the process of coordination of faith, religious components of the collective culture, and the cognitive components of public education. A teacher has to be able to contribute to the pupils' access to their own culture, bearing also immigrants in mind in order for the teacher to manage the turbulence of a multicultural society. In this respect, a clear distinction has to be made between Islam and Judaism because the *Kippa*, for example, is not an indicator of the unwillingness or inability of its bearer to manage this cultural "conflict of norms." Anyhow, first, a clear distinction should be made between the identifications of an individual, even in a public function, and the state as such. Here again we have to draw a distinction that is ignored by the dominant individualistic interpretation of the relationship between state and religion: the headscarf is, unlike the crucifix and the

[94] Bundesverfassungsgerichts [BVerfGE] [Federal Constitutional Court] 16 Oct. 1979, 52 Entscheidungen des Bundesverfassungsgerichts [BVerfGE] 223 (F.R.G.); Classen, *Religionsrecht* paras 161–3.

[95] See Bundesverfassungsgerichts [BVerfGE] [Federal Constitutional Court] 24 Sept. 2003, 108 Entscheidungen des Bundesverfassungsgerichts [BVerfGE] 282 (F.R.G.) (discussing the conflict over the "Islamic headscarf" in Germany); Huster, *Die Bedeutung* 117–18.

[96] See Huster, *Die Bedeutung* 118 (discussing the problem of the attribution of the symbolic value of the headscarf to the state).

Kippa, not really a sign but a "thing" that hides the female body (or a part of it) from the male gaze because of its supposed fascination.[97] This "thing" may of course be (and is in fact in post-modernity) recoded, but as such it demonstrates the close relationship between culture and religion because it inscribes a social status in the body, and this inscription collides with the cultural heritage of western societies.

2. *The constitutional liberty of private schools as an escape clause*

With respect to Islam, the collision has to be handled in a differentiated way as outlined above. Clearly, the evolution of a hermeneutically reflected Islam in western societies cannot be excluded for the future. However, for the time being, a rule of presumption in the procedure of decision making on the legality of private Islamic schools cannot be brought to bear on the legal evaluation. This is different again for the question of whether the individual female pupil can refer to Islamic rules of clothing for women: in this constellation, the individual option of the woman (even if it is chosen under the pressure of tradition) takes the lead over the collective dimension of the reproduction of identity in a western society, which would occur in a private school. This is the way a western society "constructs" a conflict between the elements of a collective memory and its reproduction on the one hand, and the rise of a competing collectivity on the other:[98] It can only be reduced to the domain of individual freedom,[99] although this may not seem satisfactory to Muslims. One has to add that this may be different from country to country; the "headscarf" may also become a real challenge for the pedagogical prerogatives of the state if it stands for an attitude of resistance against western education. Here, again, the differentiated "collision rules" may be brought to bear on the decision according to the status of religion in German constitutional law. One may not, as an individual parent, challenge the collective character of public education and its contents in a general way—it must be done by collectively founding a new private school, which has to be done in a public procedure. As shown above, the public privilege is reintroduced in this procedure by certain standards of education that cannot be questioned, but that do not exclude strong religious orientation.[100]

VI. Outlook

On the basis of the considerations discussed above, the famous case of the Amish decided by the US Supreme Court in 1972[101] might also find a differentiated solution. Here, we are confronted with a religious and cultural community that has existed in the United States for centuries. The "functioning" of the group within the American society is a

[97] Fethi Benslama, *La psychanalyse à l'épreuve de l'Islam* (Paris: Aubier, 2003), 195.

[98] See Naih Ayubi, *Political Islam: Religion and Politics in the Arab World* (London: Routledge 1991), 91 (discussing the theologico-political constellation in Islamic countries); also see Benslama, *La psychanalyse à l'épreuve de l'Islam* 100–1 (discussing the relationship between the state and the individual).

[99] For the right of Muslim parents not to allow girls to attend co-educational sports courses, consider Bundesverwaltungsgericht [BVerwG] [Highest Administrative Court] 12 July 2000, 94 Entscheidungen des Bundesverwaltungsgerichts [BVerwGE] 82 (F.R.G.); Oberverwaltungsgericht Nordrhein-Westfalen [OVG] [Court of Appeals in Administrative Matters] 12 July 2000, (2001) 11 *Neue Zeitschrift für Verwaltungsrecht* 77.

[100] This is also an argument for why the "Law of the Sharia" as a collective tradition cannot be accepted by a western postmodern society.

[101] *Wisconsin v. Yoder*, 406 U.S. 205 (1972).

value that has to be taken seriously; there is even a practice of opening the traditional community for an "escape" option, the so-called time of "rumspringa," which means that a young member can decide by himself or herself whether he or she prefers the traditional way of life to postmodern alternatives. This may be an illusionary "free" decision, but regardless, this is a kind of "rule of collision" that links the traditional community with a postmodern "corridor" of choice in the sense of the liberal constitution and that should be respected as a meta-rule of coordination.

In the conflict of "home education," which is legal in the United States once certain requirements concerning the capabilities of the home teacher have been met, a "collision rule" could also be formulated following the above-mentioned considerations that could avoid the popular "balancing" of interests. This approach tends to give up any effort to search doctrinal contours of the rights and competences that conflict in this case. The constitutional value of the public responsibility for schools in general (public and private alike) alone is not an argument for a general obligation to attend schools and to reject "home-education" as unconstitutional. This is all the more so because the concern about the rise of a "parallel society" within postmodern fragmentation appears to be too unstructured, in particular when it is raised against Christian or Jewish "fundamentalists" who, in fact, do not tend to turn their back completely on the postmodern fragmented society. Instead—at least in Germany—it would be possible to take recourse to a rule of collision that, in this case, is part of the constitutional order of the school system. Again, one might claim that the collective trans-subjective momentum of religion and its contribution to the formation of "identity" is to be valued in a way that is different from the mere individual choice of a "belief." The freedom to establish private (religious) schools is not only part of the plurality and openness of a postmodern culture, but also a version of the positive value of this religious freedom. Religious diversity is only acceptable when a procedural component is recognized, i.e. a differentiated requirement to lay open the elements that constitute this divergence in a process that has the character of a public reflection in itself.[102] In this respect, the right to establish private schools is itself a procedural collective right that can be invoked by groups and for groups only. This may not be convincing to everybody, but, in this case, one may claim that this is the will of the Constitution. This view would, at least, fit into the procedural framework of the Constitution and the model of a set of "rules of collision" between trans-subjective, personal, and the cognitive elements of religious freedom in a postmodern society.

[102] See the procedural conditions outlined above.

4

Preliminaries to a Concept of Constitutional Secularism

András Sajó

> ... the French people recognizes the existence of God
>
> French National Convention, 1794

Strong religion is back in the public square.[1] Constitutional arrangements are now facing new forms of religiousness due to mass emigration and, also, because the religion of both migrants and locals is changing to stronger versions that aspire to control or reclaim the public space. Strong religion is a social fact. Religious movements organize themselves politically and, in so doing, they challenge secular arrangements directly. In this regard, their chances of success vary considerably, but they are certainly capable of undermining the legal arrangements that claim to be neutral and generally applicable to all people living in the national community. This is a fundamental challenge to secularist processes including constitutionalism.

Strong religion varies among creeds and, consequently, may entail varying attitudes toward the legal order. Thus:

(a) a religious community may withdraw from the world and ask to be left alone; religious precepts would and should apply only to members of the community of believers. For them, exceptions are to be granted in the sense of being left on their own (isolationism—this is the claim of the Amish, for example); or

(b) it is believed that a divine command will apply to government action when it comes to matters affecting religious people; or

(c) that a divine command extends to conduct, including governmental conduct, outside the religious community (inclusivism); or

(d) finally, that the whole country—namely, all citizens—should identify with the precepts of the strong religion.

In this last case, we have no problem with the stable homogeneous state, but the way it is achieved and its foundations remain outside constitutionalism.

Fundamentalist religions either cut themselves off from the rest of society and live within "walls," real or virtual, or, alternatively, they aspire to impose their version of

[1] I use the term "strong religion" in the sense Almond, Scott Appleby, and Sivan use it. See Gabriel A. Almond, R. Scott Appleby, and Emmanuel Sivan, *Strong Religion: The Rise of Fundamentalism Around the World* (Chicago: University of Chicago Press, 2003). To avoid misunderstandings: the expression "strong religion" is used to avoid a one-sided concentration on the problems created by certain forms of Islam in and for Western countries. Such concentration would run the risk of unintended and unconscious bias that might undermine the equality of religious beliefs.

salvation on the rest of the society by creating general rules. The latter strategy requires the democratic cooptation of the legislative process and of the whole state apparatus. There is a constitutional version of this strategy. Here, religious legislation promises to respect constitutional values. Although solutions dictated by religion do not claim exemption from constitutional scrutiny, their proponents argue that a democratically achieved religious takeover for the purposes of legislating divine dictates is not constitutionally suspicious per se.

Strong religion may take legal pluralism to the extreme, that is, to the point of denying pluralism, insisting on the primacy of one religion's rules over and against all other normative systems. The believers and their organizations may disregard the secular dimensions of their conduct and profess a loyalty that is not to the state.

What is jurisprudentially relevant, here, is that strong religion seems to have developed strategies to overcome the resistance of secularist jurisprudence to religiously grounded claims:

(a) There is the contention that secularism as a constitutional principle is an oxymoron, and that separation of church and state does not imply secularism—that this separation is, at best, a specific technical solution to the problem of institutional cooperation among equals and does not implicate a broader principle. From this perspective, neutrality is bogus. Secularism is a militant and biased position that does not respect religion; hence it contravenes the principle of tolerance.

(b) Beyond the rejection of the legitimacy of secularism, ostensibly liberal arguments are Trojan horses used to bring religious concerns into the citadel of the secular state. Religion seeks to smuggle itself into the public and political sphere using fundamental rights language.[2]

(c) People with a strong religion agenda attack the legitimacy of the requirement of public reason giving in law and legislation. Modern constitutionalism has accepted the presence of religion and religiously inspired politics in the public space only where they have been translated, or are at least translatable, into "public reasons"—that is, where the reasons for their presence were accessible to all citizens. (It is immaterial to public reason giving what motives may underlie a public policy or constitutional position.) Strong religion denies the necessity or legitimacy of such translation.

Strong religions sometimes act as "Trojan horses," ideologies that are smuggled into constitutional doctrine in order to create a space for special practices that do not conform to constitutional values and thus undermine the social beliefs supporting the secular constitutional order. While it is not true that all contemporary religions want to conquer political institutions, such attempts are certainly quite common. A jurisprudential theory of secularism has to be able to withstand these challenges; however, most democracies are without a strong normative theory or practice of constitutional secularism. Constitutionalism seems vulnerable to some of the claims of strong religion when they are presented in terms of a free exercise of faith and of pluralism, even though the secularization of society seems to have pushed religion out of the public sphere.

[2] This increasingly popular attempt is exemplified in Michael Perry's scholarship. In his view such constitutionalism simply does not require that public and, in particular, constitutional decisions be based on public reason, as long as fundamental rights in the constitution are respected. See e.g. Michael J. Perry, "Why Political Reliance on Religiously Grounded Morality is not Illegitimate in a Liberal Democracy" (2001) 36 *Wake Forest Law Review* 217.

This is because the normative implications of this "voiding" of religion have not been instilled systematically in constitutional law; constitutional secularism remains subject to contingencies.

This chapter is based on the assumption that, for the purposes of a judicially relevant constitutional theory, one need not take positions regarding the spiritual values behind secularism. Secularism as a constitutional concept does not require agnostic background assumptions.[3] The term "secularism" is used herein to reflect no specific position regarding the truth of religion nor any preliminary position regarding the proper place of religion in society. It is not a form of atheism or secular humanism. It merely assumes a social, political, and legal arrangement that does not follow considerations based on the transcendental or the sacred. Constitutional secularism is a constitutional theory about the presuppositions or foundations of contemporary constitutional order. My concept of secularism is not a generalization of an alleged French hobbyhorse; the sovereignty of all citizens with equal mental endowment to participate in the making of sovereign decisions might recall French doctrines, but it is certainly a doctrine of *democracy* and not *laïcité*. Popular sovereignty is a reality in the United Kingdom, too, regardless of the (constitutionally somewhat) irrelevant fact that the sovereign people of England have a Queen, who happens to be the head of the constitutionally somewhat obsolete Church of England.

Given the cultural and ideological implications of the term "secularism"—especially for those Americans who identify it with secular humanism—it must be emphasized that secularism is, at the least, a half-blank slate and is not a specific (or, as some might see it, militant) position regarding religion. However, secularism assumes that—as far as law goes—humans are capable of testing their experience without reference to transcendental concepts and concerns.

As a first step toward a more robust theory of constitutional secularism, the chapter reviews some inherent difficulties surrounding the concept and identifies some core values and common practices underlying it. First, it considers the inherent weaknesses of secularism that facilitate the advance of strong religion in constitutional law. Section II discusses some normative consequences of constitutionalism that necessitate and animate secularism.

I. The Weakness of Secularism

Secularism is a somewhat unfortunate term for use in constitutional theory. It is overloaded—it refers to different, albeit interrelated, concepts in different languages and according to different disciplines. Here, I consider the term to describe certain social developments and, also, certain normative assumptions regarding the *permissibility* of religion. First, it is important to recognize the sociological implications of the term. Secularism and secularization (the second term commonly used in sociology) refer to

[3] Secularism is a term coined by George Jacob Holyoake around 1846. (*Laïcité* was coined only in the 1870s). Although the original meaning of Holyoake's terminology was not anti-religious, those who claim to be victims of discrimination directed against religions by secularism interpret it in such a way. Many of the cultural traditions, fears, and prejudices of those who are afraid of the persecution of their religious institutions, or who try to extend their autonomy on the basis of such fears and dangers, tend to refer to specific, culturally shaped meanings of secularism, *laïcité*, or *laicidad*. In many Latin American countries, e.g. *laicidad* resonates as a battle cry of anti-clericalism (which means more than dislike of the clergy: it was an oppressive practice of persecution). The present use of the term secularism is deliberately void at this stage of the analysis.

specific social realities, which cannot be disregarded in constitutional choices. The social realities captured by the term "secularization" will be important for the normative constitutional concept of secularism: it refers to those institutional arrangements and vital forces that animate the normative concept of secularism itself.

Reflected in both the concept and the reality of secularization are degrees of uncertainty and ambivalence ("Did it really happen?" "Is it going on, and, if so, in what sense?" and so forth) that must be reflected in constitutional theory. Otherwise, the legislator or the judge could insist on imposing her own esoteric and misinformed vision on society. This would be not only impermissible but also mistaken; at the end of the day, such an imposition will turn out to be irrelevant or even dysfunctional. But this is exactly the problem for law: the more uncertain the normative concept (in conformity with the social uncertainty that it expresses) the less relevant or powerful it will be when applied. This is true of the legal concept of secularism, whose weakness originates in its fuzziness. My concern is that—because of its softness and fuzziness, and because of secularization's cheap compromises in the face of politics and lifestyle varieties—secularism will fail. Of course, a laissez-faire approach is attractive since, supposedly, it leaves individuals and communities ample room for maneuvering. The French tried dress-code laissez-faire for a while: the Conseil d'État left headscarf practices to be regulated at the school level. As far as French schoolmasters were concerned, however, laissez-faire did not work, they were lost and even afraid. The French learned the hard way that, although decentralization has its virtues, it means uncertainty and perennial local conflicts, which potentially aggregate. The ECtHR has recently unanimously upheld the French "headscarf" law.[4] For the court, the centrally determined prohibition served the goals of respect for pluralism and the freedom of others.

It is often believed that European constitutional secularism is intimately related to its commitment to the Enlightenment.[5] Intellectually, European constitutions are creatures of nineteenth-century *state consolidation*—or represent an ideal of such consolidation. The idea of the modern constitution reflects a consolidation of the state based on national rather than religious identity.[6]

Secularism, both as a social fact and as a feature of constitutionalism, is vulnerable to the challenges of strong religion because of its uncertainty as a legal concept. Secularism is rooted in, and reflects, an ambiguous social reality.[7] Secularization may be operating at

[4] ECtHR, *Dogru v. France*, App. no. 27058/05; Judgment of 4 December 2008.

[5] The missionary zeal of the Enlightenment is certainly present in the current debate in the sense that by limiting the impact of religion the believers are thought to be liberated. Further, the *mission civilisatrice* of enlightened secularism is intended to protect the still vulnerable self of the modern citizen against the "backward" that exists both outside and inside the borders.

[6] This consideration applies to constitutions of the twentieth century, including the mass constitution making that began in Africa in the 1960's and in Eastern Europe after 1989.

[7] The inconclusiveness of constitutional secularism can be demonstrated by reference to innumerable concessions to religions and religious institutions in many areas of life in most countries. Speech can be restricted for religious sensitivity; there are invocations of God in constitutional preambles; and religious oaths of allegiance are common. The notion of "ceremonial deism" has been transplanted to South Africa, for example. See *In re Certification of the Constitution of the Western Cape, 1997* 1997 (4) S.A. 795 (C.C.) para. [28]. We have school prayers and insignia, which might be unconstitutional, in otherwise religiously permissive jurisdictions. See *Zylberberg v. Sudbury Board of Education* (1988) 65 O.R. (2d) 641 (C.A. Ont.). Canadian schools have to be secular but secularism allows religious considerations in school policies. Governments often support mandatory religious instruction—sometimes, however, for good secular reasons (to prevent fundamentalism). Plural legal systems reflecting religious considerations are sometimes permitted, and the employment policies of various confessions are considered matters of institutional autonomy (resulting from separation of church and state). Concordat-type contractual regimes grant special status to churches as civic organizations.

a social or cultural level, but this is not the same as public institutions becoming secular and operating under secular guidance. Constitutional law may claim that public institutions fill the public square, but this contention remains problematic and one-sided. The secularization of the state is a historical project still in the making; it is being realized by degrees. At its center, we find religion and its organizations ceding some of their power over various aspects of life in favor of the state.[8] Secularism in constitutional law means that social functions of "churches"[9] are taken over by the state or are privatized. This is the result, at least partly, of the changed self-perception of mainstream churches.

Notwithstanding its historical affinities with the Enlightenment, secularism remains uncertain and vulnerable. Prior to the Danish cartoons controversy (arising in 2005 over the publication in the Danish newspaper *Jyllands Posten* of cartoons depicting satirical images of the prophet Mohammed, labeled by some as blasphemy),[10] generations of European constitutional lawyers assumed secularism as fait accompli. But the reality was a *de facto* secularism, without constitutional entrenchment in most countries and with many exceptions even where it was constitutionalized. Its prevalence had to do with the nature of the religious beliefs that prevailed in Western democracies; even where there was widespread social demand for religion, this often amounted merely to believing without belonging[11] or even belonging without believing. In the last 50 years, religion in Europe and, in a different sense, even in the United States, has served as a point of reference only for purposes of vague identity or identification.

It was true that religions contained a particularistic element, but this was not expected to contribute, politically or culturally, to heterogeneity in a way that would have endangered social cohesion and loyalty to the state. Established religions were not a serious problem either, as long as equality was not violated. A convenience-based coexistence was made possible on the assumption that organized religions gave up, or were forced to give up, the claim to govern public life. It was assumed that the intensity of faith would diminish, and that even those who considered religion as the fundamental organizing force of life would accept living in accordance with religion only in a shielded private space. The alternative model indicated that the liberal state would allow religious activities within broad and equal limits; religious bodies would relinquish political aspirations, though not necessarily public participation, through persuasion.[12] The normative position of secularism was based on the relativity of religion.[13]

[8] Cf. e.g. Ernst-Wolfgang Böckenförde, "Die Entstehung des Staates als Vorgang der Säkularisation [The Emergence of the State as a Process of Secularization]," in *Säkularisation und Utopie: Ernst Forsthoff zum 65 Geburtstag [Secularization and Utopia: For Ernst Forsthoff's 65th Birthday]*, 75, 76 n. 5 (Stuttga rt: W. Kohlhammer, 1967).

[9] "Church" is used herein in a broad sense, referring to the gamut of organizations that run or govern religious life and are constituted according to the tenets of a religion. It is a non-denominational reference.

[10] See generally András Sajó (ed.), *Censorial Sensitivities: Free Speech and Religion in a Fundamentalist World* (Utrecht: Eleven International Publishing, 2007).

[11] "[T]he majority of the British people—in common with many other Europeans—persist in believing (if only in an ordinary God), but see no need to participate with even minimal regularity in their religious institutions." Grace Davie, *Religion in Britain Since 1945: Believing without Belonging (Making Contemporary Britain)* (Oxford: Blackwell, 1994), 2.

[12] See, for example, the "twin tolerations" model of Alfred Stepan, *Arguing Comparative Politics* (Oxford: Oxford University Press, 2001), 213.

[13] "La laïcité est [aussi] fondée sur cette irrécusable donnée de fait [qu'] aucune religion ne peut prétendre à l'universalité puisqu'elle repose par essence sur d'innombrables articles de foi, dont on ne saurait par suite exiger de quiconque, ni qu'il y croie, ni qu'il n'y croie pas. [Secularism is (also) based on the indisputable premise that no religion can lay claim to universality because each is based on innumerable articles of faith, in which one cannot demand of anyone either that they believe, or that they not

The reality is that secularization of the law has been and will remain a half-hearted compromise. Many constitutional systems have avoided arriving at unequivocal answers to the question of church-state or religion-state relations, at least in a systematic way, and have declined to take a clear and consistent position on the matter. Temporary concessions to religion have been granted in nominally secularist constitutional systems without regard to slippery-slope concerns; indeed, these concessions have been treated as consistent with constitutionalism and even secularism or even as necessary steps in providing freedom of religion.

Perhaps the most visible sign of the unfinished business of secularization in law is the existence of blasphemy laws in Western democracies. Such provisions exist in many democracies, and they are applied in exceptional and mostly trivial cases. Europe was willing to forget their existence. However, beginning with the Salman Rushdie affair, there has been increasing demand for the application of such provisions to restrict public criticism, although *not* to apply them is what constitutional and cultural conventions would suggest. Not to apply a clear rule is a serious inconvenience, as seen in both the Rushdie and Danish cartoon affairs, yet there is some reluctance to repeal such provisions.[14] In other areas of law, *de facto* compromises pervade the constitutional system, as seen, for example, in matters of religious education; even party formation and politics along religious lines are tolerated. Such negligent benevolence results from historical contingencies. Secularism exists as an unprincipled convenience.

This situation is the result of a long historical process. Beginning at the end of the nineteenth century, European Christian confessions gradually gave up their attempts to force believers to operate in civil society and state settings according to religious prescriptions. This is the factual basis for political secularization—a fragile one, indeed. The concession that various European creeds granted to the state was a matter of tacit resignation and worldly apathy, which only very gradually achieved normative recognition, as when, for example, France was defined as a secular republic, after a long political struggle, in order to consolidate the victory of the republicans. When rising religious fundamentalism once again attempts to define the public sphere, the secular powers have little normative foundation to which to refer in order to defend the achievements of the Enlightenment. (The ambiguous case of French *laïcité* is discounted here.)

The vulnerability of secularism in law is exemplified by the position of the Canadian Supreme Court, which found secularism to be compatible with religion-based policy considerations, as long as these did not preclude pluralism:

> [N]evertheless, all members of the Court interpreted the concept of secularism not to preclude at all that a public institute, like a school board, passes resolutions "motivated in whole or in part by religious considerations," while it requires that "no single conception of morality can be allowed to deny or exclude opposed points of view." The obligation of secularism placed on the school board is "aimed at fostering tolerance and diversity of views, not at shutting religion out of the arena".... [I]t does not limit in any way... the freedom of Board members to adhere to a religious doctrine that condemns homosexuality but it does prohibit the translation of such doctrine into policy decisions by the Board, to the extent that they reflect a denial of the validity of other points of view.[15]

believe.]." Raymond Boudon, *Pourquoi les intellectuels n'aiment pas le libéralisme [Why Intellectuals Don't Like Liberalism]* (Paris: O. Jacob, 2004), 100.

[14] After a 30-year campaign, the United Kingdom abolished such a law on 8 May 2008. Criminal Justice and Immigration Act 2008, ch. 4, s. 79 (Eng) (taking effect on 8 July 2008).

[15] *Chamberlain v. Surrey School District No. 36*, [2002] 4 S.C.R. 710, 2002 S.C.C. 86.

Where religious considerations at the national level do not endorse the claims of strong religion, the permissiveness of the Canadian Supreme Court will be sustainable—and this is quite telling about the conventional and unprincipled nature of secularism in many constitutional systems.

Likewise, European law is ambiguous and vulnerable in matters of secularism. This is highlighted in the jurisprudence of the European Court of Human Rights, which famously granted protection to religious sensitivity in the *Otto-Preminger-Institut* case.[16] The court states that while "those who choose to exercise the freedom to manifest their religion . . . cannot reasonably expect to be exempt from all criticism," the responsibility of the state may be engaged when the manner of opposition to those religious beliefs threatens the peaceful enjoyment of the right guaranteed under Article 9, or, in extreme cases, even "inhibit[s] those who hold such beliefs from exercising their freedom to hold and express them."[17]

What constitutes an inhibition, here, will remain contested. Who will determine what amounts to inhibition? Is it up to religious sensitivities to set the social standards of permissible criticism and disrespect? Is pluralism a sufficient justification for respecting group sensitivities? Such constitutional nonchalance was affordable on the assumption that growing secularization would contribute to rights protection, freedom, and democracy. A stronger version of the secularist constitutionalism theory would assume that there can be no constitutionalism without some level of secularism, nor can it exist outside a secularized (modern) society. In this narrative, secularization corresponds to the fundamental tenets of liberalism, namely, individualism, rationality, and universality. In order to achieve these requirements, the particularism resulting from religious (or ethnic) allegiances has to be expelled from the public space.

All models of secularist constitutionalism presume some division of the public and private spheres; even a minimalist secularism assumes that the constitutionally controlled state determines (with benevolence, more or less) the boundaries of the public. There is a high level of variance as to the openness of the public sphere to the religious, especially to organized religion, but what matters, fundamentally, is that "[r]eligion no longer structures our space, it is not handed down but chosen (in the marketplace)."[18] As Émile Poulat, the great sociologist of secularism and Catholicism in France, has written: "the public square is open to all, including churches, but is organized and functions without them, according to rules that do not depend on them."[19]

The public-private divide only superficially reflects the social dichotomy of systemic interactions and the life-world (to use the terms promoted by Jürgen Habermas). The more certain functions are provided in non-private ("societalized") and secularized systemic relations, the more religion becomes a matter for the life-world, and it might lose its importance even there.[20] Or, as the success of new religious movements indicates,

[16] ECtHR, *Otto-Preminger-Institut v. Austria*, App. no. 13470/1987; Judgment of 20 September 1994, available at <http://cmiskp.echr.coe.int/tkp197/portal.asp?sessionId=9833865&skin=hudoc-en&action=request>.

[17] *Otto-Preminger-Institut v. Austria*, para 47.

[18] Marcel Gauchet, *La religion dans la democratie [Religion in a Democracy]* (Paris: Gallimard, 1998), 107.

[19] Émile Poulat, *L'Ére postchretienne [The Post-Christian Era]* (Paris: Flammarion, 1994), 16.

[20] Here I follow the definition in Karel Dobbelaere and William H. Swatos, Jr. (eds), *Encyclopedia of Religion and Social Science* (Walnut Creek, Calif.: AltaMira Press, 1998). Clearly, the dichotomy "private-public" is not a structural aspect of society but a legitimizing conceptualization of the world, an ideological pair used in conflicts by participants. Sociologists, of course, might study the use of this dichotomy in social discourse and conflicts, but it is not a sociological conceptualization. It should be

spiritual and other needs emerging in the life-world are satisfied outside the organized forms of traditional religions and their institutions, which, at least in the past, used to have totalizing aspirations and, hence, a claim to determine systemic interactions or even to offer such interactions.

To cite an example that goes back to Max Weber, religion offered a system of interaction for banking, creating its rather limiting rules and also its mechanisms of trust building. Secularization offered the possibility of establishing creditworthiness outside one's religious community. Today, systemic interactions relying on "rational" (that is, non-personal) objective considerations supply the need in secular communities for creditworthiness. However, for relatively marginalized groups—for example, immigrant communities in Europe—systemic relations are not a solution, as they may not satisfy the "objective" criteria of creditworthiness applied by banks. Here, the assurances of the life-world will replace the systemic interaction, where religion (or ethnicity and extended family, as in the case of Chinese immigrants) again plays a functional role (consider the international money transfers by Indian Muslims in conformity with *Hawala*: the trust that is needed for the transcontinental financial transfer is, again, based on the piousness of banker and debtor).

The foundations for the legal assumptions regarding the public-private divide are problematic. The boundaries of the public are constantly shifting and renegotiated. Church-state relations are evolving in history and reflect unprincipled divisions and interferences. What is private is not simply a matter of governmental definition and fiat; meanwhile, various religions may challenge definitions of the status quo as new understandings and forms of faith emerge. The assumption that the boundaries of the public square can be shaped ultimately by secular forces disregards, to some extent, the strength of religious and spiritual needs. These needs and, hence, religion itself remain as independent variables in the process of public-private boundary shaping. As Pierre Chaunu reminds us, the history of religion follows its own rhythm and, although it is related to intellectual history and the history of emotions, it is autonomous.[21]

The public-private divide is both normative and part of a social dialogue. To a considerable extent, constitutional law is what solidifies (and, increasingly, undermines or rearranges) that divide. It is a fundamental tenet of constitutionalism that constitutional law and the political process shall determine the boundaries in regard to where religions and their institutions, as autonomous spheres, shall begin. However, in reality, these are not two neatly separate social domains. Moreover, these already fuzzy boundaries are subject to sudden internal changes and, consequently, to changes in the relations between the two imagined worlds. But constitutionalism clings to its professed ability to determine the divide, although, in the best of cases, all it does is to reflect the boundary changes and crystallize them in normative form.

replaced by Habermas' conceptual dichotomy—system versus life-world, used here in a purely descriptive sense. It is in the systemic interactions that societalization occurs: relationships became basically secondary, segmented, utilitarian, and formal. By contrast, in the life-world—the family, groups of friends, social networks, the neighborhood—interaction is communal. Primary relations are the binding forces of such groups; relationships are total, trustful, considerate, sympathetic, and personal. See Bryan R. Wilson, "Aspects of Secularization in the West" (1976) 3 *Japanese Journal of Religious Studies* 259–76; Bryan R. Wilson, *Religion in Sociological Perspective* (Oxford: Oxford University Press, 1982). The trend toward societalization is very clear in the distribution and the banking sectors—such as the replacement of neighborhood stores by large department stores, where the interactions between shopper and seller are limited to a money exchange for goods. Beyond the life-world, interactions became societalized.

[21] Pierre Chaunu, *La civilisation de l'europe des Lumières [European Civilization During the Age of Enlightenment]* (Paris: Arthaud, 1997).

The "secularist" assumption that religion is relegated to the private sphere—and will be protected there—became problematic within constitutional law not only because of the pressures from increasingly aggressive religious interests but also, in part, due to the increasing constitutionalization of the legal and, consequently, of the social system. Contemporary constitutional law in most countries seeks to penetrate spheres hitherto respected as private and, hence, off-limits to public law. The best-known techniques of such penetration are seen in such doctrines as horizontal effect, *Drittwirkung*, state action, and so forth. Much of what was once understood as private and, therefore, subject to a liberty interest, in the sense of being exempt from state intrusion,[22] is now having to satisfy constitutional considerations. Religious freedom and the autonomy of organized forms of religion, which had been thought necessary for the free exercise of religion, have been breached by this penetration. Obviously, the conflict becomes extreme where such intrusions—for example, the imposition of gender equality in private relations—come into conflict with strong religion and its different values. Religions were accustomed to finding refuge for their practices in the bastion of private life. As the new, aggressive constitutionalization enters the private sphere, new threats emerge for ways of life shaped by strong religion.

A secularism that results from convenience, carelessness, and tacit compromise remains fragile and not only because it seems to have no identifiable program or weak justiciable standards. The fragility results from the very nature of the self-understanding of the contemporary liberal state.

The logic of contemporary liberalism compels the state, even in constitutionally secular countries such as France or Turkey, to adopt a positive, benevolent attitude toward religions, mostly for good reasons. Such attitudes flow not only from the political necessity of respecting powerful groups but from the obligations of tolerance. Further, in many jurisdictions, because of the state's positive obligation to promote or facilitate the exercise of fundamental human rights, the free exercise of religion is deemed to require governmental facilitation—so long as this facilitation is not discriminatory and respects state neutrality. Such positive obligations would compel a government to extend this benevolence to strong religion generally, in light of the prohibition against religious discrimination. In addition, the modernity that animates liberalism has moved from an active form to a more reactive one,[23] rendering it less self-confident and, hence, less aggressive, more passive, even beyond mere tolerance, in the face of alternative forms of life-world, including premodern forms that are otherwise suspect. The reluctance to take vigorous, prohibitive positions is all but inevitable, where a belief in indeterminacy prevails, and this makes it difficult to insist on specific solutions that politically informed wisdom may suggest.

The uncertainty surrounding the values underlying secularism originates in the historical formation of the concept. Consider the differences between secular India and France. India experienced religiously motivated genocide at the founding moment of partition. This resulted in the ban on the use of religion in politics in the 1951 Representation of the People Act. That foundational genocide and the later violence that forcefully reminded Indians of continued genocidal threats led the Supreme Court of India to find that secularism is an unamendable principle of the Indian Constitution. The Indian experience could not be more different from the experience of France, where,

[22] Not all the constitutionally guaranteed spheres of the private were left in this condition of state non-intervention. Private property was always subjected to public interest, and it is now increasingly colonized by regulatory law.

[23] Ulrich Beck, *Risk Society: Towards a New Modernity* (London: Sage, 1992).

in the making of *laïcité*, the republicans fought a cold civil war with the monarchists and their Catholic Church allies, in a range of public areas (from marriage to education); still, *laïcité* was not inspired by massacres like a Saint Bartholomew's Eve. In both instances, constitutional secularism emerged as a set of legal practices pointing in a certain direction, namely, toward denying a public role to religion and its organized activities. Both experiences reflect an exclusion of religion from the affairs of the state, and there seems to be enough commonality for a shared principle.

In a few instances, the practices that expel religion from the public sphere—summed up as *laïcité*/secularism—became constitutional values and were written into the constitution. Sometimes only fundamental organizational arrangements were constitutionalized.[24] In many instances, only specific practices of secularism were written into the constitution, without using the expression in a general sense.[25] It makes some jurisprudential difference whether the principle behind a constitutional practice is articulated as a concept in the constitution or not. But even if secularism emerges from a set of relevant social and legal practices to find its way into the text, its meaning remains obscure. The history of the "building blocks" is controversial and cannot in itself help to bolster the principle of secularism. For example, it took 25 years of legislation in France, culminating in the 1905 law on separation of church and state, to consolidate a commitment to *laïcité*, which was constitutionalized as a concept only in 1946.[26] But the laws of these 25 years reflected very different perspectives. Some of them were anti-clerical, and even anti-religious, while others were concerned only with the influence of the Catholic Church on politics and public life.[27] The conflict had nothing to do with "believers and 'nonbelievers' but with the opposition between two visions of France."[28]

Secularism in the sense of separation of church and state, or of state-controlled and faith-controlled activities, remains fragmented even in the most secularist constitutional systems. In France, *laïcité* does not apply in Alsace-Moselle, and, all around the country, church buildings are subsidized, and municipalities determine the admittance of religious personnel to local hospitals to provide health care. Ironically, it was the same Aristide

24 The non-establishment clause of the U.S. Constitution or the separation clause in the Hungarian Constitution ("The State and the church operate separately") might serve as examples.

25 For example, in Mexico, only a statute declares that Mexico is a secular state that cannot favor or disfavor religion. The original 1917 Constitution refers to *laicidad* in the context of education as applicable to all schools, but the reference is now replaced by a reference to separation. Original: "Art. 3º. La enseñanza es libre; pero será laica la que se dé en los establecimientos ofi ciales de educación, lo mismo que la enseñanza primaria, elemental y superior que se imparta en los establecimientos particulares." The current version, as amended in 1993, states that "Freedom of religious beliefs being guaranteed by Article 24, the standard which shall guide such education shall be maintained entirely apart from any religious doctrine and, based on the results of scientific progress, shall strive against ignorance and its effects, servitudes, fanaticism, and prejudices." This anti-prejudice secular position in principle entails that religious positions be officially reviewed, criticized, and censored in the education context. Defenders of church rights and free exercise might find this anti-clerical or at least antireligious, but, for reasons to be discussed, such a position fits into a constitutional notion of secularism as long as it does not violate free exercise and neutrality.

26 "Le fond de la question est que si les Constitutions ne définissent pas la laïcité, c'est parce que, aussi bien en 1946 qu'en 1958, celle-ci est un principe déjà bien clarifié dans le droit. [The heart of the matter is this: if constitutions did not define secularism, it is because, equally in 1948 as in 1956, it was a principle already well defined in law.]" Guy Coq, *La laïcité, principe universel [Secularity, a Universal Principle]*, *Questions d'époque [Series: Questions of the Times]* (Paris: Félin, 2005), 85–7.

27 Here I follow Émile Poulat, *Notre laïcite publique [Our Public Secularism]* (Paris: Berg International, 2003). For a summary of Poulat's position in English, see <http://religion.info/french/entretiens/article_93.shtml>.

28 Jean Baubérot, "The Place of Religion in Public Life: The Lay Approach" in *Facilitating Freedom of Religion or Belief: A Deskbook* (Leiden: Martinus Nijhoff Publishers, 2004), 443.

Briand, one of the masterminds of the 1905 secular political victory, who entered into the secret Concordat with the Vatican in 1925. Turning to secularism in India, one finds that personal religious law is applicable, at least to Muslims. Meanwhile, in Turkey, there is mandatory religious instruction in public schools; moreover, such instruction is based exclusively on Sunni Islam.

In light of the above, it is no surprise that secularism, as applied in the different legal systems, remains a fuzzy constitutional concept and, as such, its constitutional status remains uncertain. In most liberal democracies, it is not expressly recognized in the constitutional text or jurisprudence. Seemingly similar references to secularism in different jurisdictions, in fact, may reflect conflicting practices, just as different constitutional terminologies may describe compatible practices. Even where "secularism" is mentioned as an accepted concept having constitutional value, it is often subject to the unprincipled wishy-washiness of balancing—or disregarded in the name of proportionality—for the sake of free exercise of religion. Constitutional secularism, even if officially endorsed, may not correspond to social realities; it may exist without corresponding social practices. Indeed, many scholars consider secularism to be no more than a convenient façade: "The terminology of state secularism, neutrality and non-sectarianism seem[s] to be little more than vague code words useful for the theoretical construction of a framework within which sensible compromises that are required in a religiously plural society, can be reached."[29]

Beyond the legal uncertainties of secularism, there are realities that must be faced. What if constitutionally advocated secularism does not reflect social practices—or, for that matter, has not reflected them for some time? What happens if the constitution and constitutional theory operate under the wrong assumptions regarding social practices? After all, secularization and the resulting secularism of social life are disputed concepts in both sociology and theology. Jose Casanova argued quite some time ago against the "secularization thesis" (that, in those societies rooted in the Christian tradition, religion has become a marginal or, at most, a private matter).[30] Church attendance may continue to diminish among the followers of Christian traditions in most Western societies; nonetheless, religion and its institutions strive continuously to bring religion back into politics. The United States and Poland offer good examples of religions regaining their position in the public space in intensely religious modern societies, although religion's role in the public sphere of the European Union remains divisive.[31] However, in many other countries of the world that were, at least for a while, candidates for constitutionalism, strong religion seems to be the fundamental ideological and perhaps social obstacle to constitutionalism. In Western democracies, strong religion—principally, Islamist and Christian fundamentalism—challenge the prevailing arrangements that are considered to be dictated by secularism or by what used to constitute secularism.

I happen to agree with those who claim on normative grounds that in order to sustain modernity, or sustain public order as ordered liberty, one needs a considerable level of secularization (in one sense or another). Constitutionalism exists only where the society does not take into public consideration transcendental concerns: people are buried in cemeteries not because it facilitates resurrection but for public health reasons.

[29] Francois Venter, *Can a Constitutional State be Really Neutral?* (unpublished paper presented at the Seventh World Congress of the International Association of Constitutional Law, Athens, 11–15 June 2007).

[30] Jose Casanova, *Public Religions in the Modern World* (Chicago: University of Chicago Press, 1994).

[31] In Joseph Weiler's view, the current European identity deficit is in itself a sufficient reason for an affirmation of religion in the European constitution. See Joseph Weiler, *Un'europa Cristiana: un saggio esplorativo* (Milano: Biblioteca Rizzoli, 2003).

It is not clear what happens if new forms of spirituality emerge or take over spirituality. Is this going to be the end of secularism and, thus, of constitutionalism? Or is it possible that such spirituality will promote the same values that animate constitutionalism? Many forms of religiosity in contemporary constitutional states tend to be personal and exist, to a considerable extent, outside traditionally recognized institutional confessions. Even where there are well-established religious organizations, their doctrines may not be decisive for the believers.[32] But where religious experience is personal, religious dictates remain important social factors in the modern world, perhaps on the rise, and need to be addressed in the constitutional construction of secularism.

At least one more fundamental complication must be taken into account in the constitutionalist equation. Émile Poulat has repeatedly reminded us that, instead of a bipolar, that is, church-state relation, today we have a triangle, as individuals position themselves *vis-à-vis* these two players in accordance with their conscience. The state is there to respect the free conscience of its citizens, whose conscience was earlier left to the good offices of their respective faiths, which might or might not have directed these consciences on behalf of the state. Some citizens expect the "state" to liberate them from the "church"; others pose the "church" against the "state." This is a matter of *personal* choice. In other times, the religious organizations provided the necessary homogeneity for the social order. However, once religions have entered into intense competition with each other, such homogeneity has become much less likely. Public order had to be established irrespective of organized religion. It is the constitutional duty of the state to provide order by government, and this may come into conflict with social conduct based on personal or religious choices.

The self-understanding of strong religion forces us to rethink the assumptions about the social order that once served as the basis for constitutionalism. Why do we need such reconsideration—and reinforcement? It is enough to look at the increased, worldwide demand to reinterpret international human rights law and domestic constitutional arrangements—to the detriment of freedom of expression and personal liberty, in particular—in favor of respect for religious sensitivities. In practice, this means not only additional restrictions on freedom of expression but also a change in the public role of religion. This entails not only religion-dictated exceptionalism that goes beyond known forms of accommodation, extending even to faith-dictated arrangements of public life, imposed on non-believers and other denominations. By this logic, religions as institutions of collective confessional existence should also be promoted by exceptions, even beyond what follows from their autonomy in organizing religious life. The exceptions would include their full participation in public life and politics *on their terms*. The cumulative effect runs the risk of balkanization and of

[32] Consider the departure of laymen from Catholic doctrines in such matters as abortion. Only 23 percent of U.S. Catholics agree with their bishops that abortion should be illegal under all circumstances and 70 percent of Mexican urban Catholics think abortion should be permitted in some or all circumstances. See *Poll on Catholic Opinion in Urban Areas of Mexico*, a survey prepared by Applied Statistics for Catolicas por el Derecho de Decidir A.C. with the assistance of the Population Council of Mexico (June 2003), cited in *Catholic Attitudes on Sexual Behavior & Reproductive Health*, available at <http://www.catholicsforchoice.org/topics/international/documents/2004worldview.pdf>. Consider also the widespread use of contraceptives. Further, in many countries the percentage of those believers who find church involvement in politics excessive or too powerful is increasing. In the United States, a 2006 Pew survey found that only 32 percent of Americans believe that the Bible should have more influence on U.S. laws than the will of the American people (against 63 percent). Meanwhile, 60 percent of white Evangelicals wanted to increase the Bible's influence. See <http://pewforum.org/docs/?DocID=153>.

institutionalizing religious intolerance while undermining other constitutional rights and secular reason.[33]

How is constitutional secularism responding to all these difficulties of ordered liberty? Constitutionalism is a theory of state. According to this theory, the state is responsible for social order and cooperative coexistence among social groups. Secularism is a form of ordered political coexistence that does not admit of according preference to, or allowing domination by, religious, social, or political groups. This requires that citizens be somewhat loyal to the state or, at least, not stand actively against it. But what if a religion denies the authority of the state to regulate matters that the religion's authorities claim are under their jurisdiction? What if there is more than one religion making such claims in a society? Believers who follow the agenda of a strong religion often challenge the assumptions of the constitutionally enhanced national community and represent a major challenge to the tolerance-based *modus vivendi*.[34]

If there were clearly legitimate strategies for action resulting from the secularist commitment, then social, political, and cultural forces that feel threatened by strong religion would, in turn, have a clear agenda and coordinated action plan. Defenders of the constitution would be able to craft legal strategies. I do not see such an arsenal available and working. Legal answers remain divisive, even when they pretend to be obvious, as was the case with the French *foulard* legislation that was passed with near unanimity and relatively little public protest.[35] From the perspective of principle, secularism, for all its pragmatism, is not immune to challenges; the danger is that there remains very little to rely on when it comes to demands for additional concessions to religious demands that are in line with the slippery slope of existing conciliatory practices. Of course, this does not rule out of the possibility of generating, or reinforcing, a toolkit of secularist responses and a growing social and legal commitment to secularism.

II. Secularism as a Dictate of Constitutionalism

It is in the foregoing context that the current challenge to secularism must be placed. The revival of religion, especially in its strong forms, and the contemporary psychological need for religious association in many Western societies challenge the individualistic understanding of citizenship. Many people construe their identity on the basis of the public standing of their religious identity.[36] The challenge to constitutional secularism comes from the emotionally charged revival of religious identity and also from religion becoming, once again, a major organizing force of collective action, at least in many parts of the

[33] In Michel Rosenfeld's view, this is not inevitable. In his dialectics, a brutally crusading religion is simply not readmitted to the pluralist universe, and radically intolerant religions are readmitted "on condition that they pose no serious threat to other religions or to nonreligious conceptions of the good." Michel Rosenfeld, *Just Interpretations: Law Between Ethics and Politics* (Berkeley: University of California Press,1998), 209. But judicial decision-making needs intelligible standards to decide the problems of the moment.

[34] Arguments of cultural pluralism are sometimes used to disregard the legal universality promoted by government. The sovereign state claims to be based on a comprehensive national community, while pluralism insists on the impossibility of such comprehensiveness. These are typically non-religious arguments, though they are used increasingly by strong religion. I address this important challenge in a separate article.

[35] Law No. 2004-228 of 15 March 2004, *Journal Officiel de la République Française [J.O.] [Official Gazette of France]*, 15 March 2004, 5190.

[36] Religion-based group considerations are recognized in EU law only as an exception, as in the case of Northern Ireland (religious preference to the underrepresented in police recruitment).

world where constitutionalism had been based hitherto on the primacy of the secular. Given the interrelations existing in a globally organized world, such developments have consequences even in countries where local religion, in itself, is unable to influence collective action.

Because of the uncertainties of secularism we have an intellectual problem in constitutional law that is not limited to one or another national jurisdiction. Part of this uncertainty results from the fact that *it has no clear standing among constitutional values*, even if certain elements of secularism (such as the separation of church and state or the autonomy of religious organizations) are stated in law as certainties. It is not clear which established constitutional category secularism fits into or what is the underlying value behind secularism. It is not an individual right that would be easy to justify, and it is not necessarily a separation-of-institutions issue. It is true that a narrow understanding of secularism would mean non-establishment, that is, non-interference of organized religion in the exercise of public power. But for what reason?

What are the foundational concepts of constitutionalism that are relevant in addressing strong religion judicially? My claim is that certain fundamental demands of constitutionalism propose and demand secularism. These demands animate the principles of secularism that can be translated into the practices that constitute secularism. From observation of the way modern societies and their cultures operate *vis-à-vis* religion, certain assumptions may be drawn regarding the preconditions and demands of constitutionally governed societies. In order to allow such empirical realities to operate fully they also need to be articulated within a broad normative concept that reflects and modifies that reality and protects it from other realities.

Apart from the empirical differences arising from contingent practices and terminological differences, there seems to be enough commonality among these to allow us to construe the shared principles that form secularism. Consider the French position: notwithstanding important later variations, as a matter of principle, the 1905 law on separation was about denials. It denied public funding to religious practices because such practices were no longer permitted to be public functions or services. A public service must be administered by the state—this removes the religious service from the public sphere. This removal renders religion a private concern—although not in the sense of a personal matter.

Of course, there are important variations in what is deemed to be public. According to the German experience, a public function (education) may be carried out with state funding by religious entities. And yet, the activity will remain public, integrated into public administration and sponsored as part of a publicly administered service. In the core area of the public sphere, namely, the political, this principle (as principle) is uncontested.

The political dimension is the one that is particularly important for secularism and secular constitutionalism. In this regard, the principle behind India's highly specific approach to secularism does not differ from that underlying the French approach or, for that matter, the German, even though German constitutional law does not recognize secularism as an independent principle.

As part of the effort to keep religion out of the public sphere, and out of the realm of politics in particular, some legal systems apply strict bans regarding the organization of the political process and election-related institutions—and specifically political parties—along religious lines. As then-prime minister Jean-Pierre Raffarin said in the debate regarding the ban of the Muslim headscarf in French state schools: "Religion cannot be a political project." This goes beyond the demand that the state shall not take sides in matters of religion. Here the religious forces that would like to use the state for faith-related purposes are prohibited from taking part, at least directly, in politics.[37]

Once again, however, the principle of keeping religion out of politics results in an unfinished process, especially where the political overlaps the symbolic and representational aspects of life. This is partly due to the nature of law, which cannot easily respond to symbols. What would be the legal remedy for alleged violations of secularism when a prime minister or president of a country attends a religious procession? Is this a violation of the demand of separation? What if he is there in a private capacity? What makes his presence private? Is not such attendance merely a fitting sign of respect for the head of state to express toward the beliefs of a large group of citizens? Who would have standing in such cases? Sometimes this is a minor issue, but not where the president will be reelected as a good Christian or the prime minister is running as someone loyal to Shinto religious traditions. Further, the presence of the head of state at such occasions sends a strong message about the proper relations between church and state.[38]

If the shielding of the political from the religious remains an unfinished project, it will be even more problematic to purge the legislative proscription of human conduct of religious considerations. This is the soft underbelly of secularism. The central demand of strong religion asserts the permissibility of behaving in conformity with divine command, even to the point of vindicating the notion that conduct shall be based on the divine command. In these more aggressive formulations, all conduct must be based on divine command, and this is not confined to believers only. Meanwhile, only a specific formulation of secularism expressly confronts this latter claim, arguing that secularism

[37] The reference to French examples shall not be understood as an identification of constitutional secularism with, or advocacy for, specific French solutions. To ascertain that secularism is not a French particularism, it would have been enough to look into a recent survey by Ronan McCrea of the London School of Economics and Political Science. McCrea demonstrates that the EU "has seen excessive religious influence in the legal and political arenas as a threat to the autonomy of the public sphere, to individual autonomy in the private sphere as well as to important values such as gender equality." Ronan McCrea, "Limitations on Religion in a Liberal Democratic Polity: Christianity and Islam in the Public Order of the European Union" (*London School of Economics Legal Studies Working Paper Series*, No. 18/2007, 2007; *New York Law School Islamic Law and Law of the Muslim World Research Paper Series*, Paper No. 08-09, 2007), available at <http://ssrn.com/abstract=1033332>. I agree with McCrea that the preferential treatment of "'established' churches," which goes back to a time before the current challenge associated with immigration, results in double standards. It is exactly for this reason that a robust secularism should be less tolerant of existing concessions that result from soft tolerance and compromise. Secularism as *laïcité* is not exceptional. More importantly, even cooperationist models of church-state relations can satisfy secularism, as long as the terms of cooperation are determined by the state. Cooperation, even in its German version, where cooperation historically has meant privileging certain denominations and their religious organizations, does not entail the acceptance of non-secular arguments nor of conducting politics along religious lines.

[38] To complicate the matter, in certain democratic constitutional communities religious parties were considered essential to the building of democracy. After World War II, the German political establishment included Christian parties, which were close to the ideology of the major denominations. Germany's Grundgesetz has incorporated the provisions of the previous, pre-Nazi Weimar constitution regarding the privileged status of established churches. The German state continued to rely on the welfare services provided by Christian churches, which continued to have privileged treatment by the state. This was a deliberate choice of Chancellor Adenauer and of the political elite; it was assumed that governmentally reinvigorated churches would be able to bring the German people closer to post-Nazi humanitarian and democratic values, more so than other, less credible social institutions. Of course, this strategy works only where the churches are ready to endorse democracy and are not antagonistic to otherwise secular projects of the state. It was only under these circumstances that the situation of "practical concordance" could have been achieved. This did not cause major problems for the constitutional state because the rapid secularization of German society did not allow the emergence of strong religion. But it was achieved to the detriment of politically more "suspect" minority religions.

means *freedom from religion.*[39] Consider the "no driving on the Sabbath" debate in Israel. For some of those who find the dictates of their strong religion constitutionally relevant, the sacred shall prevail over constitutional law, even in regard to the non-observant. Sometimes, it is professed that divine law is beneficial to human rights or offers a superior human rights regime. But, at its heart, this position finds constitutionalism for its own sake irrelevant or a matter of second order, applicable only where the sacred is silent. Likewise, constitutionalism has very little to do with such positions, which are considered constitutionally irrelevant.[40] Nevertheless, as part of the project that smuggles religion into the constitutional scheme, it is averred that positions rooted in strong religion fit well with constitutionalism. In the context of the example above, those who make this claim will argue that the ban on driving does not violate any deeply held convictions of the driver while allowing driving on the Sabbath violates the deepest convictions of religious bystanders; hence, the ban is legitimate.

One way to support such a position is to argue that the free exercise of religion should take precedence over a mere liberty interest. Here, the religious concerns are presented as free-exercise issues. This position, of course, relies on a very broad concept of free exercise, whereby the existence of violations of religious prescriptions by third parties constitutes an obstacle to one's own free exercise of religion. Proponents of such positions may further argue that religious concerns and feelings should be protected because they are balanced against interests that have lower constitutional status.

A second line of constitutional justification relies on the following argument: religion-based preferences may be constitutionally justified on apparently non-religious grounds, rendering unnecessary any arguments about expanding the requirements of the free exercise of religion. According to this logic, even if the law of the state were to adhere to religious commands, as long as such commands satisfied the democratically endorsed fundamental concerns of the majority, or local majority, this democratic support would provide sufficient grounds for such legislation, regardless of the motives alleged. Alternatively, by the same logic, the restrictions may be viewed as serving public order. The secular and the religious claims may be of equal value or the hierarchy of their values may be irrelevant: it is the democratic choice that legitimizes the imposition of restrictions on the driver, who is, in any case, subject to all sorts of restrictions relating to his driving. It is claimed that the law will be considered valid—that is, constitutional—on non-sectarian grounds, because, for example, the inconvenience of the drivers is less than the suffering of the majority believers: "the journey is not an attack on [the drivers'] integrity."[41]

With these far-fetched constructions, one can comfortably deny that it is respect for the sacred that motivates the legislation. Without a strong secularist position, such

[39] For example, some decisions of the Supreme Court of Israel consider freedom from religion to be an individual right of the non-observant: "Tolerance in religious-secular relations, for example means recognizing the existence of two important human rights—freedom of religion and freedom from religion—that require accommodation and compromise." Aharon Barak, *The Judge in a Democracy* (Princeton, NJ: Princeton University Press, 2006), 64.

[40] It is a separate consideration to what extent some dialogue with strong religion is required/permissible in a pluralistic version of constitutionalism, and whether or not the result might be some incorporation of strong religion into constitutional arrangements and if this is possible. I discuss these issues in a separate article, "Constitutionalism Facing Strong Religion" (5 Nov. 2007) (manuscript on file with I•CON).

[41] Gideon Sapir and Daniel Stratman, "Why Freedom of Religion Does Not Include Freedom from Religion?" (2005) 24 *Law and Philosophy* 467, 494. But it is exactly in order to avoid the tyranny of the religious majority, by basing a choice on religious grounds among competing interests, that the liberty interest is elevated to a right—the right of being free from religion—as a form of freedom of conscience and religion.

arguments may find their way into certain readings of constitutionalism. However, the relation between a restriction on the conduct of a third party to satisfy religious dictates and the outrage of the religious person is asymmetrical. The act of the non-believer may be disturbing for the believer as a violation of the divine order, but this distress is a lesser evil than an intrusion into the conduct of the non-believer. At least from a secular perspective, demonstrably negative impacts on conduct are, *prima facie*, more significant than alleged emotional impacts, even if it is argued that the latter are inevitable in the light of religious precepts.[42] It is fair to assume that the religious person will likely be troubled; in a normative sense, according to religious tenets, the believer has a duty to be troubled, when confronted with the knowledge that others are driving and violating the Sabbath. But this is a concern about others and about the divine order, while the mandated observance means restrictions on a person's own actions. Of course, if the conduct imperiled the *manifestation* of religious beliefs, the equation would change. But strong religion likes to claim that any departure from divine command imperils free exercise, because it forces the believer to live in an improper world.

As the Sabbath driving controversy indicates, there are a number of fundamental societal and constitutional issues at stake when the dictates of religion are turned into law, regardless of the *prima facie* reason given. These concerns implicate the crucial components of secularism, namely: (1) the epistemological preconditions of constitutionalism (in the sense of "what kind of assumptions do constitutional subjects have to have?"); and (2) the possibility of popular sovereignty and of sovereign state power. Secularism, as an institutional arrangement, provides protection to a *reason-based* polity against a social (dis) order that is based on dictates of religious doctrine and *emotions*. When constitutional law insists on secularism, it insists on the possibility of a reason-based political society.

Secularism is a doctrine of state (in the sense of being about the nature of the state) such that personal considerations are elevated to the level of public (political) assumptions. The secular constitutional state is presupposed to exist as a political community of citizens exercising their *rational* faculties. The political system operates with that assumption. This results in the nonadmissibility of revelation and faith-based knowledge, as not all citizens are endowed with the proper apparatus to understand such faith-based claims. Acceptance of religious arguments privileges the believers; rational arguments, however, are equally accessible to all.

Because I am concerned with arguments admissible in legislation and judicial decisions, I am not prepared to rely on any specific contemporary concept of public reason. The common-sense understanding of public reason (that is, accessibility to an argument without the privileged position of faith or precondition of belief) is sufficient here.[43] Rawls would not have allowed public officials to rely on religious arguments; for him, this would be simply too divisive. To which I would also add, in a robust secularist mood, that even where we have acceptable translations of religious arguments, a certain reservation is appropriate. For example, given the secular, power-related agenda of most,

[42] Secularism makes strong assumptions about the sources of, and relevant arguments in, the legal system; see below. A modern legal system is predisposed negatively toward emotions, which continue to be seen as disruptive passions to be tamed.

[43] "The public use of man's reason must always be free, and it alone can bring about enlightenment among men; the private use of reason may quite often be very narrowly restricted, however, without undue hindrance to the progress of enlightenment. But by the public use of one's own reason I mean that use anyone may make of it as a man of learning addressing the entire reading public." Immanuel Kant, "An Answer to the Question: 'What is Enlightenment?'" in Hans Reiss (ed.), *Political Writings* (Cambridge: Cambridge University Press, 2nd edn, 1991), 55.

if not all, ecclesiastical organizations and strong religions (an assertion not intended to deny that churches might be guided by moral considerations apart from their theological concerns), there is a need to look into the *consequences* of a legal decision based on arguments that are neutral but correspond to ecclesiastical positions. It might be, for example, that a secular welfare distribution policy or a public education policy could "accidentally" grant advantages to churches, with detrimental effects to neutral education. The "position of alert" is not paranoid.[44]

It is not just a convenience of modernization to rely on the—unfortunately too-often-false—promise of reason and human rationality. Basing the legal system (its laws and decisions) on secular arguments differs fundamentally from a system based on religious arguments, and not only because the secularist can tentatively demonstrate the practical advantages of reason, insofar as one prefers modernity generally. To allow non-secular arguments and grounds for legislation runs close to official support of religion, "including reinforcement of religious conduct that undermines foundational liberal principles of critical inquiry, religious and ideological pluralism, and secular reason."[45] Secular (public) reason-giving in law[46] is also crucial for the human rights component of liberal constitutionalism in the following sense: The secular character of the normative system embodied in human rights doctrine is essential to its comprehension. All its premises, values, concepts, and purposes relate to the homocentric world and to ways of thought freed from transcendentalist premises and from the jurisdiction of religious authority.[47] Of course, we all have had some negative experiences with what is called reason; indeed, it has become extremely fashionable to distrust it. But the alternative to reason is emotional politics and an arbitrary system, where the emotional dictates of religion will rule human choices. The desire to protect religious emotions[48] stands against all that modern law is about. If emotional distress becomes a decisive consideration in law, then what would matter, finally, is how angry one group can be made. Law will then be subject to the dictates of sensitivity, and highly intense religions will have a natural advantage until all social actors become passionately emotional.

[44] ECtHR Grand Chamber, *Folgerø and Others v. Norway*, App. no. 15472/02; Judgment of 29 June 2007 (Teaching of Christian religions in Norwegian public schools as part of the national Christian culture had disparate, negative effects on non-believers).

[45] See Toni M. Massaro, "Religious Freedom and 'Accomodationist Neutrality': A Non-Neutral Critique" (2005) 84 *Oregon Law Review* 943.

[46] Religious leaders and ideologues who campaign against their "victimization" by the neutral secular legal system claim that the public-reason requirement amounts to the exclusion of their arguments and concerns from public life; hence, they claim, they are treated as second-class citizens. But this claim is an impermissible confusion of permissible arguments. The secular public-reason requirement applies to legislation only. Again, this is not meant to deny the historical relation between religious ethical claims and those moral claims that serve as foundations of liberal constitutionalism. But the intelligibility of secular reasons is not symmetrical to that of religious reasons: only secular reasons are intelligible to all. See e.g. Cass Sunstein, "Beyond the Republican Revival" (1988) 97 *Yale Law Journal* 1539.

[47] Yehoshua Arieli, "The Theory of Human Rights, its Origin and its Impact on Modern Society" [in Hebrew], quoted after Frances Raday, "Culture, Religion, and Gender" (2003) 1 *International Journal of Constitutional Law* (I•CON) 663, 663. In fact, "from a liberal point of view, religion may be perceived as a way of directing human beings from the liberal ideas of self-direction, critical thinking and personal responsibility." Sapir and Stratman, "Why Freedom of Religion Does Not Include Freedom from Religion?" 472. The suspicious elements of religion, once it seeks to organize public life, do not preclude a robust protection of the *exercise* of religion. In fact, religion, like free speech, needs overprotection in the form of accommodation (a distinct protection, compared to most other needs of conscience), and receives it quite often. However, the state should be extra cautious, once such an overprotected need makes claims in the public sphere.

[48] See also HCJ 953/01 *Solodkin v. Beit Shemesh Municipality P.D.* 58(5) 595 (2004). (Barak, J., opinion, concerning the desire to protect the feelings of the Jews for whom the pig epitomizes impurity); cf. *Otto-Preminger-Institut v. Austria.*

The second consideration pointing toward a reason-based (secular) constitutional system is epistemological. Secularism—and not only because of its intimate relation with the Enlightenment—mandates a constitutional arrangement where autonomous critical reasons are to be respected as foundational for communal coexistence and self-regulation. The constitutional state is based on the assumption that individuals have autonomous morality. All state positions should be subjected to the critical examination by the reason of autonomous beings. This is obviously impossible where God's commands are to be followed.

Secularism expresses the need for legal choices to be based on secular public reasons, that is, on reasons accessible to all, quite apart from their religious beliefs. Religiously grounded reasons have to be "translated" into secular ones. For most translation theories, the requirement of a public reason is satisfied as long as the legislative reasons are presented and accepted on grounds reasonably accessible to all—that is, on grounds that do not presuppose some act of faith or belief in scripture, and without the constitutional arrangement itself being an act of faith.[49] The legislative reasons given must be honest; their honesty and accessibility are subject to judicial review.

Constitutional doctrine is the art and science of permissible arguments. Jurisprudence and legal doctrine are about deciding, authoritatively, what amounts to legally permissible, relevant argument. To paraphrase Richard Rorty,[50] in constitutional law, at least in this regard, secularism acts as conversation stopper, exactly because religious arguments tend to be conversation stoppers. This position prevents religious arguments from taking over the role of the conversation stopper. For Rorty, religious arguments were conversation stoppers in the sense of being private opinions brought up in a debate about a public matter: "[T]he ensuing silence masks the group's inclination to say, 'So what? We weren't discussing your private life; we were discussing public policy. Do not bother us with matters that are not our concern.'"[51] Religion, or religious arguments, can be and are used as conversation stoppers in a different sense, too; namely, when the religious position claims superiority and exclusive knowledge. In this scenario, the religious position accuses the secular one of a lack of understanding (of the superiority of divine command, say); while the religious position understands the public reason, it just finds it irrelevant. Relying on its constitutionally protected status, "religion" will claim that the protection shall extend to the recognition of its positions in legislation. Thus religion abuses its privileged position. It abuses an asymmetry: it offers faith-based arguments which are not accessible to the non-believers and society in general, while it accuses public reasons of intolerance for not understanding the religious argument, while rational public arguments are accessible to the religious too.

[49] These theoretical requirements were accepted in law quite some time ago. The *Lemon* test requires that a statute, to be constitutional, "[f]irst [m]ust have a secular purpose; second its principal or primary effect must be one that neither advances nor inhibits religion; finally, the statute must not foster an excessive entanglement of government with religion." *Lemon v. Kurtzmann* 403 U.S. 602, 612–13 (1971). For Canada, see *Chamberlain v. Surrey School District No. 36*, 2002 C.S.C. 86; [2002] 4 R.C.S. 710.

[50] Richard Rorty, "Religion as Conversation-Stopper," in *Philosophy and Social Hope* (New York: Penguin Books, 1999), 171.

[51] Rorty, "Religion as Conversation-Stopper" 171. It is perhaps of some interest that religions see each other as conversation stoppers when they rely on their doctrine. In an interview with the French daily *La Croix*, Cardinal Tauran said that currently inter-religious dialogue can take place "with some religions, yes. But with Islam, not at this time. Muslims do not accept discussion about the Koran, because they say it was written under the dictates of God. With such an absolutist interpretation, it's difficult to discuss the contents of the faith." "Cardinal Tauran: 'La religion fait peur, car elle est pervertie par le terrorisme' [Cardinal Tauran: 'Religion Causes Fear, Because It Has Been Perverted by Terrorism']," *La Croix*, 18 Oct. 2007, available at <http://www.la-croix.com/article/index.jsp?docId=2317870&rubId=4078>.

The use of secularism as a conversation stopper is intended to stop this abuse of a privileged position in legal discourse and adjudication, in particular. Therefore, this is not a matter of stopping conversation among social groups that are perfectly free to continue their dialogue *ad nauseam*.

The requirement of public reason giving[52] would not exclude from the world of constitutional secularism (and, I take it, somehow from the political community *tout court*) those who fail to fit into reasonable positions. Robust secularism that would not allow privileged religious knowledge to dictate public decisions does not mean that such positions cannot be held and represented in the public square. A human rights friendly secularist constitutional order incorporates fundamental values that have emerged, from time to time, in various religions—a culturally, though not constitutionally, relevant fact. Moreover, arguments and activities of ecclesiastical organizations and of believers motivated by their doctrines are illegitimate in the public square. Such activities may often be socially beneficial, sometimes even exemplary, showing the power of intense belief and the courage that might derive from it. Still, there is no guarantee that religiously motivated views and acts will be socially beneficial or right, and, therefore, they cannot be beyond criticism.

Second, nothing precludes even the atheist from learning from the religious person, and there is a lot to learn when it comes to service and humility, and from the experience of being persecuted and of being a persecutor. What can be learned from the fundamentalist aspects of religion (other than intolerance) is a completely different story. Again, the fact that someone is a member of an intolerant (religious or secular) community is not a reason not to engage in discussion with such religious *person*. Nor would I disregard personal views of the religious person and, in particular, his experiences in social discourse.

When it comes to a very specific public discourse, namely, legislative and judicial decision-making, religious people are as free as anyone else to make arguments in public. The problem with religious arguments in *law* is their reliance on divine command or other privileged, transcendentally oriented practices of the religious community. Such an attitude denies that secularism is politically entitled to impose an equal burden on legally relevant reasons which are presented to the legislator. In legal and judicial decisions, the duty of translatability of religious arguments continues to prevail.

The disregard of certain religious arguments cannot be equated with punitive governmental measures or ostracism of those who propose them. There is nothing unusual or oppressive in a legal theory that claims that some positions are reasonable and others are unacceptable according to some criteria. Contrary to Rorty, I believe that the anchoring of thought in a divine text is intrinsically wrongheaded for a democratic polity of autonomous citizens,[53] since it undermines the personal autonomy and competence needed for political decisions in any polity that is based on popular sovereignty. Like Rorty in 1999, I would argue that there is a place for conversation stoppers in a democracy, but I accept that we "should put off invoking conversation-stoppers as *long as possible*."[54] However, this moment of rupture arrives in law when the constitutional judge has to

[52] It is unnecessary to discuss at this point the differences of translation theories, e.g. early Rawls versus later Rawls, or shifts in Habermas' views. Neither of these authorities registered a change in position when it came to political and legal arguments.

[53] This does not mean that we have any problem with believer citizens. In a secularized society, with a relatively strong demarcation between the public/political and the private (which includes religious beliefs and activities), the citizen believers may act with the same assumptions as any other citizen in matters constitutionally relevant. Believers of strong religion might be different, but it is constitutionally impermissible to draw any particular conclusion from this possible empirical difference.

[54] Rorty, "Religion as Conversation-Stopper" 148.

pass judgment. I continue to believe, faithful to the tradition Rorty stood for, that—for the purposes of a judicially applicable theory of constitutionalism—only a robust secularism can resist "religious exclusivism, [and] contempt for people who should be accorded the same respect as the rest of their fellow-citizens."[55] Without this position, religious phraseology and concepts in law would give too much "aid and comfort to [already privileged] religious organizations," in the name of free exercise of religion.

I do not propose to exclude religion, an important and legitimate "agent provocateur," in order to cope with disagreement. Strong religions are not about disagreement; they seek the exclusive imposition of their divinely commanded positions. Secularism does offer space for disagreement and, indeed, this is offered against the typical unilateralism and exclusivism of religions, strong or mild. As far as constitutionalism is concerned, religions are not only free to disagree but, in fact, freedom of religion is, rightly, about the excessive protection of dissent, going so far as religious accommodation.

The requirement of public reason giving has broader social implications. Citizens must learn to think critically—otherwise democracy is meaningless. In practical terms of constitutional law, this has imperative consequences for—among other concerns—education. A departure from secularism in favor of allowing denominational education runs the risk of depriving citizens of the fundamental faculty of public reasoning, at least in the case of certain denominations. The historical link to the Enlightenment and to human rights as empirical constituent elements of constitutionalism is obvious here. It is not by accident that it was Condorcet who argued that in order to *keep* humans free and equal before the law (that is, to realize the potential of article 1 of the French Declaration of the Rights of Man and of the Citizen, namely, that people are born free) "public instruction is the duty of society in regard to its citizens,... as a means to make equality effective," which means an equal access to the facilities that guarantee access to Enlightenment.[56]

Denominational education is more a political concession by secularism than a principled act of tolerance and respect for autonomous choice. Again, denominational education, including its public support might be fully legitimate in constitutional secularism, serving fundamental rights, as long as preconditions of equal citizenship apply and the education remains open to the development of skills that enable participation in the political society. Adults, being autonomous in their private judgments, would have the right to opt out of public education. Children, lacking such autonomy, are denied the capacity to choose. But perhaps the issue does not end there. When government, reluctant to interfere in parental choices, grants parents the opportunity to opt out, it may be foreclosing children's subsequent capacity for autonomous choice as adults. It is exactly this betrayal of the children that Justice William O. Douglas complains about in his outraged dissent in *Yoder*.[57] The fight for the control of education is not only pragmatic in the sense that it has considerable impact on shaping the forms of thought and customs. In many regards, the claim of the state to be the protector of autonomous critical reason challenges the current role of many traditional religions, which increasingly define themselves as the ultimate providers of a consistent idea of the world that has the capacity to justify individual and collective human action.[58]

55 Rorty, "Religion as Conversation-Stopper" 148.

56 "... [D]'obtenir les mêmes facilités pour acquérir les lumières." Condorcet [Jean Antoine Nicolas de Caritat, Marquis de Condorcet], in Charles Coutel and Catherine Kintzler (eds), 1 *Cinq memoires sur l'instruction publique* (Paris: GF-Flammarion, 1989) 35, 75.

57 *Wisconsin v. Yoder* 406 U.S. 205 (1972).

58 Gauchet, *La religion dans la democratie [Religion in a Democracy]* 105–6.

Democratic constitutionalism (2) recognizes only one source of power, and this is the power of the people over itself. The first and foremost consideration is that constitutional systems presuppose and are created to enforce popular sovereignty. This is of fundamental importance to secularism. Popular sovereignty means that all power in the state originates from people, therefore *it cannot originate from the sacred.* This is best captured in a decree of the French National Convention from 1794, which states that "the French people recognizes the existence of God."[59] God thus exists by popular recognition. In consequence, no other entity has original powers, including the powers to legislate. All entities exist by wish of the sovereign, including religious institutions, regardless of the ontological precedence of certain entities in the state including religions. The people's power is sovereign and cannot be a delegated power; it cannot exist by God's grace. A contemporary constitutional theory that would deny people's sovereignty in the name of divine supremacy is unsustainable. Constitutional patriotism, or constitutionally endorsed nationalism, might capture constitutional identity but not religion. As Baubérot has pointed out, laicization of the state means the refusal to have religion stand as the symbol of national identity.

A particular historical interconnection exists between popular sovereignty and secularism. Secularism emerged as a denial of the divine power of the king as sovereign, in favor of popular sovereignty, at least in the French revolutionary version of this relationship. Beginning in 1789, the French revolutionaries, afraid of all particularism, prohibited intermediaries between the individual and the sovereign nation.[60] Suspicion of "cults," which took the form of private associations, continued to animate the anti-clerical forces, even up to the turn of the twentieth century.[61]

Apart from the failure to impose constitutionally attractive internal structures on hierarchical religious organizations,[62] which would go against the principle of institutional religious autonomy in any case, theoretical considerations still point to a specific concern of secularism. The collective control over the individual, which is often implicated in religious autonomy, is potentially dangerous to popular sovereignty. Popular sovereignty emanates from individuals; it exists as the aggregate of individual choices, and such autonomous individual choices serve as the foundation of democratic society.

Constitutional secularism results from popular sovereignty, but it is more than that. It reflects a deep interest in, and respect for, the free exercise of religion. Such secularism is necessary for the maximization of freedom of religion, together with other fundamental

[59] "*Le peuple français reconnaît l'existence de L'Être Suprême*..." Decree of the Convention montagnarde of 7 May 1794. Contrary to the American Declaration of Independence, the French already in the 1789 Declaration had disregarded the authorship of God in matters of inalienable rights: the rights are set forth by the Assembly "in the presence and under the auspices of the Supreme Being."

[60] The Le Chapelier Act of 1791, named after its principal proponent, the delegate Isaac René Guy Le Chapelier, prohibited all intermediary organizations between the state and the individual. Particular organizations, collectives following communal agendas, were most often hotbeds of counter-revolutionary movements and the Catholic Church, with its traditional organization, with its collective loyalty to the king, the pope, and God, was particularly suspect.

[61] The original idea of the 1905 law on the separation of church and state was to bring down the church hierarchy by granting all power of collective use of church buildings to democratic associations of believers. In practice, the lack of interest in democratization by the believers and the various governmental compromises and the jurisprudence of the Conseil d'État quickly submitted these bodies to clerical supervision. The idea of radical church democratization had to be given up, as far as the state was concerned. However, in the modernization process, the churches had to find an answer to the challenge of their democracy deficit.

[62] Today some of the religions, especially in their strong, sometimes charismatic, versions consider democratic considerations simply irrelevant, which re-creates the conflict in different terms.

freedoms, and, in particular, the absolute freedom of conscience to all and to all consciences. It is in this sense that a secular (*laïque*) republic means just the opposite of a confessional one, which, as a rule, cannot take such a stance.

The sovereignty of a people exercising its faculty of reasoning is the essence of the constitutionalism that necessitates secularism.

Are these prescriptions of secularism contrary to tolerance and respect of religious dictates in the public square? Is constitutional secularism a kind of state imposed atheism? Is constitutional secularism disregarding religious and related other pluralisms that is increasingly present in many modern societies? Certainly not. Of course, some tension with the constitutional order of secularism is inevitable because many modern constitutional systems, by virtue of the horizontal effect of the constitution,[63] interfere with the religious sphere to guarantee that certain fundamental constitutional values, such as equality are respected. Religion and religiously shaped family life are subject to constitutional control, although the state should still be respectful of religion when strong religions' influence on sensitive private spheres. But secular and religious claims on the private have direct impact on public affairs, too.

Respect for pluralism does not necessitate the recognition of plural legal systems, although tolerance suggests reasonable accommodation of religious convictions. Depending on its content, religious family law might be recognized on secular grounds and, within a single legal system, private conflict resolution can provide an alternative to state courts. It is available as a matter of expediency, in particular, where family relations are considered a private matter. Secularism has no position on this; family is a social fact, but as a private matter, an area of fundamental parental rights, does not affect popular sovereignty and its epistemological conditions, which lie at the heart of secularism. Family as a social (public) institution, where future citizens are formed, may be subject to a different approach. But religion, as an issue in family-law arbitration, might necessitate the conversation-stopping intervention of the secular legal system. A conversation-stopper role for secularism means the non-admissibility of *untranslated, purely* religious considerations in legal decision-making. When a religious arbitrator, or any other private arbitrator, would enforce values contrary to the constitution, considerations of *ordre public* must prevail. Encouraging religious family arbitration easily lends support to oppressive family arrangements, given that most religions carry the baggage of patriarchalism and tribal parochialism. But this is a risk that legislators are free to take, or not. What matters is that the admissibility of such arbitration shall not be based on the acceptance of the supremacy of a specific theological perspective. Nor should the resort to arbitration courts constitute a recognition of a doctrine of one or another religion that aggressively claims that its freedom of religion (or minority group identity) can only be sustained if the state refrains from intervening in family matters, while other religions as well as atheists are not accorded such a privilege because, on this point, at this particular moment in time, their beliefs are less demanding.

Secularism is often accused as being insensitive to religion, and to religious believers. In this (mis)representation of constitutional secularism, often described as a doctrine of religious persecution, as if it were an advocacy of positions to be found in the 1917 Mexican constitution, allegedly victimized religious organizations claim that disrespect results from secularism. An example to the point is that religious feelings are not protected from blasphemy, which is a form of hatred, while other forms of hatred directed against other groups are not tolerated in a secular system. Blasphemy is an attack on Deity and,

[63] This is comparable to the American doctrine of third-party effect. See also Stephen Gardbaum, "The 'Horizontal Effect' of Constitutional Rights" (2003) 102 *Michigan Law Review* 387.

as such, it differs from stirring religious hatred. The latter presents believers of a religion in a hateful way, with specific consequences coming from third parties; it is not about the feelings of believers (including feelings of hatred that they might feel against those whose speech they find outrageous, when confronted with critical, even troublingly disrespectful attacks on religious teachings). I see no reason why the sensitivity of communities that follow the dictates of strong religions, even when they may feel they have been humiliated, would deserve specifically privileged treatment.[64] Religious sensitivity is, in a way, related to identity. It does not command *specific* legal respect. The opposite would be an abuse of the exceptionalism of free exercise. Such claims to exceptional treatment are a favorite argument of strong religions and undermine constitutionalism as a secular political structure. According judicial recognition to the practice of crying "religious hatred" every time a disrespectful statement is made about a religion runs the risk of institutionalizing the heckler's veto in public discourse, especially where hecklers seem to rely on their well-developed anxiety and personal uncertainty.

The constitutional challenge posed by strong religion cannot be confused with the social and political problem of certain religious minorities in vulnerable social position (e.g. because they are marginalized). My chapter was written with majoritarian strong religions in mind; these politically endorsed religions increasingly claim that their arguments must be accepted in constitutional discourse as the position of the (relative) majority. Many religious minorities act in accordance with a comprehensive worldview without actively challenging the constitutional order. However, I do not intend to make a constitutional distinction dependent of the numerical power behind strong religion. The challenge is a qualitative one, originating in an all-encompassing emotional intensity. The secularist constitutional answer applies to all anti-secularist positions, regardless of the size and political place of the believers of a strong religion. As to certain European immigrant groups, they may well have genuine social and legal problems related to their minority situation, are often victims of prejudice, and may suffer from structural discrimination. All this can be and should be tackled legally ("head on") but not by confusing it with the privileged, untouchable nature of their religion, or any other religion, or any other worldview, for that matter.

Being vulnerable does not put your beliefs beyond standard criticism, and if you bet your identity on the inviolability of your way of life—well, that is your problem. Respect for sensitivity is not an ethical or professional must; moreover, I know that many people call such respect, proffered out of tact and taste, an act of hidden contempt or disrespect, an attitude of false tolerance akin to the treatment of children on the basis of their presumed cognitive immaturity. John Stuart Mill had written in this style about immature people, and for this he figures high on the "wanted" list of Orientalist malefactors. There are valid grounds for the moral position of those who claim that we should treat all adults as grown-ups; this is the way enlightenment works.

My chapter was about constitutional doctrines that can be used in deciding constitutional cases, given that constitutional tolerance traditionally has left us vulnerable in the face of fanaticism. From a strictly legal-constitutional perspective, what matters is

[64] "[R]estrictions on human rights in order to satisfy the dictates of public feeling—real or imaginary—cannot be regarded as meeting the pressing social needs recognised in a democratic society, since that society must remain reasonable in its judgement. To hold otherwise would mean that freedom of speech and opinion is subjected to the heckler's veto." ECtHR, *Vajnai v. Hungary*, App. no. 33629/06; Judgment of 8 July 2008, para. 57.

the answer to the question: What has normative authority in law? In that regard, constitutionalism and Western constitutions have made a secularist choice. Liberal constitutional law and the legal system based on it are about the understanding of law's authority as a human creation formulated in a secular process and enabling such processes to continue. Constitutional theory should find reasons for, as well as means and forms of, coexistence for dissenters. There is a debate between those who seek a coexistence in which differences are maximized and those who believe that such coexistence in a society characterized by fundamental differences is unacceptable or impossible due to its self-destructive nature. In a society where comprehensive views exist *without* agreeing on background values, people with comprehensive views will live in mutual and perpetual disagreement. (In the newspeak of Trojan horses, this is called a "dialogue for consensus.") Such disagreement on background values is not troubling per se to constitutional secularism, which has to maintain neutrality in exercises of counting the angels on a given pin and computing camel/needle ratios. Agreement on background values may not be a condition of citizenship and inclusion. However, this does not impose on the constitutional state a duty to take into legal consideration views that disregard background values of a secular order that enables co-existence to all who agree to co-exist with all other members of society. If you deny personal autonomy and gender equality, even on the grounds of divine command, you deny such co-existence, and you voluntarily disqualify your arguments in terms of the political game though you remain free, nonetheless, to hold such beliefs and worship accordingly.[65]

Constitutions in non-secular societies may make a different choice. This is legitimate from the perspective of state sovereignty, but it cannot be considered constitutionalism. What does not fit into the concept of secularism, remains (and shall remain) suspect in constitutional discourse.

[65] There is a tension, here, when it comes to public advocacy: anti-homosexual religious teaching in public (outside the protected walls of church and religious practice) is interpreted as criminal harassment in certain countries. This criminalization is somewhat parallel to the criticism of religion that I found protected from a secularist perspective. The difference is that the religion-based attack on the sinful nature of homosexuality and homosexuals is about an immutable personal characteristic, while the attack on the religion is about an idea, where believers are attacked for their problematic choices. In terms of the hatred generated, there is a difference between the accusation that one is stupid for believing in a religion that insists on discrimination, and the accusation that certain people are disgusting and damned for what they are, as far as their gender or sexual preference are concerned.

5

Recasting Secularism as One Conception of the Good Among Many in a Post-Secular Constitutional Polity

Michel Rosenfeld[1]

I. Introduction

Modern Enlightenment based constitutionalism accords secularism a privileged position: by remaining secular, the public sphere should warrant neutrality among religions and among the latter and non-religious ideologies in order to provide an optimal setting for the realization of freedom *of* religion as well as of freedom *from* religion. Thus conceived, secularism (which will be hereinafter referred to as "institutional secularism") not only protects against state preferences for religion, or for one among many of them, but also protects religion from the state—to the extent that state endorsement of a religion may entail an unwelcome state meddling into religious affairs.[2] In recent decades, however, secularism has come under intense attack from a number of different quarters intent on dislodging it from its constitutional pedestal. Some of these attacks have targeted secularism's claim to neutrality from religious as well as non-religious perspectives. Proponents of religious views have thus accused secularism of bias in favor of atheism or of the "religion" of "secular humanism."[3] On the other hand, postmodernism has built upon the "disenchantment of reason" to question secularism's coupling with reason and distancing from faith, which were meant to lend the principal support to secularism's claim to neutrality.[4] Furthermore, even if secularism were plausibly neutral, it would still be subject to attack as being pernicious for fostering relativism and a vacuum of commonly shared positive values bound to culminate in a "naked public square."[5]

Once dethroned, secularism can give constitutional way to the polity's dominant religion, to religion against non-religious conceptions of the good, to religion repackaged as a key component of culture[6] or to a vast number of possible permutations involving

[1] Justice Sydney L. Robins, Professor of Human Rights, Benjamin N. Cardozo School of Law, New York City, United States.

[2] See Michel Rosenfeld, *Law, Justice, Democracy and the Clash of Cultures: A Pluralist Account* (Cambridge: Cambridge University Press 2011), 180, n. 44.

[3] See *Smith v. Bd. of Sch. Comm'r* 827 F.2d 684 (U.S. Fed. Ct. of App. for the 11th Cir. 1987) (religious fundamentalists accuse secular public education of preaching the "religion of secular humanism").

[4] See Rosenfeld, *Law, Justice, Democracy and the Clash of Cultures* 7–8.

[5] See Richard J. Neuhaus, *The Naked Public Square: Religion and Democracy in America* (Grand rapids, Mich.: Erdmans, 1984).

[6] See Susanna Mancini, "The Power of Symbols and Symbols as Power: Secularism and Religion as Guarantors of Cultural Convergence" (2009) 30 *Cardozo Law Review* 2629, 2632–3 (discussing judicial characterization of the crucifix as a cultural symbol consistent with constitutionally mandated secularism).

competition among various religious and non-religious ideologies.[7] So long as secularism is the target and as its constitutionally privileged place is perceived as not fully eliminated, it can easily be portrayed as benefitting from an unfair advantage in the clash of ideologies. But what if secularism lost all priority, preference or advantage in the constitutional firmament? In that case, should secularism stand on an equal footing with religion? Or should it be cast as the irreligious or anti-religious in a struggle against religion? Or else, should secularism reemerge as *primus inter pares* or, on the contrary, as subordinate to all existing competing conceptions of the good?

In this chapter, I will explore the case for secularism as one of many conceptions of the good (which will be hereinafter referred to as "ideological secularism"[8]) in a post-secular constitutional polity. I will approach secularism from within or, in other words, as it would be perceived by someone who has embraced it as providing the best way of life as far as he or she is concerned. In this sense, secularism is no different than is a religion as perceived by a believer who is convinced of its truth. If within the aegis of the secular constitutional age, institutional secularism can be conceived as rising above the clash of religions, in the post-secular age, in contrast, (ideological) secularism is confined to being a conception of the good in its own right suited to coexist to a larger or lesser degree with all other such conceptions within the polity.[9]

As liberalism and its commitment to individualism and to "public reason"[10] may go hand in hand with secularism or may at least result in a strong bias in favor of the latter, I will examine the case from within (ideological) secularism consistent with a pluralist as opposed to a liberal conception of the optimal constitutional ordering of the relation between religion and the state. Whereas I have provided an extensive account of normative pluralism elsewhere,[11] for present purposes suffice it to stress the following essentials. For pluralism, in any setting in which there are a plurality of conceptions of the good—and this is the case for all contemporary constitutional democracies—the promotion of peaceful coexistence among the greatest possible number of conceptions of the good found within that setting is a paramount normative objective that must be pursued through constitutional ordering and rule as well as through other means not relevant here. Unlike liberalism, pluralism is not biased as between the individual and the group. Moreover, strictly speaking, for a pluralist *prima facie* all conceptions of the good are of equal worth, thus imposing a presumption of full equality as between secularism and all competing religious and non-religious conceptions of the good. In other words, all conceptions of the good have an *ex ante* equal claim to full recognition though they may well fare very differently *ex post* after subjection to the standard of peaceful

[7] For example, although the U.S. Constitution enshrines secularism by prohibiting the "establishment of religion," U.S. Const., Amend. I (1791), there has been a long ongoing battle aimed at suppressing state promotion of secularism, see e.g. *The State of Tennessee v. Scopes*, 152 Tenn. 424 (1925) (attempt to prohibit teaching evolution theory), and to impose state promotion of religious doctrine, see e.g. *Edwards v. Aguillard*, 482 U.S. 578 (1987) (attempt to impose teaching of creationism in science classes).

[8] "Ideology" has many different connotations ranging from the equivalent of a "world view" to that of "false consciousness" and is thus an essentially contested term. See Etienne Balibar, *Saeculum: Culture, religion, ideologie* (Paris: Editions Galilee 2012), 66–7. As used here, "ideology" is largely equated with "conception of the good."

[9] Secularism could also conceivably be absolutely incompatible with a competing conception of the good such as a fundamentalist religion imposing a comprehensive dogma that would vehemently militate against all science and all liberal rights and values.

[10] See John Rawls, *Political Liberalism: Expanded Edition* (New York: Columbia Univ. Press 2005), 212ff (political decisions of constitutional import should be justifiable under a "public reason" standard).

[11] See Rosenfeld, *Law, Justice, Democracy and the Clash of Cultures* for an elaboration of the theory of "comprehensive pluralism."

coexistence among the greatest possible number of competing conceptions of the good within the relevant polity. Thus, for example, a religion that commands holy war against the infidel, a religion that prescribes pacifism and mutual toleration above all, and a secular ideology would all start with an equal claim to recognition and respect, but the former religion would eventually fare much worse under the peaceful coexistence standard than its pacifist counterpart or than most familiar versions of ideological secularism.

In order to determine how secularism as one conception of the good among many would fare in a pluralist constitutional ordering of religion and the state and to figure out what, if any, place or function it ought to have within the constitutional ordering in question, this chapter proceeds as follows. Part I concentrates on the *ex ante* case for secularism as a conception of the good by inquiring both what secularism would need from the polity and what it would wish to impose on the latter. Part II focuses on secularism as a competing conception of the good in a setting that includes a fundamentalist religion, a non-fundamentalist non-liberal religion, or, in other words a "strong religion",[12] and a liberal religion. Part III details how pluralism's peaceful coexistence standard would mediate among the competing ideologies discussed in Part II in order to effectuate the transition from *ex ante* to *ex post* within a pluralist constitutional order. Finally, Part IV sketches out the place and function of ideological secularism in a pluralist constitutional ordering of the relation between religion and the state and contrasts that place and function to that of institutional secularism in the Enlightenment-based liberal constitutional order.

II. Secularism's Aspirations for Itself and for the World

"Secularism" is an essentially contested concept both in the context of philosophy or ideology and in that of constitutional law.[13] As it emerges from the project of the Enlightenment, secularism is epistemologically grounded in a strong split between Faith and Reason and it places exclusive reliance on the latter in terms of its own *modus operandum* while remaining tolerant of religion so long as the latter is relegated to the private sphere. Viewed as a conception of the good in its own right, on the other hand, secularism is perhaps best captured in Charles Taylor's formulation:

> I would like to claim that the coming of modern secularity... has been coterminous with the rise of a society in which for the first time in history a purely self-sufficient humanism came to be as a widely available option. I mean by this a humanism accepting no final goals beyond human flourishing, nor any allegiance to anything else beyond this flourishing.[14]

Thus, following Taylor's admittedly oversimplified, but for our purposes sufficient, characterization of religion in terms of transcendence, secularism is a conception of the good unshakably anchored in an immanent order that rejects all transcendence from an epistemological, ontological, moral, and political standpoint.[15] It is important to further specify that a secular *Weltanschauung* as conceived here does not necessarily imply atheism or agnosticism although it may seem most logically congruous with the latter. Indeed, so long as commitment to a secular epistemology and to immanent human

[12] See András Sajó chapter in this book. Sajó does not distinguish as between fundamentalist and strong religion as I do here as for his purposes they both raise similar challenges in relation to constitutional ordering and handling.

[13] See András Sajó, "Preliminaries to a Concept of Constitutional Secularism" (2008) 6 *Journal of Constitutional Law* 605, 609 ("secularism" as uncertain qua legal concept).

[14] Charles Taylor, *A Secular Age* (Cambridge, MA: Harvard University Press, 2007), 18.

[15] Taylor, *A Secular Age* 20.

flourishing remains steadfast, the mere belief in a transcendent God, so long as confined to the realm of an individual's innermost private conscience, would not be necessarily incongruous with a fully fledged secular way of life. [16] Moreover, the true relevance of this last point will become manifest in the exploration of the relationship between secularism and pluralism to be undertaken below.[17]

Secularism is compatible with many different philosophical approaches, such as monism, pluralism, and relativism,[18] and many different conceptions of human flourishing, such as those envisaged by liberalism, republicanism, and communitarianism.[19] In short, so long as the focus remains within the realm of immanence and the attachment to the epistemological foundations of secularism (e.g. reliance on science, experience, public reason) sufficiently anchored to sustain a common language–or, to use a Wittgensteinian phrase, a common language game—secularism can thrive and remain conceptually and pragmatically coherent. With this in mind, the key questions in the context of constitutional democracy become: (a) what does secularism need for itself? (b) what does it require from others, that is, from proponents of other conceptions of the good? and (c) what, if anything, would secularism as a conception of the good wish freely to spread to proponents of non-secular perspectives?

A. Secularism's needs in a constitutional democracy

Insofar as secularism is not a religion, it requires freedom *from* religion rights to pursue without unwarranted obstacles its human flourishing objectives. In this context, ideological secularism converges with institutional secularism. Just as in a modern secular constitutional polity religion cannot be allowed to interfere with freedom of belief or of conscience or of scientific inquiry, so too in the post-secular era secularism must enjoy the same rights to maintain its viability and integrity as a distinct conception of the good. Insofar as secularism as a conception of the good is akin to a religion, for example "secular humanism," on the other hand, it does also call for freedom *of* religion rights. Such rights would be largely superfluous in a genuinely secular modern constitutional democracy, such as contemporary France. But, in a post-secular polity, secularism would have to compete with other ideologies without enjoying any *prima facie* advantage within the precincts of the prevailing constitutional framework. And that could well impinge on secularism's pursuit of human flourishing much as the modern secular state may thwart religious pursuits. Thus, for example, just as freedom of religion rights would be necessary for purposes of overcoming secular bans on ritual slaughter for practicing Jews and Muslims, so too they would be for the benefit of secular humanists in a polity with a law against stem-cell research.

Contemporary polities customarily assume a very important role in providing education and in engaging in, sponsoring, and supervising scientific research. In the context of institutional secularism, government intervention in these areas ought to be unproblematic as it would naturally mesh with the basic tenets of secular ideology. In the absence of institutional secularism, on the other hand, ideological secularism would be vulnerable to majoritarian policies that are hostile to secular beliefs and objectives. Thus, for

[16] In this connection, purely private religious belief and worship would be akin to spiritual fulfillment through reading poetry, playing or listening to music, etc.

[17] See below, at 91–92.

[18] For a discussion of the differences among the three, see Michel Rosenfeld, *Just Interpretations: Law Between Ethics and Politics* (Berkeley: University of California Press 1998), 199–208.

[19] Rosenfeld, *Just Interpretations* 215–25.

example, a religious public school education hostile to any immanent perspective or religion driven restrictions on government conducted or sponsored scientific research would obviously adversely affect the vital concerns of ideological secularism. Under such circumstances, therefore, secularism would depend on constitutional protections in order to secure its paramount interests in an otherwise hostile political, ideological, and institutional environment.

Ideological secularism has a message to convey and an agenda to pursue. The message in question is that the rejection of all transcendence need not result in "an empty public square." On the contrary, from a secular standpoint, morals, ethics, and the search for fulfillment and flourishing on this earth can be enriching and uplifting for all of humanity. Solidarity, concern for the other, as well the pursuit of individual and collective self-fulfillment can result in a rich and satisfying life that looms as highly worthy and hence factually and normatively superior to all alternatives based on obedience or subordination to a transcendent or divine entity. The agenda, on the other hand, is the achievement of the greatest possible freedom to pursue all avenues that may lead to the amelioration of human life and well being on this earth.[20] This requires extensive freedom of conscience, speech, expression, and scientific inquiry and experimentation that are only subject to limitations that would be constitutionally valid only if they could be justified under a "public reason" standard[21] that excludes all arguments based on transcendent, metaphysical, or religious reasons. Thus, from an ideological secular perspective, religion-based objections to abortion, stem cell experimentation, in vitro fertilization, cloning, assisted suicide or euthanasia and the like should be unquestionably constitutionally invalid. Similarly, all religion-based arguments relating to sexual mores, gender differentiation, and sexual orientation ought to be banished from official constitutional discourse, deliberation, and decision-making. In short, ideological secularism calls for constitutionally guaranteed exclusion of all religion-based discourse and advocacy by public officials, such as judges and legislators, within the realms of law and politics.

Ideological secularism would not only require negative constitutional rights against the state, but also significant positive ones. Indeed, many of the prerequisites to human flourishing and fulfillment as envisioned by secularism, such as research and advances in the sciences, medicine, and technology, cannot be, for the most part, realistically achieved through exclusive reliance on the private sector. Accordingly, significant state subsidies would have to fill the gap produced by seemingly inevitable private sector shortfalls. Moreover, these state subsidies should become constitutionally mandated to insure against legal or political blockage by objecting religious majorities.[22] Furthermore, private education may be insufficient to guarantee inculcation of secular values to the children of adherents to secularism. In that case, a positive constitutional right to public school inculcation of the values in question would be clearly called for. There may be, of course, several other areas in which advancement of the secular conception of the good

[20] This broad secular conception of amelioration of conditions affecting or concerning humans would encompass such matters as animal protection, including animal rights, and environmental protection.

[21] See n. 10 above.

[22] It is of course plausible to object to constitutionally mandated state subsidies on purely secular grounds as would be the case in a libertarian objection to such subsidies. The latter objection would of course be fully amenable to the "public reason" standard. The upshot of this would either be a split within the secular conception of the good or a plurality of such conceptions. Be that as it may, to the extent that ideological secularism or a version of it requires state subsidies for scientific research, such subsidies should be constitutionally guaranteed against religiously motivated attempts to block or derail them through law or politics.

would require adoption of appropriate positive constitutional rights. All in all, then, it seems inevitable that ideological secularism will require both negative and positive constitutional rights in order to be in a position to meaningfully pursue its fundamental objectives.

B. Secularism's needs against proponents of competing conceptions of the good

The line between constitutional restrictions on proponents of non-secular ideologies resulting from constitutional protections afforded secularists and those stemming from direct prohibitions against opponents of secularism may be often difficult to draw. Freedom to conduct stem-cell research with the aid of state subsidies would certainly frustrate and constrain those whose religion commands a universal ban on such research. Conversely, a ban on picketing abortion clinics would enhance the rights of those who choose to have an abortion. Nevertheless, for present purposes, it is useful to rely on a rough distinction between constitutional norms and practices meant to protect or enhance someone's freedom of (or from) religion and constitutional tools primarily aimed at preventing someone from interfering with someone else's above-mentioned freedoms.[23] Moreover, whereas Section A above focused on the former, this Section will address the latter.

In terms of constitutional constraints on intended or potential interference by proponents of competing conceptions of the good, ideological secularists would particularly benefit from three kinds of distinct prohibitions. These are: first, a prohibition against slandering, denigrating, or inciting hatred or contempt against secularism; second, a prohibition against interfering with, or frustrating, a secularist's access to goods or services that ought to be constitutionally guaranteed or legally available consistent with the precepts of ideological secularism; and, third, a prohibition against interfering with the teaching of science in public schools and more generally with the integrity of scientific research and experimentation throughout the polity, except on grounds amenable to evaluation under the standards of public reason.

Secularism has been the object of many criticisms and attacks, some of them virulent and demeaning, such as accusations of amorality or immorality,[24] lack of trustworthiness stemming from a complete absence of the fear of God,[25] being the source of what

[23] A further complicating factor that will be glossed over for present purposes stems from the fact that different constitutions provide somewhat divergent mechanisms and tools to apportion constitutional rights and duties and to handle conflicts among competing constitutional rights. Thus, for example, the German Basic Law provides for individual rights as well as duties—e.g. Art. 14 guarantees a right to property that also entails obligations—and has been interpreted as applying to transactions among private parties. See Norman Dorsen et al, *Comparative Constitutionalism: Cases and Materials* (2nd edn, Minneapolis: West-Thompson, 2010), 896 (discussing *Drittwirtung* which extends application of constitutional norms to horizontal relationships). In contrast, the U.S. Constitution is overwhelmingly oriented toward the grant of negative rights that can be asserted against the state. These differences can certainly lead to problems relating to practical applications of certain of constitutional norms, but need not be taken into account in a theoretical discussion about plausible optimal constitutional arrangements from the standpoint of ideological secularism.

[24] See eg James McCann and Charles Bradlaugh, *Secularism, Unphilosophical, Immoral and Anti-Social: Verbatim Report of a Three Night's Debate Between the Rev. Dr. McCann and Charles Bradlaugh* (London: Freethought Pub. Co., 1881); Robert K. Garcia and Nathan L. King, *Is Goodness without God Good Enough? A Debate on Faith, Secularism and Ethics* (Lanham, Md: Rowman & Litlefield, 2009).

[25] See e.g. Jeroen Gunning, *Hamas in Politics: Democracy, Religion, Violence* (New York: Columbia University Press, 2009), 76.

Pope Benedict XVI termed the "dictatorship of relativism,"[26] and many other evils perceived as conspiring to deprive human life of all meaning and to reduce human beings to depraved hedonism or to mere calculating mutual exploitation.[27] In short, consistent with these lines of attack, any pursuit of flourishing that eschews appeal or recourse to the transcendent is bound to culminate in lack of dignity and integrity. Moreover, even in the context of institutional secularism, ideological secularists have been demeaned and cast as second-class citizens by being treated less seriously than their "God fearing" counterparts. Thus, for example, in the 1960's the U.S. Congress allowed an exemption from military service in a war zone to conscientious objectors who based their claim on religious grounds, but not to those who did so on principled secular moral grounds.[28] This particular instance of arbitrary discrimination was rectified through a judicial interpretation of the Congressional legislation in question that was so broad as to in effect rewrite the law so as to equate transcendent and secular principled grounds for objection.[29] In acting thus, the U.S. Supreme Court was operating in a secular institutional setting framed by the U.S. Constitution's Establishment Clause[30] which requires separation between the state and religion.[31] More generally, whereas the sting of the above-mentioned criticisms and attacks targeting secularism may be significantly blunted in the context of institutional secularism, it would be an altogether different matter in many other institutional settings. Indeed, it is not hard to imagine secularists without the backing of institutional secularism feeling existentially threatened by concentrated and intense attacks along the lines evoked above.

For secularists to pursue their conception of the good peacefully in surroundings where their dignity and integrity are not under serious or constant threat, "hate speech" against secularists and ideological secularism ought to be subject to legal sanction. In most constitutional democracies, hate speech that incites to hatred of its intended target group gives rise to criminal or civil liability.[32] Hate speech spreads slanderous and demeaning stereotypes against racial, ethnic, and religious groups and it not only tends to injure the latter directly, but it also seeks to gain converts among the broader audience exposed to its message. Just as falsely branding a racial minority as "criminals" or a religious minority as inherently "dishonest" or "violent" ought to be sanctioned, so too should casting secularists as "morally depraved" or "unworthy of trust," particularly if the latter constitute a besieged minority in a religion dominated polity. Furthermore, depending on the prevailing overall circumstances, it may not be enough to prohibit demeaning attacks on proponents of certain conceptions of the good, but it may also be necessary

[26] See Homily of Cardinal Joseph Ratzinger, Saint Peter's Basilica, 18 April 2005, for the Mass "*Pro Eligendo Romano Pontifice*," in "L'Osservatore Romano," 19 April 2005, available at <http://www.vatican.va/gpII/documents/homily-pro-eligendo-pontifice_20050418_en.html>.

[27] See e.g. John Paul II, *Evangelium vitae* (March 1995), paras 22 and 23, available at <http://www.vatican.va/holy_father/john_paul_ii/encyclicals/documents/hf_jp-ii_enc_25031995_evangelium-vitae_en.html>; Rajeev Bhargava (ed.), *Secularism and Its Critics* (New Delhi: Oxford University Press, 1998); Emmet Kennedy, *Secularism and Its Opponents from Augustine to Solzhenitsyn* (New York: Palgrave Macmillan, 2006); also see chapter by Gustavo Zagrebelsky in this book.

[28] Military Selective Service Act of 1967 § 6(j), 50 U.S.C. App. § 456(j) (1964 and Supp. V).

[29] *Gillette v. U.S.* 401 U.S. 437 (1971).

[30] U.S. Const., Amendment I (1791).

[31] How much separation is required by the Establishment Clause may be a matter of dispute, but even those who reject the total separation standard agree that the state cannot endorse particular religions or back any religious coercion. See *Abington School District v. Schempp* 374 U.S. 203 (1963); *Lemon v. Kurtzman* 403 U.S. 602 (1971).

[32] See generally Michel Rosenfeld, "Hate Speech in Constitutional Jurisprudence: A Comparative Analysis," in Michael Herz and Peter Molnar (eds), *The Content and Context of Hate Speech: Rethinking Regulation and Responses* (Cambridge: Cambridge University Press, 2012), 242–89.

to sanction slanderous outbursts directed at the very conceptions involved. For example, The European Court of Human Rights (ECtHR) upheld Austria's prohibition against exhibiting a film profoundly offensive to Catholics as it caricatured and disparaged their religious doctrine.[33] Also, Muslim minorities in Western democracies have claimed that disparagements of their religion, amounting to "insult to the Prophet" profoundly insulted them and deprived them of their dignity and equality rights.[34] What underlies claims such as these is a sense that, amidst virulent hostility and ridicule against a conception of the good, those committed or drawn to it—especially if they are a distinct minority within the polity[35]—will feel assailed and intimidated and thus unable to pursue what is of utmost importance to them on an equal basis with their fellow citizens who adhere to competing conceptions of the good. In a setting in which devotion to the transcendent vastly predominates, concentrated attacks on secularism as valueless and as bereft of all morality might well place unacceptable strains on secularists and dampen the pursuit and teaching of ideological secularism. For that reason, imposing restrictions on slandering and grossly ridiculing ideological secularism becomes arguably a *sine qua non* for a fair and dignified opportunity to embark and comfortably remain on a secularist path.

The second kind of constraint that ideological secularists would wish to impose on others bent on interfering with their pursuits relate to the realm of access to material goods and services rather than to that of ideas. Ideological secularism is strongly committed to complete freedom of scientific inquiry and experimentation and to accessibility to the full panoply of resulting goods and services subject only to limitations justifiable under a public reason standard. Thus, for instance, secularists wish to have unobstructed access to contraception including the "morning after pill," abortion, assisted procreation, the benefits associated with stem-cell research, and end of life options including assisted suicide. Interference with the access in question by hostile others acting on religious grounds have typically involved two kinds of conduct: obstruction and harassment, such as have been experienced at U.S. abortion clinics,[36] on the one hand, and refusal to provide government services or to sell certain stocked products in commercial establishments open to the public, such as pharmacies, on grounds of conscience,[37] on the other hand. Both kinds of conduct involved should be legally prohibited, particularly since those who feel bound by religious constraints usually have many alternative employment options that should allow them to avoid conflicts between their religion and their work obligations. Furthermore, whereas the prohibitions involved may in certain circumstances allow for certain accommodation of religious objectors consistent with secular pursuits of the good, in certain other circumstances, the prohibitions should remain strict. For example, a pharmacy with several employees may arrange for those non-objecting among them to cover for their objecting colleagues in filling a customer's request for an abortive contraceptive. In contrast, in the case of civil servants in charge of providing marriage licenses, no one who would refuse to handle same sex couple requests

[33] See *Otto Preminger Institut v. Austria*, App. no. 13470/87, Judgment of 20 September 1994.

[34] See chapter by Robert Post in this book.

[35] In this connection, it bears specifying that the Catholics concerned in the *Preminger* case belonged to the majority religion within the relevant polity.

[36] See The Feminist Majority Foundation, *1994 Clinic Violence Survey Report* (1994). Harrassment and violence by anti-abortion protesters lead Congress to adopt the Freedom of Access to Clinic Entrances law, 18 U.S.C. 248 (1994).

[37] See e.g. Joe Miles, "Propriety of Pharmacy and Pharmacist's Refusal to Fill Prescription for Contraceptives" (2009) 41 *American Law Reports 6th* 555.

should be allowed to be employed in that capacity.[38] Indeed, in the latter situation, the mere knowledge that a government official would refuse to honor a citizen's right because that official found the right in question religiously repugnant would demean the citizen involved and curtail his or her dignity and equality rights.

The third type of constraint that secularists would feel necessary to impose on religiously motivated others who object to modern science in whole or part is a prohibition against interfering or tampering with the teaching of science in public schools. As experience in the United States makes plain, certain aspects of science, such as evolution theory, arouse much opposition from certain religious quarters. This opposition has given rise to efforts ranging from banning the teaching of evolution theory[39] to instituting a coupling of such teaching with that of creationism.[40] From a secularist standpoint, all of this is objectionable, but the push for teaching creationism in science class is in a way much more pernicious than efforts to ban the teaching of evolution. In the latter case, we have a straightforward clash between religion and science; in the former, an attempt to obfuscate the crucial difference between the discourse of science and that of religion. Evolution theory is subject to the strictures of scientific inquiry whereas creationism is not. By obfuscating the clear line between the two, the religious objector intimates that empirical science coexists on the same plane as metaphysics. As the integrity and independence of science is essential to the secular way of life, it is therefore imperative that threatening and undermining these be prohibited.

C. Secularism's needs to proselytize

Many conceptions of the good, including numerous religions, consider spreading their truth to outsiders an important part of their normative mission. This is also the case for ideological secularism with its roots in the Enlightenment and its commitment to the separation between faith and reason. In some respects secularism's proselytizing is similar to its religious counterparts: the urge to convert others to one's views stems from conviction in one's truth and belief that others will be better off if they switch to one's way of life. In other ways, however, secularism differs from proselytizing religions. Most obviously, the latter ultimately rely on metaphysics whereas secularism is committed to remain within the realm of science and public reason.[41] But also, beyond that, secularism's proselytizing is both defensive and expansive and it can achieve its main aims through partial rather than full conversion of outsiders.

Defensive proselytizing involves trying to convert outsiders as a means to save or better secure one's conception of the good and the way of life associated with it. Whereas it may be advantageous for a proselytizing religion to count on a larger cohort of adherents, the main thrust of such proselytizing is likely to be expansive as the guiding motivation may typically be what is taken to be a divine command to spread the true religion to the heathen. Secularism, in contrast, may need to garner greater numbers to afford a

[38] For example, in the United States, the Supreme Court of Vermont held that the state constitutional free-exercise rights of town clerks are not violated when they are fired for refusing to issue civil union licenses to same-sex couples because of religious objections. See *Brady v. Dean* 790 A.2d 428, 435 (Vt. 2001).

[39] See *The State of Tennessee v. Scopes*, 152 Tenn. 424 (1925).

[40] See *Epperson v. Arkansas*, 393 U.S. 97 (1968); *Edwards v. Aguillard*, 482 U.S. 578 (1987); *Kitzmiller v. Dover Area School Dist*, 400 F. Supp.2d 707 (2005).

[41] Whereas there is a clear factual divide between science and metaphysics (e.g. divine revelation), no normative implications follow from that fact standing alone, and the secularist must therefore draw on more than science and public reason in attempts to gain new converts to her conception of the good.

minimum of protection to science and to public reason which are both indispensable to its conception of the good and its way of life. If, as discussed above, the teaching of evolution can be jeopardized in an institutionally secular polity like the U.S., as evinced by the fate of Copernicus' scientific discovery[42] and Galileo's loss of freedom[43] during the Renaissance, science's status can be very precarious where religion hostile to it has a firm grip on the relevant polity. Under such circumstances, increasing the numbers of science's defenders could only boost the latter's chances of survival.

Secularism's expansive proselytism is in part commensurate with its religious counterpart: it seems natural to wish to convince others of the truths and perceived virtues of one's own conception of the good. But going further, secularism's expansive proselytism complements its defensive one. Indeed, the development and deployment of science and the predominance of public reason in public discourse require numbers, and without a critical mass the full benefits that these offer to those who pursue secularism would seem beyond reach.

Finally, completely unlike its typical religious counterpart, secularism may achieve its most crucial proselytism aims through partial conversion. Thus, acceptance of science without relinquishing commitment to transcendence and filtering religious views to make them fit within the discourse of public reason may well be all secularists need from outsiders to secure the benefits of their way of life. In contrast, it seems inconceivable that a spreader of true religion could be satisfied with anything less than full abandon of false religion to embrace the true one in all its exclusivity.

In view of the foregoing, the question is what secularism's specific needs to proselytize would require from the constitutional system beyond the customary freedoms of speech and of association that allow approaching others to try to convince them to switch to one's views? The answer is that secularism needs in addition some enshrinement of protection and promotion of science in the constitution—a need that does not arise so long as institutional secularism is constitutionalized—and some constitutional commitment by the state and public officials to adhere to public reason in governance and to provide certain key services to the citizenry, such as public education. Moreover, secularists can argue that religion-based opposition to satisfying these secularist constitutional needs should be disregarded to the extent that many who oppose science on religious grounds do not hesitate to take full advantage of the benefits stemming from science or the use of public reason. Thus, many an opponent of evolution theory would not hesitate to avail himself of the full benefits of contemporary medicine should his health or that of a family member be at stake. Whereas it may not be logically contradictory to attack science while at the same time benefitting from it, it does constitute what philosophers call a "performative contradiction" as it involves conduct that undermines the depth and integrity of the professed anti-science stand.

III. Secularism in Competition Against Other Conceptions of the Good

Ideological secularism's amenability to partial conversion on matters of utmost importance to its way of life suggests that it is open to significant accommodation of competing conceptions of the good. This is not surprising as institutional secularism and liberalism

[42] See Edward Rosen, *Copernicus and his Successors* (London: Hambledon Press, 1995).

[43] See Rivka Feldhay, *Galileo and the Church* (Cambridge: Cambridge University Press, 1995).

are themselves open to inclusion of a fairly extensive plurality of competing conceptions of the good.[44] In the context of institutional secularism and of liberalism, secularism has the upper hand and is able to limit tolerance of those ideologies that pose a threat to its hegemony. Ideological secularism in a post-secular age does not possess such advantages, however, and must thus compete on an equal footing with all other conceptions of the good it encounters within the polity in order to secure a path to survival. With this in mind, I will now briefly examine how the competition between ideological secularism and three kinds of religion, namely fundamentalist religion, strong religion, and liberal religion, is likely to shape up. Before proceeding, though, I wish to make clear that the three kinds of religion just mentioned are meant as constructs designed to serve as a useful heuristic device. Actual religions are complex and dynamic and they are subject to differing interpretations and approaches. These religions may approximate one of the constructs in question or even, in part, all three of them, being fundamentalist in some respects, strong in others, and even liberal on some issues. Be that as it may, the constructs relied upon here should suffice to outline the main obstacles and opportunities that ideological secularism is likely to encounter as it seeks to carve out its place in a polity with a full panoply of the religious ideologies typically found in numerous present day constitutional democracies.

Before proceeding any further, it is necessary to address another key preliminary point. Just as religion is not monolithic, neither is secularism. For example, Nazism, fascism, and Stalinist style communism are all secular to the extent that they reject appeal to the transcendent and confine self-fulfillment to the bounds of a human community here on earth. Yet for all their secular credentials, these above-mentioned ideologies would be more antagonistic to the aims of Enlightenment based liberal secularism than a number of fundamentalist religions, and presumably all strong and liberal religions. In the context of a comparison of all existing ideologies, the most important cleavages would most likely not be between religious and secular worldviews. Indeed, it would seem much more imperative to divide ideologies according to the degree to which they provide respect for human dignity and are committed to fundamental equality among all human beings. Moreover, according to the latter criteria, it would seem inevitable that a mix of religious and non-religious ideologies would emerge as the most commendable and another mix also comprised of religious and secular worldviews as the least acceptable. For present purposes, suffice it to stipulate that ideological secularism as used throughout this chapter is understood as referring exclusively to Enlightenment based liberal, republican, communitarian and/or pluralistic secularism to the exclusion of authoritarian or totalitarian secularism as exemplified by Nazism, fascism, and Stalinism. Finally, from an ideological secularist perspective, authoritarian or totalitarian secularism is amenable to rejection as unacceptable either through *use* of public reason or *on account* of the latter's rejection of public reason. In other words, if all versions of secularism were to accept public reason, then persuasive arguments against Nazism, etc., should suffice; and if Nazism, etc., proved completely impervious to public reason, then such ideologies would not be, in the last analysis, any more secular than those worldviews wholly committed to the transcendent.[45]

[44] See John Rawls, *Political Liberalism* (New York: Columbia University Press, 1993), 64 (advocating a version of liberalism compatible with a "reasonable pluralism" of competing conceptions of the good).

[45] See Balibar, *Saeculum: Culture, religion, idéologie* 84 discussing "secular religions or political religions... such as Nazism and especially Communism (which embraced a much more profound messianic dimension)" (my translation).

With these distinctions in mind, fundamentalist religion as understood here takes its own truth as both absolute and as applying to the whole polity or the world at large without any room for acceptance or compromise with any other religious or non-religious world view.[46] As Habermas puts it,

> Fundamentalist worldviews are dogmatic... they leave no room for reflection on their relationship with the other worldviews in which they share the same universe of discourse and against whose competing validity claims they can advance their positions on the basis of reasons. They leave no room for "reasonable disagreement."[47]

As fundamentalist religion leaves no room for discussion or compromise, coexistence with it depends on the particular nature of its aims and the domain over which it feels obligated to impose them. Crusading or Jihadist religion that is bent on converting the infidel, if necessary by force, and that has worldwide aspirations seems to afford no room for any other conception of the good. On the other hand, a fundamentalist religion that forswears all violence and that shuns all contact with all those who do not share its truth may well be able to coexist with proponents of other conceptions of the good within the same polity. In the end, whether, and to what extent, coexistence will be possible depends both on inter-communal and intra-communal factors. Key inter-communal issues would be whether the non-bellicose fundamentalist religion at stake would be willing to abide by the law of the polity and whether its adherents would insist to impose part or all of their way of life through the democratic process—assuming, for example, that they constitute a majority of the population—on the rest of the citizenry. The principal intra-communal issue, on the other hand, would be whether that fundamentalist religion's prescriptions regarding the treatment of its own members would meet the minimum standards of a contemporary pluralist polity. Thus, for instance, if a completely insular and otherwise law abiding fundamentalist religion insisted on a ritual that in essence placed some of the young teenage girls within their religious community in a state of sexual slavery, and deemed that an indispensable part of its religious way of life, then it would seem imperative for the polity involved to intervene in the said community's internal affairs.

Strong religion, unlike its fundamentalist counterpart, is open to dialogue with outsiders and even to change over time, but it remains adamant and unmovable on certain dogma and practices that have important intra-communal and often inter-communal implications. For example, those religions that steadfastly keep women from entering the clergy though they may accommodate other feminist demands from within their ranks cannot approximate contemporary gender equality standards intra-communally. Furthermore, a religion, such as contemporary Catholicism, that seeks to promote polity wide legal bans on abortion which would impinge on the liberties of those whose religion does not ban abortion as well as on the secular, would in part impose its religious proscriptions inter-communally. More generally, strong religion has historically promoted the subordination of women and systematically stood in the way of gender-based equality. As Susan Moller Okin emphasizes,

[46] A distinction must be drawn, for present purposes, between religious fundamentalism as a religious matter and as a politico-constitutional one. From a religious standpoint, a "fundamentalist" is someone who interprets holy texts literally; from a politico-constitutional standpoint, in contrast, a "religious fundamentalist" is one who considers his or her religion as the repository of absolute truth and who insists that the state be ruled exclusively pursuant to the dictates of the true religion. Unless otherwise specified, "religious fundamentalism" will be used throughout in its politico-constitutional meaning.

[47] See Jürgen Habermas, "Struggles for Recognition in the Democratic State" in Ciaran P. Cronin and Pablo de Greiff (eds), *Inclusion of the Other* (Cambridge, MA: MIT Press, 1999), 224.

[T]he basic texts of Judaism, Christianity, and Islam are rife with sexism: the Torah/Bible reverses the reality of reproduction so that the first woman is made from a man, tells a history of the Jews from which women are virtually absent, and advises wives to obey their husbands. The Qur'an explicitly advocates beating women "from whom you fear disobedience," and suggests that some barrier be placed between the sexes, which has been interpreted in a myriad of ways, including heavy compulsory veiling and the "seclusion," or socially enforced imprisonment, of women in their homes, in much of the history of Muslim peoples... [Thus] the more orthodox (but by no means necessarily fundamentalist) versions of all three—including Orthodox Judaism, Catholicism and some Orthodox and Protestant branches of Christianity, and many variants of Islam—still discriminate against women and reinforce their subordination within religious practices, and within and outside the family, in numerous significant ways.[48]

Although not all strong religions are alike in terms of seeking to dominate or heavily influence the public sphere, they are all likely to leave a marked imprint on the politics and the culture of the polities in which they enjoy a significant presence. Accordingly, strong religion is bound to confront secularism at both the inter-communal and the intra-communal levels. Moreover, the conflicts between strong religion and secularism may be more daunting than those between the latter and fundamentalist religion. This is because unlike fundamentalist religion which is typically isolated and often alien to mainstream culture, strong religion may share much in common with more liberal religious traditions and with secularism thus allowing strong religion to seep into the general culture and to fully participate in the political arena.[49] In other words, in as much as strong religion looms in the minds of secularists as much less "the other" than fundamentalist religion, it may present more daunting challenges than the latter at both the intra-communal and the inter-communal levels.

From the perspective of ideological secularism, strong religion's endeavors to impose its dictates inter-communally, such as blanket prohibitions on abortion, euthanasia or divorce, must clearly be fought against. It is far from obvious, however, whether strong religion's intra-communal impositions that are squarely contrary to liberal or secular precepts, such as religious commands or practices that appear to relegate women to subordinate positions within the relevant religious community, ought to be actively opposed or whether it would be preferable to tolerate them. From a pragmatic standpoint, intra-communal religious perceptions or practices that risk to have inter-communal influence or to feed into prejudices or illiberal tendencies within the polity's general culture ought to be vigorously countered. In contrast, purely self-contained intra-communal practices might better be left alone to avoid unnecessary conflict. In short, ideological secularism would have to fight strong religion at least in part and how far such fight ought to optimally extend would depend, as we shall see below in Part III, on whether one subscribes to liberal or pluralist principles.

Liberal religion unlike its two counterparts discussed above seems largely compatible with ideological secularism. Indeed, the principal difference between religions that

[48] Susan Moller Okun, "Gender, Justice and Gender: An Unfinished Debate" (2004) 72 *Fordham Law Review* 1537, 1556. But see Bonnie Honig, "Complicating Culture A Response to Susan Okin's 'Is Multiculturalism Bad for Women?,'" in Joshua Cohen and Matthew Howard (eds), *Is Multiculturalism Bad For Women?* (Pinceton: Princeton University Press, 1999) (arguing that although Okun's linking of traditional Abrahamic religions and patriarchy is basically accurate, overall the relationship between the sexes envisaged by these religions is more nuanced than Okun assumes).

[49] It is of course possible for fundamentalist religion, particularly if it were that of the majority within the polity, to play a decisive cultural and political role. However, in a truly diverse polity, it seems more likely that a strong religion that is closer to the general culture and that can engage in "reasonable dialogue" on many important issues—e.g. the Catholic Religion's commitment to easing the burdens of poverty—would have a much greater impact on inter-communal matters.

have embraced the essential tenets of liberalism—e.g. several progressive Protestant denominations and Reform Judaism—and ideological secularism is that the former involve a commitment to the transcendent whereas the latter does not. To the extent that liberal religion is unreservedly committed to science and to the subjection of public discourse to the standard of public reason as well as to gender and sexual orientation based equality, it seems fully compatible with ideological secularism. On the other hand, liberal religion's embrace of the transcendent may, on occasion, align it with other religions against secularism's agnosticism or atheism.[50] For example, proponents of all religions may join forces to argue against atheists and agnostics that human beings are better off if they entertain some relation to the transcendent and that therefore the state should promote non-denominational devotion to a Supreme Being in all facets of public life, including public education. In such a campaign by all religions, ideological secularists might well feel threatened or belittled in their way of life, and thus compelled to combat even liberal religion's largely tolerant and seemingly readily adaptable conception of the transcendent.

IV. Comprehensive Pluralism's Mediation as Between Ideological Secularism and its Competitors

As already noted, comprehensive pluralism regards all conceptions of the good that count with adherents within the polity as *ex ante* equal in worth and dignity. Moreover, to the extent that there are conflicts and contradictions among existing conceptions of the good, comprehensive pluralism seeks to mediate among them with the aim of achieving *ex post* the greatest possible peaceful coexistence among the greatest possible number of competing conceptions of the good.[51] Given that all actual polities inevitably favor some conceptions of the good over others, the first task of comprehensive pluralism, in what I have termed its "negative moment," is to equalize all conceptions of the good. This involves a shift from *factual* inequality to *counterfactual* equality. Thus, for example, in the context of institutional secularism, comprehensive pluralism's negative moment requires imagining a constitutional and institutional reordering that would strip secularism of its existing advantages and place it on an equal footing with all its ideological competitors. Similarly, in a case of institutional privileging of one religion or of a particular instantiation of it, such as Ultra-Orthodox Judaism in Israel,[52] the negative moment in question demands articulation of the pertinent ordering changes which would make it possible to wipe out the advantages at stake. Furthermore, once all existing conceptions of the good have been counterfactually equalized, comprehensive pluralism deploys its second "positive moment" designed to foster counterfactual construction of the best imaginable plausible constitutional and institutional setting for the peaceful coexistence of the greatest possible number of competing conceptions of the good within the polity.[53]

[50] Strictly speaking, ideological secularism is wholly consistent with agnosticism, but not with atheism. Asserting the non-existence of God seems best understood as a transcendent negation. Nevertheless, atheism may also be interpreted as being based on a negation of the transcendent. Accordingly, it makes sense for ideological secularism to be inclusive of both agnosticism and atheism.

[51] For a more extended discussion of comprehensive pluralism's handling of competing conceptions of the good, see Rosenfeld, *Law, Justice, Democracy and the Clash of Cultures* 204–10. The discussion that follows summarizes the arguments elaborated in the book.

[52] See Gila Stopler's chapter in this book.

[53] As it proceeds within the realm of the counterfactual, the sequence leading from comprehensive pluralism's negative moment to its positive one is a logical one but not necessarily a temporal one.

In this second moment, the conflict among competing conceptions of the good is subjected to mediation pursuant to application of the normative standards issuing from comprehensive pluralism. That, in turn, requires that each conception and the norms it propounds, which figure as "first-order" norms, be subjected to comprehensive pluralism's own norms which emerge as "second-order" norms. Accordingly, the total ban on abortion applicable to all within the polity, which is a first-order norm officially embraced by the Catholic religion, and the conflicting advocacy for a broad constitutional right to an abortion, which is a first-order norm embraced by ideological secularism, will have to be handled through application of comprehensive pluralism's second-order norms further discussed below.

A. Comprehensive pluralism's conception of "justice as reversible reciprocity"

Comprehensive pluralism's conviction that fostering plurality and diversity is a paramount good provides the framework for its arsenal of second-order norms. Consistent with this, the first task associated with comprehensive pluralism's second positive moment is to ascertain to what extent competing conceptions of the good are actually or potentially compatible. Some citizens within a polity may insist that it is a God-given religious duty to help the poor whereas others may vehemently assert that the welfare of the poor is a most urgent humanist concern. Although the first of these positions is religious and the second secular, they can both be plausibly equally accommodated.[54] On the other hand, where conceptions prove truly incompatible, in part or whole, comprehensive pluralism subjects these to its criterion of "justice as reversible reciprocity,"[55] a centerpiece of its second-order norms. This latter criterion of justice goes beyond mere equality among persons or of persons as possessors of actual or potential conceptions of the good. It does so, moreover, in order to stress equality among actual conceptions of the good (subject only to limitations and restrictions resulting from application of comprehensive pluralism's second-order norms) as the highest expressions of the autonomy and dignity of those who embrace them. In short, justice as reversible reciprocity postulates that full equality among persons requires recognition of *prima facie* equality among the full panoply of conceptions of the good to which these persons respectively adhere.

In case of conflict between two conceptions of the good, justice as reversible reciprocity requires first that proponents of each of these switch sides and imagine the conception they oppose *from within* as if it were their own. Thus, if a committed secularist confronts a devout Catholic, for instance, and each of them seeks to imagine as best as possible how it is to live the perspective of the other from within, then they should end up with a clear understanding of the extent to which their respective conceptions may be mutually accommodated and to which they seem bound to remain mutually incompatible. Consistent with this, the secularist and the Catholic may both conclude that their respective conceptions of the good should be ultimately compatible as means to self-fulfillment and flourishing, or that they are in part compatible in the realms of social and economic policy, and in part incompatible in the realm of personal morality. Or else, they may also conceivably conclude, after trading places, that Catholicism

[54] It is of course conceivable that these two positions would be at least partially incompatible as where the religious duty demanded exclusive reliance on private acts of charity and the secular effort insisted on institutionalization and pervasive state intervention to assure complete satisfaction of the basic welfare needs of all the polity's poor.

[55] Rosenfeld, *Just Interpretations* 249.

and secularism are wholly incompatible as their search for self-fulfillment, respectively within the confines of the transcendent and within those of the immanent, render them radically irreconcilable.

Radically irreconcilable conceptions of the good with literally nothing in common should be quite rare, particularly since typical modern personhood and citizenship involves partaking in numerous different and often conflicting conceptions of the good. Take, for example, the case of a German Catholic feminist woman. As a citizen of the European Union, she is likely to share perspectives with fellow citizens from other member-state countries. As a feminist, she may seek to "feminize" her Catholicism, and conversely, as a Catholic, to "catholicize" her feminism. In this context, moreover, the different conceptions involved are more likely to be open to one another in a dynamic give and take than hermetically closed and impermeable to any outside influence. In short, the woman of our example is likely to confront inconsistencies and even contradictions due to her multiple allegiances, but this need not result in incompatibilities forcing her to choose one of her allegiances over another—e.g. Catholicism over feminism or vice versa.

Secularism is certainly not a radically irreconcilable conception of the good as it shares many first-order values and normative commitments with liberal religion and also in all likelihood with strong religion. On the other hand, ideological secularism may be confronted to a radically irreconcilable conception, such as a belligerent fundamentalist religion with zero tolerance for the infidel. In that case, even after application of the criterion of justice as reversible reciprocity, only one of the two conflicting conceptions could be accommodated and that would have to be to the exclusion of the other. Superficially, as plurality would be impossible under the circumstances, pluralism would seem indifferent regarding which of the two contenders would be accorded rule over the polity to the complete exclusion of the other. Upon further consideration, however, because of its (at least partial) openness to other conceptions of the good, enshrining secularism does not foreclose future plurality. Accordingly, as secularism accepts at least some of comprehensive pluralism's second-order norms—in this case some measure of tolerance of competing perspectives—it deserves priority over belligerent fundamentalism even if that were not to yield *ipso facto* greater actual plurality within the relevant polity.

Where partially irreconcilable conceptions of the good clash over particular first-order norms or scarce goods, justice as reversible reciprocity prescribes first of all that a comparison be drawn concerning the relative importance of the norm or good involved to each of the conceptions involved. Thus, if a good in question is crucial to one conception and only marginal to another, then all concerned should agree, after switching places, that the scarce good should go to the proponents of the conception to which it is most crucial. Thus, if there were only one bottle of wine left and a religious group claimed it for ritual use purposes while a secular group wished it available for recreational purposes, then both groups should agree under justice as reversible reciprocity that the religious group's claim should prevail.

In cases where the first-order norm or good under dispute is of equal importance to each of the conceptions of the good involved, then no priority prevails, and resolution consistent with justice as reversible reciprocity would involve ordinary political means, such as negotiation or majority rule. Thus, if both Catholics and Jews needed the only bottle of wine left for ritualistic purposes, and if the respective rituals at stake were equally important within the perspective of each of the two religions involved, then negotiation—e.g. the Catholics will concede the wine to the Jews this time in exchange for the latter yielding to the former next time—or majority rule—there are twice as many Catholics as Jews poised to benefit from the ritualistic use of the only available bottle of wine—would produce the best possible outcome under the circumstances.

Conflicts involving issues of priority of a disputed norm or good among competing conceptions of the good ought to be subjected to constitutionalized second-order norms whereas those conflicts that do not raise such questions of priority ought to be subjected to ordinary politics operating within a constitutional order elaborated in conformity with second-order norms. Moreover, in any comparison, whether at the constitutional or infra-constitutional level, there ought to be compensation *against* actually privileged perspectives—e.g. secularism in an institutionally secular setting or a dominant official religion in a religiously diverse polity—and *in favor of* a systematically underprivileged perspective—e.g. a persecuted minority religion. For purposes of the following discussion, however, it is assumed that neither secularism nor its rival religious perspectives happen to be either privileged or unfairly disadvantaged.

B. Two paramount conflicts: religions unite against secularism in name of pluralism and secularism demands complete freedom of scientific pursuits over religious objections

Starting from a counterfactual *tabula rasa* that eliminates the legitimacy of all attacks on either secularism or religion as enjoying any actual advantage within the polity, two conflicts emerge as paramount under pluralism's criterion of justice. The first pits all religions against secularism based on the claim that secularism undermines pluralism to the extent that it denigrates and fights against all transcendence. The second conflict, in turn, stems from secularism's demand that the freedom to teach, to pursue and to practice science (subject only to public reason based limitations), and where necessary to obtain state subsidies and support for those purposes, be constitutionally enshrined against all objections stemming from religion.

The first of these two conflicts that presumably unites all religions against ideological secularism can be summarized as follows. In the competition for constitutional entrenchment, all religions united on the issue of, commitment to, and promotion of, the transcendent could well argue that any constitutional recognition of ideological secularism, beyond what would be warranted under individual freedom of conscience, belief, and expression rights, would impoverish rather than enhance plurality. This would be because a large number of religions are in various ways committed to the transcendent and in case ideological secularism were to benefit from constitutional advantages, its opposition to transcendence would over time erode commitment to it and hence eventually lead to a lesser diversity of conceptions of the good within the polity.[56] Conversely, according constitutional priority to conceptions of the good that are committed to the transcendent would best serve maximizing plurality in the face of the conflict under consideration.

Granting constitutional advantages either to ideological secularism or to religions committed to the transcendent would have to be categorically rejected under pluralism's second-order norms. Indeed, there is a crucial distinction between fair competition among diverse conceptions of the good and anti-competitive or destructive conduct by proponents of one conception of the good against other such conceptions. Pluralism is satisfied regardless of whether the actual number of accommodated conceptions of the good increases or decreases so long as fair and open competition among all conceptions at play prevails. This can be best understood perhaps by drawing an analogy to the ideal of a free market economy. So long as a competitor runs a rival out of business by offering

[56] For a more extended discussion of this argument, see Rosenfeld, *Law, Justice, Democracy and the Clash of Cultures* 171–4.

a better product or by operating more efficiently, the market economy is well served and its aims clearly furthered. However, if a competitor engages in monopolistic practices or destructive competition, such as by intimidating a rival's customers or by destroying the rival's merchandise, then the market economy is thwarted, and if these evils spread, eventually in danger of being totally destroyed. Analogously, fair competition among conceptions of the good, through mutual exposure, open discussion, attempts at persuasion including religious and secular proselytizing (so long as it only addresses adults and is non-intimidating and non-coercive) is deemed a paramount good from the standpoint of comprehensive pluralism. In contrast, seeking to ban or drive away competing conceptions of the good by mobilizing the state or its institutional apparatus against them is inherently anti-pluralist as it artificially and coercively limits the choices open to all.

Actual fair competition among diverging conceptions of the good may on occasion result in a diminution in the number of available alternatives. That in itself, however, is no evil from a pluralist standpoint. Pluralism is not concerned about the total number of existing alternatives actually in play in and of itself but rather about every person or group within the polity having all the opportunities she or it deems necessary or helpful for purposes of furthering her or its course toward self-realization and self-fulfillment. Thus, for example, if certain religions of the past, such as those of the Ancient Greeks or of the Aztecs, no longer appeal to anyone within a polity, then, all other things remaining equal, that polity will have experienced a net loss in religious diversity. It would be absurd, however, to conclude that because of the consequent diminution of practiced religions the polity in question had become less pluralistic from the standpoint of comprehensive pluralism.

Based on the preceding observations, it becomes clear how a pluralist constitutional order should handle the opposition to secularism advanced jointly by a diverse multiplicity of religions. With secularism as one conception of the good among many and on the same footing as all the religious ones, pluralist constitutionalism should reject any privileging of religion or secularism and ought therefore allow legitimate free and fair competition among various religions and among the latter and secularism.

The second conflict mentioned above differs from the first because it does not involve a clash of ideologies taken as whole. It concerns instead a conflict between something, namely the free pursuit and spread of science, that is of the highest importance for secularism but that is at the same time vehemently opposed, in part or whole, also as a matter of highest importance, by certain religions. Taken in the abstract, this conflict is hard to handle for comprehensive pluralism because it involves two equally strong squarely opposed claims—e.g. for Catholics, human life starts at conception versus for secularists, science does not lend support to the claim that human life as such begins at conception—without any apparent hint relating to any order of priority that might conceivably emerge as a consequence of application of the justice as reversible reciprocity standard. However, as already indicated above, ideological secularism's claim for constitutionally enshrined priority to be given to science is not made all things being equal, but in the context of inconsistencies or contradictions in the positions of those opposing (in part[57]) the

[57] A religion that rejected science in whole and that forbade the use or benefit of any of the products of science could well avoid all inconsistency and hence all vulnerability to the secular claim under consideration. The conflict between such religion and secularism will not be considered any further here as the most populous religions in Western constitutional democracies, Christianity, Islam, and Judaism, all accept many important benefits of modern science in areas such as health, communications, or transportation.

secular approach to science. In essence, according to this claim, a religion that accepts and makes use of science in the areas of health, communications, transportation, etc., engages in a performative contradiction when it seeks to prevent, or to interfere with, the pursuit of science by proponents of other conceptions of the good, such as secularism. In other words, in the course of switching perspectives pursuant to justice as reversible reciprocity, the proponent of the religion that wishes to suppress science in part ought to realize that he cannot have it both ways—e.g. prohibit the teaching of evolution theory in public schools while benefiting from the latest medical advances in public hospitals—once he understands from within the relevant non-religious perspective that the language game of science has a unity and integrity of its own and, in a large number of cases, that his own religion requires recourse to some or all available medical means to save or prolong life.[58] As a consequence of this, secularism's pro-science and religion's partially anti-science stances are not equivalent and the latter ought to give way to the former.

The priority of secularism's pro-science commitment has important but limited consequences under pluralism. This priority requires that the protection and promotion of science be granted constitutional status and that any religious-based call for prohibition or limitation of the teaching, practice or application of science be strictly confined to the intra-communal sphere. Thus, a religion should be empowered to limit or counter science within its own community of believers, but not beyond. On the other hand, the priority at stake should not bar any attempt to limit particular scientific pursuits or applications so long as any resulting limitation is justifiable on public reason grounds. And this should be the case regardless of ultimate motivation, including purely religious ones. With this in mind, so long as secularism competes with religions that accept significant benefits deriving from science, the applicable constitutional order should protect and promote the teaching and pursuit of science subject to limitations justifiable under a public reason standard.

The pluralist handling of the two most important conflicts just discussed sheds light on how to mediate in the cases of the other salient conflicts identified above. These conflicts boil down to: the hate speech, defamation, or blasphemy conflict; the conflict over access to goods and services necessary to secure flourishing and self-fulfillment; the conflict over teaching what is essential for secularism or religion both intra-communally and inter-communally; and the conflict over the legitimate scope of the pluralist, as opposed to the liberal, reach into intra-communal affairs. I now turn to brief discussion of each of these.

C. The conflict over hate speech

As noted in Part II, secularism would wish protection against being demonized, demeaned, and defamed by religion. Similarly, religion seeks to enlist the state against blasphemy, disrespect, and ridicule.[59] These two objectives though seemingly indistinguishable often end up in conflict to the extent that each of the respective ideologies involved tends, because of its very worldview, to cast a negative gloss on the other. For secularism, religion may be highlighted by superstition and prejudice; for religion,

[58] Orthodox Judaism, for example, requires that all available means be used to save or prolong life. See George Robinson, *Essential Judaism: A Complete Guide to Beliefs, Customs and Rituals* (New York: Atria Books, 2001), 200.

[59] See above, at 86.

secularism typified by immorality, relativism, selfishness, and self-indulgence. From the standpoint of pluralism, secularism and religion stand in the exact same position with respect to this particular conflict. On the one hand, pluralism should seek to lessen this conflict by spreading the following message inspired by Spinoza's insight that reason and religion may be regarded as furnishing two distinct paths to the same truth.[60] Secularism and religion offer different means to human flourishing and self-fulfillment and as such should be inter-communally projected more in terms of their respective human potential than in that of the differences that set them apart. On the other hand, while maintaining strict equality between the two, pluralism can handle the conflict by either prescribing a high degree of censorship of expression deemed disrespectful of secularism or religion or by insisting on broad tolerance for such expression.

The first of these two alternatives is highly unattractive as it would thwart all ideological discussion and dispute and interfere with fair competition among distinct conceptions of the good. For example, under this alternative, the statement, drawing on Nietzsche's account,[61] that Christianity is religion fit for slaves would be sanctioned as blasphemy whereas any religiously based statement that homosexual sex is against nature and highly immoral would be punishable as defamatory against secularism (and those religions that share liberal secularism's position on this issue). The second alternative, in contrast, allows for wide ranging debate and criticism and is for that reason far preferable although it is by no means free of shortcomings. Indeed, there is an important difference between denigrating an ideology and defaming those who adhere to it, but the line between the two is often difficult to draw. It is one thing to say that secularism is immoral or amoral and another to proclaim that all secular persons ought to be barred from holding a high governmental office because anyone who lacks the fear of God is morally unfit. Accordingly, in spite of the difficulties involved, pluralism would ultimately protect all opinion regarding all conceivable ideologies, whether secular or religious, but would at the same time sanction hate speech or group defamation against the adherents to an ideology based on the sole grounds of their adherence.[62] In the last analysis, wherever pluralism may ultimately draw these lines, it should do so from a vantage point that remains as much as possible neutral as between secularism and religion.[63]

D. The conflict over scarce goods and services

In the conflict over access to goods and services in the pursuit of flourishing and self-fulfillment, secularism and religion should stand on an equal footing, except to the extent that the priority of science discussed above is implicated. Moreover, in the context

[60] See Baruch Spinoza, *Ethics*, in *The Collected Writings of Spinoza* vol 2 (Edwin Curley trans., Princeton: Princeton University Press, 1985), 7.

[61] See Friedrich Nietzsche, *On the Genealogy of Morality* (New York: Boni and Liveright, 1887).

[62] I gloss over many complexities that would have to be confronted in concrete situations where certain circumstances prevail. For example, the very joining of a Nazi party may well subject the latter's new adherent to condemnation and contempt. But would that involve hate speech or group defamation? Conversely, claiming falsely that Judaism requires using the blood of Christian children for ritual purposes is, strictly speaking, an attack against a religion as distinguished to one against the latter's practitioners. But when placed in its proper historical context, is not this blood libel above all a crude form of anti-Semitic hate speech designed primarily to malign Jews rather than to dispute the truth of Judaism?

[63] This does not mean of course that application of an appropriate neutral pluralist standard would necessarily result in a neutral outcome. If a new religion claimed that Nazism was divinely mandated, then, under any plausible pluralist standard, an *ad hominem* attack against adherents to the new religion would not be objectionable in the way that a similar attack would be on adherents to secularism or to a traditional strong or liberal religion.

of this conflict, pluralism commands particularly strong vigilance against both secular and religious built-in biases. For example, it may be easy to make a liberal secular case against male circumcision practiced on minors or the ritual slaughter of animals to meet the requirements of *kosher* or *halal* meat, but before curtailing these practices a thorough application of the criterion of justice as reversible reciprocity should be mandatory to determine whether the proposed limitations would be proportionate.[64] Conversely, based on a majority religion with great influence on a polity's culture and values, there may be deeply ingrained convictions against assisted procreation, same-sex couple adoption, single motherhood, and assisted suicide. Precisely because of the depth and width of these convictions, it is incumbent to subject them to thorough review under the above pluralist criterion.

The conflict under consideration encompasses questions of access as well as instances of refusal to provide, or assist in obtaining, particular goods or services as a matter of conscience. A devoutly religious person working in a pharmacy may refuse to honor a request to purchase a "morning after" contraceptive or a feminist and gay rights activist may object to dealing with a person who openly endorses a religious ideology widely perceived as misogynist and homophobic. Whereas certain existing constitutional democracies tend to defer to religion-based refusals based on conscience but not to those not derived from religion,[65] pluralism requires strict equality between religious and secular objections to provide goods or services as a matter of conscience. Accordingly, for pluralism the question boils down to determining the extent to which to equally honor religious and secular objections based on conscience.

As long as no disproportionate consequences would ensue, pluralism counsels accommodating secular and religion based conscientious objectors on an equal basis. There ought to be one exception to this general rule, however, in the case where the conscientious objector's job involves performing an official state function and refusal to do so would offend the dignity of any group within the polity. Thus, a civil servant in charge of processing marriage certificates should not be entitled to claim an objection based on religious grounds to refuse to handle a request by a same-sex couple in a jurisdiction that provides for same-sex marriage.[66] Similarly, a secular objector should not be allowed to refuse handling a similar request by a couple with an avowed commitment to a religious ideology that is misogynist and homophobic. Moreover, such prohibition is certainly justified under justice as reversible reciprocity in as much as the mere knowledge that the state allows a public servant to discriminate on the basis of sexual orientation or religious affiliation is an affront to the dignity of those who are targeted by the refusal at stake. On the other hand, the public servant affected can easily avoid the conflict in question by selecting another civil service position where no such conflict is likely to arise.

E. Conflicts over teaching religious and secular perspectives

Teaching is indispensable for purposes of preserving, growing internally, adapting, and expanding the reach of any conception of the good. Also, in most cases, the needs

[64] Although the present discussion is proceeding under the assumption that all the conflicting conceptions of the good in play operate under a (counterfactual) regime of strict equality, it bears noting that in the (actual) case in which secularism is aligned with the culture of the majority religion—e.g. Christianity—to attack minority religion—e.g. Judaism and Islam—practices, the potential for bias would appear significantly increased.

[65] See Post chapter in this book.

[66] See *Brady v. Dean* 790 A.2d 428, 435 (Vt. 2001).

and inspirations of particular conceptions of the good require teaching at both the intra-communal and inter-communal levels. It is obvious that inter-communal teaching claims by mutually inconsistent ideologies would lead to conflicts, but perhaps less so that intra-communal teaching initiatives might also. Consider, for instance, the teaching at a network of private Islamic schools in the United Kingdom, based on Saudi government-supplied textbooks, that proclaimed that Jews "looked like monkeys and pigs," that prescribed, inter alia, throwing those who had engaged in gay sex off a cliff, and that illustrated where hands and feet should be amputated as punishment for theft in accordance with the Shariah.[67] This latter intra-communal teaching involves incitement to inter-communal hatred and could well condition young minds to acceptance of violence against members of other communities within the polity. On the other hand, different kinds of intra-communal teaching may not target any outsiders, but may nonetheless raise conflicts as might the purely intra-communal teaching of religious doctrine promoting the subordination and submission of women to men.

In the case of inter-communal teaching, such as in public state schools, except for the priority of science discussed above, pluralism requires *prima facie* equality for all ideologies subject to further adjustment in terms of compliance with pluralism's second-order norms. It follows from this that there ought to be an affirmative obligation to teach inter-communally pluralism's philosophy of mutual understanding, mutual acceptance and mutual accommodation as well as its second-order norms, including belief in equal dignity and tolerance based on a Spinozistic emphasis on religion and secularism as different paths to human flourishing and self-fulfillment (while acknowledging that regarding them thus does not preclude considering each of the two from within the perspective of the other as an erroneous or less desirable means to the same end). Beyond that, the prescriptions of justice as reversible reciprocity would depend on contextual factors—e.g. how antagonistic are visions of secularism and religion and those of the different religions active within the relevant polity—and could range from extensive treatment of all competing ideologies to a virtual ban on teaching ideological secularism and religion *in their own right* inter-communally.[68] All things being equal, pluralism evinces a clear preference for thorough presentation and free discussion of all ideologies actively pursued within the polity. However, where antagonisms are too intense and exacerbation of prejudice more likely than better mutual understanding, it seems wiser to adopt a gag rule relating to the particulars nourishing the prevailing conflicts. This latter position is analogous to that prohibiting ethnic-based political parties inscribed in the constitutions of countries rife with ethnic animosity and conflict.[69] By forcing political concentration away from ethnic issues, the polity may improve its chances to maintain the minimum of unity necessary for its survival. Similarly, drawing public education away from fierce wars between secularism and religion or among diverse religions, may better serve the cause of pluralism in situations in which no realistic path to greater inter-communal opening is discernible.

[67] See John F. Burns, "Lessons of Hate at Islamic School Network in Britain," *New York Times*, 23 Nov. 2010, A8.

[68] References to secularism and religion would of course always be appropriate where pertinent in other contexts, such as the teaching of history. Thus, it would be important to discuss the respective religious ideologies that led to a particular religious war, or that influenced a policy of combating poverty as well as to discuss the link between secularism and the philosophy of the Enlightenment.

[69] See e.g. the Constitution of the Republic of Ghana, ch. 7, s. 55 (4), which states that "Every political party shall have a national character, and membership shall not be based on ethnic, religious, regional or other sectional divisions."

In the case of intra-communal education, a distinction must be drawn between teachings that are *incompatible* with pluralism, such as the propositions about Jews and Gays imparted in certain Islamic schools in the United Kingdom mentioned above, and teachings that are merely *inconsistent* with pluralism's own essential thrust, such as a non-proselytizing peaceful fundamentalist religion's message to its adherents that all other religions and ideologies are absolutely false and that it is a mortal sin to engage in any religious discussion or social interaction with any outsider. Intra-communal teaching that is incompatible with pluralism should be banned[70] whereas that which is inconsistent with pluralism should be permitted, provided there is intra-communal compliance with the teaching of a mandatory basic state imposed curriculum that includes a discussion of pluralism's own norms as they pertain to civic and political life.[71]

A more thorny difficulty arises in the context of purely intra-communal teaching that neither addresses nor targets any outsider but that nonetheless may cross the line between inconsistency and incompatibility both internally and externally. This would be the case where a self-contained religious community imparts purely intra-communally teachings and precepts that are categorically misogynist and homophobic. On the one hand, if the community in question recognizes and respects the right of exit of all its members and allows for wide raging intra-communal debate of its views, then its teachings would seem inconsistent but not necessarily incompatible with pluralism. On the other hand, if the community in question is very visible in a polity with a vigorous inter-communal struggle to achieve full equality based on sex, gender, and sexual orientation, then the potential spillover effects from the teachings and practices of the religious community at stake may well trigger a move from the inconsistent to the incompatible. Ultimately, whether pluralism should or should not tolerate such intra-communal teaching in any given instance would depend in significant part on contextual factors. Some further light might be shed on this conflict in general, however, through examination of the next and last conflict listed above, namely that concerning the contrast between the respective approaches of liberalism and pluralism toward intra-communal ways of life that are strongly illiberal.

F. Liberal versus pluralist handling of the internal life of illiberal religious communities

The conflict over how far to reach within the intra-communal affairs of a strongly illiberal community concerns the latter's way of life as well as its teachings. Moreover, the principal difference between liberalism and comprehensive pluralism in relation to this conflict stems from the contrast between liberalism's unshakable link to individualism and pluralism's *prima facie* indifference as between individual-regarding and group-regarding concerns. Liberalism's individualism requires systematic subordination of group-regarding claims to basic individual-regarding concerns, such as individual

[70] This would not prevent the Islamic schools in the example above to teach that Judaism is a false religion or that homosexual sex is a sin for Muslims and that accordingly it must remain strictly prohibited within the Islamic community.

[71] Such minimum curriculum consisting of basic subjects such as math, sciences, language, history, geography, and the country's constitution and political institutions is imposed on religious schools in several countries. Such curricular obligations, however, are in many cases ignored or circumvented, particularly where credible prospects of state enforcement are lacking. See Stopler chapter in this book (discussing systematic non-compliance by the ultra-Orthodox in Israel).

liberty, equality, or dignity. In the case of a strongly illiberal community that teaches and practices subordination of women and homophobic mores, therefore, a consistent liberal is bound to urge active inter-communal intervention into the community involved to promote gender and sexual-orientation based equality. The only constraint upon this liberal imperative would come from the freedom of religion rights of individual members within that community as opposed to any communal rights based on the operative religious ethos. Also, wherever the ultimate liberal balance between individual freedom of religion and individual equality may be drawn, at a minimum the consistent liberal would insist on imposing intra-communally liberal education requirements and the application of inter-communally based liberal constitutional and legal norms to all intra-communal dealings with a narrow exception drawn for religious worship, association, and expression. In the end, in as much as secularism and liberalism share many first-order norms in common, the spread of liberalism into illiberal religious communities is bound to result in providing a distinct advantage to ideological secularism against religion or at least all but liberal religion.[72]

From the standpoint of pluralism, on the other hand, the mere fact that a religious community is intra-communally illiberal does not justify intervention from the outside. Take for example a religious community that preaches and practices what clearly amounts to the subordination of women from a liberal perspective. Such subordination is certainly inconsistent with comprehensive pluralism's normative precepts as framed by its second-order norms, but it is not necessarily thereby incompatible with the latter.[73] Thus, if the religious community in question gives its women some voice in communal affairs and grants a general right of exit to all its members, men and women alike, then it is by no means apparent *prima facie* whether liberal intrusion or continuation of the illiberal status quo would better conform with pluralism's ultimate aims. There is a pluralist argument in favor of outside intervention and it is essentially twofold: (1) the religious group provides a bad example that may inspire some to attempt to reverse inter-communal liberal gains in the implantation of gender-based equality; and (2) most women born into the religious group and systematically fed its ideology may not fully appreciate their state of subordination or, even if they do, may be too trapped or inhibited to leave the group. These arguments are countered, however, by others militating against outside interference which are also essentially twofold: (1) what appears as subordination from one perspective may not be subordination from another, and suppression of what does not conform to the views of the majority may ultimately prove unduly inegalitarian (as between different conceptions of the good within the polity); and (2) if one seeks to deny recognition to group-regarding differences that seem unpalatable to a progressive liberal majority, one may well end up frustrating the deployment of pluralism.

The apparent subordination of women in the above example should be settled through application of the principle of justice as reversible reciprocity. Accordingly, women belonging to a group that allegedly subordinates them should consider their status from the perspective of outsiders, critics, and so on, as compared to their own, and to decide whether, when aware of all available options, they would continue with their own group or opt out. Although it is impossible in practice to fully experience the world

[72] There is a strong argument that liberalism calls for institutional secularism, which will not be pursued further in this chapter.

[73] This example is treated at greater length in Rosenfeld, *Law, Justice, Democracy and the Clash of Cultures* 88–9 in the context of the contrast between (liberal) equality-as-identity and (pluralist) equality-as-difference.

from the perspective of another, it certainly seems plausible that women living within a culture that others consider defective from the standpoint of gender-based equality would nonetheless choose to remain within that culture even if they could fully intuit all the benefits and drawbacks of all available alternatives.[74]

Beyond that, pluralist resolution of the two arguments in favor of inter-communal intervention and the two against the latter is dependent, in significant measure, on contextual factors that are likely to differ from one setting to the next. Thus, the claim that a culture that appears to subordinate women provides a bad example only seems seriously troubling in the context of a society that has not yet firmly implanted liberal equality. In one that has, in contrast, it might well be the minority culture that stands out as non-egalitarian that would appear more vulnerable to intolerance. In any event, if inter-group channels of communication are open, and if the minority culture though benefiting from a fair amount of autonomy cannot avoid openness to other groups and to institutionalized pluralist norms, then it may be subject to pressure for inner reform. This is manifest in the movements that have sprung in several religious communities that bar women from the ministry and in which they advocate change opening the way to greater gender-based equality.

Concerning the argument that those women that are subordinated may not be fully aware of their status, beyond what has already been said, it should be added that the risk of misperception is not one-sided. Indeed, the outsider's risk of misperceiving unfamiliar mores as causing subordination may be equivalent to the insider's risk of misjudging to what extent her role within her culture may conform to some acceptable conception of gender-based equality. Furthermore, if on account of the dangers of misperception one were to automatically fall back on liberalism, one would not only sacrifice the diversity of a multi-cultural polity but also possibly unwittingly restrict the reconciliation of diversity and equality in difficult or borderline cases. Suppose, for instance, that a religion proclaims men and women to be equal in the eyes of God but nonetheless provides for traditional sex differentiated roles within its community. Should the state intervene, consistent with pluralism, in the case of a woman member of that religion who is familiar with liberalism but who insists that life in accordance with transcendent equality among the sexes suits her much better than what she regards as shallow liberal gender-based parity? It seems clear that at least in some such situations comprehensive pluralism would counsel against any outside intervention.

Given the above detailed differences between how liberalism and pluralism would respectively handle purely intra-communal religious illiberalism, ideological secularism would seemingly fare better under liberalism than under pluralism. If all relevant contextual factors are properly accounted for, however, the actual disadvantage likely to be experienced by secularism looms as relatively minor. Moreover, such disadvantage would principally affect the scope of the secularist's freedom to proselytize within certain anti-secular religious communities within the polity.

[74] There are cases where the trade-offs are quite familiar as when Orthodox Jewish or Muslim women who work side by side with secular women, in a country like the United States, can compare notes, and nonetheless consciously determine that for them secularism would be a less desirable alternative. Of course, these women cannot shed their background, history, upbringing, family, etc., and thus their conclusions would only approximately satisfy the test imposed by justice as reversible reciprocity.

V. The Fate of Ideological Secularism in a Pluralist Constitutional Ordering of the Relationship Between the State and Religion

The fate of ideological secularism in a post-secular pluralist constitutional democracy is in the end not that different than it was supposed to be in a liberal Enlightenment-based polity that constitutionally enshrined institutional secularism. On a purely theoretical plane, ideological secularism fares better under liberalism than under pluralism. Under liberalism, secularism has an unwavering priority over religion in the public sphere, civil society and education—at least in public education and even to a significant extent in private education inasmuch as its spread into the intra-communal precincts of illiberal religious communities is called for as indicated above. Under pluralism, in contrast, secularism is in principle the equal of religion. Moreover, although submission to pluralism's second-order norms may on occasion *de facto* favor secularism, on other occasions, as exemplified by the case of the illiberal religious community that pluralism would exempt from state imposed liberal teachings discussed in Part III above, secularism would have to yield to religion. In the end, what makes secularism under pluralism more vulnerable than it is under liberalism is its dependence on contextual factors in terms of its prominence in the constitutional arena. If cast exclusively against a strong religion which happened to repudiate science wholesale, for instance, secularism under pluralism would fare far worse than under liberalism as, under such circumstances, pluralism would not lend any support to the inter-communal diffusion or teaching of science.

When approached from a more practical historically grounded perspective, however, not only do the advantages of liberal secularism over its pluralist counterpart largely vanish, but also in certain important ways pluralist secularism may end up topping its liberal alter-ego. The evening out of the two secularisms results principally from an important contextual factor operative in all industrialized contemporary constitutional democracies: as repeatedly emphasized throughout, all the major prevailing religions to a large extent accept or endorse science. On the other hand, in the transition from a modern to a post-modern appreciation of institutional secularism,[75] especially in a historico-political setting infused with the revival of religion, institutional secularism may well become weakened through an often disguised and in part unconscious return of previously (constitutionally) repressed religious narratives, norms, and values.

The return of repressed religious material occurs in all institutionally secular constitutional polities regardless of how strictly they impose a separation between the state and religion or how thoroughly they purport to expel religion from the public sphere. Moreover, this return of the repressed makes use of numerous different discursive strategies that include conflating religion and culture, reframing the religious as secular through displacement, and concealing religious bias in the very formulation of the seemingly most anti-religious version of institutional secularism. The first of these three strategies is well illustrated by the approval under Italy's current secular constitution of the mandatory display of the crucifix in public school classrooms. As expressed by an Italian

[75] The difference in this context between a modern and a post-modern understanding of institutional secularism is that whereas the former regards institutional secularism as being neutral among religions (and among religious and secular ideologies), the latter does not, and leaves no room for any neutral institutions. For a more extensive discussion of the overall contrast between modern and post-modern perspectives and their impact on the interplay between liberalism and pluralism, see Rosenfeld, *Law, Justice, Democracy and the Clash of Cultures* 52–6.

court, "the crucifix is the symbol of our history and our culture and, as a consequence, of our identity...and also of the principle of secularism."[76] More specifically, as the same court emphasized, there is "a perceptible affinity...between the essential core of Christianity, which...focuses on tolerance and the acceptance of the other, and the essential core of the Italian Constitution," which is based on fundamental rights. Although the court admitted that "during history, many incrustations were settled on the two cores, and especially on Christianity," it nevertheless insisted that the harmony between Christianity and the Constitution endures because, "despite the Inquisition, anti-Semitism and the Crusades," it is "easy to recognize the most profound core of Christianity in the principles of dignity, tolerance and religious freedom and therefore in the very foundation of a secular state."[77]

The second strategy has been prevalent in the United States which has incorporated various religious ideas, values, and symbols in the public sphere in spite of its constitutional "wall of separation" between Church and state.[78] Thus, the phrase "In God We Trust" is inscribed on every dollar bill, religious ministers recite a prayer at the beginning of sessions of the U.S. Congress, and, as will be briefly discussed below, the U.S. Supreme Court has designated the Christian "*crèche*" a secular symbol when displayed in a public square.[79]

In contrast to the first two strategies, the third strategy operates in ways that are largely invisible. This third strategy is pursued in the name of French "*laïcité*" which is cast as strictly neutral with respect to religion and regarded by many as even fundamentally anti-religious.[80] In spite of this, as Michel Troper's conceptual history of the term vividly brings to light, *laïcité* was the product of a particular accommodation between the French Catholic Church and the state.[81] To be sure, the deployment of *laïcité* in France required some restraints on religion, thus somewhat relativizing Catholicism within the polity. But at the same time, *laïcité* was molded in theory and practice so as to render the public space as compatible as possible with the culture associated with Catholicism, if not with the religion itself. This phenomenon is succinctly captured in the French popular term *Catho-laïque* used often to refer to a Catholicism that has adapted to *laïcité*, but that also connotes the corollary of a *laïcité* that has been fitted for harmonious coexistence with Catholicism. Moreover, consistent with this, French *laïcité* has on occasion been used to bolster Catholicism at the expense of minority religions such as Islam.[82]

To illustrate in greater detail how the return of repressed religion can undermine institutional secularism and circumvent mainstay liberal principles suffice it to focus on a single case, the already alluded to U.S. Supreme Court *crèche* decision, *Lynch v. Donnelly*, which furnishes an exemplary use of the second of the three strategies briefly

[76] TAR (Regional Administrative Tribunal) Veneto, 17 March 2005, Decision n. 1110, para. 12.4.

[77] TAR (Regional Administrative Tribunal) Veneto para. 11.6. For a thorough discussion of the handling of the crucifix as a cultural symbol in the context of constitutional secularism, see Susanna Mancini, "The Crucifix Rage: Supranational Constitutionalism Bumps Against the Counter-Majoritarian Difficulty" (2010) 6 *European Constitutional Law Review* 6.

[78] See Kent Greenawalt, "Secularism, Religion, and Liberal Democracy in the United States" (2009) 30 *Cardozo Law Review* 2383 (discussing different interpretations of the constraints imposed by "the wall of separation").

[79] *See Lynch v. Donnelly* 465 U.S. 668 (1984).

[80] See Rosenfeld, *Law, Justice, Democracy and the Clash of Cultures* 155–6.

[81] See Michel Toper chapter in this book.

[82] See Mancini, "The Power of Symbols and Symbols as Power" 2664 (discussing France's policy on the Islamic veil as at once a reinforcement of France's Catholic heritage and an attack against Islam).

sketched above. *Lynch v. Donnelly* was a 5–4 decision that concluded that the display of the *crèche* on city-owned property was not violative of the U.S. First Amendment's Establishment Clause, which erects a "wall of separation" between religion and the state that at a minimum forbids the state from officially preferring one religion over others. Consistent with this, the U.S. Supreme Court's majority had to overcome two daunting doctrinal hurdles. First, it had to find that the display of the *crèche* had a secular purpose and, second, that such display did not amount to an official endorsement of religion by the municipality involved.[83] To overcome the first hurdle, the Court's majority found the municipality's purpose to be secular as it regarded the placement of the *crèche* within a larger Christmas display that included Santa Claus and reindeer near the heart of the municipality's shopping district as an enticement to engage in Christmas shopping and thus inure to the benefit of local merchants.[84] Furthermore, to overcome the second hurdle, the court's majority reasoned that display of the *crèche* did not endorse (any particular) religion any more than does inscribing the words "In God We Trust" on U.S. coins.[85]

What the Court's majority in *Lynch* ended up doing was to merge the secular and the religious or to subordinate one of the two to the other, with the consequence of causing offence to all but proponents of mainstream (liberal) religion, who in the United States happen to be mainly those who belong to Protestant denominations that embrace a muted version of the Christian religion that blends well with principal values associated with liberalism and secularism. It is obvious that atheists and agnostics would feel left out and not taken seriously. But so would non-Christian believers, such as Jews and Muslims. Finally, even deeply committed Christians, for whom the *crèche*, which depicts the nativity, has profound religious significance, would have reason to be offended by having their religion trivialized and its sacred symbols reduced to props used for purposes of boosting retail sales.[86]

A pluralist constitutional approach, in contrast, could easily avoid all these problems. From a pluralist standpoint, the issue would not be whether the crucifix or the *crèche* could pass as sufficiently secular or sufficiently assimilable into secular culture. The concern would be, instead, whether or not these religious symbols would be so significantly divisive as to hinder rather than promote the greater self constraint and greater tolerance required to ensure the greatest possible accommodation of the greatest possible number of religious and non-religious conceptions of the good within the polity. In some settings, the crucifix, the *crèche*, or other dominant religious symbols may emerge as oppressive and exclusionary when officially embraced or endorsed by the state. In other settings, however, they may well have no such connotations and may therefore be promoted by the state alongside secular symbols without fostering significant divisiveness. More generally, what is crucial from the standpoint of pluralist constitutionalism is that the constitutional architecture and the constitutional jurisprudence of the polity involved be equipped so as to properly distinguish between inclusionary and exclusionary entanglements between ideological secularism and religion (as well as between different religions) and between the state and religion.

More generally, pluralist constitutional ordering would ideally be grounded in a counterfactual *areligious* ideal—"areligious" being understood here as neutral and impartial

[83] 465 U.S. at 679. [84] 465 U.S. at 690. [85] 465 U.S. at 676.

[86] In this connection, it is not surprising that some of the strongest advocates of a strict separation between religion and the state in the U.S. have been certain religious leaders of strong religions. See e.g. *Testimony of J. Brent Walker, General Counsel and Assoc. Dir., Baptist Joint Committee on Public Affairs Before the Senate Committee on the Judiciary*, Federal Document Clearing House, 25 Oct. 1995.

as between ideological secularism and religion and as between different religions (as opposed to "areligious" as an equivalent to "irreligious" or to indifferent to religion).[87] Furthermore, consistent with this areligious ideal, all competing conceptions of the good would pursue their respective objectives and be taken into constitutional account in the open. This would obviate the need for discursive strategies, such as the three listed above, which have proven useful in efforts to dislodge the supremacy of institutional secularism and to nullify the advantages that the latter bestows on ideological secularism. Under the areligious counterfactual, secularism and religion would start on an equal footing and would in principle coexist as full equals. In practice and subject to comprehensive pluralism's second order norms, however, in most cases ideological secularism will end up with some advantages over religion.[88] The most obvious advantage is that to be secured through a constitutional guarantee regarding the inter-communal diffusion of science. Less obvious, but important nonetheless is the advantage that secularism seems bound to enjoy by virtue of being more compatible with pluralism's second-order norms than religions, or at least fundamentalist and strong religions, are likely to be. Indeed, with secularism's advantage regarding science in hand, it seems highly probable that secularism will be more open to plurality than a large number of religions that start out as its full equals. Thus, for example, after securing its advantage regarding science, secularism may well be comfortable with a pluralism that allows, except in cases of egregious illiberalism, each ideological community to thrive and flourish intra-communally. Catholicism, in contrast could not wholeheartedly accept such pluralist regime so long as it remains committed to the inter-communal eradication of abortion.

As already emphasized, actual pluralist constitutional ordering is context dependent and accordingly bound to vary from one polity to the next. Moreover, as noted in the above discussion on the U.S. *crèche* case, pluralism can be as compatible with strict separation between religion and the state as with extensive state promotion of religion and secularism alike, depending on the circumstances. What pluralist constitutionalism does not countenance is concealed undermining of ideological secularism or, in by far most cases, the taking away of secularism's *ex post* advantages over religion. Because of its combined greater flexibility where appropriate and its greater firmness where called for, pluralist constitutionalism is therefore better suited to the aims of ideological pluralism in the post-secular polity than is its liberal counterpart.

V. Conclusion

Paradoxically, because of its exalted status in polities committed to institutional secularism, ideological pluralism has come under concerted attacks. These attacks cast secularism both as an obstacle intent on drowning out the calls for suitable recognition issuing from various religions and as an unworthy ideology that fosters relativism if not downright nihilism. In short, so long as institutional secularism endures, it can be portrayed as a colonizer that seeks to keep religions institutionally colonized. Also, as its legitimacy is increasingly challenged, secularism becomes subject to depiction as an ever more arbitrary and superfluous colonizer seeking to hold on to privileges that have become purely

[87] See Rosenfeld, *Law, Justice, Democracy and the Clash of Cultures* 150–4 for a more extended discussion of the areligious ideal.

[88] These advantages may not come into play in case of liberal religion to the extent that its commitment to the transcendent poses no threat to secularism.

abusive in a war of institutional liberation waged by religions vying for wholehearted recognition of their full dignity.

By shedding all the vestiges of institutional secularism, and going instead to the starting gate as one ideology among many (all of these being in principle equal to one another), secularism puts on an entirely different face. Ideological secularism thus becomes a conception of the good on a par with its religious counterparts in the search for fulfillment and flourishing. As such, like religion, ideological secularism seeks goods for itself and protection from others, including religions, which stand in the way of the path to the good it has set out for itself.

By abandoning the privileges it enjoys within the ambit of institutional secularism and subjecting itself to the prescriptions of pluralist constitutionalism (not necessarily out of outright conviction, but as a lesser evil to the war of ideologies), ideological secularism admittedly becomes in principle more vulnerable to disadvantage or subordination in certain conceivable scenarios. To be sure, if pitted exclusively against a single fundamentalist religion that forsakes all of science, or against an alliance of strong religions unbendingly committed to a relentless combat against the ungodly, ideological secularism may at best secure bare tolerance under the aegis of pluralist constitutionalism. Such scenarios, however, are far from the conditions that currently prevail (and that in all likelihood will remain in place for the foreseeable future) in contemporary industrialized constitutional democracies. The latter scenarios are typically characterized by a plurality of religions including fundamentalist, strong and liberal ones that are as likely to compete among one another as they are sure to do so against secularism. Moreover, in the overall picture most likely to emerge in the scenarios in question, ideological secularism would by no means only figure as the enemy of religion. Instead, there would undoubtedly be many occasions where secularism would align with liberal religion against strong or fundamentalist religion or even with strong religion against fundamentalist religion. In addition, in such a scenario, most if not all religions would at least *de facto* embrace science to a significant extent.

In the context of the latter scenario which currently prevails in constitutional democracies, pluralist constitutionalism would not only insure ideological secularism's status as an equal, but also propel it as a *primus inter pares*. And that far from relegating religions to any second rank status would provide them with the best possible accommodation and path to self-fulfillment, short of a constant war against all or permanent subordination of the many to a single dominant religion. Ironically, in the present predicament, pluralist constitutionalism turns ideological secularism's newly found vulnerability in the advent of a post-secular age into an advantage over its most likely competitors. That advantage, however, goes hand in hand with insuring the best possible conditions for peaceful coexistence among the greatest possible number of religions vying for self-fulfillment and flourishing within the polity.

PART II

RELIGION, SECULARISM, AND THE PUBLIC SQUARE

6

The Tempting of Europe, the Political Seduction of the Cross: A Schmittian Reading of Christianity and Islam in European Constitutionalism

*Susanna Mancini**

This word, *Muselmann*, I do not know why, was used by the old ones of the camp to describe the weak, the inept, those doomed to selection.

Primo Levi[1]

I. Europe, Muslims, and Carl Schmitt

In this chapter I analyze legal and political responses to the growing presence of Islam in Europe through the lens of Carl Schmitt's thought. I focus on three aspects of Schmitt's constitutional theory: the polarity of friend and enemy, the necessarily homogeneous basis of democracy, and the need to protect democracy beyond the state of exception.

To be sure, the context in which Schmitt theorized "his" model of democracy is not comparable, as a whole, with today's predicament. There are, however, undeniable assonances between the situation in the Weimar Republic and certain dynamics that are at play in today's Western democracies: plebiscitarian temptations, criticism towards parliamentarism, identity-related claims, a widespread irritation towards compromise-seeking and consensus-building, and a clear preference for legitimacy over legality, which is often depicted as a hurdle for the exercise of sovereign powers.[2] Moreover, while the Weimar Republic provided the concrete constitutional frame for Carl Schmitt's political theory, the conceptual force of the latter reaches well beyond Weimar. Carl Schmitt exposed certain loops of European liberalism and certain limits of civil society that are clearly perceivable in today's legal and political responses to the growing presence of Muslims in Europe. Schmitt's analysis of international law and international relations also provides a vantage point to understand our current predicament, particularly regarding the relations between "Islam and the West." Schmitt lucidly described the blurring of the line between war and peace, the ambiguous construction of the concept of "just war," which cannot escape digging its roots in ideology, the lack of legitimacy of international justice, and its inevitable appearing as the "justice of the winners," thus becoming the source of

* Professor of Law, Law School, University of Bologna, Adjunct Professor of International Law, SAIS Johns Hopkins University BC. I am grateful to Mattias Kumm and Reva Siegel for their insightful comments on an earlier version of this chapter. Many thanks also to Dieter Grimm for an illuminating New York conversation.

1 Primo Levi, *If This Is a Man/The Truce* (London: Abacus, 1987), 94.

2 Gaetano Azzariti, *Critica della democrazia identitaria* (Rome-Bari: Laterza, 2005), ix.

new conflicts. In sum, as the ongoing interest for his work demonstrates, Carl Schmitt still raises uncomfortable questions, exposing the fragility of constitutional democracy and challenging liberal and cosmopolitan projects of universal democracy.[3]

The purpose of this chapter, however, is not confined to use Schmitt's *diagnosis* as a prism through which to analyze the tensions triggered by the presence of Islam in the European public sphere(s). My analysis will show that legal and political responses to "cultural clashes" ingenerated by the presence of Islam in Europe often follow a Schmittian logic, thus deviating from the post-World War II pluralistic model of democracy that European countries identify with.

Carl Schmitt has deeply influenced Western political and legal thinking in the last century. Today, he still fascinates philosophers, legal and political theorists—that is, those mainly responsible for the education of future judges and legislators—on both the left and the right, as well as on both sides of the Atlantic, but especially in Europe. Jan-Werner Müller in his book *A Dangerous Mind: Carl Schmitt in Post-War European Thought*, outlines the ongoing influence of Schmitt's thought in Europe, and its transposition in different times, as well as in different political and ideological contexts (i.e. Italy in the 1970's). He shows how today Schmitt's thought is still highly influential in Europe, including in shaping contemporary critiques of globalization.[4]

To be sure, even the most enthusiastic supporters of Carl Schmitt are well aware that the implementation of his model of the constitutional state is inevitably conducive to the decline of democracy and to dictatorship. To read Carl Schmitt entails a great dose of caution; as Chantal Mouffe puts it, "the strategy is definitely not to read Schmitt to attack liberal democracy, but to ask how it could be improved. To think both with and against Schmitt—this is the thrust of our common endeavour."[5]

But there is another dark side of Carl Schmitt that the fascination with his work mostly obscures, and that is what Müller defines as his "vile anti-Semitism."[6] The latter has traditionally been portrayed as one of opportunity, rather than as a structural element of his political theory. Generations of continental European scholars (including mine) have been educated in academic contexts in which students were widely exposed to Schmitt's theory with virtually no mention, let alone any in-depth analysis, of his anti-Semitism. A slightly embarrassed, *en-passant* reference to Schmitt's involvement with the Third Reich was traditionally all most European professors would be ready to concede. More recently, however, some scholars have begun to show that anti-Semitism was actually at the core of Schmitt's work, and that his political theory found its logical fulfillment in a racist ideology. Raphael Gross in his book *Carl Schmitt and the Jews*, sustains that anti-Semitism permeated the very structure of Schmitt's theorization of the constitutional state as well as his categories, in particular his binomial friend/enemy.[7]

Obviously, Carl Schmitt cannot be reduced to his anti-Semitism. To do so would not only be a gross over-simplification; it would also carry the risk to "fall into Carl

[3] The literature concerning Carl Schmitt's topicality is enormous and it would be impossible to fully quote. A particularly insightful analysis is conducted by Saskia Sassen, in *Losing Control? Sovereignty in an Age of Globalization* (New York: Columbia University Press, 1995).

[4] Jan-Werner Müller, *A Dangerous Mind: Carl Schmitt in Post-War European Thought* (New Haven: Yale University Press 2003).

[5] Chantal Mouffe, "Introduction: Schmitt's Challenge," in Chantal Mouffe (ed.), *The Challenge of Carl Schmitt* (London: Verso, 1999), 6.

[6] Müller, *A Dangerous Mind* 39.

[7] Raphael Gross, *Carl Schmitt and the Jews: The "Jewish Question," the Holocaust, and German Legal Theory* (Joel Golb trans., Madison: University of Wisconsin Press, 2007).

Schmitt's trap."[8] By the same token, however, to entirely remove anti-Semitism from Carl Schmitt's work is an over-simplification of another kind, which distorts the terms of the discussion concerning Schmitt's topicality in exposing the limits of liberalism and universal democracy. Anti-Semitism operated as a structural element of Schmitt's theory at many levels. One the one hand, Schmitt associated "the Jewish" "with images of abstraction and dynamic social change,"[9] and reproached "spiritless, literal Jewish interpretation"[10] of constitutional law in his battle against Kelsenian normativism. At another level, Schmitt's anti-Semitism cannot be disentangled from his Christian sources of inspiration. Schmitt's work was notoriously heavily influenced by his Catholic background, as well as by fringes of German Protestantism,[11] and by the structure, the doctrine, and the historical and symbolic role of the Catholic Church. To the latter, Schmitt also attributed a fundamental and peculiar role in the shaping of European identity. Schmitt's anti-Semitism was, thus, of cultural and religious nature, rather than of a biological kind.[12]

My analysis will show that, *mutatis mutandis*, echoes of the Schmittian anti-Semitic logic are clearly perceivable in the way European democracies address, both politically and legally, cultural and religious conflicts that arise in their increasingly pluralistic polities. This is particularly evident if one compares the treatment of Christianity and Islam in virtually all European jurisdictions, in the case law of the European Court of Human Rights, as well as in European Union enlargement dynamics.

During the electoral campaign of 2007, a poster by the Swiss People's Party (SVP), the largest party in Parliament, caused a political earthquake in Switzerland: against the backdrop of a Swiss flag, three white sheep were shown kicking a lone black one out of their flock. The slogan on the poster said: "For more security." Another SVP poster, showing veiled Muslim women, was accompanied by the question: "Where are we living, Baden or Baghdad?" In 2009, more than 57 percent of Swiss voters, and 22 out of 26 cantons, supported a referendum proposal put forward by the SVP to ban the building of minarets. Martin Baltisser, the SVP's general secretary, told the BBC: "This was a vote against minarets as symbols of Islamic power."[13] Muslims in Switzerland are about 400,000, accounting to around 5 percent of the total population.

In Belgium, between 2004 and 2010, 11 bills aimed at banning full facial veils were introduced in the federal Parliament.[14] In 2011, one bill was finally approved,

[8] See the critique by Christian J. Emden, "Review of Gross, Raphael, *Carl Schmitt and the Jews: The 'Jewish Question,' the Holocaust, and German Legal Theory*," H-German H-Net Reviews, July 2009: "Without realizing it, . . ., Gross increasingly begins to fall victim to the strange logic of Schmitt's argument and even adopts what can be termed a kind of "Schmittianism in reverse," characterized by the assumption that any critique of universalism is necessarily Schmittian and continues the latter's antisemitism. Philosophers call this type of argument a category mistake: in the same way that Schmitt, especially after 1933, openly describes a normative, formal, and legalistic interpretation of constitutional law, represented by Kelsen and Hermann Heller, as "Jewish," Gross links the critique of universalism to a Schmittian antisemitism. He repeats, in other words, Schmitt's own category mistake, simply in reverse.

[9] Dan Diner, quoted by Gross, *Carl Schmitt and the Jews* 12.

[10] Gross, *Carl Schmitt and the Jews* 12.

[11] Gross highlights the fundamental influence exercised on Carl Schmitt's notions of *Volk* and *nomos* by the political theology of German Protestantism. See Gross, *Carl Schmitt and the Jews* 81 and Ch. 15 ("The Flight into Religion"), 197ff.

[12] See William Hooker, *Carl Schmitt's International Thought: Order and Orientation* (Cambridge: Cambridge University Press, 2009), 57ff., arguing that biological racism did not interest Schmitt as a political category.

[13] BBC News, <http://news.bbc.co.uk/2/hi/8385069.stm>.

[14] Parliamentary Papers, Senate 2008-09, no. 4-1460/1; 2009-10, no. 4-1689/1; 2010 SE no. 5-169/1; 2010-11 no. 5-722/1; Parliamentary Papers, Chamber 2007-08, no. 0433/001; 2009-10,

prohibiting the full veil in all public places.[15] The country was facing its worst political deadlock ever: since the general elections of December 2010, a dramatic intensification of the French/Flemish conflict had frustrated all attempts to form a government. Some feared for Belgium's very survival as a unitary state. Yet, the "burqa law" was accepted by the Chamber of Representatives with only one vote against. The ban theoretically affects only several dozen women of the 360,000 persons (3.6 percent of the overall population) who identify themselves as Muslim in Belgium.[16] In practical terms, the consequences are virtually none, as most Belgian municipalities concerned with the issue already had police regulations that prohibit face-covering in public places.

In 2010, France also criminalized full-face veils in the public space.[17] The proposed resolution drafted by the French National Assembly in preparation of the enactment of the law of 2010, relies heavily on the radical opposition between French values and values symbolized by full facial veils. For example, in one passage, the drafters of the proposed resolution stress the "power and the duty we have to oppose ideologies and ways of thinking [represented by the full-face veils] that one can only qualify as 'barbarian,' in the sense that they deny the idea of progress, of civilization, of democracy, of sex-based equality... It's our value system which is at issue... this is our Republic being tested in this way."[18] Tellingly, the word "*Lumières*" (Enlightment) recurs several times in the proposed resolution; in one occasion, it is juxtaposed with the word "barbarity."[19]

The statistics of the French Interior Ministry indicated that the number of women who wear full facial veils in France is no more than 1,900. Most of these women are French citizens, about 25 percent of them grew up in a non-Muslim family and converted to Islam as adults.[20]

In the Netherlands, as Annelies Moors puts it, "Mainstream politicians came to consider particular forms of Islam (or even Islam generally) as incompatible with European values, be it defined in terms of a secularist tradition, a Judeo-Christian heritage, or a mixture of both."[21] At the same time, new populist parties, "distancing themselves from the Dutch consensual form of governance... introduced a far more confrontational political style through which they claimed to express the emotions and sentiments of 'ordinary autochtonous (native Dutch) people.'"[22] As a result, the full face veil has become a major political issue, despite the fact that the number of women

no. 2442/001; 2009-10, no. 2289/001; 2009-10, no. 2495/001; SE 2010, no. 0085/001; SE 2010, no. 0219/001; SE 2010, no. 0754/001.

15 Loi 1 June 2001, *Moniteur belge* of 13 July 2011 (upheld by the Belgian Constitutional Court: see arrêt no. 145/2012 of 6 December 2012).

16 European Monitoring Center on Racism and Zenophobia, "Muslims in the European Union: Discrimination and Islamaphobia" (2006), 10, available at <http://fra.europa.eu/fraWebsite/attachments/Manifestations_EN.pdf>.

17 "Loi no. 2010-1192 of 11 October 2010 interdisant la dissimulation du visage dans l'espace public," *Journal Officiel* (*JORF*) (12 October 2010). Further regulation in: "Circulaire of March 2011 relative à la mise en oeuvre de la loi no 2010-1192 du 11 oct. 2010 interdisant la dissimulation du visage dans l'espace public," *JORF* (3 March 2011).

18 Assemblée Nationale, Rapport d'information no. 2262, "Au nom de la mission d'information sur la pratique du port du voile intégral sur le territoire national, 26 janvier 2010" [hereinafter "Rapport 2262"], 22ff. [my translation].

19 "Barbarity is growing. Violence and threats are frequent... conflicts degenerate... This is not acceptable... it is our living together based on the Spirit of the Enlightenment that is violated." "Rapport 2262" 14 [my translation].

20 "Rapport 2262," 264

21 Annelies Moors, "The Dutch and the Face-Veil: the Politics of Discomfort" (2009) 17(4) *Social Anthropology/Anthropologie Sociale* 395.

22 Moors, "The Dutch and the Face-Veil" 395.

who wear it is extremely small, estimated at no more than 400, or about 0.002 percent of the population, and about half of them are "ethnic" Dutch converts.[23] Various bills proposing to criminalize the burqa/niqab have been put forward by different political coalitions, and justified by the concern to protect security, Western values and gender equality.[24] In one case, a parliamentary majority consisting of mainstream as well as populist right-wing parties and the Christian Democrats, supported a bill to ban the full veil, according to which: "The *burqa*...is diametrically opposed to modernity. It expresses the rejection of essential Western values and norms, including the equality of men and women.... Hence, wearing a *burqa*... in the public space is contrary to the rule of law in a democracy."[25]

Niqabs and burqas have also been subject to legal regulation on similar grounds in a number of European countries, including Italy, Spain, Denmark, and the United Kingdom. In 2010, for example, the Italian Minister for Equal Opportunities declared that she favored the adoption of a French-style "burqa ban," because "tolerance cannot turn into a threat against our civilization."[26] Although the Italian government has never provided any data, full facial veils are virtually never seen in Italy.

As these examples from different European countries reveal, vitriolic attacks on "Islam" and "Islamic values," have become a *leit motif* of European political life. From frankly racist populist parties and social movements to enlighted defenders of women's rights, from Christian conservative circles to mainstream political actors, Islamophobia seems capable of gluing together apparently irreconcilable components of European democracies. Anti-Muslim discourses are united by a common accusation: that of adhering to a value-system (or a "culture") incompatible with Western democracy. Irrespective of whether Muslims are depicted as "black sheep," as uncivilized and barbarian, or just as not liberal enough to successfully integrate in Western societies, the crux of the matter is the "insurmountability of cultural differences"[27] between us and them. Etienne Balibar maintains that the category of "immigration" has substituted that of "race," thus enabling new racist discourses "whose dominant theme is not biological heredity," but rather the idea that "individuals are the result of their belonging to historical cultures."[28] This "differentialist racism" "at first sight does not postulate the supremacy of certain groups or peoples in relation to others, but 'only' the harmfulness of abolishing frontiers, the incompatibility of life-styles and traditions."[29] "Differentialist" (or "cultural") racism often paradoxically presents itself as a cure against "real" (biological) racism: to avoid racist upsurges, a "tolerance threshold" should be respected.[30] As Balibar points out, racism of this kind is not a new phenomenon. Modern anti-Semitism presents all the traits of cultural racism: "is that of a cultural tradition, a ferment of moral disintegration. Anti-Semitism is supremely 'differentialist' and in many respects the whole of current differentialist racism may be considered, from the formal point of view, as a generalized

[23] Moors, "The Dutch and the Face-Veil" 395.

[24] See Gerhard van der Schyff and Adriaan Overbeeke, "Exercising Religious Freedom in the Public Space: A Comparative and European Convention Analysis of General Burqa Bans" (2011) 7 *European Constitutional Law Review* 424 (analyzing European laws and bills prohibiting full-face veils in the public place in the light of their inconsistency with the European Convention of Human Rights).

[25] Moors, "The Dutch and the Face-Veil" 402.

[26] 12 October 2009, <http://www.corriere.it/politica/09_ottobre_12/carfagna-vietare-burqa-scuole_aecc319a-b726-11de-b239-00144f02aabc.shtml>.

[27] Etienne Balibar, "Is there a 'Neo-Racism?,'" in Etienne Balibar and Immanuel Maurice Wallerstein (eds), *Nation, Class, Ambiguous Identities* (1991), 17–28. London: Verso

[28] Balibar, "Is there a 'Neo-Racism?,'" 22.

[29] Balibar, "Is there a 'Neo-Racism?,'" 22.

[30] Balibar, "Is there a 'Neo-Racism?,'" 22.

anti-Semitism. This consideration is particularly important for the interpretation of contemporary Arabophobia... since it carries with it an image of Islam as a 'conception of the world' which is incompatible with Europeanness and an enterprise of universal ideological domination."[31]

Balibar's analysis dates back to 1991 and focused mainly on France. During the decades that followed, cultural racism against Muslims intensified dramatically across Europe, where, unlike in the United States, "immigration and Islam are almost synonymous."[32] This, as José Casanova puts it, "entails a superimposition of different dimensions of 'otherness' that exacerbates issues of boundaries, accommodation and incorporation. The immigrant, the religious, the racial, and the socio-economic disprivileged 'other' all tend to coincide. Moreover, all those dimensions of 'otherness' now become superimposed upon Islam, so that Islam becomes the utterly 'other.' "[33] The attacks of 11 September, "the global war on terror, and the ever more visible proliferation of global Muslim discourses and networks... turned into a panic,"[34] and "Muslims" began to be constructed as presumptively sympathetic to "the enemy," and thus as disloyal. Legally, this entailed a blurring of the line between an inimical political ideology and a religion. The consequence is that the religious freedoms of European Muslims have been heavily curtailed: what is presented by courts and legislators as an acceptable balance between religious freedoms of Muslims (e.g. the right to wear the *hidjab*) and the necessity to protect democracy, often shields what in the American judicial jargon would be defined as "invidious scrutiny." One could draw a parallel with the exclusion of Catholics in the Toleration Act of 1689, which John Locke justified on the ground that their Church "[was] so constituted that all who enter it *ipso facto* pass into the allegiance and service of another prince."[35]

Of all religion-related conflicts, the controversies over religious symbols in the public sphere are a particularly good case study to analyze this "normalization of the invidious scrutiny pattern," which mirrors the construction of "Islam" as an irreconcilable and threatening political other. Religion symbols play a key role in identity-related dynamics. On the one hand, thanks to their capacity of evoking unquestioned belongings, they allow for the construction of simplified and artificial identities, and thus provide clear-cut dividing lines. For example, the crucifix is often depicted as a symbol of a "Christian cultural inheritance," shared as a common legacy by the West, irrespective of the fact that Christian unity broke up, and not harmoniously, in the sixteenth century. By the same token, the "veil" is depicted as "Muslim," as if Islam were a monolithical structure, in which all adhere to the same set of values, and, as a consequence, to a given dress code. On the other hand, religious symbols "mark" the public sphere. Their presence and their absence symbolize the power relations between different cultures. The display of a crucifix in state schools or court rooms clearly identifies the "official culture" with that of the majority, whereas the ban on the wearing of the veil in state schools unambiguously marks the marginalization of the culture the veil is supposed to represent. Christian Jobbke refers to nationalism to mean a factual insistence on how things are traditionally done in a particular country. In this light, the opposition to the

[31] Balibar, "Is there a 'Neo-Racism?,' " 24.

[32] José Casanova, "The Long, Difficult, and Tortuous Journey of Turkey into Europe and the Dilemmas of European Civilization" (2006) 13(2) *Constellations* 242.

[33] Casanova, "The Long, Difficult, and Tortuous Journey of Turkey into Europe and the Dilemmas of European Civilization" 242.

[34] Casanova, "The Long, Difficult, and Tortuous Journey of Turkey into Europe and the Dilemmas of European Civilization" 243.

[35] John Locke, *Epistola de Tolerantia/A Letter on Toleration* (R. Klibanski and J.W. Gough (eds), Oxford: Clarendon Press, 1968), 133.

headscarf is constitutive of all the attempts at national self-definition that have been made in Europe's great debate surrounding Muslim integration.[36]

My chapter proceeds as follows: in Part II, I provide a brief overview of laws and cases regarding the display of Muslim and Christian symbols in Europe, focusing on the value judgments that justify the decision whether to restrict or whether to allow the presence of such symbols in the public sphere. Next, in Part III, I depict the exclusion of Muslim symbols from the public sphere as a contemporary and distorted implementation of a "militant" model of democracy, i.e. of a democracy that exclude *ex ante* movements that supposedly advocate non democratic political agendas. In Part IV, I show how under the pretences of removing an obstacle to democracy, anti-veil measures and pro-crucifix decisions draw on a essentialist and idealized notion of the people, and aim at artificially reinforcing the cultural and religious homogeneous character of the European public sphere, thus pursuing a Schmittian "identitarian" model of democracy. Finally, in Part V, I turn to the political use of Christianity to define and sustain European identity and conclude that the role attributed to the "Christian roots" of Europe in contemporary discourses is analogous to the role that Schmitt ascribed to the Catholic Church in representing the values which were the essence of European civilization and separated it from "uncivilized" others.

II. Friends and Enemies, Crucifixes and Veils

Between 1989 and 2010, Muslim traditional clothes became an issue in most European countries. Cases concerning the right of pupils and teachers to wear the hidjab, the jibab or the niqab were dealt with in most European jurisdictions, including Switzerland, Germany, Belgium, the Scandinavian countries, and the United Kingdom. Various cases were also decided by the European Court of Human Rights.

In all cases, and quite irrespective of the very divergent models of managing the relationship between religion and the state under which European countries operate, Islamic symbols underwent a process of semantic disarticulation and were interpreted according to the same pattern, that is, they were associated with beliefs and behavior that contradict the essential values that constitute the core of a liberal democracy. The conclusion in all cases is that the display of Islamic symbols (or certain variants of them) can be legitimately restricted because it objectively endangers democratic values.

The struggle against the headscarf started in France in 1989, when a handful of schoolgirls were suspended for wearing their headscarves in a state school in Creil, a suburb of Paris. The French Courts first opted for a soft approach according to which, in principle the right of pupils to wear religious symbols or clothing could not be the object of a general ban. They did, however, introduce the principle according to which such display could violate the rights of others or seriously jeopardized the carrying out of school activities, in which case it could be banned.[37] The intervention of the French government progressively restricted the right to wear the headscarf in the public schools, introducing the notion according to which certain symbols may be deemed "by their nature, elements of proselytism," and per se "so ostentatious that their meaning is

[36] Christian Joppke, *Veil: Mirror of Identity* (Cambridge: Polity Press, 2009), 16.

[37] See Conseil d'Etat [CE] [highest administrative court] 14 March 1994 (Fr.) (repealing the rule implemented in a high school in the city of Angers, according to which, "[a]ucun élève ne sera admis en salle de cours, en étude ou au réfectoire la tête converte"); Conseil d'Etat [CE] [highest administrative court] 2 November 1992 (Fr.).

precisely to separate certain pupils from the rules of the communal life of the school."[38] In July 2003, President Chirac set up an investigative committee, chaired by Bernard Stasi, the French State's ombudsman, with the task of reflecting on the application of the principle of secularism. In December 2003 the commission issued a report,[39] which eventually led to the introduction of a law that prohibits the display of religious symbols in state schools.[40] It had been estimated that less than 1 percent of the Muslim students in France actually worn the veil. In particular, a total of 1,256 *foulards* were reported in France's public schools at the start of the 2003–04 school year. Only 20 of these cases were judged "difficult" by school officials themselves.[41]

The Stasi Commission report subjected the headscarf to a meticulous dissection process. It concluded that it threatened public order, as "wearing an ostensibly religious symbol... suffices to disrupt the tranquillity of the life of the school."[42] The relationship between the presence of the symbols and the disruption of school studies, however, is not elucidated in the report. The Stasi Commission referred to a number of objectively disruptive practices which have nothing to do with wearing the headscarf, but are all associated with Islam, such as "course and examination interruptions to pray or fast," the refusal by schoolgirls to engage in sporting activities and the objections by pupils to "entire sections of courses in history or earth science."[43] The Commission also viewed headscarves as a threat to public order because they are associated with communitarianism.[44] The report mentions the difficult socio-economic situations of the banlieue and the risk that "communitarian groups with politics based on religion exploit this actual social unrest in order to mobilize activists."[45] The Commission does not provide any explanation of how the wearing of the headscarf in state schools could actually aggravate such situations. The only explanation one can draw is that the symbolic dimension of the headscarf suffices to threaten certain fundamental values. In other words, the mere presence of the veil in public schools is enough to challenge public order, because it "marks" Muslim women as sympathetic to the inimical communitarian ideology.

The Stasi Commission also heavily relied on the paternalistic assumption (not supported by any data) according to which women are pressured into wearing the headscarf by

[38] See act of 12 December 1989 (Circulaire of 12 Dec. 1989, of the Minister of Education, Journal Officiel de la République Française [J.O.] [Official Gazette of France], 15 Dec. 1989, [according to which pupils were free to wear or display religious symbols, but in case of a conflict, the pupil had to be convinced through a dialogue to renounce to the display of the symbol], and act of 20 September 1994 (Circulaire No. 1649 of 20 Sept. 1994, Journal Officiel de la République Française [J.O.] [Official Gazette of France], 24 Sept. 1994, [drawing distinction between ostentatious and discrete symbols]. This act overturned the relationship between rule and exception that the *Conseil d'Etat* had previously theorized, according to which the simple fact of wearing a religious symbol could not be automatically viewed as a violation of the principle of secularism or of other constitutional principles.

[39] Commission de Reflexion sur L'application du Principe de Laïcite dans la Republique, "Rapport Au President De La Republique" (2003) [hereinafter "Rapport Au President"], available at <http://lesrapports.ladocumentationfrancaise.fr/BRP/034000725/0000.pdf>.

[40] Law No. 2004-228 of 15 Mar. 2004, Journal Officiel de la République Française [J.O.] [Official Gazette of France], 17 Mar. 2004, 5190. This law is neutrally worded; however, shortly after its enactment the Minister of Education issued a decree according to which "[t]he prohibited signs and dress are those by which the wearer is immediately recognizable in terms of his or her religion, such as the *islamic veil*, whatever its name, the kippah or a crucifix of *manifestly exaggerated dimensions.*" Circulaire No 2004-084 of 18 May 2004, Journal Officiel de la République Française [J.O.] [Official Gazette of France], 22 May 2004.

[41] Elaine Thomas, "Keeping Identity at a Distance: Explaining France's New Legal Restrictions on the Islamic Headscarf" (2006) 29 *Ethnic & Racial Studies* 237, 239.

[42] "Rapport Au President" 41.

[43] "Rapport Au President" 41.

[44] "Rapport Au President" 45–6.

[45] "Rapport Au President" 45–6.

family and group members.[46] This argument recurs in virtually all cases concerning the wearing of traditional Muslim clothing.[47] The emphasis on the inherently anti-feminist nature of the various types of Muslim veils should not be surprising. Sex and gender play a key role in relation to the identity-related dynamics mentioned above. Seyla Benhabib has pointed out how the construction of the self and the other, the struggle over identity, is linked to sexual difference and the struggle over sexual identity.[48] In the struggle against the veil, sexual difference demarcates the line between the self and the other, between the Western, gender-egalitarian self against the Oriental and patriarchal other. This construction is vividly exemplified by a 2009 Swiss People's Party poster, displaying the slogan: "Maria, not Sharia!" The poster juxtaposed the image of a smiling Caucasian adolescent with long blonde hair loose on her shoulders, and that of a Middle-Eastern woman covered by a burqa, with a desperate look in her heavily made-up eyes, visible through the iron bars of a cage.

Five years after the enactment of the "headscarf law," after suffering a heavy electoral defeat in the regional elections, then President Sarkozy launched a campaign against the burqua/niqab type of veil, which, as I have mentioned, led to the adoption of the law of September 2010, banning full facial veils in all public spaces.[49] The issue had shifted from the schools to the general public sphere, where supposedly autonomous agents interact with one another on an equal footing. Public order, secularism, and gender equality, that previously required banning or limiting schoolgirls and teachers from covering their head at school, were invoked to prevent adult women to cover their face anywhere in public.

In five German *Länder* (Baden-Württemberg,[50] Saarland,[51] Hesse,[52] Bavaria,[53] and North Rhine-Westphalia[54]), laws have been enacted that prohibit Islamic symbols but specifically permit Christian ones in the public schools, including nun's habits.[55] As a

[46] "Young girls are pressured into wearing religious symbols. The familial and social environment sometimes forces on them a choice that is not theirs... The Republic cannot remain deaf to the cries of distress from these young women." "Rapport Au President" 58. The same unproven assumption also supports the "burqa law" report by the National Assembly.

[47] For an in-depth analysis of the misuse of gender-equality rhetoric in measures restricting the right to wear Muslim traditional clothing, see Susanna Mancini, "Patriarchy as the Exclusive Domain of the Other: The Veil Controversy, False Projection and Cultural Racism" (2012) 10(2) *International Journal of Constitutional Law* 411–28.

[48] Seyla Benhabib, *The Claims of Culture: Equality and Diversity in the Global Era* (Princeton: Princeton University Press, 2002).

[49] Law no. 2010-1192 of 11 October 2010 (*Journal Officiel* 12 October 2010). The Conseil Constitutionnel upheld the constitutionality of this law, stipulating only that the ban should not apply to public places of worship: judgment no. 613 DC of 7 October 2010.

[50] *Gesetz zur Änderung des Schulgesetzes* (1 April 2004) and *Gesetz zur Änderung des Kindergartengesetzes* (14 February 2006).

[51] *Gesetz Nr. 1555 zur Änderung des Gesetzes zur Ordnung des Schulwesens im Saarland (Schulordnungsgesetz)*, 23 June 2004. In the explanation to the draft law, it is stated that the regulation is not limited to headscarves, however, the wearing of Christian and Jewish symbols remains possible.

[52] *Gesetz zur Sicherung der staatlichen Neutralität*, 18 October 2004.

[53] *Gesetz zur Änderung des Bayerischen Gesetzes über das Erziehungs- und Unterrichtswesen*, 23 November 2004.

[54] *Erstes Gesetz zur Änderung des Schulgesetzes für das Land Nordrhein-Westfalen*, 13 June 2006.

[55] These laws constitute a direct reaction to a Federal Constitutional Court judgment concerning the wearing of the veil by a teacher (Ludin, Bundesverfassungericht, 24 Sept. 2003, 2BvR, 1436/02). The woman was refused a permanent civil servant post as a teacher in a primary school in the conservative *Land* of Baden Württemberg because she insisted on wearing the veil, which prompted the conclusion that she had a "lack of personal aptitude." The Constitutional Court ruled that German *Länder* had the right to ban teachers from wearing the veil as long as they passed specific laws on the matter. As a result, the *Länder* with the strongest Catholic traditions adopted specific laws on the issue.

Bavarian ministry official stated, unlike the nun's habit, the headscarf can be interpreted as a political symbol that denies the equality of women.[56]

All of these laws are structured in very similar terms. They emphasize the importance of the neutrality tenure of office by teachers, but also that of the "Christian Western and European tradition." It follows that it is "not a breach of the neutrality requirement if a teacher commits to this tradition."[57] For example, in Bavaria: "[T]eachers are not allowed to wear outer symbols... that express a religious or ideological creed, in case students or parents understand these symbols... as an expression of an attitude, that is not compatible with fundamental constitutional values and educational objectives of the constitution, including Christian-occidental educational and cultural values."[58] The Bavarian Constitutional Court upheld this clearly discriminatory law in 2007,[59] on the basis that "Christianity" does not coincide with the Christian faiths, but rather with values that, albeit rooted in the Christian tradition, have become part of the common inheritance of the Western civilization. According to the Court, religious freedom can be limited in the name of "constitutional values" that pupils must learn. In the case at hand, the Court held that the legislator legitimately gave prevalence over individual religious freedom to the need to protect the "teaching objectives" and the "credible transmission of fundamental values" from the "danger" posed by clothes that clearly mark a religious (i.e. Muslim) belonging.

The British House of Lords in the *Begum* case of 2005,[60] accepted the arguments of a state maintained school, according to which allowing a schoolgirls to wear the jilbab [which conceals the whole body but leaves the face and the hands uncovered] would have violated the religious freedom of others and made pupils and teachers feel "uncomfortable" in the presence of clothes that are generally associated with fundamentalism. Baroness Hale added that schools should provide "a place of protection from undue religious pressure from family and community."[61] "Like it or not [she stated] this is a society committed, in principle and in law, to equal freedom for men and women to choose how they will lead their lives within the law. Young girls from ethnic, cultural or religious minorities growing up here face particularly difficult choices: how far to adopt or to distance themselves from the dominant culture. A good school will enable and support them."[62]

The European Court of Human Rights (ECtHR) has also dealt with the "Islamic veil issue." In all cases, it held the ban on the veil to be consistent with the European Convention (ECHR). The main argument throughout has been that states are best placed for determining when interference with religious freedom becomes necessary in

[56] Human Rights Watch, "Discrimination in the Name of Neutrality: Headscarf Bans for Teachers and Civil Servants in Germany" (2009), 26 available at <http://www.hrw.org/sites/default/files/reports/germany0209_web.pdf> (citing the explanatory comments in the Bavarian government draft law, Gesetzesentwurf der Staatsregierung zur Änderung des Bayerischen Gesetzes über das Erziehungs—und Unterrichtswesen, Bavarian parliament, 15th election period, Drucksache 15/368, 18 February 2004).

[57] Human Rights Watch, "Discrimination in the Name of Neutrality" 28 (quoting the Gesetzentwurf der Fraktion der CDU und der Fraktion der FDP: Erstes Gesetz zur Änderung des Schulgesetzes für das Land Nordrhein-Westfalen, Drucksache 14/569, 14th election period, 31 October 2005).

[58] *Gesetz zur Änderung des Bayerischen Gesetzes über das Erziehungs- und Unterrichtswesen*, 23 November 2004.

[59] Bayerischer Verwaltungsgerichtshof [BayVGH] [Bavarian Higher Administrative Court], 15 Jan. 2007, No. Vf. 11-VII-05, available at <http://www.bayern.verfassungsgerichtshof.de/>.

[60] *Regina (Shabina Begum) v. Governors of Denbigh High Sch.* [2006] UKHL 15, [2007] 1 AC 100 (HL) (appeal taken from Eng.).

[61] *Regina (Shabina Begum) v. Governors of Denbigh High Sch.*

[62] *Regina (Shabina Begum) v. Governors of Denbigh High Sch.*

a democratic society, thus justifying the grant of a wide margin of appreciation. In the past, the ECtHR had often legitimized the interference by states with certain rights, and in particular free speech, in order to protect the cultural/religious sensitiveness of the (Christian) majority. In several cases, the Court upheld measures against dissemination of ideas in order to protect morals as defined by the majority culture.[63] Thus, for example, in *Otto-Preminger Institute v. Austria*[64] the Court upheld the seizing of a movie that disparaged the Catholic religion, on the ground that those who exercise freedom of expression relating to religious beliefs and opinions may have an obligation "to avoid as far as possible expressions that are gratuitously offensive to others, and thus an infringement of their rights, and which therefore do not contribute to any form of public debate capable of furthering progress in human affairs."[65]

The Court also relied on the doctrine of the margin of appreciation in the case of *Dahlab v. Switzerland*,[66] but in that case did not end up on the side of religion, as it decided that prohibiting women from wearing a headscarf in the capacity of teacher at state schools did not amount to interference with their right to freedom of religion. According to the Court "in displaying a powerful religious attribute on the school premises ... the appellant may have interfered with the religious beliefs of her pupils."[67] In addition, the Court emphasized: "It must also be acknowledged that it is difficult to reconcile the wearing of a headscarf with the principle of gender equality, which is a fundamental value of our society enshrined in a specific provision of the Federal Constitution and must be taken into account by schools."[68] However, the Court sanctioned a clear double standard, as it did not question the fact that "the principle of proportionality has led the cantonal government to allow teachers to wear discreet religious symbols at school, such as small pieces of jewellery [*sic.*]."[69] In short, it is now compatible with the Convention for teachers to wear "discreet" crucifixes, but not "conspicuous" veils. Said differently, the display of religious symbols by individuals threatens the rights of others exclusively if it is associated with one particular religious culture.

In contrast to the trend established in Western European cases, the margin of appreciation, has been applied by the Court in the Turkish veil case, *Sahin v. Turkey*,[70] in order to legitimize the interference with the religious freedom of the majority. The Court considered the Turkish notion of secularism—which is shaped as a militant democracy clause and meant to protect the Kemalist regime *from Islam*—to be consistent with the values underpinning the Convention.[71] Thus, the Court accepted that, in protecting the principle of secularism, the State may impose certain limitations on individual rights. The Court observed that "the principle of secularism ... is the paramount consideration underlying the ban on the wearing of religious symbols in universities."[72] The Court went on to stress that "democracy does not simply mean that the views of the majority must always prevail: a balance must be achieved which ensures the fair and

[63] *Müller and Others v. Switzerland*, App no. 10737/84, 133 Eur. H.R. Rep. (ser. A) 212 (1988); *Wingrove v. United Kingdom*, App no. 17419/90 (ECtHR 1996).

[64] *Otto-Preminger Institute v. Austria*, App no. 13470/87, 295-A E.H.R.R. (ser. A) 34 (1994).

[65] *Otto-Preminger Institute v. Austria* para. 49.

[66] *Dahlab v. Switzerland*, App no 42393/98 (ECtHR 2001).

[67] *Dahlab v. Switzerland* (quoting the Federal Court of Switzerland).

[68] *Dahlab v. Switzerland* (quoting the Federal Court of Switzerland) (internal citations omitted).

[69] *Dahlab v. Switzerland* (quoting the Federal Court of Switzerland).

[70] *Sahin v. Turkey*, App no. 44774/98, 44 Eur. H.R. Rep. 5 (2007).

[71] *Sahin v. Turkey* para. 114.

[72] *Sahin v. Turkey* para. 116.

proper treatment of people from minorities and avoids any abuse of a dominant position. Pluralism and democracy must be based on dialogue. . . ."[73] And this led the Court to the conclusion that Turkey, in imposing the scarf ban, did not overstep its margin of appreciation.[74] It is striking that the Court used the margin of appreciation doctrine to protect *minorities* when the majority religion happens to be Islam. If we read this together with the legitimization of Turkey's militant anti-Islamic notion of secularism and with the statement in *Dahab* that the veil cannot be reconciled with certain fundamental principles, the Court seems to imply a certain degree of incompatibility between Islam and liberal democracy.[75] Islam, unlike Christianity, even when it is the vast majority's religion, can be restrictively regulated on the ground that it threatens the democratic basis of the state.

This construction was confirmed by the decision of the ECtHR in the case of *Lautsi v. Italy*.[76] Relying on the doctrine of the margin of appreciation, the Court concluded that the mandatory display of the crucifix in Italian state schools did not violate the Convention. The margin of appreciation presumes deference to a country's authoritative determination that a particular practice is consistent with the Convention. However, as the ECtHR acknowledges, Italian courts are divided over the legitimacy of the display of the crucifix.[77] Hence, the Court took sides in a domestic dispute among courts, embracing the position favoring the presence of the crucifix. Second, the Court purported to distinguish the crucifix from the headscarf, on account that the first is an "essentially passive symbol" and the latter a "powerful" one.[78] While in *Dahab* and *Sahin* the Court expressed a strong value judgment against the headscarf (its irreconcilability with secularism and gender equality), in *Lautsi*, it carefully avoided attributing any substantive significance to the crucifix.[79] The crucifix, according to the Court, confers "greater visibility" to Christianity, but this, unlike the display of the headscarf, does not produce any interference with the rights of others, neither does it challenge any fundamental principle,[80] including, one must conclude, *secularism*, which is a cornerstone of the Italian Constitution.[81]

[73] *Sahin v. Turkey* para. 108.

[74] *Sahin v. Turkey* para. 122. But see para. 99 (Tulkens, J., dissenting).

[75] This is explicitly stated in the case of *Refah Partisi (The Welfare Party) & Others v. Turkey*, App nos 41340/98, 41342/98, 41343/98, and 41344/98 (ECtHR 2001). The 2001 *Refah Partisi* judgment was later referred to the Grand Chamber, which delivered a similar decision in 2003.

[76] *Lautsi and Others v. Italy* App. no. 30814/06 (ECtHR, GC 2011).

[77] On the domestic controversies over the display of the crucifix in Italy see Susanna Mancini, "The Crucifix Rage: Supranational Constitutionalism Bumps Against the Counter-majoritarian Difficulty" (2010) 6 *European Constitutional Law Review* 6.

[78] *Lautsi v Italy* para. 72.

[79] In the case of *Eweida and Others v. United Kingdom*, App. nos 48420/10, 59842/10, 51671/10 and 36516 (ECtHR 2013) the Court does not attribute any significance to the crucifix.

[80] *Lautsi v. Italy* para. 74.

[81] Secularism is not explicitly enshrined in any article of the Italian Constitution. Nevertheless, the Constitutional Court has declared that it is to be regarded as one of the fundamental principles of the Italian legal system. According to the Constitutional Court, secularism (*laicità*) emerges from the combined interpretation of various constitutional provisions: Art. 2, which protects "the inviolable rights of man, both as an individual and as a member of the social groups in which his personality finds expression"; Art. 3, which guarantees equality before the law; Art. 7, according to which the "State and the Catholic Church are, each within their own sphere, independent and sovereign," Article 8, according to which "All religious denominations are equally free", and Article 19 which protects the freedom to profess and promote religious beliefs, individually or collectively. Thus, according to the Court, secularism as a principle has multiple constitutional referents, not only the guarantee of freedom of religion. Freedom of religion and secularism are therefore two separate fundamental constitutional provisions, and all sources of law, to be legitimate, have to be consistent with both. See *Corte Costituzionale*,

In 2005, an Italian administrative court had stated that "The crucifix is the symbol of our history and our culture and, as a consequence, of our identity... and also of the principle of secularism."[82] As a consequence, its presence in a state school not only serves to avoid a "clash of cultures," but it also teaches "non European pupils... to reject all forms of fundamentalism."[83] Similarly, in 1991, the Bavarian Supreme Court had upheld the mandatory display of the crucifix in state schools on the ground that the cross is not religious in nature, but "an essential object of the general Christian-occidental tradition and common property of the Christian-occidental cultural circle."[84] The Bavarian Court had also drowned the difference between the display of the crucifix, which is legitimate, and "cases in which the teacher through especially determined behavior—in particular through the wearing of attention-drawing clothing (Baghwan)—which unambiguously indicates a specific religious or philosophical conviction, impermissibly impairs the basic right to negative religious freedom of pupil and parent." Interestingly, both courts felt the need to draw a more or less explicit comparison between Christianity and Islam, despite the fact that in neither case was the presence of the crucifix challenged by Muslim parents, but, respectively, by a Finnish atheist mother and a German Steinerian family. Both Courts concluded that while Christianity is rooted in the state's democratic values, Islam is not compatible with them.

With *Lautsi*, the European Court *de facto*—albeit with more self-restraint—lines up with this line of reasoning, by placing the crucifix, but not the headscarf, as a "natural," or structural, element of the European public secular sphere.

One must conclude that, as Gil Anidjar puts it, "Secularization is just Christianity by another name."[85]

The escalation of the ECtHR in its construction of the Muslim religion as a threat to secular democracy reaches its highest peak with the case of *Dogru v. France*.[86] In *Dogru* the applicant was an 11-year-old Muslim schoolgirl who refused to take off her headscarf during physical education and sports classes despite repeated requests to do so by her teacher. The school's pupil discipline committee decided to expel the applicant from the school for breaching the duty of assiduity by failing to participate actively in physical education and sports classes. The ECtHR upheld this decision, noting that in a democratic society, in which several religions coexist within one and the same population, it may be necessary to place restrictions on this freedom in order to reconcile the interests of the various groups and ensure that everyone's beliefs are respected. In particular, the Court held that the state may limit the freedom to manifest a religion, for example by wearing an Islamic headscarf, if the exercise of that freedom clashes with the aim of protecting the rights and freedoms of others, public order, and public safety. Specifically,

Decisions no. 203/1989; no. 259/1990; no. 13/1991; no. 195/1993; no. 421/1993; no. 334/1996; no. 329/1997; no. 508/2000; no. 327/2002.

[82] *TAR Veneto* [Regional Administrative Court of the Venetian Region], 17 March 2005, Decision no. 1110, para. 11.6.

[83] *TAR Veneto* para. 12.6

[84] Bayerischer Verwaltungsgerichtshof [BayVGH] [Bavarian Higher Administrative Court] 3 June 1991, 122 Bayerische Verwaltungsblatter [BayVBI] 751 (751–4) (F.R.G.).

[85] Nermeen Shaikh, "The Jew, the Arab: An Interview with Gil Anidjar," *Asia Society*, available at <http://asiasociety.org/countries/religions-philosophies/jew-arab-interview-gil-anidjar>.

[86] *Dogru v. France*, App. no. 27058/05 ECtHR (2008). While the case was decided in 2008, the actual facts took place in 1999, that is, years before the adoption of the 2004 law that banned the veil in all state schools. At that time, the issue was regulated by the case law developed by the French Conseil d'Etat, according to which the wearing of religious signs was not inherently incompatible with the principle of secularism in schools, but became so according to the conditions in which they were worn and the consequences that the wearing of a sign might have had.

the Court noted that "it can be seen from the circumstances of the case that these events had led to a general atmosphere of *tension* within the School."[87] In the past, however, the Court had been clear in stating that the role of a pluralistic State is not that of removing the cause of *tension* by eliminating pluralism, but to ensure that the competing groups at least tolerate each other and respect each other's rights.[88]

The Court went on to stress that in France, as in Turkey or Switzerland, secularism is a constitutional principle, and a founding principle of the Republic, to which the entire population adheres and the *protection* of which appears to be of prime importance, in particular in schools. Accordingly, "an attitude which fails to respect that principle will not necessarily be accepted as being covered by the freedom to manifest one's religion and will not enjoy the protection of Article 9 of the Convention." Said differently, the Court legitimized France to adopt preventive measures in order to protect a fundamental constitutional value (secularism) from mere *attitudes* that fail to respect it. This is a very troubling passage, especially if one considers that the *attitude* in question is the refusal of an 11-year-old to remove her headscarf during sports class. The Court opens the door to a significant widening of the power of states to preventively remove individual manifestations of religious freedom that cause tension and are felt as not sufficiently respectful of state secularism. This brings me to my next point, that is, to the analogy between the restrictions to wear the Muslim veil and militant democracy clauses.

III. The Exclusion of Islam as the Implementation of a Distorted Model of Militant Democracy

In 1937, in two essays published in the *American Political Science Review*,[89] the German political philosopher Karl Loewenstein coined the term *Streitbare Demokratie* ("militant democracy"). Loewenstein linked the fall of the Weimar Republic and of other European democracies in the post-World War I period to the absence or to the lack of use of "militant" tools against non democratic movements. According to Loewenstein, such instruments are essential to protect democracies from political movements that conquer power through mass-mobilization and plebiscitarian methods. Democracies, Loewenstein thought, should make all efforts to preserve their basic values, even at the cost of violating fundamental democratic principles.[90] Ever since, the debate over "the right not to tolerate the intolerant"[91] periodically resurged in Western democracies. The German Basic Law of 1949 contains a specific militant democracy clause (Art. 21), according to which "Parties that, by reason of their aims or the behavior of their adherents, seek to undermine or abolish the free democratic basic order or to endanger the existence of the Federal Republic of Germany shall be unconstitutional." During the cold war in Germany, and elsewhere, the communist parties paid a particularly high price due to the deployment of militant democracy tools.

With the collapse of the Soviet empire, the interest for militant democracy rapidly diminished.[92] After 11 September 2001, however, as a new threat seemed to imperil the

[87] *Dogru v. France* para. 74.

[88] *Serif v. Greece*, App. no. 38178/97, 31 Eur. H.R. Rep. 561, para. 53 (1999).

[89] Karl Loewenstein, "Militant Democracy and Fundamental Rights" I and II, (1937) 31 *American Political Science Review* 638.

[90] Loewenstein, "Militant Democracy and Fundamental Rights".

[91] Karl Popper, *The Open Societies and its Enemies* (London: Routledge, 1945).

[92] It is true, however, that many Eastern European constitutions adopted after the transition to democracy do contain typical militant democracy clauses that outlaw political parties that pursue

world's stability, militant democracy reclaimed a central place in the political debate. The fundamental question hasn't changed: How far can a democracy go in protecting itself, without denying its democratic character? What has deeply changed, however, are the circumstances of the new threat, as well as the responses to it. In the first place, global terrorism, unlike political parties, is not clearly confined within states, as terrorists may hide virtually everywhere. As a consequence, the militant measures that many democracies have adopted to fight global terrorism, do not target only direct suspects, but end up by limiting certain fundamental rights on a universal (or quasi universal) basis.[93] Moreover, while past targets of militant democracy clauses did certainly threaten the democratic characters of Western states, global terrorism does not. In the words of Lord Hoffman of the House of Lords, "Whether we would survive Hitler hung in the balance, but there is no doubt that we shall survive Al-Qaeda.... Terrorist violence, serious as it is, does not threaten our institutions of government or our existence as a civil community."[94] What terrorism does, though, is create stress, "causing," as Michel Rosenfeld puts it, "more psychological than physical harm. Having terrorists hidden within the polity's population is undoubtedly unnerving and can easily lead to overreactions, undue suppression of fundamental rights or exacerbation of ethnic or racial prejudice."[95] The effects of such overreactions have a particularly harsh impact on Muslims, as today's global terrorism is commonly associated with Islam. It is beyond the scope of the present chapter to discuss the actual correlation between Islam and terrorism. What is important for the sake of my analysis is that, as countless studies show,[96] in the public opinion, in the media, as well as in certain political milieus, the correlation between "Islam" as such, "Muslims" in general, and global terrorism is perceived and/or presented as objective.

It has emerged from the comparative analysis of the conflicts over the right to wear the Islamic veil in Part II, that these are often structured in terms of a sharp antagonism between Islam and the "West." The primary argument for limiting the display of Muslim symbols is that they represent cultural values that are at odds with shared democratic values. At a closer analysis, however, the limitations on Muslim symbols in the public sphere, are not only structured by courts and legislators as a reaction toward the otherness of barbaric, violent, medieval, and backward Islam, but also as a way of *protecting* the British, French, Dutch, Belgian, German, and European peoples from a perniciously public Islam. On the other hand, Christianity, often in its secularized version, is characterized as a structural element of democracy.[97] The laws adopted in the most conservative German *Länder*, discussed in Part II, candidly equate Christianity with democracy and

ideologies that are at odds with the democratic foundations of the state. The Polish Constitution forbids political parties and other organizations devoted to totalitarianism or racial or national hatred. Article 13 of the Constitution of Poland of 2 April 1997. The Ukrainian constitution authorizes the prohibition of parties that threaten the independence of the state. Article 37 of the Ukrainian Constitution of 28 June 1996. The Bulgarian constitution prohibits the formation of political parties on the basis of ethnicity. Article 11(4) of the Bulgarian Constitution of 12 July 1991.

[93] Michel Rosenfeld, "Judicial Balancing in Times of Stress: Comparing the American, British, and Israeli Approaches to the War on Terror" (2006) 27 *Cardozo Law Review* 2079, 2084ff.

[94] *A(FC) v Sec'y of State of the Home Dep't* [2004] UKHL 56, [2005] 2 A.C. 68, 132 (H.L.) (appeal taken from Eng.) (U.K.) (Lord Hoffman, concurring).

[95] Rosenfeld, "Judicial Balancing in Times of Stress" 2086.

[96] See e.g. "The Annual Report on the Situation regarding Racism and Xenophobia in the Member States of the EU," EUMC 2006, available at <http://fra.europa.eu/fraWebsite/attachments/ar06p2_en.pdf>.

[97] For an in-depth analysis of the dichotomous construction of Christianity and Islam in various European jurisdictions, considering cases involving both Muslim as well as Christian symbols in the

neutrality. In France and Switzerland, "small" crucifixes are welcome, but "conspicuous" veils are not. The Strasburg Court unmistakably provides for a different treatment of Christian and Muslim values in the European public sphere, according to which Christian values can be protected at the cost of limiting fundamental rights, while the mere wearing of Muslim symbols (by children!) can legitimately be prohibited because it is an *attitude* that fails to respect secularism.

Religious freedom is a fundamental right in all European democracies, as well as in the European Convention system. Alongside political freedoms, religious freedom is essential to democracy. Taking this into account, one could argue that the exclusion of Muslim symbols shows analogies with constitutional clauses that are typical of militant democracies. Militant democracies are those that exclude *ex ante* parties that advocate non-democratic political agendas. Non-democratic parties can be disbanded only based on their agenda and ideology even in the absence of any actual effort to implement their ideology or agenda. The mere formation and existence of such parties is rendered a crime without the necessity for undertaking any criminal act. Militant democracy is based on a "slippery slope" logic, that is, on the view that, if left alone, non-democratic parties will end up destroying democracy. For example, if a Nazi party fairly wins an election, it is predictable that it will eventually abolish democracy and impose totalitarian rules.

The arguments submitted to justify the restrictions imposed on Islam and its symbols follow the same logic. The premises are that Islam is anti-democratic and that, if left free to manifest its character in the public sphere, it might constitute a threat to democracy. Traditional Muslim clothing thus symbolizes this threat, and therefore their *mere wearing* should be constrained or banned even in the absence of any effort by the those who wear them to factually implement their (supposedly) anti-democratic agenda. In virtually none of the female Muslim clothing cases discussed above has the prohibition of the symbol been the consequence of the infringement of fundamental rights and freedoms of others. The prohibition takes place because Muslim clothing is viewed as an emblem of radical Islamist politics and the oppression of women. In other words, the symbols are prohibited on the basis that they are associated with views and ideologies that are not only at odds with, but also constitute a direct threat to, democratic values. Excluding Islamic symbols can thus be interpreted as a preventive way through which European democracies defend their democratic character.

This logic however may be flawed for at least three principal reasons.

The first, and most obvious reason is that, while the targets of typical militant democracy clauses are *objectively* undemocratic political parties,[98] Islam is obviously not a political force, inherently incompatible with democracy. Islam, just like the other monotheistic religions, is open to a variety of interpretations, including fully democratic and even feminist ones. For example, in her book *Women and Gender in Islam*, Leila Ahmed argues

public sphere see Susanna Mancini, "The Power of Symbols and Symbols as Power: Secularism and Religion as Guarantors of Cultural Convergence" (2009) 30 *Cardozo Law Review* 2629.

[98] In this respect the decision by the ECtHR in the *Refah Partisi* case is ambiguous (*Refah Partisi (the Welfare Party) and Others v. Turkey*, App nos 41340/98, 41342/98, 41343/98 and 41344/98 (ECtHR GC 2003)). The Court held that the dissolution of the Islamic *Refah Partisi*, the largest party in Turkey's Parliament, by the Turkish Constitutional Court, was not contrary to the European Convention. Although Refah's means and ends were both democratic in nature, the ECtHR found that the party's advocacy of adherence to the Koran, and implementation of a millet based system, would, if successful, lead to an impermissible surrender of the people's democratic rights to religious authorities who even if backed by large majorities, would implement illiberal policies discriminatory on the basis of sex and religion. For a discussion of the implication of this case relating to the concept of militant democracy, see Michel Rosenfeld, "A Pluralist Theory of Political Rights in Times of Stress," in Wojciech Sadursky (ed.), *Political Rights Under Stress in 21st Century Europe* (Oxford: Oxford University Press, 2006), 48ff.

that Islam's "ethical vision" is "stubbornly egalitarian" but that has not been evident in the "technical, legalistic establishment version of Islam" that historically prevailed.[99] Religion is, of course, no legitimate shield for undemocratic political agendas. One can think of a religion that is inherently anti-democratic and that organizes politically and has a definitive political agenda being the functional equivalent of a political party. In that case the logic of militant democracy would be applicable to such religion. Islam, however, is a complex and multifaceted religion that comprises a great variety of interpretations, some consistent with democracy, some not. The same is true of other religions: for example, Catholic pre-Vatican II doctrine was incompatible with constitutional secularism and freedom of religion. Most observant Muslims do not pursue any political goals connected with their religion, let alone, with an objectively undemocratic interpretation of such a religion. Accordingly, it is completely unwarranted to limit the freedom of religious expression of individuals belonging to minority religious communities when there is no apparent link with anti-democratic agenda.

In the second place, whereas the targets of typical militant democracy clauses are *clearly identifiable* parties and party-members, who undeniably hold undemocratic views, the limitations to wearing the veil signify an unwarranted restriction of fundamental rights to a significant portion of the polity that is in no way connected to any undemocratic association and does not necessarily adhere to any undemocratic ideology. Merely wearing the headscarf can in no way be automatically associated with fundamentalism. Fundamental rights, such as religious freedoms, cannot be simply weighed against non-constitutional interests[100] such as a societal interest in fighting radical expressions of religion, or even in maximizing security. If a state opts for a militant democracy model in fighting radical Islamism, then the target of the preventive militant measures should be radical Islamists and radical Islamic parties and associations, not Muslims as such. Otherwise militant measures do not safeguard democracy, but rather weaken it by legitimizing religiously/ethnically-based classifications.

This brings me to the third, and most worrisome, flaw of the new militant democracy pattern. Militant democracy is based on a paradox, according to which certain restrictions to political pluralism might be necessary in order to preserve the very possibility of pluralism. The implementation of a militant democracy logic in the field of religious freedom goes the opposite way: its aim is to artificially reinforce religious and cultural homogeneity at the expenses of genuine pluralism. According to Patrick Macklem, this entails a distortion of the very idea of militant democracy, "from a principle that authorizes a state to act in a militant manner to preserve democratic processes to one that entitles a state to establish perimeters and guards against threats of a different kind. Militant democracy now authorizes a state to assume a militant stance toward the exercise of religious freedom that threatens substantive conceptions of democracy."[101] Such a conception of democracy digs its roots in Carl Schmitt's theory of the constitutional state.

IV. From Militant to Identitarian Democracy

Schmitt conceived the bourgeois Rechtsstaat as weak and deprived of material force, whereas his conception of democracy was an essentialist and absolute one. The bourgeois Rechtsstaat, he argued, "is defined from the perspective of bourgeois freedoms"

[99] Leila Ahmed, *Women and Gender in Islam: Historical Roots of a Modern Debate* (New Haven: Yale University Press, 1992).

[100] See Ronald Dworkin, *Taking Rights Seriously* (Cambridge: Harvard University Press, 1977), 92, 95–6.

[101] Patrick Macklem, "Guarding the Perimeter: Militant Democracy and Religious Freedom in Europe" (2012) 19(4) *Constellations* 575–90.

and inspired by the principles of liberalism and individualism.[102] It signifies opposition to the power state, and it identifies with the existing legal system, thus reducing political unity to mere juridical unity. The bourgeois Rechtsstaat is nothing but "the armed guarantor of... bourgeois order, peace and security":[103] according to the division drawn by Montesquieu in the *Esprit des Lois*, it tends to *la liberté*, not to *la gloire*.[104] As Schmitt opposed liberty to authority, and endowed only the latter with the capacity to express political will, the pursuit of liberty rather than glory by the state sets the premises for its dissolution, its disaggregation and its political decay.[105] In this light, liberalism ends up by becoming a hurdle for the very survival of democracy. It follows that, in the Schmittian construction, liberalism can be sacrificed in order to safeguard democracy.[106]

According to Schmitt, a democratic state is not based on equality, but on homogeneity. Carl Schmitt argued that all political communities are based on a constitutive distinction between insiders and outsiders, a polarity of friend and enemy. "Friend" and "enemy," ultimately, have no content in themselves, they are oppositional positions capable of unifying the members of a group. The enemy can be outside, but also inside the state; it doesn't have to be a grotesque monster or a moral opposite, but only be capable of sufficiently threaten a group's way of life: the enemy is the other, the stranger: *der Fremde*.[107]

Political equality, Schmitt argued, cannot be based on the non-exclusive equality of all human beings as moral persons. All political communities, including democratic ones, must rest on some marker of identity and difference that can ground an exclusive form of political equality which will only apply to insiders.[108] "Equal rights [he argued] make good sense where homogeneity exists."[109] Therefore, "Every actual democracy rests on the principle that not only are equals equal, but unequals will not be treated equally."[110] Democracy requires "first homogeneity and second [if the need arises] elimination or eradication:"[111] thus, the political strength of a democracy rests, inter alia, on the very idea of exclusion, in its capacity to eliminate or keep at a distance the stranger, the different one, he who threatens homogeneity. Schmitt was not interested in the problem of social mediation: the state should not seek agreement and compromise with outsiders, it should simply exclude them and fight them, if they threaten the political unity of a people.

[102] Carl Schmitt, *Constitutional Theory* (orig. 1928, J. Seitzer trans., Durham: Duke University Press, 2008), 172.

[103] Schmitt, *Constitutional Theory* 173.

[104] Schmitt, *Constitutional Theory* 60, quoting Montesquieu (*Esprit des Lois* I, Chs 5 and 7), and discussing the ideal concept of the bourgeois state. See also 170 and 173.

[105] Schmitt, *Constitutional Theory* 173, discussing the destruction of the "Traditional German Reich" which produced the elimination of all existing rights.

[106] Azzariti, *Critica della democrazia identitaria* 15, maintaining that the "a-historical" and "impoverished" characterization of liberalism by Schmitt serves the purpose of demonstrating its theoretical and political inconsistency.

[107] "The distinction of friend and enemy denotes the utmost degree of intensity of a union or separation, of an association, or dissociation... The political enemy need not be morally evil or aesthetically ugly... But he is, nevertheless, the other, the stranger; and it is sufficient for his nature that he is, in an especially intense way, existentially something different and alien, so that in the extreme case conflicts with him are possible." Carl Schmitt, "The Concept of the Political," in Carl Schmitt, *Political Theology: Four Chapters on the Theory of Sovereignty* (George Schwab trans., Chicago: University of Chicago Press, 1996), 27.

[108] Schmitt, *Constitutional Theory* 257–64.

[109] Carl Schmitt, *The Crisis of Parliamentary Democracy* (orig. 1923, E. Kennedy trans., Cambridge: MIT Press, 1985), 10.

[110] Schmitt, *The Crisis of Parliamentary Democracy* 9.

[111] Schmitt, *The Crisis of Parliamentary Democracy* 9.

There is no room for dialogue, no need for consensus in Schmitt's construction: the relationship between friend and enemy is based on an absolute incommunicability.[112]

Schmitt thought that the possibility for the state to identify the enemy is crucial in order to preserve the principles and the values of democracy: "As soon as democracy takes on the content of a self-sufficient value, [he wrote] then one can no longer remain (in a formal sense) a democrat at any price."[113] The binomial friend/enemy is the fundamental Schmittian political category: only by identifying and fighting the enemy the state safeguards the principles and the values of democracy. The Schmittian democracy, thus, needs to be guarded beyond the state of exception, even in ordinary times, in order to ensure stability and duration. The essence of democracy is to ensure the people's political unity, which can be achieved only if there is a clear identity between the rulers and those subject to their rule. This identity is presupposed and undisputed, and needs to be guarded. This explains why "political laws," that is, those expressing the unitary will of the people and respecting the principle of identity, should prevail over laws that stem from the procedural aspect of the rule-of-law. Law, for Schmitt, is fundamentally an act of sovereignty that no rule-of-law requirement can ignore and obscure.[114] Legitimacy, thus, prevails over legality.

Pluralism (which Schmitt saw as the consequence of historical factors common to most industrialized states), poses a particularly pernicious threat to democracy. If a state admits that individuals can have a plurality of equally respected belongings, potentially conflicting with one another, it will end up succumbing to civil society. Pluralism will end up turning the state into a realm on the same level as groups, associations, and "non-political" spheres. When a state is threatened by pluralism, it can no longer rely on a *natural* tendency towards homogeneity and political unity. Therefore, it must react and actively pursue *artificial* unity and homogeneity; and the only way a people may reach unity is through identity.

It is somewhat ironic that Schmitt put so much effort in trying to demonstrate that "existential" political questions, such as the decision as to who is the enemy and on the means to combat it, can never be constrained by law and must therefore not be dealt with by neither the judicial nor the legislative branches of government.[115] Essential decisions must come from "the political," from the subject who is able to "feel" and articulate the needs and the desires of the united *Völk*. Quite to the contrary, in today's democratic dynamics, the exclusion of the "Muslim enemy" is the product of courts and legislators. At a closer look, however, these exclusionary measures reflect the discomfort, the annoyance, the resentment, and the fears that majorities experience in European democracies in an era of globalization and mass-scale migrations. They reflect the desire of majorities to re-establish clear boundaries between the self and the other, to avoid dialogue and compromise with the other, and to reduce the visibility of the latter, in order to guard the (supposedly) homogeneous character of the public sphere. In other words, the laws and the judicial decisions banning or limiting the wearing of the veil respond to a widespread popular will to identify a group—the Muslims—as outsiders, and to exclude it from the public sphere in the name of a homogeneity which is felt as threatened.

To be sure, no European public sphere is, or has ever been, homogeneous. Homogeneity, unity and identity do not *really* exist: they are ultimately nothing more than a myth. In the Schmittian construction, unity is presupposed, it operates at a symbolic level, and it ends up by coinciding with identity. For Schmitt, identity and representation constitute

[112] Azzariti, *Critica della democrazia identitaria* 51.

[113] Schmitt, *The Crisis of Parliamentary Democracy* 28.

[114] Schmitt, *Constitutional Theory*.

[115] Schmitt, "The Concept of the Political."

the two pillars of the political form, but do not have an intrinsic value: rather, they have the finality to identify and represent the unitary will of the people, which legitimizes the constituent decision (the *pouvoir constituant*). But it is precisely in his theorization of the *pouvoir constituant*, that Schmitt makes a shift from the "real" people to a romantic totality, deprived of any internal division.[116] In drawing the distinction between "people" and "nation," Schmitt highlights that the latter indicates the people as a unity, capable of acting politically, with the awareness of its political particular features and with the will of a political existence, whereas the people that does not exist as a nation is only one among many groups of individuals with ethnical or cultural affinity, but not necessarily existing politically.[117] The theory of popular *pouvoir constituant* presupposes the conscious will to have a political existence, that is, it presupposes a *nation*.[118] This *nation*, the *people* Schmitt endows with the *pouvoir constituant*, is a transcendent subject that results from a process of abstraction and idealization. Paraphrasing Hannah Arendt, one could say that for Schmitt the condition for political life is the existence of "Man," not that of "men."[119] In this light, the principle of political representation has a particular meaning in Schmitt's theorization. Schmitt constructs the principle of political representation through a parallel with the history of the Church. The Catholic Church, according to Schmitt, takes a political form which is capable of conferring to it "the pathos of authority in its full purity" which is typical of the political. The superiority of the Church, Schmitt thought, lies in its capacity of representation, and in the strength of its representation and it is irrelevant *what*, if anything, it represents, and whether, in the end, the Church only represents the representation.[120] Representation thus becomes almost an act of faith, and political unity is accomplished only by representation.[121] The Schmittian identity, thus, is not the identity of a material people: it is, rather, pure transcendence.

Today's exclusion of Islam and promotion of Christianity, both in the name of homogeneity and unity, draws on an analogous metaphysical construction of the people, that erases all material traits. The peoples supposedly threatened by Muslim values and represented by their common Christian legacy do not really exist. *Real* people are complex, pluralist communities, that cannot be faithfully represented as a unity. Otherwise, democracy ceases to be a substantial model of government and turns, as in the Schmittian construction, into a political myth,[122] which provides an alternative to the weakness of the bourgeois Rechstaat.

In this mythical construction of a homogeneous democracy, Muslims play an analogous and complementary role to that played by Jews in the Schmittian democracy. Schmitt constructed the Jews as standing in sharp contrast to a Catholic skepticism regarding modern life and culture,[123] which stemmed from what Martti Koskenniemi defines as Schmitt's "almost visceral anti-liberalism."[124] Moreover, in anti-Semitism, "Schmitt

[116] Azzariti, *Critica della democrazia identitaria* 37.

[117] Schmitt, *Constitutional Theory* 127 et seq.

[118] Schmitt, *Constitutional Theory* 128.

[119] "[T]he fact that men, not Man, ... inhabit the world," is "the condition ... of all political life.": Hannah Arendt, *Human Condition*, Chicago: University of Chicago Press (1958), 7.

[120] Carl Schmitt, *Roman Catholicism and Political Form* (orig. 1923, G.L. Ulmen trans., Westport, Greenwood Press, 1996).

[121] Azzariti, *Critica della democrazia identitaria* 32.

[122] Carlo Galli, *Genealogia della politica. Carl Schmitt e la crisi del pensiero moderno* (Bologna: Il Mulino, 1996), 537.

[123] Gross, *Carl Schmitt and the Jews* 11.

[124] Martii Koskenniemi, "International Law as Political Theology: How to Read the *Nomos der Erde*?" (2004) 11(4) *Constellation* 492, 500.

seemed to see . . . the potential source of a new institutional identity and a new legal order for a German state that had been fractured by historical forces and the misapplication of abstract liberal constitutionalism."[125]

Muslims in Europe are accused of challenging liberal values, supposedly rooted in the "Judeo-Christian" tradition, a post-World War II rather ambiguous notion meant to (verbally) overcome the legacy of the Holocaust. This apparent contradiction should not be misleading. Both accusations are grounded on a metaphysical construction of the "people" (the French people, the German people, the European people) which denies and ultimately erases diversity, dialectic and separation. Both accusations are meant to inflict the "stigmata of otherness" [126] onto a scapegoat, upon which to build a new oppositional identity. Both accusations are ultimately based on a rejection of pluralism and on the decision to actively fight it, as the French "burqa report" suggests, when it states that "The mission unanimously agreed that the practice of wearing the full veil is the antithesis of republican values. This shared finding should incite to action."[127]

Moreover, as Gil Anidjar argues in his book *The Jew, the Arab: A History of the Enemy*, the concept of the enemy is structured by the relation of Europe to *both* Jew *and* Arab.[128] For Schmitt, the political results from secularization, that is, the separation of theology from politics. "All significant concepts of the modern theory of the state are secularized theological concepts not only because of their historical development—in which they were transformed from theology to the theory of the state, whereby for example, the omnipotent God became the omnipotent lawgiver—but also because of their systematic structure, the recognition of which is necessary for a sociological consideration of these concepts."[129] In this light, Anidjar argues that the distinction between the theological and the political originates with the construction of the Jew as a *theological* enemy and the Arab as a *political* enemy. "The Arab [he writes] came to be constructed as an external (and political) enemy of Europe and the Jew, an internal (and theological) enemy . . . [T]he division between theological enemy (the Jew) and political enemy (the Arab) also happens to replicate the exhausted, misleading and mistaken commonplace that locates Islam outside of Europe and the Jews within it (while recounting a history that often sought to exteriorize, or simply expel, Jews out of Europe, while trying—still trying, as if it meant anything, aside from replicating old patterns of violence—to prevent Islam's 'entry' into it)."[130]

V. A Christian Europe?

In 2005, during a press conference, then EU Enlargement Commissioner, Olli Rehn, commented on the status of the negotiations concerning Turkey's access to the European Union. "It will be a very long and difficult journey" he stated. "European values need to become reality in all walks of life, in all corners of the country, before Turkey can join the European Union."[131] Eight years later, despite the reforms carried out by the

125 David Bates, "Political Theology and the Nazi State" (2006) 3 *Modern Intellectual History* 415, 441.

126 The expression is used by Balibar, "Is there a 'Neo-Racism?' " 18.

127 "Rapport 2262" 123 [my translation].

128 Gil Anidjar, *The Jew, the Arab: A History of the Enemy* (Stanford: Stanford University Press, 2003).

129 Schmitt, *Political Theology* 36/G43.

130 Shaikh, "The Jew, the Arab: An Interview with Gil Anidjar."

131 "Turkey Must Embrace EU Reforms 'In all Walks of Life' " (1 July 2005), quoted by Casanova, "The Long, Difficult, and Tortuous Journey of Turkey into Europe and the Dilemmas of European Civilization" 237.

government lead by Erdogan, Turkey's road to European membership seems longer and more difficult than ever.

In the meantime, in Hungary, a fully-fledged EU member since 2004, a majority composed of right and ultra-right wing parties, adopted a new Constitution (2011), according to which the "Members of the Hungarian nation" "recognize the role of Christianity in preserving nationhood" and are "proud that king Saint Stephen built the Hungarian State on solid ground and made... [the] country a part of Christian Europe one thousand years ago."[132] A series of subsequent legal changes undermined media freedom, limited judicial independence, and weakened the power of the Constitutional Court. In March 2013, the Hungarian Parliament adopted a number of constitutional changes, disregarding a series of decisions by the country's constitutional court, which had struck down unconstitutional laws introduced by the government. The latter reintroduced the same laws through amendments to the constitution itself and ended the court's power to review substantive changes to the constitution. One of such amendments limits religious freedom, other amendments limit the broadcasting of political campaigns, permit criminalizing homelessness, discriminate against unmarried and same-sex families, cut the powers of the judiciary etc.[133] Article 7 of the EU Treaty permits the suspension of EU member states voting rights if a member state is in serious breach of the common values of the European Union.[134] As of today, however, Hungary's voting rights have not been suspended.

One cannot help wondering "what" values are really at play in determining European boundaries. Josè Casanova argues that "an outwardly secular Europe is still too Christian when it comes to the possibility of imagining a Muslim country as part of the European community. One wonders whether Turkey represents a threat to Western civilization or rather an unwelcome reminder of the barely submerged yet inexpressible and anxiety-ridden 'white' European Christian identity."[135] By the same token, a clear turn from pluralistic democracy in a country like Hungary, that increasingly identifies with a romantic understanding of ethnicity and Christianity, does not prompt the European institutions to act.

Europe is a highly secularized continent. The "World Values Surveys" indicates that "more than any other region of the world, European countries empirically fall all over the plane" and there emerge "five distinctly different, in some dimensions radically distanced European value areas: a Protestant, a Catholic, an Orthodox, an English-speaking and a Baltic-former communist one."[136]

If it is true that, as certain commentators put it, European "societal institutions and national identities... remain anchored to an important extent in Christianity,"[137] the latter in this context is not a *real* religion. It is a kind of "belonging without believing,"[138]

[132] The Fundamental Law of Hungary, 25 April 2011, National Avowal.

[133] Human Rights Watch, Hungary: Constitution Changes Warrant EU Action, available at <http://www.hrw.org/news/2013/03/12/hungary-constitution-changes-warrant-eu-action>.

[134] Article 6(1) of the TEU: "The Union is founded on the principles of liberty, democracy, respect for human rights and fundamental freedoms, and the rule of law, principles which are common to the Member States."

[135] José Casanova, "Religion, European Secular Identities and European Integration," in Timothy Byrnes and Peter Katzenstein (eds), *Religion in an Expanding Europe* (Cambridge: Cambridge University Press, 2006), 74.

[136] Casanova, "The Long, Difficult, and Tortuous Journey of Turkey into Europe and the Dilemmas of European Civilization," quoting Pippa Norris and Ronald Inglehart, *Sacred and Secular: Religion and Politics Worldwide* (Cambridge: Cambridge University Press, 2004).

[137] Nancy Foner and Richard Alba, "Immigrant Religion in the US and Western Europe: Bridge or Barrier to Inclusion?" (2008) 42(2) *International Migration Review* 360, 374.

[138] See Casanova, "Religion, European Secular Identities and European Integration" 65, quoting Davie Grace, *Religion in Britain Since 1945: Believing Without Belonging* (1994).

that translates into the unspoken "value" requirements that Turkey does not fulfill, and, at the same time, provide the ground basis for a European political and intellectual order. In today's globalized and secularized Europe, "Christianity" has absorbed the qualities that Carl Schmitt attributed solely to Catholicism, and Muslims have substituted other enemies.

Schmitt saw in the Catholic Church a model for societies struggling to reconcile conflicts of interest. He viewed the Church as an institutional embodiment of the underlying unity of European political civilization, a "political form" which revitalized the significance of national and class oppositions: a *Complexio Oppositorum*, a complex of opposites.[139] The Church was to him the inheritor of the Roman Empire, the living embodiment of the classical political civilization which all Western European peoples shared. The Church, he thought, was also responsible for the historical evolution of Europe's distinctive national cultures. In determining the boundaries of European identity—as a unity expressed in diverse national forms—Schmitt relied on a double negation: of American capitalism, on the one hand, and of Russian radicalism, on the other. Thus, the Church also represented an endangered, classical civilization.[140]

Schmitt did not understand Christianity "in the first place as a doctrine, nor as a moral system, not even (my pardon) as a religion"; rather, he viewed Christianity as a "historical event."[141] Schmitt deeply admired the Church's moral relativism, its outstanding capacity of accommodation, and its "stubborn intransigence," its "arrogance and humility."[142] He argued that "There aren't oppositions that the Church cannot embrace, not just politically but also theologically: after all, the Old and the New Testament alike are scriptural canon."[143] The Church, Schmitt thought, was remarkably flexible: "With every change in the political situation, all principles appear to change save one: the power of Catholicism."[144] Finally, the Church's infinite ambiguity is best combined with dogmatism and will of decision when it culminates in the dogma of "papal infallibility."[145] The Church's realism and capacity of compromise testified, for Schmitt, to its political nature. Ultimately, in Schmitt's thought, the Church was a representation of the *civitas humana*, the historical connection to the incarnation and crucifixion of Jesus Christ; Catholicism represented the values which were the essence of European civilization and separated it from barbarism.[146]

This construction is faithfully transposed in today's appeal to the "Christian roots," or the "common Christian legacy" of Europe. It is actually striking how the Bavarian and Italian crucifix decisions cited above in Part II, re-echo the language of Carl Schmitt, and build on his understanding of Catholicism in historical terms, and on his political theology. The Bavarian judge describes "the representation of the cross as the icon of the suffering and Lordship of Jesus Christ . . . not [as] the expression of a conviction of a belief bound to a specific Confession," but as "an essential object of the general Christian-occidental tradition;"[147] the Italian court mentions the capacity of the crucifix

[139] Gopal Balakrishnan, *The Enemy: An Intellectual Portrait of Carl Schmitt* (London: Verso, 2000), 53.
[140] Balakrishnan, *The Enemy* 65.
[141] Carl Schmitt, *Glossarium* 283, translated in Gross, *Carl Schmitt and the Jews* 218.
[142] Schmitt, *Roman Catholicism and Political Form* 7.
[143] Schmitt, *Roman Catholicism and Political Form* 7.
[144] Schmitt, *Roman Catholicism and Political Form* 5.
[145] Schmitt, *Roman Catholicism and Political Form* 8.
[146] John P. McCormick, "Carl Schmitt's Europe: Cultural, Imperial and Spatial Proposals for European Integration 1923–1955," quoted by Mary Anne Perkins, *Christendom and European Identity: The Legacy of a Grand Narrative Since 1789* (Berlin: Walter de Gruyter, 2004), 315.
[147] Bayerischer Verwaltungsgerichtshof [BayVGH] [Bavarian Higher Administrative Court] 3 June 1991, 122 Bayerische Verwaltungsblatter [BayVBI] 751 (751–754) (F.R.G.).

to "evoke the transcendent foundation" of state principles, which shape the secular character of the state.[148]

Schmitt attributed to Catholicism traditional, anti-liberal values, which represented the endangered classical European identity, threatened by "Jewish" modernity. Today, Christianity has come to represent Europe's liberal tradition, challenged by "Muslim" illiberal projects, as candidly stated by the Italian court, according to which "the crucifix is the representation of the religious origin of the values of tolerance, reciprocal respect, human dignity, fundamental rights, solidarity and non-discrimination."[149] Clearly, from a substantive point of view, it is irrelevant *what* the crucifix actually represents. Its capacity of representation, and the strength of such representation, is all that matters. Liberalism, anti-liberalism, traditionalism, the Enlightment, nothing is excluded from the Christian complex of opposites embodied in the crucifix. The *Lautsi* case mentioned above, where the ECtHR upheld the mandatory display of the crucifix in Italian state schools,[150] is emblematic of this unlimited encompassing quality of Christianity. In November 2010, the European Court in *Lautsi I*, had held that the display of the crucifix in state schools restricted the right of parents to educate their children in conformity with their convictions, and the right of children to believe or not to believe.[151] Pasquale Annichino provides a fascinating account of how this decision was reversed by the Court's Grand Chamber in 2011 thanks to a "variegated coalition of actors ranging from the strong alliance between the Vatican and the Italian Government to the Russia of the New Orthodoxy as well as to American Conservative Evangelicals."[152] Annicchino maintains that this "Holy Alliance," which promised to restore the "authentic European faith and culture,"[153] had a clear political aim, that of re-affirming the privileges of majorities within national states. This, he argues, is detrimental not only to religious freedom, but also to the "the development of healthy and strong religious communities."[154] Annicchino is correct: the "Holy Alliance" will never restore the "authentic European faith and culture," quite simply because there isn't one, and the deep cultural and theological divergences among the components of this coalition testify to that. Religion and religiosity were not at stake in the *Lautsi* case: the political use of the crucifix by state institutions does not strengthen *religion*: to the contrary, as the German Constitutional Court held in 1995, the secularization of the crucifix ultimately produces its desecration and weakens the autonomy of the Church.[155]

The *Lautsi* case mirrors the crises of the European universalistic projects. It indicates the perceived absence of shared European values, and the attempt to shape a relativistic "European identity" based on the evocative power of tradition and on political myths. This is ultimately an illiberal project, that carries the risk of undermining the very foundations of post-World War II Europe. To rely on a powerful, and yet empty representation of Europe, opens the door to marginalization and the exclusion of those who threaten the unity of the representation, to the homologation of conducts, and to the tyranny of majorities. As Schmitt himself put it, the moral relativism of the Church

148 *TAR Veneto*, para. 11.7. 149 *TAR Veneto*, para. 11.7.

150 *Lautsi and Others v. Italy* App. no. 30814/06 (ECtHR, GC 2011).

151 *Lautsi and Others v. Italy* App. no. 30814/062 (ECtHR Nov. 2009).

152 Pasquale Annicchino, "Winning the Battle by Losing the War: The *Lautsi* Case and the Holy Alliance between American Conservative Evangelicals, the Russian Orthodox Church and the Vatican to Reshape European Identity" (2011) 6 *Religion and Human Rights* 213.

153 Annicchino, "Winning the Battle" 218.

154 Annicchino, "Winning the Battle" 219.

155 Bundesverfassungsgericht [BVerfG] [Federal Constitutional Court] 16 May 1995 (Kruzifix-Urteil), 93 Entscheidungen des Bundesverfassungsgerichts [BVerfGE] 1 (F.R.G.).

allows "One [to] appropriate all freedoms of one's opponent in the name of the opponent's principles and deny them to him in the name of one's own Catholic principles."[156]

Schmitt's analysis of European identity poses disquieting questions regarding Europe's cosmopolitan vocation. His theorization of democracy poses difficult questions, as David Dyzenhaus puts it, "to those who regard constitutional democracy merely as a given, as a self-perpetuating normative order of society, without wishing to pay much attention to the fragility of this order."[157] Thus, the mainly symbolic dimension of the controversies over religious symbols in the public space should not lead to underestimate their significance in terms of the conception, the quality and the future of European democracy and of European democracies. Under the pretense of removing an obstacle to democracy, the exclusion of Islam from the public sphere aims at pursuing the idealization of a non existing essentialist European identity, and at anchoring it in a metaphysical notion of secularized Christianity. It aims at constructing an artificial and exclusionary kind of unity, at the expensive of universalism, pluralism, and fundamental rights.

The ultimate irony is that the Schmittian logic that lurks behind both political *and legal* measures reacting to the presence of Islam in Europe, by revealing certain blind spots and vulnerabilities of European liberalism, poses the problem of how to guard democracy beyond the state of exception, in ordinary times, to protect it against its seemingly irresistible tendency towards periodical identitarian derailment. To put it differently, it poses the problem of how to deal with the fact that, indisputably "The devil has his own legality."[158]

[156] Schmitt, *Roman Catholicism and Political Form* 5.

[157] David Dyzenhaus, "Why Carl Schmitt?," in David Dyzenhaus (ed.), *Law as Politics: Carl Schmitt's Critique of Liberalism* (Durham: Duke University Press, 1998), 1–20.

[158] Carl Schmitt, *The Visibility of the Church* (1914), App. to *Roman Catholicism and Political Form*, 58.

7

On the Secularization of the Public Square: Jews in France and in the United States

*Pierre Birnbaum**

Nowadays, with the vanishing of the Eastern European Ashkenazi and Arabic Sephardic worlds, one can find in the *Galut* mainly two large groups of Jews, in the United States and in France, two main paradigms of Jewish life in Diaspora. These deeply different societies within these very different types of states have had deeply different histories. Broadly seen, one is a strong nation-state, while the other belongs to the Anglo-Saxon pluralist tradition. Yet Jews feel at home in both paradigms, whatever their differences. Their long-term involvement in the different histories of these states has lead Jewish people in France and the United States to find different forms of happiness.[1] Following the Tocquevillian or Weberian traditions, in both Charles Tilly's and Stein Rokkan's comparative project based mainly on state and culture, the state can be seen as a reaction against the strong Catholic Church or strong local peripheries. Thus the State implies a process of strong differentiation, but also a process of strong institutionalization. Without these two dimensions, one would say that there is no state, and that the political power remaining is the puppet of a class, a religion, or a party. Since the end of the Middle Ages, France can be seen as quite close to the ideal type of the state; it is almost only there that the strong absolutist state was built facing an extremely strong medieval political dispersion of local powers. The attempt failed in Spain, Italy, and Germany, where local provinces and strong ruling classes were able to resist this process of statization, and in England where the representative process allowed the representation of groups within the Parliament. It did not even begin in the United States until the Civil War and, mainly, the New Deal.

In each society, the logic of the state remained more or less the same through different centuries. From the royal absolutist state to the Bonapartist or the Gaullist one, the French state, even within the democratic order, remains the crucial variable. The United States, whatever its attempts, never succeeded in building a strong administrative apparatus based on an immense public civil service founded on a meritocratic dimension. The law is not in itself a state. The state, like in France, builds its own nation through its own institutions, its public education, its public museums, its public archives, its state-led industrialization and so on. Otherwise, it is not a state.

Thus, there is a kind of paradox. How can we understand the fact that both societies, having a deeply different kind of state, were able nevertheless to establish a separation between state and religion, a "wall of separation," i.e. a process of differentiation that,

* Universit Paris I. Prof. Birnbaum has published several books on the sociology of the State and on the comparative history of Jews in various Western States.

[1] See Yosef Yerushalmi, *Zakhor: Jewish History and Jewish Memory* (Seattle: University of Washington Press, 1982).

in other contexts, never really occurred in the United States? This puzzling issue raises interesting questions dealing with the nature of the state. How can we explain that, in the weak American state, one witnesses nevertheless the building of "a wall of separation" between Church and state? How can such a process of differentiation occur in spite of the weakness of the state? Was there really a separation of Church and state in this weak state society dominated by a Protestant upper class? As we know, the French Revolution and the Third Republic created a kind of "naked public sphere" in which the state organized its own public space, almost destroying any religious values in the society, while in the United States the separation, to the contrary, was established against the state so that the different Churches would remain free to organize themselves. Furthermore, the different states within the United States remained Christian and until 1860 some of them still excluded non-Christians from their institutions. So the famous "wall of separation" remained, until 1940 and the *Cantwell* decision,[2] which still had mostly only symbolic significance. Thus, in 1905, Jews in the United States were still excluded from the "Christian nation," to quote Judge Brewer, exactly the year when the French Republican State created almost a complete public space, with Protestants along with Jewish civil servants and lawyers extremely active in favor of this strong laïcization unknown in the United States. Therefore, French Jews have always been at the forefront of "la laïcité," while in the United States, most of them, until the 1950, remained in the niches of civil society.

Therefore, when in 1978, Rabbi M. Schneerson, the head of the Lubavitch, wanted menorahs to be kindled in public squares in recognition of the legitimacy of different religions, his logic was still the one predominant from the American revolution to the 1950's until the moment of a growing secularization, from *Everson* to *Engel*. In landmark cases in which Jews were frequently crucial actors, the Supreme Court dismantled the Protestant Establishment that provided the Christian framework of the nation by forbidding various Christian expressions within the public square. Most Jews became suddenly in favor of a naked public square. Being so fond of secularization, Jews almost look like the last Habermassians,[3] the only remaining lovers of reason seeking the benefits of a public space under the protection of an enlightened Law, threatened by various religious awakenings. A strong opponent of this process of secularization in which Jewish judges like Felix Frankfurter were so active, Rabbi Schneerson, received a letter from Rabbi Joseph Glazer, the President of the Central Conference of American Rabbis and a law school graduate, telling him that placing menorahs on public property is a breach of the "wall of separation." Rabbi Glazer then "urgently" advised Rabbi Shneerson to read again Alexis de Tocqueville's *Democracy in America*, in which de Tocqueville, a Catholic, outlines the crucial dimension of the separation of church and state in the United States, which allows religions to expand freely within society. A few years later, in 1989, the Supreme Court decided *County of Allegheny v. ACLU*,[4] in which the Court determined that the display of a menorah next to a Christmas tree in a public square could be appropriate, holding that the menorah and Christmas tree are secular symbols and thus the display was compatible with the First Amendment. As a result of this decision, the issue resurfaced. Nathan Lewin, vice-president of the National Jewish Commission on Law and Public Affairs (COLPA), said, "finally... America is a country where Jews are welcome and are first class citizens." Rabbi Allan Nadler, director of the Yiddish Institute

[2] *Cantwell v. Connecticut* 310 U.S. 296 (1940).

[3] Jürgen Habermas and Max Pensky, *The Postnational Constellation: Political Essays* (Cambridge: MIT Press, 2001).

[4] 492 U.S. 573 (1989).

of Research (YIVO), considered that "the kindling of huge menorahs in public spaces across America opens a dangerous constitutional can of worms. It can easily backfire on the Jewish community by undermining the principle of freedom from established religion which has always been such a blessing for American Jewry.... There are few, if any, legal institutions, so basic as the constitutional wall separating church and state."[5]

Orthodox Jews more or less join Chabad in their negative view of this "blessing" based on the First Amendment, aligning themselves more and more with evangelical and born-again Christians in favoring prayers in public schools and state aid to parochial schools, breaking "the wall of separation," and fighting against any kind of secularization. When, in 2000, Joe Lieberman was the Democratic vice-presidential nominee, an orthodox Jew almost reached the highest elected office while officially keeping his faith, thus bringing religion into the public space. In June of that same year, in keeping with its own interpretation of the wall, the Supreme Court ruled against prayers at public events such as public school graduation ceremonies. While most American Jews applauded this decision, the prominent philosopher David Novak said, "On Torah grounds, Jews ought to encourage non-Jews to pray in public in order to show how much they believe the world, including the political order, is dependent upon God.... We Jews should be opposed to [...] de facto public atheism...."[6]

American Jewish lawyers and law professors often cite the French model as the most hateful one, France being seen as an atheist society foreign to Jewish values. For instance, in his recent book, Steven Goldberg argues that the United States should not become like Iran, a theocracy, or France, an atheist society in which the state has sought the destruction of every religion since the French Revolution and has succeeded through its *laïcité* to become a deeply secularized society.[7] He seems to agree with famous sociologists and political scientists like Michael Walzer and Will Kymlicka, who view the French model as an almost totalitarian regime in which identities are repressed. In the name of multiculturalism, they are hostile to the French state, which they view as homogeneous; they favor the strengthening of Jewish and Muslim identities within the public square.[8] To quote Reinhold Niebuhr, the famous Protestant theologian, France seems to have the most "naked public square," the one that the United States must avoid. Followers of Horace Kallen favor a hyphenated identity, with a vision of citizenship framed by different values, including religious values.

So again, how can we compare the American and French contexts in which Jews are trying to maintain some of their values while favoring a secularist interpretation of the public realm? First, one must remember that there have been many ideas exchanged between the two countries. Thomas Jefferson, the hero of American Jews and all American liberal citizens, and the person responsible for the influential metaphor that the Constitution erected a wall of separation between church and state, was in Paris from 1786 to 1789 when the Bill of Rights—including the First Amendment—was added to the Constitution. Thus, he was confronted with the French Enlightenment and its rationalist universalism hostile to religion, and witnessed the French Revolution and

[5] See Jonathan D. Sarna and David G. Dalin, *Religion and State in the American Jewish Experience* (Notre Dame, Ind.: University of Notre Dame Press, 1997), 296, 298, 300 (quoting Rabbi Allan Nadler).

[6] David Novak, "Toward a Jewish Public Philosophy in America," in Alan Mittleman et al (eds), *Jews and the American Public Square: Debating Religion And Republic* (Lanham, Md.: Rowman & Littlefield, 2002), 331, 351–2.

[7] Steven Goldberg, *Bleached Faith: The Tragic Cost When Religion is Forced into the Public Square* (Stanford, Calif.: Stanford Law Books, 2008), Ch. 5.

[8] See e.g. Michael Walzer, *On Toleration* (New Haven: Yale University Press, 1997).

its attempt to exclude the Church from the public realm.[9] At the end of the century, when anti-Semitism was spreading in the form of the accusation that Jews contested the Christian nature of the United States, Samuel Kellogg, a Professor of Theology at Western Theological Seminary, preached against American rationalist Jews conspiring to destroy Christianity, and used as an inspiration Edouard Drumont, the author of numerous anti-Semitic books, including *La FranceJuive.* Thus, "the preachers and their theories attest to the interplay of European and American thinking about the Jews."[10] And in 1905, when the separation of church and state was obtained legislatively, one could hear anti-Semitic voices of protest in the streets of New York.[11]

In fact, French Jewish involvement in secularization in the second part of the nineteenth century seems to have been imitated by contemporary American Jews since the 1960's. Still, there is a difference in means: While French Jews used Parliament and the state bureaucracy to expand the secularism initiated by atheists and deists at the beginning of the Third Republic, American Jews with their allies used the Supreme Court to dismantle the Christian institutions that had been more or less shaping the public realm since the American Revolution. Jews had an earlier involvement in secularization in France because of the French Revolution, during which the state and the dominant Catholic Church were separated and another church controlled by the state was created. This church fell, resulting, at least for a short period, in a complete disappearance of religious symbols from the public realm. After the Concordat and the new alliance between the state and the church, Jews had to fight against, for example, Catholic presence in the public realm. Within Parliament, some elected Jewish deputies spoke loudly in favor of this process. Before the turn of the century, during the Third Republic, many Jews were active political and administrative elites, elected or appointed to high administrative positions as deputies, ministers, prefects and so on in this institutionalized and differentiated strong state,[12] and they were, with the protestant elite, at the forefront of the secularization process. Being confronted by a single, huge Catholic Church in charge of the state for many centuries, their involvement in the secularist battle led to a dangerous backlash, much more so than in the United States. For instance, many well-known prefects played a crucial role in the expulsion of the church from the public realm, and the vociferous, radical Catholic right, with its populist anti-Semitic friends, led the fight against them under the banner of "France to the French." Later, in 1905, the law separating church and state was drafted by Louis M~jean, a Protestant, and Paul Grunebaum-Ballin, an assimilated Jew, against the wishes of Orthodox Jews who were afraid to leave the shadow of the state and the financial aid it provided. Nevertheless, soon rabbis and major Jewish institutions accepted this separation in the hope that it would bring new life to Jewish institutions now facing their own needs that were being paid for by the common Jewish people.[13] This open involvement of Jews and

[9] See Daniel L. Dreisbach, *Thomas Jefferson and the Wall of Separation Between Church and State* (New York: New York University Press, 2002).

[10] Naomi W. Cohen, "Antisemitism in the Gilded Age: The Jewish View," in Naomi W. Cohen (ed.), *Essential Papers on Jewish-Christian Relations in the United States* (New York: New York University Press, 1990), 127, 138–9.

[11] Jean-Louis Halpérin, "La Reprsentation de la La'cit Parmi les Juristes Franais et Atrangers," in Patrick Weil (ed.), *Politiques de la laïcité au XXE siècle* (Paris: Presses universitaires de France, 2007), 181, 196.

[12] Pierre Birnbaum, *The Jews of the Republic: A Political History of State Jews in France from Gambetta to Vichy* (Jame Marie Todd trans., Stanford, Calif.: Stanford University Press, 1996).

[13] The best book on this period is still Jean-Marie Mayeur, *La separation de l'eglise et de l'etat* (Paris: Julliard, 1991). Another important book on this period is Jacqueline Lalouette, *La séparation des Eglises et de l'etat* (Paris: Seuil, 2005). See also Pierre Birnbaum, *Jewish Destinies: Citizenship, State*

Protestants in bringing about the separation of church and state led to an explosion of both anti-Semitism and anti-Protestantism. The Catholic periodical *La Croix* and the radical right periodical *La Libre Parole* launched a violent anti-Semitic storm along with hundreds of provincial newspapers. Many anti-Semitic movements occurred all across France as the first organized mass movements involving many hundreds of thousands of members threatened the Jews, sometimes beating them, and sometimes severely. Jews were seen as the new Christ killers in a historically Catholic France. Even in the Parliament, several strong anti-Semitic statements were made with little protest: Jews were openly accused of de-Christianizing France. Even though the hundreds of deputies who voted for separation laws were non-observant Catholics, deists, or atheists, Jews became the target of large anti-Semitic leagues.

Meanwhile, in the United States that same year, Supreme Court Justice David Brewer, in the tradition of Supreme Court Justice William Strong, published his famous lectures in *The United States: A Christian Nation.* Although the United States had no established religion, Christianity was seen by Brewer as "a mighty factor in the life of the republic."[14] In this weak state society, Jews were still outside the mainly Protestant Establishment and almost none were included within the main Washington institutions. Jews were alarmed by Brewer's lectures and could only reply through their own pamphlets, such as *A Reply to Justice Brewer's Lectures* by Isaac Hassler.[15] According to George Marsden, "[i]n 1870 almost all American Protestants thought of America as a Christian nation.... [T]hroughout the nineteenth century there had seemed to be reasonable hope for establishing the foundation of something like a 'Christian America.'"[16] At the turn of the century, in the United States, as in France, populism and Christian groups encouraged Jew-baiting and the so-called "Jewish question" was clearly back again. If some Catholics did fight the Protestant Establishment, few of them were free-thinking like so many Jews. Together with liberal religious Jews, they launched the slow process of secularization to question the predominance of the "Christian America," using as their main tool the Supreme Court, which they considered to be a more efficient means than the law, thus departing from the French process of secularization. This process of secularization through the Supreme Court would finally succeed in the 1960s.

In 1916, Louis Brandeis was appointed to the United States Supreme Court. Later, Felix Frankfurter was so influential in his strategic position at Harvard Law School that he was able to turn Oliver Wendell Holmes, Jr. "into an iconic representative of the American spirit," a "cultural hero... releasing American culture from a Christian bias.... The old Brahmin was about as "American" as it was possible to get, but he had put great distance between himself and exactly those parts of Protestant culture most oppressive to Jews."[17] In 1939, Frankfurter was appointed to the Supreme Court after

and Community in Modern France (New York: Hill and Wang, 2000), Ch. 10 (discussing the Jewish dimension of this process); Sébastien Fath, "Juifs et Protestants face à la loi de 1905 sur la separation des églises et de l'etat" (2001) 9 *Les Cahiers du Judaïsme* 104; Jean Laloum, "La Séparation au Regard de la Presse Israélite," in Philippe Boutry and André Encrevé (eds), *Vers la liberté religieuse: la séparation des eglises et de l'etat* (Bordeaux: Bière, 2006); Philippe Landau, "L'Organisation Religieuse du Judaïsme Après 1905: Continuation ou Transformation," in Boutry and Encrevé (eds), *Vers la liberté religieuse.*

14 David J. Brewer, *The United States: A Christian Nation* (Philadelphia: J.C. Winston, 1905), 40.

15 Naomi W. Cohen, *Jews in Christian America: The Pursuit of Religious Equality* (New York: Oxford University Press, 1992), Ch. 4.

16 George M. Marsden, *Fundamentalism and American Culture* (2nd edn, New York: Oxford University Press, 2006), 11, 124; also see Denis Lacorne, *De la religion en amerique: essai d'histoire politique* (Paris: Gallimard, 2008), Ch. 3.

17 David A. Hollinger, "Jewish Intellectuals and the De-Christianization of American Public Culture in the Twentieth Century," in Harry S. Stout and D.G. Hart (eds), *New Directions in American Religious History* (New York: Oxford University Press, 1997), 470.

the death of Justice Benjamin Nathan Cardozo in July 1938, filling the so-called Jewish seat. In 1940, he authored the opinion in the *Gobitis* case,[18] a turning point for the Court, in which the Court held that the Constitution required the states, as much as Congress, to respect the freedom of religion. This was a painful moment for Frankfurter because, as a Jew, his opinion required students to be loyal, as he was, to the state; thus their compulsory obligation to salute the flag, a ritual of patriotism in a time of national threat. Three years later, in the *Barnette* case,[19] the Court went the other way, holding that there was no reason for the state to coerce anyone against his or her beliefs. In this decision, the Court was "faithful to the ideal of secular instruction." This was, for Noah Feldman, "the first time in [its] history that it said anything about the 'secular' character of instruction in public schools...."[20] Frankfurter's argument was rejected. In a surprising and exceptional way, he wrote in his dissent that "[o]ne who belongs to the most vilified and persecuted minority in history is not likely to be insensible to the freedoms guaranteed by our Constitution.... [A]s judges we are neither Jew nor Gentile, neither Catholic nor agnostic. We owe equal attachment to the Constitution and are equally bound by our judicial obligations whether we derive our citizenship from the earliest or the latest immigrants to these shores."[21] One can say that Frankfurter "foresaw the danger of a constitutional approach that would treat members of various religious denominations differently rather than the same. This was the lesson that he, as a Jew living in the era of Nazi persecution, believed he could understand more clearly than the other members of the Court.... Government must pay no mind to religious difference if loyalty was to be universal."[22] Frankfurter was strongly in favor of the naked public realm, a rigorous vision of patriotism requiring some kind of secularism. As a liberal Jew, he did not want any religion to be visible; citizens as such had to be loyal to the nation whatever their religion. It was an American Jewish dream close to the French Jewish dream, obvious among the republican "Jews of the State."

The rest of the story is well-known. It was only after World War II that American Jews could involve themselves openly in the process of separation of church and state, acting as Jews in a way that Frankfurter would have probably rejected. They still wanted a secular public square excluding any religious symbols, but their open strategy was to act in the name of Jewish institutions in an historical framework shaped by a new Great Awakening, a strong revival of the fundamentalist movement.[23] Also on the front lines of the struggle were other organizations like the ACLU, moving toward an "absolutist"

[18] *Minersville Sch Dist v. Gobitis* 310 U.S. 586 (1940).

[19] *W. Va. State Bd of Educ. v. Bamette* 319 U.S. 624 (1943).

[20] Noah Feldman, *Divided By God: America's Church-State Problem—and What We Should Do About it* (New York: Farrar, Straus and Giroux, 2005), 157.

[21] *Barnette* 319 U.S. at 646–7 (Frankfurter, J., dissenting).

[22] Feldman, *Divided By God* 161–2; also see Leonard Baker, *Brandeis and Frankfurter: A Dual Biography* (1984), Chs 20–1. Brandeis argued similarly that:

> This country demands that its sons and daughters whatever their race—however intense or diverse their religious connections—be politically merely American citizens. Habits of living, of thought which tend to keep alive difference of origin or to classify men according to their religious beliefs are inconsistent with the American idea of brotherhood and are disloyal.

Arthur A. Goren, *The Politics and Public Culture of American Jews* (Bloomington: Indiana University Press, 1999), 27 (quoting Justice Brandeis); also see Robert Burt, *Two Jewish Justices: Outcasts in the Promised Land* (Berkeley: University of California Press, 1988).

[23] Joel A. Carpenter, *Revive Us Again: The Reawakening of American Fundamentalism* (New York: Oxford University Press, 1997).

position on the issue of church and state separation.[24] In 1947, the ACLU supported the crucial *Everson* decision,[25] which concerned a New Jersey law that allowed the use of public funds for busing parochial school children.[26] The Court sustained the New Jersey law, though Justice Black stated in the opinion that "[t]he First Amendment has erected a wall between church and state. That wall must be kept high and impregnable. We would not approve the slightest breach."[27] Jews were crucial actors in this struggle for an absolutist interpretation of the wall of separation. The American Jewish Congress led the cause, with the American Jewish Committee[28] and the Anti-Defamation League often joining. Leo Pfeffer started working with the American Jewish Congress in 1945 and became a key actor in the secularization process. According to Pfeffer, he wrote numerous briefs for the Supreme Court and was indirectly involved in a large number of others. He was willing to file an amicus brief in the *Everson* case, but was prevented for "political reasons." Things changed with the 1948 case of *McCollum v. Board of Education*,[29] in which the Supreme Court invalidated the "released time" program as a violation of the Establishment Clause: Pfeffer filed an amicus brief for the case, and Frankfurter, still on the Supreme Court, wrote an opinion that used Jefferson's metaphor of a "wall of separation" between church and state.[30]

Then came other important cases in the secularization of the public realm, each involving Pfeffer and many Jewish and non-Jewish organizations. The most famous case was *Engel v. Vitale*,[31] decided in 1962, prohibiting all prayer, even voluntary prayer, within public schools. The Lubavitcher Rebbe, Rabbi Schneerson, was more or less alone among Jews in strongly disapproving of this decision on the grounds of "Halacha and common sense." Thus, through his actions before the Court, Leo Pfeffer can be seen as the "apostle of strict Separationism." But one can also see that, even though he had retired, Frankfurter's interpretations shaped this crucial decision. The next big case in this line was *School District of Abington Township, Pennsylvania v. Schempp*,[32] challenging the practice of Bible reading at the beginning of the school day, a decision "that would make legal secularism the law of the land."[33] Then, in 1989, came *County of Allegheny*, where the Court held that the display of a creche in a public space in Pittsburgh endorsed Christianity and was thus unconstitutional, but the Court allowed the presence of a Christmas tree, a Chanukah menorah, and a sign saluting liberty placed outside the

[24] Samuel Walker, *In Defense of American Liberties: A History of the ACLU* (New York: Oxford University Press, 1990), Ch. 10.

[25] *Everson v. Bd of Educ. of Ewing Twp.* 330 U.S. 1 (1947).

[26] *Everson* 330 U.S. 3.

[27] *Everson* 330 U.S. 18.

[28] See Marianne Rachel Sanua, *Let Us Prove Strong: The American Jewish Committee, 1945–2006* (Waltham, Mass.: Brandeis University Press, 2007).

[29] 333 U.S. 203 (1948).

[30] *McCollum* 33 U.S. 231; also see Leo Pfeffer, "An Autobiographical Sketch," in James E. Wood, Jr. (ed.), *Religion and the State: Essays in Honor of Leo Pfeffer* (Waco, Tex.: Baylor University Press, 1985), 493–9. Pfeffer gives a superb presentation of his work in his famous book, *Church, State and Freedom* (Boston: Beacon Press, 1953); also see Eric Pace, "Leo Pfeffer, 83, Lawyer on Staff of the American Jewish Congress," *N.Y. Times* (7 June 1993), D8. For more on Frankfurter and the *Everson, McCollum* and *Zorach* cases, see Clyde Edward Jacobs, *Justice Frankfurter and Civil Liberties* (Berkeley: University of California Press, 1961), 43–51.

[31] 370 U.S. 421 (1962).

[32] 374 U.S. 203 (1963).

[33] Feldman, *Divided By God* 180. The story of those decisions has been given several times. See e.g. Elisabeth Zoller and Daniel O. Conkle, *La conception Américaine de la laïcité* (Paris: Dalloz, 2005); Gregg Ivers, *To Build a Wall: American Jews and the Separation of Church and State* (Charlottesville: University Press of Virginia, 1995); Frank J. Sorauf, *The Wall of Separation: The Constitutional Politics of Church and State* (Princeton, NJ: Princeton University Press, 1976); Jay D. Wexler, "Preparing for the Clothed Public Square: Teaching about Religion, Civic Education, and the Constitution" (2002) 43 *William and Mary Law Review* 1159, 1172–91 (providing a presentation of the evolution since *Schempp*).

City County building because "both Christmas and Chanukah are part of the same winter-holiday season, which has attained a secular status in our society."[34] Since then, the decisions of the Court have been quite confusing, but "one thing is clear: only if the display secularizes the holiday does it have a chance of passing muster."[35]

Another thing is also obvious: the increasing anti-Semitic anger of some Christians. Thus, for instance, this editorial published in *America,* the national Jesuit weekly, entitled "To Our Jewish Friends":

This fall the Supreme Court will rule on a number of cases relative to religious practices in the schools. If, as they are now bending every effort to do, Leo Pfeffer and his fellows campaigners succeed in winning Supreme Court decisions that strike down the Lord's Prayer and Bible reading in school classrooms, there will be once again—as there was at the time of the *Engel* decision, only more so—an intensely unfavorable public reaction. When and if such decisions are handed down, then unless it has been made clear that Dr. Pfeffer and the American Jewish Congress do not speak for the whole of American Jewry, Jews in general will be unfairly blamed for what in fact will have been accomplished by a mere handful of militants, allied with an assortment of humanist groups, ethical culturists, Unitarians, secularists and atheists.[36]

Today, secularism is no longer the main problem. Religious pluralism[37] is becoming more important, shifting the United States from a homogeneous "Christian America." As a result, the question of Church and state separation has become less explosive. The public square is less naked, neutrality is less compatible with the equal presence of religions in the public realm, and a growing number of Jewish thinkers, following Will Herberg and Milton Himmelfarb, are openly speaking against separatism. Thus, menorahs are now seen within the public square, even if the large majority of American Jews still favor a more conventional wall of separation as protection, a neutral public space in which Judaism is limited to the private sphere. Quarrels still exist among American Jews. As an example, consider this statement:

The Jewish festival of lights ended on Monday. But before it even started, on December 12, the Tennessee chapter of the American Civil Liberties Union sent a letter to Governor Phil Bredesen urging him to remove a Hanukkah menorah from the state capitol in Nashville. The menorah display is part of an annual lighting ceremony sponsored by a Jewish organization responsible for 1,500 similar lightings worldwide.

The letter, written by the Tennessee ACLU's executive director, Hedy Weinberg, stated that "the Center for Jewish Awareness" request to place a menorah on state property and hold a candle- lighting ceremony is clearly religious. In that context, the display would violate the Constitution....

[T]here's no reason to be afraid of the word "Christmas" and its traditional accoutrements. The efforts of groups like the ACLU serve only to antagonize the vast majority of Americans—with no discernible benefits.

On the other hand, the Christmas warriors convinced of a nationwide conspiracy should also take a deep breath....

These, indeed, are the hallmarks of the American tradition of religious tolerance—an openness rooted in religiosity. The formal separation of church and state plays an important, but supporting, role by enabling our rich civil society to simultaneously express its religiosity and welcome people of all faiths—and no faith at all....

[34] *County of Allegheny v. ACLU* 492 U.S. 573 (1989), 616.

[35] Goldberg, *Bleached Faith* 76.

[36] See Pfeffer, "An Autobiographical Sketch" 515. There is often hostility and the threat of violence against plaintiffs in cases like *Schempp, McCollum* and *Zorach*. Pfeffer, *Church, State and Freedom* 185.

[37] James Davison Hunter and David Franz, "Religious Pluralism and Civil Society," in Stephen R. Prothero (ed.), *A Nation of Religions: The Politics of Pluralism in Multireligious America* (Chapel Hill: University of North Carolina Press, 2006).

Indeed, the worldwide Jewish community will continue to feel dangerously squeezed as leftist and extreme secularist groups tighten their grip on liberalism. . . .[38]

As a result, today, as at the turn of the previous century and in the 1960's, one can hear some anti-Semitic Christian voices against menorahs, seen as an intolerable symbol in a pluralist but still deeply Christian America. This is an example of the many anti-Semitic statements:

JEWS TELL US that separation of Church & State is a fundamental Constitutional decree. But they are lying. . . .

JEWS MADE UP THE LIE OF SEPARATION OF CHURCH & STATE

ALL OF THE ORIGINAL AMERICAN COLONIAL CHARTERS gave reference to the Christian religion as the raison d'etre of the settlements' purposes. . . .

HOW CAN WE STOP THE JEWS FROM JEWIFYING AMERICA?

Here are 3 options: 1) Whenever you see a Chanukah Menorah in a public area, demand that a Nativity Scene be put up next to it.

2) Start putting up Crosses on private properties, both residences and businesses, in order to show the Jews that America is a Christian nation-not a Jewish one.
3) Demand that Jews like Attorney General Michael Mukasey keep his Anti-Christ rabbi friends off of the White House Lawn & out of the Oval Office![39]

In France also, a more "open" *laïcité* has arisen,[40] with the state helping religions and funding an increasing number of religious schools, aiming even to ignore the law of 1905 so as to legally help Muslims organize themselves, now allowing diverse religions to be openly seen in the public realm. Today, maybe 20 to 25 percent of the Jewish children in France are in Jewish schools, a new Lubavitch high school has been opened in Paris, and yeshivot and visibly kosher shops are spreading. Orthodox Jews and lubavitches are now following Rabbi Schneeshon's values and displaying large numbers of menorahs. In Paris, one can walk down the Champs Elysées, the Grands Boulevards, or Place de la Sorbonne and see impressive kindled menorahs. The same occurs in other main cities. Local authorities must have accepted those displays, or else they would have brought actions against these displays in court. But the Conseil d'Etat has not handled any cases on these situations. Like in Boston, Baltimore, and Washington, *eruv* marked the streets of Strasbourg and some other French cities. The only Conseil d'Etat decision on Jewish matters was in 1995, when this highest institution did not allow a student to miss his examinations that took place on Shabbat, arguing that this competition implied the actual presence of students.[41] In general, the Conseil d'Etat has not forbidden the

[38] Michael Rosen, "And Now, the War on Hanukkah," *National Review* (3 Jan. 2006). Rosen is an attorney in San Diego and the head of the Republican Jewish Coalition's San Diego chapter.

[39] Nathanael Kapner, "Separation of Church and State is a Jewish Lie," *Real Jew News* (10 Feb. 2008). In the recent Marcus Brown case at the East Brunswick High School in New Jersey, the coach bowed his head and kneeled before a game as a member of the team led a prayer. The school board ordered him to stop in vain. The American Jewish Congress and the Jewish Social Policy Action Network won in the Court of Appeals in 2008. The case was "closely watched not only by those interested in the law regarding separation of church and state, but also by members of the local community. Virulent anti-Semitism was directed at Jewish members of the cheerleading squad by members of the community who believed that they had prompted the school board to act" against the coach. "High School Can Prevent the Football Coach from Continuing to Join with His Team in Organized Group Prayer," *Jewish Social Policy Action Network* (16 April 2008).

[40] Jean Baubérot, *L'intégrisme républicain contre la laïcité* (La Tour-d'Aigues (Vaucluse): Ed. de l'Aube, 2006).

[41] Y. Aguila, "Koen et Consistoire Central des Israélites de France," *Revue Française de droit administratif* (May–June 1995).

wearing of religious symbols in public schools,[42] but, in November 1989, it prevented students from wearing religious symbols that were openly "ostentatious" (*ostentatoire)* and "proselitic." With the distinctions between permissible and impermissible religious symbols being unclear, leading to numerous local incidents, in 2003 the Commissioner Bernard Stasi wrote a report and a law was passed in March 2004 forbidding the wearing of those signs that are openly ("*ostensiblement*") meaningful, which meant that headscarves, crosses, and kippas were not allowed in public. One is struck by the fact that, as with the secular process of the previous turn of the century, some Jews were again at the forefront of secularism: philosophers like Alain Finkielkraut and Elisabeth Badinter, and lawyers in the Conseil d'Etat, like Rémy Schwartz, who is in charge of the Commission Stasi, working on new legislation.[43]

In this strong state, Jews still favor secularism, maybe more than American Jews, who see themselves more and more as part of a peculiar religion among others whose symbolic presence in the public square, like the presence of Muslim headscarves, is legitimate. So secularism and separatism, whatever the visions of Felix Frankfurter, Leo Pfeffer, and of the American Jewish Congress, still mean something quite different in American and French societies, shaped by radically different state traditions. And if one considers that, in the context of strong anti-Semitic incidents, Joseph Sitruck, then the Grand Rabbin de France, more or less forbade the wearing of yarmulkes on the streets of Paris and its suburbs, one cannot but recognize that the United States—where Congress, to comply with *Goldman v. Winberger*,[44] passed a law requiring the armed services to allow its members to wear a "neat and conservative" skullcap if it would not interfere with their duties[45]—is still quite far from the French "*laïcité*." So-called globalization is unable to explain these crucial remaining differences.

[42] 1 Comp 1992-11-02, Mme Kherouaa et Mme Kachour et Balo et Mme Kizic, 389.

[43] See Rémy Schwartz, "Entre assimilation et communautarisme: sur le port des signes religieux à l'école" (2004) 16 *Les cahiers du judaïsme* 69 (dialogue between Rémy Schwartz and Pierre Birnbaum); Rémy Schwartz, "La Jurisprudencede la Loi de 1905," in Weil, *Politiques de la laïcité au XXE siècle*.

[44] *Goldman v. Weinberger* 475 U.S. 503 (1986).

[45] See Sarna and Dalin, *Religion and State in the American Jewish Experience* 279. Kent Greenawalt argues that teaching religious values in American public schools is increasing while not talking about specific religions. According to him,

> This completes our analysis of religion and the public schools. Does God belong in those schools? Yes, but only in some respects.... [S]chools can legally make some accommodations in their regular program to satisfy special religious claims of parents.... The schools themselves cannot undertake devotional exercises or teach that religious propositions are true or false.... The most important concerns about religion and public schools involve teaching *about* religion.

Kent Greenawalt, *Does God Belong in Public Schools?* (Princeton, NJ: Princeton University Press, 2005), 186.

8

Sovereignty and Laïcité

Michel Troper

Just as every bachelor is unmarried, every state is sovereign, because sovereignty is precisely the defining characteristic of the state. But the state is not defined by its relationship to religion. Indeed, states have very different religious policies and some claim to have none. Some states seem to be dominated by religion. Others dominate over religion. Still others are secular and separate themselves from religion. Furthermore, these relationships change over time. Some states that have been dominated by religion may become strictly secular or vice versa. Thus, it may seem foolish to try to derive some theory regarding the manner in which some political entity treats religion from the mere fact that that entity is a state.

However, because sovereignty is defined as the power of an authority that has no superior and is superior to all others, this implies that this power has no limits. It may regulate every type of human activity, from war to education, to religion. This does not mean that the sovereign State always effectively regulates all those activities, but simply that it may do so. But while sovereignty always implies the power to regulate religion, this power can be exercised in various manners. Complete separation of state and religion is one of them and domination over religion is another because, in both cases, the organization of a religion or its autonomy is regulated by laws enacted by the sovereign.

This becomes apparent when we consider the two seemingly opposite examples of Egypt and France. Article 1 of the French Constitution of 1958 reads: "France shall be an indivisible, secular, democratic and social Republic." On the other hand, Article 2 of Egypt's Constitution of 1971, as amended in 1980, proclaimed that "Islam is the Religion of the State. Arabic is its official language, and the principal source of legislation is Islamic Jurisprudence (Sharia)."

Yet, in both cases we find that the state, instead of subordinating its laws to Islamic Jurisprudence, as could be expected in Egypt, or refraining from interfering with religious practices, as could be expected in France, can indeed regulate religious practices, sometimes in very similar ways. One striking example is the prohibition of the Islamic veil in public schools in both countries.

Let us consider first the case of Egypt under its 1791 Constitution. One possible interpretation of Article 2 could have been that legislation which runs counter to sharia is unconstitutional. However, the Supreme Constitutional Court of Egypt instead developed a two-stage argument.[1]

[1] I rely on Nathalie Bernard-Maugiron and Baudouin Dupret, "Les principes de la sharia sont la source principale de la législation: La Haute Cour constitutionnelle et la référence à la Loi islamique" in Nathalie Bernard-Maugiron and Baudouin Dupret (eds), *Le prince et son juge: droit et politique dans l'Egypte contemporaine* (*Centre d'études et de documentation économiques, juridiques et sociales (CEDEJ)*,

First, it refused to review legislation prior to 1980 because Article 2 was not retroactive. This implies that sharia was only binding because of Article 2, that it derived its force not from the Koran but from the Constitution, i.e. from the will of the constituent power. It also implied that it was part of the Constitution and therefore that sharia would be interpreted not by religious authorities but by the court.

Second, in 1993, the Court considered a law adopted after 1980, as it could not avoid reviewing this law on the basis of its conformity to the sharia. The Court decided, following its own interpretation of Article 2, that the legislative power was only prohibited to go against principles whose value are absolute, because such principles are not subject to interpretation and cannot change over time. On the other hand, there are other principles that are relative and change with time and place. Following that distinction made in this case, the court has considered in all the cases it examined since that the principles of the sharia in question were only relative principles, giving very liberal interpretations of these principles. One example is particularly striking: in 1994 a decision by the Minister of Education limiting the wearing of the Islamic veil in schools was not considered unconstitutional. It is a well-known fact that a similar prohibition was enacted in France ten years later.[2]

After the revolution of 2011, Egypt adopted a new constitution in 2012, with the purpose of giving more influence to religious authorities. The wording of Article 2 remains the same, but a new Article 4 has been inserted stating that "the noble Azhar is an independent Islamic institution of higher learning. It handles all its affairs without outside interference. It leads the call into Islam and assumes responsibility for religious studies and the Arabic language in Egypt and the world. The Azhar's Body of Senior Scholars is to be consulted in matters pertaining to Islamic law (sharia)." Obviously, the writers of the new constitution wanted to prevent the court from interpreting Islamic law. However, Article 4 does not define what constitutes a case for stating or interpreting Islamic law and even if the constitutional court consults the Azhar's Body of Senior Scholars it will not be bound by the opinion of the Senior Scholars.

Moreover, the Preamble starts with a reference to the sovereignty of the people, not of God ("The People is the source of all powers. It generates the powers; they derive their legality from the People and are subject to its will"). This implies that sharia may be the main source of legislation, but the reason is not to be found in the Koran, but in the constitution as an expression of the will of the people. The constitutional court could therefore use the same type of argumentation as under the previous constitution. Whether they will actually be able to do this depends only on political factors.

But, in any case, and even if the constitution had made the opinion of the Body of Senior Scholars binding, the relation between state and religion would be the same, because that Body would have been empowered by the constitution only and would thus have been a state authority.

Thus, in two very different countries, Egypt ruled by the sharia, and France governed by the principles of freedom of religion and religious neutrality of the state, we find the possibility of the state prohibiting the same type of religious behavior.

Egypte/Monde arabe no. 2, 1999), 107; Nathalie Bernard-Maugiron, *Le Politique à l'épreuve du judiciaire. La justice constitutionnelle en Egypte* (Brussels: Emile Bruylant, 2004).

[2] "Loi n° 2004-228 du 15 mars 2004 encadrant, en application du principe de laïcité, le port de signes ou de tenues manifestant une appartenance religieuse dans les écoles, collèges et lycées publics" ["Law no. 2004-228 of 15 March 2004, concerning, through the application of the principle of laïcité, the wearing of symbols or clothing demonstrating religious affiliation in state primary and secondary schools"] (2004) 65 *Journal Officiel* 5190.

The reason for this is that when the state imposes a religious rule, it does so by means of its own law and thus immediately translates the religious rule into a secular one that will be interpreted and applied as such. Being sovereign, the state necessarily rules every field or, in Hans Kelsen's words, "Just as everything King Midas touched turned into gold, everything to which the law refers becomes law."[3] Thus, the state always holds power over religion, but we should keep in mind that what we are talking about is not real political or social influence, but merely legal power. Even if a particular state decides not to exercise an influence on religion, it always has the power to exercise it.

The case of the French principle of "*laïcité*," apparently the opposite of Article 2 of the Egyptian Constitution, illustrates the same idea. *Laïcité* cannot be completely defined by the usual idea of an absence of influence of religion on the state, or, as it is sometimes said, by a separation between state and religion. It can be characterized as an attitude of the state toward religion, decided unilaterally by the state. Indeed, most authors, when defining *laïcité* use other characters, such as freedom of religion, tolerance or neutrality. Thus, they characterize not a mutual attitude or the relationship of religion toward the state, but only that of the state toward religion, because even the decision not to interfere with religious matters is a sovereign decision.

There are other reasons not to be satisfied with the usual characterization of the relationship between the state and religion as an influence of the state over religion, an influence of religion over the state or an absence of mutual influence.

The first reason is the impossibility of giving a good account of a legal system like the French one by merely mentioning *laïcité* and saying that it means absence of influence of religion on the state, of intervention of the state in religious affairs, tolerance or freedom of religion. French law includes the two principles of sovereignty and *laïcité*. To understand their meaning in the law, one must start not from political theory, but from all the rules that are considered consequences of these principles and those that are viewed by the courts as compatible with separation of Church and state or with *laïcité*. Even a quick look at French law will show that a very strong influence of the state on religions is considered compatible with *laïcité*. For instance, subsidies to religious schools, prohibiting the wearing of religious signs, paying salaries to ministers of three religions in parts of the country, the presence in the cabinet of a Minister of the Interior who also holds the title of "minister of religions," and ownership by the state of religious buildings are all considered compatible with *laïcité*, thus demonstrating that this principle is not sufficiently characterized by an absence of influence of religion on the state and may imply at least some interference by the state over religion.

The second reason is the fact that, whereas we understand easily what an absence of influence of religion on the state can be, we need a more precise definition of what constitutes an influence or an absence of Assemblée nationale influence of the state on religion. Tolerance and neutrality may not be sufficient, because these principles can be equally satisfied, for instance, by a state that subsidizes all religions and by a state that subsidizes none.

It would not even suffice to conclude from the two examples from Egypt and France that because of sovereignty every relation between state and religion is characterized by the domination of state over religion. True, every sovereign state necessarily makes laws regarding religion, but on one hand, there is nothing special with religion in this respect, because in every other field every single policy is also expressed by laws enacted by the sovereign, just as the opposite policy is and, on the other hand, the connection here is

[3] Hans Kelsen, *General Theory of Law and State* (orig. 1945, Union, NJ: Lawbook Exchange, 1999), 160.

between the sovereign state and laws regarding religion, not with a specific religious policy of the state. In order to show a specific relationship, such that not any religious policy, but some particular policy is connected to sovereignty, we must consider not sovereignty itself but conceptions of sovereignty. While we use a notion of sovereignty that is the same for every state, we can see that, in different political and legal systems, there are different conceptions of sovereignty. And, while any sovereign power will necessarily have a religious policy, just as it has a military or an economic policy, and while there is no connection between sovereignty itself and one specific policy, it is conceivable that some specific conception of sovereignty is linked to some type of policy.

I will consider here the following hypothesis: the French conception of sovereignty has been closely related to French religious policies, since the beginning of the seventeenth century to the present day and *laïcité*, far from representing a break from the religious policy of the ancient monarchy can best be understood as the modern expression of the French conception of sovereignty.

Two further remarks are in order: First, I will consider sovereignty and *laïcité* from a purely descriptive point of view, without making any attempt to look for the way in which they should best be understood, merely trying to tell how these concepts are being used in actual discourse. Second, the discourse that I will describe is not the language of philosophy or political theory, but only the legal discourse, the language of positive law, that of statutes, of court opinions or of legal scholars dealing with positive law.

The link between a conception of sovereignty and a general attitude of the state toward religion can be perceived in the French case. It has two aspects. On one hand, the power of the state over religion in France is not just a consequence of a preexisting doctrine of sovereignty, but it is also constitutive of sovereignty, in the sense that the doctrine of the sovereign state has been conceived from the beginning as an instrument of religious policy. On the other hand, a particular religious policy, *laïcité*, is still considered in the discourse of French courts as a core element of the very definition of sovereignty. I will therefore analyze first the role played by the need to confront religious issues in the process of constructing the French conception of sovereignty, then the role of *laïcité* in the defense of sovereignty by the French courts.

I. The Role of the State's Power over Religion in the Construction of Sovereignty

In the continental tradition, sovereignty has several meanings. Raymond Carré de Malberg draws a distinction between three meanings of the word sovereignty in the French language or three concepts of sovereignty:

> In the original sense, the word "sovereignty" refers to the supreme character of the State's power. In a second sense, it refers to the whole range of the powers included in the State's authority and it is therefore synonymous with that authority. Thirdly, it is used to characterize the position occupied within the State by the highest organ of the State's authority and in that sense, sovereignty is the same thing as the power of that organ.[4]

Carré de Malberg stresses that the French language is poor and contains only one word for the three concepts of sovereignty and the same could be said of English. However, the German language has three words, one for each of these senses. *Souveranität* corresponds

[4] Raymond Carré de Malberg, *Contribution à la théorie générale de l'État*, vol. I (orig. 1920, Paris: Sirey, 1962), 79.

to sovereignty in the first sense, i.e. the supreme character of the state on the international as well as on the domestic level. *Staatsgewalt* is the power of the state in the second sense. *Herrschaft* is the power of domination *Souveranität* by an organ.

All three concepts are important for the analysis of the relationship between the state and religion: *Souveranität* because it means that the state is independent from any other power, either an external power, such as the Emperor or the Pope, or a domestic power such as a religious organization; *Herrschaft* because the highest authority in the state is not appointed by a religious authority and cannot be dismissed by one. However, I will mainly concentrate here on the third concept, *Staatsgewalt*, that is the totality of the powers possessed by the state, even though it does not exercise them all.

If one looks at the construction of the doctrine of sovereignty in France, one sees what it owes to the necessity of justifying the exercise of power over religion. It is a well-known fact that the necessity of a doctrine of sovereignty arose from the horrors of the religious wars of the sixteenth century. As a result of these conflicts, rulers felt that there must be a sovereign who would be stronger than any of the religious factions, and who would be able to use force in order to keep peace and security. It was also quite obvious that sovereignty would need to be justified by religious doctrine: thus the divine right of kings.

On the other hand, a doctrine of the divine right of kings could become dangerous for the kings, because the Church could claim a monopoly to interpret divine law and thus gain supremacy over kings, who would thereby be deprived of much of their power. The situation of kings would be particularly difficult in case of a conflict between religious and secular laws. This is precisely what happened with King Henry IV of France, who was the heir to the throne according to salic law,[5] but who had been excommunicated by the Catholic Church. In order to let salic law prevail over canonic law, the best way was to claim that salic law itself was divine and that sovereignty resided entirely in the king.[6] In order to claim autonomous power over political affairs, kings needed to subordinate religion by affirming a divine right of kings, which then allowed them to act independently of the Church's views.

If the king's power did not depend on the Catholic Church, it was therefore unlimited, *absolutus*, and could be exercised over any possible subject matter. As such, sovereignty could be defined as an absolute and supreme power, *summa potestas*, which could not be made subservient to any other power, not even that of the Church. Sovereignty therefore also would not depend upon the personal virtue of the king, but rather upon the essence of the monarchy.

In theory, only purely spiritual matters escaped the king's power, although he retained in his jurisdiction decisions regarding what was spiritual and what was temporal.[7] In practice, many questions that might be deemed spiritual were considered temporal during that period. For instance, in 1753 one commentator wrote that it is for the Church to decide whether one should pray silently or aloud, but the state may have an interest in deciding when one should pray in public or privately, and, if prayer is done in public, when it should be conducted by a priest or a body of men, and what body. The king's power thus functionally extended over religious matters. As historian Marcel Gauchet writes, "absolutism is the demand that collective authority be placed

[5] Salic law was a rule that prohibited women from ascending to the throne.

[6] Marie-France Renoux-Zagame, "Du juge pretre au roi-idole: Droit divin et constitution de l'Etat dans la pensée juridique française à l'aube des Temps Modernes," in Jean-Louis Thireau (ed.), *Le droit entre laïcisation et néo-sacralisation* (Paris: Presses universitaires de France, 1997), 143.

[7] See generally Dominique Le Tourneau, *L'Eglise et l'Etat en France* (Paris: Presses universitaires de France, 2000).

in a pre-eminent position such that that authority could legitimately subordinate the sacred to itself."[8]

This concept, called "gallicanism," was the basis for the king's attitude toward religion: he summoned councils, appointed bishops, decided on the age of marriage, etc.[9] In a 1631 treaty of rights and freedoms of the Gallican Church, scholars Pierre and Jacques Dupuy enunciate several principles: (1) that the temporal power is distinct from the spiritual power and is independent of it; (2) the Pope cannot legislate for the French Church except with the consent and confirmation of the King; (3) the King can exercise surveillance over religious orders (it is by virtue of this principle that in 1764 the dissolution of the Jesuits was announced); and (4) that the King can intervene in doctrinal matters, as he did, for example, in the Jansenist affair.[10]

One important aspect, that would be remembered in the future, was that the properties of the Church really belonged to the king. As Louis XIV said, "The kings are absolute lords and have the full and free disposition of every single property, to use as their wise economies, that is according to the needs of their State."[11]

This doctrine is not specific to the French conception of sovereignty. One finds it also in Hobbes, when he writes that in order to decide whether a miracle has happened "we are not every one to make our own private reason or conscience, but the public reason, that is the reason of God's supreme lieutenant, judge; and indeed we have made him judge already, if we have given him a sovereign power to do all that is necessary for our peace and defence,"[12] or Pufendorf, who places among the "*partes potentiales*" of sovereignty "the right to decide what doctrines ought to be taught within the State."[13] The argument is double: if sovereignty is the absolute power to decide on everything, then the power to decide over religious matters is obviously part of it; on the other hand it is perfectly justified because it is the only way to keep peace or public order. Indeed, the argument derived from the notion of public order will later be reinforced because public order refers not merely to security or the absence of material disorder, but also to all the conditions of life in a well ordered society. It can be found in an official report commissioned in 2006 by the French government [14] and again in the decision by the Constitutional Council on the burqa.[15] Citizenship is not natural but needs to be

[8] Marcel Gauchet, *La religion dans la démocratie* (Paris: Gallimard, 1998).

[9] See generally Le Tourneau, *L'Eglise et l'Etat en France.*

[10] See generally Dale Van Kley, *The Religious Origins of the French Revolution: From Calvin to the Civil Constitution, 1560–1791* (New Haven, CT: Yale University Press, 1996).

[11] "Les rois sont seigneurs absolus et ont naturellement la disposition pleine et libre de tous les biens, tant des séculiers que des ecclésiastiques, pour en user comme sages économies, c'est-à-dire selon les besoins de leur État." Cited by Marcel Marion, *Dictionnaire des institutions de la France aux xviie et xviiie siècles* (Paris: A. Picard, 1923), 491.

[12] *Leviathan*, Ch. XXXVII.

[13] Samuel von Pufendorf, *Les devoirs de l'homme et du citoyen, tels qu'ils lui sont prescrits par la loi naturelle* (Jean Barbeyrac trans., Amsterdam: Schelte, 1707), 288–9 (author's translation).

[14] 'Qu'il puisse être question des relations entre les cultes et les pouvoirs publics dans un régime de séparation des Églises et de l'État ne saurait surprendre. La République, en effet, ne peut ignorer le fait religieux qui, comme fait social, intéresse forcément les responsables de l'ordre public. L'histoire même de la laïcité en France contredit l'idée d'une étanchéité absolue entre les deux spheres' in Jean-Pierre Machelon, *Les relations des cultes avec les pouvoirs publics: rapport au ministre d'État, ministre de l'Intérieur et de l'aménagement du territoire: travaux de la Commission de réflexion juridique* (Paris: Documentation française, 2006).

[15] Decision no. 2010-613 DC of 7 October 2010, "Loi interdisant la dissimulation du visage dans l'espace public": the Council upheld the law because Parliament rightly considered that the practices of covering one's face "fail to comply with the minimum requirements of life in society" and that "women who conceal their face voluntarily or otherwise are placed in a situation of exclusion and inferiority," whereas equality between men and women is not only a distinct constitutional principle but also an

constructed by the state itself and religion, not necessarily an organized religion but the teaching of common values, is one of the tools for this construction.

Although later regimes in France pursued very different policies, from the creation of a concordat to a system of the so-called separation between the state and the Church, the power of the state to organize and police religion has been exercised with different intensities but has never been denied.

For one thing, it was widely held from the time of the French Revolution that there can be no citizenship without shared values, and that religion played an important role in the shaping of these values. Jean-Jacques Rousseau had eloquently developed this idea, arguing that there is a "purely civil profession of faith of which the Sovereign should fix the articles, not exactly as religious dogmas, but as social sentiments without which a man cannot be a good citizen or a faithful subject."[16] In other words, although the state should not interfere with the private consciences of citizens, it cannot remain completely indifferent to the existence of religious feelings and religious organizations. In 1790, the first attempt was made in France to follow this model, by organizing religion as a public service, structured on the model of other public administrations. Under this structure, there would be a bishop in every department, and priests would be elected by parishioners. This legislation was one of the factors of a long civil war between those who accepted and those who refused this new status and who sided with the monarchists.

Napoleon ended the civil war and abolished some aspects of that legislation that were most repugnant to Catholics, but he negotiated with the Holy See a concordat that would remain in force for a century and was based on similar ideas.[17] According to the concordat, priests would be civil servants, the State would pay their salaries, and the Pope would ordain bishops only after the government had appointed them. Buildings, which had been confiscated during the Revolution, were not returned to the Church and remained property of the state or of local authorities, although the Church could use them. Religion was part of the curriculum of public schools.

Napoleon also undertook to organize other religions, the Protestant and the Jews, on the same model. It was impossible to enter into a negotiation with Protestant and Jewish organizations similar to that which had been conducted with the Vatican, due to the lack of a hierarchical structure, so Napoleon organized these two religions into institutions called consistories.[18] Protestant pastors and Jewish rabbis then received a salary from the state, which allowed the government to integrate and control them. For instance, it became illegal to undertake a religious marriage without having had first a civil marriage. The various governments that followed Napoleon, the constitutional monarchy, the Second Republic, and the Second Empire, kept this same organization and policy until 1848.

The famous act of 1905 separating churches from the state, although it introduced a dramatic change in the substance of the relationship between state and religion, did not really depart from the idea that it is the state that organizes religion.

essential component of French society. The Constitutional Council follows here the jurisprudence of the Conseil d'État who decided that French naturalization could be denied to a woman who had declared that she would wear the veil in order to comply with her husband's will.

[16] Jean Jacques Rousseau, "Civil Religion," in *The Social Contract or Principles of Political Right* (1762).

[17] See Concordat of 1801, Fr.-Holy See, 15 Jul. 1801, <http://www.concordatwatch.eu> (follow "France"; then follow "Napoleon's concordat and Organic Articles (1801)").

[18] See David Feuerwerker, *L'Emancipation des Juifs en France: De l'Ancien Régime à la fin du Second Empire* (Paris: Albin Michel, 1976).

Not only was the separation a unilateral decision by the state, but the separation was far from complete. Nowhere could it be really complete because the state has to regulate the use of public space, such as streets or city squares, to authorize or prohibit religious activities, to decide whether there can be chaplains in the military, in prisons, public hospitals or public schools. But, in France there were other reasons that constrained and still constrain the state to regulate religion. One was the fact that since the Revolution and Napoleonic legislation, religious buildings, such as churches, temples or synagogues were public property and, to this day, those which are older than 1905 remain public property. The state therefore could not avoid regulating the use of those buildings. Various statutes have thus decided that they are left at the disposal of various religious institutions, but the state and local authorities may—and sometimes must—pay for maintenance. Also the mayor has the power to keep order within the buildings.

Another reason is the persistence of the idea that one of the state's most important missions is public education, not only because it is a public service, but because it is a key factor in the shaping of citizenship. This was an important argument in favor of several laws that regulate private schools, the majority of which are catholic. These schools can enter into contracts with the state, whereby the teachers are paid by the state and some other costs are covered by local authorities, but on the condition that the teachers hold the same degrees as teachers in public schools and that the basic curriculum is the same.

A third factor that constrains the state to intervene in religious affairs is the large number of Muslims in France. According to some, the constraint comes from the need to facilitate their integration in French society and to try to avoid the development of Islamic fundamentalism. Others think that such interventions are required by the principle of equality, because in 1905 there were no Muslims in the country and of course no publicly owned mosques. Thus, while Catholics, Protestants, and Jews enjoy the free use of public buildings, Muslims can only pray in their own private mosques. On the other hand, the state has constantly been an actor in its relationship to religion. For example, Protestant and Jewish religious institutions remain organized to a large extent according to laws enacted by Napoleon or bishops are appointed by the Pope but always with the advice of the French government—and there is a need to enter into a similar relationship with the Muslims. The Minister of the Interior, who is also minister of religions, has made several attempts, although not very successful ones, to organize Islam in France and to find ways, without changing the Act of 1905, to facilitate legally and financially the building of new mosques. What is remarkable is that these attempts have been made by ministers from the left as well as from the right.

A fourth manifestation of the idea that sovereignty allows for state intervention even with a "separation" is the situation in three departments of Alsace-Moselle, where the Act of 1905 could not be applied because at the time they were part of the German Reich, which had kept the system of the concordat. After the end of World War I, when the three departments were returned to France, instead of applying the Act of 1905, a conservative majority of the French Parliament decided that the system of the concordat would remain in force and adopted in 1924 a law to that effect. Thus, in Alsace-Moselle ministers from the three religions still receive salaries from the state.

What must be stressed is that all of these features, public ownership of religious buildings, subsidies to religious schools, attempts to organize Islam, special status of religions in Alsace-Moselle, which might seem to be exceptions to the principle of *laïcité*—and there are other examples—have on the contrary been considered as compatible with it or as an interpretation of that principle.

We have seen that this interpretation is the product of the French conception of sovereignty. But it is more than that: it has an influence on modern developments of the theory of sovereignty, as we can see from the jurisprudence of the Constitutional Council.

II. The Role of Laïcité in Recent Developments of the Notion of Sovereignty

As with all other powers, the power of the state to regulate religion depends on the hierarchical level of the norms that make use of that power. As a matter of fact, although this level has varied over time, it has always been and remains the highest, so that this power is truly supreme.

In the past, during the 3rd and 4th Republics, the most important norms dealing with religion were statutes. Since there was no judicial review of the constitutionality of statutes, Acts of Parliament were supreme, according to the traditional presumption that they are the expression of the general will, a presumption established by Article 6 of the Declaration of the Rights of Man, that could not be challenged.

Some constitutional provisions did deal with religion, like Article 10 of the same Declaration of the Rights of Man, "No one shall be disquieted on account of his opinions, including his religious views, provided their manifestation does not disturb the public order established by law," or Article 1 of the Constitution of 1946, "France is an indivisible, secular (*laïque*), democratic and social Republic," a provision that has been reproduced in Article 1 of the Constitution of 1958. However, since these provisions could not be used as a basis to challenge the validity of statutes, for lack of judicial review, they really could not be said to be superior and they could be contradicted. Therefore, whatever the substance of the statutes and even when they were apparent exceptions to the principle of *laïcité*, there was an absolute presumption that they were constitutional and thus compatible with the principle.

That statutes are the expression of the general will had another very important consequence: the legislative power had a quasi-monopoly on the production of law and in the view of the French Revolution there could be no such thing as judge-made law. The role of the judge was restricted to the application of the law to the case and did not even extend in principle to statutory interpretation. Naturally, the courts could not avoid interpretation altogether and they did produce some case law, but it was accessory and remained under the control of the lawmaker. The quasi-monopoly of Parliament on the production of law helps explain the apparent lack of consistency of a notion like *laïcité*. Courts are under a constraint to justify their rulings and present a coherent doctrine, but a Parliamentary majority does not need to take into account the will expressed by the majority in a past legislature and can therefore, without formally repudiating any basic principles, adopt new laws that seem to contradict them. Yet, since the principles remain, observers must assume that they had been reinterpreted. Thus, *laïcité* does not dictate the substance of laws on religion, but the laws on religion inform on the substance of *laïcité*.

The presumption that Acts of Parliament are constitutional has become relative because of the expansion of Constitutional review during the 5th Republic. Several very important developments have taken place in 1958, 1971, 1974, and 2008 that could possibly have jeopardized either the principle of *laïcité* or the very flexible and accommodating interpretation of that principle. But they have, on the contrary, reinforced that interpretation, with some important consequences on the notion of sovereignty.

The Constitution of 1958 had created a Constitutional Council with the power to review acts of Parliament, but statutes could only be referred to the Council within 15 days after the vote, and only by the President of the Republic, the Prime Minister and the two Presidents of the two Houses. At first, the Council only reviewed their conformity against the numbered Articles of the Constitution. In 1971, however, the Council decided to review statutes also against provisions of the preamble, the Declaration of the Rights of Man and the Citizen, the Preamble of the Constitution of 1946 and to the principles referred to in that preamble. After 1971, the Council was thus able to dramatically expand its power and review statutes regulating religion or freedom of religion not only against the principle of *laïcité*, mentioned in Article 1,[19] but also against all those constitutional norms referred to in the preamble, such as the Declaration of the Rights of Man or the "fundamental principles recognized by the laws of the Republic," which are norms of constitutional value, but found in a small number of highly important laws adopted as acts of Parliament during the republics prior to 1946.[20]

This power was greatly enlarged after the Constitution was amended in 1974 to allow 60 members from the minority in the National Assembly or the Senate to refer a new statute to the Council within 15 days after the vote, so that the number of cases referred to the Council increased considerably.

In 1975, the Constitutional Council gave a new interpretation of Article 55 of the Constitution, with wide consequences.[21] Article 55 reads: "Treaties or agreements duly ratified or approved shall, upon publication, prevail over Acts of Parliament." The Council decided that this did not imply that treaties have constitutional value, nor that a statute that is inconsistent with a treaty is *ipso facto* unconstitutional. Therefore, it was not for the Constitutional Council "to consider the consistency of a statute with the provisions of a treaty." The important consequence of that interpretation was that other courts, which could not review the constitutionality of statutes, were from that time empowered to review their consistency with treaties. They still could not declare that a statute was void, but in case of a conflict with a treaty, even an older treaty, they could let the treaty prevail. Treaties were thus much better protected than the Constitution because, while the constitutionality of an old statute that had never been referred to the Council could not be challenged, any court could—and still can—refuse to apply it if it found that it was inconsistent with a treaty or with law derived from a treaty.

This was the main reason why in 2008, the Constitution was amended to create a new procedure, called "priority issue of constitutionality," to allow parties to a case before a court to challenge the constitutionality of the applicable law and refer it to the Constitutional Council via one of the two supreme courts in the two court systems, the Conseil d'État or the Court of Cassation.

The Council has generally used its power with great self-restraint and deference to the lawmaker and decided that statutes on public funding of religious schools, on the veil or on the burka were not contrary to the principle of *laïcité*. But it has done so by using two different methods, one substantive, and the other formal.

Substantively, because what is included in the principle has never been perfectly clear, the Council was able to uphold most of the statutes under review by simply declaring

[19] Article 1: "France shall be an indivisible, secular, democratic and social Republic. It shall ensure the equality of all citizens before the law, without distinction of origin, race or religion. It shall respect all beliefs."

[20] Véronique Champeil-Desplats, *Les principes fondamentaux reconnus par les lois de la République* (Paris: Économica, 2001).

[21] Decision 74-54 DC, Voluntary Interruption of Pregnancy Act.

that they were not incompatible with it. It was for example debated whether *laïcité* implies a constitutional prohibition to subsidize religious schools or conversely a permission to subsidize them all, provided that they are treated equally. The Constitutional Council found for the latter. With characteristic conciseness, the decision did not discuss the principle of *laïcité* and did not even mention it *expressis verbis*, nor did it refer to the religious character of the majority of private schools but simply decided that the Constitution does not explicitly prohibit the state from funding private schools or subsidizing the training of private school teachers.[22]

Although substantive, this method is based on an implicit assumption regarding the hierarchy of norms: the decision does not make any reference to the law of 1905. True, that law is an Act of Parliament that is not part of the Constitution. However, it would have been possible for the Council to decide that it is one of the fundamental principles of the Republic, which have constitutional value, or at least to interpret the principle of *laïcité* proclaimed by Article 1 of the constitution in the light of that law. Such efforts would not have been decisive because the law of 1905 only prohibits the funding of religions by the state and the Council would still have to face the question of whether funding religious schools falls under funding religions. The reluctance of the Council to follow this path can be explained in several ways. First it would have been forced to discuss the substance of the principle of separation, without any textual support, something that it very rarely does. More importantly, raising the status of the law of 1905 to the constitutional level would have limited Parliament's capacity to amend the law, something which some believe might be necessary in the future to accommodate the Muslim community. Finally, it reflects the Council's, and more generally the French, preoccupation with the hierarchy of norms and its relation to sovereignty.

In the French view, norms are nothing but the expression of a will and the hierarchy of norms mirrors a hierarchy of organs. The hierarchy of norms has to be construed in such a way that sovereignty is preserved, but sovereignty expresses its will in several ways, at different levels and in various forms. The Constitution must remain supreme relative to international law and to statutes, but without contradicting the idea formulated in the Declaration of the Rights of Man, that the law, meaning acts of parliament, is the expression of the will of the sovereign. The principle of *laïcité* played a major role in this delicate construction.

The supremacy of the Constitution could have been jeopardized by new developments in the relation between European law and domestic law. As already mentioned, because of the interpretation given in 1975 by the Constitutional Council to Article 55 of the Constitution, statutes that contradict an international treaty can be challenged before any court. However, treaties did not prevail over constitutional norms, so that constitutional norms remained supreme. It was therefore possible for French courts willing to save a statute from the supremacy of a treaty, either by revising the Constitution or by deciding that a particular statute had recognized a fundamental principle of the Republic and had constitutional value.[23]

This doctrine conflicted with that of the European Court of Justice, which had claimed since 1964 that European law prevails over domestic law, even constitutional law.[24] Moreover, this claim had been formalized in Article 1-6 of the defunct constitutional

[22] "Si la loi prévoit la prise en charge par l'État de dépenses relatives au fonctionnement d'établissements d'enseignement privés et à la formation de leurs maîtres, elle ne contient aucune disposition contraire à la Constitution." Decision no. 77-87 DC of 23 November 1977.

[23] Conseil d'Etat, 3 July1996—Moussa Koné.

[24] Costa c.ENEL, 15 July 1964.

treaty ("The Constitution and law adopted by the institutions of the Union in exercising competences conferred on it shall have primacy over the law of the Member States"). Although the treaty has not been ratified, the substance of Article 1-6 is still considered part of European law, because of the jurisprudence of the court and because it has been reproduced in a declaration annexed to the Treaty of Lisbon.

Therefore, a French court wishing to avoid acknowledging the supremacy of European law must use another argument than the fact that some principle of French law is a constitutional norm. This is where "constitutional identity" comes into play. Without going into details, let me mention that the Constitutional Council started in 2004 to develop a two-stage argumentation:[25]

(1) The source of the obligation to apply European law is to be found not in the treaties but in the Constitution. Therefore European law prevails over the Constitution to the extent that the Constitution prescribes that European Law prevails over itself.

(2) The Constitution could not, without contradicting itself, decide to submit to a European rule that would go against its own express provisions or the principles that shape the constitutional identity of France. Therefore, it has implicitly protected such provisions or principles and European law cannot have primacy over them. Only the French constituent power could derogate those principles.

This doctrine was finally expressed in a 2006 decision: "the transposition of a directive may not run counter to a rule or principle inherent to the constitutional identity of France, except when the constituting power consents thereto."[26] What is striking in the formulation by the Constitutional Council is the extraordinary step taken to preserve the sovereignty of the national state: in case of a conflict between European law and the French Constitution, European law prevails, except when the conflict is between European law and a principle inherent to the constitutional identity of France. On the other hand, these principles do not bind the constituent power, which remains truly sovereign, to the extent that it can always expand or restrict the limits of the power of Parliament to pass statutes.

The expression "constitutional identity" has been taken from the constitutional treaty (Article 1-5) and from the Treaty of Lisbon.[27] It is obviously extremely vague, as was the phrase "express provisions." It is generally assumed that what the Constitutional Council had in mind was precisely *laïcité*, although one could argue that other principles as well could be protected in the same way.

On the other hand, while past interpretations of the principle of *laïcité* and state interventions in the field of religion were protected against international law and even European law, the protection it enjoyed against constitutional review as long as past

[25] Decision no. 2004-496 DC 10 June 2004, "Loi pour la confiance dans l'économie numérique": "Considérant qu'aux termes de l'article 88-1 de la Constitution: 'La République participe aux Communautés européennes et à l'Union européenne, constituées d'Etats qui ont choisi librement, en vertu des traités qui les ont instituées, d'exercer en commun certaines de leurs competences'; qu'ainsi, la transposition en droit interne d'une directive communautaire résulte d'une exigence constitutionnelle."

[26] Decision no. 2006-540 DC DADVSI: "La transposition d'une directive ne saurait aller à l'encontre d'une règle ou d'un principe inhérent à l'identité constitutionnelle de la France, sauf à ce que le constituant y ait consenti."

[27] Treaty on European Union, Art 3a 2: "The Union shall respect the equality of Member States before the Treaties as well as their national identities, inherent in their fundamental structures, political and constitutional, inclusive of regional and local self-government. It shall respect their essential State functions, including ensuring the territorial integrity of the State, maintaining law and order and safeguarding national security. In particular, national security remains the sole responsibility of each Member State."

statutes could not be referred to the Constitutional Council ceased to be effective after the 2008 amendment introducing the priority question of constitutionality. Since 2008, it has become possible to challenge the constitutionality of an ancient statute. In particular, it became possible to challenge the law of 1924 that preserved the status of religions in Alsace-Moselle.

This may explain a declaration in François Hollande's important speech at Le Bourget on 22 January 2012 during the presidential campaign. He announced his intention to write the law of 1905 in the Constitution and thus protect *laïcité*. At first, this was puzzling since the principle of *laïcité* was already written in Article 1 of the Constitution. On the other hand, Catholics were alarmed because the amendment would not merely repeat the principle of *laïcité* but raise the law of 1905 to the constitutional level, which meant that the special status enjoyed by religions in Alsace-Moselle would undoubtedly be unconstitutional. However, Hollande's real intentions became much clearer when a statement was issued a few days later. The proposed amendment now specifically mentioned that the Republic would "respect the separation of the churches and the State, in conformity to the title of the law of 1905" but also "the particular rules applicable in Alsace and Moselle."[28] Thus, it was not *laïcité* that the amendment was meant to save, but the Concordat in Alsace-Moselle.

Nevertheless, once elected president, Hollande had to abandon this idea, because he could not get the support of the 3/5 majority required by Article 89 of the Constitution to adopt an amendment in the Congress of Parliament. However, the special status was preserved by the Constitutional Council in two decisions, by means of two techniques. First the Council decided that the laws preserving the special status had thus recognized a fundamental principle, which had constitutional value but, unlike other fundamental principles, did not prevent Parliament from passing new legislation to change that status.[29] Then, the Council acknowledged that the principle of *laïcité* prohibits the payment of salaries of priests and ministers by the state, but decided that the constituents of 1946 and 1958 when incorporating the principle into the Constitution had not intended to change the laws that had preserved the system of the concordat in Alsace-Moselle.[30]

Thus, in its efforts to reconcile the status of Alsace with the principle of *laïcité*, the Constitutional Council has apparently followed a reasoning based on the hierarchy of norms, but in reality it has modified it in an interesting way. It has followed it by applying the theory that among constitutional norms are some fundamental principles recognized by the laws of the Republic. Therefore, if a law like that of 1924 contradicts the principle of *laïcité*, it can still be compatible with the Constitution because of the fundamental principle. On the other hand, the traditional view of the hierarchy of norms seems to have been preserved by the method of interpretation that the Constitutional Council uses in the second decision: the Council refuses to interpret Article 1 of the Constitution in the light of past statutes, be that of 1905. What is important in the eyes of the Council is not what *laïcité* meant in 1905, but what the constituent power decided. In 1905 they may very well have meant a prohibition to pay for the salaries of religious ministers. In 1946, since the law of 1924 was not repealed, it must be considered compatible with *laïcité*.

[28] "La République assure la liberté de conscience, garantit le libre exercice des cultes et respecter la séparation des Eglises et de l'Etat, conformément au titre de la loi de 1905, sous réserve des règles particulières applicables en Alsace et Moselle."

[29] Decision no. 2011-157 QPC du 05 août 2011, Société SOMODIA [Interdiction du travail le dimanche en Alsace-Moselle].

[30] Decision no. 2012-297 QPC du 21 février 2013 (Association pour la promotion et l'expansion de la laïcité).

However, the Council has been very careful to preserve some discretion for the sovereign at both levels: that of the constituent power and that of the legislative power. In the case of the constitutional identity of France, the Council found that although European law prevails over the Constitution, it does not prevail over some core principles of the Constitution. But although these core principles rank higher than other constitutional norms, they are not super-constitutional because the constituent power could still modify them.

Similarly, even though the permanence of local law in Alsace is a fundamental principle, that principle is constitutional only in the sense that it enables the Council to save the system of the concordat and justify an exception to *laïcité*, but it is nevertheless not binding on the legislative power that can always repeal it.

In order to preserve several conflicting principles of French Constitutional law, sovereignty of the constituent power and the law as expression of the general will, supremacy of the Constitution and flexibility of legislation and reconcile existing policies with the principle of *laïcité*, the Constitutional Council has thus been constrained to change the scope of the principle of *laïcité*, create new categories of norms and reconstruct the principle of sovereignty. In part because of religion, sovereignty of the constitution is thus being redefined relative to European law as the set of core principles that form its identity and relatively to domestic law as the capacity of the constituent power to explicitly or implicitly produce or authorize norms, whose content is valid regardless of its apparent conformity with stated principles. Paying the salaries of priests in Alsace is not considered incompatible with *laïcité* simply because, according to the Constitutional Council, the constituent power has implicitly considered that it is not incompatible, which brings us back to the core of sovereignty, the fact that "*auctoritas non veritas facit jus.*"

9

Egypt's New Constitution: The Islamist Difference

Lama Abu-Odeh

I. Introduction*

While most political forces outside the Islamist camp looked to the rupture caused by the Egyptian revolution of 2011 as an opportunity to restructure the state politically and economically through law, Islamists, who have participated in the events of Tahrir square only obscurely and in the most hesitating manner,[1] had their eyes set on a different rupture of a different time. It was the rupture that had occurred a century-and-a-half before that had brought the European legal transplant to Egypt in the guise of the Code and had consequently marginalized Islamic law as the law of the state cornering it in the limited field of family law. For Islamists, that rupture was nothing short of a calamity, one that had progressively undermined the institutions of Islamic law production and the privileged cultural status of its jurists, the "Ulama."[2] In the words of Rafiq Habib, the assistant to the head of the Muslim Brotherhood's Freedom and Justice Party:

> What happened was a displacement of Islam as an authoritative framework for the benefit of a secular one... The historically displaced Islamic framework however remained the natural alternative to what is currently the case, which was never the option of the masses but was rather coerced upon them from above.[3]

The Egyptian revolution, but also and perhaps more importantly, the impressive electoral victory the Islamists garnered for themselves in its aftermath, was an opportunity to remedy that earlier foundational calamity; to reverse its fortunes so that, as the Islamist camp saw it, the proper history of Egypt based on the unfolding of the authentic identity of its masses could be set in place. Or as the Salafi preacher Mazen Al Sarsawi put it rather gloatingly:

> Why should I compromise when I have won? We have an opportunity now—do we rule by French law or Sharia? Do we choose unfaith? He who chooses to rule by man-made law even though he has the option to rule according to God's law has committed heresy![4]

* This chapter was written as commentary on the Constitution the Islamists passed when Morsi was president of Egypt. Morsi has since been removed from power forcibly by the military and a new civilian government has been formed to amend the Islamist Constitution. What the new Constitution will look like and how much of the (Islamic) identity-based constitutional provisions discussed in this chapter will be changed remains to be seen.

[1] With the exception of the youth section of the Muslim Brotherhood Organization.

[2] Arabic for "Muslim jurists."

[3] Quote by Habib who had participated with several others in discussing the draft of the new Egyptian constitution on a famous TV program called "The Last Word." أخر كلام: مواد مثيرة للجدل في دستور مصر (The Last Word: Controversial Matters In Egypt's Constitution)—Youtube, <http://www.youtube.com/watch?v=Y5bBVB3pYKU>.

[4] Sarsawi lecturing on the difference between the principles of Sharia and the rules of Sharia—YouTube, <http://www.youtube.com/watch?v=-cc0YNlYEzM>.

II. Lawyer-Politicians

The post-revolutionary project of the Islamists therefore is a legal one par excellence. It is premised on the task of reversing the displacement of Islamic law that took place a century-and-a-half earlier and returning it to its "proper" place as the official law of the land. This was by no means the first time that the Islamist camp had launched a counter-structuring strategy of the legal system in Egypt's history. There indeed were historical precedents but this was the first time they could do it with their "hands gripping at the steering wheel," so to speak.[5]

Nothing could match the confidence of Subhi Saleh of the Muslim Brotherhood, arriving to his debate with the famous liberal parliamentarian Amr Hamzawi with plentiful Islamic law up his sleeve. Enough that is to remedy the problem of imported law and replace it with what is Islamic. This is how Saleh started his opening remarks in the debate:

> Islam is both religion *and* state. There are 6200 verses in the Quran, 600 of those touch on law. Those who want to separate religion from state will have to "abolish" those 600 verses!

continuing,

> Islamic Sharia covered all aspects of the law equal to Western law. What is the meaning of the Bayaa[6] with Abu Bakr after the death of the prophet; isn't that the "social contract" of Montesquieu and Rousseau?[7]

And while there was no shortage of law talk on everybody's part in the aftermath of the Egyptian revolution, for we have all seen how legalized it had proven to be,[8] for the non-Islamist camp law was primarily a means to an end: a way to radically redraw the political and economic framework of the fallen state of Mubarak to make it more free and/or egalitarian. For the Islamists, however, law's identity was foundational. Law was both an expression of where the "umma"[9] struck its cultural identification, and a tool to restructure the state and society in the direction of that identification. The identity of the law therefore was the primary issue to which all other issues had to be subordinated, for, after all, it was only with reference to *this* (Islamic) law, and in seeking the guidance of *its* doctrinal framework, that Islamists could even begin to develop a position or a policy proposal on things political and economic.

For the Islamist camp, law/jurisprudence stood as the privileged field of knowledge towering over all others and from which those others drew their guidelines. Islamist discourse was so law-laden, that law traversed the ideological in their speech whereby the strict rigid command of the legal stood in for the more malleable organization of ideas in the ideological, stunting the growth of the latter. And so the new Islamists came armed with the "law" in more than one sense since law had to perform triply for them—it was

[5] Amr Shalakany, "Between Identity and Redistribution: Sanhuri, Genealogy and the Will to Islamise" (2001) 8 *Islamic Law and Society* 201.

[6] "Bayaa" (Arabic) means "collective contract"; the reference is to the Muslim community's collective offer to Abu Bakr, one of prophet Mohammad's first disciples, to become the first Muslim ruler/successor following the prophet's death.

[7] Debate between political liberal Amr Hamzawi and Subhi Saleh from the Muslim Brotherhood that took place in the Faculty of Law of the University of Alexandria—YouTube, <http://www.youtube.com/watch?v=1rLgKJjiBa8>.

[8] Lama Abu-Odeh, "Of Law and the Revolution" (Social Science Research Network) (2012), <http://www.youtube.com/watch?v=1rLgKJjiBa8>, forthcoming in *Penn International Law Journal*.

[9] Arabic for "Muslim nation."

the place where identity was deposited, where law proper was to be found, and the place where the skeletal concepts for politics, economics, and the ethical, could be discovered and spun out into spheres autonomous from law. Talking legally and talking about law, therefore permeated so much of those Islamists' speech, especially in the Salafis's case, making them something akin to lawyer-politicians.

III. "There Are No Secularists in Egypt"

While the authoritative and towering bite of the law in the religious tradition left the Islamist camp with infant ideologies and little direction on how to run a modern state, the unrelenting discipline of the authoritarian illiberal state had an equivalent impact on the opposing camp! For all the Islamists' railing against their opponents, the non-Islamists, whom they frequently accused of defending the (alien) import "French" law, contemptuously hailing them as "the secularists" and the "liberals," "secularism" and "political liberalism" as distinct political ideologies, did not appear to have solid local articulation in Egypt. Decades of dictatorial rule (since Nasser of 1952) made articulation of political ideologies suffer its own symptoms of stunted growth, so much so that "secularism" and "political liberalism" resided only in preliminary and nascent fashion awaiting a democratic system for their "discursive launching," so to speak.

"Secularism" especially, as an expression of the "proper" relationship between church and state, appeared to have fared particularly badly in the aftermath of Egypt's revolution. Those of us who followed the debate on Article 2 of the Egyptian constitution (Principles of Sharia is the primary source of legislation) taking place on television talk shows or in public exchanges between Islamists and their opponents, could not help but feel the rhetorical trap in which the Islamists' opponents found themselves. Grappling to respond to the Islamists' camp's insistence on amending the phrasing of the article to extend its reach, opening up the possibility of Islamicizing law on constitutional grounds, the non-Islamists' retort to the Islamic reconstructive project often appeared inarticulate and somewhat opaque. Many followed the practice of prefacing their positions with the perfunctory "Nobody is opposed to Art 2" in their exchanges with the Islamists! An example of such retort was Dr. Jaber Nassar's, the Constitutional law professor from the Faculty of Law of Cairo University, who insisted in one of those exchanges,

> There are no secularists in Egypt and there is no one opposed to Sharia. Those who are non-Islamists should not be described as "secularists."[10]

Islamists had successfully turned the word "secularist" into such a dirty word that everyone was bending over backwards to deny the allegation that they might be one! For being a secularist could only mean being anti-Sharia and any hint of such exposed the person to the charge of being a heretic. A problem that the American University in Cairo (AUC) political science professor, socialist activist and famous leader of the Egyptian revolution, Rabab Mahdi, referred to with the following words "There is a problem of accusing people of heresy and treason."[11]

That is not to say that there were no attempts in the non Islamist camp, after the obligatory "we are all for Sharia," to offer an interpretation of "Sharia" that would remove it from the domain of religious epistemology and place it in one that is more secular and universalist. The fate of such attempts, however, often seemed uncertain. In his debate with the Salafi Abdel Monem Al Shahhat, Amr Hamzawi did exactly that arguing that

[10] See n. 2 above. [11] See n. 2 above.

"Sharia" for him was a doctrine that was based on "principles of justice, freedom and equality, the ruling principles of the international human rights charter, which should equally govern the Egyptian constitution."[12] Furthermore, Hamzawi asserted that Sharia-based practices constituted a background cultural fact about the country and its inhabitants woven into the very cultural fabric of Egypt that no one could possibly deny or attack. Elaborating:

> When have we ever heard of practices violating Sharia in Egypt? Why are we afraid of Egypt? We are a disciplined society that has closely followed the principles of Sharia![13]

But such accommodating if more secular articulations of Sharia and its place left Al Shahhat cold. Insisting that Hamzawi got his prioritization order straight, he retorted: "Justice is *restricted* by Sharia. Equality is *restricted* by Sharia. Freedom is *restricted* by Sharia."[14]

Refusing the accommodating gesture, he insisted:[15]

> We the Salafis, our governing framework is clear: it is the Quran, the Sunna and we consider Al Azhar[16] as our guide. What is your guide? What is your term of reference?
>
> We the Salafis adopt a method in interpreting the text of the Quran and the Sunna—it is a specific method. We ask the question: is this permitted or is this prohibited? We seek the answer in interpretations offered by the prophet and the first three successor generations of his disciples.[17]

Islamists then fared much better than their much demonized opponents for while both camps came short on the level of the ideological, Islamists moved with the upper hand of the law on their side—the law to mobilize their supporters, to discipline their interlocuters, and to experience their normative superiority over their stuttering opponents with all their disarticulated positions. It was the law to lay down the law!

IV. But Who Speaks for State Law?

And while there was this *other* "law," the official law of the state with its origin in the legal transplant, and the object of the Islamist camp's venom, it was not exactly one that the non-Islamist camp felt they "owned" as if it were *their* law the way the Islamist camp treated Sharia. Rather it was simply *state* law. The distance between this state law and the new post-revolutionary *political* "liberals" and "secularists" was the distance between them and the authoritarian state with all its punishing history.

12 Debate that took place between liberal parliamentarian Amr Hamzawi and the Salafi leader Abdel Monem Al Shahhat—Youtube, <http://www.youtube.com/watch?v=ZA-RH7HTWOs>.

13 Deabte between Amr Hamzawi and Abdel Monem Al Shahhat.

14 Deabte between Amr Hamzawi and Abdel Monem Al Shahhat.

15 It was perhaps because of this sense of rhetorical entrapment that the non-Islamist camp made the membership of the constituent assembly drafting the constitution such a big issue. The Islamists had packed the assembly with two-thirds of their followers leaving their opponents crying for more representation of other "sectors" of the society.

16 Al-Azhar is a reference to the religious institution located in Cairo that had been a center of Islamic production of law and jurisprudence (and other forms of knowledge) since the tenth century. This institution had lost its central role with the adoption of European legal transplant in the nineteenth century and its clerical membership and income had been under the control of the state since the time of Nasser in 1952. The Islamists new project is to re-center this institution and to transform its current clerical membership to one that is independent from state interests.

17 See n. 7 above.

It is true that Egyptian law per legal system embodied a certain version of legal liberalism, given its origin as a European transplant, but it had on the one hand picked up a great deal of illiberal residue over the years as a result of authoritarian governance and, on the other, it had not had the benefit of political liberalism as a background ideological formation to feed its interpretation precisely for the same reason. And while by virtue of being a European transplant that had historically displaced Islamic law by cornering it, making it an instance of "secular law," it had had to make do without the benefit of ideologized secularism to feed it interpretively.

Indeed, it is by virtue of this "lack" that law had to function as a metonym for political liberalism and secularism—perhaps a poor one at that—for if one had to look for liberalism in Egypt one would find its traces in law—to property rights, consent of contract, punishment only with proven guilt, protection of minors. And if one looked for secularism, one looked at transplanted civil, and criminal codes, evoking in their organization, structure, and rationale, far more the achievements of European enlightenment than anything related to pre-modern Islamic jurisprudence.

In other words, this was a legal system that was "liberal" without "liberals" and non-Islamic without secularists. So it was not so much that the non-Islamist camp in the aftermath of the revolution positively identified with "French Law," rather, it was that the prospect of Islamicizing such a legal system that had most alarmed this camp, quite satisfied as it was with the way the Egyptian Constitutional Court (SCC) had historically narrowed down the meaning of "Sharia principles" referred to in Article 2 of Mubarak's constitution making only the most determinate provision qualify as "Islamic."[18] By doing so, the SCC had severely limited the possibility of using Sharia to overturn laws on constitutional grounds. For a camp that was busy articulating a coherent Egyptian-style political liberalism, Islamicizing the legal system, with the culturally disciplinarian tendencies of the Islamist camp becoming increasingly manifest, would seem to only increase exactly what was most troubling about the Mubarak's system: its illiberal aspects.

That is not to say that state "French" law didn't not have its defenders. It did. But these were primarily its professional functionaries—lawyers, judges, law professors, who might or might not be religious, for whom the Egyptianizing efforts of the drafter of the Egyptian Civil Code of 1949, the famous jurist Sanhuri, were more than sufficient, and the SCC's interpretation of Article 2 had hit the exact balance between "tradition and modernity."[19] Anything further than that threatened to disrupt the professional universe they had mastered: its division of roles, its discourse, its codes and laws, its structure and rationale, and quite possibly their own status and prestige as the "field experts."

These professional anti-Islamicizing lawyers were not in a position to counter the *politicization* of the legal system's identity in the way the religious lawyer politicians were able to do. State law did not have its liberal and secular politicians, but it sure did have its lawyers! That is because if the modern state was able to do something it was to produce "law" as a differentiated field of knowledge and practice, administered by its own professionally trained functionaries. An important aspect of this professional training was the carefully policed separation between law and politics, which limited the capacity of these state-oriented lawyers to engage the Islamists and their reconstructive project "up close and personal."

18 Clark Benner Lombardi, Note, "Islamic Law as a Source of Constitutional Law in Egypt: The Constitutionalization of the Sharia in a Modern Arab State" (1998) 37 *Columbia Journal of Transnational Law* 81.

19 See n. 4 above.

For these reasons the Islamic reconstructive project proceeded without much opposition. With a majority membership in the constituent assembly drafting the new constitution, the task before the Islamist camp was clear and without much ado they proceeded. What they wanted was nothing short of a reversal of the current legal order: from one of liberal legalism with Islamist accommodation to one of Islamist legalism with liberal accommodation. A reversal that would only be complete if constitutional review was put into effect comprehensively through use of the textual tools offered by the new constitution.

V. The Textual Basis for the Islamic Reconstructive Project

The final product was quite impressive in the effectiveness of the "identity encirclement" its provisions managed to achieve. These elements included the following.

First, the new Egyptian constitution (26 December 2012) redefines the scope of the "principles of Sharia" to include "its total proofs, jurisprudential rules and sources as agreed upon by the people of Sunna and consensus" (Article 219). According to the Salafi legislator Borhami,[20] the word "sources" refers to "Quran, prophetic tradition, analogy and consensus," the officially recognized sources of the law in the Sunni tradition. What this formulation does is potentially drastically open up the domain of Sharia-based doctrine that could function as the basis to overturn positive law. This formulation was a direct response to SCC's notorious (in Islamist eyes) narrowing down of that "trumping law domain." Now, with the new constitution, all kinds of rules qualify as "Sharia," whether determinate or not, an expression of a majority or a minority of scholars, an object of consensus or not, and all such *Sharia* rules can be used to trump modern legislation as unconstitutional.

Second, the new constitution introduces Al-Azhar as the source of guidance on what constitutes Sharia giving it a supra interpretive power over and above that of the SCC.[21] The Council of Al Azhar Senior Scholars is charged with providing legal consultation on what constitutes Sharia. This too is a response to the "notorious" SCC, and a blatant attempt to "defang" it by giving it a subordinate position in constitutional interpretation. "This SCC, we really have to get rid of it" Borhami declared![22]

Third, the new constitution restricts the exercise of "rights and liberties" to what may not violate the foundations "of state and society" which in the mind of the Islamist legislator include Sharia as such "foundation." Thus, Sharia is made to stand as the supreme law over and above any universal notion of human rights—validating the quote above by Shahhat that "Equality is restricted by Sharia, freedom is restricted by Sharia, and justice is restricted by Sharia."

[20] "Women's Rights in the Egyptian Constitution: (Neo)Liberalism's Family Values," <http://www.jadaliyya.com/pages/index/11852/womens-rights-in-the-egyptian-constitution_(neo)li>.

[21] Article 4 of the new Constitution,

> Al-Azhar is an independent Islamic institution, its headquarters in Cairo and its domain is the Islamic nation, and the whole world. It shall be responsible for spreading the Islamic call and the religious scholarship. The Council of Al-Azhar's Senior Scholars shall be consulted on issues related to Islamic Sharia.
>
> The State shall ensure all the sufficient financial allocations for the achievement of its objectives and the law shall determine the section of the Rector of Al-Azhar, who shall be independent and impeachable and will be elected from among the members of the Council of Al Azhar's scholars.

[22] See n. 14 above.

According to Article 81 of the new Constitution,

Exercise of rights and liberties should not violate the section on "state and society."[23]

Fourth, the new constitution allows for declaring acts criminal legally not only on the basis of parliamentary legislation as the old constitution required but, in addition, on the basis of a constitutional text (Article 76).[24] What this means is that the Islamic style of crime and punishment can now stand to gradually replace the current non-Islamist criminal code by declaring the latter unconstitutional and replacing it with crime and punishment according to Islamic law.

Fifth, the new constitution includes constitutional provisions that allow the "state" to enforce social morality and that sanctions the same on the part of "society." Similar provisions existed in the previous Egyptian Constitution of 1971[25] but the danger in repeating such provisions, with a slightly different formulation, is the surfacing in the post-revolutionary period of self-appointed morality enforcing religious groups,[26] opening up the possibility for an Islamic style of Hisba—a delegation of powers by the state to a civilian force to enforce the moral behavior in public on behalf of the state. Article 11 of the new Constitution provides:

The State undertakes to protect public morals and public order, the high standards of social upbringing, ethical and patriotic values, scientific facts, Arab culture, the cultural and historical tradition of the people, according to the determination of the law.

Article 10 of the new Constitution reads:

The family is the foundation of society based on religion, morality and patriotism. Both the state and *society* undertake to preserve the authentic nature of the Egyptian family, its stability and internal cohesion, protect and preserve its moral values, according to the determination of the law.

With such constitutional provisions in place, and with recorded electoral victories, Islamists in Egypt stand today to transform much about the current legal system to make it more "Islamic." The domains that will be the privileged sites of the reconstructive project will surely be women, personal liberties, and literary and cultural creativity. And this is all going to be a decided march to the "right"!

VI. Rightward Egypt Marches But How Far?

Why to the "right" and how much to the "right" will these constitutional amendments push the legal relations between the state and its citizens and among its citizens, especially its men and women, would all depend. Egyptian civil society had been turning

[23] This is the section that includes reference to "Sharia as the primary source of legislation," namely, Section One of the new Constitution.

[24] Article 76 of the new Constitution, "... no penalty or crime unless by constitutional text or legislative provision...."

[25] Article 9 of 1971 Constitution reads "The family is the basis of the society founded on religion, morality and patriotism. The State strives to preserve the genuine character of the Egyptian family—with the values and traditions it embodies—while affirming and developing its character in relations within the Egyptian society." Article 12 reads "The society shall be committed to safeguarding and protecting morals, promoting the genuine Egyptian traditions and abiding by the high standards of religious education, moral and national values, historical heritage of the people, scientific facts, socialist conduct and public morality within the limits of the law. The State is committed to abiding by these principles and promoting them."

[26] Incidents of religious groups in provincial towns enforcing morality were widely criticized by the media, see e.g. <http://www.alarabiya.net/articles/2012/10/31/246901.html>; <http://al-shorfa.com/ar/articles/meii/features/2013/04/03/feature-01>; <http://sudanyiat.net/news.php?action=show&id=20479>.

to religion since the 1970's with the rise of a variety of religious movements competing with the old Muslim Brotherhood who had been around for decades for the hearts and minds of the populace. The authoritarian regime of Mubarak persecuted these movements politically but gave them free reign culturally and socially (with intermittent crackdown), allowing them to establish social bases through pulpits, social welfare networks, and apolitical social organizations, a reign that had been intensified with the proliferation of religious TV channels and the commoditization of female religious dress and fashion. If the social pact of the authoritarianism of the nationalist Nasser was based on "give me politics I will give you economic welfare," the social pact of Mubarak's authoritarianism was based on "give me politics and the economy and I will give you economic contentment and some welfare *through* religion." Religiosity proved an effective "private" to the "public" of the state and its politics.

To express the above legally, one would have to resort to the legal realist insight that non-acts are acts. The non-intervention by the state in a set of social relations amounts to an intervention in itself in that the state's passivity serves to sanction those relations as they are in their particularity. If one were to look at the Mubarak era, one could accordingly argue that the withdrawal of the state from enforcing religious identity, for the most part,[27] while allowing for the increase in social religiosity had sanctioned the intervention of religion in social relations with all the traffic of powers, privileges, and entitlements that that entailed. Arguably, a shift in gender relations, relations between dominant religions and subordinate ones, and between more religious people and those who were less so or between them and non-believers, had been allowed to occur by the "non-intervening" state. This state of "non-intervention" is of course supplemented and qualified by the multiple acts of intervention by the state in the name of "religious identity," explicitly sanctioned by law, such as when the state acted to uphold "public morality" by banning discrete acts of "speech" (allowed by the old constitution), when it moved to enforce the rules of family law that find their basis in religion, and when it used its discretion in (de)criminalizing acts, involving assault on religious minorities, their property, and their places of worship. The totality of these acts/non-acts constituted what we might call the *de facto* relationship between "state and mosque" during the Mubarak era.

Some have pointed out that there was little that was new in the new constitution from the old one insofar as the "Islamic" element was concerned.[28] Sharia was always a source of legislation, and the values of the family and public morality were always state and society sanctioned,[29] etc. The new elements of introducing "Al-Azhar" as an advisory on the "Islamic" and making the exercise of "rights and liberties" contingent on not violating the fundamentals of "society" introduced in the constitution of 2012 would not make much difference from the set of powers/privileges/entitlements settled upon during the Mubarak era. Moreover, if the non-intervention of the Mubarak state had produced religious effects, then the kind of difference in religious effect the Islamists would produce by using state power (through their own discrete selection of acts/non-acts) made no difference or not much of it anyway.[30] Egypt would still be the same old religious Egypt.

[27] There is an important exception to that which is the discrimination against the Ahmadis and the Bahais through the decisions of the Administrative Courts by depriving them of passports.

[28] See n. 19 above.

[29] Compare Art. 10 of the new Constitution with Art. 9 of the Constitution of 1971, and Art. 11 of the new Constitution with Art. 12 of the old one.

[30] Though I would suspect that no one would deny the novelty of introducing "crimes and punishments" through constitutional interpretations as the new constitution would allow "Article 76."

VII. The Difference the Islamist Difference Would Make

Even though the new constitution is quite similar to the old one, I contend that the Islamist difference will indeed make a difference. This is so for two reasons.

First, some of what is similar in constitutional provisions between the old and the new, namely those related to women, was settled upon after the Islamists proposed in earlier drafts an account of the relations between men and women that were based on complementarity of roles inside the family that were vehemently opposed. Confronted with the opposition, those provisions were withdrawn. They were withdrawn with the idea that what was included in the previous constitution was sufficient to suggest the idea of complementarity and there was no need to spell it out specifically.

Second, the determination with which the Salafis pursued the different provisions, namely those related to the new definition of "principles of Sharia" and the inclusion of Al-Azhar as having an advisory role to the SCC, is not something that can be dismissed as of little effect.

Both the above indicate that there is an intention to pursue a reconstructive project of law premised on cultural identity regulation at the center of which stand women and public morality as politics of "first instance," through the mediation of a doctrinal "return" to Sharia and the institutional assistance of a self-avowedly religious institution, Al-Azhar.

So the question is what tools and instruments does the new Egyptian constitution offer the Islamists in power to advance such a project? What kind of state interventions would such legal instruments allow and to what distributive effect? If every legal relation, whether between the state and individuals or between individuals themselves can be seen as a particular distribution of legal powers, privileges, and entitlements, what kind of re-organization of those powers/privileges/entitlements would the Islamists proceed to enact?

To identify those "tools and instruments," I identify three rule structures, one substantive, the second procedural, and the third "corporatist" the determination of which in the future will gradually give shape to those legal tools available. I say in the future because while the rules in the new constitution give us some indication of their orientation, or shall we say "distributive effect," a great deal yet needs interpretation and determination. Constitutional rules are by nature quite indeterminate and, moreover, substantive rules interact with each other and with other procedural ones that are not necessarily immediately obvious, making prediction of distributional effects exceedingly difficult. With every new interpretation of a rule, the face of the legal reconstructive project, which I contend is apace by the Islamists, will shift accordingly.

VIII. The Cluster of Substantive Rules

Above, I have identified the substantive rules related to the identity regulative project as Article 219 (defining "Principles of Sharia"), Article 4 (role of Al-Azhar), Article 81 (rights and liberties subject to state and society foundations), Article 76 (crime through constitutional provision), and Articles 10, 11 (state and society preserve family, state sanctions public morality).

It is noteworthy that in this cluster of rules, "principles of Sharia" are made operative in three different fashions.

First, it functions formally as a supra constitutional principle. Article 2 of the new constitution (exact copy of the previous one of the old constitution) provides that "Principles of Sharia are the primary source of legislation." While typically the provisions of the constitution itself function as the basis for constitutional review, here we have a constitutional provision (Article 2) that refers to extra constitutional principles that will operate constitutionally in the same manner as the formal provisions of the constitution. What are those supra constitutional "principles"? Article 219 defines them as Sharia's "total proofs, jurisprudential rules and sources as agreed upon by the people of Sunna and consensus."

On a formal level, the text of the constitution, by virtue of Article 2, expands in its scope to incorporate a "doctrinal regime" (principles of Sharia) that has yet to be identified which will have the same power of constitutional review as the constitutional provisions that have already been textually identified in the body of the constitution of 2012. On a substantive level, how this "doctrinal regime" breaks down between formal rules that can function as extra-constitutional provisions with power to overturn legislation on constitutional grounds the way other provisions do and other kinds of legal materials that cannot do the same legal work and would have to be dismissed with, depends greatly on how the court interprets Article 219.

The way Article 219 is defined is very puzzling in that it incorporates under "principles of Sharia" the whole body of what we call in modern times "Islamic law." It refers to the substantive rules of the law (jurisprudential rules), the sources from which these rules were derived (sources agreed upon by the people of Sunna and Consensus) and the rules of interpretations to be followed in deriving the substantive rules of law "total proofs."

In modern constitutional speak, only rules can perform the function of judicial review; rules of interpretation which are only second-level rules offered as guidance to those trying to implement the law, as well as the sources from which the rules are derived, which do not have the status of "rules" at all but are nothing but pre-law, the raw and rough materials from which the rules are derived, cannot do so. It is as if the Salafi constitutional legislature who has insisted on this formulation is inviting us not so much to perform constitutional review of existing legislation or one to be passed in the future but to legislate, Islamicly, *ab initio* from the ground up.

In pre-modern speak, the difference is between insisting that *siyassa sharyya (legislation passed by ruler)* not be repugnant to what is identified as some determinate set of rules identified as "Sharia" and insisting that *siyassa* be actively derived from Sharia's sources, in complementarity with its already existent rules, using its mode of rationale and argumentation. The first would limit the role of *ulama* in overseeing the ruler's legislation; the second would increase it significantly. The closest example of the latter is the doctrinal edifice that has emerged in the contemporary era in the area of Islamic finance as instance of *neo-Ijtihad*.[31]

The historic practice of the SCC is closer to the first example, Article 219 suggests the second as normative legal practice. If so, then the delineation "issues related to Sharia" per Article 4 "... The Council of Al-Azhar's Senior Scholars shall be consulted on issues related to Islamic Sharia" would increase exponentially. According to this latter interpretation, every new piece of legislation would have to be either an instance of legislation related to Sharia on its face or derivatively related to it! Al-Azhar, the modern version of the old *ulama*, will hover over the head of the modern legislature (secular ruler) as a regulative supra council, its preview of all legislation inescapable!

[31] See Frank E. Vogel, "Conformity with Islamic Sharia and Constitutionality under Article 2: Some Issues of Theory, Practice and Comparison," in Eugene Cotran and Abel Omar Sherif (eds), *Democracy, the Rule of Law and Islam* (London: Kluwer Law International, 1999).

Second, "Principles of Sharia" appears not only formally in the new constitution but also through a "nesting" operation. Article 81 makes "exercise of rights and liberties" contingent upon conformity with "principles provided for in the *section* on state and society," which section incorporates Article 2 stipulating that "principles of Shari the primary source of..." which in turn refers to Article 219 for definition of what constitutes "principles of Sharia," etc.

As opposed to the operation described above where the constitution explodes outward to incorporate a different doctrinal regime with its own set of legal instruments, styles of argumentation and raw materials, threatening to transform through this act of incorporation the positive legal system in its totality and to cause its restructuring *ab initio*, in nesting, we see the constitution imploding inward through self referentiality, an internal continual self-negation whereby the whole section on "rights and liberties," the most important one in any modern liberal constitution, is made contingent upon the ending point of "principles of Sharia." The "ending point" is, as we have seen above, a false one for it is also the beginning for a re-launching outward.

IX. The Cluster of Procedural Rules

Procedural rules are important and stand to influence greatly the way substantive rules work. Their impact on the resultant jurisprudence overall is not negligible for they define the instances, terms and conditions under which substantive rules are triggered.

In fact a distinction between a procedural rule and a substantive one is not always apparent. For instance, a rule will need to be in place that defines "issues related to Sharia" (Article 4). It will have to answer the question of what kind of legislation qualifies as a "matter of Sharia" which would trigger the advisory role of Al-Azhar and compel SCC to transfer the case to it. This rule could either be of a substantive nature (the SCC decides depending on the nature of the legislation in question) or of a formal or procedural nature (if one of the litigants evokes Article 2 of the Constitution). The first rule would greatly increase the power of the SCC (*vis-à-vis* Al-Azhar) as a gatekeeper of what would make the first cut for consideration under Article 2. It is *up to the SCC* which cases end up in Al-Azhar's "docket." The second would go the opposite way.

Another "procedural" rule would need to be in place to define the "advisory" aspect of Al-Azhar's role. There is a difference in effect between a rule that would require Al-Azhar to write more than one opinion on the case referred to it and then obliged the SCC to follow one of them, and another that would require only one opinion by Al-Azhar and then left the option to the SCC to either adopt the opinion of Al-Azhar or to reject it. If the latter case, a further procedural rule would have to determine whether the SCC should include in its judicial opinion the reasons for overriding Al-Azhar's "advisory" opinion or whether it is exempt from doing so. The difference would be in defining the ways in which the SCC will act as the final "decider" of the case.

Another procedural rule would be needed to determine whether a piece of legislation that had been referred to Al-Azhar for an advisory opinion before its promulgation could still be challenged per its constitutionality before the SCC after it had been legislated.

Finally much would depend on the interpretation of Article 222 of the Constitution (arguably of a procedural nature) that stipulates, "All laws and executive decrees passed before this constitution shall remain legally valid and effective. They cannot be modified or annulled except according to procedures provided for by this constitution." What does this article mean? Does it preclude from constitutional review all laws passed before the constitution of 2012? What is the meaning of the exception "except according to procedures provided by this constitution?"

How the SCC interprets this rule in the future will be of great significance. There is an apparent self-referential aspect to it, in that the SCC would have to decide whether its previous constitutional review would be revisited. It would need to determine which past laws would be open for constitutional review: none? All, except those whose constitutionality had already been determined by the SCC? Some other distinction?

X. The Cluster of Corporatist Rules

"Corporatist rules" here refer to the rules pertaining to the internal organization of the judicial and legislative bodies that can either evoke or review the question of constitutionality of new legislation. An example of such rules in the case of the legislature is one that determines that before a piece of legislation is referred to Al-Azhar for advice on its "Islamicity," a certain number of parliamentary votes would have to be secured for such referral or one that would alternatively treat the request by one member (or five or ten) to be more than sufficient.[32]

Both the Egyptian judiciary and Al-Azhar as corporatist entities are undergoing re-organization. Such reorganization is bound to have an effect on the jurisprudence they will leave in their trail.

The Judicial Authority Bill, debated now by the Shura Council, raises judicial salaries while lowering judges' retirement age. Article 176 of the new constitution limits the number of judicial appointments to the SCC to ten (excepting the president of the court) putting to an end the practice of court "packing" pursued by Mubarak. If we add to the above that the rule of the Brotherhood would certainly put an end to the practice of excluding from judicial appointment judges sympathetic to religious parties and organizations "for security reasons" as was the case under Mubarak, then the Egyptian judiciary is about to depart from its previous self. The judiciary is a powerful corporatist entity or "estate" as some cynically call it, that has within it a great deal of antagonists to the rule of the Islamists. There is a great deal of ongoing pushback from some of its sections to the ongoing restructuring attempt by the legislature and time will tell how deep the change will prove to be.

Given this restructuring the question is to what extent is the Egyptian judiciary open to an identity regulative project pushed its way by an Islamist legislature? How near on the way will it meet the latter and where will it split the difference between them? It is not that the judiciary was not engaged in an identity regulative project of its own before. It was, as my discussion of the turn to religion under Mubarak argued. They obviously intervened intermittently through their interpretations to "lay down the law" on identity. The Islamist project, however, appears to create a shift in the way this is organized, relying more on the direct coercive power of the state rather than relying on social transformation occasioned and fascilitated by the non-intervention of the state.

As for Al-Azhar, the new constitution awarded it autonomy as an institution, one that it had lacked for close to half a century, including an autonomous financial budget guaranteed by the state and self-appointing powers (Article 4). The *shaykh* of Al-Azhar was awarded a post for life.

No family law reforms were passed under the previous dictatorships without the official endorsement of Al-Azhar. Its leaders had provided the interpretive framework

[32] This can also qualify as a procedural rule.

supporting those reforms and lent them the legitimating weight of the institution they presided over. So one can confidently state that insofar as the SCC in the past had upheld family law reforms that were constitutionally challenged, the SCC's position on those reforms matched those of the Al-Azhar of the past, the one beholden to the dictator.

Whether this will change in the context of a newly autonomous Al-Azhar remains to be seen. Al-Azhar has historically asserted its "*Wasatiyya*" (moderation, or literally, "in the middle") ideology, and its *Shaykh*, awarded an appointment for life by the new constitution (Article 4), had occasionally berated the Salafis for their extremism and amateurish approach to Sharia interpretation.[33] Many of those religious competitors have criticized Al-Azhar for accommodating in its student and administrative bodies those belonging to questionable "sects" (Shia, Sufis, etc.), as well as for promoting doctrinal positions that do not belong squarely to those of "the people of Sunna and consensus" as now stipulated for by the new Article 219.[34] Whether Al-Azhar will insist on this position it had delineated for itself in the past in the context of the rise of electoral power of religious parties that had historically been critical of its role under the dictatorship or whether it will shift in their direction to increase its legitimacy in the eyes of their electoral base is an interesting question.

Al-Azhar confronts not just the historic antagonism of the Salafis, but also the ambivalence of the Muslim Brotherhood towards its newly awarded constitutional authority. On the face of it, the Brotherhood would welcome this role, which would validate and support its political program presented to the electorate as introducing the novel element of "Islam." "Islam" according to the Brotherhood platform should be the defining identity of the state, including its laws, morals, and policies.[35] And what better stamp of the Islamicity of state acts than that offered by Al-Azhar the most prestigious and oldest religious institution in the Islamic world, bar none?

In fact, however, the Brotherhood would be averse to the rise of Al-Azhar authority as long as it controlled the legislature with its coalition majority. Its electoral dominance gives it the power to decide the question of "Islamicity" as it sees fit, including departing from its considerations if it needed to.[36] As the ruling party, desperate to achieve political victories against the background of state implosion in a post-revolutionary transitional period, the Brotherhood would not want to have its hands tied to "identity" considerations which it may have promoted per party in opposition, but which could limit its maneuvering room as a ruling one.[37] The instruments and tools of governance available to the Brotherhood are limited enough, as it has chosen not to radically disrupt the previous power of "estates" that ruled during the reign of Mubarak (primarily the military and security establishments with the economic domains they control). The last thing the Brotherhood needed, arguably, is yet another empowered "estate," Al-Azhar, which can undermine in the name of "Islam" the last remaining tools the new ruling party had at its disposal.

[33] Rachel Scott, "What might the Muslim Brotherhood do with al-Azhar? Religious Authority" (2012) 52(2) *Egypt, Die Welt des Islams: International Journal for the Study of Modern Islam* 1.

[34] Scott, "What might the Muslim Brotherhood do with al-Azhar?"

[35] Kristen Stilt, "'Islam is the Solution': Constitutional Visions of the Egyptian Muslim Brotherhood" (Social Science Research Network) (2010), <http://papers.ssrn.com/abstract=1612482>.

[36] See e.g. the controversies over borrowing an international loan from the European Union, Sharia compliant state bonds, and Islamic prohibition of interest as discussed in the Appendix of Gianluca Paolo Parolin, "(Re)Arrangement of State/Islam Relations in Egypt's Constitutional Transition" (2013) *New York University Public Law and Legal Theory Working Papers* Paper 392, 9.

[37] See n. 35 above.

It is noteworthy that even though both Al-Azhar and SCC had supported family law reforms, both had done it through different understandings of what constituted Sharia, almost opposite ones. Al-Azhar, while sympathetic to attempts at Ijtihad to modernize Islamic law, remained conservative in its attitude towards the tradition of *Taqlid*, i.e. the doctrinal legacy of the schools of law that emerged in the pre-modern era. Many of the modern reforms of family law had been rationalized by Al-Azhar through reference to minority views of jurists coming from these schools, including those of the Shia sect.[38] The reforms, according to Al-Azhar were justified because they corresponded to a view expressed by some jurist in the past. This is to be contrasted by the more rationalist approach of the SCC in which what constituted "Sharia" was limited sharply to those "clear and determinate rules in Quran and Hadith," which would then free, in the SCC's view, the modern legislature to innovate.[39] The ideological correspondence between the SCC and Al-Azhar on the question of family law reforms despite the difference in methodological approach, one seemingly literalist and the other rationalist, shows the indeterminacy of "constitutional tests" in relation to their ideological effect.

XI. Conclusion

How the triangular relationship between a legislature with a religious majority, the SCC and Al-Azhar, against the background of constitutional provisions that are ambiguous and await interpretation and procedural delineation will unfold, and what kind of legislative and jurisprudential legacy this triangular relationship will leave in its trail, remain to be seen. The fierce intentionality with which the Salafis pursued the cluster of constitutional provisions related to Sharia, and the "foundations of state and society," warn of a future legislative push from the right of the political spectrum. The treatment by religious parties of gendered relations as a politics of "first instance" with an electoral base that is mostly rural foretells of attempts to either reverse family law reforms or to at least halt any attempts for future ones. Many such reforms find opposition from those who see themselves as "moderate" and coming from the official establishment of the judiciary who might lend support to an attempt to reverse them on the part of a mobilized legislature.[40] A bill was already introduced to the Egyptian parliament before its dissolution proposing to change the custody age of children in an attempt to limit a mother's caretaking time period in the aftermath of divorce.[41] I expect more such bills will be introduced in the near future. Furthermore, instances of self-appointed enforcers of vice and virtue have been reported in the aftermath of the Egyptian revolution. Whether such practices find constitutional cover or become functionalized institutionally, time will only tell.

Even though "gender" appears to be a politics of "first instance" for religious parties, the pressing economic needs of Egypt as well as the failure of the Brotherhood to create a coalition among various political forces to work in the name of "public interest" has pushed matters of economics and security to the forefront of its agenda as a reigning

[38] Sir James Norman Dalrymple Anderson, *Law Reform in the Muslim World* (London: Athlone Press, 1976).

[39] See n. 17 above.

[40] See Moustafa Imam's article (Arabic) on "The Coming Revolution of Modifying the Personal Status Code," ثورة التغيير علي قوانين الأحوال الشخصية قادمة, <http://digital.ahram.org.eg/articles.aspx?Serial=619841&eid=2419>.

[41] For more analysis on modifying the Personal Status Code see <http://forums.fatakat.com/thread2837374>.

party. Continuous and increasing protests against the Brotherhood suggests a deferral of "gender" questions as any attempt to move with an elaborate agenda on such matters might fuel further street protests and makes an already deteriorating situation worse. This is so especially with the Brotherhood's attempt to secure its rule domestically by appealing to international, especially US, approval.

However, the Salafis, the Brotherhood's political partners, remain unreliable. Public morality and the relations between men and women matter deeply to them. What kind of legislative agendas they will push, what kind of support they will get from Brotherhood representatives, what kind of stance will Al-Azhar take, are questions for the future to answer.

10

The Constitutional Boundaries of Religious Accommodation

Ran Hirschl and Ayelet Shachar

In recent years, the specter of litigants turning to religious or customary sources of law as authoritative guides to regulate their behavior, alongside or in lieu of secular norms, has once again risen to the forefront of constitutional battles worldwide. The reemergence of piety religion raises profound challenges for the constitutional domain, as evidenced by the spike of jurisprudence addressing these issues in literally every region of the globe. One of the outcomes of this religious resurgence is that the comparative study of constitutional law and religion has never been as relevant or exciting as it is today. This begs the question of how constitutional law and courts have been dealing with the ever-intensifying struggle over the place of religion in the public sphere. In particular, it calls for an examination of the types of diversity claims that stand, *ceteris paribus*, a better chance than others to gain support by the constitutional domain.

That courts in expressly "separationist" regimes of state-and-religion (e.g. France) take an overall religion-limiting stance is not surprising. Two notably more difficult settings for probing into how courts deal with claims of religion are: (i) countries where strong constitutional establishment of religion exists (e.g. in the predominantly Muslim world); and (ii) countries that take great pride in advancing an official multicultural agenda (e.g. Canada and South Africa). Elsewhere we explore how constitutional courts in strong-establishment settings domesticate religion and tame its potentially radical edge by bringing it under constitutional check.[1] In this chapter, we focus on the latter category, namely the world of constitutionally enshrined multiculturalism.

We identify, with broad brush strokes, two different categories of response by the high priests of constitutionalism to religious-based claims for recognition, accommodation, and exemption: those claims of religion or culture that can reasonably be construed as accepting the ultimate authority and supremacy of the constitutional order that we shall refer to, for the purposes of simplicity and analytical clarity, as "diversity as inclusion;" compared with claims for insulation, if not outright immunization, from the purview of the state's constitutional ordering and its centrifugal force, claims which are based on adherence to alternative, supposedly extra-constitutional sacred sources of authority and identity. This latter pattern we label "non-state law as competition."

We argue, in a nutshell, that as long as legal claims for accommodation are not seen as directly or indirectly challenging the lexical superiority of the constitutional order itself ("diversity as inclusion"), they stand a fair chance of success. Contrast that with the unyielding reluctance of legislatures and judiciaries to accept as binding or even

[1] See Ran Hirschl, *Constitutional Theocracy* (Cambridge, MA: Harvard University Press, 2010); Ran Hirschl, "Constitutional Courts as Bulwarks of Secularism" in Robert Kagan et al. (eds), *Consequential Courts: Judicial Roles in Global Perspective* (Cambridge, UK: Cambridge University Press, 2013).

cognizable any potentially competing legal order that originates in sacred or customary sources of identity and authority. This pattern of clamping down and refusing to accept any alternative (here, religious or customary) sources of regulation or hierarchies of authority becomes particularly visible where the legal challenge at issue is interpreted as raising doubts regarding *which* set of norms and institutions, or *what* set of high priests, should have the final word in authoritatively resolving disputes within a given polity ("non-state law as competition"). This is a challenge that no secular legal order, no matter how tolerant and otherwise open to providing exemptions and accommodations to religious believers, can accept with indifference.

The reason is as simple as it is powerful: what is perceived to be at stake here is nothing less than the very authority and source of legitimacy of the accepted civil religion. When faced with the *non-state law as competition* type of claims, courts and legislatures may loudly manifest their commitment to respecting tolerance, balancing rights, protecting the vulnerable, ensuring proportionality, and other important values. However, they may nevertheless interpret the situation as reflecting a more foundational power struggle between competing systems of knowledge and interpretation: the earthly, human-enacted constitution and the claim to speak in a vernacular of a revealed or divine authority. When faced with this kind of a challenge, even the most generous and even-handed officials of the civil religion are structurally not in a position to rule from a "point of view from nowhere."[2] Instead, as stakeholders in and enforcers of the state's rule of law, they may feel obligated to reaffirm the superiority of its sources of legitimacy, procedures of engagement, methods of interpretation, and style of reasoning that are state-driven and entrenched in the secular constitution precisely when the very foundations of the legal and social order they protect and adhere to are (or are perceived to be) at stake.

In order to substantiate these claims, we trace in the following pages the rise of a fortified wall of separation, erected in response to the non-state-law-as-competition set of claims, even in accommodating societies that are otherwise strongly committed to the diversity-as-inclusion path of response. We demonstrate these claims by focusing on recent jurisprudence from Canada and South Africa, two countries that are widely recognized in the comparative constitutional literature as progressive jurisdictions demonstrating an expansive approach to recognizing religious and cultural diversity. Both countries are committed to the core idea of multicultural or "differentiated" citizenship: namely, that public recognition of cultural identities and religious practices offers a valuable path to inclusion and equal citizenship for once-excluded and marginalized minorities.[3] They therefore represent the "most difficult," or "least favorable" cases for our argument;[4] if there is any place we would expect to find recognition by secular countries of religious or customary sources of law and authority, it would be in these diverse societies that have made an explicit constitutional commitment to promoting their citizens' freedom to preserve and enhance their multitude of backgrounds and distinctive cultural, religious, ethnic, and racial heritages as part of their "mosaic" (Canada) or "rainbow nation"

[2] This is a narrower claim than stating that *any* type of engagement between law and religion is inevitably "tainted" by the cultural dominance of liberalism and secularism, given that, in many parts of the world, religion has a strong claim for governance and might be officially recognized by the state. See generally, Hirschl, *Constitutional Theocracy*.

[3] For a now-classic defense of differentiated citizenship, see Iris Marion Young, "Polity and Group Difference: A Critique of the Ideal of Universal Citizenship" (1989) 99 *Ethics* 250.

[4] See Ran Hirschl, "The Question of Case Selection in Comparative Constitutional Law," (2005) 53 *American Journal of Comparative Law* 125, 144–6.

(South Africa) conceptions of citizenship.[5] Although both countries have made significant progress in their attempts to advance a comprehensive reading of the diversity-as-inclusion mandate, policymakers in both countries have, in recent years, vigorously clamped down on any competing, non-statist sources of regulation.

In identifying and categorizing these jurisprudential patterns—*diversity as inclusion* is about creating a shared space for members of the polity to manifest their group-based identities and practices, if they so wish; whereas *non-state law as competition* is about contracting out of the secular regime's regulatory reach as part of a demand to establish "islands of jurisdictions" that lie outside the governance of the state and its official agents—our goal is not to justify or defend them.[6] Rather, we utilize illustrative and interpretative methods to ascertain the emergence of a "new wall of separation" between state and religion within otherwise accommodating societies. We are further interested in articulating precisely where and according to what regulatory logic the high priests of constitutionalism are in effect drawing a line of resistance in their (re)engagement with some of the most ancient, yet still highly credible, alternative sources of authority and legitimacy to that of the modern state: namely, those grounded in a religious order or a customary tradition.[7]

This inquiry is urgent; all over the world, the challenges of defining the scope and limits of multiculturalism and the boundaries of accommodation in the public sphere have become pressing, leading states (especially in Europe) to rethink—and often restrict—their policies as to how much toleration is due to cultural, religious, or other recognition-based claims. Pundits and politicians have proclaimed the "death of" and "retreat from" multiculturalism. Against this background, it is helpful to disentangle the strikingly different legal response to claims for inclusion versus those of competition, which are often mingled together in popular and policy debates. The former, diversity-as-inclusion, does not challenge the ultimate authority of the civil religion. Indeed, the power to recognize (or suppress) non-statist identities through the reign of the law further entrenches the dominance of the secular religion, allowing its officials to incorporate "difference" into the state and maintain their privileged standing as ultimate arbiters of all disputes. This task of accommodation is not always easy, as articulated by none other than the Chief Justice of the Supreme Court of Canada:

> The law faces the seemingly paradoxical task of... *carving out a space within itself* in which individuals and communities can manifest alternate, and often competing, sets of commitments.[8]

[5] This commitment is officially expressed in Canada's constitutional and federal policy. See s. 27 of the Canadian Charter of Rights and Freedoms, which states: "[The *Charter*] shall be interpreted in a manner consistent with the preservation and enhancement of the multicultural heritage of Canadians."

[6] Our task here is to provide a sound assessment of what states are already doing, rather than what they *ought* to do. As a normative and institutional design matter, one of us has argued precisely against the invocation of such "either/or" responses, favoring instead a more coordinated, joint-governance approach that is grounded in the principles of multicultural feminism. See Ayelet Shachar, *Multicultural Jurisdictions: Cultural Differences and Women's Rights* (Cambridge, UK: Cambridge University Press, 2001); Ayelet Shachar, "Privatizing Diversity: A Cautionary Tale from Religious Arbitration in Family Law" (2008) 9 *Theoretical Inquiries in Law* 573; Ayelet Shachar, "What We Owe to Women: The View from Multicultural Feminism," in Debra Satz and Rob Reich (eds), *Toward A Humanist Justice: The Political Philosophy of Susan Moller Okin* (Oxford: Oxford University Press, 2009), 143.

[7] Obviously, there may be significant differences and rivalries among and between claimants and authorities that purport to speak in the name of the divine. However, the intricacy and richness of such debates are intentionally placed beyond the scope of this discussion given its focus on decisions taken by general courts and legislatures.

[8] See Beverely McLachlin, "Freedom of Religion and the Rule of Law: A Canadian Perspective," in Douglas Farrow (ed.), *Recognizing Religion in a Secular Society: Essays in Pluralism, Religion, and Public Policy* (Montreal: McGill-Queen's University Press, 2004), 16 [emphasis added].

The latter challenge, non-state-law-as-competition, is not amenable to this resolution. It begins with the proposition that both law and religion are comprehensive systems of meaning creation and obligation for the individual. If this is the case, then conflicts between these systems will inevitably ensue, raising the menace of a showdown that challenges the accepted constitutional notion of supremacy of the civil religion. In order to clamp down on this destabilizing, existential-type threat, the new wall of separation is placed upright and barricaded. Establishing it is paramount, for unchecked competition is perceived, from the vantage point of the constitutional priests, as potentially challenging the constitutional order's semi-sacred standing as the supreme law of the land. This is a test that even the most accommodating secular societies, here exemplified by South Africa and Canada, resist and respond to firmly by resurrecting the lexical priority of the civil religion over and above any competing narrative of law and authority.

I. Curbing Traditional Law in South Africa

South Africa, it would appear, poses a most difficult test to the jurisprudential pattern described in this chapter. It is one of the most accommodating jurisdictions in the world when it comes to cultural diversity. So, if there is any jurisdiction in the liberal-democratic universe that would accept alternative narratives of law and interpretation, it would be South Africa, but here we must think again. Whereas the South African Constitutional Court has been more sympathetic to the claims of difference than most of its counterparts worldwide, even such a generous accommodation regime reaches its limits of toleration when it encounters a challenge to its overarching reign over law's empire.

Consider, for example, the uneasy relationship between constitutional law and customary sources of law in South Africa.[9] The challenge of customary law has haunted the new South Africa for years. Described as the "rainbow nation," it prides itself on being multiracial, diverse, and open-minded, and, in many respects, this is true. It features one of the most progressive bodies of constitutional jurisprudence in the world in the areas of gay and lesbian rights (even involving non-South African spouses), workers' rights, and socioeconomic rights. But even here, in this haven, or even *heaven* of (formal) constitutional inclusiveness, the boundaries of accommodation are firmly drawn and enforced when it comes to customary law. The South African Constitutional Court has consistently limited the scope and application of this once-unrecognized system of legal meaning-creation. In a series of key rulings over the last decade it has emphasized that individual rights, including the right to gender equality, if not reconciled with customary law, ultimately trump it. This is not a foregone conclusion. The South African constitution requires courts to respect cultural and religious communities and, where relevant, to apply customary law, although such law is only applicable to the degree that it is consistent with the constitution itself. This delicate balancing act has been reserved primarily for the high priests of the civil religion in Johannesburg, although the chiefs and headmen of various customary and tribal groups, especially those in rural areas, see themselves as the authoritative voices in determining (or "revealing") the content of customary rules and practices. This combination of legal recognition of customary law and the competition over who has the final word to interpret it has provided the very

[9] In South Africa, the commitment to diversity runs through the Interim and Final constitution. Sections 15, 30, and 31 of the Constitution address religion, culture, and cultural, religious, or linguistic communities, respectively. Sections 39(3) and 211(3) hold that courts are required to apply customary law "subject to the Constitution and any legislation that specifically deals with customary law."

crucible in which tensions can brew. Add to this the fact that many of South Africa's customary traditions impose severe encumbrances on women's rights, and the rumbles of legal disputes over the limits of toleration and accommodation were soon to be heard. Several recent landmark rulings of the South African Constitutional Court provide a viable illustration.

In a country where roughly half of the black population resides in rural areas, African customary rules and practices maintain a significant degree of multiplicity and diversity. They vary among the traditional groups and the different regions of the country. Despite these important distinctions, it is impossible not to notice that many customary rules and traditions are infused with gender inequality and, as such, potentially stand in tension with the equality guarantees encoded in the Bill of Rights. As the Constitutional Court predicted in its landmark 1996 decision, *In re Certification of the Constitution of the Republic of South Africa*, these tensions were bound to emerge. As the Court put it, "[P]atriarchal principles which underlie much of indigenous law would be outlawed by the Bill of Rights, thereby undermining the core of indigenous law."[10] This is particularly true in the realms of marriage, property succession, and access to political power. Women were frequently prohibited from owning or inheriting property, and they are barred from holding traditional leadership positions. The South African Constitution, as part of its commitment to overcoming past racial hierarchies, specifically requires courts to enforce customary law wherever applicable. At the same time, the Constitution enshrines individual rights and principles of equality (including gender equality) and dignity, and it declares, more generally, in its founding provisions that "the Republic of South Africa is one, sovereign, democratic state founded on the... values [of] non-racialism and non-sexism."[11] How to reconcile these commitments is an obvious and inevitable challenge. A woman's right to inherit property and to own jointly accumulated property during and upon the breakdown of marriage are two major issues where these frictions have manifested themselves.

In 1998, soon after the transition to democracy, a genuine attempt was made to employ deliberative processes of law reform to generate an agreed-upon compromise between promoting gender equality and recognizing, for the first time in South African's history, customary marriages as binding and "legible" in the eyes of the state.[12] This effort culminated with the passage of the Recognition of Customary Marriages Act by Parliament. Based on a model developed by the South African Law Commission, the Act provides legal recognition to customary marriages that were never before recognized as lawful and attributes to them certain binding obligations. In this respect, the Recognition of Customary Marriages Act pays a major tribute to traditional and tribal sources of regulating the family. At the same time, the Act heavily regulates the content and structure of the recognized customary marriages, injecting "the state bureaucracy into the regulation of customary marriages, first by requiring that all marriages be registered with a government agency and second by permitting divorce only when it is granted by a family court judge."[13] The Act also changed significantly the balance of power between the spouses in a customary marriage. For instance, the Act declares women and men to

[10] *Ex Parte Chairperson of the Constitutional Assembly: In re Certification of the Constitution of the Republic of South Africa* 1996 (4) SA 744 (CC) (S. Afr.), 200.

[11] Constitution of South Africa, s. 1; see also ss. 9–10.

[12] See South African Law Commission, *Discussion Paper 74: The Harmonisation of the Common Law and the Indigenous Law: Customary Marriages* (Pretoria: South African Law Commission, 1997).

[13] See David L. Chambers, "Civilizing the Natives: Marriage in Post-Apartheid South Africa" (2000) 129 *Daedalus* 101, 113.

be formal equals within the marriage relationship, allowing women in customary marriages the power to acquire and dispose of assets, to enter into contracts, and to litigate in their own name; these are powers and rights that they did not posses under traditional customary family rules. The recognition of customary marriages has thus involved not only acceptance of customary marriages but also a major transformation of these institutions and the traditions they reflect. It replaced, as one scholar concisely notes, "a patriarchal view of marriage with a partnership view."[14] While celebrated by many urban dwellers and women's rights advocates, not everyone was pleased with this legislative reform. Some saw it as suppressing minority cultures precisely by bringing them into the fold of formal state-centered legalism, in the process taking away the most precious currency that traditional leaders held under the old order: their authority as lawgivers.

The recognition of customary marriage was part of a larger reform that was envisioned by the South African Law Commission, an advisory body appointed by the mandarins of the civil religion. The traditional leaders initially had more success, however, in protecting their turf on another front: a Bill proposed in 1998 to reform the customary laws of succession by allowing women to inherit property on the same terms as men.[15] This legal reform would have radically changed the economic, social, and gendered status quo in relation to property-holding, particularly in light of the fact that most succession customary laws in South Africa entailed a system of primogeniture that prohibited females from inheriting. The traditional leaders mobilized against the Bill, arguing that such a Bill would amount to the "westernizing" of African customary laws, that laws of succession were critical to the integrity of customary traditions, and that they were "fundamentally opposed to the Eurocentric approach which is prevalent in [our] country."[16] Legislators acquiesced, deciding not to introduce "drastic changes to the customary system" without considering whether a more gradual approach might be preferable.[17] With this compromise, the tensions encapsulated in these succession laws—between the grand constitutional commitments to respecting customary rules while at the same time promoting gender equality—did not wither away. Rather, they were merely postponed.

From 1997 to 2000, the *Mthembu v. Letsela* trilogy of decisions rocked the country. These early cases played out the drama surrounding customary succession laws and women's (and children's) rights.[18] The legal dispute was based on an inheritance claim made by Mthembu on behalf of her daughter, Tembi, against the estate of the deceased, Letsela. In the first *Mthembu* case, the court did not directly rule on the question of whether the customary rule of primogeniture was valid, instead referring the case for a ruling on whether there was a valid marriage between Mthembu and the deceased, as "illegitimate children" are barred from inheriting under customary law. The subsequent judgment, which was upheld in the end by the Supreme Court of Appeal, found that Mthembu's case had to fail on the grounds of illegitimacy, with a judgment from the Supreme Court of Appeal calling the question of the validity of the rule of primogeniture "academic."[19]

[14] Chambers, "Civilizing the Natives: Marriage in Post-Apartheid South Africa," 114.

[15] See South African Law Commission, *Discussion Paper 93: Customary Law of Succession* (Pretoria: South African Law Commission, 2000); South African Law Commission, *Discussion Paper 95: Customary Law: Administration of Estates* (Pretoria: South African Law Commission, 2001).

[16] See South African Law Commission, *Discussion Paper 93: Customary Law of Succession*, para. 1.2.2; also see Nelson Tebbe, "Inheritance and Disinheritance: African Customary Law and Constitutional Rights" (2008) 88 *Journal of Religion* 466, 467.

[17] Tebbe, "Inheritance and Disinheritance: African Customary Law and Constitutional Rights" 468.

[18] *Mthembu v. Letsela* 1997 (2) SA 936 (TPD) (S. Afr.); *Mthembu v. Letsela & Another* 1998 (2) SA 675 (T) (S. Afr.); *Mthembu v. Letsela & Another* 2000 (3) SA 867 (SCA) (S. Afr.).

[19] *Mthembu v. Letsela & Another* 2000 (3) SA 867 (SCA), para. 33.

In its ruling, which has been criticized by commentators as a "non-decision," the Supreme Court of Appeal notes that "in terms of this system of succession, whether or not Tembi is the deceased's legitimate child, being female, she does not qualify as heir to the deceased's estate. Women generally do not inherit in customary law."[20] The Supreme Court of Appeal expressed reluctance, however, to change or reform customary law, saying that this is a task best left to the legislature.

In the face of the *Mthembu* decisions, the South African Law Commission revisited the issue. The result of its investigation was a discussion paper, issued in 2000, outlining the concern that primogeniture discriminated against women and children born out of wedlock and making recommendations to amend the Intestate Succession Act that governed civil law marriages to extend its coverage to customary marriages as well.[21] Out-of-wedlock children would also be recognized as legitimate heirs. These changes would have the advantage of complying with the requirements of the constitution and of being administratively convenient, although they did not directly confront the constitutionality of the practice of primogeniture. That issue was not fully settled until roughly a decade later, when the Constitutional Court weighed in on these charged matters.

Other branches of government did not sit idle, however. Parliament enacted in 2000 the Promotion of Equality and Prevention of Unfair Discrimination Act. This Act unequivocally prohibits gender discrimination in line with the Constitution and South Africa's international (CEDAW) obligations. As several commentators noted at the time, it is hard to understand this act without accounting for the apparent ineffectiveness of court officials in "reigning in" or bringing customary succession in line with the equality provisions of the Bill of Rights, as was evident in the consideration of the issue in the *Mthembu* decisions. Seen from this angle, the act is a victory for the side of secular constitutionalism in its battle against customary law. Others tried to challenge the very terms of this debate, and their theoretical interventions are important in understanding how this drama unfolded. Instead of conceptualizing customary succession and gender equality in terms of a "traditional v. Western" clash, authors critically argued that the reliance on traditional narratives in *Mthembu* and in customary law litigation in general was itself projecting a partial view of customary traditions because it disregarded marginalized voices within the community and imposed an artificial certainty on fluid understandings of customary rules. Thus, the view from academia was that written and rule-centered customary law is itself already "Westernized."[22] Following from this approach, the tension between customary laws and the rights of women and children could be overcome, or at least be significantly mitigated, if the stories and perspectives of women and children were actually heard. This attempt to broaden the scope of *what* should be considered "customary law" and *who* speaks for a culture proved significant in the eventual jurisprudence of the South African Constitutional Court in its persistent attempt to "domesticate" and mitigate the potential competition and disruption that customary sources of law and identity might otherwise raise in a country committed to both diversity and equality.

More specifically, scholars draw a distinction between two sources of customary law. The first consists of sources such as texts, legislation, and case law, and it is referred

[20] *Mthembu v. Letsela & Another* 2000 (3) SA 867 (SCA), para. 8.

[21] The history of the Law Commission's involvement and its recommendations are spelled out in summary fashion in "Background to the Investigation" and "Summary of Recommendations" in South African Law Commission, *Discussion Paper 93: Customary Law of Succession* 11 at ix–xxi.

[22] See Gardiol van Niekerk, "Indigenous Law and Narrative: Rethinking Methodology" (1999) 32 *The Comparative and International Law Journal of Southern Africa* 208, 211, 218–26.

to as official customary law. The second is found through the stories and examples of how people actually live and is referred to as living customary law.[23] Advocates of the living-tradition argue that official customary law is not, and may never have been, truly representative of the actual workings of the community. Some further argue that these interpretive debates themselves reflect intra-cultural struggles, as suggested in the South African context by Victoria Bronstein. Although she does not look directly at the issue of succession, Bronstein suggests that clashes between customary laws and women's rights ought not to be characterized as traditional versus Western cultural disputes but should instead be interpreted as intra-cultural struggles of women confronting traditionally male-dominated power structures within their own cultures and communities.[24] The appeal of this approach is that, in a struggle against paternalism in customary law, it denies the paternalism implicit in "Westernizing" solutions. Moreover, the intra-cultural conflict approach characterizes customary law as living and thus makes room for deliberation and adaptation to the values enshrined in the new South African Constitution.[25] This permits response to the non-state-law-as-competition claim by effectively disarming its alternative claim for authority and authenticity, bringing it instead within the diversity-as-inclusion fold.

With this background in mind, let us now consider the position taken by the country's apex court. In *Bhe*, the South African Supreme Court heard a constitutional challenge to the rule of male primogeniture as it applies in the customary law of succession.[26] The two minor daughters of Ms. Nontupheko Bhe and her deceased partner argued that the customary law rule of male primogeniture unfairly discriminated against them in that it prevented the children from inheriting the estate of their late father. Not mincing words, Deputy Chief Justice Langa, writing the majority decision, held that the African customary law rule of male primogeniture discriminated unfairly against women and illegitimate children and was, therefore, unconstitutional and invalid. While ordinarily it would be desirable for courts to develop new rules of African customary succession to reflect the living customary law and bring customary law in line with the Constitution, that remedy was not seen as feasible in this matter, given that the rule of male primogeniture is fundamental to customary law and ostensibly irreplaceable on a case-by-case basis. The South African Constitutional Court in *Bhe*, therefore, issued a call for Parliament to reconcile through legislation the role of customary law under the new Constitution, with its emphasis on fairness, justice, dignity, and equity. The fate of the "competitor" worldview, namely, customary law (as interpreted by traditional leaders), was now placed squarely in the hands of the different branches of the civil religion. This time around, the legislature acted swiftly, passing a law that unified the administration of estates.

This development did not conclude the saga of craftily responding to the non-state-law-as-competition challenge; it only set the stage for the next battle, this time around in the sphere of succession to traditional offices, most prominently chieftainship. In 2008,

[23] See Chuma Himonga and Craig Bosch, "The Application of African Customary Law Under the Constitution of South Africa: Problems Solved or Just the Beginning?" (2000) 117 *South African Law Journal* 306, 319–36.

[24] See Victoria Bronstein, "Reconceptualizing the Customary Law Debate in South Africa" (1998) 14 *South African Journal on Human Rights* 388 (1998). For a detailed analysis of intragroup gender dynamics and their connection to intercultural relations, see Shachar, *Multicultural Jurisdictions: Cultural Differences and Women's Rights* 5–44.

[25] Bronstein, "Reconceptualizing the Customary Law Debate in South Africa" 403.

[26] *Bhe & Others v. Magistrate, Khayelitsha, & Others* 2005 (1) SA 580 (CC) (S. Afr.). In the earlier case of *Moseneke & Others v. Master of the High Court*, 2001 (2) SA 18 (CC) (S. Afr.), the Court ordered the government to expedite its harmonization efforts and granted it two years to accomplish that goal.

the Constitutional Court declared the patrilineal custom of chieftainship unjustifiably discriminatory and therefore unconstitutional.[27] This fascinating case concerned a dispute between Ms. Shilubana and Mr. Nwamitwa over the right to succeed Mr. Nwamitwa's father, Richard Nwamitwa, as Hosi (Chief) of the Valoyi traditional community in Limpopo. In 1968, Ms. Shilubana's father, Hosi Fofoza Nwamitwa, died without a male heir. Because customary law at the time did not permit a woman to become Hosi, Ms. Shilubana did not succeed him as Hosi although she was his eldest child. Hosi Fofoza was instead succeeded by his brother, Richard Nwamitwa. During 1996 and 1997, the traditional authorities of the Valoyi community passed resolutions deciding that Ms. Shilubana would succeed Hosi Richard, since, in the new constitutional era, women were equal to men. Her succession was approved by the provincial government. However, following the death of Hosi Richard in 2001, Mr. Nwamitwa interdicted Ms. Shilubana's installation and challenged her succession, claiming that the tribal authorities had acted unlawfully and that he, as Hosi Richard's eldest son, was entitled to succeed his father. Two lower court instances supported his claim before the case ultimately reached the Constitutional Court.

Justice Van der Westhuizen, writing for a unanimous Court, held that the High Court and the Supreme Court of Appeal failed to acknowledge the power of the traditional authorities to develop customary law, here drawing on the living customary law approach as described above. Although courts must consider the past practice of the community, they are also required to respect the right of traditional communities to develop their own law. Courts must also balance the need for flexibility and the imperative to facilitate development against the value of legal certainty and respect for vested rights. As the Constitutional Court stated, "Past practice will . . . not be decisive where the *Constitution* requires the development of the customary law in line with constitutional values."[28] Relevant factors for this balancing test include the nature of the law in question, in particular the implications of the change on constitutional and other legal rights, the process by which the alleged change occurred or is occurring, and the vulnerability of parties affected by the law. Applying this test, the Court found that succession to the leadership of the Valoyi had operated in the past according to the principle of male primogeniture. However, the traditional authorities had the authority to develop customary law, and they had done so in furtherance of the constitutional right to equality. The value of recognizing the development by a traditional community of its own law in accordance with the Constitution was not outweighed by the need for legal certainty.

On balance, a living-customary-law approach (here understood as customary law that complied with the values enshrined in the Constitution) trumps the patrilineal-succession custom, and such a "change from within" of customary law is, from the civil religion's perspective, to be applauded.[29] So, 40 years after Ms. Shilubana's father died without a male heir, his daughter was declared eligible to succeed him as Hosi. In reaching this decision, the high priests of the civil religion were clearly aided by the fact that change had already occurred *within* and *by* the relevant community (or part thereof). This lead the Court to pronounce that:

> [C]ustomary law is living and will in the future inevitably be interpreted, applied and, when necessary, amended or developed by the community itself or by the courts. This will be done in

[27] *Shilubana & Others v. Nwamitwa* 2009 (2) SA 66 (CC) (S. Afr.).

[28] *Shilubana & Others v. Nwamitwa* para. 56.

[29] Advocates of democratic deliberative processes also support such changes, as do multicultural feminists. For further discussion, see Shachar, *Multicultural Jurisdictions: Cultural Differences and Women's Rights*.

view of existing customs and traditions... and of course, the demands of the *Constitution* as the supreme law.[30]

With this vision of partnership in interpretation, the specter of non-state-law-as-competition was disposed of, and diversity-as-inclusion emerged reigning. It should come as no surprise that not all were equally satisfied with this result. In response to the press applauding the court's decision, a member of parliament said that African political leaders were protecting their "own traditions and customs and [were] opposed to their suppression by westernized norms such as equality."[31] Either way, having provided official endorsement of those interpretations of customary law that incorporate general principles of constitutional law with respect to succession of property and succession of tribal leadership—diversity as inclusion—the Court swiftly moved on to tackle a third aspect of customary law: the division of property jointly accumulated during marriage upon its dissolution.

Elizabeth Gumede entered into a customary marriage in 1968. The marriage broke down irretrievably, and, in January 2003, her husband instituted divorce proceedings. Mrs. Gumede was not employed during the marriage, instead maintaining the family household as well as the four children. The family acquired two pieces of immovable property during the course of the marriage. The Customary Marriage Recognition Act provides that a customary marriage concluded after the commencement of that Act (in 2000) is automatically viewed as splitting any jointly acquired property between spouses. The Act does not, however, provide for this property regime in respect of customary marriages concluded before the commencement of the Act, and those marriages are consequently governed by customary law. Customary law in KwaZulu Natal has been codified in the KwaZulu Act and the Natal Code, both of which provide that the husband is the family head and owner of all family property. The result of the KwaZulu Act, the Natal Code, and the lack of provision in the Recognition Act is therefore that a wife to a customary marriage concluded before the commencement of the Act will, in effect, be entitled to nothing upon dissolution of the marriage. Ms. Gumede challenged the constitutionality of these arrangements in *Gumede v. President of the Republic of South Africa*.[32]

Deputy Chief Justice Moseneke, writing for a unanimous Court, found these impugned provisions to be self-evidently discriminatory on at least one listed ground—that of gender.[33] Only women in a customary marriage are subject to these unequal proprietary consequences. Because this is discrimination on a listed ground, it is presumed to be unfair, and the burden fell on the respondents to justify the limitation on the equality right of women engaged in pre-Act marriages concluded under customary law. Moseneke found that the respondents had failed to provide adequate justification for this unfair discrimination. He held that a section of the Recognition Act, which gives a court granting a decree of divorce of a customary marriage the power to order how the assets of the customary marriage should be divided between the parties, is no answer to or justification for the unfair discrimination based on the listed ground of gender. That section, the Court argued, does not cure the discrimination which a spouse in a customary marriage has to endure during the course of the marriage. The patrimonial

[30] *Shilubana & Others v. Nwamitwa* para. 81.

[31] Tebbe, "Inheritance and Disinheritance: African Customary Law and Constitutional Rights" 469.

[32] *Gumede v. Pres. of the Rep. of S. Afr. & Others* 2009 (3) BCLR 243 (CC) (S. Afr.).

[33] In the United States, the doctrinal sex equality standard is "intermediate scrutiny" whereas in South Africa gender classification is treated, in American constitutional law terminology, as "suspect category," thus inviting strict scrutiny.

proprietary system of customary law during the subsistence of a marriage, as codified in the Natal Code and the KwaZulu Act, "patently limits the equality dictates of our Constitution and of the Recognition Act."

The unanimous Court thus confirmed the order of constitutional invalidity issued by the High Court and held that all discriminatory federal and provincial laws that maintain unequal ownership of property between married spouses, during or upon termination of marriage, must be struck down, regardless of whether the couple entered customary marriage before or after the adoption of the Recognition Act. With that decision, the whole concept of "family head" was put to rest. In the clash between official customary law as male-privileging and the equality rights of women and children, the Court has clearly sided with the latter. The triumph of general state law, most notably constitutional law, over the legacy of customary law as a competing normative order with values that stand in tension with those encoded in the civil religion, has been completed. The result is not that customary law no longer exists, or is derecognized; rather, it has been made palatable to the statist order, transformed, as it were, into a more moderate "diversity-as-inclusion" mechanism of governing difference (and reducing intra-group inequality) by disarming a potential challenge to the supremacy of the secular legal authority and its official constitutional interpreters.

II. Canada: Emerging Boundaries of Religious Accommodation

A few words are warranted about equivalent developments in Canada. Unlike the French understanding of secular citizenship (*laïcité*) or the United States' "melting pot" approach, Canada adheres to what may be described as a multicultural citizenship model (or the "salad bowl" metaphor), whereby ethnic, religious, or linguistic differences are, in principle, not seen as a threat to citizenship, but as contributing to its strength and richness. This is reflected in Canadian public discourse, in Canada's official policy of multiculturalism, as well as in the Charter of Rights and Freedoms, adopted in 1982.[34] Section 2 of the Charter protects freedom of religion, sections 16 to 23 protect language and minority language education rights, and section 27 states that the Charter "shall be interpreted in a manner consistent with the preservation and enhancement of the multicultural heritage of Canadians."[35]

Over the years, the Supreme Court of Canada has developed a rich jurisprudence in support of state-endorsed multiculturalism and generous accommodation of difference in the public sphere. In two rulings over the last few years, for example, the Court went out of its way to generously address faith-based claims falling squarely within the parameters of multicultural citizenship as advancing a vision of "diversity as inclusion." In *Amselem*—a case involving Orthodox Montreal Jews who erected *sukkahs* on their balconies in a residential condominium partly in contravention of a boilerplate tenancy contract—the majority advocated tolerating a practice where the individual sincerely believes it is connected to religion, regardless of whether the practice is required by a religious authority.[36] In *Multani*, the Court drew upon a section 1 analysis to overturn a

[34] Canada's official multiculturalism policy predates the *Charter* and finds statutory expression at the federal level as well as in several provincial acts. See e.g. Canadian Multiculturalism Act, R.S.C. Ch. 24 (4th Supp. 1985).

[35] *Canadian Charter of Rights and Freedoms*, Part I of the Constitution Act 1982, Sch. B to the Canada Act 1982, 1982, Ch. 11, s. 27 (U.K.).

[36] *Syndicat Northcrest v. Amselem* [2004] 2 S.C.R. 551 (Can).

Quebec school board decision not to allow a Sikh student to carry the *kirpan* (a ceremonial dagger) due to potential safety hazards and an apparent conflict with the school's prohibition on weapons and dangerous objects.[37] Indeed, the very categorization of the *kirpan*—as either a prohibited weapon in a schoolyard (as the school board claimed) or as an important religious symbol (the position of the student, his parents, and the interveners on behalf of the Sikh community)—was at the heart of this legal dispute. A decision to universally ban the *kirpan*, the Court ruled, was not the least drastic means to address the rather limited harm potential, especially when weighing the sincerity of the student's religious beliefs and the fact that the interference (the ban on the *kirpan*) was not trivial. The Court thus held in favor of Gurjab Singh Multani, providing a resounding statement of the "diversity-as-inclusion" theme:

> The argument that the wearing of kirpans should be prohibited because the kirpan is a symbol of violence and because it sends the message that using force is necessary to assert rights and resolve conflict must fail. Not only is this assertion contradicted by the evidence regarding the symbolic nature of the kirpan, it is also disrespectful to believers in the Sikh religion and does not take into account Canadian values based on multiculturalism.[38]

But even Canada's multicultural policy, arguably one the most accommodating constitutional regimes presently on offer, has been obliged to set its boundaries. When it comes to clashes of religion and culture, arguments that move beyond requests for accommodation (or specific exemption from general laws) to attempts to advance alternative, extrajudicial, moral or adjudicative orders appear to fall beyond the limits of tolerance. This is the dividing line where "diversity as inclusion" ends and "non-state law as competition" emerges, the latter often bringing with it the wrath of the state. Unlike the many diversity-as-inclusion cases requesting reasonable accommodation under the rule of law (as these terms are interpreted by the courts or legislatures of the secular state), arguments that pursue the claim that faith-based sources of authority and obligation are—or ought to be—completely unregulated and parallel or superior to the general rule of law are typically answered with ironclad resistance.

Early in the Charter era, the Supreme Court ruled in *R. v. Jones* that an Alberta pastor in a fundamentalist church could not educate his three children in a church's basement without having any accreditation or approved home-schooling curriculum as required by the relevant secular legislation.[39] In this case, the Alberta Schools Act required all parents to send their children to a public school unless the parent could show that the children are going to an accredited private school or the government has approved the home-school curriculum. Jones was charged with truancy under the Schools Act. In response, he challenged the very authority of general law over the matter, arguing that the rule requiring government approval to educate his children involves "his acknowledging that the government, rather than God, has the final authority over the education of his children" and so contravenes his right to freedom of religion under section 2(a) and his right to have control over how his children are educated, which is protected under section 7 ("life, liberty and security of the person"). Writing for the majority, Justice La Forest dismissed the religion-based challenge to state authority and held that there was a compelling state interest in requiring accreditation. The certification procedure was in no way manifestly unfair or contrary to any principles of fundamental justice. While the province must reasonably accommodate religious belief in accordance with Charter principles, no extraconstitutional source of authority of the kind Jones argued

[37] *Multani v. Marguerite-Bourgeoys (Comm'n scolaire)* [2006] 1 S.C.R. 256 (Can).

[38] *Multani v. Marguerite-Bourgeoys* 71.

[39] *R. v. Jones* [1986] 2 S.C.R. 284 (Can.).

for existed (in the eyes of the state). The Court therefore bluntly rejected Jones' assertion that he should not be forced to apply for exemption or certification from the government because, as he saw it, the authority to attend to his children's education comes from God, making it sinful for him to request the state's permission to do God's will. And, so, the jurisprudential tone was set at the outset of the Charter era to accept claims for accommodation that fit the diversity-as-inclusion mold but reject claims for alternative authority or inapplicability of the constitutional law or state regulatory powers, or those falling in the non-state-law-as-competition category.[40]

With this background in mind, consider the acrimonious controversy that broke out in Canada following a community-based proposal to establish a "private Islamic Court of Justice" (or *darul-qada*) to resolve family law disputes among consenting adults according to faith-based principles.[41] The envisioned tribunal (which ultimately never came into operation) would have permitted consenting parties not only to enter a less adversarial, out-of-court, dispute resolution process, but also to use choice-of-law provisions to apply religious norms to resolve family disputes, according to the "laws (*fiqh*) of any [Islamic] school, e.g. Shiah or Sunni (Hanafi, Shafi'i, Hambali, or Maliki)," potentially delimiting rights and protections that the involved women would have otherwise enjoyed in civil courts under prevailing statutory and constitutional provisions. This proposal did not emerge from the legislature process, nor did it originate from a public consultation process. Instead, a small and relatively conservative non-governmental organization, named the Canadian Society of Muslims, declared in a series of press releases its intention to establish the Shari'a tribunal, as this proposal came to be known in the ensuing debate.[42] The envisioned tribunal, according to its proponents, would have permitted consenting parties to rely on the (then existing) Arbitration Act to enter a binding, out-of-court dispute resolution process, which would have likely been subject to only minimal judicial review. Although the turn to arbitration was presented as fully voluntary, the tribunal's advocates simultaneously argued that as a principled matter once the possibility to turn to binding Shari'a arbitration becomes readily available, it should represent a clear choice for Muslim Canadians: governance of oneself by the personal laws of religion or governance by secular Canadian family law.[43] This construction of the proposal had the effect of presenting it as a frontal "non-state-law-as-competition" challenge, which even tolerant, multicultural Ontario (the largest Canadian province and arguably the country's most influential common-law jurisdiction) could not accept with indifference.

A major controversy soon erupted, both within and outside Canada's large and diverse Muslim community. Opponents argued that a faith-based tribunal of this kind would set a dangerous precedent by allowing religious communities to "carve out" certain aspects of the law and to insulate themselves from the purview of *Charter* provisions and other basic

[40] Courts in Canada have accepted jurisdiction over religious disputes in which property rights or civil rights are implicated, here following the British tradition.

[41] Briefly, the idea was to rely upon a *preexisting* legal framework, the Arbitration Act, which (at the time) permitted a wide array of family law disputes to be resolved under its extensively open-ended terms. See Arbitration Act, S.O., Ch. 17 (1991) (Ont.) ("allow[ing] the parties to choose the law applicable to their disputes.... It does so by allowing the parties to vary or opt out of the applicability and choice of law sections"), John D. Gregory, Anne Marie Predeko, and Juliette Nicolet, "Faith-Based Arbitration" (Paper prepared for the Uniform Law Conference of Canada, Civil Section, 2005), 1.

[42] Syed Mumtaz Ali, "Establishing an Institute of Islamic Justice (Darul Qada)" (Oct. 2002) *The Canadian Society of Muslims News Bulletin.*

[43] Interview by Rabia Mills with Syed Mumtaz Ali, President, The Canadian Society of Muslims (Aug. 1995), available at > (last visited 10 May 2009); see also "Darul-Qada: Beginnings of Muslim Civil Justice System in Canada" (April 2003) *The Canadian Society of Muslims News Bulletin.*

norms of statutory and administrative law. Establishing such enclaves of unregulated "islands of privatized jurisdiction" would be detrimental, it was argued, to the universality of the rule of law in Canada. Feminist activists and numerous grassroots organizations, such as the Canadian Council of Muslim Women, further emphasized that such tribunals would put undue burden on Muslim women who, for fear of being ostracized or otherwise sanctioned, would be coerced by the community to consent to such Shari'a-based arbitration processes.[44] Others were worried that these tribunals would fall prey to intra-community politics or would be dominated by community "big-men." As tensions mounted, the debate over the proposed faith-based tribunal became highly politicized and polarized. It was in this climate that former Ontario Premier Dalton McGuinty decided to conclude the debate by publicly announcing: "There will be no Sharia law in Ontario. There will be no religious arbitration in Ontario," for it "threatens our common ground." The clearest statement of this governmental position was expressed by the Attorney General, the highest civil official in Ontario authorized with developing and enforcing the tenets of the civil religion. Upon revealing the proposed legislation that amended the Arbitration Act, the Attorney General stated that "[a]ll family law arbitrations in Ontario will be conducted using only *Canadian* law." The answer to the non-state-law-as-competition challenge, then, was to declare officially and accordingly legislate that "resolutions based on other laws and principles—including religious principles—would have *no* legal effect and would amount to advice only." This change took effect in 2006 and was further elaborated with regulations published in 2007. Bringing the point home, the Attorney General reaffirmed that only those charged with securing the implementation of the civil religion have a claim to speak authoritatively on behalf of the governed, stating forcefully that "[t]here is one family law for all Ontarians and that is Canadian law."[45] Any other sources of normativity and authority, including religious principles, are relegated to the realm of "unofficial," "unrecognized" and, indeed, "non-law" status.

Arguably, the very debate provoked by the tribunal proposal was whether this ought to remain the status quo or whether alternative, non-statist (in this example, religious) principles, should gain a degree of authority in regulating certain aspects of family law disputes among voluntarily consenting adults. Without a doubt, concerns about potential coercion and duress, as well as deeply engrained gendered power inequities, were well considered in this context. However, it is difficult to explain the austere and unequivocal response of the government to the Shari'a tribunal proposal solely in terms of a commitment to promoting women's rights, especially given that Canadian and provincial family laws still permit a great degree of contractual freedom to spouses who wish to opt out of the statutory default rules of equitable division, often leaving women with far less than equitable division.[46] The spectre of witnessing the unravelling of a reality in which not all law is state law nor is it administered exclusively by its approved members of the civil religious order seemed to have played a major role, too, in this clamp down.

The government, in short, decided to respond to the Shari'a tribunal challenge by ultimately barring the operation of *any* faith-based family arbitration process. Such a

[44] See e.g. Canadian Council of Muslim Women, "Position Statement on the Proposed Implementation of Section of Muslim Law [Sharia] in Canada" (2004).

[45] Ministry of the Attorney General, "The Family Statute Law Amendment Act, 2005" (15 November 2005) *Backgrounder*. These changes were implemented with the passage of the Arbitration Act, S.O. Ch. 1, s. 1(2) (2006) (incorporated into s. 2.2. of the 1991 Arbitration Act) and Family Arbitration, O. Reg. 134/2007.

[46] See *Hartshorne v. Hartshorne* [2004] 1 S.C.R. 550, para. 36 (Can.) (confirming and reinstating the legal validity of a "domestic contract" that was defined by legal counsel as an "unfair agreement" to

universal ban ensures that Islam is not singled out as being more (or less) friendly to women's interests than any other religious or customary tradition. It further aims to realign the regulation of the family exclusively within the state, leaving no room (except for informal religious mediation, which has no legal effect in the eyes of civil courts or legislatures) for communities' own institutions and authorities to exercise any formal role in defining the parties' marriage and divorce status. In effect, this resolution draws a high and formidable wall of separation between state and religion. It also reasserts in unambiguous terms the lexical priority of the former over the latter.

Another example of the renewed emphasis on the state's authority to enforce secular provisions against expressions of pious resistance to the ground rules established by the civil religion is found in the landmark decision of *Bruker v. Marcovitz*, in which the Supreme Court of Canada rejected the claim that non-compliance with a contractual obligation becomes immune to judicial review or intervention merely by virtue of claiming religious freedom as the motivation for such noncompliance: "[t]he fact that a dispute has a religious aspect does not by itself make in non-justiciable."[47] In the *Marcovitz* case, a Jewish husband made a contractual commitment to remove barriers to religious remarriage in a negotiated settlement reached with the consent of the parties and after consultation with independent legal counsel. That agreement was incorporated into the final divorce decree between the parties (*decree nisi*); indeed, its provisions became part of the terms that enabled the civil divorce to be finalized by the relevant state authority.[48] Once the husband had the secular divorce in hand, however, he failed to honor the agreement, claiming that he had undertaken a moral rather than legal obligation. The Supreme Court of Canada, unlike its counterpart in South Africa in the *Gumede* case, refused to enter the fray of exploring competing interpretations of the religious obligation at issue. What remained undisputed between the parties was that, unless the husband granted a Jewish divorce decree ("*get*") to his wife, she could not be released from that religious marriage because the secular divorce does not terminate or affect that relationship. Mr. Marcovitz's refusal to remove these barriers to remarriage thus left Ms. Bruker in the precarious situation known as the *agunah* or "chained wife;" despite being civilly divorced, the woman is unable to remarry or have children that are recognized as members of the faith community. The Supreme Court recognized the gendered harms caused to Ms. Baker by Mr. Marcovitz's refusal to deliver the *get*, but it was not in a position to order specific performance (directing the husband to turn to a Jewish *beth din*). Instead, the judgment imposed monetary damages on the husband for the breach of the contractual promise in ways that harmed the wife personally and affected the public interest generally. This decision was made despite the ex-husband's claims that no secular authority has the power or right to enforce damages for the breach of contract in this context because his promise to remove these religious barriers was moral, not legal, and, as such, was a protected religious freedom. The Court, in a majority opinion penned by Madam Justice Rosalie Abella, rejected this claim. It held, instead, that it was fully within the Court's jurisdiction to recognize the enforceability by *civil* courts of agreements to discourage *religious* barriers to remarriage, addressing the gender discrimination those barriers may represent and alleviate the effects they may have on

the wife, allowing the parties to stray away from statutory equitable default rules found in governing family law statutes).

[47] *Bruker v. Marcovitz* [2007] 3 S.C.R. 607 (Can.), para. 41. See also paras 3, 92.

[48] Canada's Divorce Act requires parties to remove religious barriers to remarriage. See Divorce Act, R.S.C. 1985, Ch. 3, s. 21.1 (2nd Supp. 1985).

extracting unfair concessions in a civil divorce.[49] The key to understanding this decision is found, we believe, in its opening paragraphs, which conform squarely with the distinction between accepting diversity as inclusion and treating non-state law as competition as a potential threat that must be curtailed, contained, and regulated. As Justice Abella wrote:

> Canada rightly prides itself on its evolutionary tolerance for diversity and pluralism. This journey has included a growing appreciation for multiculturalism, including the recognition that ethnic, religious or cultural differences will be acknowledged and respected. Endorsed in legal instruments ranging from the statutory protections found in human rights codes to their constitutional enshrinement in the *Canadian Charter of Rights and Freedoms*, the right to *integrate into* Canada's mainstream based on and notwithstanding these differences has become a defining part of our national character.[50]

This is a classic manifestation of Canada's now-canonical policy favoring diversity as inclusion. Immediately following this declaration, in the subsequent paragraph, the Court quickly set limits to its celebrated commitment to tolerance. These restrictions were erected precisely in response to challenges in which differences are seen as failing to accept or submit to the overarching authority of the secular state and the core values enshrined in its constitution:

> The right to have differences protected, however, does not mean that those differences are always hegemonic. Not all differences are compatible with Canada's fundamental values and, accordingly, not all barriers to their expression are arbitrary. Determining when the assertion of a right based on difference must yield to a more pressing public interest is a complex, nuanced, fact-specific exercise that defies bright-line application. It is, at the same time, a delicate necessity for protecting the evolutionary integrity of both multiculturalism and public confidence in its importance.[51]

The final decision, then, on how to articulate this "delicate necessity" is not reserved for those claiming exemption or immunity from general laws through raising the non-state-law-as-competition challenge. Instead, the state's high constitutional priests retain the crucial designation as the ultimate arbiters in conflicts between the tenets of the civil religion and its competitors.

III. Conclusion

In this chapter, we identified two different interpretations of what tolerance and accommodation require in grappling with the challenges of diversity: diversity as inclusion and non-state law as competition. The focus has been on courts and legislatures in accommodation-friendly societies that now find themselves embroiled in the search for responses to the post-secularist spread of alternative (here, religious and customary) source of law and meaning. While accepting the mantra of diversity as inclusion, the high priests of the civil religion appear to vehemently oppose the non-state-law-as-competition narrative, at least in part because it challenges the very authority and superiority they hold on account of the secular order. Although operating in different contexts, the South African Constitutional Court and the Supreme Court of Canada seem to have made every effort to subject traditional legal regimes to general principles of constitutional law.[52]

[49] *Bruker v. Marcovitz* para. 92.

[50] *Bruker v. Marcovitz* para. 1 (emphasis added).

[51] *Bruker v. Marcovitz* para. 2.

[52] Similar jurisprudential trends are evident elsewhere. See e.g. the Supreme Court of Israel's ground-breaking subjection of religious tribunals' jurisprudence to general principles of Israeli constitutional and administrative law (*Bavli v. Great Rabbinical Court*, 1995).

By so doing, they have erected a new wall of separation that places non-compliance with the essence of constitutional supremacy beyond the pale of accepted accommodation, offering to those who espouse them the potential to either bring these alternative legal domains under the general rule of constitutional law or to face a precarious existence on the external side of the wall, where no exceptions or exemptions are carved out. When those charged with protecting constitutional supremacy perceive legal claims that draw upon ecclesial sources of rulemaking to unduly collide with the core commitments of the temporal, human-made constitution, it is usually a matter of time until the wrath of state fiat is unleashed.

As we have seen, even the most accommodating constitutional systems, those that are committed to a version of multicultural or "differentiated" citizenship within the boundaries of reasonable or permissible accommodation of collective identities, are not keen on autonomous, rival adjudicative systems that derive their authority and morality from sources external and prior to, and in some cases insulated from, secular law. The ideas of Max Weber (from "kadi justice" to "rational legal authority") and James Scott ("seeing like a state") point to different aspects of this deep antagonism of the modern state and its laws toward alternative schemata of meaning and authority.[53]

The bottom line is this. Although the law is not necessarily as "jurispathic" as Robert Cover had assumed many year ago[54] —for we have seen throughout this chapter that courts and legislatures prefer to extend olive branches of various kinds to non-state, alternate and potentially competing systems of orthodoxy—the high priests of the constitutional order have not hesitated, when encountering what they perceived as unruly challenges to their own standing as supreme and ultimate lawgivers, to expel their competitors to the no-man's land of legal exile, relegating them to non-law status and unofficial existence. Those who do not comply with the constitutional religion's ultimate supremacy thus come to encounter the outer limits of law's accommodation, and it is a cold place to reside on this side of the new wall of separation.

[53] See e.g. Max Weber, *Economy and Society* (Berkeley: University of California Press, 1922); James C. Scott, *Seeing like a State: How Certain Schemes to Improve the Human Condition Have Failed* (New Haven: Yale University Press, 1999).

[54] Robert M. Cover, "The Supreme Court 1982 Term—Forward: Nomos and Narrative" (1983) 97 *Harvard Law Review* 4.

PART III

RELIGION, SECULARISM, AND WOMEN'S EQUALITY

11

Headscarf versus Burqa: Two French Bans with Different Meanings

*Patrick Weil**

On 15 March 2004, after months of harsh public debates, the President of France, Jacques Chirac, promulgated a law that stated: "in public elementary, middle and high schools, the wearing of signs or clothing which conspicuously manifests students' religious affiliations is prohibited. Disciplinary procedures to implement this rule will be preceded by a discussion with the student."[1]

Six years later, on 11 October 2010, again after months of considerable controversy, a new law was promulgated, this time prohibiting the burqa in public spaces.[2] The law became effective on 11 April 2011. In the same year, it was estimated that a few hundred women out of France's five million Muslims wore the burqa,[3] and were doubtlessly the most directly affected by the law. From now on, they would not be able legally to cover their faces before taking a walk in the streets of Paris or visiting the marketplace. And yet, the French legislature insisted that the prohibition was religion-blind; that it was a matter of a new kind of public social order; that just as it is forbidden to appear naked in a public space or to practice incest, it has always been a social norm to have one's face uncovered.[4]

This new law provoked, renewed, and increased liberal academia's condemnation of the French approach to religion. Many academics were already emphasizing the

* Patrick Weil is Senior Research Fellow at the Centre national de la recherche scientifique (CNRS, Centre d'Histoire Sociale du 20ème siècle-université de Paris1 Panthéon-Sorbonne) and a former member of the Commission on the Implementation of the Principle of Secularism in the Republic (July–December 2003). He just published *The Sovereign Citizen. Denaturalization and the Origins of the American Republic* (Philadelphia: University of Pennsylvania Press, 2013).

He would like to thank Philippe Cimay, Pamela Druckerman, Valérie Lasserre-Kiesow, Etienne Ollion, Benoist Pierre, Eugene Rusyn, Adam Seligman, James Whitman, Alexander Zevin and his research assistants, Noorain Khan (Yale Law School) and Leonid Sirota (NYU Law School) for advice and help in the writing of this chapter.

[1] Article 1 of the Law of 15 March 2004 (No. 2004-228) regulating, in application of the principle of *laïcité*, the wearing of signs or clothing which conspicuously manifest religious affiliations in public elementary, middle and high schools, JORF (Official Organ of the French Republic) no. 65 of 17 March 2004, 5190.

[2] Law no. 2010-1192 to Forbid the Concealment of One's Face in Public was promulgated on 11 October 2010 and published in the *Journal Officiel* on 12 October 2010.

[3] In 2009 the estimates provided by the French Ministry of Interior regarding the number of women who were wearing the burqa varied between 367 and 2,000. See <http://www.lefigaro.fr/actualite-france/2009/09/09/01016-20090909ARTFIG00040-deux-mille-femmes-portent-la-burqa-en-france-.php>.

[4] In her report to the French National Assembly on the Bill prohibiting the concealment of the face in public, Mrs. Bérengère Poletti states: "In the Republic, reciprocity and exchange are two essential notions and the French society is deeply marked by the notion of 'civility.' Behind this term, there is the idea that, in a society, customs have to be policed and rules should be followed as to permit a

illiberalism of the French secular regime known as *laïcité* after the passage of the 2004 law. For Joseph Carens,[5] the law required "some Muslim children to choose between following their conscience and receiving a free public education" without any "strong justification." Neither the will of the majority (the law reflects and reinforces a distinctively Christian vision of religion, and there is nothing in *laïcité* that requires ordinary Catholics to act contrary to their religious obligations) nor the need to protect Muslim girls not wearing the headscarves could justify an "unjust" law forbidding some people from acting in accordance with their religious duties, especially if one considers the multidimensional meaning of the veil.

Later on, two books were dedicated to the issue. In *Why the French Don't Like Headscarves: Islam, the State and Public Space*,[6] John R. Bowen, an anthropologist interviewing numerous French participants in this drama, seeks to understand how it could have occurred and why a whole nation has fallen into a condemnable illiberal prejudice. In his view, there is no clear definition of *laïcité*, but only a French political philosophy that citizens must all subscribe to the same values in the public sphere. This law was also passed because of the "particular passion for seeking statutory solutions to social ills" and because it "would send a powerful message to the Islamists."[7] He emphasizes how the broadcast and print media "played to popular fears" of what the veil represents (such as communalism, sexism, and Islamism) and "the extraordinary symbolic weight given to a scarf worn on the head by a small number of schoolgirls."[8]

In what should be called a pamphlet, the historian Joan Wallach Scott argues that a republicanism-dominated vision of France led to the imposition of a ban on headscarves, worn by very few girls in public schools.[9] The fear of communalism, the influence of or the reaction to Jean-Marie Le Pen,[10] played their role, but less than three other factors. The first of these is a racist conception of Muslims stuck in colonial history (historically, French conceptions of Islam fit this description—Muslims/Arabs have been marked as a lesser people, incapable of improvement and so impossible to assimilate to French ways of life).[11] The second is a tradition of secularism in which "the state becomes modern . . . by suppressing or privatizing religion because it is taken to represent the irrationality of tradition, an obstacle to open debate and discussion" and whose "effect can be intolerance and discrimination."[12] And the third is a perception of the veil, conceived

civilized exchange between individuals. The concealing of the face is perceived as undermining our social code represented by a set of norms which are consensual and whose finality is to facilitate harmony in social relations" (translation mine) French National Assembly, *Rapport d'Information*, no. 2646 of 23 June 2010.

[5] Joseph H. Carens, "Démocratie, multiculturalisme et hijab," *Esprit*, January 2005, 54.

[6] John R. Bowen, *Why the French Don't Like Headscarves: Islam, the State, and Public Space* (Princeton, NJ: Princeton University Press, 2008).

[7] Bowen, *Why the French Don't Like Headscarves* 243.

[8] Bowen, *Why the French Don't Like Headscarves* 7.

[9] Joan Wallach Scott, *The Politics of the Veil* (Princeton, NJ: Princeton University Press, 2007). Joan Scott is so stubbornly opposed to alternative perspectives that she makes minor but telling mistakes where she appears as afflicted by a form of cognitive blindness. Quoting the Commission Stasi report, she translates the sentence "des substituts au porc et du poisson le vendredi doivent être proposés dans le cadre de la restauration collective (établissements scolaires, pénitentiaires, hospitaliers, d'entreprise)" as: "substitute of pork would be offered only on Friday and absolutely not on another day of the week." The trouble is that the sentence means exactly the opposite, namely that a substitute for pork (every day for Jews or Muslims) and fish (only on Friday for the Catholics) would be offered in schools, prisons, hospitals or private enterprises' catering.

[10] Scott, *The Politics of the Veil* 40.

[11] Scott, *The Politics of the Veil* 45.

[12] Scott, *The Politics of the Veil* 93–5.

not in its possible modernity but as a sign of obscurantism or of gender oppression, calling for state action to rescue the oppressed and defend French identity.

After the passage of the burqa ban in 2010, editorialists[13] along with scholars like Martha Nussbaum emphasized the connection between the two Bills and the confirmation of the illiberalism of the French *laïcité*.[14]

A few months after the passage of the 2004 law, in the fall of 2005, massive riots occurred in French suburbs. The *New York Times* reported on 5 November 2005, that the "majority of the youths committing the acts are Muslim, and of African or North African origin."[15] The BBC reported that French society's negative perceptions of Islam and social discrimination of immigrants had alienated some French Muslims and may have been a factor in the causes of the riots: "Islam is seen as the biggest challenge to the country's secular model in the past 100 years."[16]

Yet a few months later, in the spring of 2006, a Pew Research Center survey conducted across 15 nations showed France as the country with the highest respect of and interaction between different faiths. 74 percent of non-Muslim French felt that there *is not* a conflict between being a devout Muslim and living in a modern society, whereas 70 percent of Germans, 58 percent of Spaniards, 54 percent of Britons, and 40 percent of Americans felt that there *is* such a conflict. It is in France that Christians and Muslims each have the highest approval rates among the other religion. And France was the only country where a majority of Muslims (and a very large majority, at 74 percent) had a positive opinion of Jews, which is not the case in the United Kingdom, Spain, or Germany.[17] These results were confirmed in August 2007 by a more recent *Financial Times* poll conducted by Louis Harris in the United States and the five biggest European countries: France is the only country with a majority (69 percent) of people who say they have one or several Muslim friends (versus 38 percent of Britons and 28 percent of Americans). 46 percent of Britons feel that Muslims have too much power in their country, whereas only 19 percent of the French say the same thing.[18]

How can a regime and a law that are so illiberal produce (or at least fail to hamper) the most extensive interaction between people of different faiths and beliefs among western democracies? In fact, these critics fell short of understanding French *laïcité*, which in my view is a liberal legal regime, as well as the processes that led to the adoption of the two laws and, in the case of Martha Nussbaum, the differences between them.

[13] See "France's Ban on the Burqa: The War of French Dressing," *The Economist*, 14 January 2010 or T. S. Kidd, "With Burqa Ban: France Attacks all Faiths," *USA Today*, 18 April 2011.

[14] See Martha Nussbaum, "Veiled Threats?," *NY Times Opinionator*, 11 July 2010, available at <http://opinionator.blogs.nytimes.com/2010/07/11/veiled-threats> and especially Martha Nussbaum, "Beyond the Veil: A Response," *NY Times Opinionator*, 15 July 2010, available at <http://opinionator.blogs.nytimes.com/2010/07/15/beyond-the-veil-a-response>.

[15] Craig S. Smith, "10 Officers Shot as Riots Worsen in French Cities," *NY Times*, 7 November 2005, at A1.

[16] Henri Astier, "Ghettos Shackle French Muslims," *BBC News*, 30 October 2005, available at <http://news.bbc.co.uk/2/hi/europe/4375910.stm>.

[17] Pew Research Center, *Pew Global Attitude Project: 15 Nation Survey*, Spring 2006.

[18] This *Financial Times*/Harris Poll was conducted online by Harris Interactive among a total of 6,398 adults (aged 16–64) within France (1,029), Germany (1,086), Great Britain (1,111), Spain (1,061) and the United States (1,055) and adults (aged 18–64) in Italy (1,056) between 1 and 13 August 2007. The poll results are available at <http://www.harrisinteractive.com/news/FTHarrisPoll/HI_FinancialTimes_HarrisPoll_Aug2007_Tables_US.pdf> and <http://www.harrisinteractive.com/news/FTHarrisPoll/HI_FinancialTimes_HarrisPoll_Aug2007_Tables_EU.pdf>.

I. A Liberal Régime and a Liberal Law

In France, just like in the United States (see *Reynolds v. United States*), public laws trump religious practices.[19] Yet in France, like in the United States and other democracies, the status of religion is specially protected—better protected than other human rights by the law of 1905.[20]

And in France, like in the United States, Canada, the United Kingdom and in many other democracies, there is the difference—not emphasized by the authors previously quoted—between legislation and jurisprudence on the one hand, and social norms on the other. For example, blasphemy is not prohibited in the United States.[21] Yet expressing any doubt as to the existence of God by an American would invite the distrust and animosity of a considerable number of his or her compatriots.[22] If, for example, he or she is a candidate for public office, it would in all likelihood prevent him or her from being elected,[23] even though the U.S. Constitution explicitly and unequivocally prohibits any religious test for aspirants to office.[24]

Joan Scott might be right when she says that, for French militants of secularism and for a large proportion of French citizens, religion "represent[s] the irrationality of tradition." The most recent poll shows that 36 percent of the French believe in God, 34 percent are atheists and 32 percent don't know.[25] The number of non-believers is increasing.[26] It is the opposite picture in the United States, where the believers are the majority and where—for many citizens—non-believers appear as untrustworthy persons.

[19] 98 U.S. 145 (1879). In *Reynolds v. United States*, the Supreme Court of the United States unanimously denied a Mormon who believed it was his religious duty to enter into a second marriage an exemption from the law prohibiting polygamy. The Court held that "[l]aws are made for the government of actions, and while they cannot interfere with mere religious belief and opinions, they may with practices." To allow exceptions from general laws, even when these laws interfere with religious practice, "would be to make the professed doctrines of religious belief superior to the law of the land, and in effect to permit every citizen to become a law unto himself. Government could exist only in name under such circumstances." 98 U.S. 166–7 (1879). This holding was re-affirmed, although its potentially sweeping scope was somewhat reduced, in the majority opinion in *Employment Division, Department of Human Resources of Oregon v. Smith*, 494 U.S. 872 (1990).

[20] The law of 1905, for example, guaranteed to religious institutions an extremely favorable fiscal status for donations and legacies. In addition, Art. 53 of the Appropriation Bill of 17 April 1906 permitted the devolution of all goods and properties previously allocated to the exercise of faith to the new religious associations created within the frame of the law of 1905. See François Méjan, *L'organisation de l'église catholique, ses rapports avec l'Etat* (1954), 45–8.

[21] See *Joseph Burstyn, Inc. v. Wilson*, 343 U.S. 495 (1952) (holding unconstitutional as a prior restraint on the freedom of speech protected by the First Amendment a statute authorizing a censor not to license a motion picture found to be "sacrilegious").

[22] See Penny Edgell et al., "Atheists as 'Other': Moral Boundaries and Cultural Membership in American Society" (2006) 71 *American Sociological Review* 211; also see Nelse Tebbe, "Nonbelievers" (2011) 97 *Virginia Law Review* 1111 (reviewing American attitudes towards non-believers, especially in part I.B at 1122–7).

[23] See Jeffrey M. Jones, "Some Americans Reluctant to Vote for Mormon, 72-Year-Old Presidential Candidates," *Gallup News Service*, 20 February 2007, available at <http://www.gallup.com/poll/26611/some-americans-reluctant-vote-mormon-72yearold-presidentialcandidates.aspx#1> (reporting that 53 percent of respondents stated they "would not vote for . . . a generally well qualified person for president who happened to be" an atheist, even though nominated by their own political party).

[24] U.S. Const. Art. VI, para. 3 (". . . no religious Test shall ever be required as a Qualification to any Office or public Trust under the United States").

[25] Harris Interactive Poll, conducted on 24 and 25 January 2011, based on a sample of 1,051 individuals; published by *Le Parisien*, 6 February 2011.

[26] See Sébastien Fath, "36% des sondés déclarent croire en Dieu," available at <http://blogdesebastienfath.hautetfort.com/archive/2011/02/06/36-des-sondes-declarent-croire-en-dieu-france-2011-sondage-h.html>.

That said, it does not mean that French legislation and jurisprudence does not respect religion and religious people, just as American legislation and jurisprudence respect atheism. On the contrary.

For legal scholars, *laïcité* has a clear definition, with the law of 1905 having been built around three principles: freedom of conscience, the separation of State and churches, and the equal respect of all faiths and beliefs.[27]

Separation meant a break with a previous system of Concordat in which pastors, rabbis, but mainly Catholic clergymen—all representatives of the recognized faiths organized in public and monopolistic institutions—were selected and paid by the government.[28] There was no longer a distinction between recognized and non-recognized religious institutions and freedom of religion was guaranteed. Under the liberal framework put in place by the law of 1905, Judaism and Protestantism were able to develop a new diversity in the first half of the twentieth century. Public subsidies of religious institutions were henceforth forbidden.

Yet the recognition of the right of everyone to practice their own beliefs was ensured to the point where the State, in an exception to the general rule of separation, paid the salaries of chaplains of any religion in order to permit all those forced to live in enclosed areas such as asylums, prisons, the army, some schools, and hospitals to pray and practice their faith.[29]

In fact, this law represents a break from, rather than a continuation of, preceding anti-religious laws or regulations (e.g. the law of 1 July 1901, which required religious congregations and the schools affiliated with them to be authorized by law or by governmental decree).[30] It was designed by the socialists Aristide Briand, Francis de Pressensé, and Jean Jaurès, who were much more open to religious freedom than their radical colleagues in the Parliament, in a negotiating process that involved the right-wing minority of the Parliament, who did not vote for the law but did not disapprove of it either.[31] The French bishops in their majority approved of it too. But Pius X—the new conservative Pope—decided to condemn it hastily,[32] forcing the French Catholic Church to fight the law. For the Catholic Church, its acceptance occurred in stages from 1924 to 1945, leaving the issue of the subsidies to private religious schools open until the 1990s.

Under the regime of *laïcité*, neutrality towards any religious belief is not imposed upon individuals in the public sphere, as it is often and wrongly believed by editorialists and academics, but on the state and its servants, in the political arena.[33] Here is how Jean Rivero, a leading legal scholar of the post-war period, expressed it:

> [T]here is a refusal, by the State, to endorse one faith, to give to it an official seal of approval by making a religious judgment, or to give it any material aid in whatever form. Religious choice is a

[27] François Méjan, "La laïcité de l'Etat en droit positif et en fait," in *La Laïcité* (1960), Presses universitaires de France, Paris, 201–45.

[28] Law of 18 germinal, year X (10 April 1802). See Rita Hermon-Belot, "Religion, Politics and Pluralism in France: an historical and cultural gap?" (unpublished manuscript on file with author).

[29] See Art. 2 of Loi du 9 décembre 1905 concernant la séparation des Églises et de l'État, the French law on the separation of Church and State.

[30] This idea of continuity was endorsed by Nicolas Sarkozy in the speech made in Lateran, on 20 December 2007, available at <http://www.lemonde.fr/politique/article/ 2007/ 12/21/ discours-du-president-de-la-republique-dans-la-salle-de-la- signature- du-palais-du-latran_992170_823448.html>. For a critique of it, see the excellent book by Jean Baubérot, *La laïcité expliquée à M. Sarkozy-et à ceux qui écrivent ses discours* (Paris: Albin Michel, 2008).

[31] Cf. Christophe Bellon, "La séparation des Églises et de l'Etat. De la genèse à l'application de la loi de 1905" (2005) *Historiens et Géographes* 193.

[32] See Pope St. Pius X's Encyclicals *Vehementer Nos* (Issued 11 February 1906) and *Gravissimo Officii Munere* (Issued 10 August 1906).

[33] James Q. Whitman, "Separating Church and State: The Atlantic Divide" (2008) 34 *Historical Reflections* 86.

private matter; the State presents itself to all, stripped of all metaphysical symbols, distant from any trace of the spiritual. My domain is the earth, it says to all of its citizens. Manager of the temporal world, it refuses to envisage what is beyond this management.[34]

The wearing of religious signs is therefore forbidden in the state sphere for public servants, for example, but not—despite public or academic beliefs—in the public sphere.

This regime was set at the beginning of the twentieth century, when metropolitan France was a predominantly Catholic territory with very small Protestant (1 percent) and Jewish (0.2 percent) "minority" populations. A century later, France has become the European country with the largest Buddhist, Jewish, Muslim, and atheist or agnostic communities. Within this newly developed diversity, especially during the last 20 years, the presence of Islam as the second most practiced faith has raised tensions between the free exercise of religion and local or national institutions.

Unsurprisingly, the public schools where the struggle between the Catholic Church and partisans of a purely secular education was still ongoing, albeit drawing to a close, became the location of new kinds of tensions.

The arms were still smoking when a controversy over the right of female Muslim students to wear veils in public high schools attracted public attention in the late 1980's, provoking in 1989—at the request of the socialist minister of education Lionel Jospin—an ambiguous and complex legal statement by France's highest administrative court, the *Conseil d'État*.[35]

Based on the legal constraints imposed upon the government by the French Constitution, international conventions and legislative texts, the *Conseil d'État* concluded that:

> [T]he wearing by students, in the schools, of signs whereby they believe to be manifesting their adherence to one religion is itself not incompatible with the principle of laïcité, since it constitutes the exercise of their liberty of expression and manifestation of their religious beliefs; but this liberty does not permit students to exhibit [*d'arborer*] signs of religious belonging which, by their nature, by the conditions under which they are worn individually and collectively, or by their ostentatious or combative [*revendicatif*] character, would constitute an act of pressure, provocation, proselytizing or propaganda, threatening to the dignity or liberty of the student or to the other members of the educational community, compromising their health or their security, disturbing the continuation of institutional activities or the educational role of the instructors, in short, [that] would disturb proper order in the establishment or the normal functioning of public service.[36]

As Seyla Benhabib later remarked, "this Solomonic judgment" attempting to balance the principles of *laïcité* and freedom of religion and conscience, "instead of articulating some clear guidelines . . . left the proper interpretation of the meaning of wearing of these signs up to the judgment of the school authorities."[37]

On 10 September 1994, the Minister of Education, François Bayrou, instructed the French public school system that students had the right to wear subtle religious symbols, but that the veil was not among them. The instruction added to the confusion as it was not legally binding.

[34] Jean Rivéro, "De l'idéologie à la règle de droit: la notion de laïcité dans la jurisprudence administrative," in *La Laïcité* (1960), 266.

[35] Opinion of the *Conseil d'État*, 27 Nov. 1989, No. 346893, available at <http://www.rajf.org/spip.php?article1065>.

[36] Seyla Benhabib, *Another Cosmopolitanism: Hospitality, Sovereignty, and Democratic Iterations* (Oxford, New York: Oxford University Press, 2006), 54–5.

[37] Benhabib, *Another Cosmopolitanism.*

At the beginning of 2003, the controversy resumed within the political sphere. On 3 April, Prime Minister Jean-Pierre Raffarin advocated the prohibition of headscarves in public schools. On 29 April, he answered a question by François Baroin, a member of parliament concerned that in public schools "haze and ambiguity are actually the loyal allies of fundamentalists." On 30 April, Jack Lang, and on 17 May, Laurent Fabius—both former socialist ministers—advocated the ban on headscarves in public schools. Fabius did it at the Congress of the Socialist Party, and was met with significant applause. Alerted by schoolteachers' depictions of rising tensions in public schools over the hijab issue, the members of the National Assembly from both sides of the aisle created, on 27 May 2003, a Committee of Inquiry on the "question of the wearing of religious signs in schools."[38]

But on 3 July 2003, President Jacques Chirac set up an independent commission to study the implementation of the principle of *laïcité,* in a different religious landscape than the one existing when the fundamental law providing for the separation of church and state was passed on 9 December 1905.

The Presidential Commission—often referred to by the name of its president, Bernard Stasi, as the Stasi Commission—had a broader mandate than the one set up by the legislature. It was concerned with *laïcité* not only in public schools, but in society as a whole, and its composition was more varied: its 19 members included only two members of parliament, in addition to school principals and teachers, academics, civil servants, and businesspersons—together representing very diverse origins, religious beliefs, and political opinions.

On 11 December 2003, the Stasi Commission report recommended 26 measures, at least two of which required legislation in order to be implemented: the ban on conspicuous religious symbols in public schools and the recognition of the most important religious minority festivals as public holidays.[39] Other recommendations concerned the respect of the freedom to build mosques, funerary rituals, or culinary customs as well as the need to act strongly against the social factors that favor the rise of "fundamentalist influence," such as ethnic, racial, and religious discrimination, or the recognition of slavery or colonization as a full part of French national history.

In the following weeks, the French Parliament passed the ban on conspicuous religious symbols (often nicknamed "loi sur le voile") with a huge majority (494 votes in favor, 36 against, and 31 abstentions).[40]

Despite numerous criticisms, the 2004 law can be given a liberal interpretation. The proposal to ban conspicuous religious signs was not based on the meaning of the veil as a sign of the subjugation of women—an error in factual and legal reasoning made by Scott and Bowen. Even if the media were emphasizing this interpretation of the veil, it was not endorsed by the Stasi Commission and could not justify any legal restriction against wearing the headscarf. Wearing the headscarf might be the expression of the domination of women by men, but it can also be the modern expression of a free belief, a means of protection against the pressure of males, an expression of identity and freedom against secular parents or against Western and secular society or a new transcultural way of life.[41]

[38] For a detailed timeline showing the rise of the issue on the agendas of the main French political parties in April–May 2003, see T. Jeremy Gunn, "Religious Freedom and Laïcité: A Comparison of the United States and France" (2004) *Brigham Young University Law Review* 456–9.

[39] Commission de réflexion sur l'application du principe de laïcite dans la republique, Rapport au President de la Republique, available at <http://lesrapports.ladocumentationfrancaise.fr/BRP/034000725/0000.pdf>.

[40] First reading of the law by the National Assembly, 10 February 2004.

[41] See Nilufer Göle, *The Forbidden Modern: Civilization and Veiling* (Ann Arbor, MI: University of Michigan Press, 1996).

The commission recognized that banning headscarves on that basis would have been an intrusive interpretation of a religious symbol which can have different meanings. As Christian Joppke accurately remarks, "the liberal State can expect from its members external conformity with the law; it would violate the principle of liberal neutrality to prescribe [peoples'] inner convictions."[42] The liberal state has no right to interpret religious symbols. Had the headscarf been banned on the basis of discrimination against women, it would have been logical—given that equality of men and women has emerged as a human right protected by international and national legal instruments—to ban it not only in schools, but across the whole of society.

Since 1905, the legal environment of *laicité* has evolved. France has integrated with the European Union. But the most important move has been the signature of the European Convention on Human Rights,[43] which reinforced the freedom of religion, even if already guaranteed by the law of "séparation." The Convention recognizes the right to publicly express one's religious beliefs, and permits the limitation of the expression of religious faith only in the case of problems of public order or attacks on the rights or on the freedom of conscience of others.[44] It was on this basis that the Conseil d'État produced its statements in 1989 and the Stasi Commission, in 2003, submitted their different proposals.

What new developments between 1989 and 2003 could justify the ban? Mainly, the existence of pressures—including violence in the schools where wearing the headscarf had become an issue—provoked a shift in the position of some of the actors who had previously endorsed the right to wear it.

Quite rapidly, the data collected by the Stasi Commission contradicted the assessment of the ministries of Education and of the Interior: the number of female students wearing the hijab in French high schools was probably 5 to 10 times the number officially released.[45] More importantly, over the preceding two to three years—perhaps under the influence of the September 11 attacks or of the second intifada,[46] although the cause is not particularly important—in schools where some girls were wearing the headscarf, those Muslim girls who did not wear it were subject to strong pressure to do so. The daily pressure could take different forms, ranging from insults to violence.[47] In the view of some groups, composed mainly of young males, these girls could not claim that the

[42] Christian Joppke, *Veil: Mirror of Identity* (Cambridge, MA, Polity Press, 2009), 114.

[43] The European Convention on Human Rights (ECHR) was signed in Rome on 4 November 1950, and was ratified by France on 3 May 1974. But it was not until 2 October 1981, that France recognized the right of individual appeal.

[44] Article 9 of the ECHR states:

(1) Everyone has the right to freedom of thought, conscience and religion; this right includes freedom to change his religion or belief, and freedom, either alone or in community with others and in public or private, to manifest his religion or belief, in worship, teaching, practice and observance.
(2) Freedom to manifest one's religion or beliefs shall be subject only to such limitations as are prescribed by law and are necessary in a democratic society in the interests of public safety, for the protection of public order, health or morals, or the protection of the rights and freedoms of others.

[45] The data collected by the commission were sufficient to prove the important underestimation of the phenomenon in official data and statements. Yet the lack of resources at the disposal of the commission along with a short deadline did not permit it to evaluate the exact number of headscarves worn in French public schools. Alain Touraine, a colleague in the Commission, confirms that statement. See Alain Renaut and Alain Touraine, *Un débat sur la laïcité* (Paris: Stock, 2005), 79.

[46] It is the point of view of Alain Touraine and Alain Renaut that the problems were recent and linked to the second intifada. Touraine and Renaut, *Un débat sur la laïcité* 33.

[47] For the context of these pressures, see Stéphane Beaud and Michel Pialoux, *Violences Urbaines, Violences Sociales. Genèses des Nouvelles Classes Dangereuses* (Paris: Fayard, 2003), 357–64.

wearing of the scarf was forbidden as some of their "sisters" were wearing it freely. Their refusal to wear the headscarf—they were told—was their personal choice. Therefore they were often called "bad Muslims" as well as "whores," and told that they should follow the example of their sisters who respect the prescription of the Koran. The Stasi Commission heard testimony from teachers and principals unable to manage the situation and from Muslim parents who had to take their daughters out of public schools, placing them in Catholic private schools where they were not under such pressure to wear the headscarf. In the public schools, a strong majority of Muslim girls who did not wear the headscarf called for the protection of the law and asked the commission to ban all exterior religious signs.[48]

Muslim girls who do not want to wear the scarf have a right to freedom of conscience, and they constitute the large majority. Was it possible to go after the authors of the pressures against them? It is, practically speaking, very difficult to get young students, aged between 13 and 16, to denounce their peers when they are subjected to pressure, insults, or violence. The denouncer can be seen as a traitor to some of her peers in the school community, and there has been a case where a pupil who, having had his arms broken in an act of extreme violence, lied to his parents out of a fear of denouncing his peers.

Would it not have been possible, even preferable, to give school boards or principals more power to ban religious signs in case of attacks on public order or on the freedom of conscience of other students? Dealing with the scarf issue at the local level could have created a permanent tension between local school authorities and some national organizations for which wearing the scarf or imposing it upon others has become a national strategy of using public schools as their battleground. Not acting at the national level would have permitted these groups to target schools one after the other in order to attract, every week, the attention of the public and of the national media.

This is why the Commission proposed to ban exterior—that is, conspicuous—signs of religious belonging (including Jewish skullcaps and large crosses). For any limitation on the freedom to express one's religious belief, the Convention requires a law, and for this reason—rather than because of a French passion for legislation—a law passed by the Parliament was necessary.[49] The Convention also requires that any restriction be proportionate to its permissible aim.[50] This is why the ban concerns conspicuous and not subtle religious signs, and applies only in high schools, since the majority of those involved are minors.[51] There was no question of forbidding religious signs in universities or elsewhere in the world of adults: adults have means of defense that children do not. They can go to court and protect their right of freedom of conscience more easily.

The principle of freedom of conscience has to be understood in its different historical contexts, which have an impact on the discourses, the representations and the jurisprudential interpretation of a law. The 1905 law of separation between Church and the state was directed against the influence—indeed, domination—of the Catholic Church in

[48] It was the will of the 220 students of eight high schools, representing their class in a public meeting with the Commission on 4 December 2003.

[49] See eg *Sunday Times v. United Kingdom*, 2 E.H.R.R. 245 (1979); *Larissis v. Greece*, 27 E.H.R.R. 329 (1998).

[50] In a judgment *Sahin v. Turkey*, App. no. 44774/98, 29 June 2004, the ECtHR unanimously rejected the allegation that a ban on wearing the Islamic headscarf in higher-education institutions violated the rights and freedoms of a student, under Arts 8, 9, 10, and 14 of the Convention, and Art. 2 of Protocol No. 1. The Court found that the University of Istanbul's regulations imposing restrictions on the wearing of Islamic headscarves and the measures taken to implement them were justified in principle and proportionate to the aims pursued and, therefore, could be regarded as "necessary in a democratic society."

[51] Marceau Long and Patrick Weil, "Une laïcité en voie d'adaptation," *Libération*, 26 January 2004.

public affairs. It was a victory for the majority of French citizens who, though educated in the Catholic faith, wanted the Catholic Church to be put in its place—out of public education—and deprived of political influence.

The first principle of the 1905 law, freedom of conscience, concretely includes the free exercise of religion like in the United States. But in the context in which the freedom was built (i.e. against the intrusion of the Catholic Church in public affairs), it is often perceived as the necessity to protect the individual against the intrusion of a religious group. In fact, in the relationship between the individual, the religious group, and the state, the latter appears in France as protecting the individual against any pressure of the religious group, as opposed to the United States, where the individual relies more on the religious group as a protector against any intrusion of the state.[52]

French citizens were and still are divided on the issue. But they cannot be caricatured as being divided into two groups: those who opposed the law and who are the only ones "who believed that Muslims should be considered members of the nation," and the others.[53] I have tried to distinguish between different ideal types of attitudes toward the issue of the headscarf, which can be found in the political, judicial, and intellectual arenas. The first ones that are quite influential are those of the *Catho laïques*. Born and raised in the Catholic culture, sometimes in families who opposed the *laïcité*, they have adopted it, as they finally came to discover that it benefited the Catholic Church. Catholics are in favor of a status quo protecting a special and almost exclusive relation of Catholicism to the French state. The second tradition is that of the secularist anti-religionists often nicknamed "*laïcists*." The third are the pro-religion pluralists: close to the different faiths, they want to increase the role of religion in French society. The fourth are the multiculturalists. The fifth are the individualist liberals: they want each individual to be free of any pressure or influence from any groups or institutions. In 1989, the majority of the Conseil d'État was composed of individuals belonging to the third, fourth and fifth types of attitudes. In 2004, the majority of the Stasi Commission, of the Conseil d'État (which approved the Bill with an 80 percent majority[54]) and of the Parliament was composed of the first, second, and fifth types of attitudes. Between 1989 and 2003 the shift among those liberals who also believe "that Muslims should be considered members of the nation" has been determining the change in the majority regarding this issue. That was the case for Marceau Long, who was vice president of the Conseil d'État when it authorized the wearing of headscarves in public schools in 1989, as well as a member of the Stasi Commission. It is also the case of the sociologist Alain Touraine.

It is not absurd to think that the majority of Muslim families have felt relieved by the passage of the 2004 law. A minority of Muslims are anti-religious. A small minority is fundamentalist, and some even consider that the "law" of their faith should prevail over the law of the land. A large majority does not want to impose the headscarf on their daughters while feeling uncomfortable with being unfaithful in certain ways to their religious tradition. They are subject to the pressure of friends, neighbors, and family members who want to impose the wearing of the headscarf. However, they are now able to reply, "I agree with you, I was ready to follow your advice, but now it is impossible: I cannot go against the law!" In some ways, it is the same kind of feeling shared by numerous Algerian immigrants when the French nationality was imposed through birth in France on their children, so well described by Abdelmalek Sayad. Individually,

[52] This idea was born in a conversation with Peter Skerry on 3 June 2003 in Paris.

[53] Scott, *The Politics of the Veil* 103.

[54] Philippe Bernard, "Le Conseil d'État juge le projet de loi sur la laïcité conforme à la Constitution," *Le Monde*, 27 January 2004.

Algerians could never have applied for it. But when French nationality was ascribed automatically, they were quietly satisfied:

The beneficiaries of the [French] nationality, acquired without having applied for it, adapt to their situation well, and no circumstantial protests (which may be perfectly sincere, moreover) can convince of the contrary. Those around them, who would not have accepted an act of naturalization according to the ordinary procedure, turn out to be relieved, after the fact, that French nationality ("French papers," as one says) occurred by itself, like a collectively-imposed constraint: it is the common lot of all and not the result of an individual and voluntary act through which some people would be singled out and separated from the others.... Despite the protests of all sorts that it is good form to produce, despite the feeling of guilt or simple unease that continues to haunt the naturalized, naturalization that one calls "forced" ends up giving rise to something like a satisfaction that, for a whole series of reasons, seeks to remain secret, and sometimes resigned to.[55]

With a legal ban on the headscarf, the decision comes from the outside, thus allowing for the protection of children from fundamentalist pressure without a break in their religious ties.

Can the ban on headscarves be fairly placed within a continuity which includes the colonial control of Islam in French Algeria? Quite the opposite is true. Under the French Colonial Law, not only were Algerian Muslims able to practice the rituals and commandments of their religion, but they were assigned to it; one could say imprisoned in it. Algerian Muslims could only become subject to the French Civil Code by becoming fully French through "naturalization." They were deterred from doing so; therefore, between 1865 and 1962, only 7,000 Algerian Muslims became fully French. [56] Islamic authorities governed not only the religious but also the social and civil rights of Algerian Muslims, under the guidance of the Koran and the ruling of Sharia Courts. The 1905 law of separation between Church and the state was formally applicable in Algeria, but essentially was suspended permanently until independence occurred![57] Today in France, a majority of Muslims are fully French while the reminder can become so. They are subject to the Civil Code and can still refer to the Koran as a moral and religious code.

The Stasi report along with the subsequent laws and regulations, both those which have and might still follow, can even be interpreted as part of the legacy of Napoleon's action towards the Jews in 1806[58] and of the 1905 law regarding the Catholics:[59] as a moment of compromise, of interactive adaptation and recognition. In the case of French

[55] Abdelmalek Sayad, *La Double Absence. Des Illusions De L'émigré Aux Souffrances De L'immigré* (Paris : Éditions du Seuil, 1999), 352.

[56] Patrick Weil, *How To Be French: Nationality In The Making Since 1789* (Durham: Duke University Press, 2008), 207–25.

[57] Raberh Achi, "La séparation des Eglises et de l'Etat à l'épreuve de la situation coloniale. Les usages de la dérogation dans l'administration du culte musulman en Algérie (1905–1959)" (2004) 17(66) *Politix* 81.

[58] In 1806, Napoleon convened an assembly of French Jewish notables and asked them 12 questions related to polygamy, divorce, marriage with non-Jews, the election of rabbis, and relations with non-Jewish compatriots and foreigners. Satisfied with the answers which distinguished religion from civil and political laws, Napoleon conveyed in 1807 a Grand Sanhedrin, mainly comprised of rabbis from France and Europe. It set the basis of the organization of French Judaism. See Michael Gratz, *The Jews in Nineteenth-Century France, From the French Revolution to the Alliance Israélite Universelle* (J.M. Todd trans., Stanford: Stanford University Press, 1996).

[59] Joe Carens is misleading when he states that: "There is nothing in laïcité that requires ordinary Catholics to act contrary to their religious obligations." When on 20 September 1792, the "laicization" of civil status and registration and of marriage was voted on, it concretely meant the recognition of the superiority of the civil attitude towards religious law, contrary to the doctrine and the practice of the Catholic Church, which had to retreat from previous competence and power. Cf. Whitman, "Separating Church and State."

Muslims, this could mean that, for the first time in their history, the French state and French society have decided to fully integrate an important Muslim minority into their common framework.

The public controversy which preceded the passage of the law might have produced something different and better than "tolerance": respectful inclusion.[60] The harsh public debate, that split families of all beliefs and political opinions and which raised the Koran to the top of the annual bestsellers list, enabled citizens to debate matters of public importance. The process itself favoured the inclusion of all Muslims, whatever their position in the debate for or against the law may have been, within the broader community of citizens.

More than the ban on religious signs in public schools, the frustration felt by many Muslims was provoked by the feeling that there was an imbalance in the decisions announced by the government and endorsed by Parliament after the Stasi report was delivered. They had approved of the proposal to recognize the most important religious festivals of minority faiths as public holidays. Additionally approved by Catholic, Protestant, and Muslim religious authorities during the Commission's hearings, it was backed by 40 percent of citizens and provoked a very intense, fruitful, and creative debate throughout the country. But it was rejected by the government and was coolly received by the majority of Socialist representatives.

Strangely enough, Bowen was "intrigued" by the suggestion made to give a state holiday to all minority faiths.[61] In raising that proposal, the Stasi commission wanted to accommodate French tradition and the principle of equality between all faiths included in the 1905 law. Because of the anteriority of Catholicism in French society, the distribution of official holidays is strongly unequal: having 52 Sundays off favors religions that recognize Sunday as their day of rest. Among the 11 other public holidays, six are Catholic and only five are secular.[62] Today in France, Jews or Muslims can stop working in observance of Yom Kippur or Eid ul-Fitr. They only need to apply for the particular holiday with their employer. But, in doing so, they declare themselves as Jews or Muslims. Yet the custom in France since 1905 has been, and still is, to keep religious faith as a private matter. This tradition is again most likely linked to the long battle against the power and public exposure of the Catholic faith. The recognition of Yom Kippur, Eid ul-Fitr, or Orthodox Christmas as optional national holidays and as an alternative to Pentecost would have represented an official recognition of and respect for religious diversity. But it would also have been a way to fully respect the privacy of religious beliefs. If these alternative holidays were recognized, one could bet that somebody not working on Yom Kippur would be a Jew, but one would not be sure: it could be an agnostic or an atheist who had taken summer vacation in June and who chose not to work on Yom Kippur as a way of having a long weekend before the fall.

Yet since it was passed by the French Parliament in 2004, the ban on conspicuous religious signs in public schools has been smoothly implemented.[63] Indeed, the law has

[60] Tolerance, it merits mention, can be perceived as distant and contemptuous—often camouflaging the construction of institutional barriers. See Wendy Brown, *Regulating Aversion, Tolerance in the Age of Identity and Empire* (Princeton, NJ: Princeton University Press, 2008), 25–47.

[61] Bowen, *Why the French Don't Like Headscarves*.

[62] See Pierre-Henri Prélot, "Les religions et l'égalité en droit français," *Revue De Droit Public* (2001).

[63] Stéphanie Bara, "L'école sans voile depuis trois ans," *La Voix du Nord*, 14 March 2007. The mediator of the ministry of National Education reported 639 students wearing conspicuous religious signs during the year 2004–05 (out of a total of 10 million students). After the process of dialogue organized and imposed by law, 240 persisted in wearing conspicuous religious signs. Among them 143 left their

been judged in conformity with the ECHR by the ECtHR.[64] However, the unfortunate consequence of the 2004 law was that the right of Muslim girls or of young Sikhs who want to wear the scarf or the turban freely in public schools without pressuring their peers was denied.[65] In the majority of cases, they have been offered the opportunity to attend classes in private religious schools, though these have generally not been Muslim but, rather, Catholic. Catholic, Protestant, or Jewish schools have the obligation, if they are under state contract (97.5 percent of students attending private schools are in schools under contract), to accept applications from pupils of other faiths. Catholic schools have been welcoming more and more Muslim students in recent years.[66]

In the future, Muslim schools under contract with the state—which entails state control of the curriculum—will develop.[67] Whether we like it or not, it is the French tradition to have this parallel sector of the education system strongly subsidized by the state, enabling tuition fees to remain very inexpensive. And it is the right of any Muslim to create schools open to observant Muslims who want to respect all the customs and holidays of their faith while receiving religious instruction in addition to the normal curriculum.

II. Why the Burqa Law?

Yet a few years after the ban on conspicuous signs in public schools was enacted, court cases and Bills either proposed or passed in the Parliament continue to make headlines. On 17 November 2008, the appeals court of Douai reversed a lower court's decision which had authorized the annulment of a marriage on the basis of the bride's virginity. On 27 June 2008, the Conseil d'État ruled that the government could legally deny the naturalization of Faiza Mabchour, a woman who was wearing a full veil. In April 2010, a few months before the adoption of the burqa ban by a right-wing majority, a woman was fined for wearing the burqa while driving in Nantes. On July 2011, the Conseil d'Etat decided on five important cases related to the separation of church and state in favor of a liberal interpretation of the 1905 law.[68] Finally, on 17 January 2012, a few months after the ban's adoption, a draft law was approved by the French Senate's left-wing majority which would make it permissible, if adopted, to oblige childcare assistants to be neutral in religious affiliation.

All of these decisions and controversies must be placed in their proper contexts. On the one hand, courts have been confronted with marginal and extreme cases. In the majority of these cases the courts have tended to follow jurisprudential principles and to balance their judgments. On the other hand, politicians—fueled either by a majoritarian

public schools (96 spontaneously, 41 after disciplinary procedures). The same year, 28 court litigations were started (99 in 1994–95). Since the new Bill's first year of implementation, legal conflicts seem to have disappeared. See *La liberté religieuse à l'école*, by A. Castel, A. Hafid, J. Picard and O. Saby, report written for the ENA degree (2011), 9.

64 ECHR, 30 June 2009, *Aktas v. Fr ance* (and five other cases).

65 The prohibition against the sikh turban was endorsed by the Conseil d'État on 5 December 2007, M. et Mme Ghazal.

66 See Katrin Bennhold, "French Muslims Find Haven in Catholic Schools," *NY Times*, 29 September 2008.

67 Their number is still very low, even if it rose a bit from three in 2004 to seven in 2010, providing schooling to 1,000 students. Three additional schools are planned.

68 See <http://www.conseil-etat.fr/fr/dossiers-thematiques/laicite-loi-sur-la-separation-des-eglises-et-de-l-etat.html>.

anti-religious or non-religious social mood, or sometimes by Islamophobia—have tried to politicize against a rising phenomenon: the integration of Islam in France, within the boundaries of French *laïcité*.

A. The non-virgin spouse case

On 17 November 2008, the French appeal court of Douai (a city in northern France) handed down a decision that virginity could not be considered an "essential quality" for a valid marriage, overturning a lower French court's decision. The French Civil Code states that a marriage can be annulled only if an "essential quality" is missing. On 1 April 2008, a judge in the local court of Lille had previously decided to annul a French Muslim couple's 2006 union because the bride was not a virgin as she had claimed to be. The couple had agreed on the dissolution of the marriage and the judge agreed to their request, raising huge controversies and concerns that the ruling could pave the way for a wider recognition of virginity as a legal obligation for marriage if a husband or family demanded it. Under strong pressure, the French attorney appealed the lower court's decision and won: to break their marriage, the couple would have to go through a divorce where only the agreement to divorce is requested and not the examination of its grounds. Approving of the Lille verdict, Cecile Laborde argued that it:

> rested on the fact that marriage is not (or no longer) a public institution but a private contract founded in mutual consent. According to marriage law, a marriage can be annulled if one of the parties has lied about one of his/her "essential qualities." Thus it has been found admissible that being divorced, or sexually impotent, can be a legitimate cause for the annulment of a marriage, if the groom had deliberately kept it from his bride, knowing it to be grounds for her refusal. Likewise, the Lille judge restricted himself to noting that the woman's virginity was considered by both parties as essential to their union, that the bride had lied about her status, and that both demanded the annulment on the grounds of vitiated consent. Far from substituting a religious rule (never mentioned) to secular law, the judgment merely drew the logical conclusions of the contractualisation of marriage in French law.[69]

But there is no more public, legal, and solemn an act than marriage, by which a man and a woman bind themselves to one another indefinitely, before society, so as to found a family. In marrying, the spouses accept and recognize the institution of marriage and the general law which governs it and, in return, they ask the state to recognize the existence and the value of their mutual pledge and to ensure them the protection of the law.[70] This is especially the case in France, where civil marriage is compulsory before any religious one can take place, and where marriage is usually the only event in an individual's life that involves the presence and the mobilization of public officials under the auspices of a republican ceremony. The ceremony is usually held by the mayor or his/her deputies

[69] Cécile Laborde, "Virginity and Burqa: Unreasonable Accommodations? Considerations on the Stasi and Bouchard-Taylor Reports," *Books and Ideas.net*, 30 October 2008, available at <http://www.booksandideas.net/Virginity-and-Burqa-Unreasonable.html?lang=fr#nh2>.

[70] As Nancy Cott states: "At the same time that any marriage represents personal love and commitment, it participates in the public order. [...] To be marriage, the institution requires public affirmation. It requires public knowledge—at least some publicity beyond the couple themselves; that is why witnesses are required by the ceremony and why wedding bells ring. More definitively, legal marriage requires state sanction, in the license and the ceremony. Even in a religious solemnization, the assembled guests know to expect the officiating cleric's words, 'By the authority vested in me by the state of... I now pronounce you husband and wife.'" Nancy Cott, *Public Vows, A History of Marriage and the Nation* (2000), Cambridge, MA : Harvard University Press 1–2.

in the city hall; the mayor or a deputy officiates over the engagement of the spouses and reads to them the four articles (Articles 212 through 215) of the French Civil Code—the true Constitution of France, which has resisted 16 regime changes[71]—that determine the rights and duties of spouses. The city hall is a common space that all French or foreign residents living in France have to come through; the civil code is a common and paramount legal rule that all French or foreign residents living in France have to respect if they want to marry in France.

In addition, as Christine Delphy convincingly argues: (1) The law does not permit the annulment of a marriage simply by consent of the spouses; it requests the court to define what is an essential condition of a marriage. (2) Admitting an annulment due to a lack of virginity would have made this requirement lawful, and would have marked a regression for all women.[72] The consequence of the Lille court decision would have been social pressure on women: unless you marry as a virgin, your marriage will be nullified, bringing shame on you and your family, etc. It is on this basis that the Douai appeals court decided to reverse the lower court judgment.[73]

B. Refusal to naturalize a woman wearing a full veil

On 27 June 2008, the Conseil d'État ruled that the government could legally deny the naturalization of Faiza Mabchour, a woman who wore a full veil. The ruling, which was welcomed by all of the main political parties, did not refer to her niqab, which she said she adopted after arriving in France from her native Morocco, according to a report from the judge rapporteur who offered an opinion and a decision to the Conseil d'État. The Conseil d'État seems to have looked beyond the mere fact of the wearing of the niqab, and inquired into its meaning and context. Based on her statements to immigration officials, the Commissioner's report concluded that "she leads a life almost of a recluse, cut off from French society," leaving the house only to walk with her children or visit relatives. The reported noted that "[s]he lives in total submission to the men in her family... and the idea of contesting this submission does not even occur to her."

The woman and her husband told immigration officials that they adhered to Salafism, a strict form of Islam. When interviewed by immigration officials, the woman told them that she did not know anything about the French tradition of *laïcité* or the right to vote. The immigration officials asked her to remove her veil to identify herself, which she did only when no men were in the room, the report said. The Conseil d'État stated that she "has adopted a radical practice of her religion incompatible with the essential values of the French community, notably with the principle of equality of genders, and therefore she does not fulfill the conditions of assimilation," a legal requirement for gaining French citizenship.[74] The Conseil d'Etat said the decision to refuse her citizenship did not aim to "attack (her) freedom of religion." It is noteworthy that, every year, a majority

[71] Jean Carbonnier, "Le Code Civil," in Pierre Nora (ed.), *Les Lieux de Mémoire*, vol. 2 (Paris: Gallimard,1986), 309.

[72] Christine Delphy, "Des préférences personnelles peuvent-elles être des qualités validées comme essentielles par le droit? Les contradictions de la procédure d'annulation du marriage," *Mouvement des idées et des luttes*, 18 June 2008, available at <http://www.mouvements.info/Des-preferences-personnelles.html>.

[73] Appeal Court of Douai, 17 Nov. 2008 reversing the judgment of Court of Lille April, 2008.

[74] At the end of the 1990, the Council of State had already decided that belonging to a federation involving several extremist movements that advocated the "rejection of the essential values of French society" could justify a refusal. Ben Mansour decision, 5 May 1999.

of those naturalized in France are Muslims. The case did not involve a denaturalization or an expatriation, but a naturalization—rarely a right, but rather an entry into a club that imposes some conditions on membership.[75] Among these conditions to become a citizen, it is not illegitimate to request the will to share the life of other citizens, which the court could argue was not the case with Mrs. Mabchour.

C. The Nantes driver with a burqa

A few months before the adoption of the burqa ban in the fall of 2010, a woman was fined in April 2010 for wearing the burqa while driving in Nantes.[76] Brice Hortefeux, the Minister of the Interior, alleged that the husband of the fined woman was suspected of polygamy, social security fraud, and possible links to an extreme Islamist organization. The story made the headlines of television and radio programs as well as the national press. But on 14 December 2010, the traffic court canceled the €22 fine imposed on the woman. Notwithstanding the involvement of the national government and the strong media coverage and politicization of the case, the magistrate ruled that the burqa—which shows only the eyes—did not impair Ms. Moulères' vision as it "moved with her head."

D. The five Conseil d'Etat decisions in the *Assemblée du contentieux*

Lastly, on 19 July 2011 the Administrative Claims Assembly (*Assemblée du contentieux*) of the Conseil d'Etat—in which a few major cases are resolved every year—decided on five cases regarding the separation of church and state based on an interpretation of the 1905 law.[77] The assembly relied on a literary interpretation of the law that differentiates between the "worship" contained in Article 2 of the law—which states that "[t]he Republic neither acknowledges, nor pays for nor subsidizes" any faith, nor "[t]he buildings serving for the exercise of public worship, as well as the furniture they contain"—with Article 13, which states that these properties are "left to the free disposition of the associations designated to manage the religious establishments." The Conseil d'Etat decided that it was legal for cities to use public funds to subsidize the installation of an organ in a local church in Trelaze for the use of believers as well as secular inhabitants[78] and, separately, the addition of an elevator to a Catholic basilica which was also a tourist site.[79] It was also decided that the practice among local authorities of granting a long-term lease for a parcel of communal land to a federation of Muslim associations intent on building a mosque—with rent amounting to a small amount per annum—was legal, considering the fact that the leaseholder was a non-profit making organization and that, at the expiration of the lease, the building would be incorporated as one of its holdings. [80] That same day,

[75] See Patrick Weil, "From Conditional to Secured and Sovereign: The New Strategic Link between the Citizen and the Nation-state in a Globalized World" (2011) 9 *International Journal of Constitutional Law* 615–35.

[76] See John Lichfield, "Polygamy and Fraud Claims Fan Burqa Row," *The Independent*, 26 April 2010, available at <http://www.independent.co.uk/news/world/europe/polygamy-and-fraud-claims-fan-burqa-row-1954234.html>.

[77] Available at <http://www.conseil-etat.fr/fr/dossiers-thematiques/laicite-loi-sur-la-separation-des-eglises-et-de-l-etat.html>.

[78] CE, 19 July 2011, Commune de Trélazé, no. 308544.

[79] CE, 19 July 2011, Fédération de la libre pensée et de l'action sociale du Rhône, M.P. no. 308817.

[80] CE, 19 July 2011, Mme V. no. 320796. See the case note by Cristiana Cianitto and Mariagrazia Tirabassi, commenting on Conseil d'Etat: Judgment no. 320796/2011, (2012) 1 *Oxford Journal of Law and Religion* 535.

the Conseil d'Etat held that that the free disposal of a cultural center for worship—in Montpellier—was legal[81] while separately deciding that it was also in the interest of public order (public health and hygiene) to subsidize a temporary slaughterhouse which would be used by Muslims during the Aïd el-Kébir festival.[82]

These important decisions based on a liberal interpretation of the 1905 law provoked a strong reaction from the laicist radical (left) party. The Courts nevertheless decided all of these cases independently of the government and of political pressure by combining tradition, equality, and diversity in a quite balanced way. Tensions continue to exist and are the normal product of the adaptation of newcomers to new or foreign laws and social norms. For the welcoming liberal democracy it is a test of the universalism of its laws, and of its respect for cultural difference. And when formal universalism camouflages ethnocentrism (as in the case of French *catho-laïcité*), adjustment most often implies either the equal recognition of all faiths or the exit of religion.[83]

Balance was not the approach of the parliament when it seized on the burqa controversy and pressured President Sarkozy to pass a total ban. In 2004, it was already because of his fear of an excessive politicization of religious signs in public schools that Jacques Chirac had *de facto* removed the issue from the Parliament by nominating an independent commission. The latter, under the guidance of its most powerful members (such as Marceau Long, former head of the Conseil d'Etat) and of its "rapporteurs" (comprised mainly of members of the Conseil d'État) acted de facto like a court. On the burqa issue, Nicolas Sarkozy acted in an opposite manner. He was convinced of the need to act differently by his defeat at the regional elections of 2010 and the Bill was adopted by the Parliament with 335 votes in favor and one against, with the majority of the left not participating in the vote.

III. Why Did the Majority of the Parliament Ban the Burqa in 2010?

Was it because there was a rise of radical Islam in some impoverished suburbs of French metropolises, as the sponsor of the Bill—M. André Gerin—claims? Probably. But the majority of the MPs who voted for this Bill were not elected in these areas. One hypothesis is that the majority of MPs who voted in favor of the ban were frustrated by the liberalism of the 2004 law, which banned conspicuous signs of religion in public schools only. These MPs were reflecting the mood of many citizens who, following the passage of the law banning headscarves, were disappointed by the fact that the law only applied in public schools. They often complained that it *was still legal* to wear headscarves at the office, in the street, and in universities.

In fact, these complaints also reflected a recognition that the integration of Muslims had progressed and with it, the integration of Islam had continued to deepen. Before the passage of the 2004 law, a French Council of the Muslim Religion had been established, allowing for official representation of the majority of observant Muslims and the fulfillment of some duties of common interest (e.g. the choice of chaplains, the organization of Ramadan or of the Hallal market).[84] After the law passed, other proposals of

[81] CE, 19 July 2011, Commune de Montpellier, no. 313518.

[82] CE, 19 July 2011, Communauté urbaine du Mans, Le Mans métropole, no. 309161.

[83] See Patrick Weil, *Etre Français, les quatre piliers de la nationalité* (La Tour d'Aigues: Editions de l'Aube, 2011).

[84] Jonathan Laurence and Justin Vaisse, *Integrating Islam: Political and Religious Challenges in Contemporary France* (Washington, D.C.: Brookings Institution Press, 2006), 135–62.

the Stasi Commission in favor of respecting equality between Islam and other religions were implemented. Since 2004, Muslim chaplaincies have been established nationally in the armed forces, in prisons and in hospitals.[85] The religious feast of Ramadan has become a social and national event shared by many non-Muslims with their Muslim compatriots.[86]

At the municipal level, there are over 2,100 Muslim prayer spaces. New mosques and places of worship open every week.[87] Throughout this process, the different political parties have played a variety of roles at the local level. One defends a strict neutrality and separation between public and religious institutions, rejecting any help in securing subsidies for places of worship, while the other tries to put freedom of religion into practice. Right-wing and left-wing parties can play either role, depending on whether they run the city or not.

For laïcists or those opposed to Islam, there were fewer and fewer "Muslim" practices to target which would have a chance of winning support in French or European courts. Burqas thus became the main target—not without legal risks.

The prohibition of the burqa in public spaces was upheld by the Conseil constitutionnel, which found it was indeed constitutional.[88] Yet the Conseil constitutionnel also expressed a reservation which traps the government and leaves the door open to a possible invalidation of the law by the ECtHR; namely, that the general prohibition of the burqa was inapplicable in places of worship open to the public.

The sponsor of the Bill in the National Assembly thought it important to specify that the basis for a prohibition against covering one's face "is the social or intangible public order, rather than the principle of *laïcité*,"[89] and that the law would not aim at any specific belief. For he knew that the ECtHR, in ruling on a law's conformity to the ECHR, takes into account the fact that the law in question is "*prima facie* neutral towards the exercise of the freedom of worship."[90]

Yet what is a garment, banned from being worn in public while allowed in places of worship, if not one with a recognized religious dimension? By contrast, there are no exceptions to other social norms to which the prohibition against hiding one's face has been compared, such as those against public nudity or incest.

The reservation expressed by the Conseil constitutionnel revealed the true—religious—purpose of the ban.[91] Its laborious intellectual structure is thus shaken. In order to implement the general ban, the legislature defined public space as "constituted of public roads as well as spaces open to the public or used for providing a public service." It thus put hospitals, schools, town halls, and government buildings in the same category as the street, even though these are different kinds of spaces, to which French *laïcité* and the

[85] On 17 September 2006 the French Council of the Muslim Religion chose three Muslim chaplains: Abdelkader Arbi, who served in the armed forces, Moulay El-Hassan El-Alaoui Talibi, who served in the prisons, and Abdelhak Nabaoui, who served in hospitals. For further details, see <http://www.yabiladi.com/article-societe-1459.html>.

[86] See <http://www.lefigaro.fr/actualite-france/2011/08/01/01016-20110801ARTFIG00355-les-grandes-surfaces-fetent-le-ramadan-sans-le-nommer.php>.

[87] Didier Leschi, "Les lieux de culte et le bureau central des cultes," in Jacqueline Lalouette and Christian Sorrel (eds), *Les Lieux de Culte en France, 1905–2008* (Paris: Letouzey & Ané, 2008), 23.

[88] Decision 2010-613 DC of 7 October 2010 validating the law forbidding the concealment of one's face in public.

[89] Jean-Paul Garraud, Report No. 2648 on the Bill No. 2520, prohibiting the concealing of the face in public, French National Assembly, 23 June 2010, 21 (translation mine).

[90] *Vargos v. Greece*, App. no. 65501/01 (ECtHR, 24 June 2004) (translation mine).

[91] See Patrick Weil, "La loi sur la burqa risque l'invalidation par l'Europe," *Le Monde*, 23 November 2010.

ECtHR had until then applied different rules. In a decision delivered in February 2010, in the case of *Arslan and Others v. Turkey*,[92] the Court had to consider the arrest and detention of a group of people who, were wearing while in a street, "a turban, a sirwal and a tunic, all black, after the fashion, in their view, of the principal prophets, notably the prophet Mohammad."

In declaring this arrest unjustified, the Court observed that these garments were worn "by simple citizens rather than representatives of the state exercising a public office," in "public spaces open to all, such as streets and public squares," and not "in government buildings in which respect for neutrality towards all faiths can prevail over the free exercise of the right to express one's own religion." Thus the restrictions which the Court allows in the case of government buildings or civil servants are not to be carried over to the street.

Made up for the most part of former politicians, the Conseil constitutionnel did not dare confront public opinion and engage in legal reasoning. It thus delivered an unclear and contradictory decision, which sounds like an opening to a successful challenge at the European level. In addition, unlike the ban on headscarves, the Parliament was divided on the question of the burqa while the Conseil d'État disapproved of it.

In 2004, the Parliament had enacted a law supported by school principals and teachers. It had as its general aim the protection of minor children against pressures. It was limited to public schools, leaving those girls who wished to keep wearing the veil with an alternative, usually that of a private school under contract with the state. The ban on the burqa is of a different nature. It is aimed at adults, who pressure no one, in the freest public space—the street. Its radical character offers believers no alternative. Incapable of being enforced by police officers—who do not want to enforce it[93]—it now risks being invalidated by the ECtHR.

Nevertheless, conflicts continue between courts and political parties regarding the interpretation of *laïcité*, while competition has not ended between political parties as to who can appear as its strongest defender. On 19 March 2013, France's *Cour de Cassation* (Court of Cassation) overturned previous rulings on the *Baby Loup* case, declaring that the dismissal for serious misconduct of Fatima Afif, an assistant director of a daycare center, constituted religious discrimination.[94] Fatima Afif had refused to take off the headscarf she wore, in violation of the daycare center's internal regulations imposing strict compliance with the principles of religious neutrality within the premises of the center and its annexes. The French Supreme Court noted that the principles of neutrality and secularism may be invoked by the employer in the public sector, including by a private organization that performs public sector service. Yet in the private workplace, the court noted "restrictions on religious freedom must be justified by and proportionate to the nature of the work, as well as responding to an essential professional need." The Court therefore sanctioned an overly general and absolute restriction regarding religious freedom. In an unusual reaction, French Interior Minister, Manuel Valls, digressed during question time at the National Assembly to criticize the Supreme Court's ruling, stating, "I want to take a break from my function for a few seconds to tell you how much I regret the court's decision on the Baby Loup case today, which has called *laïcité* into question."[95]

[92] *Ahmet Arslan and Others v. Turkey*, 23 February 2010, M. no. 41135/98.

[93] See <http://archives-lepost.huffingtonpost.fr/article/2011/04/11/2462424_appliquer-la-loi-sur-la-burqa-ce-n-est-pas-la-priorite-des-policiers.html>.

[94] "Baby Loup case," Supreme Court, chambre sociale, 19 mars 2013, n°11-28.845.

[95] Assemblée nationale, XIVe legislature, Session ordinaire de 2012-2013Deuxième séance du mardi 19 mars 2013, <http://www.assemblee-nationale.fr/14/cri/2012-2013/20130180.asp>.

A year earlier, in January 2012, a draft law was approved by the French Senate's left-wing majority which states, "[u]nless otherwise specified in a contract with the individual employer, a childcare assistant is subject to an obligation of neutrality in religious matters in the course of childcare activity." "Parents have the right to want a nanny who is neutral from a religious perspective," the left-wing senator Françoise Laborde was quoted as saying.[96] This was simply a political coup for the news media since the Bill was formally sent to the National Assembly with no chance of being adopted or signed into law.

Unable to deal politically and socially with the presence of Muslims and of Islam in France, some French politicians have started doing with *laïcité* precisely what they reproach religious radicals for doing: trying to displace the borders between different spaces with the opposite purpose of reducing the place left to religious expression.

One of the reasons why French *laïcité* has done historically better than expected in terms of harmonizing among beliefs has to do with the separation of geographical spaces. In every liberal state, freedom of conscience is guaranteed along with the freedom of free exercise for any faith. Yet there is one question which is not so easy to resolve: how does the government concretely guarantee one the right to exercise one's faith in practice, rather than only theoretically ensuring the right to freely enter into or leave a religious group? Where is the liberty to leave one's religious group or to observe one's faith with less zeal when doing so results in the individual facing so much pressure and condemnation. This freedom seems more readily accessible in France than in other countries because of an organization of geographical space which favors cross-border encounters and exits, thereby allowing for the practical exercise of the freedom of conscience.

In the United States, a Catholic can live in the Catholic sphere, subject to Catholic customs from his or her baptism to his or her funeral; he or she can marry at the church following a priest's sermon and exercise privately or publicly his or her faith in any function or position he or she would exercise during his or her social life.

In France, this is impossible. As we have seen previously, if a person wants to marry religiously, he or she is legally obliged to first hold a civil marriage ceremony in the city hall. The city hall is a common space that all French or foreign residents living in France have to pass through. And if they wish to become civil servants or politicians they would have to fulfill a higher duty: not to publicly express their own faith or belief.

As convincingly explained by Michael Walzer,[97] liberal societies were built through the art of separation, which permits the emergence of liberties while guaranteeing their independence from political power. In each sphere—religious, economic, academic, and private—"institutions are responsive to their own internal logic even while they are also responsive to systemic determination;[98] the liberal achievement has been to protect a number of important institutions and practices from political power, to limit the reach of the government."[99] But is it not possible to apply this framework to the relations of an individual toward a religious group and religious power? Is it possible to enjoy not a formal but, rather, a real practical freedom of conscience towards religious institutions and norms without an art of separation adapted to this particular individual liberty?

[96] See <http://www.liberation.fr/societe/01012384168-le-senat-adopte-une-proposition-de-loi-controversee-sur-la-laicite>.

[97] Michael Walzer, "Liberalism and the Art of Separation" (1984) 12 *Political Theory* 315–30.

[98] Walzer, "Liberalism and the Art of Separation" 319.

[99] Walzer, "Liberalism and the Art of Separation" 321.

Referring to ancient Greece, Marcel Hénaff and Tracy B. Strong differentiate between four kinds of spaces organized by human beings in relation to deities that speak very accurately to the modern situation: private, sacred, common, and public:

> The space is *private* when a given individual or set of individuals are recognized by others as having the right to establish criteria that must be met for anyone else to enter it. [The *sacred* space is the space of the Gods, not under human rules but religious, sacred ones.] *Common* space admits of no criteria; it is open to all in the same way. It is not owned or controlled.... [A]ll can go there to extract from it what is there. Thus the sea, pastures, forests are (can be) common space. That is not a space to which one goes to speak with others. [*Public* space is open; it is] a *human construct, an artefact,* the result of the attempt by human beings to shape the place and thus the nature of their interaction. [It is also] *theatrical,* in that it is a place which is seen and shows oneself to others.[100]

In contemporary France, private and sacred spaces are similar while the Greek common space has become a public space (in which all kinds of beliefs can be expressed) and the Greek public space has become the political one (set as neutral, which means that there is no presence of religion).

But this art of separation, when applied to religious freedom and organized through centuries of conflicts involving religious powers (mainly the Catholic Church), might explain why France seems to have been more successful in building a liberal interaction between individuals raised in different faiths or beliefs. Separated spaces with different sets of rules are imposed on these individuals, thereby permitting them to experiment with different ways of relating to their own faith, the faith of others or no faith at all.

Such a framework of separation is what has created this religious liberalism in the long run. Jews learned it in 1806, Catholics in 1905, and finally Muslims have to learn it in turn. Soundly conceived and implemented, this framework is not an attack on liberty but, on the contrary, a subtle art not only of proclaiming liberty in theory but of permitting its concrete practice. However, it is this art which some French politicians seem to have decided to either neglect or forget.

[100] Marcel Hénaff and Tracy B. Strong, "Introduction: The Conditions of Public Space: Vision, Speech and Theatricality," in Marcel Hénaff and Tracy B. Strong (eds), *Public Space and Democracy* (Minneapolis: University of Minnesota Press, 2001), 2–8.

12

Veiling and Women's Intelligibility

*John Borneman**

I. Contemporary Imaginings

We are fascinated by the veiling of women. From Morocco to Iran to Indonesia, as well as in Europe and North America, veiling has come to signify unbreachable differences between the West and Islam, achieving the status of an icon similar to the Christian cross or the national flag. In the post-Cold War imagination, the veil stands for so many things in so many different cultural contexts—Muslims, women's rights, women's oppression, tradition, beauty—that it has become a classic social fact, simultaneously indexing economic, political, cultural, and religious currents. At the same time, the icon and the word have come to closely mirror each other, especially in English, leading to a further veiling of the multitude of social forms the veil takes. Rarely is it worn innocuously. In some places, wearing a veil carries the same connotations as bearing a cross or carrying a flag—grave, involuntary belonging. Today, it is most closely identified with the issue of women's status in a politicized Islam. Experiences in Iran are modular for this politicized identification, as veiling was briefly abolished by Reza Shah in 1936, only to be made compulsory under the revolutionary Islamic regime in 1980. Various political regimes have since followed suit in making it compulsory for Muslim women to wear the veil (most famously, the Afghan Taliban and the Saudi Arabian monarchy) or to not wear the veil (as in the case of schoolgirls in republican France).[1]

Reducing the veil's significance to a particular conjunction of religion and gender, or to a particular conflict between religious and secular authorities, betrays a rich history of veiling and the wide variation in its meaning. When this conjunction is used to frame contemporary issues of constitutional and legal order, it presents the veil and its regulation as a problem in need of a solution rather than asking how this symbol comes to be regarded as a problem. What makes the issue of veiling a problem for women and men, and for religion and the law?

* Department of Anthropology, Princeton University. Professor Borneman received his Ph.D. from Harvard University in 1989, and has taught and lectured widely in Europe and the Levant, where he has also conducted field research. He was also Senior Fulbright Professor at Humboldt University in 1995, and at the University of Aleppo, Syria, in 2004. He has written widely on kinship and the state in Germany, working until 1989 in the context of the political division of Germany, and after on unification processes.

[1] For feminist works on the veil and gender politics in the Middle East, see Fatima Mernissi et al., *The Vale and the Male Elite: A Feminist Interpretation of Women's Rights in Islam* (New York: Basic Books, 1992); Leila Ahmed, *Women and Gender in Islam: Historical Roots of a Modern Debate* (New Haven: Yale University Press, 1998); David Bailey and Gilane Tawadros, *Veil: Veiling, Representation, and Contemporary Art* (Cambridge, MA: MIT Press, 2003).

The understanding of the veil, or veiling, as a problem relies, at minimum, on three plausible but ultimately misleading assumptions that do not take into account what goes on at a less conscious and rationalized level before the symbols and their representations are understood as public problems.

First, it is assumed that the religious revivals of today are a problem resulting from pluralism, specifically from religious diversity. This assumption holds that formerly stable religious communities whose members now live in diasporas experience a dislocation between their religious loyalties and socio-political identities, which in turn provides the motivation for religious revivals and counter-reactions from the communities in which these "new" residents now reside. While the influence of religious revivals on current conflicts may arguably be greater than at many times in the past, the movement of peoples and ideas, including highly contentious and conflict-producing religious ideas, is in itself nothing new in human history. The Levant, in particular, from the Axial Age to the present, has been a site of constant movement and confrontation of peoples, resulting in often radical displacements but always in pluralist configurations of culture, religion, and politics. The cultural diversity of the Levant is a longstanding empirical fact. It has not always been experienced as a problem, however, and that is the point: religious diversity becomes so only when framed in certain ways. Perhaps there is something today about the particular way in which the experience of pluralism—specifically in the registers of religion and gender—is framed by actors in the legal-political and religious fields that makes it a problem. It might be more productive, then, to think of law and religion as not merely reacting to (or solving) problems associated with pluralism and global dislocation, but to ask how they frame the experience of this diversity and dislocation in ways that create or reinforce this experience as a problem.

Second, it is assumed that the larger role played by religion today in the public sphere is leading to a blurring of the distinction between public and private spheres. This assumption holds true only if this distinction was in fact at some time unambiguous, distinct, and empirically ascertainable. However, the distinction between public and private is an analytical and not empirical one. The line between these spheres has always been difficult to identify because it is empirically in flux, a site of struggle with changing ideational content. An alternative way to understand this distinction is to compare its Cold War framing with its contemporary one. If the complaint in the secular West during the Cold War, especially against totalitarian governments, was that there was too much government interference in the private sphere, then the post-Cold War debate is all about calling on the government to regulate the public sphere. This public sphere is empirically enlarged and integrated into wider networks increasingly evaluated in terms of norms of inclusion and participation that have become part of a global discourse on equality. The analytical question, then, must begin with an understanding of this enlarged public sphere and the reciprocal demands it and the private sphere place on each other. These demands often lead not to a blurring but to a hardening of the boundaries between the two spheres. In this context, there are different gendered and religio-political investments in the two spheres, and in where the line between them should be drawn. Problems arise in the attempt to regulate this public sphere not only because of boundary issues between the secular and religious, however, but primarily because both religious and secular authorities are asked to respond to the new demands for inclusion and participation, and to offer solutions and regulations that at the same time reshape the private sphere in unintended ways.

Third, it is assumed that religious revivals, or religion generally, challenges the "dictates of reason" and the Enlightenment project. To be sure, "reason" and this project have been subject to serious critique, especially following the publication of Horkheimer and

Adorno's *Dialectic of Enlightenment*.[2] Most religious critiques of this project do not differ substantially from secular-liberal ones, though they tend to propose different solutions. Only a few of the current religious critiques, like earlier Marxist ones, are revolutionary, in the sense that they seek to overturn the entire order of things and thus reject any need for rational legitimation (precisely because the old regime lacks legitimacy). The larger challenge today, irrespective of the source of criticism, is not to the dictates of reason but to finding forms of legitimation that no longer rely on a narrative of progress.

Both secular and religious critiques of the Enlightenment, including those of most forms of "religious fundamentalisms," rely on reason to formulate their goals. Reason itself dictates nothing, however, nor does it rule anything. Reason rationalizes values, which are constitutive of any cultural group. It submits values to certain thought processes. Secular thinkers, such as myself, for example, are not always paragons of reason, even when using it. We are not always rational, and never only rational, but also emotional and driven by dictates about which we are not conscious and over which reason has minimal or no control. Law, also, does not follow reason as a dictate, but is only the result of a deliberative method that requires the use of reason. The framing here is key, because neither law nor religion as activities are necessarily more deliberative than the other, and they do not necessarily exclude each other; historical examples where both have used reason, or even faulty reason, to pursue rational ends are legion. It might therefore be more productive not to oppose the rational and irrational, and not to assign the former to secular constitutional scholars and the latter to religious ones, but to understand the values proposed by each as well as the rational and irrational investments in these values.

With these three reframings in mind, the focus of this article will be quite narrow: to analyze one symbol or practice—the veil or veiling—that has been invested with great value by both constitutional and religious authorities. What is at stake in these investments? It will focus on the contributions of 20 women in a recent book, *The Veil: Women Writers on its History, Lore, and Politics*, edited by Jennifer Heath.[3] It hopes to make clear the nature of cultural conflicts around this symbol, and the place of the registers of law and religion in current conflicts about the shape of public spheres.

II. Women's Dress and Face

The women who have contributed histories, memoirs, ethnographies, and critical essays to *The Veil* make it plain that veiling can be motivated by a range of aesthetic goals, political ideologies, economic constraints, personal choices, and opportunities. Their insistence on pluralism and sociopolitical context, necessary though it is, elides important questions: why has the veil become iconic? What explains its present power and its appeal to Muslims in particular?

To begin with, the veil is about women's dress in public. Most women who veil do so in order to enter the public sphere on particular terms, though these terms may be difficult to discern. Who authorizes those terms is a major point of contention. Women who veil remove it in private, in the company of intimates. Men veil themselves too: the

[2] Max Horkheimer and Theodor Adorno, *Dialectic of Enlightenment* (orig. 1944, New York: Continuum, 2002).

[3] Jennifer Heath (ed.), *The Veil: Women Writers on its History, Lore, and Politics* (Berkeley: University of California Press, 2008). A shorter version of this article, focused solely on this book, was published in the London Review of Books. See John Borneman, "A Scrap of Cloth," *London Review of Books*, 18 Dec. 2008, 13. I thank them for the permission to reprint this material.

Berber-speaking Tuareg of West Africa, and modern resistance-fighters in Mexico and Palestine, for example. Tuareg men are reported to veil even when asleep, leaving only their eyes uncovered—it is most important to cover the mouth and nose. Explanations are both ecological (protection from desert sands) and symbolic (to ward off evil in encounters with strangers). Resistance fighters veil only in public, to hide or mask their identity. Masks distort and disguise identities, and are more likely to frighten (as in North American Kwakiutl ceremonial masks or in south Indian Kathakali dance) than to seduce (as in the masks of Zorro or Batman). Neither variety of male veiling provokes much comment or controversy.

As Jennifer Heath writes in her comprehensive introduction, veiling attracts attention to women's faces, to the eyes, the mouth, and the hair. Veils do not hide the face but frame it. They illuminate one part of the face by setting it in relief to the part they conceal. They change the perspective for the viewers from both behind and in front of the veil. At the same time, of course, concealment draws attention to the veiled object, creating a puzzle that awakens curiosity as to what might lie behind.

Only the most extreme type and most politicized of veils, the black burqa (my young friends in Syria call women who wear them "walking tents"), tries to prevent sight altogether.[4] It makes the face and other parts of the body invisible and indivisible. In one sense, it tries to remove all clues to the mysterious, as if making part of the woman distinct would provoke the unthinkable. Viewers must be radically protected from something. The many other sorts of veil—head scarf, tagelmust, parandja, niqaab, muhapatti, bridal veil, sari, hijab, chadri, batula, abaya, kufiyya—still make it possible to see and be seen. That said, a woman can see out from inside a burqa, though with darkened vision. In this respect, the burqa functions like modern sunglasses, worn prominently by movie stars and tyrannical political leaders, which aggressively foil the sight of the other. To be sure, sunglasses prevent only the eyes from being seen, and even nudists can wear sunglasses. By contrast, most veils highlight and minimally reveal the eyes, while covering other parts of the face and body.

Understanding how the eyes and the face signify today, then, may be the key to the singular passions aroused by veiling. Why is the visibility of women such a politicized issue in so many cultural contexts? Veils work solely by altering vision. They do not fundamentally affect the other senses. One sees the veiled woman, in public, and the veil frames how she is seen. The sound of her voice may be muzzled; in humid climates she may sweat a bit more. But neither effect inflames the passions. Whether veiled or unveiled, an image results from a visual objectification. When veiled, however, and depending on how fully veiled, a woman's intelligibility is initially determined by the dynamics of vision alone. These phenomenological effects are at odds with what most women want, or at least what they say they want.

III. Objectification and Lust

Only in Saudi Arabia, Iran, and among the Afghan Taliban is veiling compulsory. In the rest of the world, women can choose whether or not to veil. The reason many give for doing so is their wish to escape visual objectification: the male gaze, gawk, leer, or stare.

[4] For more detailed descriptions of some male reactions to veiled and unveiled women, see John Borneman, *Syrian Episodes: Sons, Fathers, and an Anthropologist in Aleppo* (Princeton: Princeton University Press, 2007).

"I did not want to be judged by my body, my beauty, or the lack thereof," Pamela Taylor, who wears the hijab, explains, "but as an individual, for my personality, my character, and my accomplishments."[5] Many Saudi women, Maliha Masood writes, are aware that the veil denies "men their usual privilege of discerning whomever they desire. By default, the women are in command."[6] Jasbir Jain explains that the Indian "[p]urdah as a face covering offers women anonymity and defense against sexual harassment. It also provides them with an unobserved observer's position."[7] "A girl who dresses modestly is making a significant statement," Miriam Grossman says apropos Hasidic fashion. "She's sending out a message which says: 'My body is important, but it is only the vessel for the real me—my soul. I think of myself that way, and I want people to relate to me with that in mind.' "[8] By dressing "modestly in public" and focusing "primarily on internal work and spiritual development," Eve Grubin writes, the Jewish woman can experience her own "internal richness."[9]

The desire to be appreciated for their inner selves has been a dominant strain in the thinking of modern feminists, but in many cultures outer form is understood as the expression of inner beauty. While Western feminists may not make the link between inner and outer beauty, certainly the worldwide popularity of the cosmetics industry testifies to the importance many women place on outer appearance. The argument goes, however, that the focus on outer form makes women's bodies commodities in a market in which men determine the value of women according to the way they look. By wearing the veil, women seek to remove themselves from the public gaze, especially from an economy of objectification and exchange controlled by men. But does the veil accomplish this removal? There are many reasons to expect frustration.

The veil does not prevent objectification, though it may slow the pace of exchange. It could equally be said that women wear the veil in order to enter into public exchange, not to avoid it. Aisha Lee Fox Shaheed writes that her Muslim grandmother started wearing a veil when she moved to Pakistan after Partition to "facilitate her access to public space."[10] But while the veil may limit women's visibility, it also encourages men to take a second look. It "does little to discourage male lust," Sherifa Zuhur concludes, "[n]or does it dampen flirting from the female side."[11] In my own ethnographic research several years ago in the old souq in Aleppo, young men's gazes were indiscriminately directed towards all veiled women but only to some unveiled women—perhaps precisely because they could not immediately discern the veiled woman's shape.

There are many kinds of veils, only a few of which hide everything. Take the hijab, which in the Koran refers not to an item of clothing but to a special curtain used to protect privacy. As a verb it means "to veil, cover, screen, shelter." In Arabic, the word has come to denote modest dress for women; most forms of hijab leave the face uncovered but hide the hair and the rest of the body except for the hands (which men are

[5] Pamela K. Taylor, "I Just Want to Be Me: Issues in Identity for One American Muslim Woman," in Heath, *The Veil* 120.

[6] Jasbir Jain, "Purdah, Patriarchy, and the Tropical Sun: Womanhood in India," in Heath, *The Veil* 226.

[7] Jain, "Purdah, Patriarchy, and the Tropical Sun" 242.

[8] Barbara Goldman Carrel, "Shattered Vessels That Contain Divine Sparks: Unveiling Hasidic Women's Dress Code," in Heath, *The Veil* 46.

[9] Eve Grubin, "After Eden: The Veil as a Conduit to the Internal," in Heath, *The Veil* 178, 187.

[10] Aisha Lee Fox Shaheed, "Dress Codes and Modes: How Islamic Is the Veil?," in Heath, *The Veil* 302.

[11] Sherifa Zuhur, "From Veil to Veil: 'What's in a Woman's Head is a Lot More Important Than What's On It,' " in Heath, *The Veil* 317.

also not supposed to touch). Whatever form it takes, the veil tends to invariably signify that its wearer is a woman, and so achieves the opposite of what many women want: to control the way they are seen, and to be seen as individuals, not as a type. Moreover, what is behind the veil is left to male fantasy, that is, left largely to a projection of what men want. In the late 1960's, some Catholic nuns, who had for centuries submitted to wearing the veil, rejected their traditional clothing on the grounds that it set them apart. "Adopting modern clothing demystifed the often mysterious presence," Laurene Lafontaine writes, permitting "outsiders to see the actual woman behind the habit, thus allowing for more personal interaction whereby a sister could express and experience the wholeness of her humanity."[12]

Not all women want to be seen in public as individuals. Some want to be seen as married, others as available; some want the anonymity conferred by belonging to a group. If all women veil the same way, then in public any single woman may feel relatively invisible as a woman. In all-female settings, the veil functions like a uniform, creating equality and erasing outer distinctions. Full veiling—the burqa, for example—provides the most anonymity in public, something that can be useful in all sorts of ways, especially to avoid surveillance in Middle Eastern states with authoritarian governments. I was told in Lebanon and Syria that most female sex workers cover themselves completely in public to keep their identities secret. Ashraf Zahedi reports that in Iran under the shah, compulsory unveiling met with outrage and resistance from clerics and secular conservatives, but there was widespread agreement to make an exception for prostitutes. Since the authorities did not want prostitutes to be indistinguishable from other women, they argued that they should be allowed to remove their veils only if they married.[13]

Indeed, today the look of "the prostitute" and the look of the "glamorous Western woman" are not always easily distinguished. Modesty is out. Today, young middle-class girls all over the world seek to look "adult" and "attractive," they wear makeup, super-tight jeans that show the navel, miniskirts that reveal the upper thigh, and push-up bras. In the Middle East, this look can be accompanied by a discrete veiling of the face. In Princeton, where I live, the sexualization of young girls' dress is extreme; they remind me of what Berliners in the 1990's called "Natasha," the look of the "Russian prostitute." But I see the same sort of thing in Aleppo and Damascus and Beirut, except that sometimes the girls also wear the hijab and cover their hair. Through omnipresent advertising and media attention, and the distribution of Western blockbuster films, a standardized image of the desirable woman now circulates between different cultural worlds. This does not, of course, eliminate cultural emphases—larger or smaller hips, breasts, lips, or eyes, for instance. When the enhanced visibility of the body is accompanied by a head covering, I suspect many men project, consciously or not, an image of the glamorous Western woman onto the woman behind the veil. The veil, in short, heightens men's fantasies about women, making it easier to perceive them as a generic category of desirable objects. The more that is hidden or concealed, the greater the spur to the imagination of the viewer.

Where does this imagination come from? For one, it comes from the headscarf as an archetype, which covers, at minimum, the hair. What was at stake, in 2004, when France banned the wearing of "conspicuous signs" of religious affiliation in state schools? The proponents of the ban insisted they were upholding the values of secular republicanism,

[12] Laurene M. Lafontaine, "Out of the Cloister: Unveiling to Better Serve the Gospel," in Heath, *The Veil* 84.

[13] Ashraf Zahedi, "Concealing and Revealing Female Hair: Veiling Dynamics in Contemporary Iran," in Heath, *The Veil* 255.

specifically the protection of the individual from the claims of religion, and of the state from ethnic or religious separatism. In reality, though, the law was aimed only at Muslim girls wearing headscarves.[14] If the hijab is supposed to prohibit the viewing of some parts of women (particularly their hair), why prohibit this prohibition unless there is some disturbing power in the image of the veiled woman? That image has little to do with what is hidden behind the veil—with the religious ideas inside women's heads, for example. Rather, as I will elaborate below, it has primarily to do with a challenge to ideas of transparency in the field of vision.

Within Islam, the desire on the part of some to make veiling compulsory draws on an imagination invested in the prohibition of the image itself, one that revolves around issues with sex and its power within different Islamicized cultures. For this imagination, Slavoj Zizek argues that within Islam, "there is, in a woman's exposure, an erectile protuberance, an obscenely intrusive quality... [as she] stands for the 'undecidability' of truth, for a succession of veils beneath which there is no ultimate hidden core."[15] Plenty has been written about church steeples or minarets of mosques as aggressively phallic symbols of power; much less has been written about the way that when a woman's hair is tightly wrapped in a scarf which blends into clothing extending smoothly down to the feet, her body has the look of a vertical column with a protuberance on top. Does this look mockingly create women as the phallus, as what Zizek coyly terms "the organ of paternal insemination?"[16] Western anxiety about the veil may have something to do with the notion that by veiling, women occupy the position of the phallus, allowing them to exercise power while remaining partially hidden.

The fact that veiled women draw attention to themselves as women stands in a dialectical relation to the desire to remove themselves from visual circulation. Theoretically, women who remove themselves from circulation by wearing the veil should increase their value. Sacred objects are those set aside from normal circulation. Objects in unimpeded circulation become more profane the more they circulate; they become commodities with discernable exchange value.[17] Commodity exchange rests on both putting things in circulation and removing them, temporarily, from exchange, until they can attain new value in new contexts. Vinyl records, for example, are a case in point.[18] Now that music can be downloaded in digital files, such records are no longer being produced. Anticipated scarcity makes them collector's items. Collectors withhold them from exchange for some period of time, with the expectation that value will increase once they are re-released as fetish objects.[19] Movie stars and performance artists often work with the same principle—their value increases if they withdraw from circulation for a while and later reenter the public sphere to make selective appearances. What happens to the value of women who remove themselves from visual circulation by veiling?

[14] For an analysis of contemporary debates around the politics of the veil in France, see Joan Wallach Scott, *The Politics of the Veil* (Princeton, NJ: Princeton University Press, 2007).

[15] Slavoj Zizek, "A Glance into the Archives of Islam," <http://www.lacan.com/zizarchives.htm>.

[16] Zizek, "A Glance into the Archives of Islam."

[17] See the foundational analysis of exchange by Marcel Mauss, *The Gift: The Form and Reason for Exchange in Archaic Societies* (London: Routledge, 2000). For a reanalysis of Mauss's work on exchange, see Maurice Godelier, *The Enigma of the Gift* (Chicago: University of Chicago Press, 1999), 171–99.

[18] On the influence of the digital revolution on the music industry, see David Kusek et al., *The Future of Music: Manifesto for the Digital Music Revolution* (Boston: Berklee Press, 2005).

[19] For an analysis of how value is accrued through periodic withholding, see Igor Kopytoff, "The Cultural Biography of Things: Commoditization as Process," in Arjun Appardurai (ed.), *The Social Life of Things: Commodities in Cultural Perspective* (Cambridge, MA: Cambridge University Press, 1986), 64–91.

IV. The Value of Women

The value of women as women has traditionally been determined through marital systems, in which women serve as tokens in a wider system of exchange.[20] Anthropologists have long documented the universality and diversity of these marital, kinship-based systems, and have witnessed their transformations under the pressures of capitalism and legal centralism within modern states. Historically, only particular categories of women could be exchanged: first cousins for first cousins, for example. Value, then, was not abstract but relative and contextual. The most valuable women—usually determined by their proximity to power—were exchanged for the most valuable women of other groups. Women's desirability was based less on the shape of their bodies than on their social status and fecundity.

These systems of kin exchange, though still integral to human culture everywhere, have largely broken down and been transformed into something less systematized and less bounded. For one, as the numbers of men and women who designate themselves as "singles" has grown, the capacity to bear children has lost its central value in many places. For another, men everywhere have lost much of their control over marriage systems, and women have lost much of their control over such things as choosing suitable partners for relatives. Increasingly, people locate partners through disinterested means, such as through the invisible hand of a more generalized exchange offered by Internet forums such as Craigslist. Above all, what has come to matter most in determining the value of women, and increasingly of men, is sexual attractiveness. The transformation is, of course, incomplete and uneven, but it is crucial to the passions ignited by the veiling of women.

Within Europe, one of the occasions in which modern veiling takes on iconic meaning is the so-called "honor killing," most often of a sister by her brother, sometimes by someone contracted by her brother or father. Such killings are rare but symbolically significant, as they bring into focus differences between systems of value. From a Eurocentric perspective, such killings are shocking, abhorrent, barbarian acts; they recall archaic emotions that appear incompatible with modern conceptions of the integrity and dignity of the person. I have six sisters, and the idea that my own integrity or that of my family is at stake in protecting their honor would never occur to me. Three of my sisters were local homecoming queens where I grew up, in a non-descript town in middle-western America. Homecoming queens tended to be those girls whom young boys found most desirable. Did I ever think my own honor or my family's was at stake in the kind of intercourse my sisters had with the boyfriends they dated? The question here is what has happened to limit my imagination so that I experience the killing of someone else's sisters by their brothers as a personal affront. Why, on the other hand, is dignity for some men unimaginable after one of their sisters or daughters has been compromised—i.e. had sex outside of a situation controlled by her male relatives, usually meaning outside marriage?

For men who feel their honor is at stake in the behavior of women, their sisters or daughters do not have a sexuality that is theirs to control. They are tokens in a system of marital exchange, and this system imposes on male relatives obligations to other kin or neighbors. There are duties to fulfill, such as protecting the chastity of one's sisters, enforcing codes of modesty, and reproducing the lineage or clan or tribe through controlled

[20] See the foundational work on the universality of marital exchange, published initially in 1949, Claude Lévi-Strauss, *The Elementary Structures of Kinship* (orig. 1949, 1969).

procreation. While a sister or daughter might have a say in what kind of alliance is arranged for her, that arrangement is traditionally predicated on her virginity. Today the veil often enters here as a symbol of resistance to the sirens of Western sexuality, with its generalized exchange and incitement to sex. It is a rational resistance to the sexualization of women and young girls in the global media. Men are positioned ambivalently to these sirens, both incited in their own desire to have sex with any generalized other, yet wanting to control or limit the desire of others, specifically as their sisters and daughters become its object.

V. Transparency, Choice, and Democratic Form

Veiling practices no longer operate within traditional, kinship-based worlds, but in a modern political environment shaped by the pressures of democratic public life. Democracy is predicated on a particular conception of individuality and autonomy, on freedom from the constraints of social groups such as kin, and on a degree of transparency in the workings of its institutions. Democracy requires periodic visibility, specifically of the face: when you go to vote, for example, or to pass through airport security. There is talk of fingerprints and eye scans being used instead, but these new modes of identification are unlikely to replace facial recognition, which remains integral to the negotiation of modern life. Veiling, which blocks recognition to a lesser or greater degree, would seem to be in tension with democratic transparency. Accordingly, in the contemporary contexts within which veils signify, visuality has become central to the intelligibility of women—despite the wish of many women to be seen for qualities that are spiritual, non-visible, or just inside their heads.

In *The Veil*, each of the contributors argue, to one degree or another, that they alone should be able to choose when and how to veil, and hence control their own intelligibility. "When women receive equal rights," Heath writes in her conclusion to the volume, "veils will fall away or they will stay as simple matters of *choice*. What a woman *chooses* to wear on her head should be trivial to anyone other than that woman herself."[21] This seems straightforward and reasonable. Why not let women make personal decisions about whether to veil or not? Why not settle the matter by simply letting them choose? Because the long feminist struggle for the "right to choose" builds on assumptions that are not anchored in the legal frameworks of many modern political systems. There is little worldwide agreement about equality before the law, for example, which would be a precondition for the establishment of a general right to choose. Moreover, framing equality in the language of "choice" ignores the fact that choices are already socially structured before they are made. Women's decisions about dress are rarely free of the coercion of kinship. Nor should all choices about veiling be left to the individual or her kin. Schools might require visibility for those sitting for exams, or in Physical Education lessons, and a career such as medicine may require specific kinds of clothing to be worn.

Furthermore, framing veiling practices in terms of the notion of choice can be highly misleading. Amish, Hasidic, Islamic, or Catholic veiling may be represented as a personal choice, but this coincides with these groups' interest in differentiating themselves from others. Women may be powerful within these groups, but they do not act alone nor are they an isolable group. Fights about veiling are common in families, and the divisions are not always along gender lines: it may be that a mother who unveiled in the 1970's

[21] Jennifer Heath, "Epilogue," in Heath, *The Veil* 320.

opposes her daughter's decision to wear the veil today, or children may insist that their mothers veil themselves. Moreover, the right to choose is usually exercised only after one has left a family. What of this choice within families? Who is authorized to intervene in families in order to assert, or protect, a "woman's right to choose?"

None of the contributors to *The Veil* writes about a personal decision to veil that hadn't already been authorized by one social group or another. They don't give any instances of women who veil idiosyncratically, in order to assert their autonomy. It isn't enough to argue that for some women autonomy means conformity to the group, or that freedom can be understood as the choice to fulfill socially prescribed duties. In social groups where veiling is dominant, the decision not to veil differs fundamentally from the decision to veil precisely in its resistance to social pressure. Michelle Auerbach illustrates this in an entertaining essay about her rebellion against Jewish "modesty commandments" (including covering the head) as she struggles with religious orthodoxy.[22] She claims to have resolved the conflict by deciding to wear a prayer shawl only after she attains equal authority with men, which is to say only after she is allowed to lead the ritual services in her local synagogue. To be sure, every individual should be able to opt in or out of traditional structures, but it is an illusion to think this "choice" is not highly contingent on external factors. Coercive mechanisms are brought to bear unequally on all decisions. The choice between fidelity to a kinship role and exercise of sexuality, as in the case of the honor killings discussed above, is clearly one where the coercive force of kinship and the social can be overwhelming. Auerbach appeals, as a feminist, not to her right to choose but to the importance of restructuring the social conditions in which choices are made.

Restructured social conditions will not, of course, stop men from continuing to see the veil in ways that are independent of women's intentions. The veil, in whatever form, is not and will never be "just a scrap of cloth," as Taylor wishes the hijab to be thought of, because it is worn in order to symbolize something, or many things.[23] Veiling practices often create their own phenomenal reality, have their own set of effects, unrelated to the material world. Hence veils are not, as many of the contributors to *The Veil* want to think, merely a diversion or distraction from issues of more substance to more women, such as poverty, the distribution of rights, the allocation of resources, sociopolitical disenfranchisement, and violence. Attending to these issues, important as they are, will not necessarily change the veil's contemporary iconic status.

VI. Postscript: The Authority of Men and the Law

This chapter has focused on how the veil and the practice of veiling signifies the (un)intelligibility of women generally, and under what conditions the veil has achieved an iconic status today. In this postscript I would like to suggest why this icon has become so important for male authority and the law today, specifically in the Arab Middle East. Needless to say, many men with either religious or political authority have taken a direct interest in whether women veil or unveil in public. The issue of honor killings presents an extreme case of what is at stake in private life, which can and sometimes does lead to the murder of women. The men who engage in such murders also bring about a kind of social death

[22] Michelle Auerbach, "Drawing the Line at Modesty: My Place in the Order of Things," in Heath, *The Veil* 202–12.

[23] Taylor, "I Just Want to Be Me" 128.

for themselves. Initially they may acquire the status of the martyr who sacrificed himself for the sake of a social norm. This temporary status most frequently gives way, however, to longer-term punishments, such as imprisonment, monetary fines, the end of a normatively approved and "normal" lifecourse, social ostracism, recriminations against other kin, and an immeasurable psychological toll in ambivalence and guilt resulting from having murdered someone whom one loved. Other male relatives may share in some or many of these punishments. For such men, the issue is who has public responsibility and control over how women signify? Do they act in the name of the father, kin, tradition, and justice? Or do they defer to the authority of secular law? The conflict about women's intelligibility, then, is not usually between religious and secular authorities but between norms of kinship and the autonomy of women as proposed in written state laws.

For men who live under authoritarian governments—which includes, to a large degree, the entire Arab Middle East—the law is merely exercised over subjects and hence nearly always experienced by men as submission and castration. The state rules over but does not necessarily represent him. Even if the legal system exacts just retribution for injuries to his honor, the man has difficulty experiencing this as a redress for his lost authority. From the Egyptian novelist Naguib Mafouz to the Tunisian filmmaker Nouri Bouzid, many intellectuals and artists have represented in their work this acute crisis in male authority in both secular and religious registers. In the last four decades especially, many novels and films have sought to represent the castrated man and the waning power of the father.

As a final example, take the film "Couscous" ("La Graine et le Mule") directed by the Tunisian-born filmmaker Abdellatif Kechiche, the 2007 winner of the César, France's most prestigious film prize.[24] It takes place in France, in the Mediterranean port of Setebut. The sixty-year-old Arab immigrant, Slimane Beiji, who has worked in a ship repair yard for 35 years, is having his workload reduced and fears unemployment. Slimane's conundrum is introduced via a scene of his son, who takes time out from his work as commentator on a tourist boat to have sex with a passenger, later revealed as the wife of a powerful member of the local French elite. Slimane's family is of North African origin (one daughter has a non-Arab French husband), and the film is generally concerned to show how all members struggle with being French. But the focus is on the Slimane, the father, who in response to his impending unemployment opens a restaurant that serves couscous.

In the film, couscous becomes the symbol for an Arab cultural experience of warmth, intimacy, and belonging, and at the same time a means to seduce non-Arabs into entering into a relationship of respect and wonder with the resident Arabs. Tired, weak, and visibly aging, Slimane's investment in this restaurant—in couscous as Arab tradition—is a final effort to redeem himself. Although he sees himself as a failure, he still longs to leave behind an inheritance for his sons and daughters when he dies. But in this aim he is frustrated, and ultimately sacrificed sadistically, primarily due to the failure of his useless sons who, conspiring together in their narcissism and incompetence, abandon him in the evening that inaugurates the restaurant. Any possibility for an inheritance ultimately rests with the ability of the women in the family, especially Slimane's ex-wife and current partner, along with her daughter, to make the restaurant work.

Many other films or novels repeat this representation of contemporary perceptions of the location of the father: how his waning authority has been decoupled from secular law, which in any case does little to provide him opportunity or protect him from the

[24] "Couscous" (Pathé Renn Productions 2007).

overreach of religion or other kinds of authority, including that of the global market; how he is unable to leave an inheritance for his children; how he is dependent on the women in his life. In "Couscous," kinship and the father are betrayed by the sexual behavior of an irresponsible son; women present the only redemptive possibility. In a structural sense, then, men, because they have lost their public authority, are heavily invested in how women enter into the public sphere and whether they assume phallic authority. It should not surprise us that men resent the authority women accrue through this entry in part because they are totally dependent on their success.

13

Reproductive Rights in a Jewish and Democratic State

*Daphne Barak-Erez**

I. Introduction: State, Religion, and Law in Israel

The state of Israel is, as stated in its basic laws, a Jewish and democratic state.[1] The status and protection of human rights, including women's rights, are shaped by both parts of this definition. On the one hand, inspired by its democratic and liberal values, Israel recognizes equality as a foundational principle of its legal system. In fact, the Declaration of the Establishment of the State of Israel from 1948 carried an express promise for "complete equality of social and political rights... irrespective of race, sex and religion."[2] Not long after the establishment of the state, the Women's Equal Rights Law was legislated, providing every woman the right to equality.[3] Furthermore, many other laws, mainly focused on women's rights in the context of employment, have followed throughout the years.[4] On the other hand, shaped by its Jewish ethos,[5] as inspired also by Jewish religious tradition, Israeli law has adopted gender-based distinctions that have implications for the full equality of women—especially in the area of family law, and sometimes beyond it as well.

With regard to family law, the distinction between men and women is an offspring of the traditional application of religious law to some aspects of this branch of law. The decision to apply religious law to family issues was the choice of the colonial rulers of the land of Palestine, thus accommodating the variety of religious groups in the holy land—starting in the Ottoman period (when it was established and defined as the so-called Millet system) and continuing in the British Mandate period.[6] When Israel was established

* Justice, Supreme Court of Israel. Formerly Professor of Law and the Stewart and Judy Colton Chair of Law and Security, Faculty of Law, Tel Aviv University. I thank Sharon Basan, Daniel Sinclair, and Zvi Triger for their comments and Shir Eshkol and Asaf Wiener for their research assistance.

[1] Basic Law: Human Dignity and Liberty, s. 1A; Basic Law: Freedom of Occupation, s. 2.

[2] The declaration itself does not enjoy formal constitutional superiority, but it has been traditionally considered an important interpretive source. Currently, it is even mentioned as a foundational document by the basic laws mentioned above.

[3] Women's Equal Rights Law, 5711-1951, 5 LSI 171.

[4] Employment of Women Law, 5714-1954, 8 LSI 128; Equality of Opportunities in Labour Law, 5748-1988, 42 LSI 31; Equal Wages to Male and Female Workers Law 5756-1996, SH No. 1581, p. 230.

[5] Of course, Israeli society consists also of a large Muslim minority as well as other small (mainly Christian) minorities. However, in terms of shaping the public sphere, the Jewish tradition is the hegemonic one. For an elaborate discussion of the multicultural condition of Israeli society, see Menachem Mautner, *Law and the Culture of Israel* (Oxford: Oxford University Press, 2011).

[6] This is, in principle, a personalized system in the sense that each individual is subjected to the dictates of his own religion.

in 1948 it preserved the same principle (subject to some modifications).[7] Accordingly, although Israeli law accepts the ideal of gender equality, in principle, the area of family law serves as an enclave in which the application of equality is limited due to the dictates of religion (taking the views of the relevant religions as they are currently at least in their hegemonic versions). Other areas of law also preserve some gender distinctions unrelated to religious demands—for example, the differences between men and women with regard to the scope of mandatory military service[8] and special privileges awarded to women in connection to fertility and pregnancy to women (although later reforms have broadened the application of many of these privileges to fathers as well).[9]

In addition to this pre-state history, the status of religion in Israel is often attributed to a broader historical compromise between the secular and religious parts of Israeli society, known as the "status quo." The legal status of religion in Israel was, and still is, based on what is traditionally depicted as "a decision not to decide"—that is, on preserving an existing status quo that acknowledges the priority of religious demands in some areas, including the law governing marriage and divorce.[10] This compromise was also expressed in the Women's Equal Rights Law. This law, proudly declaring the right of women to full equality (section 1), also states that it "shall not affect any legal prohibition or permission relating to marriage and divorce" (section 5).[11]

So far, forces of change have had only limited impact on the status quo. Culturally speaking, Israelis who grew up as second and third generation secular Jews feel less attachment to old traditions and are more aware of the growing gap between the standards of the status quo and the norms prevalent in the western world (for example the world-wide availability of civil marriage). At the same time, many of them regard the status quo as a constraint unlikely to be changed. From a legal perspective, the possibilities of challenging status-quo legislative compromises have significantly broadened. A major reason, though not the sole one, was the legislation of the basic laws on human rights in 1992 — Basic Law: Freedom of Occupation and Basic Law: Human Dignity and Liberty—which opened the door to judicial review of legislation. However, the potential for change is very limited as far as women's rights are concerned. First, most of the discriminatory practices are protected by a special provision which safeguards legislation enacted before the basic laws from judicial review.[12] Second, as already indicated,

[7] Rabbinical Courts Jurisdiction (Marriage and Divorce) Law, 5713-1953, 7 LSI 139, which was enacted after the establishment of the state, gave this principle additional force with regard to the Jewish population of Israel. It established the exclusive control of Jewish religious *Halakhic* law with regard to the marriage and divorce of all Jews in Israel (s. 2).

[8] The law subjects both men and women to the duty to serve, the period of service for men is longer and more exceptions to the duty apply to women. See Daphne Barak-Erez, "The Feminist Battle for Citizenship: Between Combat Duties and Conscientious Objection" (2007) 13 *Cardozo Journal of Law and Gender* 531.

[9] Employment of Women Law.

[10] Daphne Barak-Erez, "Law and Religion under the Status Quo Model: Between Past Compromises and Constant Change" (2009) 30 *Cardozo Law Review* 2495.

[11] Women's Equal Rights Law, 5711-1950, 5 LSI 171. Commentators have noted that the compromises which had been introduced by this law were not only the result of religious political pressure but rather represented also patriarchal views prevalent among secularists. See Pnina Lahav, "Conceptions of Sex Equality in the Debate over the Women's Equal Rights Law" (1994) 47/46 *Zmanim* 149 (Hebrew); Zvi Triger, "Remembrance of Laws Past: Israel's Adoption of Religious Marriage and Divorce Law as a Means for Reviving the Jewish People's Lost Manliness," in Hannah Naveh and Orna Ben-Naftali (eds), *Trials of Love* (London: J.M. Dent, 2005), 103 (Hebrew); Zvi Triger, "The Gendered Racial Formation: Foreign Men, 'Our' Women, and Marriage Law" (2009) 40 *Women's Rights Law Reporter* 479.

[12] Section 10 of Basic Law: Human Dignity and Liberty.

the new basic laws officially state the democratic and Jewish nature of the state[13] and therefore may be interpreted as tolerant to Jewish-religious norms even when they partially contradict liberal values.

The area of reproductive rights in Israeli law brings together the basic secular structure of Israeli law and those parts of it that are being informed and shaped by religious law. In principle, unlike marriage and divorce, the regulation of reproductive rights is based on modern, secular law and is not formally part of the area of family law governed directly by religious law. Abortion law in Israel has been regulated since the times of the British Mandate in Palestine as part of the criminal law legislation on the protection of body integrity and life, as explained below. The more modern laws on reproduction (both IVF and Surrogacy matters) have been shaped since the 1980's as part of the modern legislation on the ethical regulation of medical issues. In this sense, these laws do not directly reflect religious norms; but rather medical and social concerns. However, due to the proximity of these issues to family law, religious law and religious norms have served as an important factor in shaping and drafting certain important details of the secular legislation in this area. This chapter is dedicated to exploring the regulation of reproductive rights in Israel from a perspective which focuses on the way it was shaped by the state-religion relationship.[14]

Following this introduction, Part I explains the unique nature of Israel as a modern liberal democratic state that also defines itself as Jewish. Part II addresses the main religious and cultural factors that shape the regulation of reproduction and family in Israel. Part III discusses Israeli abortion law, as shaped by British Mandatory legislation as well as by Israeli cultural concerns and religious power in the political arena. Part IV discusses the regulation of IVF and surrogacy procedures, which emerged much later and was influenced by both Jewish religious culture and Israeli modern culture in different ways, most notably in connection to the centrality of the right to parenthood in society which, culturally speaking, is perceived almost as a duty. The Conclusion aims at mapping and structuring the special traits of Israeli reproduction law against the background of its complex sources of inspiration.

II. Religious and Secular Aspects of Reproduction, Motherhood, and the Family in Israel

In order to fully understand the impact of the "Jewish" factor in Israel's constitutional system on reproductive rights, it is important to take note of the attitude of Jewish culture to reproduction and its regulation. In this context, it is worthwhile to analyze not only religious doctrine, but also the culture that has been shaped around it.

In general, it is interesting to observe that the mix of values coming from Jewish religious tradition, Jewish national (Zionist) values and Israeli secular culture leads to different points of balancing in the area of abortions *vis-à-vis* the area of advanced fertilization techniques for the sake of procreation.

With regard to abortion, one can generally trace a conflict between the anti-abortion stance originating from religious tradition as well as from aspirations for national growth on the one hand and the secular inclination toward the liberalization of abortions on

[13] See n. 1 above.

[14] Accordingly, the analysis will refrain from directly addressing other important perspectives, such as feminist critiques, social critiques etc.

the other hand. In contrast, in the area of fertilization techniques, these two sources of influence generally work in the same direction. Both Jewish religious doctrine and Zionist ideology support procreation very strongly. Therefore, these traditions tend to be very open to the use of fertilization techniques, subject to some restrictions. In addition, secular Israeli culture is family-centered and supportive of procreation in a way that reflects historical traumas and political conditions. Generally speaking, throughout history Jewish civilization has developed under conditions of constant persecutions. For Jews, it has become a sacred goal to be able to preserve civilization and have a next generation. These feelings have significantly intensified after the holocaust, when the Jewish group was faced with mass genocide and the main goal of the Jewish society became survival of the family and the group as a whole. Moreover, the conditions of Israel in the Middle East, surrounded by big Islamic states, the vast majority of which do not maintain peaceful relationship with it, has intensified the psyche of procreation in the name of growth.[15]

This family-centered culture of Israeli society, even beyond the religious realm, is considered to have important implications for the social and legal status of women in Israel (which are in tension with the formal ethos of gender equality).[16]

In fact, the background forces shaping the law of reproductive rights in Israel are even more complex. In some ways, the religious and secular views of abortion are not as distinct as they may seem at first glance. Jewish religious tradition leans against abortions but is not completely inflexible about the prohibition. It allows for abortion under certain circumstances, as described below, and although it prohibits the practice of abortion it does not consider it an act of murder. At the same time, the strong family values which characterize Israeli society as well as the demographic concerns of the Jewish population in Israel have made the attitude toward abortions ambivalent even among secular people. Nuances should be offered also with regard to the influence of religious and secular views on IVF and surrogacy law. The secular perspective on these issues focuses on medical and ethical concerns, rather than on factors such as the Jewish origin of the surrogate mother, which raise questions only from the religious perspective.

III. Israeli Abortion Law

A. Jewish religious views on abortion

The normative Jewish view on the issue of abortion is based on Biblical and Talmudic sources which address the question of abortion only indirectly, and are open to conflicting interpretations, based on the fundamental religious prohibition on feticide.[17] It is, however, broadly accepted that a fetus is not a legal person (*nefesh*), and therefore abortion is not regarded as murder. The dominant view in the *Responsa* literature is that abortion is forbidden under Jewish law (*halakha*) except in cases involving a threat to the mother's life or health, and during the very early stages of pregnancy, i.e. until the fortieth day or the end of the first trimester. Contemporary authorities have also ruled leniently with

[15] See Daphne Birenbaum-Carmeli, "Reproductive Policy in Context: Implication on Women's Rights in Israel" (2003) 24 *Policy Studies* 101; Carmel Shalev and Sigal Gooldin, "The Uses and Misuses of In Vitro Fertilization in Israel Some Sociological and Ethical Considerations" (2006) 12 *Nashim: A Journal of Jewish Women's Studies and Gender Issues* 151.

[16] See also Lahav, "Conceptions of Sex Equality in the Debate over the Women's Equal Rights Law."

[17] The focus here is on the traditional Orthodox Jewish perspective, due to its dominance in the Israeli public and political arena.

respect to the abortion of a genetically defective fetus.[18] Recent studies indicate that despite the relative tolerance of Jewish thought toward induced abortions, dominant until the modern era, a radical shift can be traced during the last century toward widening the prohibitory approach to abortions.[19] This shift can be explained not merely as a religious concern, but rather as part of the strengthening of religious fundamentalism as a counter-response to modernity and liberalism.[20]

B. Legislative developments

The origins of the law of abortions in Israel are found in British Mandatory criminal law, which included an absolute prohibition on abortion.[21] This prohibition was incorporated into Israeli law together with the whole legal system that was in place in 1948 (when the British Mandate in Palestine ended), and was only somewhat narrowed in 1952, by a Court's decision to permit abortions if performed for medical reasons and without concealment.[22] Nevertheless, this prohibition was rarely enforced. This policy of non-enforcement became formal in 1952, when the Attorney General instructed to limit prosecution only to cases that involved questionable consent to the abortion, negligence, or injury.[23] As a result of this policy, a wide practice of illegal abortions had developed.

The process of reforming the law of abortions was initiated in the 1960's,[24] when the Prime Minister at the time, Levi Eshkol, appointed the Commission for the Study of Birthrate Problems.[25] The Commission was appointed due to concerns regarding the relative decline in the growth of the Jewish population. The Commission's report linked non-enforcement of the prohibition on abortion to declining birth rates. It also indicated a connection between poor socio-economic conditions and multiple birth families.

[18] See Immanuel Jackovits, "Jewish Views on Abortion" (1965–66) 17 *Case Western Reserve Law Review* 480; David M. Maeir, "Abortion and Halakhah: New Issues" (1976) 7 *Dine Israel* 137 (Hebrew); Daniel B. Sinclair, "The Legal Basis for The Prohibition in Abortion in Jewish Law" (1980) 15 *Israel Law Review* 109; Kanneth Shuster, "An Halachic Overview of Abortion" (1992) 26 *Suffolk University Law Review* 641 (1992); Daniel B. Sinclair, *Jewish Biomedical Law: Legal and Extra-legal Dimensions* (Oxford: Oxford University Press, 2003), 12–67. For other views, see Aharon Lichtenstein, "Induced Abortions—Halakhah Aspects" (2000–01) 21 *Tchumin* 93, 93–94 (Hebrew) (arguing that an abortion is considered as homicide); Mordechai Halperin, "Pregnancy Interruption—Legal, Moral, and Halakhic Aspects" (2002) 27 *Refua VeMishpat* 84 (Hebrew) (arguing that a fetus is a human being, but that an abortion is not considered homicide).

[19] Yehiel M. Bar-Ilan, "Za'ar Gufa Kodem: Induced Abortion in Halakhah and Israeli Law," in Jonathan Davies and Avraham Sahar (eds), *The Right to Life with No Malformation* (el-Aviv: Dyonon, 2007) (Hebrew).

[20] Dorraj Manochehr, "The Crisis of Modernity and Religious Revivalism: A Comparative Study of Islamic Fundamentalism, Jewish Fundamentalism and Liberation Theology" (1999) 46(2) *Social Compass* 225.

[21] Section 175 of the Criminal Code Ordinance, 1936, which was based on s. 58 of the British Offences Against the Person Act of 1861, provided: "Any Person who, with intent to procure miscarriage of a woman whether she is or not with child, unlawfully administers to her or causes her to take any poison or other noxious thing, or uses any force of any kind, or uses any other means whatever, is liable to imprisonment for five years."

[22] Cr. A. 138/52 Horovitz v. A.G. 7 PD 469 [1952].

[23] This directive was issued by the Attorney General in 1952. It was revoked in 1963 when its legality was contested. Yet, the practice of prosecution policy remained unchanged. See: DK (1975) 1318, 1320 (Hebrew).

[24] For a more elaborate survey of these developments, see Noga Morag Levine, "Abortions in Israel: Community, Rights, and the Context of Compromise" (1994) 19 *Law and Social Inquiry* 313.

[25] The Commission for the Study of Birthrate Problems, known also as the Baki Commission (chaired by the demographer Roberto Baki).

Thus, the Commission recommended, among other things, the establishment of hospital committees which were to hear abortion requests. These committees were meant to enhance governmental control over induced abortions, with a view to decrease their rate. Accordingly, "Pregnancy Termination Committees" were established in hospitals to consider abortion requests. At that time, these committees had no official status under the law and they varied widely in the criteria they used for authorizing abortions.

Though the Pregnancy Termination Committees had taken a more liberal approach relative to what the law allowed at the time, large numbers of abortion applicants were still denied. Consequently, the illegal abortions market flourished. The number of induced abortions at the time was estimated by the Minister of Health as nearly 60,000 a year, only 15,000 of which were conducted in recognized medical institutions and only a fraction for lawful reasons.[26] Illegal abortions were thus in reach of every woman who could afford one. The lack of proper governmental supervision caused not only socio-economic based discrimination but also hazards to women's health.

Later on, in 1972, another committee was appointed in order to examine the legal prohibitions on induced abortions.[27] The committee considered various aspects of abortion policy, including medical, psychological, social, moral, and religious aspects. The committee's final report included a draft of a largely amended abortions law. In 1977, 24 Knesset members from various parties presented a reform Bill based on the committee's recommendations. This Bill, which soon became an amendment to the Penal Law, introduced a significant change.[28]

The new Penal Law has preserved the criminal prohibition on abortion as its baseline principle. It states that "any person who knowingly interrupts a woman's pregnancy, either by medical treatment or in any other manner, shall be liable to imprisonment for a term of five years or a fine of fifty thousand pounds" (section 313). However, the prohibition is currently followed by a series of exemptions, which substantially narrow its scope. To begin with, criminal liability is not imposed on the pregnant woman subject to the abortion (section 320). Thus, a woman who knowingly interrupts her own pregnancy will not bear any criminal liability. An additional exemption from criminal liability for abortion is granted on the basis of immediate or unexpected medical necessity (section 317).

At the heart of the reform was the regulation of abortion policy which provided for a system of abortions approved by medical committees. More specifically, the amended Penal Law allows for the performance of abortions under certain conditions: that the abortion is performed by a gynecologist in a state-recognized medical institution upon the approval of a special committee in accordance with law (section 314). The committee is comprised of two physicians and a social worker, at least one of whom should be a woman (section 315). Most importantly, the amended Penal law sets out the grounds for authorizing an abortion in the following circumstances (in section 316(a)):

(1) the woman is under marriage age or has completed her fortieth year;
(2) the pregnancy is due to relations prohibited by the criminal law, or incestuous relations, or to extramarital relations;
(3) the child is likely to have a physical or mental defect;
(4) continuance of the pregnancy is likely to endanger the woman's life or to cause her physical or mental harm.

[26] DK (1975) 1318, 1321–1322 (Hebrew).

[27] The Commission for the Assessment of the Prohibitions on Induced Abortions, known also as the Gabay Report (chaired by Meir Gabay, a lawyer in the public service). The report was published in 1974.

[28] Penal Law Amendment (Interruption of Pregnancy) Law, 5737-1977, 31 LSI 82; Penal Law Regulations (Interruption of Pregnancy), 5738-1978, KT 3856, 1432.

A fifth sub-section, known in the public arena as "the social clause", used to allow for abortions due to poor familial or social circumstances, more specifically when the "continuance of the pregnancy is likely to cause grave harm to the woman or her children owing to difficult family or social circumstances in which she finds herself or which prevail in her environment." This sub-subsection, originally included in the 1977 amendment of the law, was abolished only a short while afterwards, due to political pressures coming from the religious parties, as described below.

C. The religious-secular controversy

The religious-secular clash over the law of abortions mainly focused on the so-called "social clause." As already indicated, the social clause was repealed shortly after its enactment. This move became possible due to the general change in the surrounding political circumstances in Israel. In the 1977 elections, the long-time hegemonic Labor Party lost its position for the first time to the Likud Party. This strengthened the position of religious parties since they were now even more valuable in creating a coalition government (when a government transition became a realistic possibility). The religious parties conditioned their support of the new government on repeal of the social clause. Accordingly, in the coalitional agreement between the Likud and Agudat Israel, an ultra-Orthodox party, the two agreed on the repeal of the social clause. By the end of 1979 the social clause was indeed abolished after a tight vote on the matter.[29]

In principle, the revocation of the "social clause" was very dramatic and meaningful. In theory it was the only provision in the law that gave the committee some discretion to define the zone of legitimate abortions (as the other clauses are either scientific or "objective"). Nevertheless, *de facto* the legislative change was less significant than expected. The repeal of the social clause did not reduce the overall number of authorized abortions. Instead, committees used their discretion to justify abortions using alternative clauses, most notably the physical or mental risk to the mother exception. Accordingly, current religious efforts are focused on getting a better hold of the process of committee authorization by limiting the number of committees authorized to approve abortion in the more advanced stages of the pregnancy etc.[30]

D. Pragmatism or rights

The most striking feature of the debate over abortions in Israel is the relative marginality of the constitutional discourse to this debate (in stark contrast to many other countries, among which the United States is a prime example). Indeed, feminist activists were trying to promote rights-talk in this area, advocating the idea of personal autonomy and the right to control one's body. However, this narrative did not get a dominant hold in the public arena, for various reasons. First, on the formal level, the major legislative developments in the area had emerged before the enactment of the new Basic Laws on human rights in the early 1990's. Accordingly, no formal challenge to the legislation

[29] For criticism on this move, see Yitzchak Kadman, "Pregnancy Termination from a Social Viewpoint" (1979) 2(3) *Society and Welfare* 320, 322 (Hebrew) (the article stresses the political motivations which promoted the repeal of the social clause, and argues for its legitimacy even according to certain *Halakhic* sources).

[30] For more details, see Dalila Amir and Niva Shoshi, "The Israeli Abortion Law—Gender and Feminist Aspects" (2007) *Studies in Law, Gender and Feminism* 777 (Hebrew).

based on the supremacy of constitutional rights could be made. Second, it was hard to develop a fully-fledged argument for abortion legislation when the reform in the Penal Law led to what was perceived by many as a reasonable compromise. Those who resisted the full-legalization of abortions succeeded in preserving this principle, whereas women who apply for an approved abortion usually get what they need: the statistical data for 2010 shows that the rate of abortions approved by the committee stands at 97 percent, and that the majority of these cases concern pregnancies which result from criminally prohibited relations, incestuous relations, or extra-marital relations.[31] This characterization of the compromise is resisted by feminist activists but it has a hold in the public.

The result has been that feminist attempts to advocate a legal right for abortions failed to gain significant public attention and support. Perhaps the most meaningful attempt was the proposed Bill for free abortions introduced to the Knesset in 1974 by MK Marcia Freedman, an American born feminist activist. The proposed Bill was aimed at allowing abortions on demand, free from governmental intervention, during the first trimester of the pregnancy. Freedman's Bill was generally considered too radical and "American" by most Knesset members, including those from Freedman's own party, and was thus rejected.[32] Even the important amendment to the Women's Equal Rights Law from 2000, which ensures every woman's right over her body, subordinates this right to any legal prohibition, namely the prohibition on abortions.[33]

The Israeli law of abortions does not speak in the language of rights—neither women's rights nor the fetus' rights. Nevertheless, from a pragmatic view, the law of abortions is relatively lenient. *De facto*, the statutory exemptions allow for a wide practice of abortions,[34] partly with state funding (for abortions made for medical reasons, based in the National Health Insurance Law).[35] At the same time, this analysis takes account of the picture only partially, because it does not reflect the experience of women who are subject to the authorization process which operates as an educational tool for "careless women"[36] as well as those who are deterred from formally applying to get an authorization to abortion.

Pragmatically, however, the discontent from the prevailing compromise is not strong enough and therefore the debate over the legal regulation of the matter is taking place mostly in the symbolic arena. Moreover, even if a new reform is enacted there is no guarantee that it will broaden the *de facto* flexibility of the current regime (alongside its numerous problems). In other words, reform proposals come with a risk. Proposed Bills in this area are tabled mainly by individual Knesset members from either the liberal side of the political map or the Ultra-Orthodox parties with a view to inspire their constituencies rather than actually reform the law.[37] In fact, since the religious prohibition

[31] Report on Pregnancy Termination by the Law: 1990–2010 (The Ministry of Health, 2011) (Hebrew). Available at: <http://www.health.gov.il/publicationsfiles/preg1990_2010.pdf>.

Note that the data regarding the reasons for the request are given by the applicants themselves. Therefore, it does not necessarily reflect the real motivations and reasons of the applicants, since it is considered a so-called effective tactic to report to the committee about an extra-marital affair in order to secure its approval.

[32] A similar Bill was proposed earlier by MK Uri Avneri and rejected three years before in 1971. See Amir and Shoshi, "The Israeli Abortion Law—Gender and Feminist Aspects" 792.

[33] Section 7A, Women's Equal Rights Law (Amendment no. 2), 5760-2000, SH No.1735, 167.

[34] See n. 31 above.

[35] Section 7(c) of the Second Supplement of the National Health Insurance Law, 5754-1994, SH No. 1469, 156.

[36] Dalila Amir, "'Responsible,' 'Committed' and 'Wise'—The Construction of Israeli Femininity in the Pregnancy Termination Committees" (1995) 7 *Theory and Criticism* 247 (Hebrew).

[37] See e.g. Draft Bill Penal Law (Amendment—restoring the social clause as a ground for authorizing abortions), 2003, HH p/1514 and Draft Bill Canceling Pregnancy Committees (legislation amendments),

regarding induced abortions in the Jewish tradition is not unequivocal, the ongoing political battle in this matter should also be understood as reflecting the political battle over power and control between the liberal and the Orthodox parties, and not merely as a religious-ideological dispute regarding abortion as a stand-alone normative issue.

IV. Israeli Law on Advanced Procreation Techniques—In Vitro Fertilization (IVF) and Surrogacy

A. Jewish religious views on procreation

From a religious perspective, it is important to stress that Jewish law strongly supports the ideal of reproduction. Having children is considered a religious duty (*mitzvah*), learned from the book of Genesis, which states the duty to *Pru and Revu* (be fruitful and multiply). In fact it is the first mitzvah mentioned in the Bible.[38]Accordingly, infertility is often described and experienced as a tragedy,[39] and in other cases a curse or punishment.[40] The strength of this ethos is expressed, amongst other things, in birthrate statistics in Israel. Currently, the average birthrate in the religious (Jewish) part of Israeli society is 6.5 for a single woman while in the secular part of society the average birthrate is 2.1 for a woman (which itself is higher than the prevalent standard in most secular western countries).[41]

At the same time, the regulation of IVF and Surrogacy also raises concerns from the perspective of Jewish religious doctrine. The first concern regards the child's religious identity. Under Jewish law this identity is determined in accordance with the religion of the mother at the moment of birth. In the context of an IVF in which the egg being donated comes from a non-Jewish woman a question which may be asked is what should the criteria for determining the religious identity of the child be. In the case of surrogacy, questions may be raised when the surrogate mother (or the egg donor when a donated egg is being used) is not Jewish.

A second major religious concern is that of the legitimacy of the new-born, known as the *mamzerut* (bastard) question. According to Jewish law, a child born from certain prohibited relations is considered a *mamzer* (a bastard), and suffers serious consequences from a religious perspective (such as a prohibition on marriage with others within the Jewish community). Such prohibited relationships include a married woman's adultery (as distinct from a married man's adultery) and relationships between close family relatives.[42] The issue of *mamzerut* has some potential implications in the context of surrogacy. One question is whether the status of *mamzerut* applies when

2011, HH p/18/3212 (liberal Bills); Draft Bill Penal Law (Amendment—Instructions for Pregnancy Termination), 2011, HH p/18/3494 (a restrictive Bill aimed at prohibiting abortions after the 22nd week of pregnancy, based on the assumption that at this stage the fetus is viable, and therefore abortion should be regarded equivalent to murder).

38 Genesis 1:28.

39 As can see in the biblical plea of Rachel to Jacob: "Give me sons, or else I die," Genesis 30:1.

40 "Therefore Michal the daughter of Saul had no child unto the day of her death," Samuel II 23:6.

41 "Fertility among Jewish and Muslim Women in Israel, by Level of Religiosity, 1979–2009," *Central Bureau of Statistics—Demography and Census Department* (2011) (Hebrew).

42 Yossi Green, "Is there a Solution the 'Mamzerut' Problem with Medical Reproductive Technologies?" (2010) 7 *Netanya Academic College Law Review* 411 (Hebrew).

the surrogate mother is married. All of the *halakhic* authorities are of the opinion that a married woman should not serve as a surrogate when the sperm donor is not her husband, although there is some disagreement regarding the consequences of such birth. Many *halakhic* authorities contend that in the absence of sexual relations the child is not a *mamzer*. A similar question is whether the surrogate mother may be a family relative. Here, too, a question which divides religious authorities is whether the substance of the prohibition is the forbidden sexual intercourse, or the mixing of genetic materials from a man and a woman who are not married to each other.

Another challenge is connected to the question of paternity. Under Jewish law paternity is established at conception, while maternity is established at birth. The implications of this view is that the surrogate mother can be regarded the mother,[43] and that in cases of a sperm donation, the legally recognized paternity is that of the biological father, i.e. the sperm donor.[44]

As described below, these challenges have significantly influenced the shaping of the law governing IVF and surrogacy, alongside medical and ethical considerations.

B. First regulatory stage: the formation of procreation regulation

In order to understand the legal regulation of procreation in Israel, it is important to start by stressing that, in accordance with the cultural background described above, the use of procreation technologies is socially accepted as moral, legitimate, and desirable, and has not been called into question in any significant way in the public arena.[45] The result is a constantly increasing public funding of these procedures,[46] and vast academic writings dedicated to IVF procedures in Israel.[47]

From a religious perspective, most of the rabbis adopt a pragmatic approach with regard to IVF procedures, which generally support it and insist only on introducing various conditions that would guarantee the Jewish and "marriageable" status of the

[43] Although there are religious arguments also in favor of the genetic mother's paternity. See Shlomit Joy Oz, "Genetic Mother vs. Surrogate Mother: Which Does the Law Recognize: A Comparison of Jewish Law, American Law, and England's Law" (1995) 6 *Touro International Law Review* 437.

[44] The vast majority of authorities agree that paternity is always determined by the sperm donor. The fact that no sexual intercourse took place is irrelevant. A minority view, expressed by Rabbi Malkiel Tennenbaum, maintains that "once the semen has been emitted and has warmth only because of the ministration of the physician and his skill with the pipette or due to the heat of the bath" the resulting child is not regarded as being that of the sperm donor. However, Rabbi Tennenbaum himself did not rule in practice on the basis of this theory. See J. David Bleich, *Contemporary Halakhic Problems* (New York : Ktav, 1995), 238–42. An additional complication rises from the fact that adoption (a concept which had originated in Roman law) does not exist as a legal construct in Jewish law, although it is certainly practiced, and it is regarded as "a great mitzvah to rear an orphan in one's home." On the halakhic position with regard to assisted reproduction in Jewish law, see Daniel B. Sinclair, "Assisted Reproduction in Jewish Law" (2002) 30 *Fordham Urban Law Journal* 71.

[45] Critiques are usually expressed by academics and feminists who are concerned about the pressure on women to obtain motherhood at almost any cost to their health. See Daphne Birenbaum-Carmeli, " 'Cheaper than a Newcomer': On the Social Production of IVF Policy in Israel" (2004) 7 *Sociology of Health and Illness* 897.

[46] Updated records publicized by the Israeli Health Ministry (from 2010) reveal an ever-growing scope and use of IVF, and growing success rates. According to this official data in 2009–10 from the total births of living babies 4.1% came from pregnancy originating in IVF treatments (in comparison to 3.3% in 2005, 3% in 2001, and 2.5% in 1997). Available at <http://www.health.gov.il/NewsAndEvents/SpokemanMesseges/Pages/19042012_1.aspx>.

[47] See e.g. Susan Martha Kahn, *Reproducing Jews: A Cultural Account of Assisted Conception in Israel* (Durham, Duke University Press, 2000); Daphna Birenbaum-Carmeli and Yoram S. Carmeli (eds), *Kin, Gene, Community: Reproductive Technologies Among Jewish Israelis* (Oxford and New York: Berghahn Books, 2010).

resulting children (through interpretative religious verdicts and rabbis' inspections in IVF laboratories).[48] Accordingly, today, Israel is considered the world's capital of IVF treatment with a rate of 1,657 procedures per million people a year that far exceeds the statistics of the rest of the world.[49]

Regulations recognizing the operation of sperm banks were first promulgated in 1979,[50] based on the broad powers given to the Minister of Health by the Public Health Ordinance 1940.[51] Later, IVF procedures (along with other assisted reproductive procedures) were authorized for the first time by regulations promulgated in 1987.[52] The regulatory process involved collaboration between medical experts and religious authorities, and expended considerable effort to accommodate the concerns of the latter. These regulations reflect several concerns—medical and anti-commodification sentiments, as well as independent religious concerns. The anti-commodification stance led to the limitation ingrained in the regulations on egg donation by women who are not going through a process of egg-extraction for their own fertility purposes (for either going through an IVF procedure or for saving the possibility to get pregnant at a later age).[53] Other important restrictions reflect Jewish-religious concerns. The most important limitation in this regard was the prohibition on an egg donation from a family relative.[54] This prohibition was explained by reference to the religious law on *mamzerut*, which was already mentioned.

The financing side of IVF treatments grants another important perspective on the strong support offered by culture and politics in Israel to procreation. Despite their significant costs and relatively low success rates, Israel's National Health Insurance Law, which came into effect in 1996, covers many cycles of treatment for the first and second children of childless women, single or married, up to the age of 45.[55] This is the case despite bitter controversies around the coverage of new life-saving treatments by the "Medications Basket" of the National Health Insurance law (updated on an annual basis).

C. Second regulatory stage: the emergence of surrogacy

Despite its strong inclination toward the support of procreation, in the case of surrogacy,[56] the first reaction of the Israeli legal system was to ban it. This ban was originally included in the same set of regulations which deal with IVF procedures.[57] As a result, many infertile couples began circumventing the law by traveling to foreign countries which already had

[48] Birenbaum-Carmeli, "Cheaper than a Newcomer" 905.

[49] Dina Kraft, "Where Families Are Prized, Help is Free," *The New York Times*, 17 July 2011.

[50] Public Health Ordinance (Sperm Bank), 5739-1979, KT 3996, 1448.

[51] Public Health Ordinance 1940, *Palestine Gazette*, No. 1093, Supp. 2, 666 (hereafter: Public Health Ordinance).

[52] Public Health Ordinance (In Vitro fertilization) Regulations, 5747-1987, KT 5035, 42 (as amended in 2001 and 2010).

[53] Regulation 4. As explained below, a new law enacted in 2010, changes this view and opens the door for egg donation also by women who are not going through the procedure for their own fertility purposes. See Part IV.D below.

[54] Regulation 12(a).

[55] Section 6(d) of the Second Supplement of National Health Insurance Law, 5754-1994, SH No. 1469, 156.

[56] Although most surrogacy procedures involve IVF procedures, surrogacy raises additional moral and legal dilemmas and therefore merits a separate analysis.

[57] Regulation 11 provided: "A fertilized egg shall not be implanted except in the woman who shall be the mother of the child." Regulation 13 provided: "An egg taken from a donor shall not be implanted in a woman unless it has been fertilized with the sperm of the woman's husband."

operating surrogacy centers at the time. Consequently, the procedure was *de facto* reserved only for wealthy couples who could afford the travel expenses, as well as the cost of the medical procedures, which were substantially higher than in Israel. In addition, these couples had to deal with the concern that the newborn child would not be considered Jewish when the surrogate mother was not Jewish, at least those for whom this aspect was important.

In 1991, a petition challenging these regulations was brought by a couple who would become very famous in the area due to later litigation—Ruti and Dani Nachmani. They argued that the regulations infringed their fundamental right to reproduction without statutory authorization.[58] The petition was settled by an agreement, which got the approval of the court. The petitioners were exceptionally permitted to carry out the IVF treatment stage in Israel.

Soon afterward, the Minister of Health and the Minister of Justice appointed a public committee of experts, known as the Aloni Commission (named after its chairman, the late former Judge Shaul Aloni) in order to examine the ethical, *Halakhic* and legal aspects of IVF treatments and surrogacy agreements. The composition of this committee reflected the diversity of interests and considerations that the regulation of surrogacy would have to address: legal experts, sociologists, a social worker, a philosopher, rabbis, and physicians. The leading principles which guided the Aloni Committee were the right to autonomy regarding decisions on reproduction and the constitutional right to privacy as applied to the area of family life. Based on these principles, the Aloni Commission recommended to only minimally limit the access to IVF treatments and surrogacy. It also stressed the vitality of informed consent, especially in the context of treatments of this sort. As for the important aspect of the financing of the treatment, the committee only expressed the opinion that the state should finance them to some extent.

Several months after the Aloni Commission issued its report, and before it was implemented, another petition challenging the original regulations which prohibited surrogacy was brought to the Supreme Court. This time, the state declared to the court that it accepted the view that surrogacy should be regulated by legislation, and not only by regulations based on its power to regulate the area of medical treatment. Accordingly, the court was asked to postpone its declaration that the regulations were promulgated *ultra vires* for six months so that the state would have time to move forward with the legislative process. The Supreme Court accepted this request,[59] and soon after, the Knesset enacted the Surrogacy Agreements (the Approval of the Agreement and the Status of the Newborn) Law, 1996.[60] The new law required that every single case of surrogacy be approved by a special statutory committee comprised of seven members (section 3): (a) two physicians qualified in obstetrics and gynecology, (b) one physician qualified in internal medicine, (c) a clinical psychologist, (d) a social worker, (e) a lawyer, as a public representative, (f) a clergyman, according to the religion of the parties involved. The law also defines several preconditions for the approval of surrogacy:

(1) a medical report which states that the intended mother is unable to become pregnant or that pregnancy is a major risk for her health (section 4);
(2) the parties are adults and are Israeli residents (section 2);
(3) the carrying mother is not a blood relative of any of the intended parents, and not married (unless the intended parents prove that they were unable, with a reasonable effort, to attach with an un-married woman) (section 2);

[58] HCJ 1237/91 *Nahmani v. Minister of Health* (unpublished) [1991].
[59] HCJ 5087/94 *Zbaro v. Minister of Health* (unpublished) [1995].
[60] Surrogacy Agreements (the Approval of the Agreement and the Status of the Newborn) Law, 5756-2006, SH No. 1577, 176 (2006) (hereinafter: Surrogacy Law).

(4) the egg is fertilized with the intended father's sperm and at any rate was not taken from the surrogate mother (section 2);
(5) the carrying mother shares the intended mother's religion (unless all parties are non-Jewish and the exception is supported by an opinion of a clergyman) (section 2);
(6) a medical and psychological assessments of the parties are provided (section 4).

When these preconditions are fulfilled the committee is authorized to approve the surrogacy if it is convinced that all parties acted with full knowledge and free will, that no medical detriment is expected to the carrying mother or to the newborn and that the surrogacy agreement does not deprive rights of the newborn or any of the involved parties (section 5). In addition, the law addresses the issue of payments to the surrogate mother for her services (section 6) and states that the approval may be reconsidered by the committee so long as the fertilized egg has not been implemented in the surrogate mother.[61]

A comparison between the Aloni Commission's report and the final text of the law reveals several considerations that shaped it, many of them inspired by religious views, which were supported in the minority opinion of the committee.

Regarding egg and sperm donations, the committee recommended that sperm or egg donations should be permitted subject to the informed consent of the donor and providing that medical tests for the detection of infectious or hereditary diseases are carried out. More specifically, the committee recommended the cancellation of the regulations which prohibited egg donations from a family relative.[62] This recommendation was in conflict with the concern that such donations would give rise to legitimacy problems attached to religious prohibitions on sexual relations between relatives. Therefore, the committee recommended that this concern be revealed to all the parties involved. In contrast, the minority opinion gave more weight to the religious concern and supported an absolute prohibition on such donation. The final law reflects the latter view.

In the matter of the eligibility of the surrogate mother, the committee had to address some religious and non-religious concerns. The main concern was the possibility that carrying mothers might attempt to renege on the agreement. Therefore, the committee recommended that the carrying mother be a woman who had previously given birth. The committee thought that such women would be more familiar with the pregnancy experience thus minimizing the prospect of such a development. In contrast, the religiously inspired minority opinion, based on the concern regarding *mamzerut*, supported the view that the carrying mother should only be an unmarried woman, who shares the same religion as the intended parents and is not related to them. The majority objected, arguing that this view denied the possibility of an act of grace by family relatives. In this context too, the minority opinion prevailed subject to an exception which allows for approving an agreement with a married woman, when sincere efforts to find an

[61] The matter of payment to the carrying mother raises serious ethical and social dilemmas concerning the prohibition on commodification and the fear from women exploitation. The Aloni committee raised the concern that surrogacy may become a recurring practice for poor women and pointed out that the physical and psychological damages to the surrogate mother are equal if not worse than those of prostitution (which is prohibited on Israel). In the final surrogacy law the committee's recommendation to prohibit a multiple surrogacy for the carrying woman (unless it's the second procedure with the same ordering parents) wasn't accepted. However, the recommendation to cast a criminal sanction on an unauthorized payment to mediation services was incorporated, mainly due to the intervention of feminist organizations.

[62] See n. 54 above.

unmarried woman failed (section 2(3)(a)). No similar exception was made regarding the prohibition on a surrogate mother who is related to the genetic parents (section 2(3)(b)).

Another controversial aspect of the surrogacy law in Israel is the unavailability of surrogacy to single persons and non-heterosexual couples, due to the provision which limits the power to authorize surrogacy only to couples (including non-married couples) consisting of a woman and a man. In 2001, a petition challenging this limitation was brought to the Supreme Court by the *Mishpacha Hadasha* ("new family") organization.[63] The petition concerned the matter of a 44-year-old single woman who suffered from a medical condition which resulted in hysterectomy (womb resection). The woman wished to use her own eggs to have a child with the assistance of a surrogacy procedure. She was denied by the surrogacy committee according to the statutory scheme. The Supreme Court agreed that the case involved *prima facie* an unjustified discrimination but eventually decided that those sensitive and complex matters should be decided by the legislature. Accordingly, it decided to abstain from intervening in the case.

So far, pragmatically speaking, the barrier created by this condition is mainly an economic one, due to the availability of surrogacy options in other countries.[64] An example that became famous in the public domain was that of a homosexual couple that filed a petition to the Supreme Court in 2010, claiming that current law constitutes illegal discrimination.[65] Finally, after several months of litigation, the couple decided to withdraw the petition and move forward with a surrogacy procedure abroad, since the Ministry of Health decided to nominate a committee (the so-called Mor-Yosef Committee) for the purpose of considering proposals for reform.[66]

D. Third regulatory stage: egg donations

Against the background described, pressure began to emerge regarding the legalization of egg donations, as the success of many IVF procedures (as well as related surrogacy procedures) is dependent on the quality of eggs used for fertilization.

The shortage in donated eggs led to the assembling of a professional committee in 2000 to examine the social, ethical, religious, and legal aspects of egg donations in Israel.[67] The committee addressed a variety of issues such as the legal status of the genetic mother, payments to the genetic mother, the anonymity of donors, and religious aspects.[68] The committee presented its report in 2001, and at the time it led to a draft Bill presented to the Knesset.[69] However, this Bill was rejected.[70]

[63] HCJ 2458/01 *Mishpacha Hadasha v. The Committee for the Approval of Surrogacy*, 57(1) PD 419 [2002].

[64] The economic barrier may be coupled by a legal one, as some legal systems put limitations on the availability of surrogacy to foreigners.

[65] HCJ 1078/10 *Arad-Pinkas v. The Committee for the Approval of Surrogacy* (unpublished) [2010]. For obvious reasons, current law constitutes a significant barrier to homosexual couples, and not to lesbian couples, who usually succeed in moving forward with a pregnancy of at least one of the partners.

[66] See Part IV.E below.

[67] "The public-professional committee to examine the issue of egg donation" was appointed by the Minister of Health in April 2000. The committee consisted of nine members: six physicians, two rabbis, and the legal adviser to the Ministry of Health. The chairman of the committee was Dr. Mordechai Halperin who is a rabbi and a gynecologist and also served as the supervisor of medical ethics in the Ministry of Health.

[68] For an elaborate review of the committee's work, see Smadar Kanyon, "Egg Donation—Social, Ethical and Legal Aspects" (2006) 35 *Refua Vemishpat* 14 (Hebrew).

[69] Egg Donation for IVF Bill, 2001, HH No. 2985.

[70] Similar Bills were rejected in the following years. See Kanyon, "Egg Donation" 146.

Eventually, a law regulating this matter was legislated in 2010—the Egg Donation Law 2010.[71] The new law allows for the donation of eggs under strict conditions: An egg donation is allowed only for the purpose of conceiving a child (section 3);[72] the receiver must be an adult under the age of 54 and be unable to be impregnated with her own eggs due to medical reasons (section 11);[73] a procedure of egg retrieval must be based on the full consent of the donor (section 6); the donation must be approved by a committee consisting of physicians, a clinical psychologist, a social worker, a lawyer, and a public-representative or a clergyman (section 12).

Similar to the Surrogacy Law, the Egg Donation Law also contains restrictions which seem to cater to religious concerns, such as the condition that the donor will share the receiver's religion (section 13(e)(3)(a)) and the condition that the donor will be unmarried (section 13(e)(3)(c)). The law allows deviation from these specific restrictions when the receiver and her spouse give their written consent (section 14(e)(4)).

The law also orders the establishment of a database which would include the donators and the receivers' details—in order to prevent donation by genetic relatives as well as to inform the receivers and the child (by his request, from the age of 18) about the religion of the donor. Regarding the matter of the child's personal status, the law declares that the newborn will be considered the child of the receiving woman, except for matters concerning marriage and divorce and the jurisdiction of the religious courts (section 42).

Interestingly, the issue of sperm donations has not yet been fully regulated in the format of a full statute, but rather remains subject to the relatively old and brief set of regulations promulgated in 1979. As a result, issues covered by the Eggs Donation Law, such as withdrawal of consent, are still not expressly regulated with regard to sperm donations, a void that has yet to be filled.[74]

E. Toward a fourth regulatory stage: more proposals for reform

The ever-expanding technological possibilities in the area of reproduction as well as the critiques targeted at the limitations posed on their use led to the appointment of the Mor-Yosef Committee,[75] which was asked to consider reform in this area. The committee, consisting of 12 experts from different fields, had submitted its report in May 2012. The committee recommended significant changes to the Surrogacy Law in the direction of opening more venues for using surrogacy, while keeping in place certain limitations. In general, the committee recommended also giving access to surrogacy to singles. It did so whilst distinguishing between single women and single men. The committee endorsed giving access to surrogacy to single women under the same conditions given to couples, including the possibility of paying the surrogate mother. However, with regard to single men it supported only the recognition of altruistic surrogacy, that is, with no payment to the surrogate mother. The committee thought this distinction to be justified since the recourse of single men to surrogacy does not derive from a medical need. Other central recommendations of the commission addressed the relaxation of current limitations on

[71] Egg Donation Law, 5770-2010, SH No. 2242, 519.

[72] Subject to limitations some portion of the eggs taken can be used for research as well.

[73] Apparently, this limitation is designed mainly to limit the scope of unnecessary egg donations. It has also collateral influence on more scenarios. For example, *prima facie*, it prevents the ability of lesbian couples to undergo an IVF procedure where one partner gives the egg whereas the other carries the pregnancy.

[74] See the text accompanying n. 77 below.

[75] See the text accompanying n. 65 above.

the choice of the surrogate mother. According to the committee, married women should also be allowed to serve as surrogate mothers. In addition, the committee recommended the relaxation of the sweeping prohibition on the choice of a relative as a surrogate mother, whilst preserving this limitation with regard to the following: mother, daughter, grandmother, granddaughter, and sometimes also a sister (with regard to an egg fertilized with her brother's semen). The implementation of these recommendations necessitates legislative amendments, and will certainly be the subject of additional controversies. Future deliberations will also have to consider new questions being brought before the Supreme Court on related matters, such as the registration of gay couples who pursued surrogacy abroad and wish to be registered as parents in Israel (as two fathers),[76] and the possibility to pursue surrogacy in a way that will enable a woman to serve as the surrogate mother with the fertilized egg of her lesbian partner.[77]

F. Pragmatism or rights

The striking difference between the development of the legal discourse in the area of IVF and surrogacy on the one hand, and the development of the legal discourse in the abortion law, on the other hand, also exemplifies itself on a rhetoric level. The growing use of procreation technologies was very much supported by recourse to the language of rights, which was already sufficiently developed in Israeli law when these issues emerged during the 1990's (after the enactment of the basic laws on human rights). When the state was slow in moving forward with legislation on surrogacy, the petitions submitted to the Supreme Court in this matter were using the language of rights, namely rights to parenthood and family life.

This feature of the discourse has been even more evident in the context of another major case which shaped the legal arena in this area—the later Nachmani affair, which involved a lengthy litigation among the Nachmanis themselves, after they separated in the midst of a surrogacy procedure. The wife, Ruti Nachmani, insisted on moving forward with the process, whereas her estranged husband, Dani Nachmani, resisted. This litigation did not touch directly on the regulation of the matter (because it concentrated on the agreement and, in fact, on the lack of formal agreement between the two on the issue of separation). However, the judicial decisions given are important to the extent to which they analyzed the case from the perspective of rights. In fact, the Israeli Supreme Court decided the case twice—using its special power to rehear a case when it raises new and unprecedented questions.[78] In a very interesting manner, the first decision of the Supreme Court sided with the husband, who resisted unwanted parenthood, by referring to the right of women to undergo abortion, without the consent of their spouses.[79] However, this reference declined to take notice of the fact that in actuality women in Israel do not enjoy a formal right to abort (but rather have a *de facto* access to abortions,

[76] HCJ 566/11 *Anonymous v. Ministry of Interior* (pending petition); HCJ 6569/11 *Anonymous v. Ministry of Interior* (pending petition).

[77] HCJ 5771/12 *Moshe v. The Committee for the Approval of Surrogacy* (1 September 2013). The petition was dismissed by a majority of four out of seven justices. The decision was published without a detailed reasoning in order to give the petitioners time to consider other possibilities outside Israel. The detailed reasoning will be published later on.

[78] Daphne Barak-Erez and Ron Shapira, "The Delusion of Symmetric Rights" (1999) 19(2) *Oxford Journal of Legal Studies* 297; CA 5587/93 *Nachmani v. Nachmani*, 49(1) PD 485, 501 [1995] (Hereinafter: *CA Nachmani*); AH 2401/95, *Nachmani v. Nachmani*, 50(4) PD 661 [1996].

[79] *CA Nachmani* 501.

due to the lenient policy of the abortion committees). Eventually, in the second round of litigation, the decision of the Supreme Court changed and the majority opinion decided for Ruti Nachmani. This majority opinion was mainly based on references to considerations of "justice," considered to be applicable when the law is unclear. It is worthwhile to note that this time the value of parenthood and the agony of barrenness in Jewish and Israeli culture had some role in shaping the understanding of justice in this case (in contrast to the first decision which focused on the burdens associated with enforced parenthood).

A later clash of rights shaped by the legacy of the Nachmani affair concerned a case which dealt with the desire of a sperm donor to withdraw his consent to use his sperm, due to a change in his worldview. His decision clashed with the desire of a single mother who tried to use his sperm, already kept for her upon her request. Previously she had a child using his sperm, and she wanted to try and give birth to another child using his sperm.[80] In this case, the Supreme Court decided for the donor, analyzing the dilemma as a conflict between a core aspect of the right to avoid parenthood and a peripheral aspect of the right to parenthood, as the woman could still go on with a fertilization process with the sperm of another donor.

V. Conclusion

The nature and scope of reproduction-related laws in Israel has been inspired not only by liberal negative rights aimed at preventing the state from interfering with reproductive decisions, but also by positive rights aimed at promoting and even encouraging reproduction. In addition, more than by anything else the law of reproductive rights in Israel has been shaped by pragmatic compromises which balanced religious and non-religious considerations and tried to give answers for pressures originating from real-life scenarios (bottom-up rather than top-down).

Religious influence on the regulation of reproduction regulation has proved to function in a complex manner. As explained, it played an important role in shaping pro-reproduction inclinations. However, these tendencies are present in Israeli law not only due to religious influence. Pro-reproduction forces are also part of Israeli secular culture, reflecting Jewish history as well as Middle Eastern politics. At the same time, it is important to realize that the lack of absolute prohibition on abortions in Jewish religion also had an important role in making compromises in this area possible. Against this background, Israeli law is an interesting case-study of interaction between secular and religious views, which often result in surprising compromises and even similar tendencies.

[80] HCJ 4077/12 *Anonymous v. Ministry of Health* (unpublished) [2013].

PART IV

RELIGIOUS PERSPECTIVES AND THE LIBERAL STATE

14

One Among Many? The Catholic Church Between Universalism and Pluralism

*Gustavo Zagrebelsky**

I. Introduction

After the breakup of Christian unity in the sixteenth century and the gradual emergence of political and religious tolerance and freedom of conscience in later centuries, one would have expected a reduction of the Catholic Church to just one of many—as important and influential—religious denominations whose doctrines bind only their followers, and exclude any universal claims (subject to the possibility of diffusion through missionary evangelization). One would have expected, that is, that what was now just a "part" would give up speaking for the "whole," once the connection between *Christifidelis*[1] and *civis*[2] was broken. One might have expected not the renunciation of its truth, and not even of the universality of such a truth, but certainly the practical acceptance of relativistic context, in which it falls on the same plane as the proposals of other religions, that is as the bearer of a partial truth—a truth "in its own point of view"—that has to be confronted and combined with other "truths." Consequently, one might have expected the loss of the claim of the Catholic Church that its ethical standards should be made into the laws of the state, and, further, the renunciation of the right to contradict, on behalf of what is today called "non-negotiable values," the laws validly adopted by state legislatures.

But this has not happened. Accepting its relative status has been seen as a betrayal of its mission, as an unacceptable *deminutio*. The Catholic Church continues to contest laws that are not in accord with its doctrine, in the name of the numerous *non possumus*,[3] implicitly confirming that there are universal values, of which the Church itself is the interpreter and guarantor, that it has to assert for all: Catholics and non-Catholics, believers and non-believers, that is, independent of the adherence to the religious faith of which it is bearer.

The question, therefore, is: how does the Catholic Church believe that it can escape the dangers of relativism? The answer is simple, but at the same time surprising: by replacing the binary of truth-faith—which inevitably separates the Church from those who do not have the same faith—with the binary of truth-reason—which necessarily embraces all human beings who are "reasonable, beyond their particular faiths." It is the following: whereas previously the Catholic Church discussed "truth" in terms of adherence to faith, making it accessible only to the elect and not to everyone, now it is spoken of in terms of a rational knowledge, which applies to all of us (elected and non-elected), as beings endowed with reason. One must understand the extent of this shift from faith

* Translation by Elena L. Cohen. Special thanks to Francesco Biagi for his invaluable work in editing and helping to prepare the original text for an international readership.

[1] "Faithful to Christ." [2] "Citizen." [3] "We cannot."

to reason: the truth of faith cannot be recognized by those who do not believe; the truth of reason, on the contrary, cannot admit exceptions or limitations, as reason is universal. It is in this way, more or less consciously, one believes to "break away from the grip of secular thought," that founds its test of truth on the exam of reason, thus going down to its same level.

II. The Magisterium of the Church at the Beginning of the Millennium: Faith and Truth

One can legitimately say that the identification of truth-reason set the tone for the entire preaching of the past two Popes, John Paul II and Benedict XVI, and the magisterium of Roman Catholicism today. Every doctrinal intervention with practical implications, whatever the object—charity and social justice, economic and political relations, relations with religions besides Catholicism, world peace, the Nazi concentration camps and the Communist gulag, sexual morals, life and death, the limits of empirical science—has been based on this dichotomy. Therefore, it is the key concept of the self-consciousness of the Church in the disorientated world of our historical moment, characterized by the "very timely" threat of "being tossed about by waves and carried away with every wind of doctrine." This evil wind has been identified with the "fashionable" ideologies of the time: Marxism, liberalism, libertarianism, collectivism, radical individualism, atheism, religious mysticism, agnosticism, and syncretism.[4]

Through this fusion of (Catholic) truth and (human) reason, and through the fusion of reason and truth, the word of the Church is projected into a dimension of absoluteness and universality that does not allow limits, contradictions, or relativizations. Historically, there is nothing new in this proposition.[5] What is new is the insistence on a principle that, while not denying "fragments of truth" in other religions, claims that Catholicism holds the full truth itself. Thus conceived, Catholicism does not have to learn from other religions, nor from other world views "that are without God." It has nothing to learn: hence its polemical targets are both religious syncretism, that is views that relativize or place less emphasis on the Christian God, from the kinds advocated by G.E. Lessig in 1779 in *Nathan the Wise* to New Age views, and the Darwinian matrix of evolution. Syncretism removes from Catholicism its pretext of exclusive and total truth; evolution makes fate the driving force of life, undermining the creative act and "intelligent design" of God, on which Christian natural law is founded, and of which the Church's magisterium is believed to be the sole authorized interpreter and therefore sovereign. Both subjective syncretism and causal evolutionism converge in a unified and pervasive effect: the sovereignty of subjectivity, a type of renewed rebellion of man against his God, against the "new covenant" that was given by Jesus Christ after the first was broken in the Garden of Eden.

It is difficult to conceptualize in friendly terms the relationship between such a self-representing Church and the rest of the world: it is about being the conqueror or the conquered, the part of a fighter against other hostile parties. It is the revival, in an

[4] Homily of Cardinal Joseph Ratzinger, Saint Peter's Basilica, 18 April 2005, for the Mass "*Pro Eligendo Romano Pontifice*," in "L'Osservatore Romano," 19 April 2005, available at <http://www.vatican.va/gpII/documents/homily-pro-eligendo-pontifice_20050418_en.html>. The image of being tossed about by waves is from Ephesians 4:14.

[5] See Joseph Ratzinger, "Nel Cristianesimo la razionalità è diventata religione," in *30 Giorni*, January 2000, available at <http://www.zenit.org/it/articles/nel-cristianesimo-la-razionalita-e-diventata-religione>.

intellectual form, of the traditional principle: *extra ecclesiam nulla salus*,[6] with the full scope of intolerance and the natural tendency of religion to become religion of the state.

What could even have been the "dialogue" that was at the center of the Second Vatican Council and its opening of itself to the world, which allowed Catholicism to express itself, together with other religions, in a common, dynamic, and universal way, is easy to see. This "dialogue" could only have been an approach that views the other in terms of conversion or assimilation, that is, elimination of oneself as "other." This elimination could be reached, according to an idea that was rather far-fetched and fundamentally offensive to every conscience that considers its first duty to be consistent with itself, when non-Catholics raised a white flag, surrendering themselves, deciding to be and act *veluti si Deus daretur*,[7] that is, denying themselves. This was the direct opposite of the invitation to Catholics to be and act according to an adaptation of Hugo Grotius's formula *etiamsi Deus non daretur*,[8] which he had expressed in a completely different context and for other purposes.[9]

The argument of the absoluteness of Catholic truth can be reconstructed and summarized in two steps. (a) Truth, under the promise that Christ—he who said of Himself "I am Truth (*alḗtheia*)"[10] —made to his disciples (i.e. to his Church) to be with them always, "all of the days, until the end of the world,"[11] is the property of the Church. It is, therefore, without a doubt the Catholic truth against which all other "truths," or rather beliefs and opinions of people, that must be validated. Thus far, this argument is limited to the circle of those within the Christian faith. But, at this point, a second argument takes over. (b) The truth of the Church, that is the truth of the Christian faith, *is also* a truth of reason. It is the *logos* spoken of from the beginning of the Gospel of John, in terms of a universal reason, eternal and divine, through which "all things were made" and without which "nothing was made that has been made"[12] and which, through Christ, "became flesh and made his dwelling among us."[13] So too human reason, which was also "made" by means of the *logos*, is part of this *logos* that, we could say in a not overly-paradoxically hyper-rationalist vision, unites God and humans into a unitary truth. Human beings, therefore, through the reason with which we are equipped, albeit imperfectly and subject to inherent error, can and must take part in the truth, which coincides with the divine truth. It thus seems possible to condense the doctrine on which the Catholic magisterium today lays special emphasis. A "reflection" of Cardinal Ratzinger from ten years ago is entitled "In Christianity, rationality became reason."[14] The terms could be flatly reversed: "In Christianity, religion became rationality."

At this point, the validity of the argument about this bond with *logos* is universalized. It is transferred from the circle of believers to all of humanity, based on the premise of shared and natural participation of human beings in the divine word, of which they are children and participants. This appeal to reason, like participation in the divine, sanctifies the human. In the same way, the appeal to secularized reason, that is, not dependent on the divine, makes it absolute in a blasphemous attempt to make itself God. This is precisely the accusation that the Church directs at the modern world that, in claiming to "do without God," it might deify itself.

So argued, this theology encounters Greek philosophy. It should be noted that the New Testament citations discussed above, so decisive in contemporary Catholic magisterium, are from the Gospel of John, fully inserted into the *forma mentis*[15] that

[6] "Outside the church there is no salvation." [7] "As if God existed."
[8] "Even if God was not given." [9] See below for more on this two-fold invitation.
[10] John 14:6. [11] Matthew 28:20. [12] John 1:3. [13] John 1:14.
[14] See n. 5 above. [15] "mindset."

this philosophy has shaped and delivered to Western culture. In his now famous speech in Regensburg,[16] Pope Benedict XVI asks himself if "the conviction that acting unreasonably contradicts God's nature is merely a Greek idea, or is it always and intrinsically true?" He responds: "I believe that here we can see the profound harmony between what is Greek in the best sense of the word and the biblical understanding of faith in God." This explains, in recognition of the ancestors of Catholicism, the replacement that is under way, of the traditional theological relationship with Judaism (the "Judeo-Christian tradition"[17]) with the relationship of "that which is Greek in the best sense" (the "Greco-Christian tradition"), at times supplemented by the Roman Stoic mediation. In this way, through the construction of a great historic-cultural setting centered on the concept of *logos* as a bridge between Christianity and classical Greece (where there was not the concept of creation that is essential in Judeo-Christian thought), there is an intellectual turn that seems to remove the revolutionary power of Christianity, as something to be revealed to the little children, as something that is the "stupidity" of men, the stupidity primarily of the wise men of this world.

The Pauline interpretation of the Christian message, which contrasts the wisdom of God to that of men—"for indeed Jews ask for signs and Greeks search for wisdom; but we preach Christ crucified, to Jews a stumbling block and to Gentiles foolishness, but to those who are the called, both Jews and Greeks, Christ the power (*dynamis*) of God and the wisdom of God. Because the foolishness of God is wiser than men, and the weakness of God is stronger than men"[18] —is abandoned, in light of new alliances and new battles in the world, from which it distances itself. Catholic Christianity, to serve as a friend and ally of the "world," even as a bearer of a message of salvation or "truth" for the whole world, must put aside the Pauline theology of the cross as folly that separates the believers in Christ from the non-believers.

The genealogies are upset: the Jewish people are no longer the "big brothers" spoken of by Paul of Tarsus, and quoted by Pope John Paul II in his *Allocution* at the Synagogue of Rome in November of 1986,[19] who saw an essential genetic link between Jews and Christians.[20] Today, the Jewish "older brothers" have been dispossessed of their primogeniture, to the advantage of the metaphysical investigators of Greek philosophy.

[16] Benedict XVI, "Faith, Reason and the University: Memories and Reflections," *Lecture of the Holy Father* (12 September 12, 006), available at <http://www.vatican.va/holy_father/benedict_xvi/speeches/2006/september/documents/hf_ben-xvi_spe_20060912_university-regensburg_en.html>.

[17] See Jean Daniélou, *Théologie du judéo-christianisme* (Paris: Desclée de Brouwer, 1995, orig. 1958), searching for a deep "orthodox" theology, focused on eschtalogy, i.e. the end of the time of man for the benefit of the time of God, before the conceptualizations of the Hellenistc cultural structures; see Henri Desroche, entry on "Jean Daniélou," *Archives des sciences sociales des religions* (Paris: Centre national de la recherche scientifique, 1958), vol. VI, n. 6, 170ff.

[18] 1 Corinthians 1:22–5.

[19] The passage is: "Jesus of Nazareth, [is] a son of your People, from which were also born the Virgin Mary [and] the Apostles.... The Church 'draws sustenance from the root of that good olive tree onto which have been grafted the wild olive branches of the Gentiles' (Rom 11: 17–24)... You are our dearly beloved brothers and, in a certain way, it could be said that you are our elder brothers." John Paul II, "Address at the Great Synagogue of Rome" (13 Apr. 1986), available at <http://www.ccjr.us/dialogika-resources/documents-and-statements/roman-catholic/pope-john-paul-ii/305-jp2-86apr13>.

[20] This is the image that inspired the title of the autobiography of the Chief Rabbi of the Italian Jewish Community, Elio Toaff, *Perfidi Giudei, fratelli maggiori* ("Perfidious Jews, Elder Brothers") (Milano: Mondadori, 1987). C. Ginzburg (in *La Repubblica* of 7 and 10 October 1997) noted, in the expressions of the Pope, an insidious allusion—evidently not the intentional result but the pressure of a difficult to eradicate tradition—to an idea of the supremacy of the Church (the younger brother) over Israel (the elder). The reference is to the Christian doctrine of the "new election," replacing the Mosaic one, and to the step of Paul where the Jewish-Christian relationship is put in the context of the story of

The versatile art of the way rabbis argue, enemies of ontological certainty, incessant questions on the law that is "with us in our place,"[21] the recognition of duality of the words of the Lord ("God hath spoken once; twice have I heard this"[22]), are precisely that which the Papal language had called "every wind of doctrine." Better is the cultivation of the rock-hard ontological certainty of the "superior" Greek tradition (Parmenides "superior" to Heraclitus, Platonic "superior" to Aristotelian).

If this configuration of Christian truth is based on the Bible (and just about everything, in truth, is "based on" on the bible), then the bible scholars and theologians will say so. Whether this is viable and fertile, history will tell. In this chapter I am interested in responding to the question that began this chapter: what was the position of the Church such that it could present itself as having universal validity, despite coming from only one particular voice.

The two arguments outlined above—(a) the Church is the custodian of truth and (b) the Christian truth is the *logos* of the world, which is applicable to all—support each other. But, it should be noted, something is missing: there is an essential step without which the Catholic claim to possess the words of truth outside of the scope of only its faithful fails miserably. This missing step was addressed explicitly by Pope Benedict XVI at an academic function, where he pointed out the natural tension between ecclesiastical reason and secular reason. In the *Allocution* prepared for (but not actually given at) the inauguration of the academic year at Rome's Sapienza University, after observing that the condition of the Roman Church, be it healthy or degraded, affects the whole of humanity, Benedict XVI wrote that "the Pope, precisely as shepherd of his community, has also become more and more a voice of the ethical reason of humanity [note that, for now, *a voice*, not *the voice*, of humanity's ethics]." He continued: "Here, however, the objection arises immediately, that the Pope, in fact, does not really speak on the basis of ethical reasoning, but that his decisions are guided by faith and, thus, he cannot pretend that these are valid for those who do not share this faith."[23] A difficult objection to overcome, yet Benedict XVI believes that it can be, through the definition and comparison between "rational-reason or theoretical reason" and "reasonable-reason or practical reason." This is a problematic solution, as the following will show.

The declared aim of this speech was to defend an ethical pluralism in which there is room for Catholicism. Its argument is a traditional one: the recognition of the value, over the course of generations, of that which constitutes "the historical background of human wisdom." In the face of an ahistorical reason that searches to construct itself only on itself, that is faced with an abstract or theoretical rationalism, the wisdom of humanity "as such," the wisdom of the great religious traditions, "is to be valued as a reality that cannot be with impunity thrown into the garbage can of the history of ideas." This is a defense against secular intolerance of the historical religions and against the monopolistic claims of truth by "exacts sciences" and "experimental reason," but is not yet a defense of the universal values of Christianity; it is not yet an exclusivist position. The Pope, who "speaks as a representative of a believing community in which, over the centuries... a determinate wisdom of life has matured," who "speaks as the representative of a community that bears within itself a treasury of ethical knowledge and experience that turns out to be important for the whole of humanity," asks only for a place, among others, for

Esau and Jacob (Genesis 25:29–33) about the value of birthright: a story enclosing the prophecy that "the older will serve the younger" (Genesis 25:23).

[21] Jose ben Kisma, Pirkei Avot, Ch. 6. [22] Psalm 62:11.

[23] Scheduled for 17 January 17, 008, but cancelled on 15 January 2008, in *Nomos* (2007), n. 3, 69ff.

his religion, among the others. In short, he is a Pope who, advocating religious pluralism, actually reveals an attitude not improperly defined as relativistic; in fact, there is no stronger argument for relativism, and for the secularism that is its child, than the spectacle of many religions, each of which asserts its own different truth. At this stage of the Papal claims, the defense is not of the presence of one religion, but of all religions, and not for a selfish reason, but an altruistic one, offering to the world the historical heritage of knowledge, part of which is Catholic, as a "purifying element"[24] of secular reason, and on a practical level as a force of moral resistance to the naked and irrational logic of today's strongest interests, which have become even more powerful and menacing on a global scale.

But this cannot be enough. Marred by relativism, this argument can make room for the idea that not solely the Church holds the key to salvation. It needs to be based on an exclusive claim, that is the claim of standing as the sole possessor of the truth, before which all human beings must kneel down: an irresistible claim for those who wish to speak in the name of truth. It is the very truth, if one does not want to be just an opinion, to ask for. In order to get this result, there must be a small step further to support the argument that the Christian faith is *the only* way to the truth, that it is the framework within which every line of research, including those of the exact and experimental sciences, must contain themselves: "Practical (or moral) reason is the reason of the highest sense, because it penetrates the specific mystery of reality more profoundly than experimental reason. This means, however, that the Christian faith is not a limitation or hindrance of reason, but rather *it alone* is capable of enabling reason for its proper task."[25] Here, the pluralism of the *Allocution* at Rome's Sapienza University becomes exclusive. But why is the Christian faith "alone" capable of this? The answer given is because "it has passed the test" of history (and here the traditional argument returns). Not only that, but the Christian faith came to be seen as a general summary of everything that is valid in our moral conceptions of the world. Reading further: "At their core, these great ethical constructions of Greece, from the Near and Far East, haven't lost any of their validity; today, however, we can consider them like watercourses that ultimately converge in the broad current of the Christian interpretation of reality. Indeed, the ethical vision related to the Christian faith is not something exclusive in the sense of being particularistic, but rather the synthesis of the major ethical institutions of humankind from a new center [the Catholic Church], that gathers all.... [In fact] the Christian faith, which helps us recognize this the creation, is not a paralysis of reason. On the contrary, it creates a living space around practical reason in which it can develop to its full potential. The morality that the Church teaches is not a particular obligation, reserved for Christians, but the defense of man against the attempt to achieve his elimination."[26]

Here, formulated in its most explicit and bombastic form, is the claim of universalism: "the defense of man" as such, bound to the truth of "practical reason." And with universalism, the claim of being everything and of denying to those who intentionally are outside of it, of being something more than a simple "tributary." One could say that the cycle is complete. One does not see how it could be otherwise, and with these most pressing

[24] This theme and expression had already been used by Joseph Ratzinger in his meeting with Jürgen Habermas at the Bavarian Catholic Academy on 19 January, 2004, which was turned into the book *The Dialectics of Secularization: On Reason and Religion* (San Francisco: Ignatius Press, 2007), 78.

[25] See Jospeh Ratzinger, "Chiesa e mondo moderno" (1992), in *Fede, ragione, verità e amore: La teologia di Joseph Ratzinger* (Torino: Lindau, 2009), 622–3 (emphasis added) (translation by translator of this chapter).

[26] Ratzinger, "Chiesa e mondo moderno" (translation by translator of this chapter).

and significant arguments, the "Catholic" claim of the church can manifest itself, in a world that, overall, is not Catholic. Human reason was, for centuries, the corrosive force of Catholic dogma, a force that toppled the world, displacing metaphysics and placing on us the task and the responsibility of governing it; it was the initial seed of secularism. Now, through the identification of the "right reason" with the logos that are "with God," the world is re-inverted and re-sacralized.

III. The "Dictatorship of Relativism"

The intention of this chapter is not to examine the foundations of Catholicism and its explicit and implicit assumptions, nor the minimalist, self-understanding of Catholicism today, as a doctrine that sums up the alpha and the omega of the best "mankind" has produced in terms of ethical intuitions and concepts. The critical assessment of this vision that the Church, in the words of its magisterium, has of itself is a matter of theology, history, philosophy, anthropology, and perhaps good sense or even common sense. This concerns a much more narrow point, that has to do with the conditions of coexistence in today's society, which is marked by its pluralistic ethics. It has to do, then, with a question that is essentially constitutional, given that constitutional science has the task of responding to the simple and, at the same time, difficult question of how to promote coexistence without physical or moral violence, amongst many diverse heads, ideas, ideals, beliefs, and interests.

Compared to the past, the present way of establishing a Catholic universalism—the binary of truth-reason—is certainly less easily integrated into an overall conception of the common life. Indeed, it is not at all integratable: it is a cause of conflict, and not of discussion and joint action. In the past, after the break of Christian unity in the society to which it addressed itself, the Church turned to the world, first with the words of *justice* (the "social doctrine" of Pope Leo XIII's encyclical, *Rerum novarum*), then with the words of *goodness* or charity to the needy (the doctrine of "human rights" of Popes John XXIII and Paul VI and the Second Vatican Council).[27] Now, without abandoning the past (the doctrinal life of the Church always proceeds by accumulation, emphasization, or attenuation, but never substitution), we find ourselves faced with the *truth* of reason as the preponderant argument.

Verum, iustum, bonum:[28] If we deconstruct this triad, we find an important difference between the three concepts. According to scholastic philosophy, *verum, bonum et iustum* "convertuntur":[29] that which is true is also good and just; that which is just is also good and true; and that which is good is also true and just. One may be skeptical of these too simple "conversions." In the moral sphere, is the "truth" always also "just" and "good"? Indeed, these three terms are not equivalent, not from the point of view of their conceptual *status*, nor ethically, nor in terms of practical implications. Let us see why.

Antithetical to *verum* is *falsum*;[30] to *iustum, iniustum*;[31] to *bonum, malum*.[32] Between justice and injustice, between good and evil, there can be gradations: there may be more

[27] On these developments, see Gustavo Zagrebelsky, *Scambiarsi la veste: stato e chiesa al governo dell'uomo* (Roma: Laterza, 2010). On the pre-World War II period, see Enrico Rosa, "La religione cattolica dal Congresso di Vienna ai giorni nostri," in Pietro Tacchi Venturi (ed.), *Storia delle religioni*, vol II (Torino: Unione tipografico-editrice torinese, 1944), 699ff.

[28] "Truth, justice, the good." [29] "Are interchangeable." [30] "the false"

[31] "injustice" [32] "evil"

or less "good," more or less "justice." Thus, one can say that in God is the supreme good and the supreme justice, without excluding that, in lower grades of being, there can be a lesser good or a lesser justice. The human beings who lie in one of these lower grades can know and act for a good and a justice only proportionate to their capabilities, since absolute justice and absolute good do not belong to this world, according to the logic of the possible, of prudence, of Aristotelian *phrónesis*, of practical wisdom, according to the angel's promise of peace addressed to "men of good will,"[33] or better, to men of a well-disposed soul, of good faith (*eudokía*), and not to the "learned" and "wise."[34] The same does not apply to the truth, like reality that reveals itself, or like *adaequatio rei et intellectus*,[35] or reflected in the knowledge of being, physical or metaphysical, like an *epistème*. The real claims to be absolute. There are no gradations between the true and the false. In a reality that is complex and divisible, one may have partial knowledge and may gradually fill in the gaps of this knowledge; but, with respect to each segment of this progressive line of knowledge, there is only the true or the false. The ideas of "more true" and "less true" are nonsensical. The progression towards the truth takes place through trial and error, successes and failures, mistakes and corrections, that is, through successions of verifications and falsifications, and not through a progressive accumulation of truth. Something is either true or false.

Moreover, the just and the unjust, the good and the evil, arise from communication and exchange.[36] They are, in other words, social products that do not have meaning outside of a relationship (if even only in the relationship that they create between themselves, that is, in the dissociation that is the loneliness that allows the rise of reflective thought or the "conversation through thought"). This is not so for the truth, at least not the version of the Church that, on this point, is firmly rooted in the tradition prior and hostile to the "post-metaphysical turn" that disbanded ontology into the discursiveness of a procedure oriented to agreement. In this adherence to being, the truth is absolute and does not make itself in exchanges or relationships: rather, it fears them, as possible disturbances.

In short, around the good and the just one can work and build together, that is, cooperate, each bringing something of themselves, because the search for the good and the search for the just can unite. Around the truth, however, one must work only deductively, "logically" and not "dia-logically," requiring separations, inclusions and exclusions, endorsements and condemnations. The truth must be separate, giving up the relationship between itself and others. At the extreme, this can require an extreme de-consolation; the absolute truth benefiting those who are solitary to themselves, because every relationship, even those that every thinking being established in the inner dialogue can result in, indeed results in, compromises.[37]

Here lies the significance of the fateful step that the Catholic magisterium takes whenever it transposes *in re sociali* arguments of truth, all of the times that it transforms practical matters of life that fall within the ambit of justice or charity (the field of the evangelical *eudokía*), in matters of truth; all of the times that matters of relationships and living together end up being treated like matters of dogma and sacraments of faith, or like matters of loyalty-reflection, with respect to divine law requirements, as is the case when we refer to Christian natural law.

[33] Luke 2:14. [34] Luke 10:21.

[35] Expression from Thomas Aquinas, *Summa theologiae*, I, 16,1 ["the intellect (of the knower) must be adequate to the thing (known)"].

[36] See Hannah Arendt, *Denktagebuch: 1950–1973* (2002), translated into Italian in *Quaderni e diari. 1950–1973* (Vicenza: Neri Pozza, 2007), 189, commenting on Plato, *Repubblica*, 371b.

[37] See the illuminating observations of Hannah Arendt in *Quaderni e diari*, 108ff.

Once this step is taken, however, another becomes inevitable: intolerance against tolerance (or at least the revival of the ancient curial notion of tolerance as a mere forbearance of the inevitable, a waiting for "better times," in which it can be put aside). Only the truth, for those who believe to possess it, can establish the law; certainly a mistake cannot do this. And there is only one truth, complete and not influenced by external circumstances. Therefore, those who depart from this truth are outside of the law.

The polemic against "relativism" is not that the actual form under which intolerance reoccurs is that which every single-*mónos* bears against others it confronts: monism, monarchy, monocracy, and, more pointedly, monotheism. On a practical level, the polemic against "relativism" is addressed to the opposite of *mónos*, that is, it is against plurality. In this way, relativism seems to be a summarizing formula that gathers polemically many diverse things: agnosticism, skepticism, indifference, nihilism, materialism, pantheism, eclecticism, historicism, pragmatism, and scientism, all united in the condemnation since they are anti-metaphysical positions, with metaphysics being the "place" of absolute truth, independent from the work and knowledge of human beings.

What Catholic magisterium means with the expression "relativism" was well stated by Cardinal Ratzinger at a solemn liturgy, in the homily delivered during the propitiatory Mass of the election of a new Pope, a Pope who might end up being himself: relativism is that attitude of the spirit "that does not recognize anything as definitive and whose ultimate goal consists solely of one's own ego and desires."[38] Here—especially in the second part of the proposition, "desires,"—relativism coincides with nihilism, even though in reality these concepts do not coincide. Relativism means that which exists, exists not in absolute but in relation to the subject, and is to the subject "relative." Nothing rules out that this "value" might be morally high and demanding, the opposite of "desires." Nihilism, on the other hand, means that nothing counts, not even with respect to the subject, and therefore there are only his "desires," that is, the drives belonging to a lower layer of human driving factors.

Instead, for the Catholic magisterium, these expressions are equivalent and are often used promiscuously to denote their similar incompatibility with the sole Christian truth. "The sole Christian truth," in the Catholic sense: this is the touchstone of "relativism." This accounts for why totalitarian ideologies that offer visions of the world no less dogmatic than the Catholic—the racism of the Nazis or Stalinist communism—can be defined as relativist, or the children of relativism. In spite of their totalitarian "supremacy," they can be classified as relativists, as they deviate from the sole truth, the Catholic one.

Naturally, for whoever proclaims to possess the sole truth, every other claim of truth is relativistic. So it is as well for the current doctrine of the Catholic magisterium. That the denial of this truth occurs through the affirmations of another truth or through the denial of another truth cannot make any difference. And, indeed, it is hard to say whether, in regards to the Catholic truth, the denial of any absolute truth (i.e. relativism) appears more dangerous than the opposition of other absolute truths. Which is perceived as more insidious: the "nothing" or the different "everything"? When one considers that the resonant denunciation against the hedonistic relativism of Western countries is often shared by the Catholic magisterium and Islamic fundamentalism, it would appear that it is the "empty," rather than the "differently full" that is, for now, the primary enemy with whom the accounts must be settled. After, the communal front can break apart and the different dogmatisms can come into conflict with each other.

[38] Mass "Pro Eligendo Romano Pontifice."

The Catholic magisterium's critique of "relativism" goes even further than this, when it denounced it as a currently-progressing "dictatorship." In an expression from the above-cited homily for the election of a pontiff,[39] not recognizing anything as definitive and the ultimate goal consisting solely of one's own ego and desires were labeled as a "dictatorship of relativism" that is currently being built. This expression was met immediately with great success and has been repeated in diverse locations, both ecclesiastical and academic. This same Pope seems to be very fond of it, to the point of making it the touchstone with which to compare two eras, that of the seventeenth–eighteenth centuries (the era of the "dictatorship of rationalism") and of today (the era of the "dictatorship of relativism"), both of which he sees as inadequate responses to the "just demand for man to make full use of his reason," the former due to an excess of "constructivism," the latter by default. Rationalism, for the current Pontiff, was inadequate because it did not take into account human limits and claimed to raise reason alone as the measure of all things, transforming it into a goddess; contemporary relativism, on the contrary, mortifies reason, because it concludes that a human being cannot know anything with certainty outside the field of positive science.[40]

This expression can have many and improvised interpretations, and if it was used by an ordinary mortal, it would seem like a clear logical short-circuit—relativism and dictatorship. On the contrary, this expression can be interpreted as follows.

If by dictatorship in the moral field one means unilateral imposition of the sole conception of truth, justice, and the good that prevails over the others, then relativism is its opposite, since it allows space for a plurality of views, within an order dominated by the supreme value of reciprocal respect, that has to be defended non-relativistically against those who deny it, in theory and in practice. To speak of dictatorship like this is more or less nonsense. This expression may make sense, though, taking a point of view that is not pluralist, but absolutist. If one assumes not only that there are universal values, which must apply to every one, in every time and every location, but also that these values are in the possession of one's own doctrine, while at the same time one notes that there is a dominant ideology that negates these assumptions and that therefore recognizes a general right to profess values, be they religious, moral, or political, and thereby denies the right to impose them on others, then one can talk of a "dictatorship," in the paradoxical sense of "imposing the prohibition of impositions."

Obviously, relativism does not exclude recourse to the "good life," because its doctrine is not nihilistic (the search for truth and goodness is not senseless) or indifferentist (it is not devoid of interest). This does not at all mean that "the relativists" are devoid of moral tensions and are exposed to the sheer force of "desire," but that the source of ethical duties is for them within a framework of freedom and responsibility, as opposed to one of obedience to any authority, be it civil or religious. The use of the expression "dictatorship" against them is but a reversal through which what is freedom, responsibility, and humanity is passed off as intolerance, arbitrariness, and brutality. This is only one amongst many examples of the instrumental uses of language, useful for polemicizing but useless for clarifying.

That said, however, one cannot but recognize that the equation of truth-reason leads to this end. This equation, more than any previous theorization, expresses the universalist vocation of the Catholic Church. It is better than any other, but at the same time

39 Mass "Pro Eligendo Romano Pontifice."

40 See his Catechesis at Castel Gandolfo on 5 August 2009, available at <http://www.vatican.va/holy_father/benedict_xvi/audiences/2009/documents/hf_ben-xvi_aud_20090805_en.html>.

more intolerant than any other. Catholic social doctrine and humanism could well share in or even compete with other conceptions of social good and neighborly love. Yet once one wields the sword of truth, one cannot have other relationships other than those of otherness and, eventually, hostility with those who are outside, that is, with a pluralist society. It is within this context that one can understand the *non possumus*, an expression fished from a tradition of political intransience that the Catholic magisterium has recently resurrected.[41]

IV. The *Non Possumus* of the Church

The union of truth and reason is expressed in the most simple and effective way in the series of *non possumus* that the ecclesiastical magisterium believes itself to be authorized to pronounce every time that problems and issues arise that it considers to be "ethically sensitive," and, therefore, within its own jurisdiction, as a custodian of morals guaranteed by truth and reason. The *non possumus* constitute a fundamental change compared to the way that the Church has placed itself within the past 150 years, with respect to civil society. Both the social doctrine and the humanitarian tendencies of the Second Vatican Council established themselves as forces capable not only of competing and fighting battles in society, but also of creating alliances for communal battles, as the historical experience of democratic Catholicism has amply demonstrated. The Church, both as an authority and as a community, represented itself as a force that acts along with others, within a context that includes plurality. The *non possumus* emerge from this vision. Truth and reason proclaimed by the Church put the Church itself in a position of antagonism. Non-Catholics faced with this antagonism could only oppose it, unless they collude out of self-interest. This is what the current situation of the relations between two parts shows us clearly: on one hand, a growing anti-clericalism, fueled, in contrast, by the same radicalism of the Church's positions; or, a slavish subservience to the Church for opportunistic reasons. Simultaneously, one reduces the possibility of comparison, a possibility that is at the heart of non-Clerical Catholic survivors and non-anti-clerical lay people. Distrust, closures and hostility are the natural consequences. Foundational principles of coexistence, the acceptance of which could have appeared widely, if not always peacefully, have been called into question anew.

The first of these principles is the non-denominational or "secular" character of the state and communal living. This means, first of all, the self-sufficiency of civil society to suffice in and of itself. In short, it means the recognition that it is *societas perfecta*, that is capable of pursuing and realizing its own purposes without dependence on other legitimation. The expression "*societas perfecta*" is an ecclesiastical term, expressing in brief the self-understanding of the Church, as an *institutio divina*, established by Christ, absolutely and originally independent of every worldly authority. It is therefore an expression of its struggle for liberation from the state. But secularism presupposes the same recognition of civil society as *societas perfecta*, that is as *institutio humana*, sovereign in working for the purposes for which it exists, which are different from the ecclesiastical ones. This reciprocal recognition of "perfection," within which each is its own, characterizes the *dualist situation* that is the essence of the non-denominational state.

[41] On the origin of this formula, initially intended as an imperative of fidelity to Christ and later as a criterion of political action, see Gustavo Zagrebelsky, *Contro l'etica della verità* (Roma: Laterza, 2nd edn, 2009), 61.

In the teaching of the Church, this dualist condition of secularism is neither recognized nor affirmed. Indeed, the opposite seems to be taken for granted, that civil society is insufficient with regards to its tasks. On the basis of Catholic dogma and, now, a political sociology that denounces the decadence of Western societies based on liberty, one can argue that the current liberal and secular state is no longer a *societas perfecta* and therefore, *by its very foundation and for its own preservation, must rest on other powers and forces.* In the meaningful formula coined by the German constitutionalist Ernst-Wolfgang Böckenförde: "The liberal secular state lives on premises that it is not able to guarantee by itself... This is the great risk that it assumes for the sake of freedom."[42] These "premises" are social ties, which the individualist and hedonist liberal state destroy. Therefore, civil authorities have to recognize, for their own good, that the Church *cannot* "retire from its role of representing a 'religious need,' but must understand itself as a place of *absolute relevance to the public*, which exceeds the state and is legitimized on the basis of a divine claim."[43] This, then, is the first *non possumus*, which translates into a *debemus*,[44] in contradiction with the dualistic foundation of secularism.

However, the expression "absolute relevance to the public" contains *in nuce* other *non possumus.* First, the unacceptability of equivalency to other denominations, and then the rejection of the principle of equality as a criterion-base of state legislation of religion (cults) and the demand to be recognized with a special status within these same civil institutions: a demand that now, after the interlude of a conciliar period, has been reignited. The state cannot be "equidistant," which is, on the contrary, the essence of the non-denominational, liberal, and democratic state, because the state that has privileged relations with a religious denomination necessarily discriminates against others.

This is certainly a difficulty, even from the point of view of today's Church, in as much as it has not expressly embraced the denominationalism of the state: "we find ourselves in an aporia: if the Church renounces this demand [for privileged public recognition], then the state will not have the Church it needs; but if the state accepts the demand, it stops being pluralist and therefore both the state and the Church lose themselves."[45] Conceptually, the difficulty is insurmountable; in reality, the way out is sought with a historical observation: "in the current general state of culture, the theocratic threat is low."[46]

This is typically a response that, when referring to history, is relativistic and historical relativism when dealing with theological issues—and here, we are fully in political theology—is condemned by the Church. The truth (the failure of civil society with respect to itself and its dependence on a religious dimension) should not have to depend on contingent assessments, like those that come from history. Moreover, from the secular point of view, this type of argument is anything but reassuring, all the more so because the same Catholic church, at the present time, is strongly committed to changing that "general state of culture" where there would be the guarantee against the "theocratic threat."

[42] Ernst-Wolfgang Böckenförde, *Die Entstehung des Staates als Vorgang der Säkularisation*, in *Recht, Staat, Freiheit: studien zu Rechtsphilosophie, Staatstheorie und Verfassungsgeschichte* (Frankfurt: Suhrkamp, 1991), 112 (translation by translator of this chapter).

[43] These quoted propositions are a synthesis of that which one reads in Joseph Ratzinger, "Christliche Orientierung in der pluralistichen Demokratie? Über die Unverzichtbarkeit des Christentums in der modernen Welt," in H. Schambeck (ed.), *Pro Fide et Justitia: Festschrift für Agostino Kardinal Casaroli zum 70 Geburstag* (Berlin : Duncker & Humblot, 1984), 747–69 (translation by translator of this chapter).

[44] "a must."

[45] Ratzinger, "Christliche Orientierung" (translation by translator of this chapter).

[46] Ratzinger, "Christliche Orientierung" (translation by translator of this chapter).

What really matters is that the roots, the historical "footprint," the *humus*[47] —as refers to the value that is attributed to the history regarding the certification of excellence of the Catholic religion, with respect to every other denominational religion—raise convincing arguments in order to achieve a differentiated *status* that (regarding religious symbols, public financing of ecclesiastical activities, the assumption of the Catholic religion as a foundational element in public education, etc.) distinguishes the Catholic religion from other denominations. The latter, as was said,[48] have to adapt themselves to "living in a diaspora," that is, in a social, political, and legal environment of others, not including them; where their arguments of a common good life do not have public relevance; where they must be satisfied with being "tolerated," or, alternately, must adapt to being "assimilated." "Diaspora" is a terrible and precise expression, in pointing out where the Catholic *non possumus* lead when invoked against all other denominations, in a common, and thus egalitarian, framework. But, nevertheless, it is an expression more explicit and honest than others, which seek to hide the reality of their claims and their consequences behind empty formulas.

With thorough reflection we can see that, behind these positions, depicted as "living within a diaspora," that is, living with pubic irrelevance, by those who profess moral convictions different than the Catholic ones, there is a renewed attempt to create the conditions for a homogenous relationship between the Church's magisterium, society and political power, through the symbol of shared Catholic membership. At one time, when there were threats of schisms, heresies, apostasies, etc., this homogeneity gave rise to bloody repression. Today this simply gives rise to the claim of obscuring what disturbs or ruffles the alleged Christian identity of society. If we look at the latter, in today's reality, we sense its distance from these claims, but not because of its different values, open to a pluralism of beliefs and faiths, but simply (and dangerously) because, for the most part, it lives in apathy. And apathy is that condition in which anything can happen, and even the most daring projects can have chances of success, not because they elicit adhesion, but because they do not elicit any reactions.

V. The Secular *Non Possumus*

So far, the Church is like other denominations that claim a *status* of public authority, as the bearer of a truth (and of a rationality) that is valid in general. From *status*, though, the claim extends quite naturally to the sphere of public *decisions* and the law. The *non possumus* multiply and address themselves to lawmakers. Every *non possumus* does not correspond simply to the dissent that is always possible with regard to any legislation, dissent that is a normal part of the essential rules of the democratic "game" and is even internalized as a useful critical factor, perhaps even necessary, in order to address the tendencies of the majority principle to denigrate into tyranny. The *non possumus* signify something different from that, i.e. the threat of using the means of the Church, directly or more often indirectly—through the actions of those who refer to ecclesiastical authority in order to define their political identities—in order to prevent the normal progress of democracy. They signify parliamentary obstructionism by "their"

[47] '*Humus*' refers to the dark organic material in soils, produced by the decomposition of vegetable or animal matter that is essential to the fertility of the earth. See "humus," *Encyclopedia Britannica*, available at <http://www.britannica.com/EBchecked/topic/276408/humus>.

[48] See Ernst-Wolfgag Böckenförde, "Lo Stato secolarizzato nel suo rapporto con la religione" (2007) *Reset* 101.

parliamentarians; *aut-aut* in terms of fidelity to the Church, addressed to those who present themselves in the political scene by exhibiting Catholic titles; and withdrawal of the electoral support of parties and candidates, to the point of operations to topple governments and to call for disobedience of the law (the latter, in today's so-called "secularized" form, of what once were, respectively, the deposition of principles and the dissolution of subjects from the constraints of allegiance).

With the means that the historical circumstances permit, the Church feels entitled to a right of veto over public life, when reasons that justify its unilateral *non possumus* come into the scene: expression that springs sincerely from a self-understanding as entity that operates as sovereign in matters that democracy, even before secularism, attributed a different source of legitimation.[49] A conflict of legitimacy, that is, a rejection of another's legitimacy, is what lurks in this explosive formula for democracy. And what is more: it is not a conflict between homogeneous legitimacies of their concept, however different from their content, but a conflict between opposing conceptions of legitimacy. On content, it is possible to compromise. On the principle of legitimacy, it is not possible. It is unclear whether the magnitude of stakes in this conflict is fully present to those who do not hesitate to raise it.

The Church's self-attribution of possessing *truth alias reason*, and therefore the claim that its contents apply "absolutely" and in general, despite the existence of a diversity of faiths, represents a great difficulty and challenge to democratic life. The presence in these same spaces of experiences of cultural, ethical, and religious pluralism, ever more marked for the quantity and for the quality of elements that compose it, has called for reflection on the conditions necessary to ensure that, in democracy, one can preserve a minimum of cohesion and can remove the specter of disintegration. "In democracy": the clarification is necessary, because the autocracies know well what they have to do. For them, the problem does not exist. It is enough to simply eliminate the problem by reducing or eliminating pluralism, by imposing a forced homogeneity, repressing dissent, mandatory conversions or assimilations, expulsions. For democracy—liberal democracy—it is different. It considers the liberty and plurality of its social bases not only as a fact, but also as a constitutive element, and, therefore, from this point of view, its "good." However, it has the obligation to take care of the disruptive factors that every pluralistic situation has within itself. The issues that concern the relationship between the Catholic Church and democracy are part of this more general problem that affects—from many points of view—our society today, which wants to live freely and democratically.

Reflection on these issues has reached the peak of lofty philosophical-political speculation, with the development of complex conceptual categories, in the process of progressive clarification through discussion and mutual refinement.[50] However, one still proceeds from a simple, obvious, and intuitive assumption: any type of society

[49] On 7 February 2007, l'*Avvenire*, the newspaper of the Italian bishops, took a position on a draft law about civil unions, with a document in which the *non possumus* are used in a truly "displomatic note," as a kind of memorandum, followed by an ultimatum. After having enunciated the reasons of the Church in opposing the recognition of civil unions based on the Italian constitution (the memorandum), the bishops warned, in the falsely disarming language used in these occasions, of the consequences that the Church could take if its position is unheeded: "if the text that at this time is circulating like a rumor becomes substantially confirmed, out of loyalty we must as of now speak of our 'non possumus.' This is not in anyway an act of arrogance, but rather it is the awareness of that which we must have—for the service of love—to our country" and of "frank and disarmed indications of a watershed that will inevitably weigh on the future of Italian politics" (translation by translator of this chapter).

[50] See mostly recently the brilliant synthesis in Claudia Mancina, *La laicità al tempo della bioetica: tra pubblico e privato* (Bologna: Il mulino, 2009), in particular the last two chapters: *La pubblicità della ragione come categoria politica: da Kant a Rawls* and *Ragione pubblica e laicità*.

can only subsist if there is widespread, spontaneous, or induced adherence to their foundational conditions, a consensus that must manifest itself in thoughts, words, and actions. This is obvious. With respect to liberal and democratic societies, this obviousness becomes more complicated. Unity is never definitively acquired, but is an always-new end that has to be pursued by the parts of its own components. These societies must find in themselves the reasons to stay together. Failure comes from a rupture of unity, or in the abandonment of freedom and democracy, to the benefit of other ways of guaranteeing unity that do away with both. Liberal and democratic societies live precariously. The precariousness and the difficulties increase in proportion to the quantitative and qualitative extension of their pluralistic categorization, until they reach a maximum point where the groups lumped within them do not only configure themselves by their diversity of interests, but also place themselves with respect to each other as sub-societies, combined within from different cultures, but strangers to each other.

The question, then, is how the parts might be able to meet, without jeopardizing the whole, and, simultaneously, how one might preserve the whole, without jeopardizing the parts. Every partial social group, in which one might want to safeguard a framework of liberty and democracy, is saddled with special burdens in respect to the larger society in all of its complexity, burdens that have to do with the respect of others and therefore with the necessity that one's identity is not defended to the point of impairing the ability of others to defend their identities. In turn, the actions of political institutions are weighed down by the burden of keeping themselves open to all, without prejudicial preferences toward anyone.

The problem does not arise exclusively because of the presence of components characterized in a religious sense. It also arises in relation to all of the social groups that bear, to use a widespread term[51] "general and comprehensive" philosophical, eschatological, sociological, ideological, or moral doctrines, that is those based on productive and self-sufficient postulates with comprehensive world views and that tend to withdraw into themselves. It arises, to use another formula, with regards to all groups that claim to posses the "whole truth." This "truth" can be the object of more varied types of "faiths," those that in a real sense have no relationship with religion,[52] faiths that, in the beginning arise as non-religious, or anti-religious, but that, if they were marked by mass fanaticism, whatever their origins and foundations, tend to often become religions.[53] It is often said that the family, work, home, freedom, etc. "become a religion." The cult of the *Être suprême*[54] of the Jacobin revolution is a striking and paradoxical example of this change of clothing, as it was born as anti-clerical and then became, in its own way, clerical.[55]

Nevertheless, it is true that today the possession of the "whole truth" seems to typically be the claim of the "revealed religions," the religions that can call a God to witness and guarantee their fixed word. On religions, therefore, the discussion of the relationship between freedom and political democracy, on the one hand, and the pluralism of society, on the other hand, is polarized.

[51] See John Rawls, *Political Liberalism: Expanded Edition* (New York: Columbia University Press, 2005), 13 and passim.

[52] Illuminating words can be found in Luigi Einaudi, "*Major et sanior pars*," in Luigi Einaudi, *Riflessioni di un liberale sulla democrazia—1943–1947* (Firenze: L.S. Olschki, 2001), 108ff.

[53] Émile Durkheim, *De la division du travail social* (1893), translated into English as *The Division of Labor in Society* (Lewis Coser trans., New York: Palgrave Macmillan, 1984), 130.

[54] "Supreme Being."

[55] Hannah Arendt, *On Revolution* (orig. 1963, New York: Penguin Books, 2006), 233–40.

In the framework of a liberal and pluralistic democracy, any claim of whichever of these revealed religions of making their ethical principles, i.e. religious principles, a basis for public decisions or of relying on them as touchstones to assess validity, would be totally unjustified. On this, we do not need to dwell. If this happens, it would violate the equal freedom of all those who do not belong to the same religion. They would be citizens with a lesser or no title. At question here is not the right of the majority to prevail over the minority, a right obviously essential to democracy. It is the question of the nature of the arguments that can legitimately enter in public debate, the debate that, in the end, will be consecrated in political decisions destined to become enforced as mandatory for all citizens. There is no majority, no matter how large it might be, that, with its strength, could validate arguments that are invalid from the point of view of democracy. In no way paradoxically, the more the majority that crushes a minority is strong, the more the political decision made on the basis of a religious belief is violent. Faced with a reasoned decision, directly and exclusively based on the precepts of one of whichever religions ("God wills it"), the secular consciousness has, in turn, the right and the obligation to raise its own *non possumus*.

The principle of majority can only be invoked legitimately as an expression of "public reason," a key concept in today's debate that represents the adaptation of liberal "public opinion" of the past to the needs of a pluralist democracy society today.

On public reason, hopes and fears concerning the retention of democracy in the composite society of our time converge. On this concept, the discussion is open with regards to numerous problematic aspects. But here, since at issue is only the self-understanding of the Catholic Church as a bearer *in temporalibus*[56] of words that are valid in general on the basis of their truth, it is not necessary to go into details. It is sufficient to note that public reason is incompatible with any particular position that claims to posses *a priori* the "whole truth" and therefore claims to impose itself on the basis of it. Public reason is compatible only with reasons that lend themselves to being discussed, compared, and evaluated relative with others. It is compatible only with "persuasive" reasons, or, better, those potentially capable of persuasion (because, in fact, they would not need to actually persuade at all).[57] Only the presence of these types of reasons can allow what would otherwise be a comparison of forces to instead be a comparison among "good reasons." The truths of faiths are obviously not "good reasons": they are optimal for some and very bad for others, depending on whether one does or does not participate in that faith. So, too, is the case for the truths of the Catholic Faith. Once one deconstructs the *civis-Christifidelis* concurrence, one must acknowledge that they belong to particular non-political, or pre-political, spheres. This means that they must halt at the threshold of institutional sites that form collective decisions that are designed to be enforced mandatorily against everyone. If they enter into these decisions, they do so unlawfully, casting a shadow of illegality on them.

This limit is, in theory, not disputed. Insofar as one wants to recognize a place for religions in the foundation of civil society, not relegated to the field of beliefs that are cultivated in private, as it is in the eminent case of Jürgen Habermas, one should not credit them unconditionally as "good reasons" for the democracy. Distinguishing the "informal public sphere"—where ideas, beliefs, and faiths circulate freely without restrictions or obligations for anyone, from the "institutional public sphere"—where

[56] "In temporal things."

[57] See on this topic Gustavo Zagrebelsky, *Intorno alla legge: il diritto come dimensions del vivere comune* (Torino: Einaudi 2009), 22ff, on the dialogue between Alcibiades and Pericles as told by Xenophon in the *Memorabilia*, about the law as persuasion or as violence.

collective decisions equipped with authority are elaborated, one should not hesitate to say that "only secular reasons count beyond the institutional threshold that divides the informal public sphere from parliaments, courts, ministries, and administrations."[58] On the other hand, even Catholicism seems to implicitly converge on this point, every time that one affirms that the positions taken, insofar as they are rooted in the Christian faith, are valid in general, as reasons for public decisions, for their reasonableness and persuasiveness independent of faith, that is for their "secular persuasion." But, if this were really the case, they would be subjected to the test of critical discussion, with the risk of an unfavorable outcome, and there would not be the *non possumus*. These are instead expressions of the fact that, for the Church, there is a unilateral reserve of principles that are impermeable to public confrontation, yet still aspire to become compulsory for all. In short, public reason and the *non possumus* are incompatible. The Church presents itself as in a dialogue and then, when it does not prevail in arguments within this dialogue, uses its vetoes, acts with duplicity, a duplicity that is determined by its relationship with the truth. It can presume, at first and abstractly, that its truth of faith might be explained through the means of the reason, which is common to all human beings. In fact, if everything comes from God, faith along with reason, then one cannot allow that God would be contradicted. This is the doctrine acknowledged and recently reiterated in the encyclicals *Veritatis splendor* (1993) and *Fides et ratio* (1998). But if, secondarily and concretely, its rational arguments succumb to other and opposing arguments, could it waive its truth and accept a reason that is by definition erroneous? Obviously not. This is the potential conflict.

VI. *Etsi Deus non Daretur*[59]: *Veluti si Deus Daretur*[60]

The two formulas that comprise the title of this section signify an attempt to break the impasse signaled at the end of the previous section. The first, with an invitation from non-believers to believers; the second, from believers to non-believers. They are two opposing formulas, but with a common goal: to create the conditions in which one will not have to figure out the "dead end" of democracy: where both can oppose each other with their own *non possumus*.[61]

Etsi Deus non daretur is a formula of ancient origin, belonging to the post-Medieval transition from divine natural law to the natural law of reason. In Section 11 of the Prolegomena to *The Law of War and Peace* (1625), Hugo Grotius writes that the law of nature would still "have a degree of validity even if... there is no God, or that the affairs of men are not of concern to him,"[62] although this would be conceding "that which cannot be conceded without the utmost wickedness."[63] This dense formula has an unambiguous theoretical meaning but a dual and opposed practical significance. First, it sets a meaning for "justice," freeing it from theological will, specifically the will of God

[58] Jürgen Habermas, *Religion in der Öffentlichkeit* (2005), translated into English as *Religion in the Public Sphere*, in Jostein Gripsrud, Hallvard Moe, Anders Molander, and Graham Murdock (eds), *The Idea of the Public Sphere* (New York: Rowman & Littlefield, 2010), 298.

[59] "Even if God was not given." [60] "As if God were given."

[61] On the Groatian "*etsi Deus*" and its place in the development of political and juridical thought in the seventeenth century and its influence in the formation of rationalistic natural law, see Ernst Cassirer, "Vom Wesen und Werden des Naturrechts," in *Zeitschrift für Rechtsphilosophie in Lehre und Praxis*, vol VI (1932--34), 3–5.

[62] In the original, "etiamsi daremus... non esse Deum, aut non curari ab eo negotia humana."

[63] In the original "sine summo scelere dari nequit."

and his theologians who refer to principles based on Divine volition. By the resolution of a great debate on the nature of law that had long divided theologians, this formula establishes that justice is what it is. The righteous is not such because God wills it, but God wills it, nor cannot will it, because he is righteous.[64] Yet *Etsi Deus* opens a dialectic of practical significance.

(a) *Even if God did not exist* can be understood within the scope of the *validity* of the rules of justice. If they are valid independent of God, it must be concluded that also those "without God" or "without the true God" are subject to them. Thus, Christian law can claim to be obligatory in general, as universal laws. Not even atheists, Jews, Saracens, Protestants, heretics in general, or humans of other civilizations, such as the indigenous people of the Americas conquered by the armies of the Cross, in Mexico or Peru, could be exempt. Since the Christian prince, in whose name these "conquests" proceeded, was the legitimate king according to that law, even the "Indians" who knew nothing of this "true religion" would have to recognize his legitimacy. Today, at least in our world, this interpretation, which contains the seeds of Imperial Catholicism, is not the current one. What is of foremost interest is not the diffusion of this formula, but its role in determining the nature or basis of the rules of justice. In this light, *etsi Deus* has a different meaning, as the following explains.

(b) *As if (ut si) God did not exist* is a small, but significant, change in translation that moves us from the scope of validity to the problem of *justification* of the rules of justice. This brings us to the heart of today's issues. Thus understood, this formula is an invitation to religious people not to enter into the sphere of public reason, or, if they enter it, not to leave behind their faith, but instead the guarantee of truth that could be based in this faith, every time that they make decisions designed for all, and not just themselves. The most radical interpretation of this "secular" formula is from a theologian, Dietrich Bonhoeffer.[65] In "our coming of age," in our situation where "God is teaching us that we must live as men who can get along very well without him," and not less well, thanks to the extraordinary scientific, ethical and artistic developments that are able to exorcise our extreme fear of death through treatments of the psyche, Bonhoeffer argues that there is no longer a place for the *deus ex machina* of religion, which was designed to give certainty to humanity and overcome its fears and unanswered questions. Because *this God* that proclaims the Truth down from the cross, "the throne of the world," failed, there opened a time of faith in a suffering God, "who conquers power and space in the world by His weakness," that we may know for free and problematically a faith purified of worldly interests, disinterested and "demythologizing": an understanding that the authority of the triumphant Truth expressed by decree

[64] *The Law of War and Peace* (n. 9), book 1, Ch. 1, X, 5: "The law of nature, again, is unchangeable—even in the sense that it cannot be changed by God. Measureless as is the power of God, nevertheless it can be said that there are certain things over which that power does not extend; for things of which this is said are spoken only, having no sense corresponding with reality and being mutually contradictory. Just as even God, then, cannot cause that two times two should not make four, so He cannot cause that which is intrinsically evil be not evil."

[65] Dietrich Bonhoeffer, a Lutheran theologian, was executed by hanging in Flossenbürg by the Nazis in April of 1945 for having participated as a member of the German "Confessing Church" in the anti-Hitler plot of Admiral Canaris. In his letters written while imprisoned (see n. 73 below), Bonhoeffer sketched the design of a theology "without God," or more precisely, a theology that, abandoning the idea of the God of a religion, personified by historic churches, turns to the God of faith and of the Gospel. This is a theology that renders possible *even if*, indeed *precisely because* the God of religion does not exist (anymore).

has replaced the fragile, humble, and responsible listening to the Divine whisper that asks to be understood, beyond any guarantee of certainty, in the sequence of human experience, the responsibility for which must be taken here and now.[66] "Even if God does not exist" is the expression that corresponds more than any other with this conception of faith: "does not exist" (anymore), obviously, in the sense of *deus ex machina*. This (in the indicative tense, instead of the subjunctive tense of the first wording) would be the expression that best corresponds to the concept. The "political performance" of *etsi Deus* in this sense is to lay the groundwork for a common discourse in the respect of differences.

Veluti si Deus daretur wants to achieve the same goal, a unique public discourse, but through the elimination of differences. This is the reversal of the Grotian formula, and is what Joseph Ratzinger offers to non-believers: that they should seek to live and direct their lives "as if God existed." "Thus," Ratzinger writes, "no one's freedom is restricted, but everything human gets the support and the criterion it so urgently needs." [67] The idea must have seemed to be a brilliant asset because it has been repeated numerous times since its introduction into the debate.

The end goals of the appeals to both *etsi Deus* and *veluti si Deus* are thus analogous: a homogeneous society. In the first case, homogeneity is found in the sharing of the secular spirit, and in the second, of the Christian spirit. However, it is not surprising that both formulations have fallen on deaf ears.

The Church has considered *etsi Deus* to be provocative. How could one propose to a believer, who places his ultimate certainties and hopes in the faith, to act as if this was not so? The philosophy of "as if,"[68] already difficult on its own, is unthinkable when applied to faith. It is an instrumental appeal, that subordinates faithfulness to God to an ethically incomparable end: coexistence between humans. In his encyclical *Evangelium vitae*, Pope John Paul II writes that:

> By living "as if God did not exist," man not only loses sight of the mystery of God, but also of the mystery of the world and the mystery of his own being. The eclipse of the sense of God and of man inevitably leads to a *practical materialism*, which breeds individualism, utilitarianism and hedonism. Here too we see the permanent validity of the words of the Apostle: "And since they did not see fit to acknowledge God, God gave them up to a base mind and to improper conduct" (Rom 1:28). The values of *being* are replaced by those of *having*.[69]

On the other hand, *veluti si Deus* is rejected by non-believers. They see it as something shocking, from the same point of view as Christians, which results in opportunism. Should not faith be a flame that transforms? Should not it be the *imitatio Christi*,[70] which every believer is called, folly for the world? Does it not imply, however, a faith reduced to the simple morality of social life, to a code of good conduct? Is there not in this *as if* something similar to the opportunism and immoral calculations of (presumed) utility of Pascal's wager (if there is a God, I win; if not, then I still do not lose[71]), but

[66] Dietrich Bonhoeffer, *Widerstand und Ergebung*, translated into English as *Prisoner for God: Letters and Papers from Prison* (Eberhard Bethge, ed.; Reginald H. Fuller, trans., New York: Macmillan, 1959), 125, 163–4.

[67] Joseph Ratzinger, "Europe in the Crisis of Cultures," *Communio* 32 (Summer 2005), 355.

[68] Hans Vaihinger, *Die Philosophie des Als-Ob (Philosophy of As If)* (Leipzig: Meiner 1911).

[69] John Paul II, *Evangelium vitae* (March 1995), paras 22 and 23, available at <http://www.vatican.va/holy_father/john_paul_ii/encyclicals/documents/hf_jp-ii_ enc_25031995_evangelium-vitae_en.html>.

[70] In Christian theology, the Imitation of Christ is the practice of following the example of Jesus.

[71] Blaise Pascal, *Pensées*, n. 682.

even more so reduced to a purely mundane level? There exists, however, an insuperable difficulty for every spirit, not only non-believers but also secular ones. What constitutes being and acting in accordance with the existence that God requests is unknown to secular people, while people of faith have been fighting for a thousand years, each believing to know better than the others. A recognized authority is required, and this authority has to be the Catholic teaching. The calculation of utility is not in favor of God, but of the Church as an institution—and for the Church this may seem like the same thing, but it is not for the secular. How can one ask non-believers to contradict themselves so profoundly, to the point of relying on what is said about a God that they do not know? The "friendly" advice of the Church to non-believers has only a contradictory significance: follow me as an act of faith contrary to your conscience.

VII. Inevitable and Non-inevitable Conflict

Insofar as it is oriented to the good end of peaceful coexistence, or rather effective cooperation, everything leads to the conclusion that this conflict cannot be eliminated, whether it be latent or active, according to the historical moments. The calm is always only an appearance. Between the Church and civil society, each agreement is not a peace treaty, but always and only an armistice that delays the moment of conflict. This is the natural result of the Church assigning to itself a universal task, that is directed to the society as a whole, a task that, in its sole discretion, can be extended to the point where, at least on certain matters, it duplicates the task of the state. This is all the more so because this task's legitimacy is based on a transcendent principle that is conceptually and practically in opposition to the immanent principle on which the democratic state is founded. There are no surprises here. It is, precisely, the nature of things. Moreover, if this were not so, it would mean that either the Church is totally and definitively identified with the state (Church-state), or, to the contrary, that the state is identified with the Church (state-Church). Today, the sides in conflict with civil society are numerous. The distances, presumably, are destined to increase and widen hand in hand with human beings becoming objects of science, in their individual and social biological lives. To those who see in humans the image of God, it must even be repulsive that this may be studied and eventually transformed like any fact of nature. Since science is irreparably on this road, there is little illusion about a future without conflicts.

In light of the new possibilities opened up by science that move the limits of nature for the benefit of individual liberty, the idea that this difficulty can be gotten past through "permissive laws" that enable Catholics, like any member of a particular faith, to make their own choices based on their own faith, does not seem particularly productive.

"One can think," it is said, "of laws that make it totally optional to use certain institutions; so that, according to moral convictions of different orientations, churches can dissuade their followers from using the remedies set up by these laws that are permissive in the true sense, . . . in the sense of the jurist Modestino, according to the formula specified in the Digest: '*Legis virtus est imperare, vetare, permittere, punier.*'"[72] It is true that these laws have been used in obvious cases (divorce, abortion, perhaps soon euthanasia—cases for which no one has ever thought of mandatory rules) and in other less obvious cases (conscientious objections by medical personnel in performing abortions). But it is no

[72] "It is the power of the Law to command, forbid, permit, punish." Leopoldo Elia, "Introduzione ai problemi della laicità," in AA.VV., *Problemi pratici della laicità agli inizi del secolo XXI*, AIC—Associazione dei costituzionalisti italiani, 26–27 October 2007, 14 (translation by translator of this chapter).

less true that this solution was accepted only as a "lesser evil," while waiting for the opportune moment to force upon all the universal point of view of which the Church is bearer. It is truly an armistice, waiting to resume the war. To accept this, as a definitive solution, would signify for the Church an acceptance of being reduced to a partial component of society, huddled in the space that the law allows, renouncing its role as universal legislator. It would signify adherence to a self-representation as a religious denomination similar to the scorned sects discussed within Catholic doctrine.

From these considerations, which certainly do not induce optimism around the possibility of friendly relations between the Catholic world and the secular world, for those who seek this relationship and work to create it, there comes a nostalgia for the spirit of the Second Vatican Council, which seems to be from a time far removed from our own. What has been changed? Why does this common ground that seemed possible then, seem now to have been lost?

In order to answer these questions, one can simply compare the distinctly doctrinal attitude of the current positions of the Catholic church, inspired by the truth-reason dichotomy, which characterizes our time, with its attitude of marked wisdom of that time. With regards to the Judeo-Christian tradition, this attitude toward the problems and dramas of life can be found not only in texts usually ascribed to this tradition (such as the Books of Job, Proverbs, Ecclesiastes, Wisdom, and Sirach, and parts of the Pslams), but also on many pages of the Synoptic gospels. These are not about philosophies of life, but of the wisdom that feeds on experience and compassion for others. It does not dominate with a true-false dichotomy which, as explained above, is inevitably divisive. On the contrary, the extremes are justice-iniquity, mercy-impiety and wisdom-ignorance, and between these extremes there are possibilities for collaboration from many points of view. The Second Vatican Council was not only this, but certainly the propensity of the Church to be a collaborator with humanity in practical or inductive research of justice, peace, and brotherhood, put in the background the enormous doctrinal apparatus from which, through progressive deductions, one has now "cold" positions about life events. Sometimes these positions are even cruel and repugnant for those who don't look solely or mainly through the lens of the "doctrine of faith."

In words, this perspective has not been entirely abandoned. When Jürgen Habermas and Joseph Ratzinger agree on the reciprocal "responsibility to learn" of the secular and Catholic worlds, of Christian faith and secular reason, in the sign of "reasonableness" and not in that of truth, we must ask: learn what? Certainly it is quite unthinkable that secular reason has to learn from Catholic dogma, or that Catholic theology has to learn from scientific thought, which is by definition secular: that it has to learn in a cognitive sense, as a passage of "truth" from one camp to another. It would be more mutually "polluting" than mutually "learning."

In fact, even in a framework notable for the ambiguity of its positions and the language used to express them, the answer to the question of what the world of reason can learn from the world of faith is expressed by Habermas, who writes:

> This is why something can remain intact in the communal life of the religious fellowships—provided of course they avoid dogmatism and the coercion of people's consciences—something that has been lost elsewhere and that cannot be restored by the professional knowledge of experts alone. I am referring to the adequately differentiated possibilities of expression and to sensitivities with regard to lives that have gone astray, with regard to the societal pathologies, with regard to the failure of individuals' plans for their lives, and with regard to the deformation and disfigurement of the lives that people share with one another.[73]

[73] Habermas, *The Dialectics of Secularization* 43.

Only anti-Catholic and anti-religious prejudice could dismiss as irrelevant this way of looking at the experiences of Christian life, typical of many communities and individuals who are inspired by the Christian message, caring little about the "truth" that over the course of centuries has been incorporated into the enormous doctrinal construction of the Church. Once these experiences have been purified, that is, have been subjected to a rigorous scrutiny that subtracts from them every element of fanaticism, ignorance, and presumptions of superiority, in light of the consciousness of the modern secular world, only prejudice could exclude that even there (*even* there) one could find a heritage open to usufruct for all.

But would this be, for a secular culture in whose name the representative of the Frankfurt school has spoken, an openness to religion in the same sense of the then-Cardinal, prefect of the Congregation for the doctrine of faith? Or, rather, would it be something like a "psychological transposition" of which Thomas Mann has written about the great philologist and scholar of myth Károly Kerény:

> What I find particularly appealing here is a certain preference for the "secularization" of the concept of religion, for its psychological conversion into the profane spheres of morality and the soul. Religion as the opposite of negligence and disregard, as taking care, respecting, considering, conscience, as a *vigilant* attitude, indeed as *metus*, and finally as a concerned, attentive receptivity to the movements of the universal spirit—what more can I wish? Suddenly I find it legitimate to call myself a religious individual, a self-estimate which, in "prudence," I would otherwise hardly dare to make.[74]

[74] Letter from Thomas Mann to Karl Kerenyi, 7 October 1936, in *Mythology and Humanism: The Correspondence of Thomas Mann and Karl Kerenyi* (Alexander Gelley, trans., Ithaca, NY: Cornell University Press, 1975), 73–4.

15

Religious Marriage in a Liberal State

Gideon Sapir[1] *and Daniel Statman*[2]

I. Introduction

That a state might enforce religious marriage on its citizens is quite obviously against the basic principles of liberalism. Yet, to define why this is so is more difficult than often thought. This chapter seeks to examine this issue in detail, focusing on the case of Israel, one of the very few liberal countries in which marital status is determined by religion.[3]

Let us start with three clarifications that may help to define the question. First, there is a range of possibilities regarding the attitude of different states towards religious marriage. In some countries, a civil marriage ceremony is the only way to get married, while religious marriage is viewed as a private matter with no legal implications. In other countries, the only way to marry is by participation in a religious marriage ceremony. Between these two attitudes there are countries that acknowledge both religious and civil marriage ceremonies without granting preference to either.

The second clarification concerns the assumed basis for the incompatibility of liberalism with religious monopoly over marriage. The view we wish to explore contends that there is something inherently problematic in such a monopoly, regardless of the specific content of the religious law or the form of the religious ceremony. We want to exclude from our discussion other reasons for thinking that religious marriage is problematic, such as being non-egalitarian, or degrading to women. Religious marriage is not necessarily non-egalitarian or degrading: consider, for example, a marriage ceremony carried out by a reform rabbi, where the female partner has equal status, taking an active role and voicing her agreement. The question that will concern us, then, is whether religious monopoly over marriage is problematic simply because of its religious nature.

What exactly is meant by saying that some marriage arrangement is "religious"? This brings us to the third clarification. The term "religious" might refer here to any one or all of three elements: (a) the nature of the marriage ceremony. A ceremony is considered to be religious when it includes elements such as prayers, citations from the scriptures, religious symbols, etc.; (b) the laws regulating marital status. These are considered religious when they are derived from a religious code, such as the Jewish law (halakha); (c) the body in charge of administering and implementing these laws. Such a body would be considered religious when it is composed of clergymen (or, atypically, clergywomen) who would be in charge, *ex officio*, of implementing state marital law. Each of these elements raises different questions and there is no reason to assume *a priori* that they rise and fall together.

[1] Faculty of Law, Bar-Ilan University.

[2] Department of Philosophy, University of Haifa; Shalom Hartman Institute, Jerusalem.

[3] According to a comprehensive database on religion and state from 2008, only two other countries belong to this category, Greece and Sweden. See <http://www.religionandstate.org>.

II. Religious Marriage and Public Reason

With these initial clarifications in mind, let us turn now to the question regarding religious monopoly over marriage within a liberal state. One reason to think that the state should not grant such a monopoly is based on the idea of state neutrality, according to which a liberal state is committed to neutrality between competing conceptions of the good and is not allowed to prefer one conception over others.

The neutrality thesis is under dispute, but, for the present discussion we need not take a stand because the very institution of marriage expresses a *non*-neutralist attitude. It expresses a preference for marital relations over other sorts of cohabitation. One cannot oppose religious monopoly over marriage on the basis of its incompatibility with the idea of neutrality while granting preference to the institution of marriage over other forms of cohabitation.

Neutrality, then, is not a promising way to explain the problem with religious monopoly over marriage. A different way would be to argue that though the state need not be neutral with regard to different concepts of the good, religion is different, hence while the state is allowed to promote other concepts of the good, it may not promote religion (by granting special status to its marriage ceremony). The basis for this argument is the idea of "public reason," according to which restrictions on liberty must rely on reasons that are universally accepted, or at least accessible to all.[4] Rawls and his followers contend that religious arguments are the paradigmatic case of arguments that cannot satisfy this condition, hence reliance on them in the public sphere is ruled out.

Whether the doctrine of public reason is convincing or not is controversial. Our own view, which we defend elsewhere,[5] is that it is not, but for the sake of the present argument let us assume that it is. This seems to imply that from a liberal point of view, religious monopoly must be ruled out as it amounts to imposing constraints on the liberty of non-believers on the basis of religious considerations. We believe, however, that the picture is more complex. To see why, we need to refer to each of the three elements mentioned above. Let us start with the identity of the body that is responsible for the implementation and administration of the marriage laws. Suppose that in a given state, marital law itself is not religious. Could one still argue that the very fact that the bodies in charge of its implementation and administration are religious is a violation of autonomy? In our view, the answer is negative. Provided that the content of the law is not religious, we see no threat to autonomy by the fact that secular citizens need to face religious clerks (in court or in the City Hall). Such a monopoly on the administration and implementation of marital law might be problematic on other grounds, but not on grounds of (violation of) autonomy.

[4] See e.g. John Rawls, "Lecture VI: The Idea of Public Reason," in John Rawls, *Political Liberalism* (2nd edn, New York: Columbia University Press, 2005), 212; John Rawls, *The Law of Peoples* (Cambridge, MA: Harvard University Press, 1999), 131–80 ("The Idea of Public Reason Revisited"); Stephen Macedo, *Liberal Virtues: Citizenship, Virtue, and Community in Liberal Constitutionalism* (Oxford: Clarendon Press, 1990), 40–1 ("The moral core of [a liberal] order is a commitment to public justification: the application of power should be accompanied with reasons that all reasonable people should be able to accept"); Charles Larmore, *The Morals of Modernity* (Cambridge: Cambridge University Press, 1996), 125; Amy Gutmann and Dennis Frank Thompson, *Democracy and Disagreement* (Cambridge, MA: Belknap Press of Harvard University Press, 1996), 50.

[5] Gideon Sapir and Daniel Statman, "May a Liberal State Rely on Religious Considerations?" (2009) 25 *Bar-Ilan Law Studies* 599 [Hebrew]. Our analysis owes a lot to Christopher J. Eberle, *Religious Conviction in Liberal Politics* (Cambridge: Cambridge University Press, 2002).

Let's turn to the second element mentioned above. Assume that marital law is based on religious teachings such as those of halakha. Suppose that the content of the marital law raises no special problem from a liberal point of view and could be reached via non-religious reasoning too. Suppose that it is egalitarian, fair and efficient in advancing the social aims of marriage (whatever these are). Does the fact that it originated from a religious code imply that the law infringes the autonomy of the secular citizens? The answer depends on how one interprets the principle of public reason, namely, what kind of reliance on religious considerations violates it. Three possibilities come to mind:

(a) Reliance on religious considerations violates the principle of public reason even if it is explicitly combined with additional, non-religious considerations.
(b) Reliance on religious considerations violates the principle of public reason only when the body involved relies exclusively on religious considerations. The shortcomings of relying on religious considerations are not offset by the fact that non-religious ones *could* be produced and applied.
(c) Reliance on religious considerations violates the principle of public reason only when there are no non-religious considerations that could support the relevant decision.

An example may make this point clearer. Assume that some minister enacts regulations for removing carrion and cemeteries from the city precincts, expressly relying on the halakhic provisions in that regard.[6] According to possibility (a), the regulations are an infringement of autonomy and hence illegitimate, even if the minister relied explicitly on non-religious, environmental considerations as well. Since religious considerations must be ruled out in public discourse, the very use of them contaminates the relevant legislation. According to (b), since the involvement of religious considerations does not in itself contaminate legislation, the fate of the regulations depends on whether the minister was motivated exclusively by religious considerations or whether there were non-religious ones as well. According to (c), the legitimacy of the regulations depends on whether or not they could be grounded in non-religious considerations, regardless of whether the minister was actually guided by such considerations. Since the regulations in the example under discussion *could* be grounded in non-religious considerations, no infringement of autonomy occurs, because secular citizens can identify with these regulations.

It might help to present the differences between these three possibilities in the following table. In each rubric, the case under discussion is one in which the decision was actually based on religious considerations:

	Legitimacy of decision		
	(a)	(b)	(c)
The decision could not be justified on non-religious grounds.	Illegitimate	Illegitimate	Illegitimate
The decision could be justified on non-religious grounds too, and indeed was.	Illegitimate	Legitimate	Legitimate
The decision could be justified on non-religious grounds too, but was not.	Illegitimate	Illegitimate	Legitimate

[6] *The Mishna* (Jacob Neusner trans., New Haven: Yale University Press, 1988), 561–2.

Which of these three possibilities is the most convincing as an interpretation of the demands of public reason? In our view, it is the last one, (c). The principle of public reason requires that restrictions on liberty must be such that any citizen could, in principle, accept, or at least understand. The requirement is met when there are non-religious arguments that support the required restriction, even if they are not the arguments actually relied upon. Interpretations (a) and (b) pose unreasonable constraints on the use of religious arguments that do not follow from the idea of respect to autonomy embodied in the principle of public reason.

What follows with regard to the question at hand is that so long as state marital law can be supported by non-religious reasons, the very fact that it has its roots in religion, or that it was motivated by religious aspirations, is not enough to disqualify it. *If*, in terms of its content, the religious law relied upon is not problematic—if it is egalitarian, fair, and so on—there is nothing illegitimate in relying upon it.

We turn now to the third element, i.e. the nature of the marriage ceremony. The question we raised was whether the fact that this ceremony contains religious symbols, prayers, etc. is problematic from a liberal point of view. Following the previous discussion on the notion of public reason, the answer depends on whether one could come up with non-religious considerations to ground the imposition of such a religious ceremony. One might argue that such considerations exist and have to do with the importance of ceremonies. The acquisition of marital status is a very significant moment in the life of an individual and, arguably, the way to express this significance is to anchor it in a *ceremony* which would make use of the symbols inherent in any given tradition. Taking into consideration the long religious character of Western culture, it is natural that marriage ceremonies in Western states would contain religious elements. Therefore, even if some couple were to object to the religious character of the marriage ceremony imposed by the state, they could understand fully the interest of the state in preserving its cultural heritage by imposing such a ceremony, and could appreciate its importance. In this respect—so the argument proceeds—the marriage ceremony is no different than other ceremonies shaped by the state, such as the inauguration of presidents or of other high officials.

One should add that what endows ceremonies with meaning, and enables them to fulfill their social and cultural roles is the fact that they reflect traditions with an historical depth, traditions that are shared by an entire people or collective. In this sense, ceremonies are essentially conservative—they are grounded in the past. This implies an inevitable tension between the conservative aspect of ceremonies and the desire to update them to fit current trends or culture. Concessions to these trends might end in throwing out the baby with the bath water, i.e. completely losing the inspiring and uniting power of the ceremony.

This is an appealing argument, yet it is overstated. Admittedly, if too many components of traditional ceremonies are altered during too short a period, ceremonies might lose their meaning and force. But if the reform is sensitive and gradual, ceremonies could retain their force without creating an unnecessary clash with the values and attitudes of contemporary citizens. What follows is that while secular citizens could identify with a ceremony that includes some elements from their religious tradition, hence the imposition of such a ceremony would not necessarily go against public reason, they could not identify with a ceremony that was religious in a more distinct and undisguised way, like the Jewish *chuppah*. This seems to be like the difference between the ceremony held at the inauguration of a president in the United States and a wedding held in a church. In the former, the ceremony in its entirety is not a religious one, although it includes some reference to religious belief in the words "so help me God" that conclude the presidential oath, while in the latter the ceremony is religious through and through. To conclude, if by "religious marriage ceremony" one refers to a ceremony with only minor religious components, then imposing it upon secular citizens who wish to get married would not be objectionable on the basis of the doctrine of public reason. If, however, one refers to a ceremony of a *comprehensively* religious nature, then imposing it would be objectionable.

III. Religious Marriage, Conscience, and Respect

In the previous section we argued that respect for autonomy does not necessarily rule out marital law that relies on religious codes, nor does it rule out the possibility of religious clergymen administering or implementing, *ex officio*, state marital law. But respect for autonomy does rule out the conditioning of marital status on participation in ceremonies replete with religious practices and symbols. This captures one major reason why imposing such conditions is wrong from a liberal point of view, but it is not the only one. Another reason that seems to play a role here is respect for conscience. The notion of conscience we have in mind refers to deeply held normative convictions, those that constitute the personal identity of individuals. Such convictions might be false, but nonetheless they are a matter of conscience for the individuals holding them and, as such, merit special respect. Why so? The standard answer is that coercing people to act against their deep normative beliefs amounts to an attack on their integrity, an attack that brings about a sense of self-alienation and loss of identity. It is this sort of argument that underlies the exemption from military service granted to pacifists. More relevant to the present discussion is the grounding of various exemptions to religious individuals from laws which violate the dictates of their religion, or, at least, the desire to find a way to accommodate their needs.

If coercing believers to violate their principles is wrong as it is an affront to their consciences, one might argue that the same affront would be suffered by non-believers if coerced to violate *their* principles, in other words, that freedom *of* religion entails or includes freedom *from* religion. An illustration of this line of thought can be found in Kathleen Sullivan:

> The right to free exercise of religion implies the right to free exercise of non-religion. Just as Caesar may not command one to transgress God's will, he may not command one to obey it. To do either is to run afoul of free exercise. As the Court put it in Wallace v. Jaffree, "the Court has unambiguously concluded that the individual freedom of conscience protected by the First Amendment embraces the right to select any religious faith or none at all." The "conscience of the infidel or the atheist" is as protected as any Christian's . . . [T]he affirmative right to practice a specific religion implies the negative right to practice none.[7]

But exactly which principles of the non-believer might be violated by religious legislation? Surely no such principles are violated simply by the fact that some law was motivated by religious concerns. Assume, for example, that some public route is blocked to traffic on the Sabbath because it runs through an ultra-orthodox Jewish neighborhood and, as a consequence, drivers have to take a detour that lengthens their journey by three minutes. While some drivers may resent this imposition, it would be strange and artificial if they presented their complaint as one against a violation of *conscience*. The reason

[7] Kathleen M. Sullivan, "Religion and Liberal Democracy" (1992) 59 *University of Chicago Law Review* 195, 197.

is that there is nothing in the secular value system that is opposed to taking a circuitous drive, and therefore the additional journey cannot be seen as an attack on integrity.

On the face of it, this would imply that non-believers would hardly ever have a conscience-based claim against laws based on religion. After all, very few people have a principle not to act in ways that accord with those of religion. But this would be too hasty. It seems to us that conscience does add a separate reason against some kinds of religious legislation, in addition to the issue of public reason. To understand this, we need to distinguish between cases in which the content of the religious law is not, strictly speaking, "religious," like in the example of traffic limitations, and cases in which the content of the law is of a clearly religious character, as in religious ceremonies. In the former case, it is indeed hard to see in what sense the conscience of the secular individual might be under attack. By contrast, in the latter, such an attack seems evident. Think of a secular couple forced to get married in a religious ceremony in a church. These two people live in a world very different from that of the church. Their way of thought, their values, the symbols they find meaningful are all far from those expressed in the church ceremony. But here they are, participating in a ceremony that is foreign to them and that arouses in them a sense of absurdity and self-alienation. They feel they are betraying their way of life, their authenticity, in a way that resembles the feelings sensed by the believer when required to violate the precepts of religion. Thus, non-believers seem to have a conscience-based argument against *some* laws based on religion, i.e. laws enjoining participation in religious ceremonies.

But this does not put an end to the matter. We mentioned above that hardly any secular people subscribe to a principle that *prohibits* them from behaving in a way that accords with the demands of religion. But this seems to imply that even participation in religious ceremonies is not against their principles. For most secular people, participation in religious rituals—reading a chapter from the Psalms, attending a church service, reciting a blessing, holding a Torah scroll—is not perceived as problematic in itself. They are willing to carry out any of the above religious duties if a relative or a friend asks them nicely. In this respect, there seems to be a huge difference between believers and non-believers. The observant Jewess will refuse to eat non-kosher food at her best friend's birthday party, even if asked very nicely to do so. Furthermore, the friend's very request would be considered inappropriate and offensive. Doesn't this difference cast doubt on the proposal to ground the non-believer's objection to participation in religious ceremonies as protection of her right to freedom of conscience?

The answer seems to be that forced participation expresses an especially profound disrespect for secular citizens. To force non-believers to participate in religious rituals is, in a sense, *to force them to be religious*, at least for a short time. It is like a partial and temporary forced conversion.[8]

This answer has implications regarding the legitimacy of marriage ceremonies that are governed by religious law but are devoid of any explicit religious symbols or expressions. According to Jewish law, for instance, one way of getting married is for the groom to give the bride a document that declares some version of the formula "You are hereby my wife."[9] The document does not contain any religious content, nor does the act of

[8] Elsewhere we pursued a different answer that now seems to us less promising. See Gideon Sapir and Daniel Statman, "Why Freedom of Religion Does Not Include Freedom from Religion" (2005) 24 *Law and Philosophy* 467.

[9] The common formula is "Behold, thou art consecrated unto me (*harei at mequdeshet li*) [by this ring, according to the Law of Moses and of Israel]," but the Jewish law recognizes the validity of other formulae too, such as the one mentioned in the text. See BT Kiddushin 5b and Shulkhan Arukh, part Even Ha-Ezer Ch. 27, s. 1.

handing it to the bride. No blessings need to be recited and no religious authorities need to be present. Assume, then, that the state of Israel determines that all marriages between Jews have to comply with this procedure which would be carried out—let us further assume—before witnesses in the City Hall, not in the Rabbinate. Since such a ceremony could not plausibly be described as a religious one, enforcing it by law (as a condition for marriage) would constitute no attack on the conscience of the participants and no disrespect for their secular worldview.

Let us turn to the question of whether the fact that the body in charge of administering or implementing marital laws is religious expresses disrespect toward the non-believers that are forced to use its services. One is tempted to answer in the affirmative because the presence of clergymen colors the ceremony with a religious hue even if there is no explicit reference to religious content. If the marital court is comprised of priests wearing their cassocks, clerical collars and other appurtenances of their role, those appearing before them might feel that they are participating in a religious ceremony even when no religious content is explicitly referred to.

We concede that, in cases like these, appearing before the relevant judicial or administrative body is close to participating in a religious ceremony and is, therefore, problematic for the reasons just mentioned. However, not all religious officials don such explicitly religious attire while executing their various roles or activities, and even those who do, often choose less distinctive apparel. Our point is that the very fact that the relevant body is comprised of religious people, *ex officio*, does not in itself express disrespect towards those appearing before it and using its services.

Let us summarize the conclusions of our discussion so far:

(1) Religious monopoly over marriage is problematic from a liberal point of view mainly when it implies that in order to get married, citizens must undergo a ceremony of a comprehensively religious character. Such an arrangement violates the autonomy of the secular citizens: it forces them to participate in an activity that cannot be grounded in non-religious reasons. Although participation in ceremonies with some religious components could be understood and appreciated, this is not the case in ceremonies that are explicitly and clearly religious, demanding full participation and identification. Forcing secular citizens to participate in such ceremonies expresses disrespect towards them, disrespect bordering on a (temporary) forced conversion.

(2) The fact that state marital law is derived from religious beliefs and practices is not in itself problematic. Insofar as such law can be grounded in non-religious arguments, it meets the requirement of public reason and, therefore, involves no disrespect.

(3) The fact that the bodies that administer and implement the state marital law are religious is problematic only if their appearance is manifestly religious in a way that makes the proceedings too close to those of religious ceremonies.

IV. Religious Marriage in Israel

Let us now examine the implications of the above conclusions to the case of Israel which is a liberal democracy that nonetheless grants religion a special status in the domain of marital law. Historically speaking, this arrangement is a relic from the Ottoman millet system that granted autonomy to each religious community over issues of marriage and divorce. The religious character of marital law in Israel is not unique to Jews.

Each citizen is classified according to his or her religious affiliation (Jewish, Muslim, Christian, Druze) and the affiliation in question dictates the relevant marital law.[10] In the discussion below we focus on a critical discussion of the laws that govern the marriage of Jews though much of what we say applies, *mutatis mutandis*, to the laws pertaining to the marriage of non-Jews.

The special status of religion in marital law is expressed in sections 1–2 of Rabbinical Courts Jurisdiction (Marriage and Divorce) Law 1953, which state as follows:

(1) Matters of marriage and divorce of Jews who are Israeli citizens or residents will be under the exclusive jurisdiction of the rabbinic courts.
(2) Marriage and divorce of Jews will be carried out in Israel according to the laws of the Torah.

These two sections seem to entail a complete monopoly of religion over matters concerning marriage and divorce. To use the terminology mentioned above, state marital law fully adopts religious law, and the body in charge of its implementation is religious as well, namely, a rabbinical court. However, according to the analysis offered above, these implications need not be troubling. The fact that the state law is grounded in religion is not problematic if the religious law relied upon is acceptable in terms of its content. Similarly, the fact that the implementing body is a religious court is not in itself problematic, unless religious symbols are conspicuous in the court to the extent of making the secular discussant feel alienated.

Though the above monopoly of religion over marriage is not *necessarily* problematic, the actual situation in Israel is pretty troubling from a liberal point of view. The Jewish laws of marriage and divorce run against liberalism in two ways: First, they pose significant limitations on eligibility to marry, e.g. a Jew is not allowed to marry a non-Jew, limitations which violate the universally recognized right to marry.[11] Second, Jewish law is not egalitarian, hence if Israeli marital law relied on Jewish law, it will be so too, thereby violating the requirement that "[s]tates . . . shall take appropriate steps to ensure equality of rights and responsibilities of spouses as to marriage, during marriage and at its dissolution."[12] Regarding the monopoly of rabbinic courts over matters of marriage and divorce, the problem is that the atmosphere created in the court room is manifestly religious. A powerful illustration of this atmosphere is expressed by the regulation requiring any man appearing before the court to cover his head[13] in accordance with religious practice.

[10] Israeli law requires the registration of each citizen's religious affiliation, though in some cases citizens requested and were granted the option of being registered as having no such affiliation ("lacking religion"). See HCJ 58/68 *Shalit v. Minister of the Interior* [1970] Isr SC 23(2) 477, translated in Selected Judgments of the Supreme Court of Israel: Special Volume 35 (Asher Felix Landau and Peter Elman (eds), 1971). However, for the purpose of marital law, this registry is irrelevant because each recognized religion has authority to determine who its members are. For example, those who see themselves as belonging to no religion might be considered as Jews for the purpose of getting married, and those registered as Jews in the registry might be regarded as non-Jews by the Rabbinate. The important point for the present discussion is that a person's self-definition as non-Jewish is insufficient to evade the marital laws that apply to Jews if, according to the Rabbinate's definition, the person is Jewish (and the same applies, *mutatis mutandis*, to other religions).

[11] The right to get married is recognized in international law. See United Nations Universal Declaration of Human Rights Art. 16, 10 Dec. 1948, available at <http://www.un.org/Overview/rights.html>, and International Covenant on Civil and Political Rights, G.A. Res. 2200A (XXI), para. 17 (16 Dec. 1966), available at <http://www.un-documents.net/iccpr.htm>.

[12] International Covenant on Civil and Political Rights, G.A. Res. 2200A (XXI), para. 23 (16 Dec. 1966), available at <http://www.unhchr.ch/html/menu3/b/a_ccpr.htm>; Ruth Halperin-Kaddari, *Women in Israel: A State of Their Own* (Philadelphia: University of Pennsylvania Press, 2004), 227–62.

[13] HCJ 1912/97 *Rish v. Chief Rabbinate of Israel* [1998] IsrSC 52(5) 650.

Turning now to the third component of religious marriage, i.e. the ceremony. Given that the marriage of Jews in Israel is supposed to follow Jewish law, section (2) of Rabbinical Courts Jurisdiction implies that all Jews seeking to get married in Israel must participate in a religious ceremony, which, as argued above, is an attack on the autonomy and dignity of non-believers. Even more troubling, regarding the attack on dignity, is the prerequisite made by the Rabbinate according to which women cannot be married unless they first immerse themselves in a ritual bath (a *miqveh*). Full immersion in the waters of the *miqveh* is supposed to purify the future bride from the impurity of her menstruation period, thereby making it permissible for her future husband to have sexual relations with her. As a rule, rabbis will not perform a marriage ceremony (a *chuppah*) for an impure woman (*niddah*). Needless to say, forcing a woman to immerse herself naked in such a bath, under the supervision of an orthodox woman (a *balanit*), whose task is to ensure that the ceremony is carried out in accordance with the rules of halakha, is a serious violation of privacy and dignity.

Despite these features of Israeli law, saying that secular couples are *coerced* to undergo a religious marriage (with all of its problematic aspects) needs more elaboration given that, at least on the face of it, there are other, non-religious avenues to get married available to them. We explore these avenues in the next sections.

A. Acknowledgment of civil marriage

Formally speaking, the option of civil marriage does not exist in Israel, though, in a landmark decision almost 50 years ago, the Supreme Court opened the door to it. In the Funk-Shlezinger case,[14] the court discussed the case of Ms. Funk, a Christian resident of Israel, who married Mr. Shlezinger, a Jewish citizen, in a civil marriage ceremony conducted in Cyprus. Upon their return to Israel, the couple applied for their marriage to be registered in the Population Registry. The Ministry of Interior refused their request, claiming that civil marriage is not an available option to Israeli citizens. The couple filed a petition in the High Court of Justice[15] against this refusal, which, surprisingly, was accepted by the High Court. The main reason given by the court for its decision was that the registry merely collects statistical information, "which could either be true or false."[16] The records of the registry are no evidence of the veracity of the data they contain. Hence, by registering the Funk-Shlezinger couple as married, the registry does not thereby recognize the validity of their marriage.

This might have seemed to be a minor formalistic decision with no significant ramifications, but in fact it marked a revolution in Israeli marital law. As a result of this decision

[14] HCJ 143/62 *Funk Shlezinger v. Minister of the Interior* [1963], Isr SC 17, 225.

[15] In addition to its role as an appellate court (criminal and civil, both by right and with leave), s. 15 of the Basic Law: Judicature grants the Israeli Supreme Court discretionary power as a first (and final) instance to hear petitions against the various government agencies. In these cases, the Supreme Court presides in the capacity of "The High Court of Justice." The decisions dealt with in this article belong to this category. For a description and evaluation of the work of the Supreme Court, sitting as the High Court of Justice, see Yoav Dotan, "Judicial Review and Political Accountability: The Case of the High Court of Justice in Israel" (1998) 32 *Israel Law Review* 448; David Kretzmer, "Democracy in the Jurisprudence of the Supreme Court of Israel" (1996) 26 *Israel Yearbook on Human Rights* 267; Meir Shamgar, "Judicial Review of Knesset Decisions by the High Court of Justice" (1994) 28 *Israel Law Review* 43.

[16] HCJ 143/62 *Funk Shlezinger v. Minister of the Interior* [1963] Isr SC 17, 225. For a discussion of the judgment, see Asher Maoz, *Who is a Jew? Much Ado About Nothing, in Law, Judicial Policy and Jewish Identity in the State of Israel* (Binghamton, NY: Global Publications, State University of New York at Binghamton, 2000), 75, 105–10.

"civilly married couples are just as eligible for all economic benefits from the state as are those who were formally married in religious marriage in Israel, their inheritance rights are the same, and in principle the same marital property laws apply to both groups."[17]

Given this decision in the Funk-Shlezinger case, it is no longer true that the only way Israeli Jews can obtain the status of marriage is via a religious ceremony. Moreover, by *de facto* accepting the civil marriage of Israel citizens carried out abroad, the Supreme Court introduced a way to sidestep the Jewish laws regarding eligibility for marriage. Any marriage document obtained abroad would satisfy the registry and would grant the couple all marital benefits. Recently this principle was applied to gay and lesbian couples too: the Israeli Supreme Court ordered the registration as married of a homosexual couple who obtained a marriage certificate abroad.[18]

For many years the Supreme Court kept saying that its recognition of civil marriage was merely for statistical reasons and that the registration carried with it no official recognition of such marriage. A decade ago, however, the Court took that step further after receiving support for this move from an unexpected source. We refer to a revolutionary decision of the Grand Rabbinical Court, issued in Jerusalem in 2003. The Court discussed the case of a Jewish-Israeli couple who obtained a civil marriage in Cyprus, following which they were registered as married in accordance with the Funk-Shlezinger precedent. A few years later, the husband sought a divorce. Since, according to section 1 of the Rabbinical Courts Jurisdiction (Marriage and Divorce) Law of 1953, marriage and divorce of Jews are under the exclusive jurisdiction of the Rabbinic courts, the husband turned to the regional rabbinical court to sever the marital relationship. The court accepted the request and declared the termination of the marriage. Yet the court did not require the husband to go through the halakhic procedure of divorce which requires the issuance and public handing over of a divorce document (a *get*).[19] The declaration of the court that the marriage was dissolved was regarded as sufficient to terminate the marriage and to enable both husband and wife to remarry.

The wife appealed to the Supreme Court against the decision of the regional rabbinical court[20] and the Supreme Court turned to the Grand Rabbinical Court for clarification. The latter issued a detailed clarification in which it justified the decision of the regional court.[21] To explain why no *get* was required, the court relied on the halakhic opinion according to which if a Jewish couple freely chooses to obtain a civil marriage although the option of a religious one is open to it, the Jewish law of marriage does not apply to their union. One might say that they are not "Jewishly" married, or, in the technical

[17] Halperin-Kaddari, *Women in Israel: A State of Their Own* 244.

[18] See HCJ 3045/05 *Ben-Ari v. Ministry of the Interior* (unpublished). While in the United States there is a very hot public debate on this matter, in Israel no such debate really exists and the matter has been settled by a quiet decision of the Supreme Court. The court introduced same-sex marriage into Israel through the back door, so to say.

[19] According to Jewish law, a marriage is dissolved only when the husband delivers a bill of divorcement to his wife (and not vice versa). Jewish law goes into great detail about the rules concerning the writing and handing over of the get, but, as emphasized in the text, none of these rules is religious in its content.

[20] Though the rabbinic court system enjoys significant autonomy within the Israeli court system, the decision of rabbinic courts can be challenged at the Supreme Court in its role as a High Court of Justice. See s. 15(D)(4) of Basic Law: Judiciary, Sefer Ha-Hukkim [1984] 78. In the course of the years, the Supreme Court extended the grounds for its intervention in the decisions of the rabbinic courts. See Ran Hirschl, "Constitutional Courts vs. Religious Fundamentalism: Three Middle Eastern Tales" (2004) 82 *Texas Law Review* 1819, 1839–42.

[21] See file no. 4276/2003 from 11/11/03. For the full text of this decision, see 5 Ha-din Ve-Hadayan 5-9 (2005) [Hebrew].

words of Jewish law, they are not married "according to the religion of Moses and of Israel" (*k'dat moshe v'yisrael*). But if no *get* was required because the couple had never been "Jewishly" married, why was a divorce required at all? To solve this puzzle, the court relied on the laws of halakha which refer to the behavior of non-Jews ("Noahides," as they are technically called). Jewish law has something to say about the appropriate norms for non-Jews too. In particular, since adultery is forbidden for Noahides too, it is necessary to define the conditions for being married and the ways to undo the marriage. The court refers to Maimonides,[22] and concludes that Jewish law recognizes the marriage and divorce of non-Jews today provided they are carried out in a way that is accepted in civilized societies. A wife obtaining a (civil) divorce from a court in Paris or in Chicago would not violate the Noahide prohibition against adultery if she then moved in with a new partner, because this civil divorce is recognized by Jewish law.

Yet how are these Noahide laws relevant to the marriage and divorce of *Jews*? Here comes the innovative part of the decision. The court suggested that Jews can get married in two ways: qua Jews and qua human beings, i.e. Noahides. The much preferred way is of course the former, but the latter is valid as well. This means that a Jewish couple that obtains a civil marriage is regarded by Jewish law as fully married, though not "Jewishly" so. This explains why in the case at hand the rabbinic court regarded the couple as married even though they only went through a civil procedure. It also explains why the court had to *undo* their marriage (in order to make it possible for them to remarry) rather than declare that the couple had never been married in the first place.[23]

Shortly after the High Rabbinical Court issued its opinion, the Israeli Supreme Court warmly embraced it, thereby upgrading the acknowledgment of marriage between Israeli Jews from formal registration to full recognition. Moreover, the Supreme Court said that because Jewish law had not developed a legal corpus regarding the monetary aspects of Noahide, i.e. civil marriage, the jurisdiction over such aspects had to be granted exclusively to the state courts.[24]

What follows is that alongside the official option of religious marriage in Israel, there is recognition of civil marriage (performed abroad) as well. If a Jewish couple chooses to get married abroad and then return to Israel, the couple can avoid the Jewish limitations on eligibility, the religious marriage ceremony (including the pre-requisite of bathing in a *miqveh*), the Jewish laws governing the monetary aspects within marriage, and the Jewish laws of divorce. The only religious aspect that such a couple would not be able to avoid is appearance before a rabbinic court in case of a divorce. But recall that this situation would be religious only in the sense that the judges would be religious *ex officio* and the men required to cover their heads. In terms of content, neither the considerations applied by the court nor the procedure would be religious in any meaningful (and disturbing) sense.

Nonetheless, this option of civil marriage is unsatisfactory from a liberal point of view because it demands that couples go abroad to get marital status. This is problematic in

[22] Laws of Kings, 9, 8.

[23] The High Rabbinical Court's decision accords well with the view according to which the Mosaic laws supplement the Noahide laws rather than replace them. For an elaboration of this view and the Jewish sources supporting it, see Suzanne Last Stone, "Sinaitic and Noahide Law: Legal Pluralism in Jewish Law" (1991) 12 *Cardozo Law Review* 1157, 1161 (while the Rabbis did not view the Torah law solely as a theoretical construct, they did not consider it a fully functional legal system either, but rather required its supplementation by the Noahide Code that "served as a residual source of law for Jews, a bridge between the ideals of formal Torah law and the realistic constraints of maintaining a legal community over time.").

[24] *HCJ 2232/03 Plonit (anonymous) v. Tel-Aviv-Jaffa Regional Rabbinical Court* (yet unpublished), s. 31 of Chief Justice Barak's opinion.

two respects: first, in practice this route is not open to all citizens because it depends on resources and know-how which are not available to many citizens. For such citizens it would be correct to say that they are coerced into participation in a religious ceremony. Second, if, as argued above, forced participation in religious ceremonies is unacceptable from a liberal point of view, a state cannot evade its responsibility to its citizens by referring them to the marriage arrangements of some *other* jurisdiction.[25] An example from freedom of expression might help. A state that respects this freedom cannot justify limitations imposed on speech on the basis of the claim that those whose speech is limited in their home country could express their views via channels in neighboring countries, even if, on a practical level, doing so would be no less effective or costly in terms of spreading the views of the dissenters.

This last consideration explains the limited advantage that might accrue if consular marriage is ever validated in Israel, namely, marriage of an Israeli couple conducted by a foreign consul in Israel, within the territory of the consulate, in accordance with the law of the relevant country. Currently, this option is available only for couples where at least one of them is a citizen of the same country as the consul,[26] but one could imagine that in the future this limitation would be removed and foreign consulates would open their gates to any couple seeking civil marriage. If this were ever to happen, the burden of obtaining a civil marriage in Israel would be no heavier than that of obtaining a religious one, but the second objection mentioned above would still apply. States cannot fulfill their obligations to their citizens by relying on the goodwill of other countries.

B. The recognition of non-marital cohabitation

In the course of the years, the Supreme Court of Israel has created and developed a category of family life without marriage to include couples who live together, share a household, often have children, but were never formally married. The Supreme Court has made the status of such couples equal to that of "normal," married couples.[27] As pointed out by scholars working in this field, although this is a world-wide phenomenon,[28] Israel's approach to the legal status of Non-Marital Cohabitation (NMC) is one of the most radical among liberal countries.[29] The question we seek to explore is what the existence of NMC, as actually shaped by the Supreme Court, entails with regard to the tension between liberalism and the religious monopoly over marriage.

Since couples choosing this route are not officially married, sections 1 and 2 of Rabbinical Courts Jurisdiction (Marriage and Divorce) Law of 1953 do not apply to them. This means that at no stage would the rabbinical court have any kind of jurisdiction over their joint life, nor would religious law be enforced upon them in any way.

[25] This argument was made by the Supreme Court of Israel in HCJ 51/69 *Rodnitsky v. High Rabbinical Court of Appeals* [1970] Isr SC 24(1) 713 ("What kind of a solution is it for the Israeli legislator and the Israeli courts to send the Israeli citizens outside of the country's borders in order to solve their problems?").

[26] See HCJ 2888/92 *Goldstein v. Minister of the Interior* [1994] Isr SC 50(5) 89.

[27] See Halperin-Kaddari, *Women in Israel: A State of Their Own* 245–6; Shachar Lifshitz, "The External Rights of Cohabiting Couples in Israel" (2003–04) 37 *Israel Law Review* 346; Ariel Rozen-Zvi, "Israel: An Impasse" (1991) 29 *Journal of Family Law* 379.

[28] On Europe, see Kathleen Kiernan, "The Rise of Cohabitation and Childbearing Outside Marriage in Western Europe" (2001) 15 *International Journal of Law, Policy and the Family* 1.

[29] Another country with such a radical approach is New Zealand. See e.g. Grace Gunz Blumberg, "The Regularization of Nonmarital Cohabitation: Rights and Responsibilities in the American Welfare State" (2001) 76 *Notre Dame Law Review* 1265, 1300–1; Yuval Merin, *Equality for Same-Sex Couples* (Chicago: University of Chicago Press, 2002), 173–4.

Earlier we suggested that although Israel recognizes civil marriage abroad, this alternative does not fully relax the tension between Israeli marital law and liberal values. The worries we expressed in that context, however, do not apply to NMC. First, the burden of obtaining this status with its privileges (and duties) is no heavier than that involved in obtaining the status of being married via the Rabbinate. Hence, it cannot be claimed that some people are *forced*—because it comprises such an extra burden—to get married via the Rabbinate. Second, NMC is a solution *within* the Israeli legal system that does not rely on other legal systems. Given the fact that this arrangement is not religious in any of the meanings alluded to earlier, this seems a satisfactory solution to the problem arising from the religious monopoly over marriage.

Or is it? Although this recognition guarantees couples joined by this legal construction all the benefits and privileges granted by law to married couples, at the end of the day it does not make them equal. Unlike couples obtaining a civil marriage, couples joined by NMC are not *married*. For those who have no interest in obtaining the official status, this would be a perfect solution and would dilute any claim to the effect that they are forced to undergo a religious marriage. But for those who do want "the real thing," who wish to get the full social recognition of their relationship under the heading of marriage, NMC is far from satisfactory. That Israel nonetheless makes the obtaining of such recognition contingent on participation in a religious ceremony amounts to religious coercion of the kind that cannot be justified.

In light of all the above, there seem to be two main ways to deal with the problems involved in the religious monopoly on marriage and divorce in Israel. One way, which merits more attention than it gets, is to maintain the monopoly but make a serious effort to minimize its problematic aspects. We refer mainly to the disrespect towards the conscience of the secular individual when being forced to participate in a manifestly religious ceremony. As indicated earlier, for a marriage to be valid in Jewish law there is no need for a Rabbi, nor for the recitation of prayers or verses. It is enough for the groom to give the bride some modest present (not necessarily a ring) and say to her in the presence of two witnesses something like "You are hereby my wife," or sign a document which says the same. If this were to be the procedure enforced by law in order to get married, there would be no room for complaint about disrespect for conscience. That would still leave us with the violation of dignity involved in the requirement of bathing in a *mikveh* as a pre-condition for marriage, a requirement that can and should be relaxed.[30] Such reforms in the current practice of religious marriage would definitely constitute an improvement from a liberal point of view. Many will nonetheless find them unsatisfactory because of the non-egalitarian character of the marriage (and more so the divorce) and because of the limitations on eligibility, i.e. the fact that those belonging to one religion cannot marry a partner from a different religion.

The other way of dealing with the problems listed above is by reforming the law and adding the option of a civil marriage for those who do not want to or cannot get married in a religious ceremony. Like other writers on this topic,[31] we too are inclined to see this

[30] It is generally accepted that a marriage carried out when the bride was impure (*niddah*) is nevertheless valid. See Moshe Be'eri, "The Validity of a *Chuppat Niddah* in Case of a Secular Couple" (2009) 29 *Techumin* 196 [Hebrew]. In our view, the same reasons that support this validity can be developed to release secular couples entirely from this condition.

[31] See Yuval Merin, "The Right to Family Life and Civil Marriage under International Law and Its Implementation in the State of Israel" (2005) 28 *Boston College International and Comparative Law Review* 79; Shahar Lifshitz, "Married Against Their Will—Toward a Pluralist Regulation of Spousal Relationships" (2009) 66 *Washington and Lee Law Review* 1565; Ariel Rozen-Zvi, "The Rabbinic

as the preferred solution. Religious citizens would thus be respected by having the state approve of religious marriage as a legally valid way to obtain marital status. Secular citizens would be respected by having the state enable them to get married in a way that is consistent with their own beliefs and way of life. It is hard see how anybody who accepts the fundamental liberal requirement of equal respect to all citizens could object to such an arrangement.

Courts, The Halakha and the Community: A Very Narrow Bridge" (1995) 3 *Law and Government* 173, 211–20.

16

Are Secularism and Neutrality Attractive to Religious Minorities? Islamic Discussions of Western Secularism in the "Jurisprudence of Muslim Minorities" (Fiqh Al-Aqalliyyat)[1] Discourse

Andrew F. March[2]

I. Religious Minorities in Liberal Justifications of Secularism

It is a basic aspect of the liberal justification of secularism qua state religious neutrality as the most appropriate constitutional framework for a complex, morally diverse society that it gives especially firm guarantees to religious and other minorities. In its (perhaps intellectually dominant) "justificatory" form, contemporary liberalism tends to hold that this form of public secularism is required by the ultimate political-moral obligation to justify coercive laws in terms which can be presented as acceptable or reasonable to all persons subject to them. Those terms must not be derivations from the "comprehensive" rationality or moral reasoning of any single religious or secular doctrine that reasonable people might reject. Rather, they must reflect values and standards of evidence which are accessible in principle to all reasonable members of a diverse society.

This conception of public reason reflects a certain range of social goals, including the goals of advancing justice, legitimacy, and social unity. What is implied by all of these goals is a particular concern with persistent minorities. If the concern is to limit the democratic authority of religious or other moral majorities, then it stands to reason that the presumptive beneficiaries of such limitation will have special reasons to endorse and be grateful for liberal, secular institutions.[3] Minorities are not forced to abandon most religious practices, to convert, to culturally assimilate, or to profess something that essentially requires the repudiation of basic theological beliefs. They benefit (at least from the perspective of the outside observer) from a system which does not see society primarily as uniting citizens in a single common purpose but rather as the just management of multiple private purposes, insofar as a public philosophy of shared ends and values would most likely be more antagonistic to their religion than a public philosophy of neutrality.

[1] In all contexts, Arabic titles have been transliterated without the use of diacritics. References to verses in the Qur'an are cited in the following format: Q. sura #:verse #. For example, Q. 5:48.

[2] Yale University. D.Phil. (Oxon., 2006) Assistant Professor, Department of Political Science. I would like to thank my fellow panelists and especially the organizers of the panel, Sadiq Reza and Asifa Quraishi.

[3] See e.g. Martha C. Nussbaum, *Liberty of Conscience: In Defense of America's Tradition of Religious Equality* (New York: Basic Books, 2008), 2 ("[I]f government announces a religious orthodoxy...

But what is a minority, and how do we draw the lines between social groups according to their respective "comprehensive doctrines?" A simple assumption, which would seem attractive to theorists of political liberalism, is that all groups (for present purposes we are only concerned with groups defined according to their religious or secular comprehensive conception of the good or truth) view themselves as more or less insular and equally closed *vis-à-vis* other groups. In a closed society consisting of only Catholics and Protestants, Catholics see Protestant reason as exclusive and thus potentially threatening. In a more complex society, Catholics see Protestant reason as equally exclusive as Jewish, Islamic, Mormon, or secular reason. In both of these societies, according to this simple assumption, where Catholics are a minority and their own reason cannot prevail they do not prefer the comprehensive reasoning of any of the other groups over any other, and thus have reasons to endorse some form of public reason.[4]

Of course this simple assumption is too simple—and I am not attributing it to any particular theorist of political liberalism or secularism.[5] (The obvious problems with basing justificatory arguments on conjectures or assumptions about how real-world actors would calculate their interests or preferences are, after all, why we need the veil of ignorance.) But it does focus our attention on just why groups that are in the minority when counted one way (as an insular group exclusive of all others) are not necessarily in a persistent minority status for the purposes of endorsing secular public reason. Groups who are anxious about one another's power may be all too eager to form coalitions against common antagonists.[6] What may be minority groups in theological matters may easily see themselves as belonging to a broader and more important majority of the faithful in political matters. And what may be crucial disputes in theology or hermeneutics may have no bearing on a broader political consensus. Put simply, there is no obvious reason why a religious minority should automatically sign on to Rawls' overlapping consensus rather than an overlapping consensus of the religiously devout. This latter possibility is all

[e]ven if such an orthodoxy is not coercively imposed... [i]t means, in effect, that minorities have religious liberty at the sufferance of the majority and must acknowledge that their views are subordinate, in the public sphere, to majority views.") Further, "[r]eligious minorities know what the denial of that separation [of church and state] usually leads to: the imposition of the ways of the majority on all—or, at least, the public statement that the majority is orthodox, who 'we' are, and that the minority are outsiders." Nussbaum, *Liberty of* Conscience, 15. Further statements to this effect can be found at 20, 24–5, 37, 116–19, 153.

[4] Clark Wolf offers this interpretation of Rawls' statement that the liberty of intolerant ("fundamentalist") religious minorities should be restricted "only when the tolerant sincerely and with reason believe that their own security and that of the institutions of liberty are in danger," John Rawls, *A Theory of Justice* (orig. 1971, rev. edn, Cambridge, MA: Harvard University Press, 1999) (1971), 193:

> Surely there are good reasons to think that political regimes that deny the fundamental liberal rights will be much harder on rational and conscientious dissenters and that illiberal minorities may still prefer to be minorities in a liberal state than in an authoritarian state built around values that are neither liberal nor their own. Thus, theocratic Christian fundamentalists may prefer living under liberal institutions rather living in a theocratic Muslim state. This provides at least some justification for the claim that liberal values are not "on all fours" with those of illiberal regimes.

Clark Wolf, "Fundamental Rights, Reasonable Pluralism, and the Moral Commitments of Liberalism," in Victoria Davion and Clark Wolf (eds), *The Idea of a Political Liberalism: Essays on Rawls* (Lanham, MD: Rowman & Littlefield Publishers, 2000), 102, 122.

[5] Even the above interpretation of Wolf stresses that theocratic Christian fundamentalists may prefer living under liberal institutions.

[6] Indeed, we find evidence of this in no more central of a text in the canon of liberal tolerance than Locke's *A Letter Concerning Toleration* (1689); his arguments for toleration and an exclusively secular ambit for the state do not prevent him from excluding atheists and Catholics from his list of tolerated subjects.

the more plausible given the psychology of political competition between groups. Who is my political friend and who my enemy is not always a function of the objective difference between us but of the relative difference given the alternatives. In a diverse, complex society where secularism is strong not only as a political doctrine of public reason but also as a comprehensive doctrine of how to live in the world, there is no necessary reason to assume that religious groups will see the differences between themselves as greater than, or even equally great as, the differences between their respective "comprehensive" reasoning and neutral, secular, "public" reasoning. This is not to say that political liberals (or other secularists) do not have strong arguments to present to religious minorities, but it is to say that those arguments are hardly the final word. Between liberal neutrality and an opposing religion's oppressive theocracy there are many alternative political possibilities.

In this essay, I want to focus on this question as it pertains to Muslim minorities of existing secular, liberal polities. Are secularism and religious neutrality attractive to Western Muslims for the reasons of fairness and equality liberals would claim? Do Western Muslims see and appreciate a distinction between a public reason that is non-Islamic and one that is anti-Islamic? Do they perceive secularism in the form of religious neutrality preferable in principle to a religious public language of justification which would allow for traditionally Christian societies to promote and advantage Christianity? Does secularism at all add to the legitimacy of the implicit social contract between believing Muslims and their wider non-Muslim state and society?[7]

II. Fiqh al-aqalliyyat: The Jurisprudence of Muslim Minorities

In addressing these questions, I am interested in the views expressed within the framework of traditional Islamic legal and ethico-political doctrines.[8] Of course, the identification of the traditional, the "orthodox", and even the scholarly is never a matter of locating fixed and uncontroversial sources of authority. This is particularly the case for Muslim communities in the modern period after colonial and other ruptures with traditional institutions.[9] It is naturally even more so in the countries of the West where Muslim communities are still in the process of negotiating the balance of authority between local Muslim intellectuals and scholars from the Muslim majority heartland, all while being frequently called upon to publicly proclaim their endorsement of Western liberal, democratic institutions.

Bearing all of this in mind, I do not think it is impossible to track the discourses of certain Muslim scholars and intellectuals who display a particular concern with the integrity and continuity of Islam as a legal and theological tradition, or what Rawlsians might call a "comprehensive doctrine." In particular, I wish to focus on the discourse

[7] On the idea of such a social contract, see Andrew F. March, "Islamic Foundations for a Social Contract in Non-Muslim Liberal Democracies" (2007) 101 *American Political Science Review* 235.

[8] For a good introduction to this dilemma as Muslims confront it, see Khaled Abou El Fadl, "Muslim Minorities and Self-Restraint in Liberal Democracies" (1996) 29 *Loyola of Los Angeles Law Review* 1525. Abou El Fadl presents some informal survey data on whether Muslims would feel more alienated by explicitly Christian justifications of legislation or adjudication or neutral-secular justifications. He also presents his own arguments as to why Muslims should prefer the latter to a coalition with other monotheists. His argument proceeds, however, on the basis of public reason arguments of fairness, reciprocity, and Muslim self-interest, so is itself not really an example of "Islamic reason" providing grounds for or against secularism and public reason.

[9] See Wael B. Hallaq, "What is Shari'a?" (2005–06) 12 *Yearbook of Islamic and Middle Eastern Law* 151.

within contemporary Islamic juridical (fiqhi) and ethical thought on the "jurisprudence of Muslim minorities" (fiqh al-aqalliyyat al-muslima).[10] Over the past decade or so an increasing number of Muslim scholars both in the West and in Muslim majority countries have attempted to interrogate the Islamic ethical-juridical tradition in light of the myriad novel challenges faced by Muslims living as minorities, with particular concern, I believe, for the challenges faced by Muslims living in Western liberal democracies. It is largely these texts from which I will draw, although I will also refer to other texts addressing the Muslim minority condition not self-consciously part of the more recent fiqh al-aqalliyyat discourse.[11]

As would be expected with a discourse emanating from a religious legal tradition, fiqh al-aqalliyyat works deal with a wide range of matters related to ritual and personal morality. In some cases, providing solutions to the day-to-day problems of living within a morally alien society, rather than theorizing and theologizing political attitudes toward non-Islamic systems of rule, appears to be the main task of "Islamic minority jurisprudence." Here one finds the whole spectrum of attitudes, from "Salafi" calls to remain as segregated from and as uncontaminated as possible by the wider infidel society[12] to the preference on the part of prominent Muslim Brotherhood-affiliated scholars such as Yusuf al-Qaradawi and others[13] for making the ethical lives of Muslims easier rather

[10] See Khalid 'Abd al-Qadir, *Fiqh al-aqalliyyat al-muslima* (Tripoli: Dar al-Iman, 1998); Yusuf al-Qaradawi, *Fi fiqh al-aqalliyyat al-muslima* (Cairo: Dar al-Shuruk, 2001); 'Abd Allah Ibn Bayya, *Sina'at al-fatwa wa-fiqh al-aqalliyyat* (Jedda/Beirut: Dar al-Minhaj, 2007); Sulayman Muhammad Tubulyak, *al-Ahkam al-siyasiyya li'l-aqalliyyat al-muslima fi'l-fiqh al-Islami* (Beirut: Dar al-Nafa'is, 1997) (author's name has been transliterated from the Bosnian of "Sulejman Topoljak"); Isma'il al-Hasani, *al-Ikhtilaf wa'l-tafkir fi fiqh al-aqalliyyat* (Marrakesh: al-Matba'a wa'l-Waraqa al-Wataniyya, 2006); Salah 'Abd al-Razzaq, *al-Aqalliyyat al-Muslima fi'l-gharb* (Beirut: Dar al-Hadi li'l-Tiba'a wa'l-nashr wa'l-Tawzi', 2007); Salih ibn Muhammad al-Shithri, *Hukm al-luju' wa'l-iqama fi bilad al-kuffar* (Riyad: Dar al-Habib, n.d.); Taha Jabir al-Alwani, *Towards a Fiqh for Minorities: Some Basic Reflections* (Herndon, V.A.: International Institute of Islamic Thought, 2003); Shaykh Ibn Baz and Shaykh Uthaymeen, *Muslim Minorities: Fatawa Regarding Muslims Living as Minorities* (Hounslow, UK: Message of Islam, 1998); 'Abd al-Mun'im Mustafa Halima (Abu Basir al-Tartusi), "Man dakhala diyar ghayr al-muslimin bi-'ahd wa aman ma lahu wa ma "alayhi," <http://www.abubaseer.bizland.com/>. Also of note are the fatwas of the European Council for Fatwa and Research and the Islam Online website, <http://www.islamonline.net>, as well as Majdi 'Aqil Abu Shamala (ed), *Risalat al-Muslimin fi bilad al-gharb* (Irbid, Jordan: Dar al-Amal, 1999), which includes important essays by Qaradawi and Lebanese scholar Faysal Mawlawi, amongst numerous others. For a Shi'ite perspective, see Muhammad Husayn Fadl Allah, *al-Hijra wa'l-ightirab: ta'sis fiqhi li-mushkilat al-luju' wa'l-hijra* (Beirut: Mu'assasat al-'Arif li'l-Matbu'at, 1999), and 'Ali al-Husayni al-Sistani, *al-Fiqh li'l-mughtaribin* (London/Beirut: Mu'assasat al-Imam 'Ali, 2002).

[11] I believe that the writings of certain prominent Muslim intellectuals writing at least partially in European languages, such as Tariq Ramadan and Rashid al-Ghannushi, can be treated in the same context as fiqh al-aqalliyyat texts as long as the proper distinctions are drawn. This is because these writers have a basically positive attitude towards Islamic law as a framework for discussing ethical questions, and many of their main concepts (such as public interest (maslaha) or the "objectives of divine law" (maqasid al-shari'a)) are either drawn from or are shared with fiqh al-aqalliyyat. The less technical writings of Ramadan or Ghannushi are doubtlessly part of a broader conversation within Islamic circles about how traditional of a Muslim one may be while being integrated into a non-Muslim, secular, liberal society. Where these writers disavow the term "fiqh al-aqalliyyat," what they are disavowing, I believe, are (a) a piecemeal approach to life in the West, (b) the implication that life in the West is essentially an aberration, the exception to the rule, and (c) the "minority" mentality. See Tariq Ramadan, *Western Muslims and the Future of Islam* (Oxford: Oxford University Press, 2004), 6. The writings I have in mind as part of a wider conversation overlapping with fiqh al-aqalliyyat are Tariq Ramadan, *Radical Reform: Islamic Ethics and Liberation* (Oxford: Oxford University Press, 2009); Ramadan, *Western Muslims*; Tariq Ramadan, *To Be a European Muslim: A Study of Islamic Sources in the European Context* (Leicester, UK: Islamic Foundation, 1999); and Rashid al-Ghannushi, "al-Islam fi'l-gharb wa 'alaqatuhu bi'l-anzima al-gharbiyya," in Abu Shamala, *Risalat al-Muslimin fi bilad al-gharb* 90.

[12] See e.g. al-Shithri, *Hukm al-luju' wa'l-iqama fi bilad al-kuffar*; Halima, 'Man dakhala diyar ghayr al-muslimin bi-'ahd wa aman ma lahu wa ma "alayhi."

[13] See e.g. 'Abd al-Qadir, *Fiqh al-aqalliyyat al-muslima*; al-Alwani, *Towards a Fiqh for Minorities*; Ibn Bayya, *Sina'at al-fatwa wa-fiqh al-aqalliyyat*; Qaradawi, *Fi fiqh al-aqalliyyat al-muslima*.

than insisting on obligations that are exceedingly difficult to fulfill while living lives in non-Islamic environments.[14]

However, these texts also provide the occasion for more abstract reflection on the general nature of moral relations with non-Muslims[15] and on the proper attitudes toward non-Muslim forms of rule. They are thus a good source for tracking the development of views and doctrines on a variety of questions of interest to non-Muslims (such as attitudes towards secularism) from within the kinds of internal Islamic discourses where non-Islamic institutions, practices, and values are likely to be the subject of long-standing skepticism. These are the kinds of texts where both formal and substantive fidelity to traditional Islamic law is an important value, but also texts whose authors are actively seeking to remain engaged with, and relevant for, lived experience. Fiqh al-aqalliyyat tends to be a discourse where departures from traditional Islamic commitments are not seen as desirable, and certainly not goals in and of themselves,[16] but where creative rethinking often occurs in subtle and pragmatic guises.[17] It is thus an important object of study for those interested in the ideal moral encounter[18] between a public religion like Islam and modern/post-modern secularism.

The downside of focusing on this discourse is that it runs the risk of privileging and overemphasizing the contributions of scholars in the Arab world at the expense of the quotidian practices and attitudes of Muslims actually living under Western secularism.[19] Some might say that it runs the risk of "Orientalizing" Muslims by suggesting that only those discourses in a traditional Islamic garb and in Arabic are sufficiently authentic to warrant consideration as "Islamic" attitudes.[20] The benefit to studying this discourse,

[14] This principle of facilitation (taysir) in matters of personal morality and ritual observance is one of the hallmarks of the fiqh al-aqalliyyat literature. The "taysir motif" is one of the magnets of criticism of the entire fiqh al-aqalliyyat on the part of more conservative scholars for its tendency to make the forbidden permissible, as well as on the part of more liberal scholars (such as Tariq Ramadan) for its tendency to make ethical life amongst non-Muslims appear exceptional and distasteful. To give two well-known controversial examples, Qaradawi has validated the use of interest-bearing mortgages and service in non-Muslim armies even when they are attacking Muslims on the grounds that the minority condition permits exceptions to normal rules on grounds of necessity (darura) or even mere expediency or public interest (maslaha). See Basheer M. Nafi, "Fatwa and War: On the Allegiance of the American Muslim Soldiers in the Aftermath of September 11" (2004) 11 *Islamic Law and Society* 78.

[15] See Andrew F. March, "Sources of Moral Obligation to Non-Muslims in the 'Jurisprudence of Muslim Minorities' (Fiqh al-aqalliyyat) Discourse" (2009) 16 *Islamic Law and Society* 34.

[16] This discourse contrasts with some reformist discourses, which begin with the stated objective of ushering in new methodologies, values, and ways of doing things as a prerequisite for a comprehensive revamping of Islam for modern conditions.

[17] See March, "Sources of Moral Obligation to Non-Muslims in the 'Jurisprudence of Muslim Minorities' (Fiqh al-aqalliyyat) Discourse." Khaled Abou El Fadl suggests that this is very much in keeping with the traditional practice of Islamic law, which:

> creatively responds to the socio-political dynamics of society placed within a specific historical context... [this] creative process is expressed primarily through the subtleties of language, and hence, unless one focuses on the details of the juridical linguistic practice, one would not be able to notice, much less appraise, the dynamics of the legal discourse.

Khaled Abou El Fadl, *Rebellion and Violence in Islamic Law* (Cambridge, MA: Cambridge University Press, 2001), 322–32.

[18] For my notion of an "ideal moral encounter," see Andrew F. March, *Islam and Liberal Citizenship: The Search for an Overlapping Consensus* (Oxford: Oxford University Press, 2009), 5–10.

[19] Although I believe that caution applies here. Many Islamic religious authorities living in Europe and North America are very much part of the fiqh al-aqalliyyat project, and the boundaries between European Islam and Middle Eastern Islam are often hard to identify.

[20] For example, we might focus instead on survey results or anthropological accounts of the attitudes of Western Muslim communities, with "Muslim" here taken to mean nothing more than "culturally Muslim," i.e. bearing a Muslim-sounding name. Or we might look at the views of outright reformers

I believe, is that because these texts emerge from within the mainstream of traditionalist Islamic legal scholarship (itself a spectrum with fuzzy borders), one avoids treating the Islamic ethical tradition in a hasty or functionalist matter, either by downplaying[21] or by exaggerating the gravity of the moral encounter between Islamic political ethics and liberal secularism. This encounter is a complex one, even when specific political antagonisms are bracketed. To claim that all conflicts over public values are merely the shadows on the wall cast by a more fundamental conflict generated by capitalism and Western imperialism is facile and has the effect of depriving Islam of any autonomy as a source of value and motivation. To claim, on the other hand, that all conflicts over public values are the inevitable outcome of allowing "Islam" into a new political space is in turn both apolitical and also unscholarly in its understanding of how religious traditions operate in reality. Focusing on specific religious debates and conversations (of which fiqh al-aqalliyyat and its adjacent discourses are one set which we might study) is a way of taking the ideal moral encounter between Islam and liberalism seriously. Far from "Orientalizing" Muslims, one is merely being precise and disciplined about how one speaks about Islam and Muslims. One does not speak about the Islamic attitude towards secularism, but rather the Islamic attitude towards secularism as manifested in particular discourses that are important to follow.

III. Secularism as an Added Objection to Citizenship in a Non-Muslim State

It is, of course, well-known that amongst world religions, Islam has perhaps the most unequivocal claim to a public, political vision. This is expressed most simply and least controversially in the close identification between political legitimacy and the application of Islamic law. In the post-colonial setting, with the reassertion on the part of Islamists of the need for an Islamic foundation for the state, the rejection of secularism is explicit. Consider the reflections of Yusuf al-Qaradawi:

> For Muslim societies, as Islam is a comprehensive system of worship ('ibada) and legislation (shari'a), the acceptance of secularism means abandonment of shari'a, a denial of divine guidance and a rejection of God's injunctions. It is indeed a false claim that shari'a is not suitable to the requirements of the present age. The acceptance of a legislation formulated by humans means a preference for humans' limited knowledge and experiences over the divine guidance: "Say! Do you know better than God?" (Q. 2:140).

For this reason, the call for secularism among Muslims is atheism and a rejection of Islam. Its acceptance as a basis for rule in place of shari'a is clear apostasy. The silence of the masses in the Muslim world about this deviation has been a major transgression and a clear-cut instance of disobedience which have produced a sense of guilt, remorse, and inward resentment, all of which have generated discontent, insecurity, and hatred among committed Muslims because such deviation lacks legality. We Muslims believe

writing in the West, such as Abdullahi An-Na'im. See Abdullahi Ahmed An-Na'im, *Islam and the Secular State: Negotiating the Future of Shari'a* (Cambridge, MA: Harvard University Press, 2008).

21 My claim is that the tendency to rush into a search for outright Muslim "moderates" or "reformers" runs the risk of downplaying the gravity of the moral encounter if it does not consider how widely held, central, or popular such views are. It risks suggesting that all we need to do is find certain voices claiming that Islam and X (modernity, secularism, human rights) are compatible in order to satisfy ourselves that only radicals or fundamentalists have deep moral objections to modern liberal institutions.

that God is the sole Creator and Sustainer of the Worlds. One Who "... takes account of every single thing" (Q. 72:28); that He is omnipotent and omniscient; that His mercy and bounties encompasses everyone and suffice for all. In that capacity, God revealed His divine guidance to humanity, made certain things permissible and others prohibited, commanded people observe His injunctions and to judge according to them. If they do not do so, then they commit disbelief, aggression, and transgression.[22]

However, the context for the present chapter is that of Muslims living as minorities in existing secular liberal democracies. While one possible Muslim response to life as a minority is the demand that internal Muslim affairs (especially family law and education) be managed along shari'a lines, or that the wider society accommodate legally the sensibilities and sensitivities of Muslims by limiting the freedom to offend through speech and art, the assumption that Muslims are living in a society where Islamic law cannot be generally applied requires Muslim legal and political theorists to think about political life outside of the normal assumptions, categories, and debates of Islamic political and legal traditions.

This, of course, does not mean that the terms of life in those conditions are unproblematic or beyond the concern of religious legal reflection. For Islamic legal doctrine, there are two broad problems with citizenship in non-Muslim liberal states: one, in those states being non-Muslim in character, both socially and politically; two, in those states being liberal and secular in character. As to the distinct ethical problems raised by the former, one can readily find within classical and modern legal discourses prohibitions on submitting to the authority of non-Muslim states, serving in their armies, contributing to their strength or welfare, participating in their political systems and, indeed, even residing within them. These prohibitions are not mere medieval legalisms, but rather reflections of a range of more general Islamic beliefs, including those that Muslims must always strive to live under Islamic law and political authority, that Muslims have obligations of loyalty (perhaps exclusively) to Muslims and Muslim polities, and that non-Muslims are not eligible for relationships of social and political solidarity.[23]

Thus, membership and belonging in any non-Muslim polity is often treated as problematic by Muslim scholars. The question, then, is whether the particular form of liberal secularism found within contemporary European and North American states (*mutatis mutandis*) figures as a mitigating or an aggravating feature of the minority condition. The answer, of course, is "both."[24]

[22] Yusuf al-Qaradawi, *al-Hulul al-mustawrada wa-kayfa janat 'ala Ummatina* (Beirut: Mu'assasat al-'Arif li'l-Matbu'at, 1971), 113–114.

[23] On these topics in classical jurisprudence, see Khaled Abou El Fadl, "Islamic Law and Muslim Minorities: The Juristic Discourse on Muslim Minorities from the Second/Eighth to the Eleventh/Seventeenth Centuries" (1994) 1 *Islamic Law and Society* 141. On the question of participation in a non-Muslim political system, see March, "Sources of Moral Obligation to Non-Muslims in the 'Jurisprudence of Muslim Minorities' (Fiqh al-aqalliyyat) Discourse" 242–58; Wasif Shadid and Sjoerd van Koningsveld, "Religious Authorities of Muslims in the West: Their Views on Political Participation," in W.A.R. Shadid and P.S. van Koningsveld (eds), *Intercultural Relations and Religious Authorities: Muslims in the European Union* (Leuven: Peeters, 2002), 149; and Dilwar Hussain, "Muslim Political Participation in Britain and the 'Europeanisation' of Fiqh" (2004) 44 *Die Welt des Islams* 376.

[24] For the sake of comprehensiveness, it must also be noted that the answer is sometimes "neither." For those scholars and thinkers who side with the tradition in Islamic thought that Muslims may not live in infidel lands, or that if they do live therein they may not integrate into them, neither secularism-as-neutrality nor shared monotheism and Abrahamic fraternity with Jews and Christians point to any possibility for a mitigation of the eternal non-Muslim hostility towards Islam. As an illustration of this view, consider the position of Sayyid Qutb advanced to explain why Muslims must not live in infidel lands if they can avoid it:

Some contemporary scholars do not regard the modern freedoms guaranteed by liberal regimes, and especially the aspiration to neutrality of some liberal states, as a mitigating factor on non-Muslim hostility to Islam. In fact, it is coherently argued that liberal states may in fact be worse for Muslims than avowedly Christian or Jewish states because they relegate religion to the private sphere, banish God from public morality, and give protection to immoral acts, or because of the special regard for "the People of the Book" accorded Christians and Jews in the Qur'an. These views point towards an interest in an overlapping consensus with other conservative, religious doctrines in modern secular societies on either general inclinations (more religion in public) or specific points of doctrine and policy (resistance to legal protection for homosexuality, opposition to abortion, securing funding for religious schools, etc.), given the belief that secularism poses a greater threat to Islam than other faiths.

The obvious flashpoints for evoking (perhaps unavoidable) Islamic scholarly reprobation for the consequences of Western secularism are homosexuality and blasphemy or other offensive speech. Here Qaradawi addresses an online fatwa request (istifta') on the subject of whether "it permissible for Muslims to align themselves with other faith groups to fight against the homosexual movements":

> Together we can stand to confront the enemies of religious faith and those who call for atheism, promiscuity, materialism, abortion, homosexuality, unisex marriages, bloodshed, misappropriation of others' property, and enhancing materialistic trends in man at the expense of his spiritual elevation.... All of us need to stand together as one forum against those who want to ruin humankind by their calls and action and to reduce it from humanity to animalistic levels. Allah Almighty says: (Hast thou seen him who chooseth for his god his own lust? Wouldst thou then be guardian over him? Or deemest thou that most of them hear or understand? They are but as the cattle, nay, but they are farther astray!) (Al-Furqan 25: 43–33)... [W]e witnessed Al-Azhar and the World Muslim League come together with the Vatican to stand as one front during the conference on Population, held in Cairo, in 1994 and in the Women's Conference in Beijing 1995 to oppose the non-religious sentiments, and the attempt of breaking the family ties, destabilizing the natural instincts that Allah Almighty has created to guide human beings to the straight path.[25]

Similar questions are often treated with more abstract reflections on secularism as the root cause of the West's problems:

> If I were asked for a solution [to the problem of secular tolerance for homosexuality]—a solution that deals with this root problem and can at least create a mode helpful to cure all others—, I would believe in my heart as a convinced Muslim that the answer must stem from the totality of metaphysical, legal, mystical, intellectual, and ethical parameters and ethos of Islam. I am sure a convinced Christian or Jew would definitely feel the same about their faith.

> A Muslim is required to show tolerance in dealing with the people of earlier revelations, but he is forbidden to have a relationship of alliance or patronage with them. His path to establish his religion and implement his unique system cannot join with theirs. No matter how kind he is to them, they will never be happy to implement his faith and establish his system. Nor will it stop them from entering other alliances to scheme against and fight the Muslims. It is too naïve to think that we and they can ever join forces to support religion in general against unbelievers and atheists. For whenever the fight is against Muslims, they join forces with the unbelievers and atheists.

Sayyid Qutb, *In the Shade of the Qur'an* (Markfield, Leicestershire: Islamic Foundation, 2001), 144. Khalid 'Abd al-Qadir also insists that the tolerance and decent treatment required towards Jews and Christians does not imply the possibility of a "single front to resist atheism." 'Abd al-Qadir, *Fiqh al-aqalliyyat al-muslima* 646.

[25] IslamOnline.net, "Cooperating with Non-Muslims in Fighting Evil—Ask the Scholar," <http://www.islamonline.net/fatwa/english/FatwaDisplay.asp?>.

. . . I genuinely believe that the moral predicament that our world undergoes is but one manifestation of our acute spiritual crisis. This spiritual crisis, I would argue, is related to two main causes: either the complete disbelief or disregard of the spiritual and metaphysical order of our being, or the alternation of it with another one of lower reality.

Across all three monotheistic faiths—theological, legal, and scriptural particularities set aside, of course—, the key theme is the belief in the centrality of the divine and the consequential surveying of the relations between humankind, God, and the universe.

As a consequence of dismissing God and metaphysical reality, it is but natural for all non-religious worldviews to place humankind in the center of the universe, with all its dispositions, desires, needs, and limitations. That step in itself necessitated either reduction of our reality, and hence morality, to an empirical one—hence the materialist and pragmatic positions coming from atheist or agnostic beliefs; or secular mysticism and spirituality, like all new-age spirituality. . . .

. . . It is also here where I believe the collective efforts of all three traditional monotheistic faiths should come to help humanity's condition in general. All three religions have far more valid answers and guidance that are wisely designed by God with His incomparable knowledge.

Absolutely yes; in the face of secularism, mundane morality, consumerism, crime, and hedonism, the three monotheistic faiths have great influence in relieving our moral dilemma.[26]

Similarly, liberal secularism is often not viewed as making it "possible for two million Muslims to live in Britain and for Islam to thrive[, for] if British society was a religious society as Christianity, in particular Protestantism, would be given preferential treatment and special privileges."[27] Rather,

[i]n constantly trumpeting the idea that all religions are equal, while at the same time showing religion to be irrelevant, the effect is that all religions are made to seem equally unimportant.

The secularists have done their job well. The voice of faith has been made to seem a private matter, a matter of conscience, a matter for the individual alone. In this sense, it has become a generally accepted view in the UK that anyone can believe whatever he wants, as long as he doesn't harm anyone else. It wouldn't really matter if you worshipped a monkey, because religious beliefs, according to this agenda, are all irrelevant.

This has happened very subtly over many years in the UK, but it has been achieved because the secularists have worked very hard at achieving it. . . .

There is much more at stake here than supporting this or that religion. I believe that what is at stake is the very role of faith itself. . . .

It is true that Islam and Muslims are under the spotlight at the moment in the UK. But this is more symptomatic of a general trend.

At the moment it is Islam. But when the media train moves on, it will be another group. As I have said, the secularists have done their job well and all but silenced the Christian voice in Britain. They are now at work on Islam, but there will always be a faith group being targeted. Faith is under attack, not any particular religion.[28]

At times, the argument is not only that social mores and cultural practices will be more permissive than in Muslim societies, but that the problem lies precisely in the liberal legal protections for those Muslims who would revise their conception of the good:

But even more dangerous than [exposure to sin] is that the children of many of these Muslims living amongst the unbelievers have deviated and the parents look at this and find that they are

[26] Reading Islam, Ask About Islam, "Should World Religions Unite Against Immorality?," <http://www.islamonline.net/servlet/Satellite?pagename=IslamOnline-English-AAbout_Islam/AskAboutIslamE/AskAboutIslamE&cid=1173695384292>.

[27] This is the positive interpretation of liberal secularism suggested by the lay Muslim requesting a fatwa (mustafti). Islamonline.net, "Live Dialogue, Is Britain a Secular Society?," <http://www.islamonline.net/livedialogue/english/Browse.asp?hGuestID=ZYwaK5>.

[28] Islamonline.net, "Live Dialogue, Is Britain a Secular Society?." The mufti in this passage is a former Catholic priest turned Muslim scholar, Idris Tawfiq.

unable to do anything about it because the system of these unbelieving states permits sons and daughters to do as they please. Indeed it is the norm that the third generation of Muslims in these countries apostatize from Islam.[29]

Here the implication is that given the choice between different terms of life within a non-Muslim polity, Muslim scholars might prefer some forms of "corporatism" (à la the former Dutch pillar system or the Ottoman millet system), even if this means an advantage for the local religious majority, over a system of universal citizenship where neither a particular religion nor religion in general is advantaged.

In the preceding we have a simple case of Islamic echoes of the familiar conflict between secularism-as-neutrality and the goals which conservative religious citizens might wish to pursue even in a diverse society. That such views exist (and myriad more examples could be offered) should not be surprising, and the above presentation is only meant to reiterate the point that, in the conditions of religious and moral pluralism, it is far from obvious that even religious minorities will prefer the protections of liberal secularism over some form of coalition with other believers.

IV. Secularism as a Redeeming Feature of Liberal Citizenship

In what follows, I will present some alternative, more positive, attitudes toward Western secularism from within the juridical discourse on Muslim minorities. What becomes clear from these examples is that, for those scholars earnestly seeking to find a way for the life of Muslim minorities to be regarded as Islamically just,[30] liberal secularism (secularism as religious neutrality) solves a certain set of problems posed by the Islamic sources.

A. "A secularism for them, but not for us"

The first recurring theme on the question of secularism is that, while secularism is a rejection of God's guidance for Muslims, for Christians (and to a lesser extent, for Jews) it is a natural and logical consequence of both their religion and their experience with clerical rule.

[29] al-Shithri, *Hukm al-luju' wa'l-iqama fi bilad al-kuffar* 5.

[30] As noted above, this reflects the pragmatic nature of fiqh al-aqalliyyat, perhaps consistent more broadly with the Muslim Brotherhood approach to politics. By contrast, the purpose of certain "Salafi" pronouncements is to insist on the fundamental illegitimacy of non-Muslim rule and its irresolvable incompatibility with Islamic commitments. For example, in a 6,000 word fatwa on the US pledge of allegiance, the Assembly of Muslim Jurists of America (AMJA) makes clear that their objections to the pledge are not to any formal iconography or to wording but to the fundamental political commitments at stake:

Islamic objections to the Pledge of Allegiance pertain to the following concepts:

> Absolutely and entirely renouncing and abjuring any allegiance and fidelity to any foreign prince, potentate, state, or sovereignty; Support and defense of the Constitution and laws of the United States of America against all enemies, foreign and domestic; Bearing arms on behalf of the United States when required by the law; Performing noncombatant service in the Armed Forces of the United States when required by the law; Performing work of national importance under civilian direction when required by the law; Declaring on oath, all of the above, taking this obligation freely, without any mental reservation or purpose of evasion; so help me God.
>
> These objections are raised because there is a basic conflict between a Muslim pledging allegiance to Allah and Allah"s Messenger Muhammad ibn Abdullah--peace and blessings of Allah be upon him--as the final prophet of Allah to mankind, and between pledging

In the above-quoted passage by Qaradawi on why secularism is tantamount to apostasy for Muslims, he elaborates on the distinction.

> Secularism may be accepted in a Christian society but it can never enjoy a general acceptance in an Islamic society. Christianity is devoid of a shari'a or a comprehensive system of life to which its adherents should be committed. The New Testament itself divides life into two parts, one for God, or religion, the other for Caesar, or the state: "Render unto Caesar things which belong to Caesar, and render unto God things which belong to God" (Matthew 22:21). As such, a Christian could accept secularism without any qualms of conscience. Furthermore, Westerners, especially Christians, have good reasons to prefer a secular regime to a religious one. Their experience with "religious regimes"—as they knew them—meant the rule of the clergy, the despotic authority of the Church, and the resulting decrees of excommunication and the deeds of forgiveness, i.e. letters of indulgence.[31]

This is an important point to address for some Muslim scholars. In traditional Islamic public law, Jews and Christians, as "People of the Book," were given special rights to live legally under Islamic law while adhering to their ancestral religions. Alongside the arguments that liberal states may in fact be worse for Muslims than avowedly Christian or Jewish states because they relegate religion to the private sphere, banish God from public morality, and give protection to immoral acts, it is sometimes suggested that the reason Muslims may enter into relationships of civil solidarity with non-Muslims in the West is because of the special regard for the "People of the Book" accorded Christians and Jews in the Qur'an, and because the shared foundation of monotheism and Abrahamic fraternity. This, thus, raises the question of whether modern secularism means that Western "post-Christians," having rejected their Book, are no longer People of the Book. This question goes right to the heart of the nature of modern citizenship and has at least two dimensions. First, what kind of moral consensus and commonality is required for civic solidarity? Of course, for modern Muslim scholars and publicists writing on Muslim majority societies, the level of consensus sought is absolute.[32] As seen above, it is perfectly logical for Muslim scholars to conjecture that they may only establish deep bonds of solidarity with non-Muslims who share a sufficient amount of religious commonality, just as liberals conjecture that without a shared conception of justice social unity will be impossible. Second, if it is the case according to Islamic doctrine that Jews and Christians have

> allegiance to any entity, secular or religious, that does not recognize the supreme authority of Allah and Allah"s Messenger--peace and blessings of Allah be upon him—in all affairs that guide and govern man's existence: religious, political, economic and social.

Assembly of Muslim Jurists of America, "Islamic Considerations on the USA Pledge of Allegiance," <http://www.amjaonline.com/en_d_details.php?id=140>.

[31] Qaradawi, *al-Hulul al-mustawrada wa-kayfa janat 'ala Ummatina* 113.

[32] By way of one example, consider Syed Abu'l-Ala al-Mawdudi's famous defense of the traditional Islamic punishment of death for the apostate:

> An organized society which has chosen the form of a state can hardly provide a place within its sphere of activity for people who differ from it in fundamental matters. Differences of lesser significance can more or less be tolerated. But it is very difficult to give people a place in society and make them a part of the state if they completely oppose the foundations on which the order of society and the state are established. In this matter Islam has practiced a degree of tolerance which no other order in the history of the world has ever practiced. . . . But the sole treatment for the person whose hard heart, once transformed, has again hardened [i.e., the apostate] and who demonstrates no capacity whatever to assimilate into society's order is to cast him out. In any case, the value of the individual, however great it be, cannot be great enough to allow the whole order of society to be corrupted because of it. . . . The true position of an apostate is that he by his apostasy provides proof that he not only rejects the foundation for the order of society and state but offers no hope that he will ever accept it in the future. When such a person finds this foundation on which society and the state are

the obligation to uphold their own covenants and that Muslims must then respect them so long as they are doing so,[33] then Western secularism is not only something offensive to the Muslim sensibility, but also a sign of injustice on the part of post-Christians that Muslims would have no choice but to oppose.

Thus, it is significant that even very conservative scholars (i.e. those who reject secularism for Muslim societies) go out of their way to privilege an interpretation of Christianity which would avoid those implications. Similar to Qaradawi's remarks, in addressing the question of whether secular, post-Christian societies are no longer subject to the regard doctrinally due them as "Scripturary" (kitabi) societies, Lebanese Sunni scholar 'Abd al-Qadir argues that the secular nature of the political system is irrelevant because Moses and Jesus were only sent with temporary and partial messages anyway, so the abandoning of them is not something to worry about from an Islamic perspective: "Jesus was not sent to fix relations between rulers and the ruled, or to bring a law or identify the lawful and the prohibited." Thus, present-day secularism is not a departure from Christianity but a consequence of it.[34] These themes and arguments can be found repeated in various discussions.[35]

> constructed to be unacceptable to himself, it will be appropriate for him to move outside its borders. But when he fails to do this, only two ways of dealing with him are possible. Either he should be stripped of all his rights of citizenship and allowed to remain alive or else his life should be terminated. In fact the first form of punishment is worse than the second since in this terrible state "he will neither die nor live" (Qur'an 20:74). Moreover, alive, he becomes a greater danger for society, since his existence will be a permanent plague spreading among the people and a source of fear lest also the other whole and healthy members of society be permeated with his poison. It is therefore better to punish him by death and thereby at one and the same time to put an end to his own and society's misery.... Islam, in contrast to purely secular states, cannot tolerate [the propagation of other faiths] because to allow some creedal or ethical error to emerge under Islamic supervision and protection is to undermine decisively the purpose for which Islam grasps the reins of the nation to direct it. In this matter, purely secular governments certainly function differently than an Islamic government because the purposes of both governments differ. Secular governments allow within their borders the spread of every kind of lie, every creedal deviation and every type of evil act and immorality, as well as every religious perversity also. They offer the purveyors of these various wares a long leash as long as they remain faithful to them, keep on paying taxes to them and avoid any activity which might harm their political authority. Nevertheless, if they detect even the slightest indication of harm to their political authority from these movements, they do not hesitate in the least in declaring them illegal and in crushing them. They function this way because they are not interested in the ethical and spiritual prosperity of God's servants. For them their political authority and their material purposes are everything. But Islam has genuine interest in the spiritual and ethical prosperity of God's servants and for the sake of this prosperity takes the management of the nation into its hands. Hence, as Islam cannot tolerate movements which instigate political dissension or revolution, likewise it cannot tolerate movements which spread moral dissension and creedal deviation.

Syed Abu'l-Ala al-Mawdudi, *Murtadd ki Saza Islami Qanun men* (Lahore: Islamik Pablikeshanz 1953).

[33] Perhaps per Q. 5:48, which reads in full: "For every one of you We have prescribed a path and a way. If God had willed He would have made you all one community, but [He has not done so] that He may test you in what has come to you. So compete with each other in good works." Classical exegetes read the final phrase, which some contemporary thinkers cite in the context of cross-communal solidarity, as merely exhorting each community to implement their own laws and forms of worship, not to extend charity or welfare to one another. See 3 Isma'il ibn 'Umar Ibn Kathir (d. 1373), *Tafsir al-Qur'an al-'Azim* (Bairūt: Dār al-Kutub al-'Ilmīya, 1998), 118; 6 Muhammad ibn Ahmad al-Qurtubi (d. 1273), *al-Jami' li-ahkam al-Qur'an* (Beirut: Dar al-Kutib al-'Ilmiyyah, 1996), 137.

[34] 'Abd al-Qadir, *Fiqh al-aqalliyyat al-muslima* 23–5.

[35] Such as in the internet fatwas of Islam Online. See e.g. Reading Islam, "Islam vs. Secularism," <http://www.islamonline.net/servlet/Satellite?>. Here it is repeated that "secularism originated in Europe as a reaction to the Christian theology, which had forged shackles for the freely enquiring minds of thinking humans. As science and technology developed, the opposition to religion grew and took on several philosophical forms which were secularist in spirit," and that:

B. The secular within the religious

A more common approach to secularism is to note the great value that Islamic law places on the pursuit of worldly goods and, thus, the possibilities of substantive overlap between what secular politics seeks to secure and what Muslims want anyway. The key concepts here are those of "maslaha" (public interest), "maqasid al-shari'a" (the ultimate objectives of the religious law) and the "qawa'id fiqhiyya" (juristic maxims or rules for adjudicating ambiguous or indeterminate cases). These views tend to appear when scholars are confronted with the problem of political participation or contribution to a non-Muslim polity.[36]

The first such argument in favor of participating in non-Muslim governments is articulated by Rashid al-Ghannushi, a Tunisian Islamist opposition leader in exile in Great Britain, based on his reading of the jurisprudence of fourteenth-century Andalusian jurist Abu Ishaq al-Shatibi. The argument advanced is that the Muslim's duty is "to work towards preserving whatever can be preserved of the aims of shari'a," understood broadly as the five basic human interests (al-daruriyyat, or al-kulliyyat, al-khamsa) of life, faith, property, intellect, and lineage. This emphasis on the ultimate purposes of Divine law (maqasid al-shari'a) serves to deflect attention from both particular, technical rulings of Islamic law and the un-Islamic forms of behavior permitted in non-Muslim states. Instead, non-Islamic governments can been seen as sufficiently just because of the general human interests that they protect (for Ghannushi, such interests include both in Muslim majority and minority political contexts, "independence, development, social solidarity, civil liberties, human rights, political pluralism, independence of the judiciary, freedom of the press, or liberty for mosques and Islamic activities"), possibly realizing a legitimate form of governance that he calls "the government of rationale" as opposed to "the government of shari'a."

The crucial measure of Ghannushi's doctrine of how to share political space with non-Muslims is how he addresses the question of social coalitions with non-Muslims. Here, he sides firmly with liberal secular groups:

> Can any Muslim community afford to hesitate in participating in the establishment of a secular democratic system if it is unable to establish an Islamic democratic one? The answer is no. It is the religious duty of Muslims, as individuals and as communities, to contribute to the efforts to establish such a system.[37]

This goes for Muslim minorities in particular, who have no hope of establishing Islamic rule.

> The best option for such minorities is to enter into alliances with secular democratic groups. They can then work towards the establishment of a secular democratic government which will respect human rights, ensuring security and freedom of expression and belief—essential requirements of mankind that Islam has come to fulfill.[38]

> [T]he Christian interpretation [of "Give unto Caesar what is Caesar's"] is that Jesus through this statement was preaching secularism—that is, a separation of religion and politics—as the right policy for his followers. If this was what Jesus meant, Christians who follow religion cannot have any share in the governance or administration of a country.

Rather they should leave the affairs of the state to the whims and fancies of any brutal dictator or unscrupulous politician who assumes power.

[36] What follows is also discussed in March, "Sources of Moral Obligation to Non-Muslims in the 'Jurisprudence of Muslim Minorities' (Fiqh al-aqalliyyat) Discourse."

[37] Rachid Ghannouchi, "Participation in Non-Islamic Government," in Charles Kurzman (ed.), *Liberal Islam: A Sourcebook* (New York: Oxford University Press, 1998), 89, 92.

[38] Ghannouchi, "Participation in Non-Islamic Government" 94. Ghannushi also frequently makes the point that it is secularism and liberalism that have made the West hospitable to Muslims and not Abrahamic fraternity. See al-Ghannushi, "al-Islam fi'l-gharb wa 'alaqatuhu bi'l-anzima al-gharbiyya" 90, 115.

Like Tariq Ramadan, Ghannushi is articulating a self-consciously liberal doctrine of citizenship, and it is not clear what in his above views represents attempts to formulate Islamic doctrine on the basis of a methodology and what are his judgments about what is prudent. The more conservative juridical tradition, however, also contains powerful resources for similar forms of pragmatism. Speaking about Muslim-majority societies, Yusuf al-Qaradawi argues that the basic principle (al-asl) is that it is forbidden to participate in a non-Islamic government, but that there are certain grounds for exception: (a) reducing evil and injustice to the extent one can, (b) committing the lesser of two harms (akhaff al-dararayn), and (c) descending from the higher example to the lower reality.[39] These three grounds for participating are linked to certain general maxims of Islamic jurisprudence (principles which jurists refer to when arriving at a ruling that is not resolved by the authoritative sources[40]), including: "necessity makes the forbidden permissible" (al-darura tubih al-mahzurat); "toil brings about relief" (al-mashaqqa tajlib al-taysir); "no harm should be sustained or reciprocated" (la darar wa la dirar); and "relieve difficulties" (raf' al-haraj). The conditions that Qaradawi imposes on such participation are illuminating. They include: (a) that there be some responsibility, independence and authority, rather than merely being the executor of another's will; (b) that the regime not be characterized by injustice and tyranny, and known for its antagonism to human rights. This means that a Muslim may not participate in dictatorial regimes that tyrannize their populations, but "only in a regime based on democracy which respects human faculties"; and (c) that there be the right to oppose everything that contradicts Islam in a clear way, or at least to refrain from it.[41]

This pragmatic position has deep roots in Islamic legal thinking. While those (such as Ghannushi or Ramadan) seeking to argue for the justness of non-Islamic regimes generally quote Shatibi, those (such as Qaradawi or 'Abd al-Qadir) arguing for a more modest pragmatism refer to the authority of Ibn Taymiyya, namely his view that "the shari'a came to bring about and perfect welfare, and to reduce and negate corruption."[42] Qaradawi refers to this basic consequentialist form of thinking as "fiqh al-muwazanat," or "the jurisprudence of balancing [costs and benefits]."[43] The application of this methodology to our present question results in the fairly anodyne recommendation to Muslim minorities to develop a "disciplined openness and flexibility so that they do not become cramped, isolated and withdrawn from their societies, but rather contribute to them positively, give them the best they have to offer and take from them the best they have to offer. Thus the Islamic community achieves that most difficult balance: preservation without obscurity and participation without assimilation."[44]

This form of justifying political participation in non-Muslim states emphasizes two main themes: The duty to command the right and forbid the wrong, and the possibility of securing benefits (masalih, singular: maslaha) for Muslims. As for the first, there is little more to add to our previous treatment. While there are purely secular wrongs and injustices to be stamped out and some scholars are apt to emphasize them over questions

[39] Yusuf al-Qaradawi, *Min fiqh al-dawla fi'l-Islam* (Beirut: Dar al-Shuruq, 1997), 180.

[40] For an introduction to the place of legal maxims in Islamic law, see Mohammad Hashim Kamali, "Legal Maxims and Other Genres of Literature in Islamic Jurisprudence" (2006) 20 *Arab Law Quarterly* 77.

[41] Qaradawi, *Min fiqh al-dawla fi'l-Islam* 184–5.

[42] 20 Ahmad ibn 'Abd al-Halim Ibn Taymiyya (d. 1283), *Majmu' al-fatawa* (Beirut: Dār al-Fikr, 1980), 55.

[43] See Yusuf al-Qaradawi, *Priorities of the Islamic Movement in the Coming Phase* (Cairo: al-Dār, 2000), 47–55, 243–52.

[44] al-Qaradawi, *Fi fiqh al-aqalliyyat al-muslima* 35.

of religious morality, there is no avoiding the fact that most conservative or traditionalist Muslim scholars (and many pious lay believers) would regard illiberal legislation passed by a non-Muslim legislature which bans certain behavior noxious to a Muslim sensibility (such as offensive or blasphemous speech) as a clear-cut political victory. 'Abd al-Qadir writes that a Muslim can be elected to a non-Muslim legislature, but may not agree to anything that contradicts the law of his Lord and must demand that which that law requires.[45] Yet, within this broad consensus, there are important differences of priority and emphasis; that one can justify participating for other reasons and that one can justify participating even when a regime fails to suppress certain moral "evils" are the reasons for not regarding a scholar's interest in "forbidding wrong" as definitively incompatible with liberal citizenship.

'Abd al-Qadir also gives a particularly succinct summary of the second theme, the argument from maslaha:

> [W]orking within the institutions of unbelief is permissible if it is in defense of basic needs and necessities, or if it is to advance the interests of Islam and Muslims, for example, to combat injustice or to bring about some advantage to the Muslim community within a given country. But if it is to advance a private interest or individual ambitions then it is impermissible.[46]

He invokes another principle of jurisprudence, citing Ibn Taymiyya: "That without which something required (or recommended) cannot be realized, is itself required (or recommended)." (Ma la yatimm al-wajib (al-mustahabb) ila bihi huwa wajib (mustahabb).) The obvious question raised by this statement is what sorts of interests or benefits these scholars are imagining being advanced by political participation. There is strong reason to believe that the reference to maslaha generally signifies an interest in secular, public goods. Abu Hamid al-Ghazali (d. 1111) introduced the concept in its mature form, defining its substance as everything which helps mankind preserve the five necessary interests of life, religion, intellect, property, and lineage.[47] Shatibi in turn writes: "I mean by maslaha that which concerns the subsistence of human life, the completion of man's livelihood, and the acquisition of what his emotional and intellectual qualities require of him."[48] The use of maslaha as an ethico-legal concept obviously requires much more rigorous and technical treatment than there is space for here.[49] However, what is important to establish at this point is that the largely secular implications of the concept of maslaha[50] help answer one of our two main concerns about its use as a justification for political participation in a secular state. That concern is that the conception of welfare advanced by Muslim scholars might involve aims that are themselves incompatible with a secular political order. As opposed to the use of concepts such as "commanding right and forbidding wrong" or "reducing evil in society," the reliance on maslaha generally signifies a pragmatic approach

[45] 'Abd al-Qadir, *Fiqh al-aqalliyyat al-muslima* 618.

[46] 'Abd al-Qadir, *Fiqh al-aqalliyyat al-muslima* 609.

[47] See Felicitas Opwis, "Maslaha in Contemporary Islamic Legal Theory" (2005) 12 *Islamic Law and Society* 188 (2005).

[48] 2 Abu Ishaq al-Shatibi, *al-Muwafaqat* (1997), 20.

[49] In addition to Opwis, "Maslaha in Contemporary Islamic Legal Theory," see Wael B. Hallaq, *A History of Islamic Legal Theories* (1997), and Muhammed Khalid Masud, *Shatibi's Philosophy of Islamic Law* (1995).

[50] Opwis argues that the post-Ghazali legal theorists, most importantly Fakhr al-Din al-Razi, Shihab al-Din al-Qarafi, Najm al-Din al-Tufi, and of course al-Shatibi, all made important methodological and epistemological contributions to clarifying the place of maslaha in Islamic legal theory, but "the constituent elements of the concept did not actually change after al-Ghazali defined them at the end of the 5th/11th century." Similarly, modern polemics have focused on questions of epistemology and juristic methodology rather than the basic substantive meaning of maslaha. Opwis, "Maslaha in Contemporary Islamic Legal Theory" 197.

to the public sphere and an emphasis on goods compatible with a liberal political order. American Muslim scholar Muzammil Siddiqi claims, for example, that "it is in the best maslahah (welfare) of Muslims to participate in the system" because, as minorities,

> they must protect their lives, their properties and their rights to live in peace. In order to protect their own rights and to promote the good things in the society, if it is necessary for them to participate in the political system of non-Islamic states, then it is their duty to do so.[51]

It is also common for scholars to speak about the possibility of using political participation to change specific policies of non-Muslim states. The foreign policy of Western states towards the Islamic world is obviously a common theme.[52] It also cannot be said that most of the scholars we are quoting would in any way object to some domestic political outcomes which are incompatible with dominant understanding of a liberal-secular political order, such as the forms of "internal restrictions" which set limitations on exit from or criticism of one's community. Getting non-Muslim states to recognize Muslim personal law or ban offensive, or blasphemous speech would without a doubt be regarded as enormous victories by fiqh al-aqalliyyat scholars. However, there are two countervailing considerations: that these scholars do not limit the benefits they seek to secure through participation to such incompatible aims, and they do not speak of these incompatible aims as conditions on residence or political participation. For the most part, they have in mind either general conceptions of human welfare (as evidenced above by the emphasis on the secular as the appropriate domain for cooperation with non-Muslims) or Muslim-specific aims that are nonetheless compatible with competitive democracy. For example, there is nothing about using democratic means to direct social spending towards eligible Muslim communities, to secure recognition for religious schools, or even to support foreign policies beneficial to the welfare of Muslims in Muslim-majority countries, which suggests an illegitimately tactical attitude to democracy. Furthermore, in addition to specific policies or outcomes, there is a more interesting tendency to speak of the inherent benefit of being a community that participates politically. 'Abd al-Qadir endorses Qaradawi's sentiments quoted above ("that Muslims do not become cramped, isolated and withdrawn from their societies"), and argues that not participating leads to "marginalization and remaining in darkness."[53] Thus, the focus on Muslim welfare as a justification for participation in secular politics goes beyond mere checklists of desired policies or reforms.

C. Public speech and demands of "profession" matter: secularism as a welcome relaxation of the embrace of civic friendship

The previous two sections have shown a certain willingness to accept post-Christian secularism and to pursue secular goods though non-Muslim political systems. There is a strong tendency, however, to go well beyond this and to argue that the metaphysical and comprehensive restraints non-Muslims impose on themselves make it easier for Muslims to commit to the right level of solidarity and community with unbelievers.

[51] IslamOnline.net, "Muslims Participating in the US Local Councils," <http://www.islamonline.net/fatwa/english/FatwaDisplay.asp?hFatwaID=62236>.

[52] This is obviously a theme of countless texts, but Monzer Kahf's fatwa is interesting because it uses the question of US foreign policy to emphasize the necessity of civic involvement. IslamOnline.net, "Refusing to Pay Taxes to the US Due to its Anti-Muslim Policy," <http://www.islamonline.net/fatwa/english/FatwaDisplay.asp?hFatwaID=70581>.

[53] 'Abd al-Qadir, *Fiqh al-aqalliyyat al-muslima* 614.

The problem being solved in these arguments is the oft-cited obligation to avoid relationships of loyalty, friendship, or clientage (muwalah/wala') with non-Muslims personally and with non-Islamic forms of legal and political authority. A series of Qur'anic verses seem to prohibit this, including 3:28,[54] 3:118,[55] 4:139,[56] 4:144,[57] 5:51,[58] 5:80–81,[59] and 60:1,[60] and Qur'anic exegetes in the classical and modern period have interpreted these verses to cover a range of relationships, from legal clientage to personal friendship to political loyalty.[61] The claim is that loyalty and affiliation (wala') are exclusively between believers, while the attitude towards unbelievers is one of disassociation or moral non-obligation (bara'). Salafi and other traditionalist views that are opposed to affirming citizenship in non-Muslim polities, or even residing within them, will ultimately refer to this basic moral principle, and addressing it is crucial for any scholar seeking to theorize and theologize a permanent and principled Muslim presence in non-Muslim political space.

A tradition of contextualizing the wariness over excessive muwalah with non-Muslims extends back to the beginning of the twentieth century. In his exegesis of the Q. 3:28, the early Syrian-born scholar Rashid Rida (d. 1935) says that only

> those who are without knowledge and interpret the Qur'an whimsically claim that the verse does not permit Muslims to ally themselves or come to agreement with others, even if this is in their interest and despite the fact that the Prophet himself made alliances with certain polytheists. In fact, some religious zealots claim ignorantly that this verse forbids any cooperation or association with them, or trusting them in any matter at all.[62]

In opposition to this view, Rida argues that there are three elements to a proper interpretation of the ban on muwalah. The first is that, as with the verses on war and fighting, they refer strictly to those non-Muslims who aggress against and fight Muslims, emphasizing that the circumstances of revelation (asbab al-nuzul) of this and the other muwalah verses are the betrayal of the Muslim community by Muslims to Meccan pagans who were engaged in active combat with Muslims.[63] Decisive for him in this judgment are

[54] "Let not the believers take the infidels for their allies in preference to the believers—for who does this has nothing to do with God—unless it be to protect yourselves from them in this way. God warns you about Himself and the final goal is to God."

[55] "O you who have believed! Do not take for your intimates other than your own kind. They will continually cause you turmoil and love anything that will distress you. Loathing has already come forth from their mouths and what is concealed in their breasts is even greater. We have made the signs clear to you if you will use your reason."

[56] "Those who take unbelievers as friends rather than believers: Are they looking for honor amongst them? All honor is with God."

[57] "O you who have believed! Do not take as friends unbelievers rather than believers. Do you want to give God a clear proof against you?"

[58] "O you who have believed, do not take Jews and Christians as friends for they are friends to each other. And who becomes friends with them becomes one of them. Verily God does not guide a wrong-doing people."

[59] Can you see many of them allying with those who disbelieve? So vile indeed is what their passions make them do that God has condemned them and in suffering shall they remain. For if they truly believed in God and the Prophet and all that was bestowed on them from on high they would not take unbelievers for their allies, but many of them are iniquitous.

[60] O you who have believed! Do not take My enemies and your enemies as friends, offering them affection while they have denied what Truth has come unto you, driving away the Messenger of God and yourselves because you believe in God your Lord. If you have gone forth to struggle in my cause and longing for my blessing do you secretly hold affection for them? For I know all that you may conceal as well as what you do openly. And who does so has erred from the path.

[61] See 'Abd al-Qadir, *Fiqh al-aqalliyyat al-muslima* 626; 2 Ibn Kathir *Tafsir al-Qur'an al-'Azim* 390.

[62] Muhammad Rashid Rida, *Tafsir al-Manar*, vol. 3 (Beirut: Dar al-Kutb al-Ilmiyya, 1973), 277.

[63] Cf. Wahba al-Zuhayli, *al-Tafsir al-wasit* (*Damascus*: *Dar al-Fikr* 2001), v. 1, 186.

verses 60:7–8 ("God does not forbid you from dealing justly and equitably with those who do not fight you for your religion nor expel you from your homes, for God loves the equitable") and the fact that the Prophet himself established bonds of friendship, trust, and alliance with various non-Muslim individuals and states both before and after his migration from Mecca.[64] The second, related point that Rida emphasizes is that Q. 3:28, 4:139 and 4:144 all refer to taking non-Muslim allies rather than or in preference to believers: min dun al-mu'minin. Thus, what becomes forbidden is allying with them at the expense of Muslims and Muslim interests.[65]

Finally, Rida understands the reference to muwalah as approving of non-Muslims' unbelief and allying with them in pursuit of these false religious aims.[66] Encapsulating these latter two points, he quotes his mentor Muhammad 'Abduh, who argued that what is forbidden is anything that results in abandonment (khidhlan) of religion, harm (idha') to its people, or damage (ida'a) to their interests. "But what opposes this, such as trade or other social interactions of a secular [dunyawi: this-worldly] nature, is not included amongst that which is forbidden because it does not involve any opposition to God and His Apostle or any opposition or resistance to their religion."[67]

Contemporary Mauritanian scholar (and, along with Qaradawi, a leading scholar of the European Council for Fatwa and Research) 'Abd Allah Ibn Bayya notes that "wala' is any firm bond which ties people together in a special, close, and intimate relationship which give rise to obligations, rights and duties." Note first that there is a certain reversal of the traditional order of causality. Whereas the traditional question is whether certain relationships are eligible for wala' (and the obligations it implies) in the first place, Ibn Bayya's point of departure is that certain such relationships of wala' already exist and that certain moral obligations are thus unavoidable. He then makes the distinction between various types of such relationships, the first being based on shared creed, the second on familial ties, and the third on contract.

> The highest and most exalted of these loyalties is that based on creed which includes faith in basic pillars of religion, the shared practice of rituals and adherence to moral virtue. This relationship of loyalty is not incompatible with loyalty to a homeland which binds people together into a contract of citizenship and defends its territory against aggression.[68]

Further on, he suggests that loyalties be seen as concentric circles, or as steps in a pyramid, with religious loyalty at the summit, "but which does not exclude loyalty to a nation or homeland."[69]

Ibn Bayya clearly finds modern, liberal conceptions of citizenship and political community conducive to Islamic modes of justification of the minority condition. If anything, Ibn Bayya is more explicit in his endorsement of contemporary European norms for European Muslims than other scholars contributing to fiqh al-aqalliyyat. He begins a lengthy discussion entitled "On Citizenship" by describing the various components of the modern understanding of national citizenship and how it differs from pre-modern ones: It expresses a reciprocal, mutual (mutabadil) relationship between individuals living on a territory not necessarily bound by descent, religion, or common

[64] This argument is repeated almost verbatim in Yusuf al-Qaradawi, *Fatawa mu'asira* (Kuwait: Dār al-Qalam, 2003), 193.

[65] This argument is also noted in Ibn Bayya, *Sina'at al-fatwa wa-fiqh al-aqalliyyat* 307.

[66] Again, this exact point is advanced in Qaradawi, *Fatawa mu'asira* 194.

[67] Rida, *Tafsir al-Manar* vol. 3, 288 (emphasis added).

[68] Ibn Bayya, *Sina'at al-fatwa wa-fiqh al-aqalliyyat* 292–3. Significantly, this scholar is known to be particularly close spiritually and intellectually with an important group of scholars operating in California at the Zaytuna Institute, namely Hamza Yusuf and Zaid Shakir.

[69] Ibn Bayya, *Sina'at al-fatwa wa-fiqh al-aqalliyyat* 304.

memory; its framework is a constitution and system of laws; it is similar to a voluntary association of cooperation based on contractual belonging; and those belonging to it today have the same rights as the longest-standing members.[70] His interpretive understanding of liberal conceptions of citizenship is thus nearly identical to the liberal self-description. Ibn Bayya even cites Jürgen Habermas' conception of constitutional patriotism, or "the feelings of an individual towards his own membership in a civil society established on the basis of participation in certain basic values," as the ideal expression of the modern conception of "citizenship as a voluntary bond joined within national horizons and ruled by a constitution" and suggests that this conception "is the most important bridge to the respect and acceptance of religious values in all human societies which is compatible with Islam's conception of human coexistence. A Muslim doesn't find an objection to it but rather cooperates with it."[71]

Thus, Ibn Bayya's point about the compatibility of multiple loyalties is quite specific and interesting for this study, for his statement (quoted above) that religious loyalty does not exclude national loyalty continues by adding the qualification "according to the conception of citizenship to which we have pointed," i.e. the modern liberal conception, "for it is not incompatible with religious loyalty insofar as the contract of citizenship does not imply leaving one's religion, abandoning rituals or limitations on the freedom for a Muslim to live his faith." Ibn Bayya's endorsement of this conception of citizenship is not only negative, however. He argues that the "circle" that comprises the compact of citizenship provides much good that is "demanded by religion and desired by nature," including:

> The right to life, justice, equality, freedoms, protection of property, protection against arbitrary imprisonment and torture, the right to social security for the poor, elderly and ill, cooperation between individuals in society for the general welfare, as well as all of the duties and obligations which follow, such as paying taxes, defending the homeland against aggression, obeying the law and upholding the contract of citizenship all of which falls under the religious obligation to be loyal to contracts and their requirements which itself falls under loyalty to religion: "O you who believe! Fulfill all contracts."[72]

Of course, these goods which are "demanded by religion" and are thus encompassed by (the broader circle of) Islamic religious commitments are clearly not only secular ("political" in the Rawlsian sense) but also meant to evoke liberal self-descriptions. He is even more explicit than this, though. He takes pains to enumerate the

> great values of secularism ['almaniyya] and neutrality [al-muhayida] which are regarded positively, including: (1) respect for convictions; (2) neutrality between religions; (3) the recognition of both individual and collective human rights and the state's protection of them; (4) the right of disagreement, diversity and transformation of the characteristics of individuals and groups; (5) and the right of access to courts to realize and enforce one's rights, the setting of obligations on individuals with respect for law, paying taxes by way of participation in national efforts to construct institutions, and defense against aggression.[73]

Finally, he defends secularism against some of its Muslim critics, who put forward an interpretation of secularism as a system which "departs from neutrality and interferes in the particular characteristics of peoples and nations, and functions as a tool of control over convictions." This, he submits, is a "distortion of the basic meaning of secularism

[70] Ibn Bayya, *Sina'at al-fatwa wa-fiqh al-aqalliyyat* 302.
[71] Ibn Bayya, *Sina'at al-fatwa wa-fiqh al-aqalliyyat* 303.
[72] Ibn Bayya, *Sina'at al-fatwa wa-fiqh al-aqalliyyat* 304.
[73] Ibn Bayya, *Sina'at al-fatwa wa-fiqh al-aqalliyyat* 305.

which [does not require] submission to a single comprehensive ideological trend which might wish to impose its particular concepts constructed on its own prejudices."[74]

So here we have a quite unmistakable endorsement of secularism and citizenship on liberal terms as a system which is beneficial for Muslim minorities and which is asserted to be compatible with Islamic commitments. It is also noteworthy that this endorsement comes not from a savvy media figure living in a Western country like Tariq Ramadan but a senior, traditionalist Maliki religious scholar from Mauritania writing in Arabic; these passages cannot be dismissed as rhetoric for consumption within some "cross-cultural" or "ecumenical" dialogue.

However, it is appropriate to ask just what is "Islamic" about these arguments. As I suggested in the introduction to this article, an "Islamic argument" is not just the judgment or opinion of someone with a Muslim name or writing about Islamic themes. Of course, in the banal sense, "Islam" is just what its adherents believe it to be; however, this does not exclude a search for more concrete Islamic doctrinal demonstrations or efforts to fit these kinds of statements of judgment into broader theories of Islamic moral commitment. This search does not imply the assumption that the only authentic Islamic beliefs or values are those which can be shown to have direct textual derivation, but rather the assumption that Islamic law and ethics (like certain Western ethical discourses) are not just assertions of opinion or authority but rather "justificatory projects" which involve standards of argumentation and demonstration that establish how a moral claim can be evaluated, justified and carried from one discursive situation to another.

Ibn Bayya does not fail to draw on Qur'anic verses, although it is not obvious that they are causing the full extent of the beliefs presented above. The first verse used to ground his robust affirmation of the virtues of secularism is, as quoted above, Q. 5:1: "O you who believe! Fulfill all contracts." However, although the obligation to uphold contracts can give strong reasons for honoring secular systems, it is not clear where it gives any particular reasons to value all of the goods provided for by secular systems or, more precisely, to choose a system which limits coercive social action to these goods. A second verse introduced seems more apropos: "And never let your hatred of people who would bar you from the Inviolable House of Worship lead you into the sin of aggression: but rather help one another in furthering kindness [al-birr, which can imply religious devoutness as well as charity] and God-consciousness [al-taqwa], and do not help one another in furthering evil and enmity."[75] As Ibn Bayya notes, this verse clearly refers to the relationship with the Meccan polytheists with whom the Muslims were at war, "so how could it not permit [cooperation] with peaceful citizens?"[76] It is clear how verses such as these could give warrant to the civic principle of cooperation in worldly matters, possibly on grounds of solidarity (this verses resurfaces often in discussions of political participation in non-Islamic systems), but this still seems quite remote from the enthusiasm displayed by Ibn Bayya for secularism, neutrality, and modern citizenship. Why, for example, would this verse not also ground cooperation with Jewish and Christian fellow monotheists against strict secularism and all of the equal liberties it has been shown to protect ("...help one another in furthering kindness [al-birr] and God-consciousness [al-taqwa]...")?

Thus, another approach for Ibn Bayya is to step back from the texts and simply note the substantive overlap in broader values and aims. After enumerating the "great values of secularism and neutrality" (the five points quoted above), he observes that "all of this

[74] Ibn Bayya, *Sina'at al-fatwa wa-fiqh al-aqalliyyat* 306.
[75] Q. 5:2.
[76] Ibn Bayya, *Sina'at al-fatwa wa-fiqh al-aqalliyyat* 305.

does not contradict the great values to which the revealed religions called, especially Islam, which calls to kindness, affection and human brotherhood [al-birr wa'l-mahabba wa'l-ukhuwa al-insaniyya]" and that devotion to one's homeland and fellow citizens is validated by both reason and revelation.[77] Here it is hard not to recall Rawls' claim that, even without explicit metaphysical grounding, the values of fair social cooperation are simply "very great values" that will have intuitive appeal for persons who enjoy them.[78] Although it does not resolve the concern expressed above about concrete Islamic metaphysical grounding for such principles, it is noteworthy to hear an echo of these claims in an otherwise fairly technical work of modern Islamic jurisprudence. While Ibn Bayya does not elaborate on this here, we can recall from above the efforts to fit the pursuit of purely secular, worldly goods into a larger and longer-standing Islamic conception of the good and the legitimate purposes of law and social cooperation (to wit, the tradition of speculating on the "purposes of shari'a" (maqasid al- shari'a)).

The final perspective on the question of loyalty and belonging within a secular context that Ibn Bayya introduces by way of response to (unnamed) Islamic skeptics is what we might call the "no prohibition" ('adam al-tahrim) argument, although he chooses to frame it in terms of the obligation on Muslims to avoid evil. He begins by noting that evil has its degrees and ranks, with the evil of losing religion entirely at the top, closely followed by the evil of participating in sins and prohibited acts. The acts of forming bonds of loyalty and affection with non-Muslims only rise to the rank of an evil to be avoided when they come at the expense of such bonds with Muslims—min dun al-mu'minin.[79] Once again, he repeats his basic point that the very extensive and incontrovertible obligations that Muslims have to one another are not:

> a suspended wall keeping out all secular [dunyawi: this-worldly, mundane] relationships with other people which do not impinge upon or attack the foundations of belief; nay, cooperation with people to advance common interests [masalih] and repel harm, the mutual exchange with them of affection and cooperation with them in accordance with the law of morality is all in keeping with the words of the Exalted "speak goodness unto people."[80]

This debate finds a slightly more precise and doctrinally systematic elaboration in 'Abd al-Qadir's treatise on fiqh al-aqalliyyat. He concurs with Rida that the muwalah verses are not absolute in the sense of applying to both peaceful and warring unbelievers, but that "God has prescribed hostility and antagonism only to those who fight God, His Apostle and the believers. There is no prohibition on friendship with unbelievers who do not harm believers."[81] He arrives at this position for reasons identical to Rida's (and Ibn Bayya's[82]): the verses all emphasize non-Muslim aggression and the idea of befriending them "in exclusion of the believers" (min dun al-mu'minin); the Prophet himself turned to non-Muslims for help; and other generally held rulings, such as the permissibility of marrying Christian and Jewish women, show that the ban on befriending non-Muslims cannot be general in application.

[77] Ibn Bayya, *Sina'at al-fatwa wa-fiqh al-aqalliyyat* 305.

[78] Rawls, *Political Liberalism* 139, 157, 169, 218.

[79] Ibn Bayya, *Sina'at al-fatwa wa-fiqh al-aqalliyyat* 307. He cites the exegesis of Q.3:28 of twentieth-century Tunisian scholar Muhammad al-Tahir ibn 'Ashur (d. 1973) as his authority for these views. Ibn 'Ashur is interesting as a modern exponent and theorist of the doctrine of "the purposes of shari'a" (maqasid al-shari'a) developed in the medieval period by al-Ghazali, al-Shatibi and others.

[80] Ibn Bayya, *Sina'at al-fatwa wa-fiqh al-aqalliyyat* 308.

[81] 'Abd al-Qadir, *Fiqh al-aqalliyyat al-muslima* 630.

[82] "The disassociation [bara'a] discussed [in surat al-Tawba of the Qur'an] is directed at the polytheists in a limited, restricted context connected to treaties, war and peace." Ibn Bayya, *Sina'at al-fatwa wa-fiqh al-aqalliyyat* 301.

'Abd al-Qadir's remarks are interesting, however, because he makes more of an effort to consider what forms of alliance are permitted and to apply these views to a contemporary political context. Therein, we encounter what are by now rather familiar views. In terms of alliance between political entities, he writes that there must be an overwhelming need for this and the "word of unbelief" may not be dominant, but that alliance is "not muwalah unless it is to the benefit of the unbelievers and their word is ascendant. Such a situation is humiliation for religion and its adherents." Non-Muslim lands are permissible as refuges if Muslims are in danger and no other Muslims are in a position to help, as with the case of those whom Muhammad sent to Abyssinia during the first Meccan period. Within this context it is permissible to cooperate with them in the spheres of economics, science/knowledge, and even military "coordination" (tansiq) under the supervision of Muslim authorities. This covers also treating unbelievers with kindness (al-ihsan, bi'l-lutf), tolerating them, being charitable, hospitable and equitable towards them, exchanging gifts, loaning and borrowing, visiting them, etc.[83]

Possibly drawing from 'Abduh's and Rida's treatment, he reserves the term muwalah for situations in which there is a form of setback, subjugation, disappointment (khidhlan) for religion, harm to its people and a neglect of their interests, as well as an aggrandizement of unbelievers and a strengthening of them over Muslims, without regard to whether the unbelievers in question are peaceful or warring. This can happen in two ways: (a) being pleased with their unbelief or having affection for them because of it; or (b) "relying" on them.

The first, (a), involves associating too intimately with them on a religious basis, ascribing truth to their doctrine or seeing no difference between it and Islam in regards to their respective truth-claims. "This includes approving of their doctrines or religious rituals, or ascribing truth to them, as well as aiding them in ways which strengthen and affirm them in their unbelief. This results in a defeat for religion and belief." He refers to this, quoting Ibn Taymiyya, as "muwalah bi'l-qalb"—"allying one's heart [to them]"—and emphasizes that the only hatred a Muslim feels is towards what the unbeliever holds by way of error and idolatry, not towards him personally.[84] However, various forms of special consideration, approval, and recognition of unbelievers with good characters/morals, or personal relations with unbelieving children, wives, or other relatives, do not constitute muwalah.

> The second, (b), involves not merely forming bonds of trust with unbelievers, but being pliable or submissive to them, flattering them, being obsequious, etc., as well as asking them for help or allying with them against Muslims, imitating them, or aggrandizing them and spreading their doctrines and ideas.[85] The crucial element for him and others is clearly how intimately linked the political and the religious are in a given alliance or friendship. For 'Abd al-Qadir,tolerance consists in inter-personal treatment, not in the doctrinal concept or in the social system. Good treatment does not mean loyalty or assistance in religion, or recognition that the religions revealed before Muhammad's prophecy are accepted by God and that Islam can stand with them in a single front against atheism.[86]

Others have also recently interpreted the ban to refer to adopting unbelievers' characteristics related to their religion, doctrines, beliefs or rituals, not as neighbors or citizens.[87]

[83] For this paragraph, see 'Abd al-Qadir, *Fiqh al-aqalliyyat al-muslima* 634–5.

[84] 'Abd al-Qadir, *Fiqh al-aqalliyyat al-muslima* 637.

[85] 'Abd al-Qadir, *Fiqh al-aqalliyyat al-muslima* 638–9.

[86] 'Abd al-Qadir, *Fiqh al-aqalliyyat al-muslima* 646.

[87] Mustafa al-Tahhan, "al-Muslim al-da'iya yuhsan al-ta'amul ma' al-muslim wa-ghayr al-muslim," in Abu Shamala, *Risalat al-Muslimin fi bilad al-gharb* 283 (citing Qaradawi).

There are at least two very strong reasons for arguing that secularism, as understood by political liberalism, comes as close as possible to avoiding the dilemmas of excessive loyalty and public "profession" which Islamic theorists find unacceptable.

The first main condition which was seen to constitute the unacceptable form of muwalah was the forming of political alliances to the exclusion of (min dun) and in opposition to fellow Muslims. Mustafa al-Tahhan, for example, was cited above as having no objection to living with non-Muslims as neighbors and citizens, but (citing Qaradawi's authority) "it is necessary that a Muslim's loyalty not be to another community at the expense of his own." The second condition was if Muslims were required to ally with non-Muslims in expressly religious or doctrinal matters, advancing the aims or prominence of another creed.

Political liberalism can advance a case that requires neither of these from Muslim citizens. Even in cases where a Muslim entity or force is clearly the aggressor against a Muslim's state of citizenship, one can argue that the liberal state can in good conscience accommodate the Muslim citizen's desire not to kill fellow Muslims.[88] As to the second condition, we again have reason to point to the advantage of political liberalism's commitment to neutrality and "epistemic abstinence." In disavowing any claim to metaphysical truth as the basis for justice, in requiring of citizens no such affirmations in order to participate politically, and in establishing no collective goals that require adherence to a controversial metaphysical doctrine, political liberalism can retort that it requires of Muslim citizens no statement whatsoever about the truth or superiority of any one religion, doctrine, or way of life. Given that Muslim jurists are prepared to allow residence even in states that exhibit no such restraint, their very discourse on muwalah reveals Islam-specific reasons why Muslims should be more willing to take a step beyond resident alienage towards citizenship in a politically liberal state than in any other non-Muslim regime.[89]

With this theoretical perspective, we can now return to the question of political participation. The discussions surrounding this question are particularly supportive of the view that a politically liberal regime is best placed to gain the support of non-liberal communities. While we have encountered the view that the secularism of liberal states poses a challenge for Muslim loyalty to those states, an equally common view—introduced above in the discussion of the "muwalah verses"—is that the religious neutrality of liberal political institutions alleviates Muslim concerns about offering loyalty to non-Islamic comprehensive, metaphysical doctrines.

In a fatwa by Texas-based American Muslim scholar Mohamed El-Moctar al-Shinqiti, he writes:

> Taking part in the US elections... is not a sign of affiliation [muwalah] to the polytheists, nor is it a kind of support for the oppressors... [J]udging parliaments to be gatherings of disbelief and polytheism is inappropriate, as this does not take into account the complicated nature of such parliaments. The US Congress, for instance, is not a religious organization, as the American constitution neither supports a certain religion nor restricts another. The US Congress is not, thus, a gathering of disbelief, even though its members are disbelievers. Also, it is not a gathering of belief, even if there are Muslim members in it. It is a neutral political body in relation to matters of religion, according to the American constitution.

[88] I have argued for what I regard as the "equilibrium" between the concerns of political liberalism and Islamic law on these matters in March, "Sources of Moral Obligation to Non-Muslims in the 'Jurisprudence of Muslim Minorities' (Fiqh al-aqalliyyat) Discourse" Ch. 4, 135 (chapter entitled "Identifying Equilibrium: An Ideal-Typical Islamic Doctrine of Citizenship"); and Andrew F. March, "Liberal Citizenship and the Search for an Overlapping Consensus: The Case of Muslim Minorities" (2006) 34 *Philosophy and Public Affairs* 373.

[89] This interpretation of how the Islamic conception of loyalty bears on the question of citizenship is, in fact, quite commonplace amongst the better-known neo-classical scholars active in the West.

The US Congress can only tackle issues related to public welfare, which a Muslim is enjoined to participate in achieving, whether for the favor of Muslims inside or outside America, or even in relation to non-Muslims.[90] Sheikh Muhammad Al-Hanooti, a member of the North American Fiqh Council, echoes these views:

> In the US, religion is not a priority in politics. On the contrary, politicians are secular in demonstrating what they are targeting. Of that secularism, we have perhaps more than 60% of our welfare and interests to be run through a polling system. Schooling, sanitation, zoning, social services, police, court, medication, finance, business, sports, recreation, etc. are run by people that are elected to office.... Are you going to tell me that I am loyal or giving allegiance [muwalah] to the kuffar [infidels] because I want to lead myself in the way that can get a school for my children, good sanitation for my neighborhood or good cooperation with the police to protect me?[91]

This is also the official position of the European Council for Fatwa and Research, which uses the example of the Prophet's behavior in cooperating with non-Muslims, to argue that:

> [i]t is permissible for Muslims to engage with non-Muslims in commercial transactions, peace treaties and covenants according to the rules and conditions prevalent in those countries....
>
> Mutual cooperation in worldly affairs goes far to encompass all citizens who share a common destiny, neighborhood and sometimes kinship. This may be extended to include economic and commercial fields.[92]

Furthermore, as to the application of this principle to democratic elections,

> elections in the modern world systems have become a means through which people choose candidates and judge the programs they adopt. Muslims living in such societies enjoy rights and are bound to do some duties. If they fail to meet the duties obligated on them, they are no more entitled to receive the rights, for the rights meet the duties.
>
> Thus, Muslims' participation in elections is a national duty; in addition it falls under cooperation on that which is good and righteous for society and warding off harms from it.[93]

This awkwardly articulated position in fact probably goes well beyond the most common liberal conceptions of civic duty in the direction of positive participation.

V. Conclusion

It is not surprising that there should be both favorable and unfavorable views towards Western secularism in a discourse like fiqh al-aqalliyyat. This is, after all, a fundamentally pragmatic discourse, rather than a systematic-philosophical one. Internal consistency and overall coherence may be valued, but they are valued alongside many other things, including the struggle for the adherence and support of lay Muslims. While mainstream scholars who consume and contribute to fiqh al-aqalliyyat take great care to play by the rules of post-9/11 (and post-3/11 and post-7/7) European and American religious politics, the fact is that the costs for publicly—yet non-violently—opposing homosexuality and blasphemous speech are relatively low (isn't this what we expect of religious figures?), and

[90] Sheikh Mohamed El-Moctar al-Shinqiti, IslamOnline.net, "Muslims' Participation in US Elections," <http://www.islam-online.net/fatwaapplication/englishdisplay.asp?hFatwaID=106769>.

[91] Muhammad Al-Hanooti, IslamOnline.net, "Voting in a Majority non-Muslim Country," <http://www.islamonline.net/fatwa/english/FatwaDisplay.asp? >.

[92] IslamOnline.net, "Elections in non-Muslim Countries: Role of Muslims," <http://www.islamonline.net/servlet/Satellite?pagename=IslamOnline-English-Ask_ >.

[93] IslamOnline.net, "Elections in non-Muslim Countries: Role of Muslims."

the costs with the laity of supporting them in the name of some higher commitment to secularism and neutrality possibly very high.

Indeed, the costs of opposing "secularism" at large in the name of natural law or higher spirituality are also not that high, certainly not the United States. Why, then, the elaborate theoretical apparatus that emerges in fiqh al-aqalliyyat to show that religious neutrality is something which Muslims should endorse? The fact is that public religious neutrality solves a great problem for Muslim scholars, namely that of the appearance of excessive loyalty and subjugation to none other than an alien religious or comprehensive doctrine. A frequent critical remark on Rawls' "political-not-metaphysical" turn was that merely altering the public language of justification will do nothing to assuage religious citizens, since it leaves in place the same set of institutions, laws, and fundamental secular bias in the public language of justification.[94] Indeed, as seen in the cases of homosexuality and speech, there is nothing stopping religious citizens from opposing policies they detest, and even mobilizing anti-secular language to do so.

However, it does not follow that the concern with the symbolic, with the "demands of profession" we place on fellow citizens, is shallow or mere hiding of the comprehensive liberal ball. What we have seen is that often religious scholars are as much concerned with the language employed by a state—are Muslims being asked to profess something contrary to Islam or even to endure quietly the glorification of a contrary truth?—as they are with the actual policies enforced. Religious jurists are experts at redescribing reality so as to avoid violations of the law (see the above discussion on Qaradawi's infamous fatwa permitting service in the US-Afghanistan war); secularism removes humiliating realities which are exceedingly hard to redescribe. At the same time, it is undeniable that some of these scholars perceive in liberal neutrality many of the same virtues that its theorists insist on: its desire to accommodate the consciences of as many citizens as possible, the desire to include minorities, and accountability for the secular welfare of those subject to it.

94 Will Kymlicka, for example, writes that, because adopting autonomy as a purely political value has effects on the private pursuit of the good that liberalism is supposed to endorse Rawls' strategy of endorsing autonomy only in political contexts, rather than as a general value, does not succeed. Accepting the value of autonomy for political purposes enables its exercise in private life, an implication that will only be favored by those who endorse autonomy as a general value. Rawls has not explained why people who are communitarians in private life should be liberals in political life. Will Kymlicka, *Multicultural Citizenship: A Liberal Theory of Minority Rights* (Oxford: Clarendon Press, 1995), 162.

PART V

THE CONFRONTATION BETWEEN SECULARISM AND RELIGION IN SPECIFIC CONTEXTS: EDUCATION AND FREE SPEECH

17

The Ultra-Orthodox Community in Israel and the Right to an Exclusively Religious Education

Gila Stopler

I. Introduction

The right of parents, and of the communities in which they live, to educate their children according to their own beliefs is a fundamental one, and educational pluralism is an essential aspect of respect that states must show to their diverse citizenry. Accordingly, section 18 of the ICCPR states that: "The States Parties to the present Covenant undertake to have respect for the liberty of parents... to ensure the religious and moral education of their children in conformity with their own convictions." Nevertheless, while respect for parents' and communities' decisions with regard to the form and content of their children's education should be the rule, there are instances in which the liberal democratic state is allowed and indeed required to assert its authority in educational matters in order to protect the rights and interests of others as well as the public's interests. One such case which I wish to discuss in this chapter is the case of the education of ultra-Orthodox boys within the ultra-Orthodox (UO) community in Israel.

In 2008 the Israeli parliament passed a law entitled Unique Cultural Educational Institutions Act (the Act).[1] The Act legalized an existing, albeit until that time illegal situation, which has continued for many years, in which UO high schools for boys did not teach their students any part of the mandatory state core curriculum, but were nevertheless given generous state funding. These schools have for years restricted their curriculum strictly to religious studies, since according to UO ideology the study of the Torah is every man's highest obligation and is the equivalent of all other religious commandments.[2] The Act was passed in order to circumvent the expected outcome of petitions to the Israeli Supreme Court against the illegal funding of UO schools that do not teach the core curriculum.[3] In the explanatory notes for the proposed Act it was stated that the purpose of the act is to enable the existence of the educational institutions of the UO community and similar unique cultural communities, in view of the need to respect the rights of such unique cultural communities and to enable them to maintain their own educational institutions.[4] The Act defines a "unique cultural educational institution" as

[1] The Unique Cultural Educational Institutions Act 2008, s. 1.

[2] Ehud (Udi) Spiegel, *Talmud Torah is Equivalent to All: The Ultra-Orthodox (Haredi) Education System for Boys in Jerusalem* (Jerusalem: Jerusalem institute for Israel studies 2011), 32 [Hebrew].

[3] H.C. 4805/07 *The Center for Jewish Pluralism and Others v. The Minister of Education and Others* (27 July 2008).

[4] Proposed Act: Unique Cultural Educational Institutions, 2008, 239 Proposed Acts (23 June 2008), 350.

an educational institution which gives systemic education that originates from the way of life of the unique cultural group and is in accordance with the unique characteristics of the group.[5] The Act grants UO high schools (Yeshivot Ketanot) 60 percent of the funding awarded to public schools, regardless of whether they teach the core curriculum, thus enabling them not to teach their students any basic skills, such as math or English, or citizenship education. Although the Act applies only to high schools the *de facto* situation is that UO schools for boys have for years been teaching almost only religious studies at all levels of schooling while still receiving extensive state funding.[6] Thus, the model of autonomy for UO education which the Act establishes, and which has existed de facto even prior to the act, is one which combines generous state funding with an almost complete lack of state supervision over the content of education.

The purpose of this chapter is to question the soundness of the Act from comparative and theoretical perspectives and especially in light of the unique circumstances of the UO community in Israel, and the distinctive relations between religion and state that exist in this country. While it is customary to compare the situation of the UO minority in Israel to that of religious minorities in western liberal states, I will argue that although such a comparison may expose some of the shortcomings of the Act, only a deeper analysis of the illiberal nature of religion state relations in Israel and of the central role that the UO community holds in the Israeli religious establishment and in its politics can fully capture the flawed nature of the Act.[7] Consequently my analysis will proceed in two stages. In the first stage, after giving a brief description of the UO community and its unique position in the Israeli polity in Part II, I will conduct, in Part III, a comparative analysis of the autonomy granted to religious education in three liberal countries in which controversies over religious education have erupted in recent years. I will claim that in liberal countries, as well as in the writings of liberal theorists, it is possible to identify two models of autonomy in religious education—one model which can be found in countries such as Britain and the Netherlands, which combines a relatively high degree of supervision over the content of education with the grant of state funding, and the second model which can be found in the United States and which combines almost no state funding with rather lax supervision. I will argue that the situation in Israel which combines a high degree of funding with no supervision is neither required by liberal theory, nor comparable to the situation in other liberal countries.

In the second stage of my analysis I will show that the shortcomings of the Act are further exacerbated by the illiberal nature of religion state relations in Israel and by the position of the UO community within the Israeli religious establishment and Israeli politics. Since Israel deviates considerably from the liberal model with respect to the role that the Jewish religion plays within the state, its treatment of UO education should also be compared to the measures that non-liberal countries which exhibit similarly close ties between religion and the state take with respect to the education of religious groups within them. Consequently, in Part IV I will discuss religious education in Malaysia, in

[5] Proposed Act: Unique Cultural Educational Institutions. The only group to which the Act explicitly applies is the UO community. The Minister of Education has the authority to recognize other groups as unique cultural groups for the purposes of the act, but thus far no other group has been recognized as such.

[6] Spiegel, *Talmud Torah is Equivalent to All* 33.

[7] It is important to note at the outset that the analysis in this chapter will focus on the rights and interests of the UO parents and community *vis-à-vis* the state, and will not deal with the rights of the children, which deserve separate treatment. Since my analysis will conclude that the UO community does not have the right to an exclusively religious education funded by the state, any analysis of the harm caused to UO children by such limited education will further support the outcome.

which Islam is the official state religion, and show that contrary to the situation in Israel, in Malaysia private religious education, and especially Muslim education, is closely supervised by the state regardless of its funding. I will argue that this close supervision results from the power and importance that the Muslim religion holds in the life of the nation. Because the Malayan state uses the Muslim religion as an important source of authority it restricts the educational autonomy of Muslim religious groups within it as a means of preventing challenges to its own religious, and hence—political, authority. Thus, Malaysia is an example of a third, non-liberal model, where precisely because religion is powerful and has considerable state authority, the autonomy granted to private religious education is restricted.

In Part V I will show that Israel, which does not fit any of these three models, emerges as a unique hybrid which on the one hand gives extensive religious autonomy in education to the UO community, on misguided liberal grounds, while on the other hand, it allows the same community to retain control over the Israeli religious establishment and to enforce its increasingly radical religious ideology through this establishment. In Part VI I will claim that far from being a disempowered enclave community, the UO community in Israel emerges as what I will call a *prodigious enclave community*, which is politically strong and highly influential, and that therefore the multicultural discourse used to justify the Act and the accommodations that it offers is misplaced. My conclusion will be that the right to an exclusively religious state funded education that was granted to the UO community by the Act is the result of a political power play that cannot be justified theoretically or comparatively, and constitutes a challenge to the rights of others as well as to the already shaky liberal democratic foundations of Israel.

II. The UO Community in Israel

The UO community, or in its Hebrew name—the Haredi community, or the Haredim—gets its name from the proverb in Isaiah 66:5 "Hear the word of the Lord, you who tremble (haredim) at His word."[8] The UO are a radical segment within Orthodox Judaism, and while there are many subgroups within the UO community they all distinguish themselves from other Jews by their dress, attitudes, world view and the character of their religious lives.[9] The UO are fundamentalists who believe in the fundamental truths of their religion, which they assume are unchanging from the time of Abraham, and who view the past as "the great teacher."[10] A crucial feature of their existence is their refusal to endorse contemporary Western culture and their entire lives are dedicated to fortifying their form of traditional Judaism in opposition to modernity.[11] Thus, while UO fundamentalism is built on a commitment to an idealized past, this past has in fact never existed and is constructed and reconstructed by UO sages in opposition to developments in modern culture and society.[12] The UO community has objected to the establishment of the state of Israel and still retains an anti-Zionist ideology to this very day.[13] Furthermore, the UO consider themselves, and are often perceived by others, as a

[8] Samuel Heilman and Menachem Friedman, "Religious Fundamentalism and Religious Jews: The Case of the Haredim," in Martin E. Marty and R. Scott Appleby (eds), *Fundamentalisms Observed* (Chicago: University of Chicago Press, 1994), 197, 198.

[9] Heilman and Friedman, "Religious Fundamentalism and Religious Jews" 197, 199.

[10] Heilman and Friedman, "Religious Fundamentalism and Religious Jews" 197.

[11] Heilman and Friedman, "Religious Fundamentalism and Religious Jews" 198.

[12] Heilman and Friedman, "Religious Fundamentalism and Religious Jews" 257.

[13] Menachem Friedman, *The Haredi (Ultra-Orthodox) Society—Sources, Trends and Processes* (Jerusalem: Jerusalem Institute for Israel studies, 1991), 19–20.

secluded enclave community, and have on that basis successfully secured multicultural accommodations such as the Unique Cultural Educational Institutions Act.

The UO community is the fastest growing community in Israel, with an average fertility rate of almost 7.7 children per woman.[14] One out of every four Jewish students in the Israeli primary school system is educated in an UO school. The continuous study of Tora (Talmud Tora) has always been a central ideal in Jewish tradition and in contemporary UO society in Israel the full realization of this ideal has become the sole goal of the education system.[15] Consequently, the UO education system centers on teaching all boys rigorous religious studies throughout their school years with almost no secular subjects.[16] This paves the way for boys in the UO community, after finishing Yeshivot Ketanot (the UO equivalent to high school), to continue their full time religious studies in Yeshivot Gdolot (until their marriage) and later in Kolelim.[17] As a result almost half of UO men dedicate their time to studying religious studies and live off stipends they receive from the government in return.[18] Because of the combination of very high fertility rates with very low workforce participation the UO community's mode of existence is heavily dependent on state funding and on donations.[19]

III. Religious Education in Liberal Democracies

Education plays a crucial role in shaping world views and the identities of children and of young adults. As philosopher Elizabeth Minnich argues, "education is of critical importance. It is in and through education that a culture, and polity, not only tries to perpetuate but enacts the kinds of thinking it welcomes, and discards and/or discredits the kinds it fears."[20] For this reason educational autonomy is highly important for religious minorities. Nevertheless, for the same reason partial state control over private education seems necessary to ensure that important interests of the liberal democratic state are not jeopardized.

When assessing autonomy in religious education the rights and interests of three actors should be taken into account.[21] First, the interest of the parents, whose right to decide the education of their child is part of their religious freedom.[22] Most often the parents belong to a religious community and aspire to inculcate in the child the community's religious values and way of life, an interest which they share with the community.[23] The second actor is the child, whose right to an enabling education and to equal opportunities can be jeopardized by her parents' educational choices for her.[24]

[14] As of 2001. Hagai Levin, "The Haredi Sector in Israel: Empowerment through Workforce Integration," *The National Economic Council* (2009), 10 [Hebrew].

[15] Levin, "The Haredi Sector in Israel" 33.

[16] Levin, "The Haredi Sector in Israel" 33.

[17] Yaacov Lupu, "Haredi Opposition to Haredi High-School Yeshivas," *The Floersheimer Institute for Policy Studies* (2007), 30.

[18] Lupu, "Haredi Opposition to Haredi High-School Yeshivas" 13.

[19] Lupu, "Haredi Opposition to Haredi High-School Yeshivas" 41–43.

[20] Elizabeth Minnich, *Transforming Knowledge* (Philadelphia: Temple University Press, 1990), 53.

[21] Rob Reich, *Bridging Liberalism and Multiculturalism in American Education* (Chicago: University of Chicago Press, 2002), 148–57.

[22] Galston refers to this right as their right to expressive liberty, see e.g. William Galston, *The Practice of Liberal Pluralism* (Cambridge, UK : Cambridge University Press, 2005).

[23] The right to instill their values and lifestyle to their children is also part of the parents' right to culture.

[24] As will be discussed below, different theorists have different perspectives as to what an enabling education entails.

Finally, the third actor is the state; as we will see, many theorists argue that the continued existence of the state as a functioning democracy depends on its citizens' ability to participate in the life of a modern democratic state, an ability that can only be acquired through education. Liberal thinkers disagree on how the balance should be struck between these different sets of interests, and consequently about the extent to which the state should allow the existence of private religious education, the extent to which it should finance such education, and the extent to which it should intervene in private religious education in order to ensure that these schools maintain an adequate level of civic education. This disagreement roughly matches the distinction between the autonomy-based conception of liberalism and the diversity-based conception of liberalism.[25]

A central proponent of the autonomy-based conception of liberalism is Brian Barry. Barry is a strong believer in the right and duty of the state to have a say in the way parents and communities educate their children, in order to safeguard both the interests of the state and the rights and interests of the child.[26] As far as the interests of the state are concerned, Barry argues that all citizens have an interest in the future of their society, and that the future of society "depends on the way in which those who are now children turn out."[27] A major aim of education should, according to Barry, be to develop in the child a capacity for autonomy.[28] Barry supports a multicultural education insofar as it means that the curriculum is inclusive and pays attention to the various groups that exist in society.[29] Nevertheless, he insists that all schools must have a common curriculum, since it is impossible for society to function if it is divided into mutually exclusive groups whose separate schools follow different curricula.[30] While he supports state funding for suitable private religious schools,[31] he insists that other private religious schools, such as the Christian fundamentalist schools in the United States, which teach only creationism and whose biology textbooks explain that evolutionary theory is a creation of Satan that is used effectively against Christians, must be shut down.[32]

A position which is arguably even more uncompromising is expressed by Will Kymlicka, who holds that requiring separate religious schools to teach a core curriculum that includes citizenship education may not be sufficient to provide the appropriate sort of citizenship education.[33] Kymlicka posits that inculcating essential traits such as civility and public reasonableness in our interactions with others can only be done in a pluralistic, non-homogenous, environment in which children can interact with those who have different religious beliefs and ethnocultural backgrounds than their own.[34] Consequently, while he supports the existence of private religious schools, he believes that in later stages of education, all children, including those belonging to separate religious groups, must attend public schools. As will be discussed in Part VI of this chapter, the only exemption from attending common schools should, according to Kymlicka, be given to small isolationist religious groups, such as the Amish, who completely withdraw from society and do not exercise their political rights.[35]

[25] William Galston, "Two Concepts of Liberalism" (1995) 105 *Ethics* 516.

[26] Brian Barry, *Culture and Equality* (Cambridge, MA: Harvard University Press, 2001), 209. According to Barry there is no group right to the education of children, only the right of the parents (207) nevertheless, the group to which the parents belong has a crucial influence on the education that the children receive.

[27] Barry, *Culture and Equality* 207.

[28] Barry, *Culture and Equality* 224–5.

[29] Barry, *Culture and Equality* 238.

[30] Barry, *Culture and Equality* 237.

[31] Barry, *Culture and Equality* 204–5.

[32] Barry, *Culture and Equality* 249.

[33] Will Kymlicka, *Politics in the Vernacular: Nationalism, Multiculturalism and Citizenship* (Oxford, UK: Oxford University Press, 2001), 303–4.

[34] Kymlicka, *Politics in the Vernacular* 304.

[35] Kymlicka, *Politics in the Vernacular* 305–7.

On the other side of the spectrum, a most avid supporter of diversity liberalism, Chandran Kukathas, posits that since two core principles of liberalism are toleration of diversity and limited government, the liberal state should not educate its citizens or shape their thinking.[36] The state should allow communities to educate their children according to their own beliefs, although it need not subsidize such education.[37] He criticizes the position which insists that a liberal polity must educate citizens to participate in a shared political framework and to affirm shared political principles, such as the obligation to respect the rights of fellow citizens regardless of their religious convictions.[38] To the contrary, he argues, "what characterizes a liberal political order is not shared political commitments but institutions which enable people whose moral, religious, cultural and political commitments differ."[39] According to Kukathas, it is hard to see how the same political order which allows people to hold illiberal, and even anti-liberal views and allows them to proselytize those views, and even run for office on their basis, can justify inculcating particular liberal values or virtues in its citizens. As he succinctly puts it "Liberalism does not run re-education camps."[40] Kukathas is very clear in his emphasis on toleration and in his critique of the limits placed on communities. Nevertheless, while failing to qualify the swiping toleration he advocates, he is careful to note that such qualifications are due,[41] and that his theory is probably not feasible for any actual liberal state.[42]

Proponents of the Israeli Unique Cultural Educational Institutions Act maintain that granting the UO education system extensive state funding while exempting it from the duty to teach the national core curriculum is required by liberal and multicultural precepts. However, neither of the theorists discussed above seem to advocate such an arrangement. While Barry advocates tight control over private education but allows for state funding, Kukathas rejects any state control over education, but at the same time rejects demands for funding. Furthermore, an examination of the autonomy granted to religious education in the United States, the Netherlands and England, three countries which in recent years have debated the relationship between religious education and the state, also reveals the existence of these two models. One model, which combines a relatively slack supervision of private religious education with no funding: the American model. And a second model, which combines a much closer supervision of religious education, with a more generous funding: the European model.

A. The American model

In the United States the right of parents to send their children to private religious education has been recognized by the American Supreme Court as early as 1925.[43] While parents have a fundamental liberty to give their children private religious education,

[36] Chandran Kukathas, "Education and Citizenship in Diverse Societies" (2001) 35 *International Journal of Educational Research* 319, 321–2.

[37] Chandran Kukathas, *The Liberal Archipelago: A Theory of Diversity and Freedom* (Oxford, UK: Oxford University Press, 2003), 162.

[38] Kukathas, "Education and Citizenship in Diverse Societies" 326–7.

[39] Kukathas, "Education and Citizenship in Diverse Societies" 328.

[40] Kukathas, "Education and Citizenship in Diverse Societies" 328.

[41] Kukathas, "Education and Citizenship in Diverse Societies" 329–30.

[42] Kukathas, *The Liberal Archipelago* 267. In this book Kukathas puts forth a liberal theory based on the primacy of toleration, which he calls the liberal archipelago. Nevertheless, in the conclusion of the book he concedes the impracticability of his theory for actual liberal states.

[43] *Pierce v. Society of Sisters* 268 U.S. 510, 535 (1925).

the constitutional "wall of separation" between church and state was held to prohibit any direct government funding for private religious education.[44] Although the state cannot fund private religious schools the Supreme Court held that it retains the power to reasonably regulate them. [45] The Supreme Court has never specified what kind of state regulation of private schools constitutes "reasonable" regulation, but in general the regulation in the United States is less intrusive and less comprehensive than the regulation in Europe.[46] Nevertheless, most of the states impose various curricular requirements on private schools, regardless of their religious character or of the fact that they are not funded by the state.[47]

The strict prohibition on state funding for religious private schools has been somewhat narrowed in 2002. That year the US Supreme Court paved the way to indirect government funding of religious schools when it held that a voucher program which gives parents tuition aid through vouchers they can use towards tuition costs in any private school of their choice, can be used for tuition in private religious schools.[48] However, the program approved by the Supreme Court required participating private schools to meet statewide educational standards, to agree not to discriminate on the basis of race, religion, or ethnic background, and not to "advocate or foster unlawful behavior or teach hatred of any person or group on the basis of race, ethnicity, national origin, or religion."[49] Finally, a third form of private religious education that exists in the United States and which is not funded is homeschooling. While homeschooling is the least supervised, most states do supervise it to various extents, and several state and federal courts have rejected the claim that homeschoolers are constitutionally entitled to complete freedom from state supervision.[50] Nevertheless, the level of supervision of private religious education in the United States is on the whole much lower than it is in Europe.

B. The European model

In contrast to the American model, the European model can be generally characterized as combining funding for private religious schools with close supervision of these schools. Two European countries in which the number of religious schools is particularly high, and which in recent years have debated the relationship between religious education and the state, especially in the context of Muslim religious education, are the Netherlands and England.

In the Netherlands only about a third of the primary schools are public, while the other two-thirds are private schools, mostly religious, that are fully funded by the state. The vast majority of these private schools are Protestant and Catholic and very few

[44] For example, *Everson v. Board of Education of Ewing Tp.* 330 U.S. 1 (1947).

[45] *Everson v. Board of Education of Ewing Tp.* 330 U.S. 534.

[46] Richard W. Garnett, "Regulatory Strings and Religious Freedom: Requiring Private Schools to Promote Public Values," in Patrick Wolf et al. (eds), *Educating Citizens: International Perspectives on Civic Values and School Choice* (Washington, D.C.: Brookings Institution Press, 2004), 324, 329. See also Rob Reich, *Bridging Liberalism and Multiculturalism in American Education* (Chicago: University of Chicago Press, 2002), 147.

[47] Catherine J. Ross, "Fundamentalist Challenges to Core Democratic Values: Exit and Homeschooling" (2010) 18 *William & Marry Bill of Rights Journal* 991, 992. For a court case rejecting a challenge to state supervision of private schools see *Fellowship Baptist Church v. Benton* 815 F.2d 485 (8th Cir. 1987).

[48] *Zelman v. Simmons-Harris* 536 U.S. 639 (2002).

[49] *Zelman v. Simmons-Harris* 536 U.S. 645.

[50] *Zelman v. Simmons-Harris* 536 U.S. 993.

belong to other denominations, including Muslim.[51] The freedom of education is guaranteed in the Dutch constitution, but is subject to the right of the authorities to supervise the schools and the teachers, and to set educational standards.[52] The constitution further stipulates that supervision of private schools must be done with due regard to the freedom to provide education according to religious or other belief, and that private schools that meet the standards set by parliament are entitled to public funds equal to those received by public schools.[53]

Although private schools have rather extensive autonomy in determining what is taught and how, this autonomy is restricted by qualitative and quantitative standards that they have to meet, including teacher qualifications, curriculum requirements and in secondary schools the examination syllabus and the national examinations.[54] The strict conditions that have to be met in order to establish a fully funded private school have made it difficult for the Muslim community to establish Muslim schools and only a small percentage of Muslim primary school children attend Muslim schools.[55] Islamic Studies teachers are required to obtain teacher diplomas,[56] and all Islamic schools teach the official Islamic teaching curriculum.[57] Dutch law requires all state funded schools, including religious ones, to offer education that is aimed at developing active citizenship and social integration.[58]

The same model of close supervision with generous funding to those schools that meet the standards also exists in England. One-third of the state-maintained schools in England are religious schools, but the overwhelming majority of them belong to Christian denominations, while only around 50 are non-Christian.[59] All state-maintained schools must fully incorporate the national curriculum.[60] Muslim children comprise more than 5 percent of the total school population in Britain, but the vast majority of them attend public community schools or Church schools, and only around 1 percent of them are educated in independent or state-maintained Muslim schools.[61] Muslim independent schools do not receive any state funding and consequently they are usually small and suffer from severe financial limitations.[62] While Islamic independent schools may apply for state funding the process is long and complex, and often depends on political power relations, and consequently very few have managed to gain such funding.[63]

[51] Geert Driessen and Micheal Merry, "Islamic Schools in the Netherlands: Expansion or Marginalization?" (2006) 37(3) *Interchange* 201, 203.

[52] Article 23, ss. 2, 5 can be found at <http://www.servat.unibe.ch/icl/nl00000_.html>.

[53] Article 23, ss. 5, 7.

[54] Ben P. Vermeulen, "Regulating School Choice to Promote Civic Values: Constitutional and Political Issues in the Netherlands," in Wolf et al., *Educating Citizens* 46.

[55] Driessen and Merry, "Islamic Schools in the Netherlands" 204. As of 2006 only about 10 percent of Muslim pupils attended Muslim schools.

[56] Inga Niehaus, "Emancipation or Disengagement? Islamic Schools in Britain and the Netherlands," in Aurora Alvarez Veinguer et. (eds), *Islam in Education in European Countries* (Münster: Waxmann, 2009), 113, 120.

[57] Lisa Baughn, "Islamic Education in Europe," *Euro-Islam.Info*, can be found at <http://www.euro-islam.info/key-issues/education/>.

[58] "Inclusive Education in The Netherlands," *SLO • national institute for curriculum development* (2007), 44.

[59] Rob Berkeley, *Right to Divide?: Faith Schools and Community Cohesion* (London: Runnymede Trust, 2008), 11. Thirty-seven of the non-Christian maintained schools are Jewish.

[60] Damian Breen, "A Qualitative Narrative of the Transition from Independent to Voluntary Aided Status, A Problem for the Concept of the 'Muslim School,'" in Alvarez Veinguer et al. (eds), *Islam in Education in European Countries* 95, 105.

[61] Inga Niehaus, "Emancipation or Disengagement? Islamic Schools in Britain and the Netherlands," in Alvarez Veinguer et al. (eds), *Islam in Education in European Countries* 113, 114.

[62] Breen, "A Qualitative Narrative of the Transition from Independent to Voluntary Aided Status" 101.

[63] Niehaus, "Emancipation or Disengagement?" 114–15.

Unlike state-funded schools that must fully incorporate the national curriculum, independent Muslim schools can determine their own curriculum. Nevertheless, they too have to meet academic standards that are checked through periodic inspections and compulsory national tests.[64] Among other things, independent schools are required to provide their students with an education that "gives pupils experience in linguistic, mathematical, scientific, technological, human and social, physical and aesthetic and creative education," that ensures "adequate preparation of pupils for the opportunities, responsibilities and experiences of adult life," and that "promotes tolerance and harmony between different cultural traditions."[65] Following the 9/11 attacks and the increasing concerns that Islamic schools might isolate Muslim children from the larger society, a new citizenship curriculum was introduced in British schools and state-funded schools were required to actively promote social cohesion.[66]

IV. Religious Education in Democracies with a Thickly Established Religion

While it is customary to compare Israel to liberal states, Israel is in fact a hybrid whose legal system combines certain liberal protections of human rights with a thick establishment of religion, and especially of the Orthodox Jewish religion, that has close ties to the state and coercive authority over its citizens.[67] The close ties between the Orthodox Jewish religion and the state make Israel similar in various ways to other countries with thickly established religions, and especially to those that attempt to combine thick establishment with a more than symbolic protection of human rights, such as Malaysia.[68] It is therefore worthwhile, before engaging with the Israeli case, to examine how countries such as Malaysia deal with the religious education of citizens, and especially with the religious education of citizens who belong to their dominant religion.

Malaysia is an Islamic federation that has a non-Muslim population of around 40 percent.[69] Religion and ethnicity are closely intertwined in Malaysia and though the country maintains a façade of interracial harmony and religious pluralism, clear preference is given in the constitution and in federal law to the Malay ethnic group, who are Muslims.[70] While the constitution guarantees individual religious freedom and the right of every religious group to manage its own religious affairs, it includes special provisions for Islam.[71] For example, the constitution allows state and federal law to restrict "the propagation of any religious doctrine or belief among persons professing the religion of Islam."[72] The control over the propagation of Muslim religious doctrines granted to the

[64] Niehaus, "Emancipation or Disengagement?" 115.

[65] The Education (Independent School Standards) (England) Regulations 2010 (SI 2010/1997), Sch. 1, Parts 1 and 2.

[66] Niehaus, "Emancipation or Disengagement?" 121–2.

[67] I use the term thick establishment to denote an establishment of religion which is more than merely symbolic and which gives the established religion both authority and coercive power over citizens.

[68] For a detailed description of the Malay combination see Ran Hirschl, *Constitutional Theocracy* (Cambridge, MA: Harvard University Press, 2010), 127–39.

[69] Article 3 of the Constitution of Malysia; Farish A. Noor, "From Pondok to Parliament: The Role Played by the Religious Schools of Malaysia in the Development of the Pan-Malaysian Islamic Party (PAS)," in Farish A. Noor et al. (eds), *Madrasa in Asia: Political Activism and Transnational Linkages* (Amsterdam: Amsterdam University Press, 2008), 191, 192.

[70] Hirschl, *Constitutional Theocracy* 128.

[71] Article 11(1)–(3) of the Constitution of Malaysia.

[72] Article 11(4) of the Constitution of Malaysia.

government in the constitution has enabled the government, among other things, to clamp down on dissident Muslim organizations and shut down their schools.[73]

While all religious groups have the right to establish and maintain religious schools, the government runs and funds only Muslim religious schools.[74] The close ties between Malay identity and Islam, and the government's resolve to affirm Malay hegemony, have led to the increasing importance of Islamic education and to attempts to systematize it within the national system.[75] A separate religious education division was established in order to gradually turn all Islamic schools into national Islamic schools with a uniform curriculum.[76] Although private Islamic schools are allowed to operate, and some are even partly funded by the state, after 9/11 the pressure on private Islamic schools to conform to national authorities has increased, and funding has been withdrawn from hundreds of schools.[77] Some of these schools have closed for lack of funding, while others have forgone their independence and become fully aided government Islamic schools.[78] The government accused private Islamic schools of stocking Islamic extremism and of teaching a deficient non-religious curriculum that left the children graduating from them virtually unemployable.[79] The funding cut combined with the government's campaign against the quality of private Islamic schools and the parallel expansion of the Islamic education curriculum in national schools have led to a sharp decline in enrolment to private Islamic schools.[80] By 2010 all private Islamic schools in Malaysia were required to adopt the official Islamic education curriculum, thereby creating a homogenous Islamic education curriculum in all Malaysian schools.[81]

Thus in Malaysia, because Islam forms such an important part of the Malay state, both in terms of identity and in terms of structure and authority, the state exercises close supervision over Islamic education. Not being committed to liberal principles the state does not hesitate to restrict the propagation of Islam and to enforce an official Islamic education curriculum in all schools in order to prevent extremist religious challenges to its political and religious authority.

V. UO Education in Israel—An Analysis

Three models of the treatment of religious education by the state emerge from the above analysis. In liberal countries two models can be detected—the American model which combines a relatively lax supervision of private religious education with no funding, and the European model, which combines a much closer supervision of religious education, with a more generous funding. In view of these two liberal models it seems plausible to say that the situation in Israel in which UO education receives considerable funding

[73] For example the government has banned the Darul Arkam movement in 1994 and closed down its schools. Ahmad Fauzi Abdul Hamid, "Islamic Education in Malaysia" (2010) 18 *RSIS Monograph* 60.

[74] Hamid, "Islamic Education in Malaysia" 25.

[75] Hamid, "Islamic Education in Malaysia" 29.

[76] Hamid, "Islamic Education in Malaysia" 29.

[77] Hamid, "Islamic Education in Malaysia" 45; Noor, "From Pondok to Parliament" 209. According to Noor, funding was cut to 260 schools.

[78] Hamid, "Islamic Education in Malaysia" 4, 45.

[79] Jonathan Kent, "Malaysia's Doubts over Muslim Schools," *BBC News* (4 March 2003), available at <http://news.bbc.co.uk/go/pr/fr/-/2/hi/asia-pacific/2913565.stm>.

[80] Richard G. Kraince, "Reforming Islamic Education in Malaysia: Doctrine or Dialogue?," in Robert W. Hefner (ed.), *Making Modern Muslims: The Politics of Islamic Education in Southeast Asia* (Honolulu: University of Hawaii Press, 2009), 106, 124–5.

[81] Hamid, "Islamic Education in Malaysia" 46–7.

but retains an almost complete autonomy is neither practiced by liberal countries nor required by liberal precepts. Moreover, the distinctiveness of the treatment of UO education in Israel becomes even more evident when considering the thick establishment of the Orthodox Jewish religion that takes place in Israel, and comparing Israel to countries with a similarly thick establishment of religion. Like Israel, Malaysia has a thickly established religion, which exercises coercive power and authority over the country's citizens. Consequently, in Malaysia the education of Muslims is closely monitored by the state to ensure that the authority given to religion is not turned against the state by extremist Muslim groups. In contrast, in Israel the state gives extensive funding and autonomy in education to the UO community, while at the same time allowing it to control the state's religious establishment and to use it to enforce its radical religious ideology on all citizens, thereby eroding Israel's already shaky liberal democratic structure.

Thus, while giving the Orthodox Jewish religion both state power and state budgets, Israel refrains from exercising direct control over religious ideology. Israel's reluctance to control religious ideology in the way that Malaysia does stems from the fact that such control would go against another important component of Israel's ethos—the liberal component. Consequently, Israel emerges as a unique hybrid which attempts to reconcile two irreconcilable ideals: on the one hand it gives considerable state power and state funds to its preferred religion—Orthodox Judaism (and is therefore an instance of what Hirschl calls a constitutional theocracy), but on the other hand, and at the same time, it purports to respect liberal ideals such as religious freedom in all areas not directly subject to religious law. The result is that the UO community is given state coercive power and state funds through its control over Israel's religious establishment, but at the same time it is given extensive autonomy to pursue its own deeply conservative way of life. The Unique Cultural Educational Institutions Act is but one example of this problematic mix. On misguided liberal and multicultural grounds it guarantees funding for UO boys' schools without any state supervision of their curriculum, while at the same time also it ignores the fact that the same UO boys, who are not taught any secular subjects or civic education, and whose religious education is dictated solely by UO sages, will later become public officials in the state's religious establishment, and enforce the dictates of their radical version of Orthodox Judaism on all Jews in Israel.

In order to understand the depth of the problem a more detailed description of the religion state relations in Israel is required. Israel was defined in its Declaration of Independence and later in its Basic Laws as a Jewish and Democratic state, and while there is an ongoing debate whether the reference to "Jewish" in this definition denotes the Jewish religion or merely the Jewish nation, the Orthodox Jewish religion was partially established in the state through laws and administrative decisions from Israel's early years.[82] The most important aspect of the partial establishment of Orthodox Judaism is that all Jews in Israel are subject to Orthodox Jewish religious personal laws. At the same time, members of other recognized religious communities such as Muslims and various Christian denominations are also subject to the personal religious laws of their particular

[82] Basic Law: Human Dignity and Liberty, 1992, SH No. 1391, 60; The Declaration of Establishment of the State of Israel (Israel, 14 May 1948) available at <http://www.mfa.gov.il/mfa/go.asp?MFAH00hb0>; see Avigdor Levontin, "'Jewish and Democratic'—Personal Reflections," in Yossi David (ed.), *The State of Israel: Between Judaism and Democracy* (Jerusalem: The Israel Democracy Institute, 2000), 251 (taking a position against interpreting the term Jewish in the Basic Laws as including the Jewish religion). Cf. Menahem Alon, "Constitution by Legislation: The Values of a Jewish and Democratic State in Light of Basic Law: Human Dignity and Personal Freedom" (1993) 17 *Iunei Mishpat* 659, 668–70 (taking a position supporting the inclusion of the Jewish religion in the term "Jewish").

religions.[83] The imposition of the religious personal laws of the various religious communities on all residents and the lack of an alternative civil marriage, constitute a violation of the right to freedom of conscience and belief, as well as a violation of the rights of women, who are subject to the discriminatory patriarchal religious laws of the various religious communities.[84] While establishing an exclusively religious system of laws in matters of marriage and divorce is probably the most serious entanglement of religion within the Israeli state, there are other areas in which the Orthodox Jewish religion is given a preferred status by the state. The state has established a chief rabbinate and has given full control over it to Orthodox Judaism.[85] The chief rabbinate is a powerful state organ which enjoys large budgets and which controls the religious services given by the state to the Jewish population such as marriage and divorce, burial, kashrut, synagogues, conversion to Judaism and so forth, through organs such as the rabbinical courts and the regional religious councils.[86]

What does all this have to do with the UO? Despite the UO community's anti-Zionist ideology and its enclave mentality, the UO community holds key positions in Israel's religious establishment. UO rabbis have been serving as judges in the Rabbinical Courts system, to which all Jews are subject in matters of marriage and divorce, from its inception, and have full control over it.[87] Through their positions the UO judges are authorized to impose their version of ultra-Orthodox Jewish religious law on all Jews in Israel. In recent years, with the increasing radicalization in the UO community the rulings of rabbinical courts have become more conservative and more detrimental to the rights of women and to the rights of converts.[88]

In addition, the influence of UO political parties, which has started as early as the establishment of the state, has strengthened considerably ever since. This influence has allowed UO politicians to obtain considerable budgets for the UO community, which support their Yeshiva studies and their increasing families.[89] It has also allowed them to have significant impact on general issues affecting the Israeli society at large, by securing appointments to key state and municipal positions such as the Minister of Interior, the Minister of Religion, the head of the Israeli Parliament's Budget Committee, and the mayor of Jerusalem. In their capacities in the government, in the Knesset, and in the local municipalities UO politicians and public servants strive to implement their ultra-Orthodox religious ideology on the public at large, in contravention of the liberal values of the state. To give one example, in Jerusalem UO politicians controlling

[83] The authority of the various religious communities was established through legislation from the period of the British Mandate that was later incorporated into Israeli law, Sign 51(1) of the King's Order in Council, 1922. The detailed authority of the Jewish Rabbinical Courts is set out in the Jurisdiction of Rabbinical Courts (Marriage and Divorce) Act 1953. The detailed authority of the Muslim religious courts can still be found in Sign 52 of the King's Order in Council, 1922.

[84] See e.g. Frances Raday, "On Equality," in Frances Raday et al. (eds), *Women's Status in Israeli Law and Society* (Jerusalem and Tel Aviv: Schocken, 1995), 19.

[85] The Chief Rabbinate of Israel Law, 1980, SH No. 965, 90.

[86] The Jewish Religious Services Law, 1971, SH No. 628, 130.

[87] Nissan Slominslki, "The Appointment of Rabbinical Court Judges—An Ultra-Orthodox State or a Zionist State?," available at <http://www.toravoda.org.il/node/584>.

[88] To give just one example, in 2011 a rabbinical court has ruled that a wife who sued her husband for damages because of his refusal to release her from their marriage for ten years, is herself to blame for his continuous refusal to divorce her. It further ruled that until the wife consents to her husband's financial demands she is not entitled to the divorce. Rivka Luvitch, "Rabbinical Courts, Raise the Anchor," *Ynet* (8 February 2011), available at <http://www.ynet.co.il/articles/0,7340,L-4025574,00.html> [Hebrew].

[89] Friedman, *The Haredi (Ultra-Orthodox) Society* 189.

the municipal government have for years been denying municipal budgets to the Homo-Lesbian community in Jerusalem despite repeated court rulings holding that such denial is discriminatory and illegal.[90] Another example is a religious ruling issued in 2010 by 50 municipal rabbis forbidding the sale and rental of homes to gentiles, particularly to Arabs.[91] These examples all involve UO public servants who receive their salary from the state and claim to be acting within their authority.

The above account demonstrates how UO state officials, representing the UO community, are engaged in strengthening the hold of ultra-Orthodox religious ideology in the Israeli government and in the Israeli public sphere and have significant impact on the lives of all Israelis. At the same time these officials contend that the UO education system is entitled to full autonomy as part of the freedom of religion and of the multicultural respect owed to the UO community as an isolated religious minority, which is dedicated to its deeply religious (yet deeply illiberal) way of life. This position was adopted by the Israeli parliament in the Unique Cultural Educational Institutions Act which exempts UO high school students from studying the core curriculum. As will be discussed in the last part of this chapter, in light of the considerable political and state power that the UO community yields through its representatives, this allegedly multicultural accommodation is not supported by multicultural theory.

VI. Multiculturalism and the UO as a Prodigious Enclave Community

In multicultural theory there are typically two types of groups that require multicultural accommodations. One type is the integration seeking group: this type of group is usually a newly arrived immigrant group that comes from a different cultural and religious background and requires multicultural accommodations such as the right to deviate from school or workplace dress code for religious reasons, or the right to have a different day of rest. Most often these groups do not question the liberal democratic structure of society and require multicultural accommodations in order to enable them to integrate in the larger society on an equal footing while still retaining their religious and cultural practices.[92] Many Muslim immigrants to Europe fall under this category. The other type of group is the isolationist group: this would typically be an old minority, which shuns the larger society and demands to be left alone to lead its own way of life and run its own affairs. An example of such a group is the Amish in the United States.[93] While the Amish lead an illiberal way of life, they are completely withdrawn from society, do not discriminate against others in civil society, and do not participate in politics. According to Kymlicka, as long as such groups are small and sincerely committed to their self-imposed isolation, they pose no threat to liberal citizenship and to a stable liberal order and can therefore be exempted from requirements such as sending their children into common public schools for part of their education. Kymlicka emphasizes that such groups should not be encouraged since they are free riders on a stable liberal order which they do not help maintain, but as long as they remain small the liberal state can afford to

[90] See A.A. (administrative appeal) 343/09 *Open House v. Municipality of Jerusalem* (14 September 2010).

[91] Kobi Nahshoni, "50 Municipal Rabbis: Don't Rent Flats to Arabs," *Ynet* (12 July 2010), available at <http://www.ynetnews.com/articles/0,7340,L-3995724,00.html>.

[92] Kymlicka, *Politics in the Vernacular* 162–72.

[93] Kymlicka, *Politics in the Vernacular* 305–7.

accept them.[94] A similar argument is made by Jeff Spiner-Halev who suggests referring to groups such as the Amish as *partial citizens*, that may be exempted from certain duties of citizenship, as long as they are completely self-reliant and do not participate in politics.[95] Spinner Halev distinguishes between the Amish and another old and arguably isolationist minority—the Satmar Hasidim of Kiryas Joel in NY. According to him, while the former do not ask the state to help them maintain their isolationist way of life, the latter depend on public funds to maintain their illiberal and isolationist way of life and use their voting power in order to get politicians to cater to their needs. Consequently, the Satmar Hasidim should not be considered *partial citizens* or enjoy exemptions from the obligations of citizenship.[96]

Despite the fact that the UO are portrayed by supporters of the Unique Cultural Institutions Act as an isolationist group such as the Amish, who should be entitled to exemptions from the obligations of citizenship, they are very different from the Amish. The UO are deeply involved in state and municipal politics and their community is heavily funded by the state. In fact, perhaps ironically, the UO's extensive involvement in politics and their extensive funding by the state are what enabled UO leaders to create and maintain the semi enclave for which they are now claiming multicultural protection. The large state funding for religious education from early childhood through late adulthood has enabled the transformation of the UO community into a community of learners in which an unprecedented number of adult men study religious studies and do not need to work for a living. This enables these men to lead most of their lives without having to step out of the UO community. In addition, state funding of UO men's religious studies has enabled the UO education system to shun any secular studies, since many of its graduates continue their religious studies into adulthood and consequently do not have to find jobs. The shunning of any secular education and the exclusive focus on religious studies made possible by increasing state funding has led to the growing radicalization of the UO community.[97]

Due to their size, the UO community cannot even be compared to the Satmar Hasidim of NY, despite the fact that both communities subsist mainly on public funds and use their political power to obtain them. The UO are by no means a small minority whose free riding can be easily absorbed by the larger Israeli society. One out of every four Jewish students in the Israeli primary school system is educated in an UO school and the number is continuously increasing owing to the UO community's high fertility rates. This means that the number of school children who are not taught basic skills and civic education and are given an exclusively religious education is very high, and creates serious concerns as to Israel's continued economic sustainability and democratic stability.

Furthermore, because of the unique religion-state relations in Israel the power that the UO community holds over other citizens, and its ability to undermine the liberal democratic structure of the state, are considerable. The establishment of the Orthodox Jewish religion in the state has enabled the UO community through its representatives in the religious establishment to become the official interpreters of the Jewish religion, determining the legal status of other citizen's marriages and divorces, of their conversions

[94] Kymlicka, *Politics in the Vernacular* 305–7.

[95] Jeff Spinner-Halev, "Extending Diversity: Religion in Public and Private Education," in Will Kymlicka and Wayne Norman (eds), *Citizenship in Diverse Societies* (Oxford: Oxford University Press, 2000), 68–97, 71–2.

[96] Spinner-Halev, "Extending Diversity" 79–80.

[97] Friedman, *The Haredi (Ultra-Orthodox) Society* 80–6.

and of their children's religious status on the basis of their own radical religious ideology.[98] In addition, the lack of separation between religion and the state coupled with the UO's extensive political power enables them to deepen the hold of their radical interpretation of the Jewish religion over the Israeli public sphere. Consequently, one could argue that far from being a disempowered community, the UO is a *prodigious* enclave community that uses its political and state power both to guarantee its own flourishing and expansion, and to enforce its ideology on the rest of society. Thus, unlike the isolationist groups discussed above, the UO do not isolate their members from mainstream society merely as a means of maintaining their separate way of life, but also as a means of fostering a radical religious ideology which they can then impose on others. This points to a final important distinction between the UO and both isolationist and integrationist groups; while both isolationist and integrationist groups do not challenge the liberal democratic structure of the country within which they reside, the UO do challenge the liberal features of the Israeli state structure and are striving to change them to conform to their radical religious ideology.[99]

VII. Conclusion

One out of every four Jewish children in Israel is educated in the UO education system, which is heavily funded by the state, but at the same time does not teach boys almost any secular studies. This state of affairs poses a serious challenge to the continued sustainability and stability of Israeli democracy. Those who support its continuation claim that it is required by the right of UO parents and community to freedom of religion and to multicultural accommodation. The comparative and theoretical perspectives discussed in this chapter refute this claim. Furthermore, supporters of the continued exemption of UO education from the core curriculum regard the UO community as an enclave community and fail to take into consideration both their extensive political power and their hold over Israel's religious establishment, which due to Israel's state religion relations yields considerable power over the lives of all Israelis. Thus, they fail to take into account the violation of rights that women, Arabs, homosexuals, converts, and others suffer as a consequence of the application of deeply illiberal ultra-Orthodox religious ideology by UO politicians and state officials who are the products of an UO education system that shuns any civic education. Since the right to an exclusively religious state-funded education was given to the UO minority on the basis of misguided liberal and multicultural grounds, and constitutes a challenge to the rights of others as well as to the already shaky liberal democratic foundations of Israel, it should be revoked.

[98] It should be noted that another group which is influential in the Israeli religious establishment are the religious Orthodox Zionists, but the UO are the more powerful of the two groups.

[99] On respect for liberal democratic values as the basis for multicultural policies see Kymlicka, *Politics in the Vernacular* 172–6.

18

Religion and Freedom of Speech: Portraits of Muhammad

Robert Post

On 30 September 2005, the Danish newspaper *Jyllands-Posten* solicited and published twelve cartoons depicting the prophet Muhammad.[1] By American standards, the cartoons were prosaic. One is a child's portrait of Muhammad in the desert; another shows Muhammad's face intertwined with Islamic symbols like the crescent and the star; several poke fun at the *Jyllands-Posten*, calling the cartoons a "PR Stunt" and the journalists a "bunch of reactionary provocateurs." Some contain ordinary, rather anodyne satire.[2] One shows Muhammad with a turban in the shape of a bomb; another confuses Muhammad with St. Peter, portraying the prophet at the entrance to a cloud-filled heaven facing a long line of suicide bombers saying, "Stop, Stop. We ran out of virgins."

The consequence of publishing these cartoons was truly dreadful. There were riots throughout the world. According to one estimate, 139 people died.[3] A fatwa was issued offering a million dollar bounty for the death of the cartoonists. Newspaper editors were fired and imprisoned, newspapers closed, and an Italian minister forced to resign for displaying the cartoons on his T-shirt. The Swedish foreign minister was forced out of office for attempting to close a website that wished to display the cartoons.

Islam contains a rich history of portraying the prophet Mohammed, but the modern fundamentalist sects who now claim to speak for Islam assert that it is forbidden to publish any representation of Muhammad, or, in some versions, of any prophet recognized by Islam. "Merely publishing the image of Muhammad is regarded as blasphemous by many Muslims."[4] For this reason the violent riots protesting the publication of the cartoons no doubt included numerous persons who were "undeniably outraged by what they perceive as blasphemy."[5] The question I shall address in this chapter is how the law ought to have responded to this outrage. How should the law mediate between the demands of religious sanctity and freedom of speech?

[1] The cartoons, along with much useful information about the controversy, can be seen at <http://www.zombietime.com/mohammed_image_archive/jyllands-posten_cartoons/>.

[2] The cartoons are certainly a good deal less vicious and racist than the anti-Semitic cartoons that routinely appear in the Arab press, see e.g. *Major Anti-Semitic Motifs in Arab Cartoons*, <http://www.jcpa.org/phas/phas-21.htm>; *Cartoons From the Arab World*, http://www.tomgrossmedia.com/ArabCartoons.htm, or the anti-Semitic>, anti-Holocaust cartoons recently solicited by Iran. See <http://www.irancartoon.com/>. Not to be outdone, the Israeli-based Dimona Comix announced its own anti-Semitic cartoon contest, <http://drawn.ca/2006/02/14/israeli-anti-semitic-cartoon-contest/>, proclaiming that "We'll show the world we can do the best, sharpest, most offensive Jew hating cartoons ever published! No Iranian will beat us on our home turf!" See http://www.boomka.org/>.

[3] See <http://www.cartoonbodycount.com/>.

[4] Craig Smith and Ian Fisher, "Temperatures Rise over Cartoons Mocking Muhammad," *New York Times* (3 Feb. 2006), A3.

[5] "Silenced by Islamist Rage," *New York Times* (25 Feb. 2006), A14. It is clear that the riots were also fomented in part by secular anti-Western Arab governments, like Syria, and by Islamic extremists

This is a very narrow question, which concerns only the coercive power of the state. It is quite distinct from the ethical issue of when and how one should speak. All that is legally permitted is not ethically advisable. Carsten Juste, the editor-in-chief of *Jyllands-Posten*, later said that "If I had known that the lives of Danish soldiers and civilians would be threatened, if I had known that, as my finger hovered one centimeter above the send button for publishing the drawings, would I have hit it? No. No responsible editor in chief would have done."[6] Juste was plainly correct to distinguish legal right from ethical propriety. Even if *Jyllands-Posten* were legally entitled to publish cartoons that were offensive, provocative, and likely to lead to violence, it may have been ethically inappropriate to do so. In this chapter, I analyze only the question of legal right.

In the United States this question could be easily and accurately answered by any first-year law student. Since 1940 our First Amendment has been held to protect from legal sanction all religious polemic, even expression that aims deliberately and provocatively to assault the religious sensibilities of the pious. "In the realm of religious faith, and in that of political belief," our Supreme Court has held,

> sharp differences arise. In both fields the tenets of one man may seem the rankest error to his neighbor. To persuade others to his own point of view, the pleader, as we know, at times, resorts to exaggeration, to vilification of men who have been, or are, prominent in church or state, and even to false statement. But the people of this nation have ordained in the light of history, that, in spite of the probability of excesses and abuses, these liberties are, in the long view, essential to enlightened opinion and right conduct on the part of the citizens of a democracy.
>
> The essential characteristic of these liberties is that under their shield many types of life, character, opinion and belief can develop unmolested and unobstructed. Nowhere is this shield more necessary than in our own country for a people composed of many races and of many creeds.[7]

It is recognized that "a first great principle of consensus" in First Amendment doctrine is that "In America, there is no heresy, no blasphemy."[8] The American Constitution protects speech in "public discourse," which is to say speech about public figures or circulating in the national media, that seeks intentionally to violate religious sensibilities by causing emotional pain, distress, and outrage.

The American First Amendment, however, is unique. Alongside our commitment to the death penalty, it stands as an outstanding exemplar of American constitutional exceptionalism. In Europe, where the Danish cartoons were published, there is a long history of regulating blasphemy, and as a consequence the question of subjecting the cartoons to legal sanction was not a dead letter.[9] It is that question which I shall analyze

seeking to discredit moderate Arab governments. In an astute discussion of the cartoons, which includes their only reproduction in the American print media, cartoonist Art Spiegelman observed that "the most baffling aspect of this whole affair is why all the violent demonstrations focused on the dopey cartoons rather than on the truly horrifying torture photos seen regularly on Al Jazeera, on European television, everywhere but in the mainstream media of the United States. Maybe it's because those photos of actual violation don't have the magical aura of things unseen, like the damn cartoons." Spiegelman, "Drawing Blood: Outrageous Cartoons and the Art of Courage" (2006) 312 (1873) *Harper's* 47. Spiegelman noted that "none of the millions of protesters saw any of the images. It was enough to be told that insult was intended. The *Jyllands-Posten* could have saved the $129 it paid to each of its 12 cartoonists and simply printed a front-page headline in 64-point type that shouted Yo' Prophet Wears Army Boots!" (46).

[6] Quoted in Alan Cowell, "Cartoons Force Danish Muslims to Examine Loyalties," *New York Times* (4 Feb. 2006), A3.

[7] *Cantwell v. Connecticut* 310 U.S. 296, 310 (1940).

[8] H. Kalven, *A Worthy Tradition: Freedom of Speech in America* (New York: Harper & Row, 1988), 7 (emphasis in original).

[9] On 23 October 2008, the Venice Commission, the Council of Europe's advisory body on constitutional matters, issued a report about blasphemy, religious insult, and incitement to religious hatred. In its conclusions, the report stated "it is neither necessary nor desirable to create an offence of religious

in this chapter, with particular emphasis on decisions of the European Court of Human Rights (ECtHR), which has set minimum European requirements for the suppression of religiously provocative speech. There are of course many distinct justifications for protecting freedom of speech,[10] but because all European nations are committed to democratic self-governance, I shall in this chapter seek to explore the compatibility of blasphemy regulation with the requirements of democracy.

I. Speech and Democracy

All agree that states aspiring to democratic legitimacy must extend some protection to freedom of speech. The extent and nature of these protections will depend upon many factors, including, most centrally, the meaning of democracy.

I begin with what I take to be the unobjectionable premise that democracy refers to "the distinction between autonomy and heteronomy: Democratic forms of government are those in which the laws are made by the same people to whom they apply (and for that reason they are autonomous norms), while in autocratic forms of government the law-makers are different from those to whom the laws are addressed (and are therefore heteronomous norms)."[11]

When we use this definition, we must immediately distinguish democracy from majoritarianism, in which a majority of the people exercise control over their government. Although it is frequently said "any distinct restraint on majority power, such as a principle of freedom of speech, is by its nature anti-democratic, anti-majoritarian,"[12] it is plain that majorities can implement rules that are inconsistent with democracy, as for example by voting a monarchy into office. Although majoritarianism may be intimately associated with the practice of democracy, democracy is not defined by majoritarianism, which is why it is intelligible to conclude that particular majoritarianian enactments are anti-democratic.

Democracy is distinct from majoritarianism because democracy is a normative idea that refers to the substantive political values of self-government,[13] whereas majoritarianism is a descriptive term that refers to a particular decision-making procedure. Essential to democracy are the values that allow us to determine whether in specific circumstances particular decision-making procedures are actually democratic. Governments, for example, do not become democratic merely because they hold elections in which majorities govern. Such elections are currently held in North Korea. To know whether these elections make North Korea democratic requires an inquiry into whether these elections are implemented in a way that serves democratic values. It is a grave mistake to confuse democracy with any particular decision-making procedure,

insult" and "the offence of blasphemy should be abolished." The report urges that only incitement to hatred be punishable by criminal law in member states. See *European Commission for Democracy through Law (Venice Commission), Report on the relationship between freedom of expression and freedom of religion: the issue of regulation and prosecution of blasphemy, religious insult and incitement to religious hatred, 17–18 October 2008, Doc. No. CDL-AD(2008)026.*

[10] For a good summary of the major positions, see Frederick Schauer, *Free Speech: A Philosophical Enquiry* (New York: Cambridge University Press, 1982).

[11] Norberto Bobbio, *Democracy and Dictatorship: The Nature and Limits of State Power* (Peter Kennealy trans., Cambridge, UK: Polity, 1989), 137.

[12] Schauer, *Free Speech* 40–1.

[13] On democracy as a substantive value, see Frank Michelman, *Brennan and Democracy* (Princeton, NJ: Princeton University Press, 1999).

and thereby to fail to identify the core values that democracy as a form of government seeks to instantiate.

What does it mean for a people to fulfill the value of self-governance? The practice of self-government is often interpreted to mean that a people must be ultimately responsible for governmental decisions, either by making such decisions directly or by electing those who do. This is the view, for example, of Alexander Meiklejohn or Owen Fiss.[14] But this is an insufficient account of the practice of self-government. For reasons that I shall explain, I think it preferable to say that the practice of self-government requires that a people have the warranted conviction that they are engaged in the process of governing themselves.[15] The distinction is crucial, for it emphasizes the difference between making particular decisions and recognizing particular decisions as one's own. Self-government is about the authorship of decisions, not about the making of decisions.

We can test this distinction by imagining a situation in which the people retain their collective capacity to decide issues, but in which individuals within the collectivity feel hopelessly alienated from these decisions. Suppose, for example, that in state X citizens are provided with interactive computer terminals that they are required to use in the morning to register their preferences about various issues. Each morning an agenda for decisions (composed by an elected assembly) is presented on the terminal. The citizens of state X must decide what color clothes should be worn; what menu should be served for lunch and dinner; the boundaries of the attendance zones for the neighborhood school; whether a stop sign should be placed at a local intersection; and so on. Assume that citizens of state X can get from their computer whatever information they believe is relevant for their votes, including information about the likely views of other citizens.

Imagine, further, that state X has no public discourse. There are neither newspapers nor broadcast media. The state bans political parties and associations. It proscribes public demonstrations and prohibits individuals from publishing their views to other citizens. Each citizen must make up his or her mind in isolation. Decisions in state X, however, are made on the basis of the majority vote of the collectivity, and all individuals are henceforth required to comply: to wear blue, or to serve chicken for lunch, or to attend a particular school, or to stop at the local intersection. Individuals in state X feel completely alienated from these decisions. They do not identify with them and instead feel controlled and manipulated by the external force of the collectivity.

Would we deem state X an example of a society that engages in self-determination? Although in state X the people retain their ability, "as a collectivity, to decide their own fate,"[16] which is to say to make decisions by majority rule, I very much doubt that we would characterize state X as a democracy. We are much more likely to condemn it as a dystopian tyranny. Rousseau long ago diagnosed the reason for this condemnation: collective decision-making is merely oppressive unless there is some internal connection between the particular wills of individual citizens and the general will of the collectivity.[17]

[14] See e.g. Alexander Meiklejohn, *Political Freedom: The Constitutional Powers of the People* (New York: Harper, 1948).

[15] The concept of a "warranted conviction" is meant to signify that a subjective conviction of self-government is not a determinative and preclusive condition for the realization of democratic values. The conviction must withstand scrutiny, which means that it must always be open to third parties to attempt to convince a citizen that his or her experience of self-government is delusory.

[16] Owen Fiss, *Liberalism Divided: Freedom of Speech and the Many Uses of State Power* (Boulder, Colorado: Westview Press, 1996), 37–8.,

[17] Jean-Jacques Rousseau, *The Social Contract* (Maurice Cranston trans., Baltimore: Penguin Books, 1968), 58–62. Ironically, Rousseau seemingly contemplated that the general will would be formed through just such an alienated process as I have sketched. "From the deliberations of a people properly informed, and provided its members do not have any communication among themselves, the great

It is implausible to claim, as Rousseau might be thought to claim, that there can exist a complete identity between the particular wills of individual citizens and the general will of the democratic state. It is enough that individual citizens can recognize in that general will the potentiality of their own authorship.[18] When this occurs, collective decision-making is democratic because it is experienced as self-determination. But when citizens feel alienated from the general will, or from the process by which the general will is created, voting on issues is merely a decision-making mechanism, a mechanism that can easily turn oppressive and undemocratic.

It follows that the value of democracy can be fulfilled only if there is continual mediation between collective self-determination and the individual self-determination of particular citizens.[19] If democracy requires that citizens experience their government as their own, as representing them, they must experience the state as in some way responsive to their own values and ideas. How is this theoretically possible under modern conditions of diversity, when the citizens of a state are heterogeneous and disagree with each other? The focus of analysis must shift from specific state decisions to the process by which these decisions are authorized. Citizens must experience that process as responsive to their own values and ideas.

Modern democracies conceive this process in terms of communication. They seek to make the decisions of the state responsive to public opinion, and to protect freedom of speech so that citizens can participate in the formation of public opinion. They hope that the opportunity freely to participate in forming public opinion will allow citizens to experience their government as their own, even if they must live in common with citizens who hold diverse views and otherwise disagree. That is why in the United States we say that the First Amendment, which is anti-majoritarian, is nevertheless "the guardian of our democracy."[20] Hans Kelsen, speaking of democracy, puts the matter this way:

> A subject is politically free insofar as his individual will is in harmony with the "collective" (or "general") will expressed in the social order. Such harmony of the "collective" and the individual will is guaranteed only if the social order is created by the individuals whose behavior it regulates. Social order means determination of the will of the individual. Political freedom, that is, freedom under social order, is self-determination of the individual by participating in the creation of the social order....
>
> The will of the community, in a democracy, is always created through a running discussion between majority and minority, through free consideration of arguments for and against a certain regulation of a subject matter. This discussion takes place not only in parliament, but also, and foremost, at political meetings, in newspapers, books, and other vehicles of public opinion. A democracy without public opinion is a contradiction in terms.[21]

number of small differences will always produce a general will and the decision will always be good" (73). This suggests that Rousseau may have had a finer grasp of the analytic prerequisites of democracy than of the sociological dynamics necessary for its realization.

[18] For a full explication of this argument, see Robert Post, "Meiklejohn's Mistake: Individual Autonomy and the Reform of Public Discourse" (1993) 64 *University of Colorado Law Review* 1109.

[19] I have elsewhere argued that "[t]he essential problematic of democracy...lies in the reconciliation of individual and collective autonomy." Post, *Constitutional Domains: Democracy, Community, Management* (1995), 7. Harvard University Press, Cambridge For a full discussion, see Post, "Between Democracy and Community: The Legal Constitution of Social Form," in John W. Chapman and Ian Shapiro (eds), *Democratic Community: Nomos* XXXV (1993), 178–9.

[20] *Brown v. Hartlage* 456 U.S. 45, 60 (1982).

[21] Hans Kelsen, *General Theory of Law and State* (Anders Wedberg trans., New York: Russell & Russell, 1961), 285–88.

A democracy must protect the communicative processes by which its citizens work toward an "agreement" that is "uncoerced, and reached by citizens in ways consistent with their being viewed as free and equal persons."[22] Of course, under conditions of modern heterogeneity, actual agreement is impossible, so the notion of agreement functions merely as a "regulative idea" for the formation of public opinion. If we use the term "public discourse" to refer to the communicative processes by which public opinion is formed, we can say that public discourse continuously but unsuccessfully strives to mediate between individual and collective self-determination to produce "a common will, communicatively shaped and discursively clarified in the political public sphere."[23]

In a modern democracy, therefore, citizens are free to engage in public discourse so as to make the state responsive to their ideas and values, in the hope that even if the state acts in ways inconsistent with those ideas and values, citizens can nevertheless maintain their identification with the state. Freedom of speech is thus a necessary condition of democratic legitimacy, but not a sufficient condition. If the state prevents citizens from participating in public discourse when they would otherwise desire to do so, the state loses democratic legitimacy with respect to those citizens, for it prevents them from attempting to make public opinion responsive to their views.

The Danish cartoons of Muhammad that we are considering are plainly part of public discourse.[24] They concern matters of intense public controversy. When Danish author Kåre Bluitgen complained that he could not find an artist brave enough to illustrate his forthcoming children's book about the life of Muhammed, the culture editor of *Jyllands-Posten* decided to test the "fear of violence from Islamic radicals" by inviting members of the Danish Cartoonist Society to depict their interpretations of the Prophet.[25] As Kurt Westergaard, author of the "incendiary but dignified drawing" of Muhammed with a bomb-shaped turban that "has become the metonym for the whole controversy," subsequently explained in an interview: "The cartoon is not directed against Islam as a whole, but against the part of it that obviously can inspire violence, terrorism, death and destruction."[26] Fear of these aspects of Islam is relevant to matters of important public policy, like immigration. If public policy is to be directed by an intelligently informed public opinion, and if citizens are to feel that public policy is potentially responsive their views, they must be free to express and discuss their perspectives on the matters satirized in the *Jyllands-Posten* cartoons.

[22] John Rawls, "Justice as Fairness: Political Not Metaphysical" (1985) 14 *Philosophy and Public Affairs* 229–30.

[23] Jürgen Habermas, *The Theory of Communicative Action* (Thomas McCarthy trans., Boston: Beacon Press, 1987), 81.

[24] Exactly how to draw the boundaries of public discourse is a complex and complicated matter. For a discussion, see Robert Post, "The Constitutional Concept of Public Discourse: Outrageous Opinion, Democratic Deliberation, and *Hustler Magazine v. Falwell*" (1990) 103 *Harvard Law Review* 667–84.

[25] Craig Smith, "Adding News Print to the Fire," *New York Times* (5 Feb. 2006), 5. A *New York Times* columnist has characterized the "callous and feeble cartoons" published by *Jyllands-Posten* as "cooked up as a provocation by a conservative newspaper exploiting the general Muslim prohibition on images of the Prophet Muhammad to score cheap points about freedom of expression." Michael Kimmelman, "A Startling New Lesson in the Power of Imagery," *New York Times* (8 Feb. 2006), E1.

[26] Quoted in Spiegelman, "Drawing Blood," 48. Spiegelman shrewdly observes of this cartoon that "the irate artist successfully discharged himself of the political cartoonist's duty to bring matters to a head. If the drawing had simply not appeared under the rubric of 'Muhammad's Face,' it would have been more immediately seen to specifically represent the murderous aspect of fundamentalism, the one that . . . made this drawing a self-fulfilling prophecy" (48–9).

II. The Suppression of Blasphemy

It follows that if free speech is to serve the value of democratic legitimation, the Danish cartoons ought to be immune from legal censorship. This conclusion, however, is merely the beginning of analysis. We must ask whether there are state interests that might nevertheless justify suppression of the cartoons. In the context of the cartoons, there are three such interests that have been advanced: the suppression of blasphemy, the protection of religious groups, and the prevention of discrimination. I shall discuss each of these in turn.

The state has an interest in suppressing blasphemy insofar as it has an interest in protecting the respect properly due to God.[27] Samuel Johnson defined blasphemy as "an offering of some indignity unto God himself."[28] English law made blasphemy a crime based upon "the plain principle that the public importance of the Christian religion is so great that no one is allowed to deny its truth."[29] In 1841 the English Commissioners on Criminal Law reported "that the common law of England punishes as an offence any general denial of the truth of Christianity, without reference to the language or temper in which such denial is conveyed."[30]

About the middle of the nineteenth century, British blasphemy law began to evolve. Instead of protecting the respect due to God, it sought to protect the feelings and sensibility of religious groups. In 1883, for example, Lord Coleridge explained that whatever the "old cases" may have said "the mere denial of the truth of Christianity is not enough to constitute the offence of blasphemy."[31] He defined the crime of blasphemous libel instead as the publication of communications "calculated and intended to insult the feelings and the deepest religious convictions of the great majority of the persons amongst whom we live." The point of blasphemy was altered to prevent "outrages to the general feeling of propriety among the persons amongst whom we live."[32] "If the decencies of controversy are observed, even the fundamentals of religion may be attacked without the writer being guilty of blasphemy."[33]

[27] For a discussion, see Robert Post, "Cultural Heterogeneity and Law: Pornography, Blasphemy, and the First Amendment" (1988) 76 *California Law Review* 297. In England, blasphemy was a common law crime. It was one of the four branches of criminal libel, the other three being obscenity, sedition, and defamation. See J.R. Spencer, "Criminal Libel—A Skeleton in the Cupboard," *Criminal Law Review* (1977). All four branches of libel sought to ensure that speech did not violate established norms of respect and propriety. The particular province of blasphemy was to prevent disrespect toward God, which according to Blackstone could be manifested "by denying his being or providence; or by contumelious reproaches of our Saviour Christ." William Blackstone, *Commentaries* (1769), vol. 4: 59.

[28] Samuel Johnson, *A Dictionary of the English Language* (1756). Benjamin Norton Defoe defined blasphemy as "vile or opprobrious Language, tending to the Dishonour of God." Defoe, *A Compleat English Dictionary* (1735).

[29] James Fitzjames Stephen, *A History of the Criminal Law of England* (1883), vol 2: 475. The English law of blasphemy was successfully used to prosecute individuals for publishing such works as Thomas Paine's *Age of Reason* (471–3), *Rex v. Williams, Howell's St. Tr.* 26 (K.B. 1797), 653; *Rex v. Carlile (Richard), St. Tr. N.S.* 1 (1819), 1387; Shelley's poem "Queen Mab," *Regina v. Moxon, St. Tr. N.S. 4* (1841), 693; and the popular Discourses of an early Deist, a minister and Fellow of Sydney Sussex College at Cambridge, which urged that the miracles reported in the New Testament be interpreted allegorically, rather than literally. See *Rex v. Woolston, Eng. Rep.* 94: 112, *Barn. K.B.* 1 (1729), 162.

[30] Commissioners on Criminal Law, *Sixth Report* (1841), 83.

[31] *Regina v. Ramsay and Foote, Cox C.C.* 15 (1883), 231, 236.

[32] *Regina v. Bradlaugh, Cox C.C.* 15 (1883), 217, 230, 231.

[33] *Ramsay and Foote*, 238.

This was essentially the status of the crime of blasphemous libel in Britain until it was abolished in 2008.[34] The crime prohibited "any contemptuous, reviling, scurrilous or ludicrous matter relating to God, Jesus Christ or the Bible," but provided that opinions hostile to Christianity may be expressed in a "decent and moderate" manner.[35] I trace this development in order to emphasize the distinction between a state interest in protecting the respect due to God, and a state interest in protecting the feelings and religious convictions of religious groups. I shall address the former in Part II, and the latter in Part III.

Even today there exist blasphemy laws that seek to protect the sacred by enforcing the respect due to God. Pakistan, for example, prescribes the death penalty for anyone who "by any imputation, innuendo, or insinuation, directly or indirectly, defiles the sacred name of the Holy Prophet."[36] One teacher at a medical college was prosecuted for speculating that Muhammad's parents might not have been Muslims. Pakistani Christians are particularly vulnerable to legal sanction.

Some who claim that the Danish cartoons ought to be legally suppressed argue that they are blasphemous because they disrespect God or Muhammad, his Prophet. King Abdullah of Jordan, for example, announced that "With all respect to press freedoms, obviously anything that vilifies the Prophet Muhammad, peace be upon him... needs to be condemned."[37] A communiqué from the Organization of the Islamic Conference (OIC), a group comprised of the world's 57 Muslim nations, denounced the "desecration of the image of the Holy Prophet Muhammad in the media."[38] A Hamas legislator proclaimed that "We are angry—very, very, very angry.... No one can say a bad word about our prophet."[39]

The question is how a state interest in safeguarding the respect due to God and his prophets can be reconciled with the freedom of speech necessary to serve the function of democratic legitimation. There is an obvious and immediate contradiction between keeping public discourse open to all opinions and excluding from public discourse those who would deny what a particular religion regards as sacred. With respect to those who do not share the religious beliefs protected by a particular blasphemy law, and who are therefore excluded from public discourse, the state is rendered heteronomous. The state loses democratic legitimacy with respect to those who do not believe in the truths protected by a law of blasphemy.

This loss in democratic legitimacy may be acceptable if a state does not aspire democratically to govern those of differing religious beliefs. But most modern states define their jurisdiction in terms of a geographical territory that includes persons of many different beliefs. To the extent democratic legitimacy is important with respect to persons who do not share the beliefs enshrined in a state's blasphemy law, any such loss of democratic legitimacy should be unacceptable.

[34] On 5 March 2008, an amendment was passed to the Criminal Justice and Immigration Act of 2008 that abolished the common law offenses of blasphemy and blasphemous libel in England and Wales. See Criminal Justice and Immigration Act 2008, Part 5, s. 79, available at <http://www.legislation.gov.uk/ukpga/2008/4/part/5/crossheading/blasphemy>.

[35] *Wingrove v. United Kingdom* (1996) 24 E.H.R.R. 1, 7.

[36] For a discussion, see Donna E. Arzt, "Heroes or Heretics: Religious Dissidents under Islamic Law" (1996) 14 *Wisconsin International Law Journal* 349.

[37] David E. Sanger, "Bush Urges Nations to End Violence; Rice Accuses Syria and Iran," *New York Times* (9 Feb. 2006), A14.

[38] Hassan M. Fattah, "At Mecca Meeting, Cartoon Outrage Crystallized," *New York Times* (9 Feb. 2006), A1.

[39] Smith and Fisher, "Temperatures Rise over Cartoons Mocking Muhammad" A3.

III. The Protection of Religious Groups

It is no doubt for something like this reason that British blasphemy law evolved in the middle of the nineteenth century, changing from a law designed to protect the sacred into a law designed to protect religious groups. British law was anomalous, because it protected the religious feelings of only one religious group, Anglicans.[40] But it is easy to imagine a non-discriminatory prohibition on all speech offensive to the religious feelings of any religious group. Many states currently have laws of this kind. Oriana Fallaci, for example, was charged with the crime of blasphemy in Italy because her attacks on Islam "offend a religion acknowledged by the state, by defaming those who profess it."[41]

The objective of a blasphemy law that seeks to protect the honor of God is to uphold a certain version of religious truth. By contrast, the objective of a blasphemy law that seeks to protect religious groups from outrage is to prevent these groups from suffering the harm and indignity of offense. The law commonly protects groups from such harm.

The second form of blasphemy law was considered in 1993 by the ECtHR in the case of *Otto Preminger Institute v. Austria*. Austrian law imposed criminal penalties on anyone who, through behavior "likely to arouse justified indignation, disparages or insults a person who, or an object which, is an object of veneration of a church or religious community established within the country, or a dogma, a lawful custom or a lawful institution of such church or religious community."[42]Austrian authorities had invoked the statute to justify the seizure of a film, *Liebeskonzil*, that offensively satirized Christian beliefs, portraying "God the Father... both in image and in text as a senile, impotent idiot, Christ as a cretin, and Mary Mother of God as a wanton lady."[43]

In upholding the seizure, the ECtHR invoked "the right of citizens not to be insulted in their religious feelings by the public expression of views of other persons." It reasoned that "in extreme cases the effect of particular methods of opposing or denying religious beliefs can be such as to inhibit those who hold such beliefs from exercising their freedom to hold and express them," and it accordingly held that "provocative portrayals of objects of religious veneration... can be regarded as malicious violation of the spirit of tolerance, which must also be a feature of democratic society."[44]

40 *R. v. Chief Metropolitan Stipendiary Magistrate ex parte Choudhury* (1990) 3 W.L.R. 986; Anthony Chase, "Legal Guardians: Islamic Law, International Law, Human Rights Law, and the Salman Rushdie Affair" (1996) 11 *American University Journal of International Law and Policy* 419–20. On 16 February 2006, Britain enacted the Racial and Religious Hatred Act of 2006, which provides that "A person who uses threatening words or behaviour, or displays any written material which is threatening, is guilty of an offence if he intends thereby to stir up religious hatred" (s. 29B). The Act defines "religious hatred" to mean "hatred against a group of persons defined by reference to religious belief or lack of religious belief" (s. 29A). The Act thus prohibited threats that stir up religious hatred against any religious group, not merely Anglicans.

41 Margaret Talbot, "The Agitator: Oriana Fallaci Directs Her Fury Against Islam," *The New Yorker* (5 June 2006), 61.

42 *Otto Preminger Institut v.Austria* (1994) 19 E.H.R.R. 25; citing s. 188 of the Austrian Penal Code.

43 *Otto Preminger Institut* s. 16; quoting the judgment of the Austrian Regional Court.

44 *Otto Preminger Institut* ss. 48, 47, 47. In a subsequent decision, the European Court of Human Rights upheld British censorship of a film showing a Catholic saint in a state of sexual ecstasy. *Wingrove v. United Kingdom* (1996) 24 E.H.R.R. 7. The Court's reasoning, however, was far less substantive than in *Otto Preminger Institut*. The Court turned its decision on the conclusion that "a wider margin of appreciation is generally available to the Contracting States when regulating freedom of expression in relation to matters liable to offend intimate personal convictions within the sphere of morals or, especially, religion" (s. 58):

The logic of the court was essentially that persons have a right not to be insulted in their religious beliefs because offense of this kind inhibits the right to practice a religion. Something like this rationale was evident in the controversy over the Danish cartoons. The OIC denounced the cartoons as offending "hundreds of millions of Muslims around the world" and as "meant to disturb and infuriate Muslims." For this reason, OIC argued, the cartoons "could not be considered as an innocent behavior falling within the scope of freedom of expression in which everyone believes."[45] Ayatollah Ali Khamenei condemned the cartoons for "insulting the beliefs of 1.5 billion Muslims."[46] Doudou Diene, the United Nations Special Rapporteur on Contemporary Forms of Racism, Racial Discrimination, Xenophobia and Related Intolerance, urged that the United Nations "treat cases such as the Danish cartoon situation... as a debate on the balancing of two rights, freedom of expression and freedom of religion."[47] The Rapporteur is reported as stating that "the cartoons are absolutely insulting" and that "beliefs should not be humiliated under the veil of freedom of expression."[48]

If suppressing speech in order to protect the sacred excludes from public discourse those who would dispute a particular conception of the sacred, so suppressing speech

> Moreover, as in the field of morals, and perhaps to an even greater degree, there is no uniform European conception of the requirements of "the protection of the rights of others" in relation to attacks on their religious convictions. What is likely to cause substantial offence to persons of a particular religious persuasion will vary significantly from time to time and from place to place, especially in an era characterised by an ever growing array of faiths and denominations. By reason of their direct and continuous contact with the vital forces of their countries, State authorities are in principle in a better position than the international judge to give an opinion on the exact content of these requirements with regard to the rights of others as well as on the "necessity" of a "restriction" intended to protect from such material those whose deepest feelings and convictions would be seriously offended.

But see *Affaire Giniewski v. France*, judgment of 31 January 2006.

[45] Patrick Goodenough, "Growing Anger over Mohammed Cartoons," *CNS News* (3 Jan. 2006), <http://web.archive.org/web/20060204220445/http:/www.cnsnews.com/ViewForeignBureaus.asp?Page=%5CForeignBureaus%5Carchive%5C200601%5CFOR20060103b.html>.

[46] Quoted in Nazila Fathi, "Contest for Cartoons Mocking the Holocaust Announced in Tehran," *New York Times* (8 Feb. 2006), A10. Dr. Abdulaziz Othman Altwaijri, Director General of the Islamic Educational, Scientific and Cultural Organization, called for "enacting an international law incriminating offences to religions and prophets" because of the need "to reinforce tolerance among the followers of the divine religions, the aim being to remove the causes that lead to hatred and discrimination and contribute to stirring up conflicts among civilizations and cultures" (Saudi Press Agency, *At the Congress of Imams and Rabbis*, U.P.I., March 21, 2006, available at Lexis, At the Congress of Imams and Rabbis Saudi Press Agency March 21, 2006 Tuesday 11:03 AM EST.) Two months previously Altwaijri had called upon the Danish Center for Culture and Development "to protest in the manner you deem appropriate against this newspaper as well as against every other information means in your country that damages the image of Islam and Muslims, following in that the policy of tolerance that rejects the contempt of religions and the profanation of religious sanctities in which believe a billion and a third people on this earth." (<http://web.archive.org/web/20060219093123/http://www.isesco.org.ma/English/press/viewpage.asp?Lien=9996992+++++++++>).

[47] Press Release, "Special Rapporteur on Racism tells Committee that Racism and Racial Discrimination Are on the Upswing," 7 Mar. 2006, <http://www.unhchr.ch/huricane/huricane.nsf/view01/5F30A01100D70D67C125712A006FBE18?opendocument>.

[48] Quoted in Hasan Cucuk, "UN: Denmark Acted Irresponsibly in Cartoon Crisis," *ZamanOnline* (19 Mar. 2006), <http://www.zaman.com/?bl=international&alt=&trh=20060319&hn=31079>. This Turkish paper quotes Diene to the effect that the "defense that freedom of speech is limitless contradicts international rules. There is a great need to establish a balance between freedom of speech and freedom of faith. This publication explicitly shows a lack of understanding and emotion for believers. The newspaper also helped Islam and terror to be likened." See also "The Volokh Conspiracy, Another U.N. Official Demanding Speech restrictions, and faulting Denmark for Protecting Speech Too Much," available at <http://volokh.com/posts/1142989233.shtml>.

in order to protect the sensibility of religious groups is also inconsistent with freedom of speech because it excludes from public discourse those whose convictions are offensive to religious groups. The ECtHR offered several arguments for attempting to ameliorate this contradiction.

The first was to claim that a "spirit of tolerance... must... be a feature of democratic society."[49] This strategy strikes me as inadequate. The toleration required by democracy refers to action. Democracy demands that we refrain from acting toward each other in ways that are inconsistent with the social order. We must not riot or murder in defense of our beliefs. We must allow others peacefully to practice their beliefs. But democracy does not require toleration in the sense that persons must abandon their independent evaluation of the beliefs and ideas of others. Democracies encompass groups that dislike and even detest each other, sometimes on religious grounds.[50] To the extent that democracy suppresses my expressions of disapproval or condemnation for the actions of groups that I dislike, it excludes me from the formation of public opinion.

A second strategy adopted by the ECtHR for minimizing the anti-democratic consequences of suppressing religiously offensive speech was to assert that speech critical of religious beliefs may be suppressed only if it is "gratuitously offensive to others" and thus does "not contribute to any form of public debate capable of furthering progress in human affairs."[51] This argument turns on the distinction between "gratuitous" offense and other forms of offense. We must thus ask when offense is merely "gratuitous" and hence not necessary for public debate.

Consider the example of Dr. Wafa Sultan, a Syrian-American psychiatrist who was raised a Muslim but who has strongly denounced the violence associated with Muslim

[49] *Otto Preminger Institut*, s. 47. Recently the Court attempted to explained this principle of tolerance as requiring the Court in prosecutions for blasphemy to weigh "the conflicting interests of the exercise of two fundamental freedoms, namely the right of the applicant to impart to the public his views on religious doctrine, on the one hand, and the right of others to respect for their freedom of thought, conscience and religion, on the other hand" (s. 55). Case of *İA v. Turkey*, 13 September 2005, s. 27. In *İA* the Court upheld the blasphemy conviction of a novelist for publishing a novel that contained this paragraph: "Look at the triangle of fear, inequality and inconsistency in the Koran; it reminds me of an earthworm. God says that all the words are those of his messenger. Some of these words, moreover, were inspired in a surge of exultation, in Aisha's arms.... God's messenger broke his fast through sexual intercourse, after dinner and before prayer. Muhammad did not forbid sexual relations with a dead person or a live animal" (s. 13).

[50] The ECtHR implicitly recognized this principle in *Kokkinakis v. Greece*, Judgment of 19 April 1993, which struck down a Greek law prohibiting proselytism, by which was "meant, in particular, any direct or indirect attempt to intrude on the religious beliefs of a person of a different religious persuasion (*eterodoxos*), with the aim of undermining those beliefs, either by any kind of inducement or promise of an inducement or moral support or material assistance, or by fraudulent means or by taking advantage of his inexperience, trust, need, low intellect or naivety" (s. 16). The ECtHR held that "a distinction has to be made between bearing Christian witness and improper proselytism. The former corresponds to true evangelism, which a report drawn up in 1956 under the auspices of the World Council of Churches describes as an essential mission and a responsibility of every Christian and every Church. The latter represents a corruption or deformation of it. It may, according to the same report, take the form of activities offering material or social advantages with a view to gaining new members for a Church or exerting improper pressure on people in distress or in need; it may even entail the use of violence or brainwashing; more generally, it is not compatible with respect for the freedom of thought, conscience and religion of others" (s. 48).

[51] *Otto-Preminger Institut*, s. 49. In *İA v. Turkey*, the Court explained that freedom of speech "carries with it duties and responsibilities. Amongst them, in the context of religious beliefs, may legitimately be included a duty to avoid expressions that are gratuitously offensive to others and profane (see for example, *Otto-Preminger-Institut v. Austria*, judgment of 20 September 1994, Series A no.295-A, pp. 18–19, s 49, and *Murphy v. Ireland*, no. 44179/98, s 67, ECHR 2003-IX). This being so, as a matter of principle it may be considered necessary to punish improper attacks on objects of religious veneration (ibid.)" (s. 24). See also *Case of Murphy v. Ireland*, 12 March 2003, 65.

fundamentalism. She has characterized recent controversies as "a clash between barbarity and rationality." Sultan has since been denounced by Muslim clerics "as an infidel" who has "done Islam more damage than the Danish cartoons mocking the Prophet Muhammad." An Egyptian professor of religious studies charged that "she had blasphemed against Islam, the Prophet Muhammad and the Koran." Sultan "has received numerous death threats."[52]

Sultan's remarks are clearly offensive. But are they gratuitously offensive? They refer to the same issues of violence and sectarianism as do the Danish cartoons. They equally stereotype Muslim attitudes and actions. Sultan's denunciations are probably more offensive than the cartoons because they are more reasoned, comprehensive, and hard-hitting. But should the law regard them as "gratuitous"? To do so would of course turn the law into an instrument for deciding which opinions it will recognize as legitimate. For the reasons I have already discussed, this is not compatible with the use of freedom of speech to establish democratic legitimation.

There is a hint in the ECtHR decision that the concept of "gratuitous" offense refers to the style of speech rather than to its substance. Speech like Sultan's can offend religious groups and nevertheless receive protection as contributing to public debate if it is sober and rational. But speech that is expressed in an offensive manner, like *Liebeskonzil* (or perhaps the Danish cartoons), is not deemed to contribute to public debate. This is essentially the position of late nineteenth century British blasphemy law, which permitted anything to be said, so long as "the decencies of controversy are observed."[53]

Insofar as this is the position of the ECtHR, it necessarily follows that the Court was incorrect to invoke "the right of citizens not to be insulted in their religious feelings by the public expression of views of other persons." The position we are now considering assumes that citizens must tolerate insults from speech that is sober and rational, like Sultan's, but that citizens do not have to tolerate insults that flow from a certain style or manner of speech that is condemned as intrinsically offensive.[54] The question is how the law should distinguish between styles of speech that are intrinsically offensive and styles

[52] Sultan writes: "We have not seen a single Jew blow himself up in a German restaurant. We have not seen a single Jew destroy a church. We have not seen a single Jew protest by killing people.... Only Muslims defend their beliefs by burning down churches, killing people and destroying embassies. This path will not yield any results." Quoted in John M. Broder, "For Muslim Who Says Violence Destroys Islam, Violent Threats," *New York Times* (11 Mar. 2006), A1. Sultan continued, "The clash we are witnessing around the world is not a clash of religions or a clash of civilizations.... It is a clash between a mentality that belongs to the Middle Ages and another mentality that belongs to the 21st century. It is a clash between civilization and backwardness, between the civilized and primitive, between barbarity and rationality."

[53] The British distinction between style and substance was meant to maintain the openness of public debate. See e.g. Peter Jones, "Blasphemy, Offensiveness and Law" (1980) 10 *British Journal of Political Science* 142–3:

> The intention behind the distinction is plain. Granted that it is possible to distinguish manner from matter, a law restricting only forms of expression need not prevent the assertion of any substantive point of view. The usual conflict between freedom of opinion and prevention of offense is therefore largely avoided.... The failing of the matter-manner distinction is that it supposes that statements are capable of more or less offensive formulations which are nevertheless identical in meaning. The manner of an assertion is treated as though it were so much verbal wrapping paper whose features had no bearing upon the content of the parcel. In certain cases this assumption may not be unjustified.... More often, however, manner and matter are so integrally related that it is impossible to distinguish the offensive manner from the offensive matter of a statement.

Even the ECtHR has recognized the ultimate difficulty in any effort to enforce a hard distinction between the style and substance of speech. See e.g. *Jersild v. Denmark* (1994) 19 E.H.R.R., s. 31: "The Court recalls that Article 10 protects not only the substance of the ideas and information expressed, but also the form in which they are conveyed."

[54] In *İA v. Turkey*, the Court upheld a blasphemy prosecution because "the present case concerns not only comments that offend or shock, or a 'provocative' opinion, but also an abusive attack on the

of speech that are inherently protected.[55] If freedom of speech is to serve its function of democratic legitimation, any such distinction must be drawn in such a way as to minimize damage to public debate.

This suggests that the distinction cannot be drawn simply on the basis of the beliefs of discrete religious groups. What any given religious group finds offensive is a matter of contingent history. Before the European religious wars of the seventeenth century, Catholics found deeply offensive the mere existence of Protestants in their community, and vice versa.[56] It would seem that the law cannot transparently apply the beliefs of religious groups without becoming entangled in endless and insoluble contradictions.

More importantly, the beliefs of particular religious groups may be more or less compatible with the maintenance of the kind of public sphere required for democratic legitimation. One religious group might experience any negative reference to its founding Prophet as intolerably offensive; another might find outrageous and blasphemous any aspersion on the character of its religion or of its followers. As different religious groups experience subjects for public discussion and commentary to be differently inadmissible, the public sphere may shrink in ways that are incompatible with democracy.[57]

The distinction between speech that is consistent with "the decencies of controversy" and speech that is unacceptably offensive, therefore, must be drawn by reference to social norms of dialogue that are endorsed by a democratic state, in part because they are deemed compatible with the function of democratic legitimation. It follows that if a state's interest in the protection of religious groups is to be rendered compatible with freedom of speech, the state must at a minimum distinguish between "gratuitous" and

Prophet of Islam. Notwithstanding the fact that there is a certain tolerance of criticism of religious doctrine within Turkish society, which is deeply attached to the principle of secularity, believers may legitimately feel themselves to be the object of unwarranted and offensive attacks through the following passages: 'Some of these words were, moreover, inspired in a surge of exultation, in Aisha's arms.... God's messenger broke his fast through sexual intercourse, after dinner and before prayer. Muhammad did not forbid sexual intercourse with a dead person or a live animal' (s. 29)."

[55] In England in the nineteenth century, Lord Denman sought to draw this distinction in the following way: "[U]pon the question whether it is blasphemous or nut I [make] this general observation... namely, that the question is not altogether a matter of opinion, but that it must be, in a great degree, a question as to the tone, and style, and spirit, in which such inquiries are conducted. Because, a difference of opinion may subsist, not only between different sects of Christians, but also with regard to the great doctrines of Christianity itself; and... even discussions upon that subject may be by no means a matter of criminal prosecution, but, if they be carried on in a sober and temperate and decent style, even those discussions may be tolerated, and may take place without criminality attaching to them; but that, if the tone and spirit is that of offence, and insult, and ridicule, which leaves the judgment really not free to act, and, therefore, cannot be truly called an appeal to the judgment, but an appeal to the wild and improper feelings of the human mind, more particularly in the younger part of the community, in that case the jury will hardly feel it possible to say that such opinions, so expressed, do not deserve the character [of blasphemy] affixed to them in this indictment." *Regina v. Hetherington*, (1841) 4 St. Tr. N.S. 590–1.

[56] Consider, for example, Oliver Cromwell's famous directive regarding religious liberty to the Catholics in Ireland: "As to freedom of conscience, I meddle with no man's conscience; but if you mean by that, liberty to celebrate the Mass, I would have you understand that in no place where the power of the Parliament of England prevails shall that be permitted." Quoted in *McDaniel v. Paty* 435 U.S. 618, 631 n. 2 (1978) (J. Brennan concurring).

[57] As an historical matter, toleration in the Christian West only began "when the advocates of competing religious orthodoxies failed to impose their doctrines and standards on the population at large," so "that they began to accept, reluctantly at first, an ideology which legitimated the reality created by their own failures." Steve Bruce, *A House Divided: Protestantism, Schism, and Secularization* (London, New York: Routledge, 1990), 99–100. It has thus been said that "Religion, any religion, is the enemy of liberal democracy as long as it has not been defanged and privatized. Religion, any religion, is quite explicitly about election and exclusion." Benjamin Beit-Hallahmi, "The Return of Martyrdom: Honour, Death and Immortality," in Leonard Weinberg and Ami Pedahzur (eds), *Religious Fundamentalism and Political Extremism* (London, Portland, OR: Frank Cass, 2004), 32.

"non-gratuitously" offensive speech on the basis of general secular principles that protect all members of society and reflect universally applicable standards of civility. Speech cannot be suppressed merely because it is inconsistent with the religious principles of particular sects.

It does not follow that a democratic state cannot discipline public discourse by enforcing basic norms of civility. European states typically possess laws that prohibit outrageous, indecent, or offensive forms of speech that violate social norms and thereby convey insult, infringe upon honor, or violate dignity. It is clear, however, that although such laws *purport* to enforce civility norms that are universally shared, they *in fact* express the mores of dominant groups. During debates 76 years ago in the British Parliament about the revision of blasphemy law, for example, it was well recognized that "what it really comes to is that, where opinions are strongly held by an educated man, those opinions will be expressed in a way which the law cannot touch, while those expressed by an uneducated man, simply because he is uneducated, will come under the penalties of the law."[58]

American law differs in this regard. In America, the First Amendment is interpreted to create a "marketplace of communities" as well as a marketplace of ideas.[59] The First Amendment precludes the state from imposing the norms of any one particular community onto the common space of public discourse, which is the arena in which all communities have the right equally to compete for the allegiance of public opinion. Respect for the equality of diverse communities underlies the American constitutional conclusion that civility norms, which always reflect the view of some particular community, may not be used to regulate speech within public discourse.[60] That is why First Amendment doctrine cautions against condemning "one man's vulgarity" on the ground that it may be "another's lyric."[61]

European states, by contrast, are more normatively hegemonic than America, and are therefore more comfortable enforcing civility norms that distinguish permissible from impressible speech. Hate speech is commonly regulated in Europe. The suppression of speech that is deeply offensive to religious groups is sociologically and theoretically analogous to the suppression of speech that is deeply offensive to racial groups. But whereas in the latter context it is plain that law must ultimately define the boundaries of permissible speech on the basis of civility norms that a secular state is prepared to endorse as its own, in the context of blasphemy there is the suggestion that these norms might be established simply by the religious values of particular groups. This is untenable, for the reasons I have suggested, and as a consequence the ECtHR was incorrect to uphold the censorship of *Liebeskonzil* on the ground that the "unwarranted and

[58] Parl. Deb., H.C. (5th Ser.) 234 (1930), 535 (remarks of Mr. Kingsley Griffith); also see 499: "We have writers today who can commit the offence of blasphemy with impunity, if the offence of blasphemy is an attack on the Christian religion. There are men like Sir Arthur Keith, Mr. H. G. Wells, Mr. Bertrand Russell, Mr. Aldous Huxley and others who are able to attack the Christian religion without any danger whatever of their being prosecuted, while poor men, expressing the same point of view more bluntly and crudely, expose themselves to fine and imprisonment. That is a thoroughly unsatisfactory state of the law. After all, if one concedes the right to attack religion . . . one has to concede to the people who care to do this thing the right to choose their style of doing it. Different styles are needed for different circumstances and different audiences. I do not suppose the kind of style that would go down in a select circle in the West End would be effective amongst the democracy of the East End" (remarks of Mr. Thurtle); see also 558 (remarks of Mr. Lansbury).

[59] Post, "The Constitutional Concept of Public Discourse" 634–5.

[60] See Robert Post, "Community and the First Amendment" (1997) 29 *Arizona State Law Journal* 473.

[61] *Cohen v. California* 403 U.S. 15, 25 (1971).

offensive" nature of the film was to be determined merely by reference to the "religious beliefs" of "the overwhelming majority of Tyroleans," who were Roman Catholic.[62]

This conclusion, of course, rests on the priority of using freedom of speech to maintain democratic legitimacy. The conclusion does not follow if a state does not especially prize such legitimacy, or if it believes that the need "to ensure religious peace"[63] trumps in particular circumstances the necessity of democratic legitimation, or if a state's population overwhelmingly shares religious norms so that the state is indifferent to losing democratic legitimacy among religious minorities.

IV. The Prevention of Discrimination

A third theme that emerges from the controversy surrounding the Danish cartoons does not concern the protection of religion or religious sensibilities, but instead focuses on the prevention of discrimination.[64] This theme is explicit in Doudou Diene's response to the cartoons. The UN Special Rapporteur linked the publication of the cartoons to "the development of Islamophobia" and to racial discrimination. He asserted that the cartoons "illustrated the increasing emergence of the racist and xenophobic currents in everyday life."[65] Those who condemned the cartoons argued that they were "a new sign of Europe's growing 'Islamophobia'" because they reinforced "a dangerous confusion between Islam and Islamist terrorism."[66] Civil rights lawyers in Denmark argued that there ought to be "a balance here between freedom of speech and the right not to be subjected to racial discrimination."[67]

States have a significant interest in prohibiting and preventing discrimination against Muslims. This objective is distinct from the interest in prohibiting and preventing speech that Muslims find offensive. Prohibiting discrimination means, in the first instance, forbidding conduct that discriminates. Preventing discrimination, however, might also mean altering the social conditions that cause discrimination. Among these conditions are a fear and dislike of Muslims, which is captured by the term "Islamophobia." It is not implausible to conclude that speech that promotes Islamophobia is causally connected to discrimination. The nature and strength of this causal connection is a question of contingent, historical fact.

In America the First Amendment would prevent the state from prohibiting speech for this reason. Content-based restrictions on speech cannot be imposed on the ground that the speech might cause a future harm unless the speech "is directed to inciting or producing imminent lawless action and is likely to incite or produce such action."[68]

[62] *Otto-Preminger Institut*, s. 56, see also s. 52. The conclusion in text must have formed the basic premise of the reasoning of the ECtHR own judgment in *Kokkinakis v. Greece*, on the not implausible assumption that the Greek Orthodox Church, which is the "the dominant religion in Greece" (quoting the Greek Constitution of 1975), found the proselytism protected by the Court to be "morally reprehensible." *Kokkinakis* s. 17; quoting the judgment of the Supreme Administrative Court of Greece in *Symvoulio tis Epikratias*.

[63] *Kokkinakis* s. 56.

[64] See e.g. Ruti Teitel, "No Laughing Matter: The Controversial Danish Cartoons Depicting the Prophet Mohammed, and Their Broader Meaning for Europe's Public Square," *Findlaw*, 15 Feb. 2006, <http://writ.news.findlaw.com/commentary/20060215_teitel.html>.

[65] "Special Rapporteur on Racism tells Committee that Racism and Racial Discrimination Are on the Upswing."

[66] Smith and Fisher, "Temperatures Rise over Cartoons Mocking Muhammad" A3.

[67] Alan Cowell, "More European Papers Print Cartoons of Muhammad, Fueling Dispute with Muslims," *New York Times* (2 Feb. 2006), A12.

[68] *Brandenburg v. Ohio* 395 U.S. 444, 447 (1969) (*per curiam*).

This severe restriction is deemed necessary because a more lax causal connection would invite the government to use the pretext of a causal connection as an excuse to prohibit speech. Classic historical examples of this abuse were statutes prohibiting the advocacy of Communist doctrine on the ground that the advocacy might cause a future revolution.

European states have on the whole allowed speech to be prohibited on the basis of far looser causal connections between speech and potential future harms. This may be because the legitimacy of European states is typically far more secure than that of the American state, which is constantly battling a deep libertarian streak in the American character. In America it is uniformly said that the "people" are sovereign; in Europe it is more common to say that the "nation" or the "republic" is sovereign. The consequence is that in the United States, as distinct from Europe, the government is continuously deprecated by the people it seeks to serve. The demand for democratic legitimation in the United States is more persistent and insistent than in Europe, and so restrictions on public discourse are correspondingly more disfavored.

Nevertheless, even in Europe the ECtHR has held that there are some restrictions on the capacity of member states to prohibit offensive racist remarks,[69] even though there might be some connection between such remarks and subsequent racial discrimination. National courts in Europe typically impose a requirement of proportionality on such regulation, which means that states must show that the harm of discrimination cannot be ameliorated by means other than the suppression of protected speech. Such alternative means might include educational initiatives about the nature of Islam, affirmative efforts to insure that Muslims receive adequate access to jobs, housing, health care, and food, the regulation of offensive speech that is *not* public discourse (such as speech in the workplace or in schools), and so on.

Assuming that these conditions are satisfied, there still remains the question of the kind of speech that a state might properly prohibit in the interest of preventing racial discrimination, and whether the Danish cartoons would qualify for proscription. Some of the cartoons do invoke stereotypic criticisms of Islam. They comment on Islamic repression of women; on the use of Islamic fundamentalist doctrines to foster violence; on the fear of violent reprisal for publishing criticisms of Islam.[70] These are ideas that have been and will be used by those who would discriminate against Muslims.

But they are also ideas about real and pressing public issues. The relationship between Islam and gender is a lively and controversial question. Fundamentalist Islamic violence is a public worry throughout Europe. Fear of reprisal for violating Islamic taboos is omnipresent, as can be seen in the contretemps about a German production of Mozart's opera *Idomeneo*.[71] To cut off all public discussion of real and pressing public issues would be unthinkable. And if such issues are to be discussed, the expression of all relevant views must be protected.

[69] *Jersild v. Denmark* (1994) 19 E.H.R.R.

[70] One cartoon shows Muhammad with a slit covering his eyes in front of two women who are covered everywhere by a veil except for a slit over their eyes; another Muhammad with a turban in the shape of a bomb; a third shows the cartoonist frightened at the thought of drawing a portrait of Muhammad.

[71] See Judy Dempsey and Mark Landler, "Opera Canceled Over a Depiction Of Muhammad," *New York Times* (27 Sep. 2006), A1:

> A leading German opera house has canceled performances of a Mozart opera because of security fears stirred by a scene that depicts the severed head of the Prophet Muhammad, prompting a storm of protest here about what many see as the surrender of artistic freedom. The Deutsche Oper Berlin said Tuesday that it had pulled "Idomeneo" from its fall schedule after the police warned of an "incalculable risk" to the performers and the audience... Political and cultural figures throughout Germany condemned the cancellation. Some said it recalled the decision of European newspapers not to reprint satirical cartoons about Muhammad, after their publication in Denmark generated a furor among Muslims.

How to draw the line between protected expression and speech that can be suppressed because it is likely to cause discrimination is thus a difficult and complex issue. The most obvious way to make this distinction would be to rely on the traditional difference between hate speech and ordinary expression, a difference that is incorporated into the positive law of many countries, like France and Germany.[72] French author Michel Houellebecq, for example, was charged with violating France's Pleven Law, which prohibits words that "provoke discrimination, hatred or violence against a person or group of people" on account of ethnicity, nationality, race, or religion. Houellebecq had called the Koran "mediocre" and had asserted that "The dumbest religion, after all, is Islam." He was acquitted on the ground that his comments "constituted mere criticism of Islamic doctrine."[73]

Measured by this standard, the Danish cartoons seem to me rather far from legally prohibited hate speech. They take a position on issues of obvious public moment, but they do not advocate discrimination or oppression or violence; they do not threaten; they do not use racist epithets or names; they do not attack individuals; they do not perpetuate an obvious untruth; they do not portray Muslims as without human dignity. They may exacerbate stereotypes and exaggerations, but that is not the same as hate speech. As Walter Lippmann noted almost a century ago, that is simply the nature of most popular ideas.[74]

The Deutsche Oper Berlin rescheduled and staged the opera later that year without incident. See "Berlin Police Protect Mozart Opera," *Aljazeera* (19 Dec. 2006), available at <http://www.aljazeera.com/news/europe/2006/12/2008525125811305741.html>.

[72] For a discussion, see Michel Rosenfeld, "Hate Speech in Constitutional Jurisprudence: A Comparative Analysis' (2003) 24 *Cardozo Law Review* 1523.

[73] See Susannah C. Vance, "The Permissibility of Incitement to Religious Hatred Offenses under European Convention Principles" (2004) 14 *Transnational Law and Contemporary Problems* 202–3. Houellebecq quoted in Sara Rimensnyder, "Sins of the Author: Hate and Free Speech," *Reasononline*, Dec. 2002, <http://reason.com/0212/ci.sr.sins.shtml>.

[74] Walter Lippmann, *Public Opinion* (New York: Harcourt, Brace & Co., 1922).

Index